W9-AMT-952

Children in Family Contexts

Children in Family Contexts

PERSPECTIVES ON TREATMENT

Edited by
LEE COMBRINCK-GRAHAM, MD
Institute for Juvenile Research and
University of Illinois at Chicago

Foreword by Salvador Minuchin, MD

THE GUILFORD PRESS
New York   London

© 1989 The Guilford Press
A Division of Guilford Publications, Inc.
72 Spring Street, New York, NY 10012

Printed in the United States of America

Last digit is print number: 9 8 7 6 5 4 3 2 1

Library of Congress Cataloging-in-Publication Data

Children in family contexts: perspectives on treatment / edited
    by Lee Combrinck-Graham.
        p.   cm.
    Includes bibliographies and index.
    ISBN 0-89862-732-X
    1. Child mental health.   2. Child psychiatry.   3. Family
psychotherapy.   4. Family—Mental health.   I. Combrinck-Graham,
Lee.
    [DNLM: 1. Family.   2. Family Therapy.   3. Psychotherapy—in
infancy & childhood.   WM 430.5.F2 C536]
RJ499.C4894   1989
616.89'156—dc19
DNLM/DLC
for Library of Congress   88-5108
                                                              CIP

Contributors

Joan C. Barth, PhD. Private practice, Doylestown, PA.

Jeanette Beavers, ACSW (deceased). Southwest Family Institute, Dallas, TX.

Susana Bullrich, PhD. Department of Mental Health Sciences, Hahnemann University, Philadelphia, PA; Centro di Terapia Sistemica e di Ricerca, Milan, Italy.

Iris C. Butler, PhD. Minneapolis Psychiatric Institute, Minneapolis, MN; Abbott Northwestern Hospital, Minneapolis, MN; University of Minnesota Medical School, Minneapolis, MN.

Richard Chasin, MD. Family Institute of Cambridge, Watertown, MA; Department of Psychiatry, Harvard Medical School at Cambridge Hospital, Cambridge, MA.

Lee Combrinck-Graham, MD. Institute for Juvenile Research and Department of Psychiatry, University of Illinois at Chicago, Chicago, IL.

Stuart Copans, MD. Department of Clinical Psychiatry, Dartmouth Medical School, Hanover, NH; The Brattleboro Retreat, Brattleboro, VT.

David Greenwald, PhD. Private practice, Philadelphia, PA.

Herta A. Guttman, MD. The Sir Mortimer B. Davis–Jewish General Hospital, Montreal, Quebec, Canada; Department of Psychiatry, McGill University, Montreal, Quebec, Canada.

Jill Elka Harkaway, EdD. Departments of Psychiatry and Pediatrics, Tufts Medical School/New England Medical Center, Boston, MA; Brookside Hospital, Nashua, NH; Private practice, Cambridge, MA.

B. Janet Hibbs, MFT, PhD. Center for Contextual Therapy at Philadelphia, Philadelphia, PA; Department of Mental Health Sciences, Hahnemann University, Philadelphia, PA.

Ann Itzkowitz, MA. Philadelphia Child Guidance Clinic, Philadelphia, PA; Private practice, Philadelphia, PA.

David V. Keith, MD. Family Therapy Institute, St. Paul, MN.

Douglas A. Kramer, MD. Atlanta Psychiatric Clinic & Institute for Experiential Growth, Atlanta, GA.

Judith A. Libow, PhD. Children's Hospital Medical Center of Northern California, Oakland, CA.

Marion Lindblad-Goldberg, PhD. Philadelphia Child Guidance Clinic, Philadelphia, PA.

Paul A. Mansheim, MD. Center Psychiatrists, Portsmouth, VA.

Dusty Miller, EdD. Brattleboro Family Institute, Brattleboro, VT.

Myrtle Parnell, MSW. Private practice, New York, NY; New York University Graduate School of Social Work, New York, NY.

Mary Jane Rotheram, PhD. Division of Child Psychiatry, Columbia University, New York, NY.

Jo Vanderkloot, MSW. Private practice, New York, NY; New York University Graduate School of Social Work, New York, NY.

Linda Webb-Watson, EdD. Salesmanship Club Youth and Family Centers, Dallas, TX.

Tanya B. White, PhD. Private practice, Lexington, MA; Department of Family Studies, Wheelock College, Boston, MA.

Mary F. Whiteside, PhD. Ann Arbor Center for the Family, Ann Arbor, MI.

Joan J. Zilbach, MD. Fielding Institute, Santa Barbara, CA; Boston Psychoanalytic Institute and Society, Boston, MA.

Foreword

Systems theory was heady stuff to family therapy. In a world where differences have meant strife, wars, and isolation, the esthetics of patterns that connect had tremendous appeal. By taking a metasystems position we would enjoy the formal similarities of ecological niches, and the family would become as one with other systems: the marsh, the grasslands, the digestive system, the welfare system, and the earth as a small planet.

If you become an expert in any of these fields, it is the idiosyncratic dimensions that take the fore. But it was marvelously exciting to embrace a theory that allowed us to function as polymaths, studying and comparing universes seemingly so different. Bateson's voice gave to family therapists, as practitioners, theorists, and participants in the human exchange, a vision of belonging, interconnectedness, and caring, a mystical sense of being a part and yet whole, and the hope that the logic of systems does indeed transcend the irrationalities of mankind.

But the irrationality of the particular kept making demands on practitioners. As usually happens in the development of human science, deviancy skulked in shaded corners, disguised in the words of the accepted model of truth. Therapists working with families with young children, for instance, had to address the idiosyncratic aspects of a given developmental level, or respond to the particular demands of contexts. They attended in practice to the differences in function and style of husband and wife, father and mother, and the cultural determinants constraining gender function. But they ranked that at the level of technique; in theory they continued giving salience to the isomorphic characteristics of different subsystems. In this world of universals a young child triggers and controls parental responses, the concept of parental responsibility has no descriptive power (since it puts a beginning to a recursive process), and the cultural determinants of gender responses can't be computed because they are products of social history.

In the ecological niche of the prairies, the balance of deer, wolves, and grass is essential. More wolves will kill more deer but endanger the survival of the wolves, less grass will limit the growth of deer and in turn the growth of wolves. Nobody makes an ethical statement about wolves or grass. The wolves are not perpetrators or the deer, victims.

But when we move to families, ethical concepts intermingle with general systems grammar. In family therapy it was actually the feminist group who challenged the isomorphism of patterns as obfuscating moral issues and supporting the cultural status quo. Child-oriented family therapists working with child abuse had difficulties in maintaining at the same time a systems and a child-oriented perspective. But the power of theories is such that we were able to maintain a correct practice and a pristine theory by keeping them separated by language.

This volume attempts to change this state of affairs. It is a book written by practitioners who unabashedly accept that the particular is valid and that its knowledge is essential for good practice and good therapy. They know that family therapists must know and understand the idiosyncracies of families and children, the singularity of different contexts, the multiplicity of techniques, the power of ideologies and ethnic containers, and the texture of toys. All these experiences of participation need to be packed along with theory. They will constrain its range, but they will also act as ballast, holding the balloon at a median height where the constructor of theories can gaze at connections and patterns, but will be humbled into including as valid the frustrations of the always-fumbling tasks of being a family with children.

Salvador Minuchin, MD

Introduction

This book is based on the premise that the family is a child's primary resource system. Children are born into, grow up within, and learn a fundamental world view within their families. The socializing influence of the world outside the family is secondary to that of the family, and at first is experienced only through the filter of the family. Because this is so, no response to a child requiring assistance should be considered adequate unless family members can be, if not the givers of aid, at least assistants to the process. If the ecology of childhood is visualized as a series of concentric circles in which the child is the center circle, the nuclear family is the next one, and the mental health system is at least one more circle removed from the child, then it becomes obvious that the family itself will have the most significant effects upon the child, as it does on all of its members.

Although the statement that the family is a child's primary resource system may appear to be a truism, a study of education, child welfare, and child mental health practices will demonstrate that many child advocates do not believe this. In fact, many families are very troubled, and when their availability to their children is not immediately apparent to avid protectors of children, families may be overlooked or dismissed as primary resource systems.

The authors in this volume have examined this premise in a variety of situations, especially situations in which families experience hardship or have exceptional stresses to manage while they are raising their children. The questions posed to all of the authors were these: How do families raise children in these situations? What are the means by which they handle the situations and care for their children? What are the dangers? When help is needed, what are some ways to involve a family in the solutions to the problems?

We have addressed some circumstances that might otherwise have been taken for granted. For example, it is usually assumed that the two-parent family is the healthy configuration in which most well-adjusted children grow up. It is the norm. But what exactly is it about the two-parent family context that makes it the norm? The two-parent family context needs to be characterized. The single-parent-headed family, on the other hand, has often been regarded as abnormal and pathogenic. Problems of children from single-parent-headed households may be easily explained as stemming from the "motherless" or "fatherless" environment. What we can learn by examining each type of environment is that each has its particular advantages and liabilities.

We have also addressed many situations that are commonly assumed not to be good environments for children, such as violent families, families with mentally ill parents, and families in poverty. Without making judgments about the goodness or badness of the conditions, we can acknowledge that children do grow up in such circumstances. Usually they cannot be removed to better circumstances, for a number of reasons. For one thing, there are not enough "good," secure homes to replace the "undesirable" ones; for another, displacing children has its own ill effects, disrupting ties that exist by blood and by attachment. The questions are, then, as follows: (1) How can these families provide their children with the basic resources required to grow into healthy adults? (2) What can we as mental health professionals do to help things along, if necessary?

That children's families are their primary resource systems is illustrated over and over again in maps and diagrams of children's ecology. The system that immediately encloses a child is the child's family. It is important to emphasize this, because it means that other child advocates, including teachers, doctors, and mental health professionals, are always at least one ecological level removed from the child, and when they move into an individual relationship with the child, they violate the child's ecology. Ecological systems are delicately and elaborately interconnected. We know that when we make a seemingly simple and straightforward move, such as removing a child from an abusive situation, the ramifications and reverberations of this move are far-reaching—both in space and interpersonal impact, and in time (children do not recover from such incidents for a very long time, and sometimes they never do). This book invites child advocates to take another look at the attachments, to assess and catalogue the strengths of families' coping mechanisms, and to weigh the relative benefits or liabilities involved in treating children in families as opposed to treating them apart from their families. If all this is done, a basic respect for the fundamental attachments in families will enable both children and their helpers to move forward in a safer and more coherent fashion, even when children must be removed from their families.

The systematic investigation of and treatment of troubled children in the United States began with the founding of the first public institution for children, the Institute for Juvenile Research, in 1909. At that time, children who were entering the juvenile justice system were the focus of interest; these children often came from disrupted and desperate situations. It might appear that child mental health took a turn for the worse when psychoanalysis dominated the field as the primary explanatory theory, because in addressing only the internal life of the individual child, and his or her drives and conflicts, it directed attention away from children's contexts. I have already commented on the ecological implications of this. Indeed, for a period of time this singular method of addressing children's emotional lives directed attention away from many populations of children, particularly those who were poor, members of cultural and racial minorities, and/or handicapped.

Several lines of inquiry and expertise have brought children's ecology back into the mental health field. One is the introduction of education as a primary milieu for children's growth and development. Bettelheim and Redl were leaders in this area. Another was the development of family therapy as a modality for treating troubled children. Ackerman was the pioneer in this area; however, Minuchin and colleagues were really the first to work with the families of children who were at this point not being addressed in any form of psychotherapy—delinquent children. Later, Minuchin and colleagues addressed another refractory group of children—those with psychosomatic illnesses. A third line leading to a contextual framework for understanding and treating children is the interest in infant psychiatry, which is really an exploration of infant development in the context of primary relationships. Pioneered by Bowlby in his original synthesis of work on attachment and separation reactions, this movement has led through the studies of Mahler, on the one hand, and of the Kleinians, on the other, to the development of object relations theory and formulations of child development in context. All of these movements have converged within the matrix of the community mental health consciousness to provide a generally richer understanding of children's development within a variety of important contexts.

Until the early 1980s, very little family systems literature specifically addressed young children. On the other hand, work with children such as that of Ackerman and Minuchin actually facilitated some of the major developments in the family systems movement; some of the important contributors to these developments were child psychiatrists, or psychiatrists who had extensive training in working with children. The list is impressive, including Ackerman, Whitaker, Minuchin, Bloch, Kramer, Zilbach, Chasin, Grunebaum, Andolfi, Byng-Hall, and Selvini Palazzoli. Important ideas about child mental health ecology can be found in the work of Auerswald and of the Palo Alto group, as well. The many authors in this volume who are psychologists and social workers amply illustrate that children's functioning in family and other contexts is an area of expanding interest and innovation.

Since 1980, children as a special population have entered the literature, with a special emphasis on development. When this book was first conceived in 1985, the contributors felt that justice had not been done to the substantial advances made by the family systems professionals who were working with children. Yet many of the major areas of child difficulty had been addressed using an ecological framework. We decided to assemble some of this work in a book that would reflect knowledge and experiences ranging from the practical matters of how to get children into family therapy, to the broadest questions of how important preoccupations of our age affect our children and how this effect can be mitigated by other resources in children's ecosystems.

It turned out that it took a considerable effort to formulate what we were practicing in a way that relates especially to the lives of children. Many family systems theories deal more with abstractions about human systems, such as symmetry and complementarity, boundaries, or systems functions, than with specifics, such as differences between adults and children (or, for that matter, between men and women). A common way of thinking about a family in which a child presented as a problem was that there was probably a problem in the marriage for which the child's problem was a distraction, a symbolic representation, or a way of getting attention for the family. This way of thinking did not help when children experienced any numbers of personal insults (e.g., disabilities or physical illnesses) or relational insults (e.g., losses, abuse, placement, or poverty). Although working with the way parents related to each other may have helped them to manage or comfort a child better, it did not directly address the child's distress as something suffered by the child, nor did it address the impact the child's behavior and feelings had on the family and the way other family members related to each other. Attention is paid to the specific experiences of children in this volume at three different levels:

1. The child is the focus of concern, as when a parent dies: How can families help children manage this loss?
2. The child's symptoms are the focus of family therapy that results in major reordering of the family relationship system.
3. The child's experience is understood as a part of a larger system dysfunction that is replicated at different levels of the system, so that if larger system configurations are not addressed, neither the child nor the family will be adequately helped.

The book is organized into five sections. The first is comprised of overview chapters discussing what happens to traditional ideas and practices when children are brought into conjoint therapy, or when family theory is applied to concepts of child development and psychopathology.

The second section addresses some of the different forms of the nuclear family. We may be criticized for leaving out so many, but we believe that the chapters in this section are conceptually grounded in such a way that professionals working with other family forms may gain some useful frameworks from them. For example, Kramer's assertion in Chapter 5 that there are two natural parents in all families is a useful rule to keep in mind—not only with adoptive, single-parent-headed, and remarried families, but also with gay and lesbian families, grandparent- or aunt-and-uncle-headed families, and so on.

The third section concerns families who have an atypical challenge affecting one of their members. The chapters in this section give suggestions for assessing how this challenge shapes the family context, how families adapt and cope with these challenges, and how children may or may not be compromised in such situations. Finally, each chapter, in providing an ecological assessment of family functioning, offers guidelines for treatment when the adaptation is so difficult that the children do suffer.

The fourth section moves out of the nuclear family domain into the domains of interaction between the nuclear family and larger systems. Each interface has its own characteristics. Of course, in choosing the ones we have, we have not given others as much attention. Interfaces with neighborhoods, peer groups, and religious communities have not been addressed specifically, although they are mentioned throughout the volume. We have also not addressed the mental health care system in a specific chapter. Since we are attempting, with this book, to expand the concept of the mental health care system to include many contexts and many different kinds of professionals, we hope that the systematic reader of this book could write his or her own version of that chapter after completing the reading.

The fifth section includes issues that seem to involve agencies, attitudes, and families and seem to shape both beliefs and management in very specific ways. Many of these issues cut across cultures and even nations in their significance.

The authors have different backgrounds and approach their tasks from very different disciplines. Some have presented research findings, and this is the first collection of this kind of research concerning family environments focused on children. Others have presented syntheses integrating a variety of research and conceptual contributions with a systemic approach. Still others offer a framework derived entirely from clinical experience. We have tried to present material from all of the prevalent frameworks of family systems thinking, as they involve children in this thinking. These frameworks have different emphases and lead to different techniques for intervention; they are communicated in different styles as well. What unites these varied contributions, of course, is the basic premise: that families are children's primary resources. What we can conclude from this multimodal examination of the implications of that premise is that assessing and working through the family relationship system constitute a powerful means of supporting and sustaining child development, often succeeding where other efforts have been dismal failures.

Each of the authors has a list of individuals to whom he or she owes gratitude for the contributions and support of the work. In addition to those, who are acknowledged directly in the individual chapters, thanks go to Betty Karrer, Douglas Breunlin, and Richard Schwartz, who read several chapters and offered substantial suggestions, and to Sharon Panulla, our editor at The Guilford Press, who maintained an extraordinary balance between rigorous demands and warm encouragement. Secretaries in my office, including Bernadine Vana, Iris Diggs, and Joyce Farries, typed many of the chapters and offered incidental critique along the way. Of course, we all must thank our families and our clients, especially the children, who really inform the work and give us our best ideas.

One final note is a sad one. Shortly after completing her chapter, Jeanette Beavers was diagnosed with advanced cancer, and she died after a short illness;

also, in the summer of 1987, Michael Borus, huband of Mary Jane Rotheram, died suddenly. These irreplaceable losses have touched this project and its subject matter with an important note of reality. This work on helping children and families cope with life's challenges and grievous situations so that they may thrive is presented in the context of our own coping with illness and death—a context that makes this work all the more vital.

Lee Combrinck-Graham

Contents

Children in Family Contexts

Central Issues for Children in Family Therapy

The central issues for children in family contexts and in family therapy are the same as those for children in any mental health setting (or at least as these are viewed through the lenses of mental health)—development, psychopathology, and treatment. We believe that a conceptual shift needs to take place in order that the importance of context in child development, dysfunction, and treatment may be adequately considered; this shift requires a reassessment of familiar ways of thinking in the light of new ideas that expand possibilities. Traditional theories and practices must be carefully reviewed and reintegrated in such a way that they relate meaningfully to each other as well as to the relationship matrix of the family as a primary unit of child development and therefore of treatment.

This section (and the book itself) opens with Chasin and White's discussion of how to engage children in family therapy. Despite the fact that children's place in families is not disputed, inclusion of children in family therapy is still a problem. Several reasons for this include desires to protect the children from information or hurt, as well as a difficulty with addressing adult and child modes in a session at the same time. These impediments can be overcome, and the chapter goes on to spell out structural, equipment, and conceptual steps that can be taken to involve children actively in their own and their siblings' healing.

Chasin and White's space design for an office appears to require a lot of square footage and renovation; given the limitations of space under which many therapists work, it is important that the reader consider the functions of the space, to include adult activity, children's activity, and joint activity. Instead of having separate areas for each different type of activity, one space could be made to be convertible, for example. In defining the space as they do, however, Chasin and White point out that in therapy, as at home, family members do not simply sit and talk to one another. Constructive family activity involves a variety of levels of activity and interactions, from independent exploration to dyadic collaboration to family games. Family therapy with young children should benefit from this variety as a range of choices for activity, investigation, and therapy.

Chasin and White favor an expressive form of therapy, but employ approaches derived from strategic and structural forms. Underlying their approach is the assumption of a basic functional structure to the family with young children: Parents should be in charge of a family with young children, and the therapists should be careful not to undermine this parental authority with their charm or apparently greater competence at managing the children. They stress the importance of a clear structure for the sessions, as well as a clearly articulated set of rules and expectations for the family that addresses discipline and safety, in addition to the personal rights of individual participants.

The particular resources that children bring to a therapy setting are illustrated with delightful vignettes; these also demonstrate the therapist's own playful enhancement of the children's imaginative contributions, which invites adults in the family to join in as well.

In Chapter 2, Hibbs provides the first piece explicitly applying contextual family theory to children. Contextual theory has always had children as its primary interest. The work in contextual therapy is done to relieve suffering in the present and also for posterity, as reflected in the children, but few authors writing about contextual treatment describe working with children in this way. Here, however, Hibbs has considered real children in different stages of development, and has described the interaction of developmental issues of children and parents along a dimension rarely addressed in the family literature—the ethical dimension.

A lot of ground must be covered in this chapter, because these important theories about relational ethics are still relatively unfamiliar to many mental health professionals. Hibbs combines a discussion of the concepts of loyalty, justice, and entitlement in family relationships with concepts of human development derived from Kegan, and particular development descriptions of children by Kagan and Elkind. She observes that family theories have been largely interpersonal, and have been distinguished from individual theories, which are largely intrapersonal. Furthermore, within the family field there is a distinction between those theories suggesting that inner experience derives from family organization and those suggesting that family organization is the outcome of inner experience. Hibbs offers relational ethics as a bridge to connect these different approaches. She emphasizes "meaning making" as a developmental process that occurs in the process between parents and children—and that of course is shaped by the process occurring when the parents were children, and so on.

David, a toddler whose mother's concerns could easily be dismissed as those of the "worried well," is an object of concern and an illustration of the implications of relational ethics as experienced in both his mother's and father's families;

in their relationship to each other; and ultimately in the interaction of David's personal development with the particular developmental challenges experienced by his parents. The situation of three children in foster placement facing another change in their attachments and living situation is assessed in relation to their different states of development and their loyalties. In both instances, Hibbs illustrates the relieving effects of this contextual analysis and interventions made on this basis.

The family life cycle has been a focus of interest and model making for almost 20 years. In Chapter 3, Zilbach presents her particular model and demonstrates its usefulness in evaluating problems experienced by families of young children. This general approach assumes that difficulties, whether experienced by individuals or families as a whole, have some kind of meaning, and often arise in the context of some developmental stresses on the family. Zilbach's model is a stage model. Most models of the family life cycle are based on individual development; the stages of the family are defined by one generation's activities. Zilbach's model emphasizes primary focal activities of the family members, and the stages are defined by explicit family movement rather than by individual developmental stages. Thus, Stage I, "coupling," can and does occur at many different points in individual lives, and there are central coupling issues that must be addressed, regardless of the individual developmental issues. Zilbach illustrates this fact with a vignette of a couple with children from previous marriages joining households. By the same token, Stages VI and VII of family development, categorized as "finishing," may also occur in families with young children, as Zilbach indicates in an example reported by Murray Bowen of children experiencing the loss of a parent.

This is, then, a particularly valuable perspective on the life cycle when working with young children, because it integrates all of the issues of joining and parting that occur in families, rather than using the development of the children themselves as the exclusive focus for family preoccupation and organization. An assessment of how a family is functioning in this framework is a useful part of the evaluation of any family with young children that is experiencing difficulties.

Chapter 4 deals with the question of child psychopathology and shows how the concept of psychopathology does and does not fit into a systems perspective. The argument examines psychopathology as a metaphor borrowed from medicine and pathology and questions its usefulness as a systemic concept. Efforts to explain dysfunction in relation to family functioning are traced from the family as pathogen to the family as a pattern context. The chapter concludes that, for the purposes of treatment, dysfunction in young children may be more usefully understood as a part of patterns of family interaction—and, in some cases, the family's interactions with larger systems—than as psychopathology in the youngsters. Some of these patterns and their treatment implications are illustrated.

The section itself, then, covers a range of topics relating to child and family development, dysfunction, and treatment. It invites the reader into a process of examining children and families together; it asserts that although theories about child development, psychopathology, and therapy have evolved about children in isolation from their family relationships, reviewing these concepts while keeping the family relationships in mind adds a richness that provides more options for a healthy intervention and a better chance for a satisfactory outcome of therapy.

1

The Child in Family Therapy: Guidelines for Active Engagement across the Age Span

RICHARD CHASIN, MD, AND TANYA B. WHITE, PhD

Over the past 30 years, the field of family therapy has made great strides in developing well-articulated theories and a rich repertoire of interventions. Less impressive is its development of techniques and practical guidelines for conducting sessions with families—*whole* families, including young children. In fact, in actual practice, children are more frequently excluded than included in family therapy.

This condition prevails even though some of the earliest family therapists had a special interest in children, and though over the years frequent reference has been made in the literature to the value of including latency-age and preschool children in family treatment (Augenbaum & Tasem, 1966; Bloch, 1976; Dowling & Jones, 1978; Keith, 1986; Zilbach, 1986). One clear advantage cited for the inclusion of children is that it makes them available to the therapist for direct intervention. Also, it is generally agreed—at least in principle—that the family cannot be well understood if some members living under the same roof are known only by hearsay. Moreover, those who include young children in sessions testify that each child brings to the session not only a separate viewpoint, but also uniquely evocative and contributory modes of communicating, often characterized by immediacy, spontaneity, and refreshing candor.

Many reasons have also been given for excluding children from therapy sessions. Children are omitted to protect them from information or actions that might

Richard Chasin. Family Institute of Cambridge, Watertown, MA; Department of Psychiatry, Harvard Medical School at Cambridge Hospital, Cambridge, MA.

Tanya B. White. Private practice, Lexington, MA; Department of Family Studies, Wheelock College, Boston, MA.

harm them (e.g., when the session is likely to focus on adult sexual relations or when the adults involved are in poor control of destructive impulses).[1] Children are excluded as a matter of course by therapists whose theoretical persuasions justify their working principally or entirely with adults and their families of origin (Bowen, 1978). Yet many who espouse approaches that call for direct observation and intervention with members of all generations omit children from most sessions in practice. Perhaps the most popular explanation they give for this omission is that the heart of the problem and the ultimate key to the solution lie in the parental subsystem; therefore, seeing the parents alone is the most efficient way to help the family.

All these reasons for excluding children seem sound. However, in many cases the explanation simply rationalizes the therapist's fear that effective simultaneous engagement of adults and children in therapy sessions is impossible. Therapists who work primarily with adults may worry that young children will become bored and resort to distracting behavior to gain adult attention (Villeneuve, 1979). Therapists accustomed to work with young children may worry that their repertoire of play techniques will engage the children but alienate the adults, who may fail to appreciate, for example, the value of finger painting in a family session. Moreover, some practitioners may be concerned that parents will feel demoralized by a therapist's expertise at understanding and relating to children. In fact, the more skillful the therapist is with the children, the more inadequate the parents may feel. Worse, some child therapists may bring to their work with families a stereotype about parents—for example, as destructive or as well-intended but inept at meeting their children's needs. Such a bias is likely to contribute to therapist anxiety and to parent alienation. Finally, some therapists are experienced and confident working with children *and* with adults, but not in the same session. They may resist including both because the techniques they use with adults and with children have so little common ground.

Our aim in this chapter is to provide practical guidance to therapists interested in developing techniques within that common ground—techniques with which active engagement of all family members, regardless of developmental level, can be promoted. We begin with practical suggestions about physical space and equipment. Next, we discuss play techniques that have served us well in our family work with young children. Finally, we present a model opening interview for families with young children. This model is intended not as a rigid procedure, but rather as a guiding support for therapists in their efforts to engage children and adults together in the therapeutic process.

Space

Most settings for family therapy are poorly designed for work with whole families. Generally, consulting rooms are furnished for either adults or children, but

---

[1] Ackerman (1966) and Dowling and Jones (1978) suggest reasons for including children even in these situations.

not both. In adult-oriented spaces, the chairs are often ideal for insight-oriented psychotherapy; they are large, immobile, and well-cushioned. In family therapy, however, such furnishings give the therapist little flexibility for moving people around. Moreover, small children may feel paralyzed when they sink into big soft chairs. Their feet hang in the air, and they can barely reach over the huge arms that surround them. The chairs make a child feel anxious about being a child. Making matters worse is the delicate dictating and recording equipment that is just one lurch away from the naturally curious child. The vulnerability of the equipment makes the therapist worry that the child may act like a child.

By contrast, some consulting rooms are designed for traditional play therapy. There, adults are sometimes cramped in child-sized chairs and may feel menaced by the presence of clay, paints, and other potential hazards to the fine clothing they may have worn to impress the interviewer. (For most children, the cornucopia of exciting toys typically provided in such an environment is likely to be more fascinating than the interview process!) The room is often too small for individuals and subsystems to establish comfortable distances from one another; crowding can be persistently stressful for disengaged families and can impede boundary formation with enmeshed families. Finally, walls are often tissue-thin; thus the therapist may inhibit useful but raucous communication during the family session, so that those in the adjoining room are not distracted, irritated, or frightened by the intruding noise.

The point here is that therapists must apply their sensitivity about context to the physical layout and materials of their working space. Too often, a therapist will assume an attitude of denial and passivity about these conditions and will neither comment on them to the family nor attempt to do anything about them. Even when little can be done about the physical circumstances, it will help to build an alliance with the family if the therapist points out the problems of the space and works with the family to minimize its hindrances.

Furnishings and play materials should accommodate both full family interaction and separate subgroup activities. An ideal physical space has four areas—one each for observation, time out, discussion, and play (see also Bloch, 1976; Chasin, 1981; Zilbach, 1986). A complex of four such areas affords many options: full togetherness, distance without physical isolation, observation without interaction, and total physical separation. The discussion and play areas should be composed of one large space partially divided by a movable screen. This space should be sparsely furnished with simple objects, such as movable chairs and large pillows. The flexibility of such furnishings allows the therapist to clearly shift focus from one subsystem to another; it also allows for a "stage" to be set for play enactments. The observation area should be big enough to accommodate professionals and family members simultaneously. Its one-way mirror should provide a good view of the discussion and play areas. Video equipment that can be controlled from either side of the mirror is extremely useful. A waiting room with an adjacent bathroom can serve as a time-out space. It should be cut off both visually and acoustically from all other areas, so that family members can temporarily withdraw from the interviewing activity.

The play area should be equipped with toys meeting the following criteria. First, they should be safe and nondistracting (i.e., not *too* fascinating). Toys should be excluded if they are dangerous to swallow, have sharp points or edges, or make loud, frightening noises. Second, the toys should lend themselves to play that children and grownups can all interpret. Generally, it is easier to make sense of what a child does with mother and father hand puppets than it is to decipher what he or she does with an open sack of marbles. Third, toys should lend themselves to active and creative play rather than obsessive, repetitive routines. Although any toy can be used spontaneously or obsessively, some toys, such as magnetic darts or even doll houses, tend to draw children away into evasive rituals. By contrast, a bataka (a fat, soft, harmless bat) rarely engenders that risk. Fourth, toys should allow for interaction between children and adults. Baby dolls will usually better serve that purpose than will puzzles that are designed for children to work with alone.

Perhaps even more important than the reservoir of toys one has is the choice one makes about which are to be made available for the session and which are to be left out of sight. The therapist should select toys according to the developmental stages of the children and to the issues being addressed by the family. For example, if the parents have been unable to manage the anger and neediness of a 3-year-old following the birth of a new sibling, the therapist might provide a baby doll, a blanket, family puppets, and a bataka or two to serve as harmless weapons. As the session moves along, more playthings can be offered; as any first-grade teacher can attest, it is easier to offer more later than to remove toys from a vast and delightful handy array.

Play

Therapists who work with young children rely on the revealing and therapeutic nature of the child's most natural activity: play. Yet they clearly appreciate the fact that not all types of play are equally revealing and therapeutic for all purposes. In this section, we describe the types of play that we have found to be most illuminating and engaging in sessions with families with young children, and we emphasize those forms of play that tend to be underutilized.

For the purposes of this discussion, we classify play along three continua: "distanced–involved," "nondirected–directed," and "imaginative–factual." Child therapists are typically trained to employ play techniques on the "left side" of these three continua (distanced, nondirected, and imaginative). Although these techniques have great value and are not to be abandoned in family work, we argue that techniques representing the "right side" have been insufficiently used.

Child therapy in the psychoanalytic tradition (Axline, 1969) tends to utilize drawing materials, clay, doll houses, and small rubber dolls in distanced play— play in which objects are often held at "arm's length," literally and sometimes experientially. Their manipulation by the child is interpreted by the therapist as revealing projection of intrapsychic and/or interpersonal issues. This interpretation then serves as the basis of intervention on the part of the therapist and the parents. In the less used involved play, on the other hand, the child *is* the toy and the action usually requires little interpretation. The child may play a role in an enactment using no toys, or perhaps (in a slightly distanced form) using only hand puppets. Such play is particularly well suited for work with families, as it can be used by both children and adults, and it ordinarily communicates emotionally engaging information in an intelligible way. Yet, like other forms of play, it provides a comfortable alternative to using words—a medium that is often ill suited for robust and clear communication across developmental levels.

Child therapists with a psychodynamic orientation typically employ nondirected play techniques. Such a therapist may offer the child materials (e.g., a crayon and paper) or may simply make available a stockpile of materials and tell the child to do whatever he or she pleases. Less frequently used directed play is clearly guided by the therapist. For example, a child might be asked to draw a particular picture (e.g., kinetic family drawing; Burns & Kaufman, 1972) or to enact a particular scene and play a particular role in it (e.g., "You're Dad at the dinner table and your brother is Mom, who has just arrived home late from work. Make up a skit that shows us what would happen if your parents got along exactly the way your mother wants them to").

Imaginative techniques generally involve the playing out of fantasies. Children may become kings or queens, monsters or animals; they may travel to nonexistent planets or brave wild, terrifying jungles. By contrast, factual play documents the actions and feelings of real people as they are now or could realistically be in the future (e.g., "Dad, be your daughter, and Mom, be the doctor. Show us what will happen at her checkup next week"). Factual play can be an easily comprehensible alternative to using words to explore real events.

The more traditional distanced, nondirected, and imaginative types of play are certainly valuable in many therapy contexts, including that of family therapy. Free drawing, as outlined by Zilbach (1986), is an example. The children work on their drawings while the adults are engaged in conversation to which the non-participating children may be closely attuned. Through the drawings, children may express their concerns about family relationships and "communicate family issues that might otherwise remain underground, or at least take much longer to be raised by adults" (Zilbach, 1986, p. 98). The drawings are interpreted both diagnostically and as clues to progress in family work.

However, there are many virtues to recommend the less traditional involved, directed, and factual types of play in the context of family therapy. To the extent that play is involved, families become actively engaged and display high levels of energy. To the extent that it is directed, it is efficient and to the point. To the extent that it is factual, it is directly informative about everyday life. Role playing usually exemplifies all three: It is always involved, it is usually directed, and it is often factual (although it can also be imaginative). Particularly notable among its virtues are the enthusiasm with which family members impersonate each other and the honesty with which they represent everyday life as it affects them. Of course, in these impersonations each family member may develop empathy for the person he or she plays, and may gain fresh perspectives by observing his or her own behavior as it is played by those affected by it.

Many family therapists employ role playing in some form or another, and its virtues are well documented in the literature—in Haley (1976), Minuchin (1974), Neill and Kniskern (1982), Papp (1980), and Satir (1964), to cite a few examples. In fact, role playing has been used by representatives of most approaches in family work. Behavior therapists have used it to shape parental responses to child misconduct (Bernal, Williams, Miller, & Reagor, 1972; Forehand, 1977). Even though systemic therapists rely heavily on questioning to increase family awareness of its own patterns, role playing (in the form of ritual) is sometimes prescribed as a homework assignment. Some systemic therapists (e.g., Coppersmith, 1985) direct elaborate symbolic rituals within the session to expand the family's awareness of its patterns and beliefs and to trigger family change. Strategic therapists generally do not include role playing in their sessions. A luminous exception is Cloe Madanes (1984), who may engage the family in a vivid dramatic enactment with a clear strategic purpose in mind. Most family therapists have one or two role-playing devices in their repertoire; some never use it at all. We believe it can be usefully employed in a wide range of ways in virtually any approach to family therapy, especially in sessions where children are included.

The following vignette is an example of an involved, directed, factual role play:

In the initial contact with the parents, the therapist was told that the identified patient, Pat, aged 9, was suicidal and was intensely jealous of and competitive with her younger sister, Sue, aged 6. Pat told her recently separated parents that she would remain silent in an individual or family session. After an initial interview with the parents, which established an urgent need for accurate assessment, the therapist chose to see the girls together, assuming that Pat could not resist talking in the presence of Sue.

After joining with both girls, the therapist introduced the idea that puppets could play the roles of family members. The girls became involved with the puppets immediately. At first the tone of the play was humorous, with much joking about the puppets' messy hair. "I'm not looking my best today," Pat said on behalf of the puppet, giggling. Eventually, each girl had a chance to enact the mother's response to Pat's unhappiness. Then the therapist, playing Pat, asked:

THERAPIST (as Pat): You know what I'm especially not happy about? Daddy's going away. Why did he go away?
SUE (as Mommy): I don't know. You'll have to ask him.

Pat later played herself, and spontaneously stated that Daddy went away because he fought with Mommy too much. The therapist suggested that the girls do a "Mommy and Daddy fight."

PAT (as Daddy, with a deep, pompous voice): Did you see anything in the paper today about acid rain?

SUE *(as Mommy, in an annoyed tone):* Don't ask me that, I never look at the paper. You should know that by now!

PAT *(as Daddy):* Well, you'd better start looking.

SUE *(as Mommy, angrily):* Don't tell me what to look at.

PAT *(as Daddy):* You're my wife.

SUE *(as Mommy):* You shouldn't tell me what to do even though I am your wife. We're not related except by marriage.

(The parent puppets hit each other throughout the scene.)

THERAPIST: That was very good. Want to do another one?

At this point Pat decided to be Mommy. Sue stated that Mommy should start the fight this time.

PAT *(as Mommy):* What were you doing last night?

SUE *(as Daddy, in a deep, long-suffering voice):* Working at the office.

PAT *(as Mommy, in a sarcastic tone):* With Carla?

SUE *(as Daddy):* No, I was working with Bill.

PAT *(as Mommy):* He doesn't work there any more.

SUE *(as Daddy, obviously evasive):* I mean I was working with what's-his-name.

PAT *(as Mommy):* I'm going to get my hair done tomorrow. I expect you to stay with the girls.

SUE *(as Daddy, importantly):* No. I've got an appointment.

PAT *(as Mommy):* I'm going right now. Goodbye.

SUE *(as Daddy):* Pat, I want you to take care of Sue. I have to go to a conference.

PAT *(as herself, with original little girl puppet, speaking in a high-pitched, panicky voice):* No, you have to stay here.

SUE *(as Daddy):* Well, get Sue. We'll all go to the conference.

PAT *(as herself):* No.

SUE *(as Daddy):* Well, I'll have to put you in bed. *(The father puppet angrily stuffs the girl puppets in a box)* Get in your bed. *(Starts to leave)*

PAT *(as Mommy, just coming home, accusingly):* What are you doing?

SUE *(as Daddy, defensively):* Ah, just going to check on something outside. Now that you're here, mind if I go to the conference?

PAT *(as Mommy):* I do mind! I just came back for my purse.

The girls were highly attuned to the parental battle. Their mutual awareness that they had been abandoned by their angry, self-involved parents was now obvious. Pat's distress about having to care for her younger sister when she was not getting sufficient nurturing herself was also apparent. This role play was highly informative to the therapist and to the parents, who saw a videotape of it. It also served to unite the sisters through helping each become aware that the other knew what was going on in the family; neither was alone with her distress. The bonds between them were strengthened by this method of revealing their shared misery.

Of course, role playing need not always be factual to be of value in family therapy. We offer here an example of an intervention (informed both by psychodynamic and structural theory) that used wildly imaginative play.

Bobby, aged 4, was the identified patient. Much to the disgust of his older brothers, he was encopretic. His language was immature and he spoke in a high-pitched register. An initial evaluation session had taken place with his parents, but for this second session, intended to be an intervention, only he and his brothers, Josh, 9, and Paul, 13, were included. The three boys were quite distanced from one another; they were hardly a team. Age differences were exaggerated. The youngest seemed immature, and the oldest acted as though he were further along in adolescence than he was. The older boys, who were struggling against expressing any of their own regressiveness, stated that they wished for Bobby to communicate better so they could play with him, so he could be a "member of their club." The therapist asked them if Bobby got more attention when he acted like a baby. Bobby exclaimed defensively, " I am not a baby," and said that he wanted to be 6 feet tall. The therapist stood him on a high stool, and Paul cooperatively measured himself against Bobby, demonstrating that Bobby was now the taller of the two.

The therapist, squatting beside Bobby, suggested that Bobby act as though he were the oldest brother who could tell the others what to do because they were smaller. He coached the other boys to do as Bobby ordered. Bobby, enjoying this new experience, ordered his brothers: "Poop in your pants!" They pretended to do so. Bobby went on, "Now poop in the toilet!" Both older boys made believe they were following Bobby's directions. Liberated from their fear of childishness, they laughed hysterically and then began to hit each other with batakas, but stopped obediently when Bobby yelled, "Hold it! Hold it!"

Through this enactment, enjoyable to all three boys, the brothers' status had been somewhat equalized. The therapist now suggested playing a game called "Poops." Each boy was asked to hold an object (a pillow or bataka) symbolizing a "poop," and jump into the sewer and find out what happens to poops as they swim through the drainage. With the intention of further demystifying the toileting process for Bobby and unifying a disengaged sibling subsystem, the therapist remarked, "I bet you didn't know your poops had this much fun together. I'm gonna interview each of these poops. What happened to you?" The boys offered wonderful stories about the years they'd spent in the sewer, and the therapist exclaimed, "Look at all these other poops, brother poops. A whole family of poops!" Bobby then excused himself, saying, "I have to go pee."

These are but two examples of the diverse uses of role play in family work with children.

A Model Opening Interview

In their attempts to incorporate adults and children into the therapeutic process, many therapists may understandably feel anxious: The sheer number of clients in the room places greater demands on them, not to mention the range of developmental abilities and concerns to which they must attend. Our purpose in outlining the structure of a model opening interview is to alleviate some of that anxiety—to provide a simple map for a therapist's journey. Undoubtedly, when therapists become highly familiar with the terrain, they will map out their own routes in accordance with their own styles and theoretical persuasions.

Before the Family Session:
Preliminary Contact with Parents

If at all possible, the initial phone call should involve both parents. Together, they can best provide information on which to base decisions about the first session. Most importantly, no matter who is the index patient, the therapist will need to decide during that phone call whether to begin by seeing the parents alone, the whole family, or some other individual or subgroup.

More often than not, we begin with the parents (or other responsible adults). If symptoms are mild and acute, a single session with parents may be used to empower them, through support and advice, to experiment successfully with fresh approaches to the problem. If so, the child will not be seen and thus will be spared the feeling that he or she caused the family to seek outside help. If symptoms are severe or long-standing, a preliminary meeting with parents can be used to take a careful and extended history of the family and its past attempts to solve the problem. This information is most efficiently gathered without young children present. A preliminary meeting with parents also provides an opportunity for the therapist to assess the parents, particularly with respect to their commitment to the work that may lie ahead, and gives the parents an opportunity to ask questions and express concerns about the expected course of assessment and treatment.

There are many important exceptions to the parents-first rule. We will see the family first if the initial phone contact or referral has indicated (1) that it is the family's wish to be seen first as a family; (2) that adequate background information has been, or can be, transmitted over the phone, obviating the need for an initial parent interview; and/or (3) that the parents feel secure enough to present the family directly to us. We may see a child first if the child so requests. Finally, we will see a child or children without parents first in an emergency situation in which the parents are unavailable.

The Family Interview

In presenting our model, we distinguish among six sequential phases: orientation, joining, goal statements, goal enactments, problem exploration, and advice to the family (Lee, 1986; Chasin, Roth, & Bograd, 1988). It may not prove possible to progress through all six phases in one session, especially in one 50-minute session. If two sessions are used, a natural breaking point between them is after goal statements and enactments, and before problem exploration. We recommend scheduling opening interviews for 1½ to 2 hours. Even then, it may prove difficult to complete all six phases in one meeting.

ORIENTATION

The first part of the interview, the orientation phase, involves the therapist sharing previously obtained information with the family and establishing rules and expectations. Since it is as important to engage young children in this phase as it is to engage older family members, the therapist must take care from the beginning to use language accessible to all participants. If at this stage (or any other stage) the parents or older children talk over the heads of the younger ones, the therapist can indicate that full engagement of the children is important by translating the remarks made by older family members into appropriate child language. This can be done by simplifying phraseology and altering voice pitch and volume; brevity, repetition, and phrasing questions to require only simple answers (Snow, 1972) are all useful strategies. The therapist can also take cues from the parents, many of whom understand quite well what type of language provokes responses from their children (Garnica, 1977; White, 1982). In general, we strive to make a habit of speaking in a family session in a manner that a 3-year-old with average language abilities can understand. We have included some examples of such language in our presentation of the model interview.

At the beginning of the interview, the therapist should introduce himself or herself and have family members introduce themselves by the names they prefer to be called. We suggest that parents offer their names first. This will affirm their authority and establish an appropriate tone for children, who may get anxious and silly if asked to start.

Next, some background information should be offered by the therapist about prior contacts with the parents or others (e.g., school personnel), the purpose of the meeting, and, in general, what may be expected in the session. Precise, carefully prepared information offered by the therapist at this juncture clarifies the nature of the meeting and makes it less threatening. Moreover, the therapist's openness can serve as a first intervention, modeling a standard of candor and clarity for the family.

In some cases, stating the purpose of the meeting will require reference to a child's "bad deed," but in those cases the therapist can demonstrate an interest in understanding all sides of the story. For example, a therapist may say to a child, "Your mother says that you have no friends, but she says that your father thinks you have friends and are kind to others practically all the time. So it might be important to talk about how to enjoy other children. It might also be important to find a way for your parents to agree." In describing his or her own goal, many therapists emphasize "learning more about the problem." We recommend a more forward-looking and corrective emphasis on "finding ways to make things better for everyone in the family."

We are dismayed that many therapists begin a first session by asking children, "Why do you think you are here?" This question often produces anxiety and defensiveness, since children may well feel blamed for whatever difficulties have brought the family into treatment. Such feelings should not be reinforced. Worse, the therapist may uncover that the parents have misled (or lied to) the children about the session. It is rarely a good idea to start a relationship by catching someone in a lie.

The second major part of the orientation phase is particularly important in work with family members of many developmental levels. It involves the establishment of rules. In work with young children alone, the therapist, as the only adult in the room, is assumed to be keeper of the rules. In work with adults or older children, most rules are implicitly understood. When parents, a therapist (or two), and young children work together, ambiguity about "who's in charge" can sabotage the meeting by disabling the parents and provoking (ostensibly) disruptive behavior on the part of young children. Therefore we strongly recommend that rules be clearly stated and that the authority for enforcing these rules be clearly delegated. Just as we counsel parents to provide clear limits in their daily parenting practice—secure boundaries within which their child's growth can proceed—we must also provide a similar space for growth through clear limits during therapy sessions.[2]

There are three types of rules that must be established in every case. These are rules of discipline, safety, and noncoercion. Parents and children often assume that the therapist will take responsibility for discipline. We recommend, however, that parents be asked to enforce the rules the family uses at home. Assigning the major responsibilities for discipline to parents emphasizes the boundary between the parental role and the therapeutic role, strengthens the parental position in the family hierarchy, and gives the therapist an opportunity to observe the way in which discipline is carried out in the family. The following example demonstrates the importance of clear delegation of authority.

A single mother, her 2½-year-old daughter, and her 6-month-old son arrived for their first family session at a pediatric clinic. Both children endured a few formal exchanges between the mother and the therapist. Then the baby began to scream and the little girl began to complain loudly ("I'm hungry," "I'm thirsty," "Let's go," etc.). She was offered a cup of water, which she spilled on the rug. She appeared to lose all control as she began to throw things around, and the mother did nothing to stop her.

A videotape of this part of the session was shown to a group of students, who were asked to comment on what they had observed. All expressed a deep concern

---

[2] There are only a few resources available to the therapist who is interested in limit setting as a safeguard. In his writing about the psychoanalytic treatment of children, Moustakas (1959) encourages definitive limit setting to provide a sense of security to the child, stating that limits provide the structure within which growth can occur. He suggests time limits, rules about safety, physical abuse, and leaving and returning to the room. Satir (1964), in discussing her conjoint work with parents and children, mentions a number of rules that should be stated during treatment to protect office equipment, as well as to provide structure for the sessions. Zilbach, Bergal, and Gass (1972) comment that the obligation to enforce standards of behavior must be reinforced. It is clear that a preliminary statement of expectations about conduct is valid in both child psychoanalytic and family therapy traditions.

for the mother's lack of intelligence, sensitivity, and executive control. When shown the next few minutes of videotape, the students were humbled.

The mother, referring to the noise and chaos in the room, asked the therapist, "Do you want me to get this under control?" The therapist said, "Yes." The mother instructed the girl to get the baby's bottle from the diaper bag and then to either draw with crayons or build with blocks. The baby drained the bottle. The little girl played with blocks—a model of composure, creativity, orderliness, and active concentration.

The mother's handling of the situation, her tone, and her language were all what would be expected from an honors graduate of Parent Effectiveness Training. Contrary to the students' hypotheses, she exercised effective control with intelligence and sensitivity. New explanations of the previous chaos emerged: The mother was in a pediatric setting, in which parents are frequently encouraged to stand back passively and let the doctor—the expert—take over. No wonder she expected the expert on child behavior to be in charge! How much simpler it would have been had the therapist begun by explicitly giving the task of discipline to the mother.

Safety ought to be established as a joint responsibility; that is, it should be the duty of every individual present to intervene to protect the physical safety of every other individual.

A noncoercion or "pass rule" gives each individual the right to decline to answer any question or follow any suggestion without giving a reason. This rule can be particularly comforting to children, who fear being "put on the spot," defenseless against intrusion by adults (Zilbach et al., 1972).

Other rules will need to be made, depending on the circumstances of the case. It may be important to establish with parents that no one is to be punished after the session for what is said and done in the session. In some cases, the therapist will want to make an agreement about confidentiality—for example, if he or she would like permission to discuss the case with school or court officials. In many cases, the therapist will suggest that family members agree not to share with others what happens in the session; family members can be offered an opportunity to review that commitment at the end of the session after they know what has transpired.

Finally, if the therapist wishes to tape the session, he or she should secure permission to make the tape and should offer the family an opportunity at the end of the session to discuss whether the tape is to be kept, and for what purposes it may be used. If a session with a family subsystem is taped, the participants should be allowed to determine which other family members, if any, may be allowed to view it. One should exercise common sense in these decisions, of course, and not let a 2-year-old veto a sensible parental decision.

In our experience, the proper establishment of rules and expectations at the beginning of a session need not be time-consuming, nor need it inspire feelings of inhibition. On the contrary, it takes little time and seems to be a very wise investment toward a therapeutic process that is highly productive, liberating, and comfortable for all involved.

The purpose of the joining phase of the interview is to establish an alliance with the family as a whole, with the key subsystems, and with each individual. When joining with children, it is important to avoid asking the sort of questions that children suffer through at gatherings of distant relatives: "How old are you? What is your favorite subject at school? You're in the first grade already—how nice!" Rather, the therapist should take clues from the child as to what the child is trying to express about himself or herself through clothing, jewelry, or hairstyle, for instance, and comment about these things. A well-worn pair of sneakers and a He-Man T-shirt are likely to be more important expressions of individuality for an 8-year-old boy than his preference for spelling over math. In this case, one might ask the boy, "Are you good at sports? Are you strong?"

Even better than a series of such comments and questions is an exercise that highlights the unique qualities or strengths of each family member. Such an activity will promote each individual's sense of feeling both esteemed and distinctive in the eyes of the therapist. Specifically, the therapist may say, "I'd like to hear from each of you something good about yourself—something you're good at doing or something you are proud of." Ordinarily, it is wise to ask the parents to comment first. If they boast, it will make everyone less shy.

STATING GOALS

Once rules have been agreed upon, and rapport has been established through joining, the interview may take one of a number of directions. Some interviewers prefer to work in an organic, seamless way, without predesigned, well-demarcated, explicit steps. They may use something that has happened in the rule-setting or joining phase as a springboard to the next topic. We prefer to maintain clear expectations and state precisely what we are attempting to do in each phase of the interview. Although it probably does not much matter just how obviously the interviewer shifts gears, the choice of the next step is vital for the success of the evaluation.

At this point, most clinicians ask the family to say what the problem is. Others give the family a general, exploratory, standardized task that is designed to reveal some aspect of family functioning or self-perception. For example, the family may be asked to do a kinetic family drawing to reveal how the family activity is perceived by all its members. Or the family may be asked to use blocks to show how the home is laid out. There are many such exercises available to therapists.

We believe that even after effective joining, many family members still feel quite unsafe. By focusing on the problem at that point, the therapist may foster a negative set in which people feel blamed, guilty, demoralized, and inept. Such a negative set, especially at this delicate juncture, endangers hopefulness and may undermine the family's exercise of its strength.

If a problem focus is too risky at this point, what is the difficulty with a general exploratory task? Since the family has had no opportunity to name its problem or its goal, its members may not grasp the object of performing a task that may seem totally unrelated to their distress. Also, the rapport established during joining may be diluted by the family's confusion and boredom.

A less risky step than moving to problem exploration, and one that is more obviously pertinent than most standardized tasks, is to ask the family members to specify their goals. Experienced clinicians know that such a task is often extremely difficult to accomplish. Families are much more likely to be obsessed with their distress than they are to have specific objectives in mind. Furthermore, many members are eager to complain to the therapist and to attack one another. In short, they may not be in a mood to be constructive. Some therapists think that unless one starts with and maintains a focus on "the problem," the family will lose its motivation. Undoubtedly this is true for some families. Nonetheless, seeking out family goals at this point in the evaluation has so much to recommend it that we think it is the best next step in most situations.

One of the virtues of making goal statements is its positive quality as an activity. Emphasizing what the family desires in the future, rather than the problems it is experiencing in the present, tends to circumvent blaming, discouragement, and deflation of the family's self-confidence. It also avoids giving the family the opportunity to attack a scapegoat; if this occurs at an early phase of the evaluation process, it can alienate the scapegoat and make other family members feel guilty and insecure. If the discussion of problems is subordinated to the subject of goals, then the troubled areas will reveal themselves less offensively as the unspoken, but often obvious, obverse of the goals.

A second virtue of stating goals is that it can be accomplished by anyone over the age of 3, particularly if one allows younger children to depict goals that seem trivial and private (e.g., "I want a stuffed bear"). This permissiveness frees older members from an obligation to sound intelligent by being abstract. For example, it allows the father to state that he "wants everyone to help to clear the table after dinner" rather than to state that he seeks an "atmosphere of cooperation."

Since eliciting goals is more easily said than done, we offer a few guidelines: First, the instructions should be clear and the task simple to fulfill. For example, the therapist may say, "I am going to give each person a chance to tell me one or two ways the family can be better than it is now. Remember what I said about the rules. You don't have to say anything if you don't want to. But each of you will have a chance if you want it. Who would like to start by saying one way the family could be better?"

Second, statements of goals are most helpful when they are concrete enough to be imagined, and general enough to have some breadth of meaning. The therapist may need to reframe the young child's overspecificity ("So you want a stuffed animal, something warm and cuddly like a stuffed animal"). The therapist may also lead adults from the general toward the specific (''Could you try to tell us what would happen if, as you say, harmony were to prevail?'').

Third, the therapist should encourage each family member to turn any complaint or blaming into a goal. For example, a complaining sibling may be told, ''You don't want your brother to hit you. OK. What do you want him to do instead?''

Fourth, the therapist should remove all pressure for comprehensiveness, as in this example: ''You don't have to say all the ways things could be better now. You'll have plenty of chances to tell me about other things later.''

And fifth, the therapist should not pressure the family for completion of the task if:

a. They seem incapable of putting anything in a positive frame, due to an overwhelming fixation on their pain and their problems.
b. The task seems to undermine their motivation—for example, if a peripheral father says, ''How can we talk about this junk when these savages are just destroying the family?''
c. The family is experiencing overwhelming stress (e.g., due to the recent death of one of its members) and it seems insensitive or disrespectful to talk about ''desires.''
d. The resistance to the task does not yield to gentle encouragement, even if the reason for the resistance is obscure.

In such situations the therapist should move on to problem exploration—for example, by saying, ''I don't think it was such a good idea for me to ask you first about what you want. What I think we should do instead is find out what it is that you are not happy about in your family. Afterward we can talk about what will make you happier.''

GOAL ENACTMENT

Once goals have been stated, the therapist can direct enactments of those goals. Ideally, separate enactments will be directed for each member's goal. The enactment of goals has distinct advantages. First, it promotes specificity and concreteness of objectives. When it is demonstrated what the family might look like and sound like when the goals are met, everyone can have exactly the same image of what each person wants. That image will be ''worth a thousand words.'' Second, it gives the family members a chance to rehearse how they want to be without necessarily feeling pressured to change in that way. For example, the therapist may say, ''Remember how your son showed us the way he wanted you to help him make things. Of course, this may not have anything to do with the problem you came about, and it may not be anything that we are going to work on in therapy, but let us complete the exercise anyway. So sit next to him and show him how he can put puppets on his hand as an example of your helping.'' After they do it, the therapist may say, "Johnny, is he doing it all right? Is this what you meant?"

Suppose Johnny's goal is for the family to get him a stuffed animal. The therapist can encourage enactment by saying, "Johnny, it's OK not to be fancy. You think the family would be better if you had a stuffed animal. That's a fine goal. Here is a pillow. Make believe it is a stuffed animal. Can you show me who would give it to you, what you would to with it, and how the family would be better if you had it? Let's start with who would give it to you." If he points to his mother, the therapist may say, "Make believe you are your mother and that your mother is you. Give her the animal just the way you would want her to give it to you."

In some situations the therapist may decide against separate enactments, and instead design and direct the family in a single role-played minidrama that incorporates the goals stated by each family member. The following vignette provides an example of such an integrated enactment.

George, 11, the index case, seems depressed to his parents and teachers. In the second phase of the interview, each family member states goals:

FATHER: I want George to show more enthusiasm. It would demonstrate that he isn't depressed.
MOTHER: I want mealtimes to be calmer, with no fighting, and I'd like the boys to help me with it. After it is served, everyone should discuss current events while eating. I want Alice to sleep through the night instead of having nightmares and coming to my bed.
BILL (14): I want George to be more enthusiastic.
GEORGE (12): I wish Bill would want to do more with me.
ALICE (4): I want not to be afraid at night. I want to feel good and sleep at night.

The therapist constructs and directs a scene in which the family's goals have been achieved. He does this by explaining privately to each family member the role he would like them to play. For example, Bill is instructed to show interest in George's ideas if they can include him. No family member knows what the whole scenario will look like until it is played out. The enactment proceeds as follows:

The whole family is at home. George has arrived and is expressing to his father and Bill wild enthusiasm about his recent visit to a computer fair. Bill says he is eager to go there with George the next day. The mother, with that cue, announces dinner and thanks the boys for preparing it. During dinner the father mentions a newspaper article about someone who attempted murder and was released on $500 bail. Everyone has something to say about the event.

The therapist dims the lights for bedtime. Alice lies down on a couch with a blanket, as if safe in her bed. The therapist assures her that she is very comfortable. She now overhears the rest of the family talking softly about how nice it is that she has been sleeping through the night recently. Her father jokes that the electric bills are lower; her mother and both brothers comment upon how good it is that they can all get a good night's sleep now, and that Alice is so grown up.

When the therapist turns up the lights and announces that it is morning, Alice bounds excitedly from bed and rushes to her mother to tell her about the wonderful dream she had that night about swimming without her water wings.

When the enactment is over, the family members seem light-hearted and pleased with themselves. Following some further exploration of family problems, the therapist tells them that there is no need for further meetings as this point. At follow-up 4 months later, George's and Alice's symptoms have disappeared. The father seems depressed and unenthusiastic about his work, however; he has been putting off a career decision for a year.

PROBLEM EXPLORATION

By the time this phase occurs, the therapist already has a great deal of information. Family members have discussed their strengths, expressed their wishes, and experienced their goals psychodramatically. Thus, the phase of problem exploration can begin with a sense that the therapist is informed and the family feels understood. Furthermore, the therapist is in a good position to determine which manner of problem exploration will be most likely to succeed with the family.

The object of this phase is for the therapist to fill in whatever gaps of information remain after the prior phases. By the end of the problem exploration phase the therapist should have answers, or at least good hunches, about the following:

1. Whether there exists a problem requiring urgent attention.
2. What principal cycles or redundant sequences of behavior are associated with the family's distress and/or developmental impasse.
3. When and in what context these problems emerge.
4. What attempts have been made to solve problems, with what results.
5. What belief systems seem to prevent the family from discovering a solution.

The problem exploration phase involves two steps.

Step 1. In most instances, this phase should begin either with a relatively nonthreatening but revealing family task, or with a series of descriptions and enactments that depict the "dreaded future" (i.e., what the family members fear might happen if things do not improve). Nonthreatening standardized tasks are a good choice when the family has preschool children who can easily and fruitfully join in such activities, or when it is already obvious what the family most fears about the future. The "dreaded future" task may be selected with families in which there are older children, and with families whose fears about the future are obscure.

Examples of nonthreatening tasks are the kinetic family drawing task, in which each family member sketches a picture of the family doing something, and a building task, in which the family makes a structure together using blocks. Such tasks and a brief open discussion of them will ordinarily provide the therapist (and the family) with abundant information without creating much stress.

The second alternative can be painful, but is almost always worth the strain. In role-playing the "dreaded future," the same principles and practices of enactment apply as in the enactment of an improved future. The principal virtue of enacting the dreaded future is that it provides detailed information about the family's current problems without blaming anyone for past or current misdeeds. It is a nightmare fantasy, not a damning, well-documented indictment. A secondary benefit is that explicit visions of a dreaded future defeat denial and stimulate motivation for change.

However, in a few cases, the therapist may feel that such enactments are implicitly so maligning to a scapegoated family member that the therapist may wish to give each family member an opportunity to set the record straight. Ordinarily, however, it is best to allow these "enacted fears" to stand unchallenged and to remind the family that these worries are simply concerns about the future and *not* portrayals of actual current or past events. If the therapist does permit protests about "unfair representations," then corrections should be briefly and simply stated and not pursued unless they seem to be a fitting subject for the second step of this phase.

In the following vignette, fears about the future were of paramount concern. Only a few symptoms of anxiety existed at the time the family sought therapy.

The mother requested a consultation for herself and her anxious 3-year-old daughter, Beth, who in the next few weeks would be facing several events, each one of which the mother felt Beth could handle; in combination, however, these events threatened to overwhelm the little girl. Beth was to witness her (single) mother giving birth to a sibling; lose a grandparent to illness; visit her (divorced) father, who had just moved to another city; and face a few other new and potentially frightening experiences.

At first the mother played Beth going from one event to the other, getting increasingly frightened and flustered. Beth laughed, but showed interest and curiosity. Beth said she would like to try playing out these occurrences. The therapist suggested that she use toys and puppets to enact her role in each event, in the order in which the events were likely to occur. The therapist used different parts of the room to symbolize each event and walked Beth through them in sequence. Beth then re-enacted each one by herself, with a sense of relaxation and mastery over her anticipated itinerary. It was like learning a nursery rhyme.

Step 2. The second step of the problem exploration phase involves focused questioning of family members by the therapist or still further simple enactments designed to gather any remaining data the therapist needs to arrive at a provisional assessment of the family predicament. This step is likely to be brief, as few gaps of crucial information are apt to persist at this point.

If one uses verbal inquiry at this point, simple and direct questions may be perfectly adequate. However, those therapists familiar with circular questioning

(Penn, 1982) will ordinarily use that mode of investigation for the extra richness of information it gives to the therapist and family.[3]

A sharply focused directed enactment may also be helpful in this stage of the problem exploration. The following vignette provides an example of problem exploration through simple enactments of the past and present, and also demonstrates the value of our earlier recommendations that the consulting room be large and flexibly furnished.

In attendance at the session were 10 family members: the mother and her three children from a previous marriage; the father and his four children from a previous marriage; and the father's mother, who lived with the family. The presenting problem was hostility between the father's 8-year-old son and the mother's 9-year-old son, who, with great bitterness, shared a bedroom. Problem exploration in this case involved, among other things, investigating the costs to the children of the new "blended" family.

The therapist said, "Let's go back to see what your households looked like 2 years ago [before the meeting of the parents]." He asked each original family to use separate sides of the room and a collection of pillows to map out their homes and to depict relationships within each of the original families through enactments of typical activities. Then, in a third part of the room, the family laid out their current living arrangements, with children grouped not by family of origin, but by age and sex. When asked to depict relationships in the blended family, it was clear to everyone that an enormous amount of strain and conflict had arisen from the abrupt reshuffling of roommates and the abandonment of each separate family's traditions in favor of a new image created by the new couple. It was evident that the children were still loyal to the values of their original families, and were struggling mightily against the couple's new family image.

ADVICE TO THE FAMILY

In the final phase of the interview, the therapist should offer the family a synopsis of findings and a recommendation about further evaluation or treatment. No therapist should feel obligated to deliver this statement without pause for private reflection. There is no harm done if the therapist leaves the room for a few minutes to prepare this summary statement. A therapist who is not working with

---

[3] Some therapists will want to use action "probes" to supplement this phase. These tasks, given by the therapist to the family, are designed to test the therapist's hypotheses about what age-appropriate, constructive behavior patterns are *outside* the family's repertoire. For example, if the family appears to have disabling problem-solving patterns, the therapist might say, "Talk together about where to eat on the way home." No matter how the family performs, it can be congratulated for completing the task. Even if the family members talk irrelevantly and angrily, pay no attention to each other, and in general fail to make any progress with the task, the therapist can still say, "Thank you for doing what I asked you to do. It was very helpful." It *was* helpful: It confirmed a hypothesis about the family's limited repertoire of problem-solving techniques, and provided information about how the family failed in its attempts to carry out the task.

a team should at least give himself or herself (and the family) the benefit of self-consultation.

The summary statement should include the following:

1. A respectful acknowledgment of the family's strengths.
2. A brief summary of the family's wishes and fears.
3. One or two hypotheses that benignly connect the family's current problems with well-intended and wise traditional (but currently ineffective) family patterns of thought and behavior.
4. A clear recommendation for future action, with a very brief rationale for it.

Conclusion

Our aims in this chapter have been to encourage therapists to recognize the virtues of including *whole* families in family therapy sessions, and to provide practical guidelines and techniques to support their attempts to do so. We expect that as therapists increasingly venture into this challenging area of practice, their work will become more rewarding.

Many of our recommendations speak directly to the issue of "active engagement." We recommend that consulting rooms be large and flexible so they can function as stages on which wishes, fears, and factual family interactions can be played out. We recommend that materials be offered that encourage intelligible play—play that can be interpreted not only by the therapist, but also by the family members. We recommend assessment and intervention techniques that are as boredom-resistant as possible: Who will be bored watching himself or herself being played by another family member? We recommend clarity of rules and expectations—boundaries within which truthfulness can freely, safely, and actively unfold before the eyes of family members and therapist alike. And, finally, we offer a model for assessment interviewing to guide clinicians who feel eager but unsure about conducting engaging and effective family sessions with children.

REFERENCES

Ackerman, N. W. (1966). *Treating the troubled family.* New York: Basic Books.
Augenbaum, B., & Tasem, M. (1966). Differential techniques in family interviewing with both parents and preschool child. *Journal of the American Academy of Child Psychiatry, 5,* 721–730.
Axline, V. M. (1969). *Play therapy.* New York: Ballantine Books.
Bernal, M. E., Williams, D. E., Miller, W. H., & Reagor, P. A. (1972). The use of videotape feedback and operant learning principles in training parents in management of deviant children. In R. D. Rubin, H. Festerheim, J. D. Henderson, & L. P. Ullmann (Eds.), *Advances in behavior therapy.* New York: Academic Press.
Bloch, D. A. (1976). Including the children in family therapy. In P. Guerin (Ed.), *Family therapy* (pp. 168–181). New York: Gardner Press.
Bowen, M. (1978). *Family therapy in clinical practice.* New York: Jason Aronson.

Burns, R. C., & Kaufman, S. H. (1972). *Actions, styles and symbols in kinetic family drawings (K-F-D)*. New York: Brunner/Mazel.

Chasin, R. (1981). Involving latency and preschool children in family therapy. In A. Gurman (Ed.), *Questions and answers in the practice of family therapy* (pp. 32–35). New York: Brunner/Mazel.

Chasin, R., Roth, S., & Bograd, M. (1988). *Dramatizing ideal futures and reformed pasts in systemic family therapy*. Unpublished manuscript.

Coppersmith, E. I. (1985). "We've got a secret!": A nonmarital marital therapy. In A. S. Gurman (Ed.), *Casebook of marital therapy* (pp. 369–386). New York: Guilford Press.

Dowling, E. & Jones, H. (1978). Small children seen and heard in family therapy. *Journal of Child Psychotherapy, 4,* 87–96.

Forehand, R. (1977). Child non-compliance to parental requests: Behavioral analysis and treatment. In M. Hersen, R. M. Eisler, & P. M. Miller (Eds.), *Progress in behavior modification* (Vol. 5, pp. 111–143). New York: Academic Press.

Garnica, O. (1977). Some prosodic and paralinguistic features of speech to young children. In C. Snow & C. Ferguson (Eds.), *Talking to children: Language input and acquisition* (pp. 63–88). Cambridge, England: Cambridge University Press.

Haley, J. (1976). *Problem solving therapy: New strategies for effective family therapy*. San Francisco: Jossey-Bass.

Keith, D. V. (1986). Are children necessary in family therapy? In L. Combrinck-Graham (Ed.), *Treating young children in family therapy* (pp. 1–10). Rockville, MD: Aspen.

Lee, R. (1986). The family therapy trainer as coaching double. *Journal of Group Psychotherapy, Psychodrama and Sociometry, 39*(2), 52–57.

Madanes, C. (1984). *Strategic family therapy*. San Francisco: Jossey-Bass.

Minuchin, S. (1974). *Families and family therapy*. Cambridge, MA: Harvard University Press.

Moustakas, C. E. (1959) *Psychotherapy with children*. New York: Harper & Row.

Neill, J. R., & Kniskern, D. P. (Eds.). (1982). *From psyche to system: The evolving therapy of Carl Whitaker*. New York: Guilford Press.

Papp, P. (1980). The use of fantasy in couples' group. In M. Andolfi & I. Zwerling (Eds.), *Dimensions of family therapy* (pp. 73–90). New York: Guilford Press.

Penn, P. (1982). Circular questioning. *Family Process, 21*(3), 267–279.

Satir, V. (1964). *Conjoint family therapy*. Palo Alto, CA: Science & Behavior Books.

Snow, C. E. (1972). Mothers' speech to children learning language. *Child Development, 43,* 549–565.

Villeneuve, C. (1979). The specific participation of the child in family therapy. *Journal of the American Academy of Child Psychiatry, 18*(1), 44–53.

White, T. B. (1982). *A developmental sociolinguistic study of the doctor register*. Unpublished doctoral dissertation, Boston College.

Zilbach, J. J. (1986). *Young children in family therapy*. New York: Brunner/Mazel.

Zilbach, J. J. Bergel, E., & Gass, C. (1972). Role of the young child in family therapy. In C. J. Sager & H. S. Kaplan (Eds.), *Progress in group and family therapy* (pp. 385–399). New York: Brunner/Mazel.

2

The Context of Growth: Relational Ethics between Parents and Children

B. JANET HIBBS, MFT, PhD

David was 20 months old when his mother first requested a therapy appointment for advice about him. She was concerned about David's apparent preference for the babysitter, rather than his parents. Bess was an older woman who had been with David 3 days a week since he was 3 months old. Both Mr. and Mrs. Gold were attorneys in their mid-30s, and David was their only child. David, his mother, and his father attended the family session. David was quite at ease, and spent the time playing and going from the mother to the father with toys, finally resting in his mother's lap.

David's father did not agree with his wife that David's attachment to the babysitter was unusual, and he was not worried by it. However, when asked whether he or his wife would be upset if their son had a strong attachment to either grandmother, Mr. Gold replied, seriously, "We'd kill her."

Although this may appear to be a simple case of the "worried well," an instance to be managed with reassurance and advice, it is an excellent example of the delicate and continuous process of balancing relational ethics in the family of a young child. For David, there were important implications of his obligation to please and complement his mother on her terms, while still free to develop other relationships. The mother wondered with whom she had ever been "first"—with her parents, her spouse, her child? To whom could she turn for acknowledgment

B. Janet Hibbs. Center for Contextual Therapy at Philadelphia, Philadelphia, PA; Department of Mental Health Sciences, Hahnemann University, Philadelphia, PA.

of her efforts and her pain? The father, for his part, had to ask himself how he could satisfy his wife's needs and maintain his own sense of well-being.

Another area of concern was that of the Golds' distant relationships with their own parents. The Golds wanted to "protect" David from having too close a relationship with his grandparents. What about the avoided grandparents? What was their side, and how did their right to get to know their grandson and his right to receive care from them figure in this? Questions such as these are some of the practical problems of relational ethics—ones that demand an understanding of the process of development in the context of relationships between parents and children across generations.

This chapter focuses on the give-and-take between parents and children that shapes meaning; this is the contextual approach. This approach, developed by Ivan Boszormenyi-Nagy (Boszormenyi-Nagy & Krasner, 1986; Boszormenyi-Nagy & Spark, 1973) and colleagues (Cotroneo, 1986), incorporates systemic interactions and the intrapsychic activity with the dialectic of relational ethics between persons. From this perspective, relational ethics, which is a unique contribution of contextual therapy, shapes the meaning-making activity of development.

The construction of meaning occurs within the individual in making sense of the realm "between" persons. Kegan (1982) has suggested that the primary evolutionary task of development is the ongoing task in which both children and parents are simultaneously engaged: the meaning-making activity of growth. Every individual psychology (with the possible exception of strict behaviorism) "directs us in some way to this zone of mediation where meaning is made" (Kegan, 1982, p. 2). That zone may be more sharply defined as "within" the person (the intrapsychic) or viewed from the outside (the cognitive activity of meaning making). As Kegan (1982) observes, child development has been examined from the Freudian, developmental perspective of individually experienced meaning from within, and the Piagetian, constructivist perspective of subject-object balance from without. He concludes that despite their different emphases, Freud and Piaget each were interested in the development of meaning making.

Family theory, invested in freeing developmental from a static, linear notion of growth, has also struggled with the zone of mediation of meaning. Family therapy began with a rejection of its heritage of finding meaning "within," and advocated for finding meaning "between" individuals in the system. This took the form of addressing the experience of present made meaning "between" persons in the multiperson system, rather than "within" the intrapsychic sphere. Systems theory has taught us that both a child and his or her family members will change in response to each other. This is illustrated in the attachment studies of the family therapy literature (reviewed by P. Minuchin, 1985), which enlarged their scope from the traditional individual and mother–child dyad to encompass the triad of father or siblings and the larger family system.

Yet, like individual psychologies, family therapy has also divided into constructivist and developmentalist camps. Constructivists in family theory (most notably S. Minuchin, 1974) emphasize the "here-and-now," horizontal experience of relationships. Minuchin focuses on the outside activity that generates the form, asserting that family structure organizes internal experience and behavior. This approach resembles Piaget's emphasis on the mastery of outside experience leading to the making of individual meaning. Like Piaget's, this approach obscures the "within" for each family member. Developmentalists, on the other hand (such as Bowen, 1978), have investigated the origins and processes by which the individual's meaning within the family has come to be. This honors the inner experience of meaning making, yet does not fully offer an integration of the spiral of the within and the between. We are left with polarities of present and past: activity generated from outside the individual, in the social and family system, and activity generated from within the individual. Another organizing principle is needed to incorporate the meaning making of the individual within a dialogic systems model.

This chapter proposes that contextual theory offers such a metatheory, which can serve as a bridge for the stranded family theories. This bridge addresses meaning making within the developmental dialectic between parents and children, and how that dialectic is informed by relational ethics between the generations. This approach takes a resource-oriented stance, which recognizes that some made meanings are more growth-producing or growth-inhibiting than others.

This chapter integrates the dialectical, ethical tasks of growth for the child and the family, as posited by Boszormenyi-Nagy and colleagues. The ethical dimension of contextual theory incorporates fair claims and balances between family members. Here the growth of an individual (whether adult or child) is seen as inseparably related to his or her capacity both to give and to receive care, in a way that leaves no one (whether adult or child) burdened by either chronic overgiving or overtaking. A description of the major concepts of the contextual approach is followed by a discussion of the implications of these observations for therapy in families with young children. From the contextual point of view, growth (or impediments to it) is shaped by the relational context of the individual, which serves as the starting point.

The Context of Growth: Claims and Balances

Relational Context

An infant is born into a unique 'relational context." This concept refers to more than the mere family arrangement in which an infant is raised. Children grow up in many types of family constellations. Some are raised by both biological parents to maturity. Others are raised primarily by one parent, or by a grandparent or relatives; they may have a visiting relationship or no relationship with other family members. Others are adopted or raised for a time in foster care. Yet all children, despite later circumstances are linked both horizontally and vertically by birth to their relational context.

Here the use of "context" differs from its common meaning of social circumstances surrounding an action or behavior (Cotroneo, 1986). Rather, the term used in the relational sense refers to the facts and circumstances we inherit by being born male or female, first or last, black or white, and so on, into a particular family, with its inherent resources and limitations. It includes what is unique to each of us and what we have in common with our familial, ethnic, cultural, and religious rootedness. This connection, based on birth, is built up by the balances of give-and-take between family members, and by the consequences of actions or behaviors, whether these acts are trustworthy or exploitative. The child's relational context will be the source, not only of life, but of meaning itself. It is "meaning-making" in the sense that present experience unfolds as the continually expressed result of past and present relational context. As such, context lays the foundation for future relating. Its dimensions are the factual, the psychological, the systemic, and the ethical.

The infant is entitled to his or her biological family relationships simply because the infant has been born into those relationships. This is an ethical axiom.

> Family relationships are empowered by the fact that members *are* connected by birth. They are empowered only secondarily by what family members *do* for each other. . . . Existence itself speaks to the meaning and significance of the connectedness between parent and child, which constitutes an actual or potential resource for care for a child. (Boszormenyi-Nagy & Krasner, 1986, p. 8)

Regardless of the arrangement in which a child grows up, the care or lack of care the child receives from his or her biological parents and family will be part of his or her meaning making and is likely to express itself developmentally. This premise, which underscores a child's reality, is not sufficiently acknowledged either in the literature on child development or in the problem-oriented treatment of families with children. Instead, basic resources for a child's growth are viewed as intrapsychically dependent on attachment to a primary caregiver, or as systemically dependent on an adequate parental subsystem. In either instance, the caregiver or the parental subsystem may or may not be part of the child's primary, biological reality. Why is this important?

Theoreticians (Boszormenyi-Nagy & Krasner, 1986; Cotroneo, 1986;) have proposed a nonconditioned, inherent mechanism, which is expressed early in life and may be growth-producing or inhibiting. This mechanism, which Nagy calls "filial loyalty," refers to the child's early and growing recognition that he or she has received parental care (even if it is limited to the acts of conception, pregnancy, and birth) and to the child's corresponding efforts to discharge loyalty commitments. Research confirms this mechanism, as Kagan (1981) reports that children as young as 2 years of age "invent an obligation" to meet an adult's standard. This self-obligation can be expressed instrumentally or affectively. Loyalty speaks to the connectedness (whether robust or tenuous) to one's relational context, and has implications for growth.

Loyalty

The concept of "loyalty," as first defined by Boszormenyi-Nagy and Spark (1973), refers to expectations shared by the family, the community, and society at large, which are transmitted from generation to generation through the family. Its referent is not the psychological feeling of allegiance to country or group membership, or even to an individual, as Cotroneo (1986) has articulated. Its referent is ethical. Loyalty speaks to a person's obligation to care about those who have made investments in him or her, which have resulted in the person's birth and rearing. Loyalty commitments take the form of expectations shared by family members for reciprocal care and consideration due another family member, based on the balance of care, both given and received. These expectations are passed on from generation to generation, from parent to child. We are born into, develop, and transmit loyalty expectations.

The basis of loyalty commitments is the fact that we are born in need of care (Cotroneo, 1986). Loyalty is the means of repaying our indebtedness for the massive investment of care we need and have received for survival, however imperfect that care may have been. If filial loyalty emanates from the act of our birth and the facts of our care, then parental expectations for filial devotion arise from the one-sided investments made in our care. Parents' expectations of what children owe them are also rooted in the circumstances of what parents were expected to give (and did in fact give) their own parents, and whether those loyalty expectations were fair or unfair.

Loyalty expectations can be growth-enhancing or growth-inhibiting. If parents can appropriately invest in a child's well-being, that child will be free to invest in his or her own continued growth, as well as to offer age-appropriate consideration to his parents. That child will also be free as he or she matures to make loyalty commitments outside the immediate family—to other relatives, to peers, and later to mate and children. This is an expression of positive loyalty. If for some reason parents cannot make appropriate investments in the child's well-being, that child will develop a growth-inhibiting, negative loyalty. Negative loyalty expressions can be seen both in overdevoted, sacrificial giving and in "acting-out" behavior. Loyalty, then operates positively if a child has received enough care and negatively if a child has not.

A child's loyalty commitments take into account the child's relational context, of biological parents and family, as they constitute part of his or her "shared self." Whether this self is "good" or "bad" is partly based on the meaning a child is able to make regarding whether he or she received sufficient care and offered (age) appropriate care to the people who invested care in him or her. A child's assessment of the care he or she has offered and received is an important part of meaning making, which is subject to developmental cognitive and emotional shifts. This assessment, based on factual events of give-and-take and perceptions of fairness, finally cannot be based solely on any one individual's definition; it requires a dialectical integration of each person's terms for fairness, for parent and child or adult child alike. Next, an understanding of the justice system in the family helps in determining the claims to which parents and children are entitled (i.e., who has a right to expect what from whom).

The Family Justice System

Loyalty is based first on the connection of birth, and second on what family members do for each other. The expression of loyalty (whether positive or negative) is based on the balance of give-and-take between family members. The capacity to make fair claims for oneself while considering the well-being of others is an expression of earned "entitlement." Entitlement is earned by the offer of due care in relationships. It gives a family member the right to make claims for care for himself or herself. Whereas a child's birth entitles him or her to claim caring from the parents, the parents' investment in the child entitles them to loyalty expectations. Whereas a parent earns entitlement by his or her acts of care for the child, that child is obligated by filial loyalty, which takes the form of the child's caring about the parent. Efforts to discharge filial loyalty commitments flow from child to parent. The family justice system is this management of the balances of give-and-take between family members.

A premise of growth that Erikson (1968) makes explicit is that the child has a "claim" on "the next average expectable environment" in a "sequence of 'expectable' environments" (p. 222). To the extent that parents are responsible for providing that next expectable environment, this premise may be applied to justice issues between parent and child. What is owed between parent and child? Kegan (1982) metaphorically refers to parent and child as "host" and "guest." This less emotionally charged referent allows us to engage in a little imaginative play. What does a host owe a houseguest? A warm welcome? Dinner? Some privacy? A farewell in the morning? Many books of etiquette have been written on the topic. All are in basic agreement that when hosting begins as a unilateral offer of care, it carries responsibilities to attend to the guest. The guest also has some reciprocal, though different, responsibilities to offer consideration to the host. In the family, this etiquette between parent and child is a matter of justice: "The justice system of the family is the configuration of giving and receiving that takes its shape from family relating, either through actions that benefit others or actions that exploit them. . . . In terms of simple justice each of us is required at times to be giver, at times receiver" (Cotroneo, 1986, p. 418).

The focus on the facts of give-and-take, as well as on the relational consequences of benefit or burden, takes justice out of the illusory realm of perceived differences or competing individual needs. Justice between family members is based on the reality that no one can keep giving without receiving in return. Justice also requires that family members cannot indefinitely accept care without reworking this imbalance by offering care in return. The continual give-and-take between family members registers as individual accountings of what one has given and what one has received. The balance of giving and receiving can be positive and interpreted as a trust resource for the future, or negative when exploitation has occurred.

Why, if the balances of give-and-take register in both children and adults, do we see people acting in apparently destructive ways? When we have expended ourselves offering care, we are entitled to receive care. If we do not receive care within the context in which it was offered, this registers as an injury: "Care manifests itself in the physical and emotional tasks of caretaking. . . . Someone's concern for us is the magnet of our reciprocal concern. When we do not experience another's concern for us, we tend to withdraw from the attempt of reciprocity in order to 'take care of ourselves' " (Cotroneo, 1986, p. 416).

Depending on the nature of the injustice suffered and its consequences, children, as they grow up, will develop justice-seeking behavior, which reflects and attempts to right prior imbalances of give-and-take. This quest for justice takes place first within the original relational context, then, failing the restoration of justice, outside of it. The intersection of cognitive maturity, prior loyalty expectations, and the nature of justice within our own families shapes our expectations of what we deserve for ourselves. If one has experienced injustice within the family, injustice is likely to continue as a "norm for relating outside the family," as Cotroneo has indicated (1986, p. 418) This norm of injustice may take the form of low entitlement—expecting that one is obliged to give and not to receive. Here the self becomes the object of exploitation. It may also take the form of destructive entitlement—expecting that one can receive with no obligation to give in return. Here others become the objects of exploitation.

To the extent that a person exploits care, that person loses the freedom to ask for himself or herself, as trust is diminished. Often justice-seeking behavior is directed outside the originating family context onto new trust resources, whether mate, children, or peers. It becomes apparent that justice issues in the present (between two generations of parent and child) often have a referent to a third generation.

Thus the balance or imbalance in the family justice system is reflected in how each individual experiences his or her entitlement to give and receive care, both within and outside the family. The imbalance of give-and-take in relationships can turn trust resources into mistrust. In contextual therapy, a primary action component involves the rebuilding of trust resources between family members.

Trust Resources

The internalization of basic trust has been considered a fundamental stage in a child's development (Erikson, 1963). However, trust is not a static commodity, gained in infancy and stable for life. It is continually earned, based on the fair exchange between relating partners, which flows between parent and child from one generation to the next. This conceptualization of "trust" as ethically linked to fairness between family members differs from its psychological, individual meaning of whether someone can be believed or relied upon. In the contextual approach, a resource orientation offers options for mobilizing trust. Trust is shaped by acts of care, both given and received. It is also dependent on one person's crediting the other person for actual offers of care, however small that investment may seem. Care or the lack of care creates the dynamics of trust and balances of justice, which can facilitate or inhibit growth. The contextual orientation to growth attends to the resources for trust building. Here the term "contextual resources" refers to those relationships in which trust has been invested for care, or exploited in mistrust. It presumes that resources for care exist in any relational context, even those characterized by mistrust.

This raises the question of where resources come from: self, spouse, grandparent, child? What trust resources do parents have to meet children's claims, as well as their own? To what claims are children entitled, at what age or stage of growth? To what claims are parents entitled? The next section of this chapter examines the implications of contextual theory for the therapy of families with young children.

Early Childhood

Although it is not the purpose of this chapter to describe in detail developmental stages (see Kegan, 1982), it is important to keep in mind that each family member, parent and child alike, is simultaneously in his or her own evolutionary loop, crisis, or truce at any given moment of development. These loops are always intersecting, uniquely shaping how loyalty is expressed and how the balances of fairness are established between individuals in the family, and so adjusting and readjusting the family justice system. The first intersection of child and parent development occurs with the infant's task of differentiating himself or herself while remaining attached to the mother and father.

The first formative experience has been described variously as the establishment of basic trust (Erikson, 1963) and the "incorporative balance" (Kegan, 1982). Broadly outlined, the task is for the infant to simultaneously emerge from this state and be successfully held within it by the parents. This is an excellent example of the consequences of the relational issues of fair exchange. The infant's survival depends on the total care he or she receives. The parents cannot receive back "in kind" in this asymmetrical relationship, but they do earn entitlement by giving, while receiving the benefit of helping their child survive and grow. As the child matures, they will be the recipients of the child's loyalty. Through their earned entitlement, the parents will also pass along loyalty expectations. Relational ethics are already being negotiated in this early exchange between infant and parents.

The balance between infant and parents and the system of justice requires a healthy attachment of the infant, reliable nourishment from the parents, and a parenting culture that does not "overhold" the infant in this helpless, incorporative state. Such overholding would represent the parents' investment in remaining primary for the child, which would exploit the child's trust. This overholding is recognized as "parentification," an exploitation of the child's need for nurture in order to meet the parents' needs.

This constitutes the child's first evolutionary truce. But what about the parents? How do their own experiences relate to their child's growth? And how does the child's growth shape their own development? What motivates the parents to offer fair treatment in this asymmetrical relationship? What happens when a parent's own needs are distressed by the infant's growth into the next expectable sequence in its development, that of forming new relationships? Here we have at stake the collision of entitlements between parent and child. This was the situation of David Gold and his parents, described at the beginning of this chapter.

David Gold, the 20-month-old youngster whose mother expressed concern and jealousy about his attachment to the babysitter, was embarking on the age-appropriate cognitive and affective task of forming new attachments and differentiating from his mother. David was beginning to expand his attachments, creating a rivalry where none existed before. This evolution was greeted by his mother's alarm, signaling her investment in his demonstrating an exclusive attachment to her.

As readers will recall, Mr. Gold did not agree with his wife about the importance of David's attachment to the sitter. Mrs. Gold became deeply upset when her chance to be "first" with her son did not rise to her expectations. On further questioning, it was learned that she had never been first for anyone—not as a child, not as a spouse, and now not as a parent. She came to therapy hoping for a way in which her son David could be made "right" (i.e., first) for her.

A situation such as this is hardly an unusual circumstance: An individual seeks to reverse an injury sustained in another relationship. This phenomenon, which is often seen between parents and child, has been called "displacement" (intrapsychically) and "parentification between parent and child" (systemically). It is a situation in which "the evolutionary host is drawing upon the guest as if the guest were a culture of embeddedness for the host. The host is deriving a kind of support from the guest [that is] dangerous to the development of the client or guest" (Kegan, 1982, p. 127). Why does a parent parentify his or her child? This age-inappropriate expectation of receiving care from one's child is a consequence of the parent's distorted family justice system. Typically the adult is depleted within his or her own relational context, and so turns to the child. Why does a child allow himself or herself to be parentified? The child's overresponsible stance is a negative (growth-inhibiting) loyalty expression. Here the obligation to care about the parents overrides the child's own entitlement to take care of himself or herself.

In such situations, a therapeutic priority is to lessen the child's inappropriate burden of failing to satisfy an unrealistic parental standard (whether that standard is behavioral or emotional). Yet few therapists working with children honor the dialectic—that not only is the child's development in jeopardy (the more so because he is the most vulnerable in this assymetrical relationship), but the parents' development is also in evolutionary jeopardy. This calls for a recognition of the fact that the burden is being placed upon the child in the context of distorted relational ethics, and that proper corrective intervention involves attending not only to the child, but also to the parents—indeed, to the relational context.

In the case of David, the transactions are easy to see. One strategy that would alleviate the symptom would be to side with the father, helping him to reassure the mother that the behavior was not abnormal, and perhaps encouraging him to offer comfort in place of the desired comfort from her son. This would allow David to pursue his current project of differentiation. But this approach, which might shift systemic behavior and free David for the moment, would miss the intersecting meaning of the relational context that triggered the mother's and father's responses and that had to do with the avoided grandparents and other family members. This strategy would address what Piaget (1936/1952) referred to as "learning in the narrow sense." Learning in the narrow sense is akin to training for a specific reponse. It disregards the inner structure that justifies the "wrong" response. It is aimed at changing behavior, not premises.

If the parents could not be shown a new possibility for themselves, they might be helped to change the offending behavior, but might remain "stuck" with imbalances of fairness that would be growth-inhibiting for parent, child, and grandparent alike. For learning in the broad sense to occur, an intervention would have to address the present and the prior contexts in which imbalances of fairness occurred. Here, relational context and the family justice system could provide a key to the intersecting meaning of the individual's and the family's development. Let us look at this intersection for each family member.

MRS. GOLD'S SIDE. Mrs. Gold was the oldest of three daughters of middle-class, Jewish parents. She described her mother as physically and emotionally undemonstrative, and unlike other mothers. Mrs. Gold reported being closer to her father, while her mother tended to her younger sisters. Mrs. Gold tried hard through her academic achievements to win her mother's approval, yet her mother was never enthusiastic. Though she felt loved by her father, she felt betrayed by the times he beat her when her mother yelled at her. In recognizing the parallel between past and present, she reflected, "I didn't have the mommy everyone else had, and I didn't have the kid everyone else had."

Like all children, Mrs. Gold expressed her loyalty in trying to please her parents. When her mother still did not seem pleased, she tried harder. Eventually Mrs. Gold became discouraged and resentful about her mother's lack of demonstrative attention. In adulthood Mrs. Gold handled these injustices, as many adults do, by a retreat, both internally and from the actual parental relationships. This retreat was an expression of negative loyalty between herself and her parents. In order to still comply with old, intuited parental loyalty standards, Mrs. Gold avoided dialogue with her parents. Although she identified areas of mistrust with her parents (particularly her mother), she only asked for fairness in an internal monologue with "imaginary" parents (the parents in her head), not her actual parents. Unable to come to terms with what she owed her parents and what they owed her, she was unable to make a fair claim for what she was owed. The breakdown of trust had no place to go but forward. She drew on trust resources in the present, especially David; this represented an exploitation of his care. This growth-inhibiting loyalty affected the interactions with her son, husband, and actual parents in the present, as well as her peer relationships. In terms of the family justice system, Mrs. Gold felt entitled to claim from her son what she did not get from her own parents. Mrs. Gold distanced herself from her family of origin, but still felt as if she were "odd man out." The babysitter was a metaphor for these old injuries.

MR. GOLD'S SIDE. Mr. Gold was clearly angry at his wife's distress, which he perceived as unreasonable. He accepted David's displays of independence and other attachments as part of his development. However, Mr. Gold's impatience with his wife's feelings rested on his own relational context and the meaning it had for him. He deeply resented his own mother for pushing him to achieve, and his father for not mitigating his mother's pressure. Like his wife, he distanced himself from his mother and father in the present because of his resentments from childhood. He was invested in protecting his son from a controlling mother, and thus attempting to correct his old injuries. But this stand actually maintained the estrangement with his mother and his son's mother. Like his own father, Mr. Gold now contributed to his own injuries by remaining relatively mute, and in so doing, he passed on his own ledger of injustice to his son.

DAVID'S SIDE. David's dilemma was this: Did he have to inhibit his own growth in order to meet his mother's loyalty expectations? Was it fair to him to limit his access to his grandparents because of his parents' unresolved family justice issues? He was at a real loss in terms of trust resources for himself, since his mother decided, unilaterally, to fire the babysitter. More important were the present and lifelong implications of the avoided grandparents. Would he begin to suffer the same consequences that his father did, if his mother remained overinvested in him while his father withdrew into an angry silence?

For David, the initial expression of the loyalty dynamic would be emerging in this period. This emergence coincides with the learned acquisition of standards, and the representations of good and bad states. Kagan's (1981) research suggests that children, from the age of about 18 months onward (once they have developed the cognitive structures to form representations, and identify good and bad standards), "invent an obligation to meet an adult's standard" (p. 127). Kagan concludes that this self-imposed obligation is not based on behavioral conditioning. He has also found that children are cognitively appreciative of what parents offer them as early as 3–4 years of age: "The child constructs a 'tote board' of the respective values of various parental gifts, whether embraces, privileges, or presents" (Kagan, 1984, p. 268). In exchange, children intuit and attempt to contribute what they can offer their parents. Because children are limited in what they can instrumentally "do" to give back, loyalty expressions often take the form of attempts to please the parent or to invest in the parent's emotional well-being. A child's early recognition of having received parental care is expressed by his or her efforts to discharge loyalty commitments. Like empathy, loyalty appears to be a primary psychological phenomenon. It is also an ethical phenomenon, which seeks expression in the dialectical mechanism of offering fair exchange.

Kagan (1984) has noted that modern parental standards are primarily affective and later become oriented to competency and academic achievement for the child. The child will attempt to meet intuited parental standards, and become distressed when he or she cannot. These standards are unique within each family, and the child cannot evaluate (until a much later age) whether the emotional or instrumental standards were reasonable to expect. For example, if David's parents kept him from knowing his grandparents, the meaning of this loss would take years for David to register. There are, then, several different situations in which filial loyalty commitments will be discharged. There is a growth-enhancing match between parental standards that are supportive for the child's growth, and the child who meets them. There is also a growth-inhibiting match between a child and demanding standards that the child may not be fortunate enough to meet or may act out over.

These discrete categories seem to call merely for a realignment of reasonable parental standards suited to the particular limits of a child, so that the child can meet self-obligated filial loyalty commitments. However there is a danger here for the child who meets present demanding standards that are inhibiting for future growth. This was David's situation. This situation reflects the loyalty dynamics that maintain parentification.

Kegan (1982) has suggested that a child will inhibit growth in order to avoid unrecoverable loss. The perception of what that loss will be changes as the child matures. In early childhood, the fear of the real, physical loss of the parent is later replaced by the fear of the psychological loss or the loss of love, as the child attempts, although imperfectly, to meet parental standards.

The loyalty dynamic between parent and child is internalized through the overt as well as intuited standards that the child (even into adulthood) experiences, and interprets as either the freedom to grow or the obligation to remain in the old balance that child and family unwittingly construct. As we have seen with David's parents, it is not only the intuited standards, but also the real relationships between the adult child and parents, that may be avoided or rejected. Rejection then serves the pseudoprotective function of maintaining the old self and the old, remembered family. This growth inhibition, whether it takes place at age 2 or 32, is an expression of the negative, binding loyalty of unsuccessful attempts by the child to reintegrate intergenerational mandates within a family of what children and parents owe each other.

It has already been stated that a simple intervention based on the present family transactions does not address the intergenerational issues of relational ethics, and will leave the family members vulnerable to further developmental challenges. The contextual approach to family therapy requires that fair consideration be offered to each family member. Otherwise, in situations like David's, we can expect that the child will continue to be pulled by the polarized balances the parents stand for, and will eventually replicate the growth-inhibiting loyalties that are evident in the parents' families of origin.

The thrust of contextual therapy is to balance areas of injury while attempting to move each family member toward a more trustworthy position. In the Golds' case, it would mean helping Mrs. Gold get more of what she deserved, while not inappropriately expecting her son to make up the difference. This not only would relieve the child of too great a demand on his loyalty, but also would free the mother from her own negative loyalty to her parents. It would mean helping Mr. Gold stand up for himself and consider the sides of both his parents and his wife. This would afford him an opportunity to rebalance his relationships and to relate to David in a more directly protective and caring way. David deserved his parents' acknowledgment of his devotion to them, and also deserved to receive care from as many significant people in his context as possible, including his grandparents.

In the five sessions with the Golds, the implications of their unreworked injuries from their own families were spelled out. Mr. Gold chose not to pursue work with his own parents, but Mrs. Gold accepted help in working with her mother. She was encouraged to return to her mother, both to elicit her mother's side (by putting her mother's resources and limits in relational context) and to articulate her own side. Had her mother given her more than she had herself received? Did her mother know how hard Mrs. Gold had always tried to please her? Had she pleased her? If so, why was it so hard to show? The trust resource that enabled Mrs. Gold to return to her mother was her acknowledgment that her mother was very loving to David. By inquiring into her mother's side, and offering her the possibility for dialogue, Mrs. Gold earned entitlement to make a claim to have her mother care about her own pain. When Mrs. Gold returned from this visit, she was surprised and relieved that her mother had been so receptive.

In a subsequent appointment, Mrs. Gold reported that things were much easier with David. She no longer looked to him as the only trustable resource, the only one from whom she could claim care. Mrs. Gold's retested assumptions, brought from the imaginary audience to dialogue with her mother, offered the possibility of her own growth.

The Golds stopped therapy at this point. Untested for Mrs. Gold were the areas of mistrust with her father and with her husband. During the therapy, she had become more aware of and distressed by her husband's "crisp" and businesslike relationship with her. Mr. Gold had been encouraged to ask others to consider his needs and preferences, rather than withdrawing into resentful silence. He was satisfied that the crisis of the moment had passed. Mrs. Gold correctly perceived that if she invested more in her own growth (and Mr. Gold did not), the marriage would be threatened.

Despite the premature closure, short-term gains and long-term benefits for both parent and child were recognized. Mrs. Gold was offered a bridge to dialogue with her own mother, which allowed her to make claims for fairness for herself. This freed her to lift the inappropriate loyalty expectation that David should inhibit his own growth to meet her needs. This renewed trust resource held the promise of benefit for David, both in terms of his own development and interpersonally. He was freer to expand his own attachments—to positively express his loyalty toward and to receive caring from both his parents and his grandparents. Because Mrs. Gold was able to rework some of her judgments and disappointments with her mother, she was less likely to "protect" David from his grandparents. Although Mr. Gold chose not to pursue avenues to dialogue with his parents, he was not done the disservice of being made a therapeutic ally against his wife and her problems. This would have reinforced his destructive entitlement toward a "controlling mother."

Here, the mobilization of trust resources was not dependent on stage of development, or even on personality characteristics. The implications for growth did not reside merely in mandating what Mrs. Gold owed David, or what husband and wife owed each other. Instead, the practical problems of relational ethics required a rebalancing of areas of unfairness, as they were informed by the unique relational context as well as stage of development. Let us now follow this dialectic of growth over the middle years of childhood.

Middle Childhood

As Kegan (1982) observes, the broad developmental task of middle childhood requires the family to help promote the child's self-sufficiency. This primary task is largely applied to competency in school and to the life of rules, cooperation, and competition with peers. The child needs to be engaged with family, peers, and school in a balanced way. In encouraging the overdifferentiated stance normal to this period, parents need to promote age-appropriate personal responsibility, whether about time, money, personal choices of clothing, activities, or the like. The contradiction that the family and school cultures must provide for the child in helping him or her evolve is a denial of the validity of total self-sufficiency, of only taking one's own perspective into account. In return for their efforts, parents derive pleasure from their child's progress in school and his or her growing capacity to respect limits and be helpful within the family.

A stumbling block in this developmental balance can be found in the case of children who are not able to meet parental or school standards for competence. Another bind for a child arises when there is a mismatch between or among parental, school, and peer expectations. Here the child is subject to "split loyalties" (competing loyalty standards) on a systemic level. The growth of capability and achievement is also linked to whether the child is free to invest in his or her own well-being or is expending energy over time in the self-invented loyalty obligation to offer care to strengthen a parent. There is a carryover tendency for the child in this period to see himself or herself as responsible if things go well, and also responsible if things go badly. Why is this? The interplay of cognitive development and loyalty may result in a child's overresponsible tendency. This dilemma is highlighted in the following vignette.

Three siblings, aged 11, 9, and 7, had been put in the same foster home 2½ years earlier, following incidents of physical abuse by their father. Both parents were substance abusers, and both were court-ordered to receive treatment in order to maintain visiting rights. Their father, Mr. Brown, did not comply. Subsequently, Mrs. Brown separated from her husband and worked in therapy on maintaining her sobriety in order to regain custody of her children. Mitch, the youngest, had recently returned to his mother's care, but the girls had refused to see their mother for 9 months. Soon either her daughters would be returned to her care, or her parental rights would be terminated. A contextual family evaluation was requested at this point, as the three supervising agencies could not agree on a plan for the children's custody and faced a legal fight.

The siblings' ways of expressing loyalty were different, reflecting their respective stages of growth, as well as their unique relational contexts. The oldest, Polly, told the child therapist that she wanted a "divorce" from her biological mother, in order to be adopted by her foster parents. Mitch tried to reassure his sisters that "Mom doesn't hit any more" and that "You'll be OK." The middle sister, Jane, let Polly speak for her. What did these differences reflect?

Loyalty expressions change with the maturing cognitive structures of childhood. Elkind (1970) proposes that children and adolescents develop "assumptive realities," or hypotheses that are irrefutably held, despite contradictory evidence. One such assumption of the first decade is that adults are benevolent. This belief is reinforced by children's willingness to assume responsibility for events. Children, in learning parental standards, interpret failure in meeting these standards as their own fault. They believe that they have violated a parental standard if their efforts do not please their parents. The children will then try harder, which from the children's side might be described as loyalty overpayment. This sacrifice by the children is an exploitation of their care and depletes their trust resources. They will expend their energy in offering their parents care, with little left over to make investments in their own well-being or growth.

This paradox was reported by Bowlby (1969) when he asked an abused child whether she wanted a new mommy. The child replied, "No, I want my own mommy." This illustrates filial loyalty despite inadequate care. The loyalty dynamic explains why children assign responsibility to themselves for the loss or deprivation of parenting. Over time, if this injustice is not addressed within the original context of depleted parent–overgiving child, that child will seek justice outside that relational context, which may lead to a similar kind of demand from his or her own children. This is what Boszormenyi-Nagy and Spark (1973) refer to as a "revolving slate." Clearly, this was the situation in the Brown family. Mrs. Brown had herself been abused as a child, and reported that her mother still hit her on occasion in the present.

As a child matures, the concept of "parental benevolence" is replaced by the assumption of the "imaginary audience," which is an internal forum where the older child (and, later, the adolescent and adult) can rehearse the anticipated thoughts and responses of others. This shift often results in a new assessment of "what's fair." It can lead to a new assumptive reality—that parents were not necessarily fair, and if they were not, they did not care if they did harm. Kagan (1984) has noted that children (into adulthood) universally interpret whether their parents' responses to them were essentially caring. The conclusion that "I was hurt because my parents didn't care" becomes a negative binding loyalty between parent and child (or adult child). The child (from about age 11 or 12) may retest his or her earlier assumptions regarding parental benevolence. Now the child begins to assess the family justice system on his or her terms. In the Brown family, the siblings' loyalty expressions reflected these differences.

Mitch, as the youngest, was most firmly lodged in the assumption of parental benevolence, and at this point was expending his energy in supporting his mother (as does the child who overinvests in parental expectations that are inhibiting for his or her future growth). Polly, who earlier had been parentified in the Brown family, was beginning to reassess the notion of parental benevolence. She took a more judgmental stance and refused to see her mother. Her younger sister, Jane, silently supported her. Mitch and Polly were beginning to polarize in the positions of "Mom cared" and "No, she didn't." Siblings often continue this polarization into adulthood, rather than directly addressing parents with their injuries. In addition to this polarization, Polly carried a terrible burden of split loyalties in having to choose one set of parents (foster or biological) and betray her loyalties to the other.

Split loyalty is literally "split self." Split loyalties represent cutoffs from actual or potential trust resources for a child. The child, in a triadic relationship to both parents, feels that in order not to lose one parent, he or she has to choose against the other. In a situation of split loyalties, the child owes some loyalty to each parent, but is faced with two (or more) competing sets of loyalty expectations. When the child chooses one standard, he or she automatically disappoints the other (and cannot discharge the loyalty commitment in that context). It is a "Catch-22" situation that diminishes trust resources by fragmenting options for care. A child who is subject to split loyalties as an infant may suffer consequences that he or she is not yet able to assess. As he or she matures, the child will begin to intuit and make meaning out of these pulls and reassess the fairness of parental actions. Adults, then, need to order relationship priorities so that, if possible, children are not cut off from their full context; this is often a concern in cases of divorce and foster care. Children are more vulnerable to split loyalties when they sense that the adults they care about have anger or contempt for each other, which was the case here.

One hypothesis in the Browns' case is that the girls' exaggerated protests against seeing their mother were an expression of a split loyalty bind between biological and foster parents. This split only intensified as a forced choice became imminent. Both sets of parents were competing for the girls' loyalties, and not wanting to see their mother served a pseudoprotective function for the girls. They did not want to hurt their mother by their wish to remain with their foster parents.

In such situations, how do we simultaneously advocate for what is fair to the

children, fair to the foster parents, and fair to the mother? Are the children entitled
to "divorce" their mother, as Polly Brown put it to her child therapist? Has their
deprivation of care earned them the right to disengage from their mother? What is
a fair balance between the children and the biological mother? Some might even
question why the mother deserves fair consideration. If relational ethics were not
our criteria, we might judge the case on ego strength, family functioning, or even
a moral abhorrence for what the children endured. By these criteria, the foster
family is the clear winner. But if we look down the road, will there be a hidden
cost in ignoring loyalties that the children retain, regardless of estrangement? Here
the question for each child is not " 'Shall I be loyal or disloyal?' for loyalty is
the glue for parent–child relationships" (Boszormenyi-Nagy & Krasner, 1986, p.
145). Instead, it is "How can I consider my parents and invest in my own growth?"

In the Browns' case, the children clearly needed a more secure environment,
and the foster parents needed assurance that they could retain custody. But the
mother also deserved consideration. Despite her limits, she had given more to the
children than was ever given to her. She had chosen for them against the wishes
of her husband, and her own mother and father, who refused to see the children
or her. In the long run, it would not further healing to support the girls' avoidance
of their mother; this would only bind their negative loyalties further. It would
finally leave the girls with the conclusion that their mother did not care. In fact,
they had suffered injustices. However, from Mrs. Brown's side, she had struggled
heroically to offer her children more consideration than she ever received. Although the children could not be asked to deny their reality (i.e., that on their
terms they received inadequate care), they also could not afford to deny the fact
that on their mother's terms, she invested in their care. In the long run, the children's true freedom lay in making rightful claims for their welfare while offering
their mother due consideration. The intergenerational spiral of loyalty and intergenerational justice issues required fair consideration to each family member.

These hypotheses were tested in four family evaluation sessions, in which
mother, children, and foster parents met together, along with members of the
social service agencies. Despite her protest that she did not want to see her mother,
Polly's dilemma was clearly expressed in a family meeting where children and
mother met for the first time in 9 months. In her mother's presence, Polly was
clearly concerned that her wishes to remain in foster care were "heartbreakin' her
mother." The children's evident care for her enabled Mrs. Brown to move from
a highly competitive stance with the foster mother to one of overriding concern
for the children's well-being. She acknowledged that her daughters loved their
foster parents, and accepted their wish to remain in their care. Mrs. Brown's
evident investment in her girls moved the foster parents from their previous judgmental attitude toward her and eased their own proprietary pull on the children.
Because the adults were helped to take more trustworthy stances, the children
were relieved of their split-loyalty dilemma and gained the freedom to express
their caring to each parenting adult.

In this case, the therapist asked, "What does anyone stand to gain by a forced-choice situation?'' Here, a recognition of the children's loyalties worked toward integrating all parenting resources, rather than fragmenting parenting and diminishing the children's trust base. A long-term foster care arrangement, in which Mrs. Brown retained parental rights, was agreed to in this case.

Although this vignette was not designed to address the complexity of foster care situations (see Colon, 1978), it raises questions about the connection between adult and child development and how children and parents renegotiate what they owe each other over the course of life. Renegotiation will again occur as a child moves through adolescence, and questions, as Polly was beginning to, the family justice system on his or her own terms. A renegotiation is also critical in adulthood, as was indicated with the Gold family. Now the adult child has the task of handling past and present injuries in dialogue with primary others within the relational context to which they belong. Many adults opt to contain their experienced injustices (and maintain negative loyalties) with their parents, as Mr. Gold did. Typically, this failure to reintegrate the balances of fairness with our actual parents has consequences for the justice we are able to offer our own children. Justice accountings then necessarily require a three-generational focus, because we embody two generations within ourselves as we act on a third generation. As we have seen, the tasks for parent and child shift as the child matures. Although the main focus of this chapter has been on the family with young children, the implications for this approach span the generations.

Summary

This chapter suggests that reintegration of issues of fairness at every stage of development is an ethical task of development. It is ethical in the sense that it requires a reintegration of the past relational context, rather than mitigation of the past context (and actual relationships) by interpreting it or acting on it through the present third generation of children. This premise is crucial in an intergenerational model, in which the parents of the child may be blocked in their own quest for justice; if this blockage is not fed back to the original context in which imbalances occurred, it will be inappropriately fed forward to the present relational context. Children always benefit when their parents have faced their own parents in order to rebalance family injustices as they experienced them. How we as clinicians resolve this question of what we owed and owe, and what we deserved and deserve, within our own families has important implications, not only in our own relational context but also for the families we see.

In requiring a reintegration of issues of fairness, the contextual therapist is not invested in facilitating any given ''stage'' of development, but in offering a bridge for growth to each family member. This differs from therapies that place a value on the health of one member above the health of another; this weighting of values often results in a focus on one person's development isolated from relational context. The contextual therapist functions as a multilateral advocate to the multiple sides of the dialectic of three generations of family justice, and of positive and negative loyalties. It is my experience that family-of-origin work is a primary tool in the training of the therapist who wants to do this kind of work.

The contextual approach to child and adult development incorporates the dialectic of growth for an individual within a dialogic systems model. The contextual paradigm can be employed with parents and children regardless of their "stage" of development, intelligence, or psychological-mindedness. Relational ethics of growth go beyond these characteristics. These ethics are rooted in the balance of give-and-take between parents and children, and in the universal attempts by children to return care to their parents and to make sense of whether their parents were essentially caring to them.

This approach calls for an assessment of future consequences for posterity, whether the child is or is not the identified patient, and whether an individual or a couple is seen. It attends to the positive and negative loyalty implications of a child's full relational reality, including but going beyond the present household membership. It entails the capacity to assess which situations are most wholesome for growth; it is not merely the detecting of pathology. This approach requires a therapist to help adults order relational priorities, rather than making the child's behavior the only focus of treatment. It calls on the therapist to extend a balance of trust and accountability to all family members, even those who have been exploitative.

The contextual approach provides a metatheoretical bridge for family theories. It honors how meaning is made of the individual and the family, both in the here-and-now and in its prior context, intergenerationally. It places the developmental tasks of parent and child in the organizing framework of relational ethics. It calls for a recognition of the fact that resources for development for parent and child alike are in dialectical relationship to each other, within a given relational context. An individual's growth and made meaning are informed by the balance of fair treatment he or she has received and offered. The context of growth between parent and child operates as an intergenerational meaning maker that is shaped by the balance of give-and-take between primary family members throughout life. It provides, as well, a frame for the ethical tasks of development.

ACKNOWLEDGMENTS

I wish to acknowledge Dr. Lee Combrinck-Graham's investment in this chapter and Dr. Barbara R. Krasner for her ongoing personal and professional contributions. Appreciation is also extended to Dr. Krasner for her permission, as primary therapist, to include material from the Brown family in this chapter.

REFERENCES

Boszormenyi-Nagy, I., & Krasner, B. (1986). *Between give and take.* New York: Brunner/Mazel.
Boszormenyi-Nagy, I., & Spark, G. (1973). *Invisible loyalties: Reciprocity in intergenerational family therapy.* New York: Harper & Row.

Bowen, M. (1978). *Family therapy in clinical practice*. New York: Jason Aronson.

Bowlby, J. (1969). *Attachment and loss: Vol. 1. Attachment*. London: Hogarth Press.

Colon, F. (1978). Family ties and child placement. *Family Process, 17*(3), 289–312.

Cotroneo, M. (1986). Families and abuse: A contextual approach. In M. Karpel (Ed.), *Family resources* (pp. 413–437). New York: Guilford Press.

Elkind, D. (1970). *Children and adolescents: Interpretive essays on Jean Piaget*. New York: Oxford University Press.

Erikson, E. (1963). *Childhood and society*. New York: Norton.

Erikson, E. (1968). *Identity: Youth and crisis*. New York: Norton.

Kagan, J. (1981). *The second year*. London: Oxford University Press.

Kagan, J. (1984). *The nature of the child*. New York: Basic Books.

Kegan, R. (1982). *The evolving self: Problem and process in human development*. Cambridge, MA: Harvard University Press.

Minuchin, P. (1985). Families and individual development: Provocations from the field of family therapy. *Child Development, 56*, 289–302.

Minuchin, S. (1974). *Families and family therapy*. Cambridge, MA: Harvard University Press.

Piaget, J. (1952). *The origins of intelligence in children*. New York: International Universities Press. (Original work published 1936).

3

The Family Life Cycle: A Framework for Understanding Children in Family Therapy

JOAN J. ZILBACH, MD

Although the arena of human passion is ordinary family life, only recently has this context come under actual observation and been taken seriously. It is becoming more evident that families undergo a developmental process over time, and human distress . . . symptoms appear when this process is disrupted—Haley, 1973, p. 42

The birth of a child is a momentous event that captures the attention of all family members. At the moment of birth (and perhaps before), as the newborn child becomes a family member, the infant also begins to traverse the familiar path of individual human development. Family development, however, does not begin with the birth of the infant, because the child is born into an already existing family unit whose development is already in progress. Simultaneously, as the family receives a baby, the individual development of the infant becomes manifest and the development of the family unit continues, incorporating the event of the child's birth and the child's development in its evolution. The family life cycle and phases of family development are, however, different from those of the individual family members.

The focus of this chapter is not on individual development, but on the family as a unit over time, with particular emphasis on the implications of this process for children in family therapy. In the course of ordinary life, some families encounter difficulty, impediments, or arrest in traversing their family life cycle. Family development does not always proceed smoothly. A family developmental framework will underscore family therapy as the treatment of choice when serious impediments to family development occur.

There are now several models of family development, some using the idea of a cycle or spiral (Combrinck-Graham, 1985), and others using the more familiar

Joan J. Zilbach. Fielding Institute, Santa Barbara, CA; Boston Psychoanalytic Institute and Society, Boston, MA.

concept of stages (Carter & McGoldrick, 1980b; Duvall, 1977; Haley, 1973; Minuchin & Fishman, 1981; Zilbach, 1968, 1979). The model proposed here is a stage model, focusing on the progression that begins with the formation of a couple independent of the partners' families of origin, and ends with the deaths of these two individuals. Events that occur in the beginnings of new, related families during the life cycle of this nuclear family can be understood in terms of this nuclear family as well as in terms of the new families themselves. For example, a primary couple with children may divorce and marry others, forming new primary families. The relationships of the children and parents of the original nuclear couple, however, will continue to evolve, and there will continue to be primary family functions in relation to this group, even when they are not living in the same household (i.e., do not continue to live together as a family). Furthermore, as we shall see, a family with grown, independent, and married children continues to have primary family functions even as these new primary families have their own progressions through the life cycle. Thus in any family there are at least three levels of development: the individual; the nuclear or household family; and the related families, those of each of the parents or children in a nuclear family. For simplification and presentation of the conceptual model, I concentrate here on the stages in the development of a single unit, a nuclear family.

Every family passes through beginning, middle, and late stages of development. The beginning of the family unit is defined when a couple establishes a household with the intention to form a family. Middle phases are characterized by rearrangements of the family relationships due to various family members' interacting more with the extrafamilial world. Late stages are those taking place after the children have left, leading to the death of the couple that formed this family unit in the first place, the end of this family.

After the end of one family unit, family history provides continuity for ensuing family units over the generations. Multigenerational family history accumulates within each separate unit in the course of its own family life span. Children are both the recipients and users of this history, and the potential change agents for the next versions of family history. The accumulation of many generations of family history is the natural context for the children in any family unit with its immediate and unique family history.

Defining the Family and Basic Family Functions

What is meant by a family? . . . the very omnipresence of the family renders it almost invisible. Because we are immersed in the family we rarely have to define it or describe it to one another—Degler, 1980, p. 3

As we live immersed within our families, we experience their "omnipresence," as Degler has noted, often without an immediate necessity to define or even knowingly comment on this. But in order to understand the intricacies of development and the power of the family, it is useful to disentangle ourselves from the family presence sufficiently to achieve an observational stance—to understand, to define, and, as therapists, to treat the family as a whole enveloping unit.

The family is a basic biopsychosocial unit, a unity of interacting personalities that surrounds and encompasses all of its members from birth to death (Burgess, 1926/1976). In addition, and as a more specific definition, I offer the following: "A family is a small natural group in which members are related by birth, marriage, or other form which creates a home or functional household unit" (Zilbach, 1986, p. 6).

Like any other infant organism, every family, from the moment of its birth or beginning, has fundamental needs that must be met for its existence to be maintained and progress. These needs of the interacting family entity are met in specific ways that become more and more characteristic of a particular family unit, even though they also evolve, adapt, and change over time. There are basic functions of each family unit, which include providing space, shelter, food, and other supplies, money, and basic health. These basic functions are so fundamental that they are often overlooked as the defining functional activities of a family unit in favor of more esoteric observations.

A functional household unit is created through the operation of these basic family functions. All family members (i.e., the family as a unit, a whole, a family group) participate in the performance of basic family functions. Thus the family unit's work in the implementation of basic functions is greater than the work of any individual family member. Most of the functions that form an operational substrate to the family have their origins early in family life; others emerge later. As they develop and change over the course of the family life cycle, they adequately, partially, or inadequately serve the integrity of the family unit. One critical function—caring for children and other dependent members, and attending to all aspects of individual development—is the concern of all family members in the course of the entire family life cycle.

When one examines how families address these basic family functions, two aspects of the process become apparent. The first is mainly intrafamilial: the creation and enhancement of closeness and intimacy between family members. The second is mainly extrafamilial: the creation and enhancement of bonds outside the family, and the fostering of familial expansion into the community and the larger society.

Intrafamilial processes include the provision of family psychosocial interior space and boundaries, supplies, finances, and health. These family functions are "primary," because without accomplishing these tasks in some form or another, a family cannot continue to exist as a functional unit. The primary intrafamilial processes begin their mutual establishment in Stage I (see below). They continue throughout the family life cycle with necessary changes at each subsequent stage.

Extrafamilial processes involve various familial aspects of socialization and enculturation. This group includes provision of education, transmission of values, provision for leisure activities, and others. The extrafamilial family functions start their operations at the outset of the establishment of the family unit, but gain momentum and more importance in the middle and later phases of the family life cycle (Zilbach, 1979, pp. 64–68).

Family Development and the Family Life Cycle

Family development is an orderly sequence of changes that take place over time in the ever-changing unit of the family. Developmental progressions have been described in many kinds of units, cells, groups, and organizations. Like these units, the family undergoes a series of expectable stages with specific stage markers. Moreover, as in other developmental models, "expectable" family stages are inevitable in the course of the family life cycle. In each family stage, family development proceeds through family task accomplishment, and family characteristics of the previous period are carried into the subsequent stage. If family task resolution is incomplete, impeded, or disturbed, these difficulties also are carried into the next stage of family development.

A model of family development that examines the shifts in the management of these family functions highlights this important internal activity of the family and reveals how troubles can develop in managing these tasks as the family situation evolves. Furthermore, such a model provides a general sense of direction that will be taken by most families as they develop. This is the model to be presented here.

The Family Life Cycle: Stages and Stage Markers[1]

There are three major subdivisions of the family life cycle:

- Early stages: Forming and nesting (Stages I and II)
- Middle stages: Family separation processes (Stages III, IV, and V)
- Late stages: Finishing (Stages VI and VII)

At the outset, any attempt to organize the complex and seemingly inchoate forces that operate within the family may seem inadequate to the task. And yet the early stages are dominated by centripetal forces, or, in plainer language, by "joinings"; the middle stages are dominated by centrifugal or outward movements, or "separations"; and the late stages seem to be intricate combinations of both. (One author has used the figure of the spiral in her attempt to capture these larger movements in families; see Combrinck-Graham, 1985.) A more detailed description of Stages I–VII will amplify these brief descriptive captions.

Early Stages: Forming and Nesting

STAGE I: COUPLING

The beginning of a family unit is marked by the establishment of a common household by two people who may or may not become married. The central fam-

---

[1] See the Appendix for a table of family tasks and central issues at each stage.

ily task is to facilitate psychological movement from individual independence to couple/dyadic interdependence. Accompanied by increasing affectional bonds, "joining" or couple/family interdependence occurs in the course of the initial establishment and subsequent performance of the basic family functions.

STAGE II: BECOMING THREE

The second phase of the early years of the family life cycle is marked by the arrival and subsequent inclusion of the first dependent member of the family. The central/core family task at this stage of family development is to progress from coupled dyadic interdependence to the incorporation of triadic dependence.[2]

To keep the model as broad as possible, it is noteworthy that the first dependent member to enter a family may be an adult rather than a child (e.g., a parent, a sibling, or a non-family-related adult). There has been an understandable emphasis in other descriptions of the family life cycle on the importance of the birth of the first child and its inclusion within the family. Undoubtedly, this is an important family event; however, it may not be the Stage II marker event. In this more general family model, the first dependent family member is age-unspecified, and an older person may be the first familial inclusion and Stage II marker, prior to the birth of a first child.

Middle Stages: Family Separation Processes

Family separation processes occur in small steps, beginning in Stage III. Early outward movements or small separations eventually lead to the establishment of subsequent family units in the next generation. This final, obvious shift appears as a big leap, but is really the culmination of the steps begun in the middle stages, where the outward movements of family members begin and increase. Family separation processes are to be differentiated from the better known and recognized individual separation/individuation processes that occur within the individual embedded in the mother–child dyad.

Family separation processes include the stages of "launching" that have been described by other authors (Haley, 1980) "Launching" is only a part of this larger middle period of family life and family separation processes. Individuals become launched and may establish separate family units in the last of these middle stages of family development (Zilbach, 1982).

STAGE III: ENTRANCES

Although family pathways are complex and varied in the middle stages of family development, family stage markers and universal core family tasks can nevertheless be identified.

---

[2] In some recent alternative family structures, where there is only one parent from birth on, this phase is more accurately called "becoming two."

The third stage is signaled or marked by the first entrance of a dependent family member into the larger extrafamilial world. This entrance is, at the same time, a small or partial exit from the immediate world of the family. The family task is to facilitate progression from triadic dependence to recognition and incorporation of partial independence and the beginnings of separation from the family.

When the family development model being discussed is primarily child-focused, then the entrance into the extrafamilial environment is an entrance into an institution that takes care of young children (e.g., day care center, nursery, kindergarten, or school). However, since in this general family model the first age-unspecified dependent family member is not necessarily a child, then the first entrance into an extrafamilial environment may be to a nursing home, another kind of residential institution, or other receiving and care-giving facilities.

STAGE IV: EXPANSION

The next junction point is marked by the entrance of the *last* dependent member of the family into the larger extrafamilial community. At this stage of family development, the central task of all family members is to foster the continuing expansion of partial separations by family members. As this last dependent member expands his or her functional, social, and emotional ties beyond the family, basic family functions, as in previous stages, must change. Although the family remains a critical base for all members, some family functions greatly expand and develop as family members' active lives spill beyond the confines of the immediate family.

STAGE V: EXITS

The next family milestone, the final phase of the middle stage of family development, is marked by the first complete exit of a dependent family member from the family unit. In this phase, one of the partial separations is completed by the establishment of an independent household that may or may not include marriage. The central or core family task is to facilitate and support the completion of partial separation and to assist in the expansion of independence. This is the stage of the family life cycle that may properly be called "launching." Here, a family member is "leaving" the family as a household unit in order to establish an independent household. "Launching," in the sense of individual family members' establishing independent family units, extends into the next phase of family development. In this next phase, the completion of "launching" is accomplished.

Late Stages: Finishing

STAGE VI: BECOMING SMALLER/EXTENDED

Ultimately, the phase of late family life is reached with the exit of the last dependent member/child from the family and the establishment of an independent household entity by this member. The core/central family task is the fostering of continuing independence by various family members. Grandparenthood may begin in this phase or earlier. The emphasis in the family work of this phase is on expansion of family processes, rather than on diminishment, shrinking, or emptying. The terms "shrunken family" or "empty nest" have a negative cast. Although they have been used quite frequently as primary descriptions of this phase, they are not accurate for a normative, nonpejorative, and nonpathological general family model. Potentially, expansion and creative growth are important aspects of family experience in this phase of the family life cycle. When emptiness, narrowing, and shrinking predominate, nonoptimal negotiation of the family task is occurring at this time of family life.

STAGE VII: ENDINGS

The family lives as long as interaction is taking place and only dies when it ceases.—Burgess, 1926/1976, p. 7

The last stage of family development includes the death of one spouse/life partner and continues on to the death of the other life partner. The "sibling" family, consisting of the children of this nuclear couple, continues until the death of the last sibling. At that point, a family unit has come to an end. Family history, myths, and traditions continue to exist and expand in the new family units that have been spawned and created in the course of family life.

Many joinings and separations occur in the course of the family life cycle—from singleton independence to couple interdependence, incorporation of triadic dependence, partial separations, and exits with achievement of full independence. In this last stage, final separations occur with closure and completeness. Death of a family member may have occurred earlier in family life. The death of one spouse/partner also may have occurred earlier, but the death of a second life partner marks the closing of a family cycle. By this time, in some families, new family units with children will be in various stages of their own family development. Each in their own way will resolve the end of the original nuclear family.

Family grieving, including children of all ages, is the central family task in this stage. Family mourning is the powerful context for individual mourning. When any part of this process is incomplete, all family members suffer in some long-lasting, poignant, and sad manner (Paul, 1967). The core family task is the resolution of final separations. Some families experience downward motion with extremes of complication and pain, and during these last years of family life, there are many changes in the direction of decreases and diminishments. Fortunately, negative changes are not the only possibilities for late family life. There are also remarkable enhancements and (too infrequently recognized and appreciated) pleasure and happiness when resolution of long-standing family difficulties occurs in these late stages. Some families do experience resolution of family issues and family integration only in this late stage of daily development. In others, resolution may require the passing of a generation or more for resolution.

Most professionals who utilize a developmental framework in their work concentrate on and emphasize the early stages of the family life cycle. Even the middle stages may be addressed as family life cycle events, especially those that involve the painful processes of moving out and differentiating (particularly Stage V). But it is most important not only to include but perhaps even to give added emphasis to the late stages, in order to achieve the full understanding and expansion of our knowledge of families' and family members' experience that the family life cycle perspective offers.

Children and the Family Life Cycle

To the small child, the family ways and the parents' ways are THE way of life and THE way for people to interact with one another. . . . The family influences are so pervasive and transpire so naturally. . . . The family forms the first imprint upon the still unformed child and the most pervasive and consistent influence that establishes patterns that later forces can modify but never alter completely—Lidz, 1963, p. 1

The pervasive, intensive, and powerful influence of the family upon the child is emphasized in this quotation from Lidz, one of the early writers who took the family unit as a central organizing theme. Having just traversed the stages of the entire life cycle, and defined family stage markers and central family tasks at each stage using this same theme of the family unit as an organizing context for individual development, I now return to the beginning of the family life cycle and comment by example on aspects of each stage with particular relevance to children.

Early Stages: Forming and Nesting

STAGE I: COUPLING

Since this chapter has an explicit focus on children, it might seem that Stage I, the joining of the primary parental couple and the establishment of the basic family functions, should be bypassed or at least given minimal attention. But since the family as an entity, an organizational whole, establishes the foundations for performing the basic family functions in Stage I, and since each of these basic family functions will impinge on children in all the subsequent phases, Stage I is a critical phase to examine.

On the other hand, children also directly influence the Stage I development of the primary couple. How? When children are present before the couple forms, as when previously married individuals with children marry each other. Children are critical in the development of stepfamilies. The Stage I development of such a couple involves the interaction and simultaneous existence of Stage I and whatever stage(s) the other, earlier family units may be in. As the "new" primary couple inevitably traverses Stage I, the necessary establishment of the new basic family functions is influenced by the other family members, including the stepchildren. An example involving stepchildren highlights some common experiences in Stage I when young children are involved. The basic family function of providing shelter/housing establishes the psychophysical external boundaries and interior living space of a family unit:

When after a period of "going together" Arthur and Barbara decided to "join" their households, they bought a house. Arthur and Barbara both had joint custody of their respective school-age children. There were many discussions about allocation of space, particularly play space and bedrooms, that were quite repetitive. The new couple felt puzzled about the "stuck" quality of these discussions and the difficulty of making these family decisions. There had been fairly agreeable resolution of various other issues (e.g., money, space, and taste involved in buying the house, as well as the house itself), and they had expected that this relatively nonconflictual process would continue after the actual purchase was completed. But in the area of space allocation, the couple encountered the stepchildren.

Arthur and Barbara were able to recognize that their desires as a new couple for their "nest" in the choice of space for the master bedroom in the new home had to be combined with the play space and other needs of the various stepchildren units. The impasse occurred as one or the other set of needs—for the Stage I "new nest" or the Stage IV stepfamily home—threatened to dominate. Resolution and decision making occurred when both sets of needs were recognized:

Both Arthur and Barbara had been in individual treatment prior to and during the course of their subsequent divorces. Their puzzlement as they were joining families did not seem to them to be a serious problem, but they decided to go for a joint consultation. Since both "families" were involved, they chose a family therapist, who asked them to bring in all the children. During the evaluation about the present state of the basic family functions, the information about the couple's difficulties in organizing the space in their new house was developed. The therapist observed that the whole family unit was in developmental transition, and focused on these needs generated by this state. The parents and children had an animated discussion about various aspects of their developmental transition and difficulties. Consultation was terminated after a few sessions, and later resolution took place without further treatment.

STAGE II: BECOMING THREE

This stage, marked by the entrance into the family of the first dependent member (often the first child), has received considerable attention. In fact, this stage has been entitled "birth of the first child" in other family life cycle models (e.g., Carter & McGoldrick, 1980b). In order to emphasize that the infant's dependent state and subsequent individual development are not the only events in this stage, I discuss examples that demonstrate how all the basic family functions change. The entrance of the first infant, child, or older member into the family is the beginning of "being depended upon" for all other adult family members.

The extent of family change in all basic family functions equals and usually even surpasses the adjustments already achieved in Stage I. There is a flurry of intense activity within the household. The intensity is often attributed to the needs of the baby, this may not seem so obvious or compelling at first to an outside observer. There may be a move just prior to the birth or shortly thereafter, which may not seem, on the surface, to be well timed or based on actual space needs. This change, often enlargement, in the physical boundaries appears to be a familial psychophysical response to the impending birth of the first baby. There is a felt urgency within the whole family that propels change.

"We must have a place for the baby," Mrs. B said a bit desperately and with considerable intensity. Within their house there was an existing room that seemed to have good space possibilities for the needed nursery. This room was small but adequate and sunny, although in disarray at that time, containing a collection of overflow books, clothes, and other adult sundries. The practicalities of making extensive interior architectural structural changes in order to accommodate nursery space for the new baby were reviewed and seemingly dismissed. But, still, the need for making interior space change persisted and became a big project that dismantled large areas of the house and required considerable attention just before the birth, and physical displacement and discomfort in the immediate postdelivery period. However, the enthusiasm of both Mr. and Mrs. B remained high and fairly constant with the expressed theme of "making things new and different, spanking clean and shiny, for this special time in our family life!"

The space within the family abode is the psychosocial functional interior of the family unit. The intensity of the process and the need for explicit change in the interior space of the family seem to coincide with the inevitable change that occurs in the expanding interior space of the pregnant mother. Thus, the need for change in interior housing space is not necessarily propelled by concrete "reality," but rather by a family developmental force expressed in this area of basic family functions. Within the framework of family development, these physical manifestations of psychosocial developmental family change become both observable and understandable.

All of the other basic family functions—household supplies/food, finances/employment, and family health—also undergo inevitable change. These changes may not be as obvious as the housing space change described in the preceding example. In addition, each function has complex relationship to all the others. In the following example, it appears that as one family function changed, others seemed to follow. But this is an artifact of description, in which it is difficult to describe family developmental occurrences intermixed, intertwined, and with some simultaneity.

A young artist and his graduate student wife had lived together for several years. The basic family functions of shelter/housing, finances/employment, household supplies/food, and family health were well established in Stage I. In this stage, as the couple established a joint household, changes occurred as they worked out the development of their interdependent functions. The wife moved into the husband's art studio/apartment. Their external family boundaries of shelter/housing were essentially satisfactory in his art studio, though they moved some internal walls. These internal changes, rather than a total physical move, seemed to satisfy the need for new space. She had steady employment, which provided sufficient basic family finances. Additional income from his art work was sporadic, but allowed them some monetary and economic flexibility. She pursued her chosen graduate studies on a part-time basis, which meshed well in their mutual lives with the extensive time demands of his demanding creative and artistic pursuits. Provision of household supplies/food, cooking, and so on were done by either one, depending on who was not occupied with other work or school.

Before the birth of their first baby, the couple discussed and came to a mutual agreement as to how their "new" family would function. They planned that the wife would return to work shortly after the birth of the baby, since she provided the stable income, and the husband would do the major portion of early primary child care.

The delivery was uneventful, and the baby was healthy. But in the first months of life the baby developed a number of protracted, troublesome, and somewhat serious infections, and there was some additional concern about the baby's overall development. There seemed to be some evidence of developmental lag or possible retardation.

What was the status of the basic family functions at this phase of family development, Stage II, with particular attention to the baby? The inclusion of a baby, a dependent family member, had of course increased the needs in all the primary family functions. The basic income supplied by the mother's employment remained stable, though the supplementary income from the father's art work had decreased, since his artistic production time was now partly taken up with child care. There was also increased financial need because of the additional family member, and particularly because the baby had numerous lengthy infections requiring frequent and expensive medication. Due to these and other increased expenses, there was increased pressure on the artist father to sell more of his art work. This had not been an issue in the earlier phase. He was not immediately willing to do this, since it required marketing time, and he preferred to create during the time he was not spending in child care. These hours were sparse, though available, and were designated as solely for artistic working hours.

Superficially, at first it appeared that the basic family functions of shelter/housing and household supplies/food were adequate at this time. However, further discussion of these areas revealed that the father often lost track of time when involved in his artistic work. In addition, the baby's space, the nursery, had been constructed and placed at some distance from the work area of the father, in order to protect the baby from some of the toxic materials that the father used in his art work.

When the father was fully absorbed in his creative endeavors, the cries of the baby went unheard, and provision of adequate food, medication, and stimulation were neglected. The father (and mother), though willing and agreeable, had not made the necessary adjustments to the needs of the new and totally dependent family member, the baby.

All of these family functions had been discussed before the birth of the baby and mutually agreed upon. The baby was planned—the mother wanted to "produce" also, and they had agreed that this was important for both of them. The family's difficulty in developing satisfactory patterns for adjusting to and meeting the needs of the early phase of Stage II were not revealed spontaneously, but through specific family developmental inquiries:

When different arrangements for baby care were arranged to supplement the father's primary care, the recurrences of the baby's infections diminished in amount and length. The development of the baby proceeded and caught up when adequate nutrition and simulation were provided by other caretakers and the father. He was also able to devote some time to selling his art work, and their finances improved. Along with these interlocking changes, the mother decreased her out-of-the-home employment and assumed some primary child-rearing responsibilities. An incipient case of failure to thrive was prevented, and the issue of developmental lag or retardation was resolved.

Finances/employment, household supplies/food, and family health had been addressed up to this point. But there were to be changes in shelter/housing as well. An auxiliary space was made in order for the baby to be closer to the father on "safe" days (i.e., when he was using nontoxic materials). Changes and readjustments thus occurred in all of the basic family functions, and the family developmental difficulties of Stage II were thereby resolved.

Family referrals are not common at Stage II. This case involving a child was seen in a family consultation at a health agency. Stage I referrals are more frequent for marital or couple therapy. Children are often not mentioned in the referral, but will appear if the whole family is considered essential in the evaluation process. When children become the focus, then the context of "treatment" facilities widens and includes health clinics (as in the preceding case), "well-baby clinics," schools, and other places that "treat" children.

Middle Stages: Family Separation Processes

Family separation processes begin long before there are adolescent "separating" children as family members. When there are teenagers in the family, the adolescents' developmental phase, the second (individual) separation/individuation phase (Blos, 1979), interacts vigorously with the family developmental phase of "launching" (Haley, 1980).

However, taking the first little steps in the family separation processes begins much earlier than a child's adolescence for the entire family, as when the very young child, infant, or toddler moves out of the immediate family world to day care, nursery, or kindergarten.

STAGES III AND IV: ENTRANCES AND EXPANSIONS

The reverberations of the first entrance into the extrafamilial world by a young child may become more apparent in retrospect, well after the initial experience, as in this example:

Mrs. Baxter had many concerns abut the adequacy of her first child's future elementary school. He was about to enter kindergarten. She talked and worried at length about the teachers, the curriculum, and the immediate neighborhood of the school. "But," she said with some relief in her voice, "I can see him walk all the way—the whole two blocks." She mused, "I remember how we felt when we had to put him into day care [the actual first separation] in order for me to go back to work. It was so wrenching we almost couldn't do it, but we had to."

That first family transition (Stage III) had been handled in this way: Both Mr. and Mrs. Baxter had become very active participants in their cooperative day care center. Initially, both of them spent considerable time at the center—fixing, painting, repairing, and so on. They were in contact during these activities with their child during this first separation.

"This time," she said, "he is really gone. Once he's inside that school yard, I can't see him or be with him. He's in the real world outside our family with all its influences."

Stage III, the first exit, had been eased by the parent's adoption of the first extrafamilial environment, the day care center. Now, although the Baxters were actually in Stage IV, some of the family developmental work of Stage III was being completed. This example is not one of troubled family development, but rather of everyday, ordinary family developmental processes.

The family members' responses to the extrafamilial world begin to develop in Stage III and continue throughout the middle stages of family development. Emphatic pleasure in outward family movement at one extreme, and suspicion and excessive family closeness at the other, are the endpoints of a spectrum of family responses. To highlight the importance of these processes in all family members, including the young children, here is an example of a family in Stage IV of the family Life cycle with considerable family separation difficulties, at the closed end of the spectrum.

The Taylors' 7-year-old child was referred to a mental health clinic by a school psychologist for evaluation for "school phobia." In this clinic, including all members of the family in an interview was a standard part of their evaluation procedures. The family insisted at first that it was not necessary to include all the children, because the nonreferred ones, the other children, were "quite normal." In the course of the interview, however, the following self-descriptions emerged.

The oldest son, aged 21, had recently returned from brief and unsatisfactory military service. He described himself as "staying home and doing nothing"; he was neither employed nor in school. The other family members showed little indication of any concern with this nonactivity or nonproductivity. The next sibling, a 15-year-old girl, described herself as "sick." She spent long periods of time out of school with "rheumatic fever"; however, this diagnosis had not been medically substantiated, and her vague signs and symptoms were not questioned by the parents or other family members. She remained at home now with her brother since his return from his brief military service. The next child, the 7-year-old identified patient, also spent considerable time at home with "colds." These frequent and protracted states of "illness" were not questioned or investigated; rather, they were accepted at face value by the parents. They considered his being at home "normal—all children are mostly sick in the early years of school."

Mrs. Taylor was herself mostly housebound, though not entirely. She was unable to drive and went into the community at large only with Mr. Taylor, on whom she depended for any outside-the-home activity or errand. He enthusiastically took care of the entire family. His job allowed him considerable flexibility; he could do his "work" on a self-made schedule. His "free time" was spent performing many functions for family members, whom he described with pleasure as "always being around." Outside the family, the school authorities had identified only the 7-year-old as a "problem." The family functioned in a series of syntonic, interlocking nonseparations, and the members depended heavily on the father for almost all extrafamilial contact. In essence, the father brought home not only "the bacon," but almost everything that this family needed for the sustenance and maintenance of the basic family functions.

The referral for the 7-year-old with "school phobia" occurred after the oldest son had attempted a unsuccessful separation from the family by going into the military service. The youngest son was the only family member without somatic symptoms, so that his protracted and numerous absences from school were not acceptable to the school authorities. School history revealed that none of these children had gone to any form of preschool, though these were prevalent in their social group and community. In this family, the little early steps—exploratory, partial, and expanded separations from the family—were absent, diminished, or otherwise unsatisfactory.

The Taylor family was in Stage IV, when the core family task is the continuing support of partial separations and fostering of independence. But family task resolution in Stage III—the stage of beginning separations and support of partial independence—had been markedly incomplete and carried as such into Stage IV. Exits and completion of "launchings" had not yet arrived. The identification of need by the school authorities allowed therapeutic entry into this family. The work with this family in this middle phase, which included all the children, was timely and influenced the progression of all family members into the next phase.

A referral for family treatment after the evaluation met with considerable opposition by the parents. At the outset, arrangements were made with the school authorities to assist the 7-year-old's prompt return to school. After this immediate goal was met, the entire family re-evaluated the idea of treatment. This family had many strengths and settled in to work on their unfinished family developmental issues of separation. Fears about separation were expressed, and each family member was surprised at the fear of the other. Material from the parents' families of origin was helpful in elucidating some of the background of these present-day family concerns.

A later phase of treatment occurred when the parental couple came by themselves to reassess their marriage through reviewing their experiences in Stage I.

This family provides a striking example of the usefulness of a family life cycle emphasis in family therapy, particularly with children. It was the task of the initiation and pursuit of family separation processes in the middle phases of the family life cycle that in this family enlarged the scope of treatment beyond the 7-year-old identified patient to the entire family, including all the children.

STAGE V: EXITS

The first complete exit from the primary family and establishment of an independent household is a major step in the normal progression of family development. This step, like other family processes, may take place over considerable time and always involves all family members.

An "independent household" is established when each of the four primary or intrafamilial basic family functions is established, maintained, and controlled by the new family unit. As this transition is taking place, each of the basic family functions must be established by the "launching" family member. This does not usually occur in giant steps; many little steps are frequently necessary.

As the children in the Smith family grew into young adulthood, each of them moved out to college, progressing from dormitory living to apartments with several roommates. These moves were supported by the parents, as is the pattern now a days in many families. One of the children, David, attended college only briefly, establishing an "independent" business as his work. This business initially required considerable family financial support. For business purposes, an old building was bought in which there was potential living space. Thus one of the primary basic family functions, shelter/housing, was in the process of transformation with the purchase and subsequent rehabilitation of this building.

It became "his" as David worked on it, creating new internal space. Gradually, family financial support decreased. However, during these many months he continued to eat all of his meals at the family home. The kitchen, with all the accoutrements necessary for basic functioning, was the last room to be completed in the new building. When this was accomplished, all the functions of shelter/housing, finances/employment, and supplies/food were now established separately and were independent of the primary family unit.

What about the fourth basic family function—family health? One day shortly after the kitchen was finished, David called and said with nonchalance, "I haven't been in touch because I've been sick, but I'm better now. When can we get together?'' This was a marked change from the previous pattern of dealing with everyday illness. In the past the parents were called immediately for advice and/ or simple medication. Chicken soup was often the result! Now David's health was separate from that of the rest of the family still living at home.

All four of the basic family functions were now established by the new family unit. An independent household, the first in David's family, was in existence after many large and small steps over time were accomplished and completed.

There would not be much apparent change that an outside observer could have noted in this process, except over a considerable period of time and with the status of basic family functions as indicators of change. This is an example of everyday, ordinary family development in Stage V.

Late Stages: Finishing

STAGE VI: BECOMING SMALLER/EXTENDED

[A]s it will be the right of all, so it will be the duty of some, to prepare definitely for a separation, amicably, if they can; violently if they must.—Quincy, 1811

This quotation, though from another context, captures significant emotional aspects of the late stages of the family life cycle. All families struggle with the late stages of family life and family separation processes. At the time when the last child leaves, is finally launched, and has established an independent house-hold, there is a major normal disruption of the family unit. Minor residues of this struggle may continue to exist without much apparent change within the primary family house for some time. For example, a relatively untouched bedroom or two may continue to be called by the ''launched'' child's name. These rooms, con-taining closets stuffed with left-behind but not discarded clothes and other stored treasures, attest to normal difficulties and pain of resolution of Stage VI, the stage of becoming smaller/extended.

More major residues of struggles and difficulties with this phase, the accom-plishment of final launchings and separations, may be noted in mild to severe estrangements within families. Here is an example of mild difficulties.:

The six members of the Jones family weathered the ordinary stresses and strains of their years together as a family in Stages I–V.

Over a number of years, separations and exits occurred in the family, with anticipatory pleasure and joyful participation by all family members. The Joneses were ''midrange,'' neither extremely closed nor very open in the spectrum of family cohesion.

As independent household units were established, the family station wagon moved many items to and fro. Some items moved from one household to the next as ''upgrading'' occurred. These well-used items were greeted with recognition and reminiscences as they moved into the next ''new'' household.

The first move out of the primary family to an independent household by the oldest sibling was accomplished with some accompanying enthusiastic fanfare from the younger members. This sibling family member never moved back. The second oldest sibling moving back and forth several times, accompanied each time by a "significant other." During the "away" moves, close contact with the primary family remained intact, as it did with the oldest child in the already well-established independent household. The third child's exit and separation were uneventful.

However, the fourth and last child's move was stormy (Stage VI). This sibling had always been regarded by the others as very independent. An initial peaceful separation turned into a family crisis and rescue of this member from a difficult situation. All family members participated in the many activities of this crisis. Following the resolution of the crisis, this youngest family member moved home. When subsequently she decided to move out, she went farther away geographically than any of the others. Visiting was thus not easy in either direction.

Periodically, unlike the others, she needed financial help. The other siblings noticed these periods with concern and attempted to keep in contact with their youngest sibling. She remained "independent," and there was a long time period when the close and continuing contact of the oldest three was in sharp contrast to the lessened contact and isolation of the youngest. She was missed at family celebrations and holidays, but serious estrangements did not develop.

More serious difficulties are illustrated in the next example.

The Stevens family had a family business in which two siblings and a mate worked in steady productive employment. Mr. Stevens had a central position in the establishment of the business, as he advised and invested but did not do the actual day-to-day work of the business. He suddenly became seriously ill and died after a short, painful illness. Shortly after his death, the two siblings began an intense fight that included nasty business accusations. The business fell apart and went bankrupt. The two siblings became and remained seriously estranged; they did not speak for many years. However, their children had grown up together and remained very close friends. All communication took place through this younger generation. When one of the siblings moved far away, this caused more estrangement in the primary family. When the two close cousins were geographically separated, communication within the entire family diminished further. Though each household unit functioned well, there was persistent sadness in all family members about the primary family. Periodically one of them would muse, "It's not been the same since Dad died." After a Thanksgiving Day with only part of the family present, unlike earlier years, Mother commented, "Our family fell apart when Dad died. I wonder if we'll ever be better."

The precipitant for further separation and exits was the death of the first spouse. But this was accompanied by serious alienation and family splits, which were signs of serious difficulties with finishing and ending in the late stages of their primary family life cycle.

As families become smaller by exits, they may become larger by the formation of new related units. Young children often appear in these stages as grandchildren. Thus, in these late stages a mixture of outward and inward family movement occurs in any number of combinations.

It should be noted that at this stage we begin to speak of other family units that have been created out of the primary family unit. These families develop at their own speed, and on a family tree several units will exist simultaneously in their own phases of family development. There is a combination and intricate interweaving of family influence in these last phases.

STAGE VII: ENDINGS

By the time we are adults we have said a great many good-byes, often knowing long periods of minimal contact with parents. . . . When parents die, all of the partings of the past are re-evoked with the realization that this time they will not return, and the distances of separation . . . become infinite. And yet the familiar experience of reunion persists, expected beyond the accustomed separation.—Bateson, 1984, pp. 259–260

The death of the second parent completes a cycle for the children and creates a "sibling family." The sibling family continues until the last one of the siblings dies. Each in turn mourns for the particular loved one and for the entire family. Young children and old are part of family mourning. Incomplete or partial mourning affects all members of the family and may not be resolved until the next generation or beyond. Hesitancy or concern about the inclusion or presence of children in the rituals of mourning is common. But their inclusion is vital as part of the resolution of grief and loss for the entire family.

In order to include young children, variations of traditional mourning and funeral rites may be needed. In his paper "Family Reaction to Death," Murray Bowen (1976) gives a beautiful description of the reactions of three young children, aged 10, 8, and 5, in the aftermath of the sudden death of their mother. Bowen encourages direct and open talk, exemplified by the use of the words "death," "die," and "bury," rather than "passed on," "deceased," and "expired." He encourages close and personal contact with death in the funeral rituals by the children. He states unequivocally, "Children are commonly excluded from funerals to avoid upsetting them. This can result in a lifetime of unrealistic and distorted fantasies and images that may never be corrected. . . . I have never seen a child hurt by exposure to death. They are 'hurt' only by the anxiety of survivors'' (p. 345). In this family, Bowen encouraged the father to have a private session at the funeral parlor with the children and the dead mother. He warned the father that others would try to interfere and disapprove. The father reported back to Bowen after the family had their private session with the mother in her casket; he related many details of the children's asking questions, and his dealing with them directly and immediately. Children do not intellectually fully "understand" death. These young children went up to the casket and felt the dead mother.

The youngest, the 5-year-old, kissed her and then said, ". . . She could not kiss back." The 5-year-old found some pebbles to give to the mother and placed them in her hand. The other children then did likewise. They announced the end of the visit by saying to their father, "We can go now, Daddy." The description continues and includes a follow-up some years later.

Conclusion

The family is an ever-changing unit into which children are born, in which they develop, and out of which they create new family units in the course of time. This developmental model of the entire family life cycle is a framework for organizing some of the complexities of family functioning. The model has undergone several revisions from the initial formulation and will continue to change over time, as families do. For example, the development of alternative family structures will modify and vary the shape of basic family functions in Stage II, "becoming three." Some families accomplish both Stage I and Stage II at the birth of the first child, when the family forms in a birth household. On the other hand, when a child is born to an uncoupled and independent mother, the stage of "becoming three" is really "becoming two." Other functional changes will modify aspects of this model, perhaps some of the definitions and descriptions of basic family functions.

The unit of treatment in family therapy is the whole family, and children are always integral members of this family unit. The complexities of every stage of the family life cycle, as encountered in family therapy, become more understandable when a model of family development is utilized.

This model of the family life cycle encompasses many changes over time that impinge upon all members, including children within families. This model is useful in facilitating understanding of children within their most important context— their immediate and developing family, which surrounds them and facilitates their growth over the entire span of the family life cycle.

Appendix. Family Development: Stages of the Family Life Cycle

Gestational: "Going together," courtship, engagement	
Early stages: Forming and nesting	
Stage I: Coupling	
Family stage marker:	The family begins at the establishment of a common household by two people; this may or may not include marriage.
Family task:	Individual independence to couple/dyadic interdependence.
Stage II: Becoming three	
Family stage marker:	The second phase in family life is initiated by the arrival and subsequent inclusion/incorporation of the first child/dependent member.
Family task:	Interdependence to incorporation of dependence.
Middle stages: Family separation processes	
Stage III: Entrances	
Family stage marker:	The third phase is signaled by the exit of the first child/dependent member from the intrafamilial world to the larger world. This occurs at the point of entrance into school or other extrafamilial environment.
Family task:	Dependence to facilitation of beginning separations—partial independence.
Stage IV: Expansion	
Family stage marker:	This phase is marked by the entrance of the last child/dependent member of the family into the community.
Family task:	Support of facilitation of continuing separations—independence.
Stage V: Exits	
Family stage marker:	This phase starts with the first complete exit of a dependent member from the family. This is achieved by the establishment of an independent household which may include marriage or another form of independent household entity.
Family task:	Partial separations to first complete independence.
Late stages: Finishing	
Stage VI: Becoming smaller/extended	
Family stage marker:	Ultimately the moment comes for the exit of the last child/dependent member from the family.
Family task:	Continuing expansion of independence.
Stage VII: Endings	
Family stage markers:	The final years start with the death of one spouse/partner and continue up to the death of the other partner.
Family task:	Facilitation of family mourning. Working through final separations.

Revised from Zilbach (1968, 1979, 1982, 1986).

REFERENCES

Bateson, M.C. (1984). *With a daughter's eye*. New York: Simon & Schuster.
Blos, P. (1979). *The adolescent passage*. New York: International Universities Press.
Bowen, M. (1976). Family reaction to death. In P. Guerin (Ed.), *Family therapy: Theory and practice* (pp. 335–350). New York: Gardner Press.
Burgess, E.W. (1976). The family as a unity of interacting personalities. In G.D. Erickson & T.P. Hogan (Eds.), *Family therapy: An introduction to theory and technique* New York: Jason Aronson. (Original work published 1926)
Carter, E.A., & McGoldrick, M. (Eds.). (1980a). *The family life cycle*. New York: Gardner Press.
Carter, E.A., & McGoldrick, M. (1980b). The family life cycle and family therapy: An overview. In E.A. Carter & M. McGoldrick (Eds.), *The family life cycle* (pp. 3–21). New York: Gardner Press.
Combrinck-Graham, L. (1985). A developmental model for family systems. *Family Process, 24*, 139–151.
Combrinck-Graham, L. (Ed.). (1986). *Treating young children in family therapy*. Rockville, MD: Aspen.
Degler, C. (1980). *At odds: Women and the family in America from the Revolution to the present*. New York: Oxford University Press.
Duvall, E. (1977). *Marriage and family development* (5th ed.). Philadelphia: J.B. Lippincott.
Haley, J. (1973). *Uncommon therapy*. Toronto: Norton.
Haley, J. (1980). *Leaving home*. New York: McGraw-Hill.
Lidz, T. (1963). *The family and human adaptation*. New York: International Universities Press.
Minuchin, S., & Fishman, H.C. (1981). *Family therapy techniques*. Cambridge, MA: Harvard University Press.
Paul, N.C. (1967). The role of mourning and empathy in conjoint marital therapy. In G. Zuk & I. Boszormenyi-Nagy (Eds.), *Family therapy and disturbed families*. (pp. 186–205). Palo Alto, CA: Science and Behavior Books.
Quincy, J. (1966). Abridgment of Debates of Congress, 14 January 1811 (Vol. IV, p. 327). In *Oxford dictionary of quotations* (2nd ed., p. 404). London: Oxford University Press. (Original work published 1811)
Zilbach, J.J. (1968). Family development. In J. Marmor (Ed.), *Modern psychoanalysis* (pp. 355–386). New York: Basic Books.
Zilbach, J.J. (1979). Family development and familial factors in etiology. In J.D. Noshpitz, J.D. Call, R.L. Cohen, & I. Berlin (Eds.), *Basic handbook of child psychiatry* (Vol. 2, pp. 62–87). New York: Basic Books.
Zilbach, J.J. (1982). Separation: A family developmental process of midlife years. In C. Nadelson & M. Notman (Eds.), *The woman patient* (Vol. 22, pp. 159–167). New York: Plenum Press.
Zilbach, J.J. (1986). *Young children in family therapy*. New York: Brunner/Mazel.

4

Family Models of Childhood Psychopathology

LEE COMBRINCK-GRAHAM, MD

The title of this chapter suggests that it will answer questions posed to family therapists by those who favor a biomedical model of psychiatry. But the title is a misnomer. Three words, "models," "family," and "psychopathology," are misleading. All are words that are common to the scientific technology of the biomedical sciences, but do not fully express the complexities of an ecosystems approach. In a sense, then, the title is an invitation to move beyond the dimensions of the biomedical model into those of a biopsychosocial perspective on childhood, child development, and exceptional children.

The biopsychosocial influence of a child can be represented by a series of concentric spheres creating a continuum of three-dimensional domains encompassing or being encompassed by others. Each one of the domains will thus both shape and be shaped by the relationships of events in other spheres of the ecology. An example of how these spheres might be named is given in Figure 4-1.

Behavior science has constructed models to explain events at each of the levels of this continuum. We have biological models to explain events *within* the individual, psychological models to explain events *of* the individual, and family models to elaborate upon events *around* the individual. Models at each of these levels incorporate much information, but each is limited to the extent that it does not integrate modifying influences of several other levels, both internal and external to it. According to this illustration, clearly "family models of psychopathology" would focus only on the family sphere of influence around the individual.

Lee Combrinck-Graham. Institute for Juvenile Research and Department of Psychiatry, University of Illinois at Chicago, Chicago, IL.

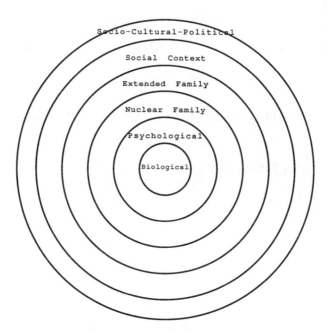

Figure 4-1. Biopsychosocial systems of childhood.

"Family" is a misleading term, because when it is used in relation to "family theory" it represents more than the family sphere. Currently, family systems theories are being applied to larger and smaller systems than the family, so that the important word is "systems," not "family." Furthermore, many of the family systems theories are derived from biological models, such as those of Cannon, involving regulation and homeostasis, and those of von Bertalanffy, involving general systems theory. More recently, another biologist, Maturana, has made significant contributions to understanding the operations of biological systems (see Dell, 1986).

Family systems theories have also borrowed from larger spheres of study, such as sociology, anthropology,and political science. Recently family systems theorists have described themselves as "ecosystemic," showing their perceived connection to the biological discipline that studies relationships between different forms of life and their environments.

So, in many cases, when family therapists talk about their views on emotional dysfunction, they are usually talking about a broader concept than the family. Unfortunately, many whose interests focus them at other levels of the biopsychosocial continuum expect that a discussion of family models of psychopathology will neglect contributions of the other levels, especially the biological and psychological. They expect that all problems will be explained within the context of family interactions, and that we will claim that the treatment to all problems should therefore be family therapy.

I do not believe that family therapy is the only way to treat children, and I do not believe that it is always indicated. I do, however, believe that it is always indicated to assess a child's problem at more than one level of the biopsychosocial continuum, and to integrate the information from these levels in formulating an understanding of the problem and a treatment plan. Thus I include in my assessments a consideration of brain pathology, cognitive functioning, temperamental patterns, genetic predisposition, and developmental vulnerability. But I maintain that these areas of evaluation yield data that should be viewed only in light of the context in which they occur.

The tendency to see things only one way or another, such as either biological or contextual, polarizes the study of individuals and does them an injustice. As I attempt to rebalance this study, so that individual function is understood in its context, I present some models. These are not models to be applied in every similar case; they are examples of a process of creating a map for each situation that functions as a guide through several layers of the biopsychosocial continuum at once.

The third and most complex misnomer in the title of this chapter is "psychopathology." A problem with this should be immediately obvious, in light of the preceding discussion, because the name suggests a focus on the biological and psychological levels of the continuum, usually excluding larger contexts.

For example, a case of a child of almost 3 was presented (Kashani & Carlson, 1985) in which it was wondered whether her irritability, moodiness, difficulty sleeping, expressions of unworthiness, and self-destructive thoughts could be evidence of a major depressive disorder. The fact that the child lived with her abused and abusive mother, who had been a drug user, had been treated for depression, had been suicidal, and was seen as impatient with and unprotective of the child, was also presented, but was not considered sufficient explanation for the child's behavior to dispel the consideration of major psychopathology inside the child.

To give another example, a 13-year-old boy whose diagnosis of attention deficit disorder with hyperactivity (ADDH)) at 7 was supported by a good response to methylphenidate became paranoid and irritable, withdrew, and manifested psychotic symptoms. This is not the usual course of ADDH and thus surprised his therapist.

The concentration on identifying psychopathology in both cases broke a cardinal rule of child psychiatry—that *development is transforming*. Historically, this rule has affected the ways in which clinicians have explained the expression of symptoms in children. For example, early in child psychiatry's own development, Anna Freud (1960) argued that young children lack the psychological mechanisms to experience depression. From our current perspective, in which childhood depression is very much recognized (indeed, possibly overidentified), Anna Freud's point of view seems to reflect both an interpretation derived from the study of adult psychological mechanisms and then superimposed on children, and a protective sentimentality about childhood. It is likely that this kind of sentimental belief about the innocence of children was behind the denial of the presence of suicidal or deliberate self-destructive thoughts in young children, as well as the reality of the high rate of incest. This example shows, however, that the practice of identifying psychopathology is influenced at another sphere of the biopsychosocial continuum, the professionals' context.

Times have changed. Perhaps the pendulum has swung too far in our readiness to identify psychopathological processes in children. More and more children are being diagnosed as having conditions from which there is very little hope of their full recovery, and they are being subjected to more drastic treatments as a consequence. Biological inherited affective disorder is considered a diagnosis for life, even though with treatment one can expect to have good periods.

The therapist's wonder about the unusual course of the boy with ADDH illustrates another problem with the attachment to a psychopathological model. Here there was a problem of looking for continuity when perhaps there was none, either within the child alone or within the diagnostic category of ADDH. Long-term follow-up of adults who had minimal brain dysfunction or hyperactivity (now assumed to be due to attention deficit) as children shows that certain symptoms persist and find particular expressions in adults. The most common of these is restlessness (Weiss, Hechtman, Milroy, & Perlman, 1985). Other reported behaviors, such as antisocial behavior and substance abuse, may not be the outcomes of the brain function of ADDH, but of other influences at other levels of the biopsychosocial continuum. Some of these influences might include having been identified as "different" (as a "patient," as a "problem") and depending on medication to manage behavior (many children on methylphenidate have told me, "The medicine makes me good"). Furthermore, a child's parents and teachers are often in a quandary about whether to set limits on some of the irritating behaviors or to excuse them on the grounds that they cannot be helped because of the brain dysfunction. Incidences of the development of psychosis in such children may be more understandable in terms of the confusion about how to react to these children, and the youngsters' own confusion about their worth, place, accountability, and control, than in terms of the process of ADDH alone. Furthermore, as such an example illustrates, ADDH is a diagnosis that is descriptive of a complex of behaviors and has no proven underlying brain pathology common to all children who bear the label. There is nothing in making the diagnosis that requires that every child's onset, treatment, and course will be like the others. In fact, experience tells us quite the opposite.

Finally, if we look at contexts of ADDH outside the child, we must acknowledge that "attention deficit" is a value judgment based on some undefined standards for what is an acceptable amount of attention. Such standards will differ according to the situations in which the child's attention is being assessed. The diagnosis of ADDH may also be properly reflective of the child's parents, teachers, and others in the environment having intolerance for the amount of the child's activity. It is conceivable that in some settings, perhaps where wariness has a function, a child's shifting focus of attention could be regarded as an asset.

Following this preamble, I examine the process of expressions of emotional and behavioral dysfunction in childhood in relation to family context. First, I discuss the metaphorical meaning of "psychopathology" and the difficulties this metaphor presents for examining childhood conditions, especially in the context of development. Second, I present a historical view of the evolution of models of family influence on individual emotional and behavioral adjustment. Finally, I present three models of family–child interaction to illustrate how certain child symptoms occur in particular family contexts. I conclude that a contextual view of childhood difficulties is more consistent with the emphasis on development than is the psychopathological view.

Development and Psychopathology

Establishing a diagnosis is a basic first step in medicine. It accomplishes many things: It allows one to communicate both with the patient and with colleagues at a level of consensual understanding; it allows one to apply consensually established treatment; and it gives one an understanding of both the expression of the condition and the mechanism of action of the treatment. A hypothesis about underlying pathology is implicit in this last aspect of diagnosis (Maxmen, 1986). Most of adult psychiatry is concerned with establishing a pathology-based diagnosis that will operate as a guide to treatment.

"Psychopathology" is a metaphor. Derived from the Greek word *pathos,* "pathology" means, literally, "able to elicit sympathy." In this literal sense, pathology is an expression in one individual that evokes a response in others—a definition that clearly illustrates the interpersonal context of pathology. Common usage of the concept of pathology is taken from medicine, where it is associated with postmortem examinations or the study of tissue removed from a living organism that is now fixed, frozen, or dead.

If the brain is the anatomical location of the source of behavior, it is reasonable to expect to find identifiable structures of the brain that are associated with deviance. These structures, being abnormal, could properly be called "pathological." Individuals who have deviations in brain function, however, are described as having brain pathology, but not psychopathology. When individuals with brain pathology also manifest psychopathology, they are called "dually diagnosed." Clearly, psychopathology is not an outcome of brain pathology.

Perhaps the problem in the word "psychopathology" is not with pathology, but with "psyche." In mythology, Psyche, the beloved of Eros, represents relationships. Psyche is the metaphorical mediator of internal drives and external constraints. She is not associated with a physical locus, such as the brain, but with a metaphorical representation, the mind. Though we may talk about psychological mechanisms and psychological apparatus, these are conventions from another era of science.

Psychopathology as a concept represents an effort to reconcile intellectual constructs about psyche with the physical. Unfortunately, psychopathology usually refers to fixed or frozen psychological processes. These perceptions have the unfortunate consequence that psychopathology is usually regarded as fixed in adults; once the character is formed, or malformed, there it is.

There is a contagious pressure on child psychiatrists to operate by the same principles—that is, to associate deviant emotions and behavior in children with psychopathology. But any child psychiatrist who has followed a child for more than a decade knows that the ways in which the child expresses deviance, or whether he or she expresses deviance at all, changes over time. The concept of psychopathology, in its fixed, frozen, and dead nature, is contrary to the concept of plasticity in the child. In spite of the recent interest in adult development, the adult psychiatrist is concerned with psychopathology; the child psychiatrist is concerned with development. Psychopathology and development are not alternatives to each other, however. In fact, they are different logical types: Psychopathology is a name that implies a state; development represents a process. If one thinks of the brain as being the seat of psychopathology, one might say that the brain functions differently in children and adults—that by the age of 18 or so "hardening of the neurons" has set in, the personality is formed, and its maladaptations are now identified as psychopathology.

What is the brain equivalent of development? "Growth," meaning accrual of restraint, maturity, and wisdom, is implicit in psychological development. But, as Kagan (1985) points out, modifications of the brain after birth do not reflect accrual of neurons, but are better understood as a kind of pruning, shaping, refining, and eliminating of excess. The one instance of apparent growth in brain size that is known to take place after birth is completed some time during early school age. This occurs in the cortical areas, particularly in the frontal lobes. "Growth" here does not represent the addition of neurons, however, but the completion of myelinization, a further refining of neuron channels (Shapiro & Perry, 1976).

So "psychological development" is also a metaphor, describing a journey associated with growth, meaning accrual—in this case, of attributes such as restraint, wisdom, and maturity. von Bertalanffy (1968) proposed that the development of systems is associated with elaborating more refined and varied subsystem behaviors, and this seems to provide a more useful biological model of development than does the growth model. More recently, Nobel Prize winner llya Prigogine's (1978) model of "order through fluctuation," referring in another way to the changing organization of systems as they move through time, gives another view of how systems develop in unique and finely patterned ways.

There are normally certain patterns in the pruning process we call development, so, at this level of inquiry, we cannot account for differences between children. Abnormal brain function or structures, such as brain pathology, may account for variations from normal patterns of development. But most variations are not due to identifiable variations in physical structures, but to differences in that ephemeral area of the psyche. To account for individual differences of this sort, Thomas and Chess (1957) came up with the idea of "temperament." Temperament, they said, is not the "why" or the "what," but the "how" of behavior. It is an aggregate of what they called "primary reactive patterns." Temperament is a pattern of patterns; it is a way of describing traits, or natural tendencies brought by the child. Chess and Thomas (1984) have diligently traced the persistence of these traits into adulthood, and have also described how they are manifested differently at different stages of development and in different contexts.

Another model for inborn traits that are modifiable in context comes from work with the monkey colony at the National Institute of Mental Health (Suomi, 1986). Because of the annual birth of a new generation of rhesus monkeys, it has been possible to select for monkeys genetically predisposed to shyness, withdrawal, and depression, and, conversely, for those who are disposed to sociability, curiosity, and extraversion. High-risk monkey infants reared by extraverted mothers (after being switched in the fist 24 hours of life) develop exploratory and prosocial behaviors in the same time frame as their extraverted age mates. In these ways, they look identical to their age mates. Yet, when separated from their mothers, these high-risk youngsters immediately withdraw; when kept away from the mothers for a period of time, they may develop an affective disorder. This affective disorder responds both to antidepressants and to the restoration of the mothers. Thus the genetic predispositions can be thought of as traits that give character to the way a monkey responds to new experiences and challenges, which lead at certain moments to states, which can be modified in a variety of ways.

These observations about trait, which is intrinsic and often perhaps genetic, and state, which is an outcome of response to circumstance, raise this question: When does a state merit a *Diagnostic and Statistical Manual of Mental Disorders,* third edition, revised (DSM-III-R) Axis I or II diagnosis? When a state is thought to be permanent, is that when we call it psychopathology? That the age of 18 is the turning point is an increasingly unsatisfactory answer in light of the study of adult development, which recognizes significant modifications of behavior and psychological expression throughout the life span. Perhaps trait has been fixed into state when the behavior becomes so repetitive that it appears to be independent of context. At this point, perhaps helplessness is what leads us to hypothesize that there are actually identifiable brain processes reflecting the behavior characteristics, and that these processes can be identified through biopsy, postmortem, assessment of brain electrical activity, integrated visualization techniques, or analysis of brain metabolites.

Family Context as Explanation for Emotional Dysfunction

The first well-known family model of psychopathology was developed by Sigmund Freud. I am sure that if Freud had lived in the mid-1900s he would have been a family therapist. Victorian mores probably prevented him from confronting the real family members he believed to exist behind the psychological dysfunction he found in his patients. He had to settle for working with the projection of these family relationships on the individual. Because of the social limitations of his time, Freud was not a family therapist. He actually had no model of family interaction; his description of the treatment of Little Hans (1909/1963) illustrates this. Never were the parents' relationships with each other explored. Nor was the father's greater involvement with Hans as a consequence of the child's phobia examined, as it related either to the child's relationship to his mother or to the father's relationship to the mother. The Oedipus complex, although it describes a small boy's feelings about his parents, is not a family theory; it is a theory about what goes on in small boys' heads. Thus Freud's theories about the family did not include real relationships at the family level, but remained at the psychological level.

Over the 80 years since Freud gave up on changing families, "family" has become a convention for referring to the interpersonal context of behavior and emotions. The family is the most portable interpersonal context, and, at least when the child is very young, it is the most influential one. As Sullivan (1953) observed, it is not until the child reaches school age that he or she has a chance to modify the influences of the family through contacts with society (the next level). The family, however, is not the only context of influence; there are other contextual spheres outside the family. And context alone does not make the individual. Individuals in a context have traits, and individual traits will influence the context as the context will influence the expression of these traits. This reciprocity or mutual modification is critical to the family systems viewpoint.

A History of Family Models of Psychopathology

I have said that if Freud lived in the mid-1900s he would have been a family therapist, because some time in the 1940s professionals overcame their reticence about dealing directly with family members. Actually, in the 1930s, Nathan Ackerman began including families in his work with children because he recognized that families were critical to children's functioning, and he felt ready to work with the family group. Since the 1940s there have been three distinct approaches to understanding individual dysfunction in its relationship to the family: the mechanistic notion of the pathogenic family; the faulty-communications position; and understanding of the family as an organism.[1]

In the radical environmentalism of the postwar period of the 1940s, sources of emotional weakness were sought within the family. Professionals have since come under severe criticism for their attacks on families. Lasch, in *Haven in a Heartless World* (1977), among others, cites professionalism for undermining family competence. More recently still, the families themselves have taken to task the professionals who have blamed families.

Back in the 1940s, however, "family" was synonymous with "mother." Wylie (1942) led the way by referring to "a generation of vipers" and coining the term "Momism." Kanner referred to the mothers of autistic children as "refrigerator" mothers, reflecting his belief that their cool detachment was associated

---

[1] These three paradigms were actually characterized by Levenson in his 1973 book, *The Fallacy of Understanding*, which described his observations about changes in the nature of psychoanalytic inquiry in the years since Freud's earliest introduction.

with the autistic symptoms. Fromm-Reichmann is credited with the term "schizophrenogenic" mother. This trend to see mothers as crucial to the emotional development of their children persists into the present, despite numerous scientifically based protests.[2]

The approaches to families implied in these terms mechanistically blame families for the problems in their children. The environment is held totally responsible, and the inquiry based on these premises is to find the causative elements in the environment and to eliminate them.

In the second phase of the history of family models of psychopathology, family communication was found to be the villain. This approach had its heyday in the 1950s and early 1960s. At first it was a subtle modification of the mechanistic theory, locating the causative element in the communication—at first, in the mother–child communication. This was true of the original version of the double-bind theory (Bateson, Jackson, Haley, & Weakland, 1956/1972), which was subsequently revised to include fathers. Lidz, Cornelison, Fleck, and Terry (1957) identified communications problems they called "marital schism" and "marital skew" in the parents of schizophrenics, and Wynne, Ryckoff, Day, and Hirsch (1958) posited a form of misleading communication reflected in their terms "pseudomutuality" and "pseudohostility." Each of these models (and they are quite different from each other) held that schizophrenia occurs in the context of pathogenic communications. Each was another way of blaming the family for the patient's dysfunction.

The third phase of this history began in the 1970s and is being elaborated even now. The family is now seen as a context for the expression of dysfunction, and dysfunction is also seen as influencing the family context. The models in this era are referred to as "organismic," being organized through interactional, cybernetic, and general systems principles, rather than mechanical (cause-and-effect, or communication) message transmission principles.

It has been argued that the current era of family systems thinking reflects a different basis of idea construction than that which underlies more traditional medical/psychiatric thinking. Dell (1980) tried to characterize these differences in his vividly titled article, "The Hopi Family Therapist and the Aristotelian Parents." Dell pointed out that the Hopi language, which is filled with predicates and has few objects, represents an outlook based on expectation and preparation for evolution and change—an outlook clearly consistent with our developmental view of

---

[2]Once again, the idea that a child's traits are brought into the family context and shape the parents' responses as the parents shape the child was proposed in the mid-1950s by Chess and Thomas, when they initiated their longitudinal study of temperament and sent out the encouraging message that each child is a person in his or her own right. Rutter's (1972) famous work on maternal deprivation questions the premise that the child survives or fails on the basis of good mothering, while Kagan (1985) proposes that the mother–infant bond issue seems to be a "moral imperative" clung to in spite of little supportive scientific evidence. That it is clung to in spite of the changing status of women is reflected in Caplan and Hall-McCorquodale's (1985) review of "mother blaming" in the child development literature. They found that there was no substantial shift in the focus on mothers as instrumental in their children's emotional health and adjustment, even with the changed emphases brought about by the women's movement.

children. Aristotelian English, on the other hand, emphasizes nouns and focuses on things and the names of things as they are. The differences in world views shaped by these linguistic differences could result in major misunderstandings if a Hopi family therapist were to treat the child of an Aristotelian parent.

Frameworks for organismic models include games and rituals, general systems theory, and cybernetics. A brief description of each one will clarify how symptomatology or dysfunction is understood within these frameworks.

Game theory as a clinical model was popularized by Eric Berne's book *Games People Play* (1964); it refers to the observation that people engage in repetitive, rule-bound, and seemingly pointless interactions. Berne described a number of interpersonal games without end. My favorite is "Why don't you; yes, but." This is commonly played between professionals and clients and is a game whose only conceivable goal is to perpetuate the relationship. Basically, the professional orders, demands, exhorts, or begs the client to try something, and the client responds, cooperatively, "I tried to, but . . . ," or "I would if I could, but . . ." Actually, this is a kind of feedback cycle: The professional is triggered to be helpful by the client's need, and the client responds by trying and failing, and therefore continuing to depend upon the professional. The usefulness of the game concept is that if the game can be named and the rules can be teased out, the players may be able to decide whether the activity they are engaged in is or is not accomplishing what they want. Family games and family rituals are concepts applied often in the systemic school of family therapy (Selvini Palazzoli, 1986). They operate on the same principles as Berne's games. Less mechanical and more metaphorical, and tailored to the special instances of each family, the game model also introduces the playful element in these otherwise deadeningly repetitive situations.

General systems theory was first applied to human systems by von Bertalanffy (1968). He proposed that human systems function like open systems, in that they act in some ways like independent organisms by generating rules and regulations for behavior within the system, but are subject to modifications from without. Open systems have a direction, in that they are evolving more complex, intricate, and differentiated mechanisms of activity. The family as an open system generates its own rules and rituals, which evolve and are modified as the family develops and as its members become more differentiated from each other and more integrated with the surrounding society (Combrinck-Graham, 1985).

As I have already mentioned, Prigogine's (1978) notions about the effect of entropy—randomly stirring systems, which then find entirely new and unexpected ways of organizing—have added to the basic ideas about human systems' functions. For clinicians, the humbling observation pointed out by Prigogine is that changes in systems are not predictable or controllable. Each system adapts and adjusts (i.e., develops) in its own particular way.

Cybernetics supplies a third approach to human systems. It begins with the simple feedback model of the house thermostat or steam engine governor. Two levels of cybernetics are illustrated by the thermostat: first-order, which describes the negative feedback cycle itself, and second-order, which defines the setting of the first-order cycle. A klutzy child may be observed to have his clumsiest moments when his mother and father are heating up for a good fight. Suddenly Johnny crashes into the TV set, it breaks, and Mom and Dad, in their exasperation with Johnny, forget their fight. Later, Mom wants to watch the news, becomes exasperated at the broken TV set, and begins to criticize her husband because he won't let her take Johnny for a neurological exam. The fight heats up and Johnny has another accident. This can be understood as a cybernetic system—not as neat as the thermostat—furnace system, but similar. It is also called a symptomatic cycle. The recursive and repetitive nature of the behaviors can be characterized in this way. Although some might say that the child's symptoms have the function to regulate the parents' fights, others would simply notice the repetitive sequences without attempting to explain them.

A second-order adjustment in this system could occur in a number of ways. Mom and Dad may decide that they hate fighting and go to a marital therapist. They then readjust their setting for fighting, which changes the setting for the system in which Johnny has accidents. Or Dad may finally agree that Johnny seems to be excessively uncoordinated, and they all go to the neurologist, who recommends physical therapy for Johnny. This readjusts the family's expectations of Johnny, and thus it changes the setting of the system's response to Johnny's accidents. These are second-order cybernetic possibilities. One can see that these second-order changes can occur naturally through developmental changes, through changes in family status, or through therapeutic interventions.

All three family models—mechanical, communications, and organismic—exist in the present. There are still many family therapists who use a family to correct or to mediate difficulties in an individual family member, believing that the individual's symptomatology is caused by the family. These clinicians will identify and label the individual biological or psychological characteristics of all relevant individuals in the client system. The identified patient's symptoms will be seen as the consequence of diagnosable psychopathology in significant family members, and causative processes, such as projective identification, will be thought to explain the pathogenesis. For example, the fact that a mother has a severe depression or borderline pathology may be used to explain her child's borderline personality organization. These clinicians understand the process of family therapy in terms of the transference phenomena between family members and between each family member and the therapist. Unfortunately, the family members tend to be negatively evaluated, because they are thought to suffer from psychopathology.

The communications-oriented family therapist works on improving and clarifying communications. The popularity of this approach is expressed by many couples in marital therapy who say that they are learning to communicate better. The emphasis in neurolinguistic programming (NLP) on clarifying differences in how people send and receive messages is an example of this. Practitioners of NLP point out that one spouse uses primarily feeling and kinesthetic imagery, whereas the other uses primarily visual imagery. The message about feelings sent by one spouse cannot be ''seen'' by the other, whereas how the other sees the problem cannot be ''felt'' by the first. Recognizing these perceptual differences is a first step in NLP therapy toward straightening out communication.

The organismic family therapist works with an understanding of the symptomatic behavior as intrinsic to the operations of the entire ecological system, of which the family is a most significant level for children. To illustrate some conceptual and practical uses of the organismic approach to family systems, I consider three areas of child diagnosis: anxiety disorders; the borderline syndrome of childhood; and failure to thrive in infancy.

Uses of the Organismic Models

Anxiety Disorders

In assessing a child presenting with complaints of anxiety, the family-oriented therapist's first question will be about the context of the anxiety. Inquiries will be made about all relevant contexts, including the family system, the school, the extended family, and the social systems of the child and the family. The child's experience of anxiety is real and painful for him or her. It is the child who has the foreboding, the nightmares, the distracting worry, the physiological symptoms (palpitations, diaphoresis, and diarrhea or nausea), and probably the accompanying identifiable disturbances in neurobiology and endocrine functions. These symptoms are upsetting internally, and their effects are compounded by the fact that they interfere with normal school and peer development.

Yet these symptoms in a young child must be examined in context, particularly in terms of how they resonate within the family. On a logical level, the persistence of anxiety occurs when there is inadequate reassurance. This is true whether the anxiety itself is logical or not. It is not always possible to provide reassurance to an overanxious child. The child's discomfort itself tends to focus family concern on the child in a way that reinforces the symptoms rather than providing reassurance; thus efforts to reassure the child may actually produce greater anxiety. The child's increased anxiety reflects back on those who sought to reassure, making them less able to reassure and also resulting in greater anxiety on the part of the child. The parents may plead with the child to calm down, to which the child will usually respond by not calming down. A cycle develops: child anxious, parent offering support, child not accepting support, parent feeling inadequate, child anxious in the context of parent inadequacy, and so on.

There may be a lack of parental sureness in relation to the child. The child may have traits or vulnerabilities, such as a temperamental misfit, that contribute to this lack of parental sureness. I want to stress that a parent's unsureness does not cause the child's anxiety and that the child makes his or her own contribution to the parent's unsureness. Effects in the system go in all directions.

Parental unsureness may be expressed in differences between the parents—differences that reinforce their unsureness. In the case of school avoidance due to separation anxiety disorder, a child who refuses to go to school may do so while one parent orders him or her to go to school and the other begs the first not to be so hard on the child. These patterns of unsureness and worry may also be observed between the parents and their own parents in relation to the child. Very often they will be seen between the parents and the professionals from whom they seek help. In fact, the act of seeking help is often a reflection of parental feelings of inadequacy, which can induct the therapist into the symptomatic cycle.

We now have several models of childhood anxiety in a family context. The first is an internal symptomatic cycle (Figure 4-2). The second is in the context of parental disagreement (Figure 4-3).The third is a symptomatic cycle in which professionals outside the family participate (Figure 4-4).

Why elaborate these hypotheses in this graphic way? Treatment, regardless of the modality chosen, will have to disrupt these symptomatic cycles. Anxiolytic medication given to the child may interrupt the symptomatic cycle by diminishing the child's anxiety, but it will not change the second-order characteristics of the symptomatic cycle. Each time the medication is given, the greater expertise of the prescribing psychiatrist will be recalled, thus reinforcing the expert cycle (Figure 4-4), and the cycle is likely to resume in a different form. New symptoms appearing in this system may be understood as "symptom substitution": First-order changes reduce the presenting symptoms, but unless changes are introduced at the second-order level, the symptomatic cycles are likely to persist.

A brief example of a 6-year-old boy with a separation anxiety disorder is presented from the *DSM-III Casebook* (Spitzer, Skodol, Gibbon, & Williams,

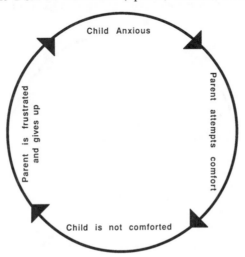

Figure 4-2. Anxiety: Internal symptomatic cycle.

Figure 4-3. Anxiety: Two-parent involvement.

1981, pp. 167–168). The child, Michael, will not sleep in his own bed and has terrible stomachaches in the morning before school. A fuller description of the treatment has been presented elsewhere (Combrinck-Graham, 1986); this is summarized here.

In interviewing the family, the therapist may discover that the mother encourages the child to get dressed, but when the father is more forceful, she pleads with him not to be so hard on Michael. The father leaves in a huff, and the mother finally gets Michael off to school; he arrives late, thus being very obtrusive to his classmates, creating embarrassment, and adding to his experience of anxiety. The

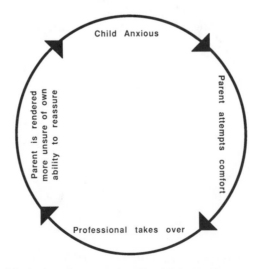

Figure 4-4. Anxiety: Symptomatic cycle with professional intervention.

parents will have similar arguments about bedtime. To break the symptomatic cycle, the therapist might first ask the parents to choose whether they want to begin working on getting Michael to sleep in his own bed or on getting him to school in the morning. They argue about this and seem deadlocked. The therapist reminds them periodically that she is waiting for their decision. Finally the father gives in and agrees to start with the bed problem, since that is what his wife wants. The therapist then explores the bedtime routines with them and asks for their thoughts about what changes they might make.

In each of these steps, the therapist is not taking control of the symptom or making suggestions about the solution, but is guiding the parents to a position of greater authority in their own family by her respectful expectation that they will come up with some decisions and solutions. The child is present and experiences his parents' struggle to become more decisive. He may appear to try to sabotage their efforts, perhaps by complaining about feeling poorly in the session, or by observing that this is not helping him. The therapist will have to prevent the child's symptoms from co-opting the therapeutic system, which, since it is not following the pathway of the symptomatic cycle, is likely to be truly therapeutic, operating by changing the setting of the system and allowing new interactions to occur.

The Borderline Syndrome of Childhood[3]

The diagnosis of borderline syndrome of childhood has not reached the DSM-III, as has its more established relative, borderline personality disorder, which is to be applied only to individuals 18 and over. The idea of a borderline classification emerged in the 1950s (Shapiro, 1983); it originally referred to conditions that seemed to be ''on the border'' between clearer regions of nosology and descriptive phenomenology. Currently, the borderline syndrome more fully represents a psychodynamically hypothesized personality structure that explains the phenomena of impulsivity, affective storms, and fluctuating emotional states.

Current theories of the genesis of borderline characteristics depend largely on object relations theory and the nature of the infant's internalization of objects to build a secure and reliable sense of self and nonself. This process is thought to depend on the quality of the infant–mother interaction, a ''good enough'' mother, and the mother's capacity to provide an adequate holding environment (Winnicott, 1965) within which the infant can sort out the world of affectional objects.

Like many adult syndromes whose origins are supposed to be rooted in childhood experience, the borderline syndrome takes on a different and rather confusing shape in childhood. Though the descriptive characteristics of impulsivity, af-

---

[3] My thoughts on the borderline syndrome of childhood and family systems are more fully presented elsewhere (Combrinck-Graham, in press).

fective storms, and fluctuating relationships with reality may be described in both the childhood syndrome and the adult syndrome, clinicians differ about the qualities of the borderline child, the origins, and the outcome of the syndrome in adulthood (Kestenbaum, 1983).

Since family systems theory focuses on the contextual aspects of behavior rather than the intrapsychic aspects, borderline phenomena, as they have come to be described in contemporary literature, take on different meanings. When the family-systems-oriented therapist considers treatment of what others refer to as the "borderline child," it is necessary to reassess the child in terms of his or her family context.

The word "borderline" evokes notions of borders and boundaries, which in turn evoke pictures of actual boundaries such as fences, hedges, walls, and doors, which delineate spaces and demarcate functions. And since "boundary" is also a family systems concept, we can explore this aspect of the interpersonal functioning of "borderline" children, in order to obtain a clearer picture of the family context of this condition. "Boundary" is an important abstraction about multiperson structures, referring to the negotiation of space and distance between individuals, subsystems, and systems. Furthermore, boundaries differentiate roles and functions within family systems. Thus boundaries, as family systems concepts, refer both to proximity and to hierarchy.

Wood (1985) has defined family boundaries in terms of family proximity and family hierarchy. A wholistic expression of excessive proximity is "enmeshment," which describes a high degree of family closeness, resonance between individuals and subsystems, and unclear hierarchical functions as well. In addition to proximity, enmeshment also refers to role diffusion, poor hierarchical distinctions, and cross-generational coalitions.

An example of a child described as borderline, from the literature, can illustrate how this way of understanding symptomatic behavior in the family context will lead to different ways of viewing the behavior and treating it. Velia (Kestenbaum, 1983) presented at age 7 with poor academic achievement and poor social relationships with both teachers and peers. Her problem behaviors including lying, stealing, fighting, and truancy. Her symptoms met the consensus criteria for borderline syndrome (Vela, Gottlieb, & Gottlieb, 1983) She was born when her mother was 16 and her father was 17. Velia lived till age 5 with her maternal grandparents. Velia's mother had left home when she was 15; the grandfather was an alcoholic, and the grandmother was described as a martyr-like member of a group that helped wives of alcoholics. Velia's own mother remarried when she was 5, and Velia then left her grandparents' care to live with her mother and stepfather. Adjustment difficulties were manifested in rages and sleepwalking. She also had severe difficulties getting along with other children.

Velia had 2 years of intensive individual therapy, during which she manifested ambivalence toward the therapist, blocking progress. Therapy ended when the family moved away, but a follow-up more than 15 years later found that Velia

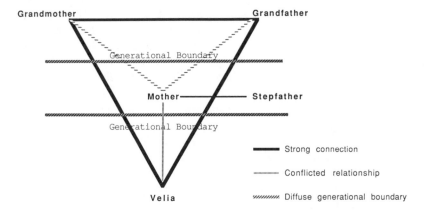

Figure 4-5. Structural diagram of a "borderline system."

had continued to have a rocky course. As an adult, she was diagnosed as having a borderline personality disorder.

Because of the structural language implicit in the name of the syndrome, I use a structural model (Figure 4-5). I have developed the following hypotheses about the family. First, Velia was very attached to her grandparents and they to her; this is represented in the bold lines connecting Velia and this generation. Having the infant to care for had very possibly organized the grandparent household in a functional way. The grandfather may even have reduced or stopped his drinking to care for his infant granddaughter. When she went to live with her mother, both Velia and her grandparents experienced a sense of loss. The grandparents also had little respect for Velia's mother, who had left when she was very young. This is represented in the diffuse generational boundary between grandparents and parents. Since Velia had been born prematurely, was sickly as an infant, and was clumsy and wore leg braces till 18 months of age, her mother was even more uncertain of her competence as a parent. Futhermore, Velia's stepfather was unclear about his role in relation to both the child and her mother. These parental uncertainties are represented in the diffuse generational boundary between parents and child. Velia's behavior maintained the diffuseness of roles and boundaries in the system by reinforcing her mother's uncertainty and the stepfather's confusion while sustaining her loyal attachment to the grandparents, whose attachment to her further undermined the mother and stepfather's functioning. Thus Velia's behavior functioned in the context of strong cross-generational coalitions and diffuse generational boundaries, both as a cause and as an effect, recursively.

Again, the purpose of the diagrammatic hypothesis is to plan treatment. Individual therapy in a situation in which the grandparent–child coalition is undermining the parental function of the mother and stepfather is doomed to failure for several reasons. The first is what the therapist experienced. Velia's desperate attachment to others did not permit her to commit herself to the therapeutic relationship. Another is that a relationship with the therapist that excludes the mother and stepfather will increase their removal from effective management of this child.

With these observations in mind, family treatment would be designed to strengthen the effective function of the parents while maintaining the child's relationship with the grandparents. In order to do this, it would be necessary to clarify the boundaries between the grandparent system and the parent system. This could be done, in sessions, by asking the parents to manage Velia's behavior, restraining the grandparents if they tried to take over or criticize the parents, and praising the grandparents for the parents' success, thus attributing to them the effectiveness of their own daughter, Velia's mother. In sessions with only Velia and her parents, the therapist would continue to work on the boundaries of role definition. This could be accomplished not only through management and structure for Velia, carried out by the parents, but also through encouraging play and suggesting that the parents could learn about play from Velia. Management, limit setting, and boundary marking are parents' roles. Play is a child's role and contribution to the family. The parents would continue to be supported in a parenting function by discussing Velia's school performance and developing relationships with peers. These discussions would point them toward other areas they would need to manage as parents.

Failure to Thrive

"Failure to thrive" is a condition in which an infant fails to gain weight or to grow, despite the availability of adequate nourishment. Originally, failure to thrive was associated with marasmus, an extreme emotional withdrawal described in institutionalized babies by Spitz (1945). The notion here was that failure to thrive is a physiological representation of emotional distress and giving up. More recently, it has been asserted that there is no such thing as marasmus on an emotional basis, and that the babies in the institutions observed by Spitz were actually neglected. More recently still, the search for the vegetative signs of depression in very young children has encouraged clinicians to reconsider the affective component of failure to thrive. Nevertheless, failure to thrive has been most commonly understood as failure to be fed—a formulation of the problem that often led to the immediate accusation of mothers for neglecting their infants. These infants were often admitted to the hospital, where it was said that, rocked in the ample lap of a maternal nursing assistant, they eagerly fed and gained weight rapidly, but then, upon discharge and return to their mothers, would lose the weight once again. A careful study performed by Bell and Woolston (1985), however, demonstrated that the only factor that was associated with the relative ability to renourish infants with nonorganic failure to thrive was the nutritional status of the infant.

Observation of the mothers feeding their infants yielded more information about the failure-to-thrive system. The infants were listless and often turned their heads away from the mothers attempting to feed them. The mothers would readily conclude that the children were not hungry. Wasn't this a repetitive cycle? A mother would attempt to feed; the child would refuse or act listless; the mother would give up; the child would become weaker and more listless; and so on.

Experience has shown that one cannot break the symptomatic cycle by bringing such an infant into the hospital and feeding it, even though this changes its nutritional status. It becomes necessary to look beyond the mother–child dyad to a larger system. Many of these dyads are failing to thrive in a social environment. Cut off from family of origin, from neighbors, and often from the baby's father, a mother and child are isolated and without social nourishment. Child welfare workers are often perceived as critical or as spying; thus they are not included in the inner system and do not fill the hungry social void (Figure 4-6).

Sonya M, a 6-month-old infant, had had two hospital admissions for failure to gain weight. On each admission she gained weight, but on returning home she lost the weight again. Sonya lived with her mother, aged 21, and her 2½-year-old brother. Ms. M's mother lived in the same city but had no contact with her own daughter or grandchildren. Both the children were at home with the mother full-time, and the family was on welfare. Ms. M, her two children, and the hospital social worker arrived for the first session. They came half an hour late because the mother forgot the time of the appointment. The children's father and grandmother were also invited, but did not attend.

They came into the room and stood until the social worker invited the mother to sit down. She was holding Sonya, while Derrick, the toddler, clung to her coat,

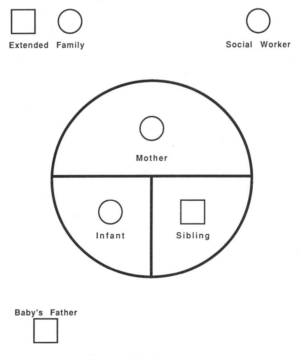

Figure 4-6. Failure to thrive.

whimpering slightly. The social worker helped Derrick off with his coat. He cried a little and looked searchingly at his mother, who said, "Shut up." Sonya was asleep, precariously balanced on her mother's lap, while Ms. M tried to sooth Derrick, who was now nearly hysterical. When he calmed down, the therapist asked about the problem. The mother replied that the baby was never hungry, cried during the feedings, and went to sleep in the middle of a feeding. She appeared distressed and concerned for her infant. Sonya woke up, crying weakly, and the mother decided to feed her. This was not a regular feeding time, but there did not seem to be a regular feeding time. Ms. M produced a bottle of formula and put the nipple into the baby's mouth. The toddler was playing noisily with some toys in the room, and his mother shouted at him, "Stop that." Sonya did not suck, but allowed the nipple to sit in her mouth. A little of the formula dribbled down the side of her face, and her mother carefully wiped it up. Sonya eventually became fretful and cried. Her mother withdrew the bottle, saying, "She's not hungry now." The infant continued to cry; the mother changed her diaper and finally laid her on the couch while she turned her attention to the therapist. Derrick stood next to his mother, sucking his fingers and staring at the therapist.

The therapist asked about Ms. M's situation, and she responded defensively, refusing to talk at all about her relationship with her own mother. She reported that the children's father was no good, as he took no responsibility and came around just when he wanted to.

At a later point in the session, the therapist asked the social worker to take care of Derrick while Ms. M was encouraged to try to feed Sonya again. The therapist moved very close to Ms. M and Sonya so that she could study their faces and actions as Sonya fed. She encouraged Ms. M to look at Sonya and to talk to her, placing the baby's face in front of her mother's. When the baby turned away, Ms. M was encouraged to follow her gaze and get her attention again. Sonya began to suck, and Ms. M was pleased, while the therapist complimented her on her involvement with the infant.

Treatment, as it proceeded, was based on the hypotheses at two levels: The first was the symptomatic cycle in regard to feeding; the second was the social starvation of the little family. The mother and children were admitted to a family apartment on a child inpatient psychiatric unit (Combrinck-Graham, Gursky, & Brendler, 1982). There, feeding sessions were attended by a staff member, who continued to encourage the mother to play with the baby and to report her observations about the baby's response, particularly during feedings. The staff member "fed" the mother by calling her attention to the baby's attributes, the brightness of her eyes, the cute smile, the way she expressed herself. The mother was given credit for Sonya's attractiveness while her attention was being focused on the infant. When Sonya was listless and unresponsive in feedings and let the food dribble out of her mouth, Ms. M was praised for sticking with it during a time when the child wasn't helping very much. When Sonya perked up and ate, she herself rewarded her mother. (This kind of intervention can be done in the family's home by a visiting nurse or social worker.)

After Sonya had begun to gain weight through her mother's feeding, Ms. M was asked to invite the children's father in. She was more willing to do this when she was feeling successful. The father babysat for the children while Ms. M went out to look for a job. Before she left, she gave him careful instructions about caring for the children and supervised his feeding of Sonya, giving him pointers about looking at her and stimulating her while she ate. Later, she invited her own mother in, and demonstrated her competence with her own children. Ms. M's mother was very busy herself, but did offer to take care of the children on occasion. When the M family was discharged, Ms. M had a small but responsive network of resources to help her with the children. She chose not to work outside of the home until Sonya was walking, but did arrange to go out with friends from time to time, sometimes with the children, and sometimes leaving the children with their father or grandmother. Sonya continued to thrive.

Within the family, the symptomatic cycle was interrupted, and between the family and extended family relationships, boundaries were diffused to create a competent and nourishing system in which the whole family could thrive.

Summary and Conclusions

I have presented three examples of ways in which family contextual observations can be organized to understand child symptoms. If they appear simplistic, it is because I have schematically reduced them to "models." The execution of such systemically conceived plans is not always straightforward, because the therapist's plans and formulations are always being modified by the family's responses. The principle, however, of including several systems levels (especially the therapist) in the formulation will always yield a useful working hypothesis that can be worked into a model or map, a guide to action.

If there really were child psychopathology, these could be called family models of child psychopathology. But I have also argued that childhood is such a fluid experience that describing the states of childhood in pathological terms may actually interfere with the momentum of development. Assessing and treating childhood problems in their family contexts permit interventions that support the competent functioning of both child and family in larger contexts. In this way, the momentum of development may be restored.

REFERENCES

Bateson, G., Jackson, D. D., Haley, J., & Weakland, J. H. (1972). Toward a theory of schizophrenia. In G. Bateson, *Steps to an ecology of mind* (pp. 201–227). New York: Ballantine Books. (Original work published 1956)
Bell, L. S., & Woolston, J. L. (1985). The relationship of weight gain and calorie intake in infants with organic and nonorganic failure to thrive syndrome. *Journal of the American Academy of Child Psychiatry, 24,* 447–452.
Berne, E. (1964). *Games people play.* New York: Grove Press.

Caplan, P. J., & Hall-McCorquodale, I. (1985). Mother-blaming in major clinical journals. *American Journal of Orthopsychiatry, 55*, 345–353.

Chess, S. & Thomas, A. (1984). *Origins and evolution of behavior disorders: From infancy to early adult life.* New York: Brunner/Mazel.

Combrinck-Graham, L. (1985). A model of family development. *Family Process, 24*, 139–150.

Combrinck-Graham, L. (1986). Family treatment for childhood anxiety disorders. In L. Combrinck-Graham (Ed.), *Treating young children in family therapy* (pp. 22–30) Rockville, MD: Aspen.

Combrinck-Graham, L. (1988). The borderline syndrome in childhood: A family systems approach. *Journal of Psychotherapy and the Family.*

Combrinck-Graham, L., Gursky, E. J., & Brendler, J. (1982). Hospitalization of single-parent families of disturbed children. *Family Process, 21*, 141–152.

Dell, P. F. (1980). The Hopi family therapist and the Aristotelian parents. *Journal of Marital and Family Therapy, 5*, 123–130.

Dell, P. F. (1986). Understanding Bateson and Maturana: Toward a biological foundation for the social sciences. *Journal of Marital and Family Therapy, 11*, 1–20.

Freud, A. (1960). Discussion of Dr. John Bowlby's paper. *Psychoanalytic Study of the Child, 15*, 53–62.

Freud, S. (1963). Analysis of a phobia in a five-year-old boy. In *The sexual enlightenment of children.* New York: Crowell-Collier. (Original work published 1909)

Kagan, J. (1985). *The nature of the child.* New York: Basic Books.

Kashani, J. H., & Carlson, G. A. (1985). Major depression in a preschooler. *Journal of the American Academy of Child Psychiatry, 24*, 490–494.

Kestenbaum, C. J. (1983). The borderline child at risk for major psychiatric disorder in adult life. In K. S. Robson (Ed.), *The borderline child: Approaches to etiology, diagnosis, and treatment* (pp. 49–82). New York: McGraw-Hill.

Lasch, C. (1977) *Haven in a heartless world.* New York: Basic Books.

Levenson, E. A. (1973). *The fallacy of understanding: An inquiry into the changing structure of psychoanalysis.* New York: Basic Books.

Lidz, T., Cornelison, A. R., Fleck, S., & Terry, D. (1957). The intrafamilial environment of schizophrenic patients: II. Marital schism and marital skew. *American Journal of Psychiatry, 114*, 241–248.

Maxmen, J. S. (1986). *Essential psychopathology.* New York: Norton.

Prigogine, I. (1978). Time, structure, and fluctuations. *Science, 201*, 777–785.

Rutter, M. (1972). Maternal deprivation reconsidered. *Journal of Psychosomatic Research, 16*, 2412–250.

Selvini, Palazzoli M. (1986). Towards a general model of psychotic family games. *Journal of Marital and Family Therapy, 4*, 339–349.

Shapiro, T. (1983). The borderline syndrome in children: A critique. In K. S. Robson (Ed.), *The borderline child: Approaches to etiology, diagnosis, and treatment* (pp. 11–29). New York: McGraw-Hill.

Shapiro, T., & Perry, R. (1976). "Latency" revisited: The age 7 plus or minus 1. *Psychoanalytic Study of the Child, 31*, 79–105.

Spitz, R. A. (1945). Hospitalism: An inquiry into the genesis of psychiatric conditions in early childhood. *Psychoanalytic Study of the Child, 1*, 53–74.

Spitzer, R. L., Skodol, A. E., Gibbon, M., & Williams, J. B. W. (Eds.). (1981). *DSM-III casebook.* Washington, DC: American Psychiatric Association.

Sullivan, H. S. (1953) *The interpersonal theory of psychiatry.* New York: Norton.

Suomi, S. (1986). *Family therapy for high risk monkeys.* Paper presented at the annual meeting of the American Family Therapy Association, Washington, DC.

Thomas, A., & Chess, S. (1957). An approach to the study of individual differences in child behavior. *Journal of Experimental and Clinical Psychology and Quarterly Review of Psychiatry and Neurology, 18*, 347–357.

Vela, R., Gottlieb, H., & Gottlieb, E. (1983). Borderline syndromes in childhood: A critical review.

In K. S. Robson (Ed.), *The borderline child: Approaches to etiology, diagnosis, and treatment* (pp. 31–48). New York: McGraw-Hill.

von Bertalanffy, L. (1968). *General system theory.* New York: Braziller.

Weiss, G. Hechtman, L., Milroy, T., & Perlman, T. (1985). Psychiatric status of hyperactives as adults: A controlled prospective 15 year follow-up of 63 hyperactive children. *Journal of the American Academy of Child Psychiatry, 24,* 211–220.

Winnicott, D. W. (1965). *The maturational process and the facilitating environment: Studies in the theory of emotional development.* New York: International Universities Press.

Wood, B. (1985). Proximity and hierarchy: Orthoganal dimensions of family interconnectedness. *Family Process, 24,* 487–507.

Wylie, P. (1942). *A generation of vipers.* New York: Rinehart & Company.

Wynne, L. C., Ryckoff, I. M., Day, J., & Hirsch, S. I. (1958). Pseudo-mutuality in the family relations of schizophrenics. *Psychiatry, 21,* 205–220.

Family Shapes Confronting the Therapist

Anthropologists report that there are scores of family structures in which children grow up. Chapters in this section address a range of therapeutic possibilities with different family structures.

Kramer, in Chapter 5, asserts that growing up in a two-parent family is a complex affair because it involves learning to love and hate a "two-headed monster." Through his evocative style, he presents the family as a context for the management of the psychological experiences of duality and balance, and then goes on to illustrate the psychological continuity between the individuals and the family. Thus he illustrates a comment made to a young music student who was studying a score: "The black is the notes; the white is the music."

But *all* families are two-parent families. This is a fact of biology, and if other parenting figures have been introduced, the two original parents are still there in the family mind. Often, for the purposes of therapy, it is better to coordinate the family mind than to leave open the possibility of so many conflicting views of these essential family figures. This view of the family as being largely a fantasy of itself derives from the "symbolic–experiential" school of Carl Whitaker and leads to the methods of provoking the family's symbolic experience. At the core of the experience are the two-headed monster and getting comfortable with loving and hating.

Chapter 6 is the first publication of some very important research on poor, minority-group, single-parent-headed families. Lindblad-Goldberg's investigation of competence in families with this composition derives from the school of structural family therapy, in which family organization, executive functioning, and role assignment and flexibility become significant in differentiating competent from clinical families. In her study, further significant factors were found in the family-of-origin experience of the parent and in the parent's sense of herself as an adult relating to adults. Moreover, an optimistic, problem-solving approach to the frequent stresses that plague poor families enabled the competent families to survive these stresses.

The roots of such competence in the histories of these families, going back at least one generation, might induce the therapist to be pessimistic about treating those families who do not manage so well and need to involve outside agents. But Lindblad-Goldberg gives a fine illustration of treatment in which the helping system's perpetuation of the crisis orientation of the family is gently approached in such a way that the family assumes responsibility for itself and the mother eventually becomes a helper herself. Thus, attitudes and coping styles inherited from a previous generation can be revised in the present one. An understanding of the factors that define competence in these families is crucial to formulating and executing treatment with those who are struggling.

Chapters 7 and 8 deal with two family forms that I like to call "made-up" families. I find that this is a useful way of thinking about both remarried and adoptive systems, because it takes the pressure off their expectations that they will function like a family.

In Chapter 7, Whiteside leads us through the complexities of remarried family formation by presenting a model that combines family development (which is viewed much as Zilbach views it in Chapter 3) and child development. The roles of different adults and of the "add-on" siblings are described, in a presentation based on Whiteside's extensive clinical and research experience with remarried family systems. Systems in different stages of formation interact with children in different stages of development; each cell in Whiteside's chart of possible interactions (see Table 7-1) has its own characteristic problems and solutions, which she describes with vivid clinical examples. The issues of the remarried system for the child vary, then, with the complexities of these interactions, often in two separate households.

Whiteside stresses that children do better when the adults in the two households coordinate their efforts. She points out that even when one parent fears that bitterness and acrimony will interfere with such coordination, contact between the parents usually produces a surprising amount of relief. To bring this about, a therapist committed to the notion that families are children's greatest resources will firmly insist on involvement of both parents as a condition of therapy. The therapist's firmness and conviction that such an encounter will benefit the child serves as an encouragement, and the actual encounter, while not necessarily resulting in comradeship and close collaboration between the parents, probably dispels some of the nasty myths that have fostered conflict and have bound the children within the conflict (much in the way Kramer proposes that discussing things as a family has its own effects without the therapist's doing much else).

Chapter 8 focuses on the acceptance and management of the differences as the healthy task of the adoptive family. Butler wonders about the disproportionate numbers of adopted children in clinical settings, and examines the particular characteristics of the adoptive family that may contribute to this finding. She notes that adoptive families may be more ready to seek assistance than other families, because it is often through community assistance that they have adopted their children. That is, they are used to dealing with social systems. The dysfunctional aspects of these families seem to derive from factors that are intrinsic to adoption: The child and the family are genetically different from each other. Sometimes, as when they are of a different race, this is more apparent than at other times. But this difference always exists in the minds of the family members, and can become a sticking point when either side is unhappy with the other.

In addition to the genetic difference is the recognition of loyalties. Butler cites Boszormenyi-Nagy's assertions about filial loyalty (described in Chapter 2), and alludes to the observation of Kramer (Chapter 5) that the biological parents must be acknowledged and the child's connection to them accepted (though not pushed) if the family is to function well. These observations lead to a notion that adoption, beyond the execution of bureaucratic and legal requirements, represents a contract between adoptive parents and adopted child—one that states implicitly that the parents will act *as if* they were the child's parents, and the child will act *as if* he or she were their child. Sometimes it is useful to make the contract explicit so that parents and child can work on it and negotiate it. Butler gives some examples of contracts that evolve more comfortably when the child lives somewhere else, on the one hand, or when the parents move more in the direction of the child's racial and ethnic heritage on the other.

Despite all the possible problems, adoption can be a highly successful experience for both parents and children. And this is lucky, because adoption is one of the oldest mechanisms by which animals and people have taken care of abandoned and parentless young.

The section as a whole, then, represents a variety of different family shapes; it also presents families as biological organisms, as competent systems, as cooperating systems, and as deliberate systems. These different views of families offer a richness to the family therapist working with young children. The therapist can keep focused on the functions of the family in the present, while recognizing the influence of its heritage and that of the child as factors that shape the present, producing impediments and offering solutions to present difficulties.

5

Two-Parent Families, or
How to Love a Two-Headed Monster

DOUGLAS A. KRAMER, MD

Two-Headed Monsters

Can they both be hated and I continue to have a home? Will I end up in an orphanage? How many children have murdered both their parents anyway? Do they hate me too? Maybe I should make friends with one of them to protect myself from the other. Someday when I grow up, she may want me to kill him. She hates him, you know. He hates her just as much. I guess they hate each other. Maybe I can make friends with both of them separately. Neither can be completely trusted. After all, they are adults. They seem to enjoy it when I hate both of them. Even when I leave them notes on their bed telling them how much I do. They act like this is a good thing. I am not sure, but they seem to be snickering to themselves about it. They go into their bedroom and laugh. They try to hide it, but I can hear them. They even seem closer as a result of my hatred. This isn't working out quite right, but it does feel good somehow. Maybe my murderousness gives them a common enemy. Maybe it reminds them of their own murderousness. Why did my Mommy have me if she wanted him for a friend anyway? I love you, Daddy. He sure smiles a lot when I say that. My blankee is calling me. He tells me to finish all my cereal before getting more with the marshmallows in it. Mommy, more cereal. I didn't say "please." This sure is fun. I'm smiling. No bed. Big brother go to bed. I'll smile some more. I wonder how I'm going to be a Mommy and a Daddy at the same time?

The unique problem for the child in a family with two functioning parents is the necessity of having to hate two parents at the same time, equally and fairly.

Douglas A. Kramer. Atlanta Psychiatric Clinic & Institute for Experiential Growth, Atlanta, GA.

This requires extra effort on the part of each child so afflicted. It means something akin to growing two necks with a head attached to each and learning to breathe fire through all four nostrils simultaneously. It requires a special commitment to hating. It insists upon the courage to be.

I have a green two-headed monster on my desk, among numerous other items, and it is often the first thing noticed by children entering the office for the first time with their families. When they ask about it, I always answer, "That's what it is like to have two parents. Having to hate two people at the same time." At first there is some confusion. Do I mean that the parents are monsters, each breathing fire on the children? Therapy has already started. I explain that having two parents doubles the number of people to be hated. A knowing smile occurs, and then we move on to something else.

Sendak's (1963) *Where the Wild Things Are* is about safety in hating one's parents, and about the equivalence of love and hate. The object in my office that next catches a child's eye is usually a stuffed "Wild Things" creature. The remark is almost always "I have that," not meaning, interestingly, the stuffed creature, but the book. Children are very aware of the issues of love and hate and are pleased that an adult is going to confront these issues.

The family in therapy very quickly discovers that we are going to look at their loving and hating. Winnicott's (1949) statements, "A mother has to be able to tolerate hating her baby without doing anything about it," and later, "and certainly the patient cannot see that the analyst's hate is often engendered by the very things the patient does in his crude way of loving," and Sendak's ". . . and into the night of his very own room where he found his supper waiting for him . . . and it was still hot," are very close. The child in the two-parent family has the possibility of hating both parents at the same time, and therefore, of course, loving both parents at the same time—and of being hated and loved by two parents simultaneously as well. Loving and hating two parents at the same time is the child's first experience with dualities.

It is easier with the two-functioning-parent family to identify a separate parental generation, as two people are present to carry that flag, just as it is easier in families with more than one child to identify a separate and second generation for the children to occupy. A confusion of logical types occurs in single-parent families between the class of persons (of the single parent) and the class of parents. So, implied in my answer to children regarding the two-headed monster on my desk is the idea that the parents are both a single entity and two people, and that this is one of the arenas in which we are going to play.

Also implied in that answer is the idea that a child is a person.

This is a story . . . of a couple who are driving from up North down to Florida, and it's mealtime, and it's somewhere in South Carolina, and they find a restaurant along the road. They walk in. And they have a five year old boy, and they sit around this table, and this waitress comes by and takes the order from the mother, and the father, and then turns directly to the five year old son and says, "And what will you have?" He said, "I'll have a hot dog with everything on it, and a Pepsi Cola, a big one.'' The mother smiled at the waitress, and said, "Just bring him a piece of chicken, and some mashed potatoes, and some peas, and a glass of milk.'' The waitress said nothing and walked away. Shortly afterwards, she returned with their meals, and set down the plate in front of the father and mother, and then in front of the five year old son, she set a large hot dog with everything on it and a very large Pepsi Cola, and turned around and walked away. There was a very very quiet silence, and then the five-year-old, looking up from his plate toward his parents said, rather wistfully, "You know, she must think I'm a real person." (Story told by Thomas P. Malone, MD, January 5, 1987, and repeated in Malone & Malone, 1987, pp. 14–15).

Conversely, parents are people too. It needs to be emphasized that one has to be a person to be a husband or wife, and one has to be a person and a husband or wife to be a father or mother in a two-parent family. Single-parent families never work unless the single parent has the capacity to have a multiple personality disorder. A contemporary complaint is that nowadays people are doing everything backwards, becoming mothers or fathers, then husbands or wives, and then persons.

Victoria announced early in family therapy that she was the "bad kid." Her tone implied not so much that she believed it, but that it seemed to her that she was blamed for everything. She was adept at changing the subject every time the anger of her mother toward her father or vice versa was about to be discussed. Vivian was considerably overinvolved with her daughter. When I asked her why, she responded, "Vernon has a tendency to overreact." She explained that she was worried that he would become violent.

THERAPIST: You don't trust Vernon's love for your daughter?
VIVIAN: Well, he has been physical with her in the past.
VICTORIA *(interrupting)*: Remember that time he held me up against the wall? He might kill me.
THERAPIST: Let's take this to the extreme. Why would you want to be married to a murderer?
VIVIAN: I don't want to take it to the extreme.
THERAPIST: Well, what should be done about this problem? How about if you and Vernon talk about it?
VIVIAN: I raised her for 42 weeks a year while he traveled. *(Victoria interrupts again)*
THERAPIST: You're angry about that and maybe you don't want to talk to him? *(Victoria interrupts some more)* Vernon, it sounds like you are angry at Vivian for the way in which she has raised your daughter. *(More interruption)* You seem to change the subject, Victoria, every time your parents are about to talk about something.

The Xaviers began family therapy after the sudden suicide of their son. Mrs. Xavier spoke of wanting to be able to talk to another person—for instance, her husband—honestly about their relationship. The irony of Mrs. Xavier's wish with regard to being a peer with another adult, to talk honestly with someone about their relationship, is that this is something that any 3-year-old is quite capable of doing. Adults become psychologically retarded. An adult learns to be dishonest just as thoroughly as a child learns to ride a bicycle. In the end, family therapy with the two-parent family can be about the possibility of the two parents' being people. A distant implication of my answer to the question about the monster is that if the children can be people, perhaps the parents can be also.

Also implied in the answer about my two-headed monster, and clearly one of the themes central to the parents' and the children's being people, is that feelings are going to be part of this project. It may be that from a communicational viewpoint feelings are like play. By this, I mean that they are not owned by anyone. How can a feeling be something I own, like my appendix, or my coffee cup? Because it is something that cannot be volitionally changed. I can give my coffee cup to a friend, or have my appendix removed, but I cannot will my feeling. Feelings are always "right." If a woman hates her husband because he wears brown shirts, that is not right or wrong, crazy or sane; it is just a fact. It does not change anything. It does not necessarily lead to any particular action. It does not mean that the husband and wife have to get divorced. It is just between two people, like play—owned by neither, occurring in the transitional space (Winnicott, 1953/1971). Furthermore, there are no "bad" feelings and no "good" feelings.

All Children Have Two Parents

I discovered in the process of writing about two-parent families that the experience of being with them does not differ from the experience of being with all families. It struck me that all families are two-parent families.

In mammalian species, most parents children do not appear to recognize each other once adulthood is reached. In primates, the "father," being the group of mature adult males in the community, is sociological rather than biological (Bowlby, 1969). Even so, there are always two biological parents, and therefore always two-parent families.

Because all children have two parents, all families are two-parent families. In any two-generational biological system, each offspring has no more or less than two parents. This is true even if the father is unknown. This is true for pregnancies resulting from artificial insemination. This is true for test-tube babies. This is even true for the title character in *The World According to Garp* (Irving, 1976). His father has a name, even a military rank. Jenny Fields has a sexual encounter with Technical Sergeant Garp in his hospital bed at Boston Mercy; his name lives on in Garp.

From the child's point of view, the child has two parents. Interestingly, the original birth certificate for many adopted children often lists just a mother. The statement, "I do not have a father," is impossible and ridiculous. It usually means "My mother does not have a husband." Does this lead to fantasies of a virgin birth? Do subsequent delusions of grandeur develop? Despite all of the human variations in parenting and family structure, the biological truth is still the truth. There must be two parents, one male and one female. This will be true until cloning becomes possible.

Children develop various ways to classify their parentage. Often the word "real" is used (Kramer, 1982). An adopted child will refer to his or her biological mother and father as "real" and to the consciously experienced parents as "adoptive," or will sometimes say, "You know, my parents, the ones I live with." A child's family is like the mythological Hydra: When one of its heads is cut off, two more may grow in the place of the one amputated.

Adoption and the Two-Parent Family

Many adopted children wonder, whenever meeting adults who chronologically and ethnically could be their biological parents whether those persons might actually be their parents. The only two people they can be sure are not their biological parents are their adoptive parents. Almost everyone else is a candidate.

Alex, who was exploring the idea of searching for his biological parents, said, "I better call my mother first, before going to her front door, and make sure her husband knows about me." Strangely, in describing a possible scenario of the events surrounding his birth and subsequent adoption, he referred to himself as "the baby." That therapy session went on to become the first time he thought of himself in a biological mother–infant relationship. He had relegated these events to a third-person experience prior to this and viewed them in a detached way, almost administratively, from a adult-like point of view. Part of his confusion may have been relational. Even though his parents had always been "honest" about his being adopted, his mother once commented, "A friend asked me if Alex had been breast-fed, and I couldn't remember." A suggestion was made at that time for the family to celebrate separately Alex's birthday and his adoption day (2 days later). It was also suggested that periodically, perhaps annually, perhaps on his adoption day, the information and stories about his adoption be retold so that as he developed both psychologically and cognitively he could reintegrate the information at higher levels. This would simultaneously encourage the family to do likewise (Kramer, 1982). The family had been behaving as if the fact of Alex's adoption was irrelevant; by extension, therefore, the fact that he had biological parents elsewhere also seemed irrelevant.

The experience, the fantasy, the memory, and the reconstructed memories of the biological mother–infant relationship are highlighted by the sociological experiment of adoption. Another family was referred by an adoption agency after they had inquired about returning their 13-year-old son to the agency. Bo had been adopted at age 4. A major difference between his family and Alex's family was in the area of the fantasies surrounding the adoption process. Bo's was a large Irish-Catholic family, and Bo was black. Presumably, there was a minimal confusion about the fact of his being adopted. The family, of course, had no memory of Bo's mother–infant experience, and Bo had no conscious memory of this either. They could not visualize him as ever having been cute, vulnerable, or cooing. No pictures or home movies were available to help reconstruct such memories for either the boy or the family. It was suggested that together they read several books on early development, such as those by Brazelton (1969) and Harris and Levy (1977), to stimulate such fantasies—not so that they would ever or should ever lose sight of the reality of Bo's being adopted, but so that he and they could experience him in a more profound way as a biological being, and therefore as more "real" and "alive" than they had previously. The family's descriptions of Bo's relationship to them were characterized by a quality that was administrative, legal, and church-connected, and this had tended to depersonalize him.

Totally denying reality, a family raises a relative's child as its own. A teenage mother's mother will raise her daughter's baby, or a married sister will raise an unmarried sister's baby, and everyone in the family knows except the baby himself or herself. Once, perhaps twice, the growing child asks a relevant question. The child is told (nicely) that he or she is crazy, and thereupon accepts the family myth and agrees to be delusional.

Often the truth comes out, for better and worse. It turns the universe upside down for the person involved, and for the family's mythology and basis for relating: "You mean my sister is really my mother?" . . . "my father is really my grandfather?" . . . "my brother is really my cousin?" "No wonder my aunt was always so nice to me." I have treated (unsuccessfully, on the surface) two marriages where one of the partners in each marriage came out of such a situation.

Being adopted in itself need not be problematic. The kind of honesty that Alex's family was encouraged to develop—an honesty that is true factually, developmentally, cognitively, and relationally—prevents most major problems with adoption from occurring.

"Factually" refers to the legal, administrative, and biological reality as consensually understood by those involved. "Developmentally" refers to the need to explain this reality in terms and with concepts that are consistent with the child's psychological development, and also to do so periodically in order to add the possibility of enhanced understanding at each new level of development achieved by the child. "Cognitively" refers to the importance of understanding in such an explanation the particular aspect of development that is cognitive, and of being aware of the child's capacity for abstraction. "Relationally" refers to the concepts of "biological parent" and "psychological parent" and the importance of clarity about these issues, especially as other aspects of development allow. The term "real" confuses this issue, as it is most often applied to the biological parents, but could just as easily refer to the psychological parents. Adopted children are as much at risk of becoming stepchildren or foster children as other children, and therefore relationally can have biological parents, psychological parents, stepparents, and foster parents about whom this honesty is quite relevant.

Another reason for relational honesty is the difficulty in treating any two children the same, let alone one child who is biological and one child who is adopted.

In each situation, the parents can say, "We attempt to treat you equally." When the inevitable discrepancies occur, the child may be able to understand that sometimes these are facts of relational reality, rather than interpreting them in terms of his or her own supposed goodness or badness. The same issue always comes up in blending families between the mutual stepparents and stepchildren. Lurking in the Hydra family's relational unconscious is the original two-headed monster, multiplied once again by the numbers of turnovers in parenting responsibility.

A woman in her 30s told me that as a child she assumed she was adopted. Elizabeth was the third daughter, the youngest, and had noticed an absence of baby pictures of herself in family albums. She did not mind that she was adopted; she just assumed it was a fact. Her factual reality was incorrect as a result of her interpretation of her relational reality, which was based upon the family's photographic behavior. Her mother overheard her telling another child, who actually was adopted, that she was adopted too, and then corrected this "fact" for her. Relational reality requires factual reality.

Children who have been adopted or who become stepchildren at a very early age probably become, for better and worse, members of the relational family in a very real sense—that is, in a biological sense. In the vast number of possible facial expressions, verbalizations, and actions (especially the more subtle ones), those that characterize a family, that identify "this is us," are most likely, but unknowingly, reinforced: "That laugh sounds just like Uncle Al's." In reality, the reinforcement process probably consists of a thousand slight smiles and twinges of recognition for every thought or statement as conscious as in the example. Through this process, the child may actually begin to look like a member of the family. This can confuse the reality of adoption in one sense, and serve to perpetuate any denial the family has developed, but at the same time it enhances a sense of belonging that in a different way is also very real.

Many times I have had the experience of seeing the facial and other nonverbal characteristics of one or both parents in an adopted child. Of course, many adoption agencies attempt to match children with families along ethnic and racial lines. But it may be also that facial shape is to some extent a product of facial expression, and to the extent that certain expressions are noticed and therefore reinforced, the child's face may change in the direction of the functional family's. As time and experience go on, the identification process further adds to this belonging in a psychological way.

Stepfamilies present the most common variation on the idealized norm of the same parents' being both the genetic and the functional parents. Children whose parents were separated at a young age have the most cognitive difficulty with this factual reality, as their conscious memory of ordinary day-to-day experience with the absent biological parent is so lacking. This may be magnified if further contact with the noncustodial parent has been minimal. Verbal (and to some extent preverbal) experience tells that child that one person is the father (or mother). Biology tells a different story. What about the unconscious? Is there memory for the voice of a different parent early in life, or even *in utero?* Is there an unconscious experience of a difference between one's genetics and one's experience with one's parents? Some children have learned the word "biological." This may not mean much to a child until perhaps age 8 or 9, but it helps establish the existence of a difference. It establishes a classification of the two or more "fathers" (or "mothers").

Fred, a 9-year-old boy, said to me that his stepfather was his "real" father because his biological father would not have divorced his mother if he had loved him (Fred). Since his stepfather had not deserted his mother, and was both parental and loving to him, he was the "real" father. He was referred to as "my dad." The biological father was "my father."

Experiential Reality

But what of this and the "two-parent" family? "Mother" and "father" are constructs in the Piagetian sense. To the child, there is the mother-experience and the father-experience. To the child, all of the parental experiences with people, male or female, legally related or not, become part of the mother-experience and father-experience constructs. The child still and always has two parents. The child defines the mother and the father. The adults, and the child as he or she begins to enter the reality-oriented adult world, have difficulty conceptualizing the mother and the father as not necessarily residing in one person. The real parents are within the child. Categories are invented by adults to describe different types of parents: "step-," "adoptive," "foster," "real," "biological," "psychological," "god-" and so on. The intent is to define the child's world in terms of the adult world. The adult world prefers that the parents be external to the child rather than constructs within the child, so that they can sort through the Hydra heads and assign their own parental importance. But an experience cannot be divided up, no matter how many categories are found. As a more left-brained socialization occurs, there is more of a need to incorporate all of a particular category of experience into one living person. This process parallels the development in history of predominantly monodeistic religious beliefs from the pantheistic beliefs of Greco-Roman mythology. Ontogeny recapitulates phylogeny. Child development recapitulates theological or cultural development.

Erikson (1950) has said that the competent child elicits from the parents what that child needs. It is somewhat egocentric, if not narcissistic, to assume that this implies one parent of each gender. The competent child gets from the world of mothers and the world of fathers what experiences it needs. Experientially, there is one mother-construct and one father-construct. People of each gender have masculine and feminine aspects (Jung, 1964; Pittman, 1985; Sanford, 1980). Therefore, in theory, these maternal and paternal experiences can be gained with people of either gender.

Along with the need of the typical adult to be in control, to be the parent, and even thereby to own the child, moral issues are also important in the genesis of the idea that there are families other than two-parent families. A child "without a father" is often seen as the product of a promiscuous relationship. How can a child not have a father? A child born out of wedlock is usually viewed as different to a married couple. The factual reality is that there is nothing inherently different about that child. That child began just like all others, in an experience between two people, one of each gender, and carries a genetic complement from each. The child has had experiences with both men and women, and has mother-experience and father-experience constructs.

When Alex first saw his original birth certificate, the one issued prior to his adoption, he discovered that he had been legally named by his biological mother. She had given him a first name along with her last name. Discovering this at the age of 19, he said, felt "weird." He had expected the rest of the information, but had not expected to have had a name other than "Baby Boy." There is another side to this story that deserves mention—his biological mother's. The first name on his birth certificate was the male version of her first name. This prompted the suggestion in a family interview that she had truly loved him to have given him her name even as she was about to lose him. Alex was first able to contact his maternal biological grandfather as a result of obtaining the certificate. The grandfather immediately called Alex's mother and said, "I found your blue and yellow blanket." The last thing that Alex's mother had said to her father 19 years earlier as Alex was carried out of the hospital was "There goes my blue and yellow blanket." The transitional object works in both directions.

Many parents do not remain friends, even while married. My colleagues and I (Westman, Cline, Swift & Kramer, 1970) have described a process called the "postdivorce syndrome," in which the same relationship patterns that existed prior to divorce are found following divorce. Whitaker maintains, "There is no such thing as divorce." Spouses stay inside each other's "guts" no matter what occurs on paper (Whitaker, personal communications, 1975–1979). I frequently have had the experience of seeing families where the parents are legally divorced. At the first interview, unless I have taken detailed notes over the telephone, I am often unable on the basis of the interactions to distinguish couples who are married from those who are divorced. A not uncommon, but nevertheless eerie, experience sometimes occurs when parents and stepparents are seen together for interviews with whole families. The more intense relationship is often between the divorced couple; the original two heads of the Hydra claim priority. Of course, much of the intensity is negative, blaming, and hostile. If passion is love, then the only things that have changed in these divorces and second marriages are the names.

An interesting variation on this theme occurred with the parents of an autistic child when they presented as married but were actually divorced (Kramer, 1987). The obviously autistic child was seen for an initial interview with his parents. The interview was unstructured, as I wanted to interact with Henry primarily and to do so at the autistic level. Some formalities did occur, however, and a history was taken. It did not occur to me to ask whether the mother and father were married or divorced, as their presence and silence about the subject implied marriage. They returned for the second interview and said there was one thing they thought I should know. It was that even though they lived in the same house, they were legally divorced and slept without exception separately. During the course of therapy (not at my suggestion), they remarried and altered the sleeping arrangements.

Sometimes pointing out the reality of these relational issues can have a profound and apparently useful effect on people's lives. In the following example, the therapeutic question was resolved, and a new marriage was consummated following such an intervention.

A father, his 8-year-old daughter, Isabelle, and the father's second wife were seen in consultation. The father and stepmother were patients of another psychiatrist. Isabelle had been mistreating the stepmother and asking to move to her mother's home, which was in a different community. The referring psychiatrist had asked me to assist them in resolving the living arrangements. During the consultation interview, it occurred to me that the father still loved the mother and that his daughter, Isabelle, knew this unconsciously. Her unconscious awareness of this was probably behind her actions and the custody question as well. The interview appeared nonproductive until the intervention was made: "Your father probably didn't tell you that he still loves your mother." The tension dissipated at this point, and at the end of the interview the family was very interested in another appointment. However, the second interview was canceled, and I began to question the appropriateness of my intervention. Shortly thereafter, in a chance encounter in the waiting room, the parents told me that they and Isabelle had resolved both the behavior problem and the custody problem and that Isabelle was living with them happily. Nine months later, the father and stepmother had a new baby.

In this case, the child knew the relational truth, and probably so did the parents. Once this was "all right," the child could return to the business of being a child, and the new marriage had permission to go ahead and produce new life. Family therapy can have an impact on relational reality, both interpersonal and intrapsychic, but it cannot change factual reality or make factual reality conform to interpersonal or intrapsychic reality.

Alex's adoptive mother, faced with the imminent possibility that Alex would meet his biological mother, commented with a fair amount of feeling, "He is my son." And then, thoughtfully, "Maybe she loved him more. She was willing to give him up." Of course, she and her husband were willing to give him up as well, as they had been supportive of his search for and reunion with his biological mother. In her first statement, she was correct interpersonally; probably correct intrapsychically; incorrect genetically and perhaps in certain biological ways; but correct in other biological ways, particularly those involving the identification process and other biological events that had occurred postnatally.

The Family as Patient

Therapy with the "two-parent family" is not difficult as long as the logical types, which greatly interested Bateson, remain clear: The patient is the family. If the therapist needs to develop a relationship with a person—the spokesperson of the family, who is often the mother, or with the symptomatic person—or if he or she feels compelled by the demands of verbal communication to interact with just one person at a time, then problems may develop. If the therapist befriends the father while the mother watches, or the mother while the father watches, then the therapist's needs, or perhaps the befriended person's needs are being met rather than the family's. As an adult, the therapist can relate to the marriage and the people in the marriage. As a child, the therapist can relate to the second generation and to the people there involved—that is, the children. It is always useful to remember that he (the husband) is her (the wife's) shadow, and she his, and that each is the perfect spouse for the other, and that the therapist should not therefore be drawn into the space between them.

A team is like a family. A family is a team with biological connections. Invisible elements are present in both. These exist inside the semipermeable boundary that defines a group of people as a particular team. When the Pittsburgh Pirates won the World Series in 1979, they called themselves "The Family." The historical and mythological characteristics of a team operate in the present. For years, being a New York Yankee baseball player has been something very special. It implies connections to Babe Ruth, Lou Gehrig, and others; just being on the Yankees bring out the best, or the worst, in a player. Similarly, Wayne Gretzky, the great hockey player, recently commented, "When you're on a good team, you all look good as individuals." This comment is noteworthy, given the level of Gretzky's individual accomplishments.

When teams rise above their individual capabilities, this is often described as resulting from good "chemistry." This is probably not an accidental choice of termninology. It most likely is biological, in terms of the ethological concepts referred to in this chapter, and even biochemical at some level, although this has not yet been defined in the laboratory.

The idea of a person cannot exist without the idea of a family, just as the idea of a baseball player cannot exist without the idea of a team. Descarte's statement, "I think, therefore I am," localizes the person in the left brain, but the family lives in the right brain. The right brain is the conceptual brain. The definition of a family accordingly should be right-brained. It could involve something like the artist's technique of looking at "negative space," at the outlines of an object—drawing what is not there, rather than what is (Edwards, 1979). Imagine a family in the present. Draw the outlines of the people, and then fill in the negative space. That may be what a family is—that is, everything between the people. People are not the home; people live in the home. People are not the family; people live in the family. Bateson (1972) stressed in his discussion of the theory of logical types (Whitehead & Russell, 1910–1913) that "no class can be a member of itself.'' In other words, in the present discussion, people are members of families; people are not families. A list of people does not constitute a family.

From a pragmatic viewpoint, families include at least two generations and perhaps three; hence the importance of children in working with families as patients. Even a childless couple is a family if one conceptualizes them as children, or sees them in therapy, with their parents. They remain the children of the family in terms of family structure, not necessarily relationally or psychologically, although having children does catalyze maturation.

Whitaker (1976), and Whitaker and Keith (1980), playfully suggest that individuals do not exist, and that what we call ''individuals'' are really ''fragments of a family.'' From this right-brained point of view, treating less than two or even three generations would be pointless. The accumulation of myth from at least two sides of the family—more than two sides, if the family is a stepfamily—is otherwise unavailable for intervention. Whitaker and Keith (1980) advocate working with the three-generational system in order to have access to the ''introjected reality'' of the entire family. In this approach, the grandchildren are potentially given freedom from the accumulated mythology. An author of children's books (Blos, 1981) has suggested that in literature each character is in reality a manifestation of a particular aspect of one whole person. The Seven Dwarfs, for instance, together form one person. It would be ridiculous to treat Grumpy without Bashful and Sleepy if they are indeed part of one and the same individual. It would be biologically impossible. Freud (1900/1953) suggested that every person in a dream represents the person who is dreaming.

Whitaker (1976) asserts that it is pointless to work with fewer than three generations. It might even be argued that the average family includes five generations, since most children have parents and grandparents and can expect to become parents and grandparents (Kramer, 1981). Deciding with whom to work becomes more art than science, although more errors are made through exclusion than through inclusion.

Ken was referred for evaluation after having his nose broken in a fight at boarding school. Family therapy was suggested. The mother asked, ''Just who exactly is Ken's family?'' The cotherapist answered, ''All of the people defined by [meaning related to] Ken.'' This included his parents, their new spouses, his stepsister, and his eight grandparents.

It can get even more complicated, at least for the therapist, because the previous spouses of the stepparents are naturally going to be present psychologically in the lives of these people and probably should be considered members of the family also. A real ''biological'' divorce may be impossible. A scientist certainly cannot unravel strands of DNA from each other, and a therapist may not be able to extricate previous spouses from each other's ''guts,'' to use Whitaker's metaphor.

Marriage is a biopsychosocial disease; it has lasting psychophysiological effects. Divorce can only solve the social problem. Pittman (1987) has called serial marriage "legalized polygamy." In the example above, the parents, the stepparents, and Ken were ultimately seen in therapy.

If the difficulty in defining "family" and in determining the composition of the "whole family" lies in the existence of the family in the right brain, then perhaps the only way to approximate a definition is with art, since words are not really the province of the right brain. The medium could be drawing, as mentioned above, or possibly music, poetry, fiction or sculpture. That is, the medium should be one of the languages of the right brain.

I used to have a habit of doodling with poster paints at an easel next to my chair as I interacted with families. The artistic results were always nonobjective and always different. I thought of them as "family portraits," which is how I would answer if one of the children asked what I was painting—portraits transmitted out of my unconscious as a result of my experience with families. I would send a painting home with the children to be posted on the refrigerator door, much like artwork from nursery school or kindergarten. The apparent fallout was occasionally dramatic.

The Madisons, who had been seen for several months following referral by a neurosurgeon because of Mike's back problems, went home with a "family portrait" after an otherwise fairly routine marital interview. The same evening, they had an honest and extremely definitive discussion, in many ways their first ever (a bit more intense than I would have recommended); finished therapy soon thereafter; and had a baby daughter about a year later.

I have no way of knowing, of course, but I assume that these paintings were transmissions from my right brain directly to the families', and that the paintings interpreted the families to themselves in ways that words could not. Words were used as in any interview, but never in a context of interpreting the painting. Sometimes a child would have attended to the process and could describe what lines and what colors were applied in connection with various segments of the hour, but I studiously avoided processing such information during the time that I was painting, nor afterwards did I attempt to interpret them as in Art Appreciation 101.

I am frequently reminded of Bateson's assertion (personal communication, 1978) that "in the left brain, the wine stands for the blood, and in the right brain, the wine *is* the blood." Therefore, both words and art can be correct, and I would assume are of equal value and importance, but the right brain is often ignored in therapy. It may be that my "family portraits" responded to this to some extent. Also, I suspect that the right brain is inherently more honest, or at least less capable of dishonesty, than the left brain. From the patient's side of the conversation and perhaps from the therapist's, the right brain may be less able not to hear, to be resistant to therapy, than the left brain.

If the whole family is not present, the family is not present, and therefore the patient is not present. Perhaps Mom, Dad, and Sally are there—that is, a list of three people—but the family is not there if Dick and Jane have stayed home because they have homework to do. The surgeon cannot operate on the leg if the arms and the stomach and the heart go shopping. The whole patient has to be present.

The Biology of Family Therapy

Family therapy may be more a biological than a psychological form of treatment. It is the treatment of a biological entity—the family. True, the family is also a psychological entity, a sociological entity, a financial entity, and a legal entity; however, the underlying structure is biological. The family is the organism primarily responsible for development and reproduction. The fact of pregnancy does not occur at the psychological, the sociological, the financial, or the legal level. It occurs at the biological level. It is certainly true that pregnancy is a psychological event, and more important, a relational event. But the fact of pregnancy (perhaps it is a final common pathway for the psychological, relational, sociological, financial, and legal levels) is still biological and only biological. In *The World According to Garp,* Jenny Fields and Technical Sergeant Garp's relationship is primarily biological. Sergeant Garp dies; is almost brain-dead when Garp is conceived. Jenny, Sergeant Garp, and Garp are nevertheless a family.

Families are timeless. Families never die. If we return to the theory of logical types, and remember that people are not families, then even if the people have died, the family still exists. So, in the example above, Jenny, Sergeant Garp, and Garp *are* a family. More pragmatically, it is wise to remember that families do not just exist in the present. The family that exists in the present, or the one that was sketched earlier in fantasy, exists backward in time infinitely. So the negative space drawing of a family is also three-dimensional with respect to time. Imagine for a moment what that drawing would look like. Now, add the interweaving that ultimately connects all families through time.

One day several years ago, I was following the Newsome family out of my office when suddenly, to my extreme surprise, the members of the Newsome family and the family with the next appointment, the Oswalds, began to embrace passionately. It turned out that the women in each family were sisters. Each had been referred by entirely separate sources and had come to see me independently. The composition of the "whole family," through no particular therapeutic acumen of mine, doubled in size at that instant.

One idea that has been suggested in this chapter is that the self exists in the left brain and the family exists in the right brain. The developmental goal is for the person to be both a self and a family. Any imbalance may reveal itself as an imbalance does on the pharmacist's scale, which tips totally in one direction when the sides are unequally weighted. A dynamic equilibrium is envisioned, as in the equations of physiological chemistry. Whitaker has said, "Your divorce is really an effort to find the person of yourself" (Neill & Kniskern, 1982, p. 365). The point of therapy is to catalyze both autonomy and togetherness. Real psychological change only occurs when both occur in tandem.

If the self does live in the left brain, and the family does live in the right brain, then for family therapy to have access to the family, all of the right brains need to be involved. Access to the people—that is, the selves—is available according to their attendance, but an experience with the family may only be possible if the whole family, all of the right brains of the family, are present. A practical implication of this is that if the whole family is present, then all of the individuals are too, so that a therapy focused on treating all of the selves in a family becomes possible, even if in some way no therapy for the whole family occurs. That is probably not possible, but it is a theoretical consideration, and it may be a way in which some therapists prefer to conceptualize a course of therapy. Some families also seem to engineer a therapy experience weighted in this way.

The Parkers called for an appointment because of emerging episodes of rage involving the younger of their two boys. Paul was 10 at the time. The suddenness of onset had prompted me to suggest a neurological evaluation even before I had seen the family once. Most of the interactions early in therapy were with Paul, but his older brothers and parents were always there and were emotionally very involved in the experience. Mr. Parker, who was himself a therapist, evolved as the next "patient," in part because of a natural continuity with the issues that came up in Paul's treatment. At times, it seemed as if he and I were talking alone, almost totally unaware of the other family members. This was symbolized at one point for me by an experience with a videocamera. In order to provide the family with a videotape of their sessions, while at the same time not designating one person as the cameraperson, all of us took turns holding the camera. During one point of an interview of Mr. Parker, I was viewing his face through the zoom lens with my right eye, while simultaneously seeing the context, the whole family, with my open left eye. The superimposition of the two images was quite dramatic. Mrs. Parker became the next primary patient, and then a period of time went by when the marriage was most clearly in focus. Finally, Paul's 14-year-old brother, Patrick, who had been the most reluctant participant, stepped forward for a time as the patient.

The whole family's being present does lead to each of the individuals' being present; however, the converse is not true. Some of the individuals can be there, and the family as a whole will not be. They can be involved in therapy as individuals, or even as subsets of a family (e.g., a couple, or the parents and the child who is the identified patient), but that can never result in the family as a whole being there. Most of the time, the differences in the experience are subtle.

The Quarles were seen for two interviews. The first included the mother, two daughters from a previous marriage, a new son-in-law, and the 15-year-old son. The son had suddenly stopped going to school, created a number of minor disturbances, and was threatening to move to Oregon with his father. The second interview included the same group plus the boy's father on the speakerphone. A metaphor developed from a faulty connection, wherein Mrs. Quarles was referred to as "Jenny Lee" by her husband, but this was misheard by me as "General Lee." The latter was perceived by members of the family, and in particular by Mr. Quarles, as better fitting her personality. This led to discussions that resulted in Mr. and Mrs. Quarles's better cooperation as parents, a return to school by their son, and a diminishment in the behavior problems.

Sometimes, seeing a subset of a family is an obvious mistake. Most of the time this is not understood until it is too late. One clue is a therapy that is not progressing. Sometimes a consultant will see the obvious and point it out; occasionally, it just turns into a failure.

The Anesthesia for Family Therapy

The family therapy experience can be compared to a surgical procedure. The therapist's "love" for the patient is what allows the operation to proceed. In this analogy, the countertransference becomes the anesthesia. In seeing only a subsystem of the family, the therapist only anesthetizes part of the patient. If the whole family can be present, general anesthesia is possible, and major surgery is then sometimes allowed by the patient (i.e., the family). Perhaps the anesthesia puts the collective left brains in the family to sleep.

In a termination interview, Mr. Parker (the father of the Parker family described above) characterized his experience in family therapy: "Maybe it's just supposed to be this way, but it's like we've been in all this process for several months now, and I swear to you, I cannot tell you exactly what has happened. . . . It's both neat and sort of frustrating. I have a few friends that know that we've had some kind of difficulties, and to try to tell somebody about it is like, I feel like a dummy. At least I should understand it, I feel like I should understand it, even if nobody else does."

I commented, "I think of it as like an anesthesia. I think somehow you suspend some sort of conscious awareness, of logical process."

Mr. Parker responded, "You think that happens, that it's almost like your left brain goes to sleep?"

I agreed, "I think so, because that's what you described. You can't find the words to say what it is that we did, which is just what you said. . . . like your left brain quit working."

Mrs. Parker then noted, reminiscent of the Bateson (1972) discussion of logical types, "Well, how could you have been acutely aware of it if you were part of it?"

The idea that the family is the patient, the one patient, presents conceptual and practical difficulties. Of course, as illustrated by the Parkers, each of the individuals is a patient too. Maybe the purpose of seeing the family as a whole is for the therapist to experience the people as a family, so that he or she (or they, if the therapist is two people) can picture a particular group of people in his or her (or their) right brain as a family. When this happens, however, a complementary process probably also happens in the family, or in the right brain of the family. In some way—perhaps relating to boundary issues, both in the creation and in the experiencing of them—a healthy "I–they" or "we–they" moment occurs.

This year, our family visited the Keiths (see Chapter 15) in Minnesota by automobile, and they visited us in Georgia. Upon driving up to our respective homes, the children in each family commented, "They must be rich." Neither one of us is, but there was a sudden unanticipated experience of a we–they moment.

It may be that in just being with another human being as a family—not socially, not buying an automobile or having a picnic, but just being a family—a new sense of knowing is possible: knowing the self, knowing each other, and knowing the family. Each person can be a family, as well as a person, while not also being a function (e.g., the "mother," the "schizophrenic," the "wicked stepmother," the "daughter," or the "breadwinner").

The ethological "niche" (Tinbergen, 1958) in which paranoia developed as a human potential may have to do with the survival value of boundaries. There was at one time a definite and positive physical survival value in being able to create semipermeable boundaries around basic biological groups, such as the couple, the family, the tribe, or the community. This was true in the days of the cave dweller, and may still be true in very tangible ways today relating to food and shelter, and in psychological and developmental ways also.

The family does not need to accept the idea that the "patient" is the family, but I think it helps if they understand that this is important to the therapist. I do believe it is necessary for the therapist to allow himself or herself to experience the family as a single entity, a whole, and to know that in some way the family, as distinct from the list of people in the family, is the patient. Of course, for the therapist to be able to have this kind of experience, he or she must have access to the whole family. Otherwise, the experience can never occur.

Finally, from an interactional or perhaps communicational point of view, all of the relationships in the family are potential patients. This includes the marriage, but also includes the numerous other relationships in the various dyads and triads in a family, the relationships between various subsets of a family, and the relationships between the various generations in a family. To summarize, in different ways the "patient" may be the family, all of the individuals in the family, or all of the relationships in the family. It can and may be all three. But of the three entities, the one that has been the most difficult to conceptualize and articulate, and that often gets lost in a left-brained world, is the idea that the family as a whole can be the patient.

"Beans"

It is impossible for a person to divorce himself or herself from the biological model of family. Garp knows that he has a genetic father. Even with artificial insemination, the functional parent(s), and eventually the children so conceived, know that there is a genetic father if they are told the history of the artificial insemination. Even the Christian belief in the Virgin Birth does not entirely do away with the idea of the father, because God is so defined. The family is the lowest common denominator of a functional biological–psychological entity. Only a family can procreate. Only a family can provide a surname. If the family is the lowest common denominator, it follows that the family must be the patient. One of the most difficult family types to treat is the single-parent, single-child entity. The mother or father always has to be a parent, and therefore a function, never a person. The child always has to be the representative of the second generation, and also never a person. Even if the parent and child switch roles, there are still just two functions operative and no people.

In the termination interview described above, Mr. Parker described his personal confusion over what had happened during the family therapy experience. He concluded by saying, "I'm trying to understand what's happened in the last 9 months." Paul Parker, now 11 years old, responded: "Well, I can tell you. We all got to know each other better. All of us. Well, I mean you and Mom know each other good because you sleep in the same bed each night, you know. I mean we got to know each other like inside, at least half and half—maybe not all, I don't know. We got to know each other much better. It's like we kind of attached our insides, we kind of traded, and now we're all mixed. See, we've gotten to know our insides, what's inside; I don't mean like guts. Like I got to know what Mom, you got to know what Mom, she got know what you, all that. We all got to know each other. Then, we just kind of—all of our insides kind of gathered up in a big circle, really, and kind of just mixed up, and came back down, we all got part of each other.

"Well, you know since we've been working and finding out ourselves, we shared our insides, you know, we spilled the beans and it all mixed. It's like, we're sitting in a circle, every bean knew the other bean, it came out and mixed and talked and went back in. The beans are like the insides. But we still have our own ways, you know. That's in our head. But the beans that are like in our heart are mixed. And a couple of beans went up to your head from each. All right, three beans of mine went into my head, one, two, three, and three beans went up into your head. Well, that's what I think. . . . I don't think we threw out any bad beans. I think we still got the bad beans in us, but one person doesn't have quite as many, cause everybody has them anyway. . . . It was like me and Dad were kind of have bad beans in the family, you know, at first, you know how, and then later on everybody's beans came out, and they mixed, and now we only have a little, and ya'll only have a little, an equal amount of beans and everything else. . . . I oughta write a book called *Beans*."

Perhaps Paul could have written this chapter. The wholeness of families seems obvious to me. I have written much of this chapter to try to understand what it is that causes others to see individuals or subsets of families in therapy, rather than seeing closer approximations to whole families. It seems to me that doing therapy with these subsets can be successful but more often risks failure, or at least less success than might be possible, and is more difficult, time-consuming, and therefore expensive. A colleague who mostly treats individuals, but who knows very much about families, talks about "treating the family in the patient's head." However, I believe this approach ignores not only the reality of that family in the present, and the mutuality of their ancient introjects, but the reality of families and family systems as well.

The extent to which "family" in the broad sense permeates our thinking and our living seems to me to suggest that it should also direct our approach to therapy. Whether it be the genetic reality that all children have two parents, or the reality that we ascribe to and see in teams, or the "chemistry" that certain metaphors anticipate, or the literary model of characters' being fragments of persons, or the related family model of persons' being fragments of families, we seem to function as if "family" is integral to our living.

Conclusion

The two-parent family in general, and the two-parent family in treatment in particular, has the best opportunity of keeping the generational transferences straight. Problems sometimes develop out of the relationship between a father or mother and his or her parents, and these often get recreated in the relationship between the mother or father and one of the children. As an example, family therapy provides the possibility of working on these problems in the following ways:

1. With the child as a person.
2. With the mother or father as the function of the mother or father.
3. With the relationship between the mother or father and the child so involved.
4. With the mother or father as a person.
5. With the marriage as it has added to the problems in its attempts to help solve the problems.
6. With the problems as they have developed in the marriage as well.
7. With the mother or father as the child of her or his parents.
8. With the mother or father in relation to her or his parents.
9. With the marriages of the grandparents.
10. With the relationship between the two sets of grandparents.
11. With the family as a whole.
12. In particular, with the family as an entity greater than the sum of its parts.

A final vignette illustrates why it frightens me not to work with the family as a whole as the patient.

Paul Parker was experienced and described as "abusive" by his father during the time leading up to their treatment. Mr. Parker was paralyzed by this. He couldn't remember much about his own childhood at age 10. When he began to reconstruct it during an early session, what he primarily remembered were beatings. "What comes to mind when I think about being 10 or 11 are beatings. Being beaten. Beatings." He was crying. He had even had to get his own "switch."

When I had to restrain Paul on my office floor for attacking me, he began to spit at me, and I attempted to cover his mouth to shield myself. In doing so, I struck his lip and it bled slightly. Suddenly, Mr. Parker was wiping up the blood off the carpet with tissues, even though it was small in amount and the carpet was red anyway. Even though he was a loving and responsible father, he was not at the time angry at me for hurting his son, or particularly worried about his son's lip, or even very upset that Paul had been spitting at me. He was overwhelmingly worried, however, about the blood on the carpet.

The next time he talked of the beatings he received at age 10, he remembered the primary reason for the beatings was his dropping and breaking glasses on the concrete floor of their home at that time. "And it seemed like I was always dropping glasses."

This kind of specificity of symptoms is not usually available, and may not even usually be present, but one never gets to it if one does not consider the whole family as the "patient." Furthermore, in a very real way, the family is the "therapist" too; the professional therapist is more of a catalyst to this biological entity. Not unimportant was my love for the Parkers, as well as my knowledge of families, child development, and child psychiatry. But more important in their changing was family love—that is, whatever it is that makes a family greater than the sum of its parts. The family is the therapist in the sense that the body is its own physician. The surgeon makes incisions, removes things, moves things around, and reapproximates things. But the real magic is what the body then does to heal itself. It would leak and fall apart if it depended on the sutures and staples to hold it together. In this most important sense, the family is not only the real patient, but the true therapist.

ACKNOWLEDGMENTS

I would like to thank the "Parker" family. David V. Keith, MD, Patricia Kramer, RPT, William R. Phillips, ThM, and Carl A. Whitaker, MD, read earlier drafts of this chapter. Their comments are acknowledged and appreciated. This work was supported in part by a grant from the Institute for Experiential Growth, Atlanta, GA.

REFERENCES

Bateson, G. (1972). *Steps to an ecology of mind.* San Francisco: Chandler.
Blos, J. (1981, October 16). *Children's books and other people: Some remarks on purpose and process.* Paper presented at the 28th Annual Meeting of the American Academy of Child Psychiatry, Dallas.
Bowlby, J. (1969). *Attachment and loss: Vol. 1. Attachment.* New York: Basic Books.

Brazelton, T. B. (1969). *Infants and mothers: Differences in development.* New York: Delacorte Press.

Edwards, B. (1979). *Drawing on the right side of the brain.* Los Angeles: J. P. Tarcher.

Erikson, E. H. (1950). *Childhood and society.* New York: Norton.

Freud, S. (1953). *The Interpretation of dreams.* In J. Strachey (Ed. and Trans.), *The standard edition of the complete psychological works of Sigmund Freud* (Vol. 4, pp. 1–338; Vol. 5, pp. 339–627). London: Hogarth Press.

Harris, R., & Levy, E. (1977). *Before you were three: How you began to walk, talk, explore, and have feelings.* New York: Delacorte Press.

Irving, J. (1976). *The world according to Garp.* New York: E. P. Dutton.

Jung, C. G. (1964). *Man and his symbols.* London: Aldus Books.

Kramer, D. A. (1981, October 17). *Like (grand-)father, like (grand-)son.* Paper presented at the 28th Annual Meeting of the American Academy of Child Psychiatry, Dallas.

Kramer, D. A. (1982). The adopted child in family therapy. *American Journal of Family Therapy, 10*(3), 70–73.

Kramer, D. A. (1987). The autistic moment in psychotherapy. *Contemporary Family Therapy: An International Journal, 9,* 79–89.

Malone, T. P., & Malone, P. T. (1987). *The art of intimacy.* Englewood Cliffs, NJ: Prentice-Hall.

Neill, J. R., & Kniskern, D. P. (Eds.). (1982). *From psyche to system: The evolving therapy of Carl Whitaker.* New York: Guilford Press.

Pittman, F. S., III. (1985). Gender myths: When does gender become pathology? *The Family Therapy Networker, 9,* 24–33.

Pittman, F. S., III. (1987). *Turning points: Treating families in transition and crisis.* New York: Norton.

Sanford, J. S. (1980). *The invisible partners.* New York: Paulist Press.

Sendak, M. (1963). *Where the wild things are.* New York: Harper & Row.

Tinbergen, N. (1958). *Curious naturalists.* New York: Basic Books.

Westman, J. C., Cline, D. W., Swift, W. J., & Kramer, D. A. (1970). The role of child psychiatry in divorce. *Archives of General Psychiatry, 23,* 416–420.

Whitaker, C. (1976). A family is a four-dimensional relationship. In P. J. Guerin, Jr. (Ed), *Family therapy: Theory and practice* (pp. 182–192). New York: Gardner Press.

Whitaker, C. A., & Keith, D. V. (1980). Family therapy as symbolic experience. *International Journal of Family Psychiatry, 1,* 197–208.

Whitehead, A. N., & Russell, B. (1910–1913). *Principia mathematica.* Cambridge, England: Cambridge University Press.

Winnicott, D. W. (1949). Hate in the countertransference. *International Journal of Psycho-Analysis, 30,* 69–74.

Winnicott, D. W. (1971). Transitional objects and transitional phenomena. In D. W. Winnicott, *Playing and reality* (pp. 1–25). London: Tavistock. (Original work published 1953)

6

Successful Minority Single-Parent Families

MARION LINDBLAD-GOLDBERG, PhD

Changing Family Shapes

One of the most dramatic changes in family shapes over the last decade is the increasing number of single-parent families, particularly those consisting of a mother and her children. In 1979, over 17% of the 30.4 million families with children present were maintained by a single mother, and another 2% were maintained by the father alone (U.S. Bureau of the Census, 1980). These figures do not reflect the uncounted single-parent families where the youngest child is 18 years or older and still at home.

Births to white single women accounted for 5.67% of all white births in 1970 and 8.7% of all white births in 1978. Births to black single women represented 34.9% of all black births in 1970 and 47.5% of all black births in 1978 (U.S. Bureau of the Census, 1980). These data clearly show that the incidence of single parenting is much higher for blacks, but that the rate of increase in births to single mothers is the same for blacks and whites. This finding supports Bianchi and Farley's (1979) conclusion that trends away from family stability are not limited to the black population, as Moynihan (1965) stated earlier, but appear to be affecting whites at the same rate. Even so, the relative proportion of single-parent households among black families is so high that increased understanding of these single-parent families is essential to mental health professionals.

Births to single parents account for only some of the many single-parent-headed families in the United States. Of all single-parent families in 1979, 15%

Marion Lindblad-Goldberg. Philadelphia Child Guidance Clinic, Philadelphia, PA.

were maintained by never-married women, up from 7% in 1970. Numbering nearly 1 million families, this subgroup of single parents is no longer insignificant (U.S. Bureau of the Census, 1980). But the acceleration in the growth of American single-parent families is primarily due to increases in the numbers of mothers who have separated from or divorced their husbands. Separated and divorced single parents accounted for 63% of the single-parent population by the end of the 1970s. The number of separated and divorced mothers maintaining families in 1979 represents a larger group than the total number of single parents in 1970. In contrast, the number of single-parent families created by the death of one parent has declined. In 1970, widows and widowers headed 23% of all one-parent families, but by the end of the decade they headed only 13% (U.S. Bureau of the Census, 1980).

In a 1983 analysis of marriage trends, Espenshade (cited by Cordes, 1984) found that black women could expect to be married less than one-fourth of their lives, in contrast to white women, who could expect to be married nearly twice that long. In addition, remarriage rates have dropped among black women, while divorce rates continue to rise (Cordes, 1984). A further burden on black families pointed out by Cordes is that among black female heads of families in 1975, 31% were separated and only 19% divorced, whereas among white female heads of families the figures were nearly reversed. She attributes these higher rates of separations among blacks to the high cost of divorce. McGhee (cited in Cordes, 1984) has suggested that the high rates of separation and divorce stem from black men's difficulties in getting jobs to support families, while Simms and Betsey (also cited in Cordes, 1984) suggest that black women place more emphasis on financial stability and less on companionship than white women.

Reconsidering the Deficit Model of the Single-Parent Family

Proponents of the nuclear family have claimed that the increase in the numbers of single-parent families is a sign that "the family," as a unit of health and stability, is decaying. There appears to be a prevalent belief that single-parent families are deviant and cannot live up to the ideal standard of American life represented by two-parent families. Public opinion and the mental health literature have tended to label these families pejoratively as "deviant," "unstable," or "disintegrated," rather than viewing the single-parent family as simply an alternative family form.

Those arguing from the perspective of a deficit model conclude that children from single-parent families are at psychological risk with regard to personality development, social behavior, and school achievement (Marotz-Baden, Adams, Buccho, Munro, & Munro, 1979). Blechman (1982) summarizes three theoretical positions that equate child rearing by one parent with a risk for maladjustment. These positions are, first, the psychodymamic assumption that the mother's *and* father's presence during childhood are minimum necessities for normal sex-role identification and healthy child development; second, a position held by anthropologists, sociologists, and early social learning theorists that fathers are the "role models'' boys need in order to learn appropriate masculine behavior; and third, confluence theory, developed by Zajonc and Markus (1975) to explain familial (particularly birth order) influences on cognitive development. Confluence theory has stimulated studies suggesting that the father's absence (due to death or divorce) has a negative effect on intellectual performance. Based on the assumption from the confluence model that a one-parent family is inadequate to provide a satisfactory intellectual environment, these studies demonstrated that inferior intellectual abilities were found in children from father-absent homes as compared to children from intact homes.

Several excellent reviews (Blechman, 1982; Herzog & Sudia, 1973; Marotz-Baden et al., 1979) have criticized the methodology of those studies supporting the "deviant" model of single-family forms (i.e., divorced families, father- or mother-absent families, employed mothers, single mothers in poverty). According to Blechman (1982), confounding variables such as income and social class may explain some of the negative findings. In fact, research that compared children in female-headed families to other children at the same income level demonstrated that children do not suffer intellectually, academically, or behaviorally because the father is not in the home (Cashion, 1982). Summarizing the social-psychological research pertaining to female-headed families published between 1970 and 1980, Cashion states, "The majority of families, when not plagued by poverty, are as successful as two-parent families in producing children with appropriate sex-role behavior, good emotional and intellectual adjustment, and nondelinquent behavior" (1982, p. 83). Moreover, recent studies of low-income black single-parent families have demonstrated their success in raising healthy children (Hill, 1972; Lindblad-Goldberg & Dukes, 1981; Wilkinson & O'Connor, 1977; Willie, 1976), showing that even poverty-stricken single-parent families are not inevitably dysfunctional.

The deficit model often focuses on defective family form as the source of pathology. Marotz-Baden et al. (1979), among others, have proposed that perhaps it is not family form, but family process, that can contribute to both negative and positive personal and social development in children. That is, it is not who is in the family that matters, but how the family is organized and how the individuals interact, adapt, and cope. Marotz-Baden et al. (1979, p. 12) have emphasized the importance of "research on the mediating processes that accompany family life styles as they influence the socialization of children." Their research review of the effects of alternative family forms on a child's well-being identifies several important factors as central to understanding developmental outcomes, regardless of the form of the family unit; these include familial conflict, financial instability, quality of supervision, and role modeling. Developmental psychologists who look at interpersonal process recognize, too, that not only does the family shape the child, but the child is also an active participant in simultaneously adapting to and modifying the environment (Sameroff, 1975).

The conclusion to be drawn from these lines of research is that the single-parent family is a potentially sound family form, but we are still lacking a normative model to describe adaptive single-parent family functioning.

Defining Normal Families

Answering the question "Is this family normal?" depends on the values derived from a particular conceptual model. The structural family model developed by Minuchin (1974) views normality as the accomplishment of essential family tasks, which consist of supporting individuation while providing a sense of belonging. Just as there are many forms of family composition, there are many forms of family functioning, and many of these are compatible with healthy development. The single-parent family can be viewed as an open system in transformation, which operates within social and developmental contexts. Rather than functioning well or poorly *in toto,* the single-parent family performs specific family tasks well or poorly in certain life situations and at given points in time. To survive in a changing environment, a well-functioning family must be flexible in mobilizing alternative patterns when stressed by developmental and external change.

The Exploration of Well-Functioning Single-Parent Families

The need to develop an empirical model of "normal" family functioning in single-parent families arose in the course of clinical and community work with such families at the Philadelphia Child Guidance Clinic. Although the seminal research of Minuchin, Montalvo, Guerney, Rosman, and Schumer (1967) described the dysfunctional characteristics of such families, descriptions of optimal family functioning were lacking. Consequently, we (Lindblad-Goldberg & Dukes, 1978) designed a research program that examined normative and dysfunctional single-parent family functioning in Afro-American, low-income families headed by working and nonworking females.

A total of 126 families were studied; 70 were classified as "functional" and 56 as "clinic" cases. All families were recruited according to the following criteria: (1) The single parent living in the home was the biological mother; (2) the single-parent status had existed for at least 1 year; (3) at least two children between the ages of 6 and 18, one of whom was 10 or older, were living in the home; (4) no children in the family were diagnosed as being mentally retarded or psychotic, having severe physical handicaps, or having chronic diseases; and (5) the gross family income was at or below the poverty level. Families were accepted for study when others were living in the home. No family was eligible if an unrelated male caretaker lived in the home on a regular basis.

After 70 families who met these criteria were recruited, a screening procedure for determining "successful" family functioning was developed. This included a telephone interview, a home interview, and an interview with the school counselor. Basically, we were looking for families whose members had no history of child abuse, delinquency, alcohol or other substance abuse, poor social relations (on the part of the children), criminal charges, school problems (behavioral or academic), chronic illness, physical handicaps, or use of mental health or mental retardation services. Fifty-six families referred to the Philadelphia Child Guidance

Clinic's Outpatient Service, whose members agreed to participate in the research project at the time of their initial contact with the clinic and who met the project's criteria for family eligibility, comprised the comparison group. These families were called "dysfunctional" because they had identified themselves as needing some help. The majority of these families were self-referred to the clinic, most frequently because of a child with problems in school. Most often, the reported problem in the child was a behavior difficulty (fighting, stealing, poor peer relations).

Demographically, the two groups of families were quite similar (Lindblad-Goldberg & Dukes, 1985a). The sample was composed of mothers in their early 30s having an average of three children, with equal numbers of boys and girls, ranging from predominantly preadolescents to adults. The groups did not differ on employment status, length of time on public assistance, length of time on present job, length of time since last job, occupational level, or educational level. The mothers in both groups were most frequently semiskilled workers with 12 years of education. As for income level, 80% of well-functioning families and 70% of symptomatic families had incomes below $6000, which was far below the poverty level as defined by the Pennsylvania Department of Public Assistance in 1979.

The basic premise underlying the research study was that single-parent families are viable family units with variability in style, structure, and values. We proposed that adaptive or nonadaptive functioning would be related to the reciprocal influences of three dimensions: family resources, environmental stress, and social network resources. The first dimension, the family's internal resources, consisted of four major areas. First, the structure or organization of the family would determine how the family would organize its resources and maintain its integration while adapting to environmental events or developmental changes of family members. The importance of executive hierarchy and of boundary functioning was examined. Another family resource considered was that of family communication patterns; we looked at the ways in which family members expressed their thoughts, ideas, conflicts, and feelings. A third internal resource was the mother's own personal abilities, which included her coping skills and sense of control and mastery. Finally, in addition to our assessment of how we saw the family functioning through observed family interaction, we examined individual family members' internal perceptions of their families as adaptive and integrated units.

In assessing the second dimension, environmental stress, we evaluated the family's accommodation to extrafamilial pressures on a member; to extrafamilial pressures on the entire family; to transitional points in the family's development; and to idiosyncratic problems (illness, etc.). The frequency and severity of stressful events, and the perceived positive and negative impact of these stressful events on the family, were also ascertained.

Finally, we explored the effect of potential extrafamilial buffers on the family's functioning. We were interested in the impact of the mother's immediate social network (family, relatives, friends, coworkers) and community associations, as well as that of broader social factors, such as economics, employment, education, and housing.

In summarizing the results of this study, I present the characteristics of well-functioning families in contrast to those of symptomatic families, and I propose a model for conceptualizing adaptive functioning in single-parent families.

Forming the Single-Parent Family

Whatever the underlying events in the formation of single-parent families (e.g., death, separation, divorce, or out-of-wedlock pregnancy), each has its own unique emotional impact on the family, and each also stimulates family reorganization. As with any process of reorganization, the family will experience instability as roles are reallocated within the family.

The families we studied had been single-parent families for from 1 year to 25 years (median for adaptive families, 8 years; median for nonadaptive families, 10 years); thus, most families had had time to stabilize in the single-parent form. Two-thirds of these families had originally been two-parent families. One-third of the mothers had never married and had held single-parent status for about 20 years. Fifty percent of the mothers from both adaptive families and symptomatic families had been teenage mothers. Thus, the nature of the precipitating event per se was unrelated to successful single-parent family functioning.

Family Resources

The Mother's Personal Resources

Single mothers in poverty are susceptible to depression. Severe, frequent chronic stress creates hopelessness, which in turn engenders vulnerability to depression in low-income single mothers (Belle, 1982; Lindblad-Goldberg & Dukes, 1985b). Extreme depression may lead to a mother's abdication of the parental role through alcoholism, drug addiction, or desertion. However, even mild depression can decrease a mother's nurturant activity to her children. Adaptive mothers in our study were less depressed than mothers in symptomatic families. In contrast, less adaptive mothers were upset with the way life was going, worried more frequently, and generally felt too tired to enjoy themselves. In addition, they often spontaneously reflected that someone who was deceased was an important resource. This did not occur in the adaptive families. Fulmer (1983) has discussed unresolved mourning as a special problem in some single-parent families.

What might be some of the historical and current factors affecting these women's lives and psychological well-being? In examining historical antecedents, we were particularly interested in mothers who had grown up in single-parent families themselves, who represented about 50% of our sample in both the adaptive and less adaptive families. The most frequent precipitating events leading to the single-parent family status of the family of origin in adaptive families were separation or widowhood; the family of origin in less adaptive families was most frequently created by separation or out-of-wedlock pregnancy. Although 75% of the families of origin of both groups had been headed by mothers, there were differences between the groups when the original families had not been mother-headed. Of adaptive families, 20% were headed by fathers and 7% by "others"; in contrast, 21% of less adaptive families were headed by "others" and only 4% by fathers.

There were no major differences in the two groups in how they reported relating to their fathers, with a good spread between good and bad. But in rating the relationship with their mothers, less adaptive mothers were more extreme, rating the relationship as either "excellent" or "poor," whereas adaptive mothers more evenly rated the relationship on a continuum from "excellent" to "poor."

When these mothers reported two parents who were still living, more adaptive mothers had parents living together. But probably the most telling finding concerning families of origin was that significantly more adaptive mothers described their single-parent families of origin as "successful' than did less adaptive mothers.

We felt that a mother's ability to meet her adult needs through dating, leisure activities, and having a feeling of control in her life would have a current beneficial effect on functioning, and we found that adaptive mothers were satisfied with their dating relationships, whereas less adaptive mothers did not date and wanted this to change. Adaptive mothers controlled their schedules in such a way that they found time to engage in more relaxing leisure activities that were free of responsibility (e.g., talking on the phone, going to the movies, etc.).

Less adaptive mothers perceived the environment as controlling them, while a stronger sense of personal control was evident in the ability of adaptive mothers to create more stability in their environments. For example, these mothers were more likely to have purchased their homes. In addition, although these adaptive mothers had income levels similar to those of the comparison group and were also receiving public assistance, they had been more successful in securing jobs that they felt provided their primary source of income, and they felt more satisfied about the adequacy of their incomes than did less adaptive mothers, who more often relied on government aid and network support as primary income sources. Thus, despite the fact that adaptive mothers were living with the restrictions engendered by the welfare system, they attached importance to areas where they had authority and control.

In summary, the adaptive mothers appeared to have more personal resources available to them, which may have enhanced their coping effectiveness creating feelings of well-being and mastery.

Family Organization

The hundreds of discrete tasks involved in carrying out basic family functions comprise two full-time jobs. Maintaining a household and caring for children constitute one job, and income production represents another. Thus a potential problem for all single-parent families is task overload. A family's level of organization is critical in determining whether tasks will be performed effectively. Of the subsystem organization of the family, the most crucial in a single-parent family is the executive subsystem. This unit is defined by implicit and sometimes explicit rules (i.e., boundaries) indicating who may engage in parental executive behavior (and when), and who is required to obey those in charge.

There is considerable variability regarding who is on the executive team and how tasks are divided. In families where the single parent is the only parental figure actively involved, the probability of overload increases. When this executive structure prevails and the family maintains the cultural ideal of the two-parent family, the parent may try to become both mother and father in an attempt to have the family feel complete as a unit. This can often lead to overdependence in both parent and child(ren). The maintenance of generational distinctions is a major difficulty in most single-parent families (Weltner, 1982). This is particularly true in those families where the single parent is the only adult involved, and the parent has limited contact with peers. Here the feeling that "we have only each other" organizes family behavior and promotes overly involved relationships between parent and child(ren). Essential parenting functions such as discipline are often compromised, due to the difficulty in creating the emotional distance required to set limits.

In other single-parent families, parental responsibility is shared with one or more adults and/or children. These executive members may live in or out of the household, and they may or may not be biologically related to the children in the family. Membership in the parental subsystem is less important than the effectiveness of the unit's functioning. The single parent either takes the authority role or delegates it clearly. Executive functioning is not effective when people compete for the role of primary parent or when the mother abdicates her authority either to another adult or to a parental child. When the single mother and another adult have not formed a workable alliance, the child(ren) may not know which adult is in charge.

Probably the most problematic executive structure exists when a child assumes more responsibility than the parent. This structure may develop when parental functioning is severely impaired through alcoholism, psychosis, severe depression, or the like.

In our research sample of single-parent families, the executive team was generally composed of a mother and one or more of the children. It should be noted that in our sample over 86% of the households studied consisted of mothers living with an average of three biological children. However, less adaptive families had more people living in their homes than did adaptive families. Although family size was comparable for both groups of families, less adaptive families had more of their adult children living at home. Despite the extended-family living arrangement frequently mentioned in literature on the black family, households in this study rarely contained other adults, except for the mother's adult children. Wilkinson and O'Connor (1977) also report that relatives were rarely members of the household in their study of 101 low-income, black, female-headed families.

Well-functioning families had more effective executive authority than did the clinic sample. There was a balance between children doing what they were told to do and mothers providing structure and discipline. These findings are in contrast to observational studies of mother–child interaction in a laboratory setting, which have found that low-income mothers are more authoritarian (e.g., making demands without explanation or obvious reason) and less responsive to their children's requests than middle-class mother (Hess & Shipman, 1965; Kamii & Radin, 1967). Our findings suggest that low-income status does not, in itself, result in predictable child-rearing beliefs and practices. Many of the attitudes held and techniques used with their children by the adaptive mothers resembled what have traditionally been viewed as "middle-class" values. For example, they used reasoning and emotional appeal when their children needed to be disciplined.

There was also evidence that a more effective executive hierarchy existed in these families. The critical factor regarding family structure was that the mother was always ultimately in charge within the family. In addition, she was continually responsive to the needs of all her children. Executive authority was hierarchical, and the mother frequently delegated authority and responsibility in an age-appropriate manner within the sibling subsystem. Next to the mother, the oldest daughter was usually the most responsible family member in carrying out family jobs. Male children were also expected to demonstrate helpfulness in the family, and the oldest boys in these families had a high degree of awareness of the family's necessary job functions. When a maternal grandmother was living with the family, she never assumed primary authority; rather, she worked in a supportive alliance with her daughter.

The communication process in these families was clear; family members participated equally, and consequently they were better able to work as a group in accomplishing tasks. Related to effective functioning was the clarity of subsystem boundaries. In essence, these family structures were better organized along lines of responsibility and authority. There was a tendency for adaptive families to have clearer communication about the jobs to be done and more differentiation of subsystems in terms of "who does what." Although adaptive families had more rules about respecting others and safety, the two groups of families did not differ in the number of rules concerning obeying/respecting the mother, sharing, morality, self-control, honesty, cleaning house, or curfew.

The affective relations between adaptive family members were positive; individuals were able to generate a lot of discussion about what they liked in each other. There was less conflict in these families, even though they easily discussed any negative feelings about a family member's behavior.

In marked contrast, less adaptive families demonstrated weaker executive authority. Children in these families requested less executive behavior from their mothers, and mothers were also less responsive to their children's requests for authority. When they did respond to their children, however, they used the same kind of verbal directives (i.e., leadership, behavior control, and guidance) as the adaptive mothers. It should be noted that for the entire sample, few requests for executive authority were made to children in the family or by other adults when they were present.

Although these symptomatic families had an executive hierarchy, it was less effective than that of adaptive families. The mothers and oldest daughters in these families assumed less responsibility than those in the adaptive families. The position of male children in these families was particularly difficult: Not only were they not given responsibilities, but they were frequently scapegoated and seldom had a voice in the family.

The communication process was at times vague and often disruptive, and tasks were not completed as successfully in the clinic sample. Boundaries between subsystems were more diffuse, and a quality of intrusiveness prevailed among family members. The two most common dysfunctional patterns in the less adaptive families were these: (1) The mother was too involved with one of the children, or (2) the mother's executive authority was undermined by the maternal grandmother, whether or not she was living with the family. Impairment of family functioning was greatest when a mother was disengaged from her children because of the mother's depression and/or alcoholism.

Family Concept

While "observed family interaction" describes external family functioning, "family concept" reveals how the family members perceive themselves to be managing. Successful single-parent families in our sample viewed themselves as integrated, support-giving units that valued loyalty, home-centeredness, consideration, communication, and closeness. Less adaptive families had the opposite perception of themselves. Their internal relations were characterized by lack of fondness for each other, lack of separateness and communication, conflict, and estrangement.

Adaptive families saw themselves as dealing effectively with the world outside, having a sense of control over their own destiny, and having an action orientation. Less adaptive families, on the other hand, felt controlled by external forces. Of importance is that members of the adaptive families were more congruent in their self-perception than those in the clinic sample, in which there was obvious discrepancy among family members. These findings are similar to those in Van der Veen and Novak's (1974) work with families of disturbed and nondisturbed children.

Environmental Stress

All families inevitably encounter stresses in their attempts to cope with developmental and societal demands, but the impact of social and economic trends is most severe for female-headed families living in poverty. Stress is more probably best understood not as inherent in a situation, but as a product of the interaction between the situation and a family's capacity to deal with it (Eckenrode & Gore, 1981). How a family experiences stress relates to the interactions between and among the following elements: (1) characteristics of the stressful situation (frequency and magnitude of the event); (2) the family's definition of the event (positive, negative, or neutral); (3) characteristics of the social support system (amount of support and reciprocity within one's social network); and (4) a family's internal resources (Lindblad-Goldberg and Dukes, 1988).

Although all families in the sample experienced a similar high frequency of stressful life events, the nature of these events was different in the two populations. For example, symptomatic families were experiencing more legal problems: Mothers and children were often in court as victims, and children were in court as perpetrators. They had more short- and long-term physical, emotional, and behavior problems; unplanned pregnancies; menopause occurrences; and worsening of children's personal habits, such as grooming, manners, and choice of friends. More family arguments, in-law problems, and trouble coping were also found in less adaptive families. Interestingly, there were no differences with regard to frequency of problems with finances, jobs, education, home management, environment, social activity, or family configuration (i.e., pregnancies, births, marriages, separations, divorces, deaths, and gaining or losing household members).

A crucial factor in evaluating the impact of stressful life events is a family's perception of these events. It is this cognitive process that determines the nature of the stress reaction and subsequent coping abilities. The coping process begins with the cognitive appraisal of an event as to whether it constitutes a threat to one's self or family. Cues from both the immediate situation and an individual's belief system also affect this assessment. One critical difference between adaptive families and symptomatic single-parent families in our sample was that adaptive families tended to highlight positive events and to place less emphasis on the negative aspects of stressful events than did less adaptive families.

Social Network Resources

Social networks are hypothesized to provide resources to enhance coping capacity. The existing hypotheses about participation of black families in support networks have been summarized by Malson (1983) as follows: (1) the Afro-American tradition of doing for others, (2) the need for economic support, and (3) the functional network of support systems and the services provided. In addition, for many Afro-Americans, the definition of a family has always reflected embeddedness in extended-family networks (Foster, 1983; Hays & Mindel, 1973). Implicit in all of these hypotheses is the concept that reciprocity exists between persons who participate in the exchange. Although several studies (Hill, 1972; Malson, 1981; McAdoo, 1981) have viewed support systems as a major resource to the single parent, others have indicated that not all social ties provide support, especially among low-income mothers (Belle, 1982, 1983; Wahler, 1980).

In our study, there were many similarities in the structural features of social networks developed by adaptive and symptomatic families (Lindblad-Goldberg & Dukes, 1985a). A variable differentiating well-functioning and symptomatic families was that boyfriends or fiancés were usually more central in less adaptive mothers' networks; in examining the clinical records of symptomatic families, we found that the relationships between and among boyfriends and/or fiancés, mothers, and identified patients were always problematic.

Examining the relationship between social support and stress revealed several interesting patterns in symptomatic families (Lindblad-Goldberg & Dukes, 1988). In general, those single-parent families that had higher stress tended to be more involved with family and relatives; conversely, higher stress also occurred when there was more frequent contact with relatives, when more emotional help was given to relatives, and when mothers had more intense emotions about relatives than relatives had about them. Mothers' perceptions of giving more concrete assistance than they received in return was strongly related to stress in these families' lives. Thus, the social networks of less adaptive families seemed to be more stress-producing than supportive.

A Model of Adaptive Functioning in Black, Low-Income, Single-Parent Families

Conceptually, the black single-parent family is viewed as an open system in transformation (Minuchin, 1974), which operates within specific social contexts. As a dynamic open system, it continually receives and sends information to and from the extrafamilial environment, while at the same time it adapts to changes in its own internal processes. What processes lead to adaptive functioning in some families and to symptomatic functioning in others? I propose that adaptive functioning relates to reciprocal processes influencing how single-parent families experience and manage stress, how social network resources become supportive or stress-producing, and how family resources and the coping process facilitate or impede adaptive functioning.

There is, then, a link between stressful life circumstances and adaptive functioning that is affected by a family's resources, by its appraisal of stress and coping responses to stress, and by the effects of the social network. Stressful life circumstances include (1) relatively discrete events of short-term duration (e.g., plumbing breaks down; son has an argument with teacher), as well as (2) combinations of these discrete events (e.g., family changes residence; son is suspended from school), and also (3) chronic life conditions—the steady, unchanging or slowly changing oppressive conditions that must be endured daily (living with poverty, racism, discrimination, and limited educational and occupational opportunities). Include in the definition of "stressful environment" is the impact of the broader social factors—namely, neighborhood, community, and social policy. The social network can be both a source of stress and a possible mediator of stress.

Our model also considers the role of family resources, including (1) family members' personal resources, especially the mother's coping philosophy, sense of well-being, health status, and problem-solving skills; and (2) the internal resources of the family as a unit, especially the family's level of organization and the family members' internalized perceptions of the family as an adaptive and integrated entity. The model suggests that life stressors and the family's resources related to such stressors can shape social network resources, cognitive appraisal, and coping responses, as well as their effectiveness (i.e., adaptive or nonadaptive functioning). In a reciprocal fashion, adaptive or nonadaptive functioning can influence the coping process, family resources, social network resources, and life stressors.

The following example of an adaptive single-parent family is used to illustrate the model.

Carol is a 32-year-old, never-married, black single parent; her five children, ranging from 5 to 13 years of age, are doing well at home and school. Living on an annual income of $7000, she supplements her welfare allotment by working part-time as a domestic. She lives in public housing but spent 3 years negotiating with the housing authority for an apartment in the best-managed housing project in the city. Carol has just told an interviewer that she had been in the hospital very recently for her own health problems. In addition, her adolescent daughter has been recently diagnosed with arthritis; her telephone service was cut off; her automobile's transmission needed major repairs; and the washing machine broke down. She is asked by an interviewer to describe how she and her family have coped with these difficulties.

CAROL: I don't know—just take it one day at a time, just deal with one problem at a time. I guess I have a spiritual belief that carries me through a lot. And I guess I was raised—I work better under stress. Sometimes my best performance is when I'm under a lot of pressure. I say to the kids, "OK, now we're going to do this, this, and this." And the kids will say "OK," and then we get it done. The kids know when things are going downhill. It seems they work better when we're all trying to work together to do something. And they all help out—especially Danielle, since she's the oldest.

Like, yesterday, the washing machine went out in the middle of the wash! And me with five kids! It was a mess! The kids came home—by this time I had taken to the couch! But I was giving orders—I was supervising. I told Danielle to take the clothes out, Shana rinsed them, Daryl took them outside, and Barbara helped him to hang them up. I called housing. They said they'd come and pick up the washing machine. I called my sister who's moving to Georgia, and she's going to give me her washing machine. It's old but works. Last year her youngest lived with me while she worked a night shift, so she owes me.

I think I have a lot of faith that things will work out, and my children do too. It's like a pendulum—like nothing runs smoothly all the time. There has to be a downswing sometimes. So now I'm in a downswing. But I'm content because the family pulls together. I'm content. I have an apartment I've always wanted. It seems that we're kind of happy, despite everything that's going on. We've got bad times, but we'll get through it.

INTERVIEWER: Do you see anything negative about your situation?

CAROL: Well, most of my family [extended] has also had hard times, but we help each other out. Sometimes a few of my relatives look at us like we're going through it. I've got an aunt who seems to thrive when things go bad for me. I don't see her very much and I guess she doesn't have much happening in her life.

This vignette illustrates that stressful life circumstances (the washing machine breaking down), when met with strong family resources (effective executive behavior; workable executive hierarchy; clear differentiation of sibling responsibilities; mother's problem-solving skills, ability to attend to her own needs, sense of control, and positive coping philosophy), can lead to an empowering cognitive appraisal (definition of stress event as nonthreatening to mother and family's integrity as a unit, but requiring action). It also shows how an effective coping response (successfully resolving the washing machine problem) can transform a potential negative stress event and reduce the probability of experiencing a future stress event (having no clean clothes for six family members). In addition, the reciprocity within the mother's social network (the mother gets help from her sister in proportion to her giving help to her sister), the mother's ability to distance herself from potential stress in her network (her aunt's critical attitude), and the social network's validating the mother's interpretation of the stress event (the extended family has "hard times" too) all serve to maintain the supportive features of the mother's social network.

This example is of a single coping episode. In reality, low-income single-parent families cope daily with stressful situations involving multiple threats and multiple coping strategies. Adaptive functioning is the outcome when the family and social context maintain flexibility in mobilizing alternative patterns and resources when dealing with stress. Evolving belief systems develop within the family and social network that motivate what Antonovsky (1979) has described as the desire for a "sense of coherence." In his words,

> The sense of coherence is a global orientation that expresses the extent to which one has a pervasive, enduring though dynamic feeling of confidence that one's internal and external environments are predictable and that there is a high probability that things will work out as well as can be reasonably expected. . . .
>
> This does not mean there are no ups and downs. . . . But such changes occur around a stable location on the continuum. . . . A sense of coherence does not at all imply that one is in control. . . . The critical issue is not whether the power to determine such outcome lies in our own hands or elsewhere. What is important is that the location of power is where it legitimately is supposed to be . . . and that issues will, in the long run, be resolved by such authority in one's own interests. (1979, pp. 123–124, 128)

Working with Less Adaptive Single-Parent Families

We have learned so much from adaptive single-parent families—not only about the possibility of effective functioning, but also about how to function effectively—that we now have a framework for treatment of families who have been overwhelmed in their situations.

Mrs. Wilson, a black, never-married, 36-year-old single parent, was referred to the university outpatient family therapy service through her caseworker at the Department of Human Services. Two of her three children, Tory, 11, and Kim,

9, had returned to the home 4 months previously. The Department of Human Services had placed the two children in a residential home for 3 years while the mother received counseling and medical treatment for alcohol abuse. The youngest child, Stacey, aged 6, had been allowed to stay with her mother. The caseworker was concerned because Tory had recently been truant from school.

The caseworker, a 25-year-old, white, Jewish woman, greeted the therapist, Dr. Lester, when he came to the reception area to meet the family. She pulled him aside to tell him secretly of her concern that the mother would begin drinking again. She then introduced the children to Dr. Lester. Mrs. Wilson greeted the therapist in a friendly but tentative manner. In the interview, the mother complained loudly that she did not understand Tory's behavior. On the one hand, she pointed out, he was extremely helpful to her. He would stay home from school and take care of his sisters when she had to go out. He helped with the cooking and cleaning, and kept his two sisters "in line." She expressed frustration and felt she couldn't get through to him about his truancy: "Doesn't he know how upset I get to have the school on my back?" Mrs. Wilson complained that if she couldn't handle Tory, she would have to send him back to the residential home. The mother sat with each daughter on either side of her; Tory sat across the room. She would frequently stroke Kim's hair, tie Stacey's shoelaces, and relate in general to her daughters as if they were much younger children. Tory sat quietly, but with an unhappy expression, during his mother's complaints.

Mrs. Wilson's only social contacts were with her sole living relative—a sister who was a well-respected school teacher in the community, but who was critical of her drinking and child-rearing practices—and her caseworker. The children's father had left town while the mother was pregnant with Stacey, and the mother did not know his whereabouts. The caseworker had been assigned to her in the past month. The previous caseworker, a 50-year-old black woman "who I owe my life to," had been instrumental in referring the mother to the alcohol treatment program. This previous caseworker had driven Mrs. Wilson to all her therapy appointments, and she had encouraged and supported her during the past 3 years. Whenever Mrs. Wilson was upset, she had called this caseworker. She had become a part of the family's significant resource system.

In assessing this single-parent family system, factors were considered that might be inhibiting adaptive functioning. First, the family resources were assessed. Mrs. Wilson did not have a coping philosophy that gave her confidence that things would work out. Her method of handling stress previously had been to abuse alcohol. Her current method was to call her new caseworker and request that she remove the children. The caseworker would calm her down over the phone, and then come to the house and tell the children not to upset their mother. Thus a sequence was enacted wherein when the mother was out of control, an external agent was brought in to take charge. This perpetuated the mother's feelings of incompetence. A low-level stress event, such as the children's not washing dishes when asked, was perceived by the mother as harmful to the family's functioning.

This sequence also engendered alternate feelings in the children as to whether they should protect their mother or be angry that she was abandoning them to an external agent. Tory tended to assume a position of authority in the family to protect his mother; Kim and Stacey tended to withdraw and regress, thus prompting her to infantilize them. The haphazard hierarchical organization in the family was nonadaptive. As the mother relinquished authority to the caseworker, Tory magnified his "parental child" role at home. He felt more responsible for the family's functioning than for his own performance at school. Consequently, he would leave school to check on the home situation. Kim and Stacey did not assume age-appropriate responsibilities because they were encouraged to be young by their mother. She continued to relate to them as if they were 3 years younger than they were (i.e., the ages they had been when the family was split up 3 years earlier).

Expression of feelings was also inhibited in the family. All family members were uncertain as to whether the family would continue as a viable group or whether it would be fragmented again. The constant tension that existed diminished the opportunity for a trustful atmosphere to develop wherein feelings could be expressed.

The social network resources available to the family were then assessed as stress-producing rather than supportive. Mrs. Wilson felt judged by both her sister and the new caseworker. She was dependent upon the caseworker, yet resentful at her intrusiveness. Her unresolved sadness and anger at her previous caseworker's departure contributed to her difficulty in developing a workable relationship with the new caseworker.

Based on the assessment, treatment goals were developed to facilitate adaptive functioning in the Wilson family. The 90-minute treatment sessions were split between 45-minute individual meetings with Mrs. Wilson and whole-family sessions. Thus several treatment goals could be addressed simultaneously within a given treatment session.

The first treatment goal to be addressed was the perceived fragility of the family unit during this reorganization stage; Tory and Kim had returned home only 4 months previously. The therapist normalized the Wilson family's phase of reorganization by sharing a story about his grandmother's family, which had been fragmented by the Holocaust, and the realistic challenges of reforming as a family unit. While telling the story, he identified the uncertainty family members had felt during this process and how those feelings had changed as the family's life became more predictable. He emphasized how his grandmother initially contacted the rabbi every time she became uncertain about her ability to succeed, and how her children resented the rabbi's telling them what to do. He related how the family members eventually worked to solve their own problems without involving the rabbi. Mrs. Wilson and her children strongly identified with this story and began to share the parallels between that situation and their own.

A new sequence was created wherein Mrs. Wilson agreed not to contact the caseworker until she first sat down and tried to work out difficulties privately with each of her children. If she could not resolve the problem, she was to call the therapist, and the two would decide whether to contact the caseworker.

The family sessions were used to empower the mother in her executive role as she negotiated conflict within the family, and to help her develop a more appropriate executive hierarchy among the children. Tory, Kim, and Stacey began sharing in the household responsibilities, and this decreased Tory's "parental child" role. A balance was achieved in the family between responsibility and play. Many play experiences were created between the mother and each of her children, especially Tory. Thus Tory could be both a "child" and a responsible young male at home. Mrs. Wilson stopped keeping Tory out of school to help her; his truancy ceased.

Mrs. Wilson's success in her executive role during sessions generalized to experiences at home, and the caseworker no longer was asked to assume the mother's executive role. Instead, the caseworker was invited to attend various family sessions as an observer, and thus had the experience of observing Mrs. Wilson being effective with her children. An important session occurred wherein the mother expressed her feelings of missing the old caseworker and her resentment at the new caseworker who had replaced her. This session allowed the new caseworker to become more empathic and to understand Mrs. Wilson's loss of that relationship, rather than her difficulty in abstaining from alcohol, as underlying some of her distress. The caseworker soon recommended that permanent custody of the children be transferred back to mother.

After strengthening the family's internal resources and improving the social network linkage with the caseworker, treatment focused on augmenting other network linkages and continuing to empower Mrs. Wilson. She was asked to help the therapist with another black female client in need of treatment for alcoholism. A new group counseling program had begun in the community for black clients; Mrs. Wilson was asked to accompany the therapist's client to the group and to inform him whether she felt this new program would be more helpful to the client than the program she had attended. She undertook this assignment with enthusiasm and a strong sense of responsibility toward the client. They became friends, and both continued to attend the new program, feeling that it was more responsive to their needs as black women than the other program.

In an attempt to challenge the perceptions of Mrs. Wilson's sister, the therapist gave Mrs. Wilson an official certificate from the university's family therapy center to hang visibly in her living room. This certificate proclaimed Mrs. Wilson as the "mother of the year" in achieving success in the reorganization of her family; it also acknowledged her accomplishments as a "teacher and guide" in helping another to achieve sobriety. Mrs. Wilson was encouraged to invite her sister for dinner at least once a week. Since the sister's teaching certificate was from the same university, she regarded Mrs. Wilson's certificate with great respect.

A 3-year follow-up with the family indicated that the children were doing well at home and at school. Tory, Kim, and Stacey were described as "mature, responsible" family members who appeared to enjoy making contributions to the family's functioning. Mrs. Wilson had become a coleader in the alcohol counseling group. She and her sister had worked out a child care arrangement wherein they took turns caring for each other's children so that they could take time for themselves.

Conclusion

The single-parent family is an increasingly prevalent family form. It is also, as this chapter has demonstrated, a viable family form, able to function well and to promote education and a sense of relationship and responsibility in its children. Because most single-parent families are female-headed, and because women generally have lower earning capacities, single-parent families are generally beset by poverty and the kind of social supervision (or interference) that families of poverty are subject to. Thus these families often have to cope with a multiplicity of interferences and opinions that threaten their integrity and sense of competence. Nevertheless, many such families are successful in raising children to be effective adults.

Our study of poor, single-parent black families has provided guidelines for how these families do cope, and should supply therapists with a framework for assessing families who have difficulties and for providing them with direction for reorganizing effectively. As our study looked to the families themselves for the answers to questions about how they managed, we advocate that therapists seek out the resources within even the most desperate family for the first steps in building a new confidence.

REFERENCES

Antonovsky, A. (1979). *Health, stress, and coping.* San Francisco: Jossey-Bass.
Belle, D. (1982). Social ties and social support. In D. Belle (Ed.), *Lives in stress: Women and depression* (pp. 133–144). Beverly Hills, CA: Sage.
Belle, D. (1983). The impact of poverty on social networks and supports. *Marriage and Family Review, 5,* 89–103.
Bianchi, S., & Farley, R. (1979). Racial differences in family living arrangements and economic well-being: Analysis of recent trends. *Journal of Marriage and the Family, 4,* 537–552.
Blechman, E. (1982). Are children with one parent at psychological risk? A methodological review. *Journal of Marriage and the Family, 8,* 179–195.
Cashion, B. (1982). Female-headed families: Effects on children and clinical implications. *Journal of Marital and Family Therapy, 8,* 77–85.
Cordes, C. (1984, August). The rise of one-parent black families. *APA Monitor,* pp. 16–18.
Eckenrode, J., & Gore, S. (1981). Stressful events and social supports: The significance of context. In B. Gottlieb (Ed.), *Social networks and social support* (pp. 43–68). Beverly Hills, CA: Sage.
Foster, H. (1983). African patterns in Afro-American families. *Journal of Black Studies, 14,* 201–232.
Fulmer, R. (1983). A structural approach to unresolved mourning in single parent family systems. *Journal of Marital and Family Therapy, 9,* 227–234.

Hays, W., & Mindel, C. (1973). Extended kinship relations in black and white families. *Journal of Marriage and the Family, 35*, 51–56.

Herzog, E., & Sudia, C. (1973). Children in fatherless families. In B. Caldwell & H. Ricciuti (Eds.), *Review of child development research* (Vol. 3). New York: Wiley.

Hess, R., & Shipman, U. (1965). Early experience and the socialization of cognitive modes in children. *Child Development, 34*, 869–886.

Hill, R. (1972). *The strengths of black families*. New York: Emerson Hall.

Kamii, C., & Radin, N. (1967). Class differences in the socialization practices of Negro mothers. *Journal of Marriage and the Family, 29*, 302–310.

Lindblad-Goldberg, M., & Dukes, J. (1978). *Single parent family functioning: Normative and dysfunctional patterns* (ACYF Grant No. 90-C-1775/02). Washington, DC: Department of Health and Human Services, Office of Human Development Services.

Lindblad-Goldberg, M, & Dukes, J. (1981). *Single parent family functioning: Normative and dysfunctional patterns*. Paper presented at the meeting of the American Orthopsychiatric Association, Toronto.

Lindblad-Goldberg, M., & Dukes, J. (1985a). Social support in black, low-income, single-parent families: Normative and dysfunctional patterns, *American Journal of Orthopsychiatry, 55*, 42–58.

Lindblad-Goldberg, M., & Dukes, J. (1985b). Stress and social support in black, low-income single parent families: Normative and dysfunctional patterns. In A. Gurman (Ed.), *American Family Therapy Association Proceedings* (pp. 30–31). Washington, DC: American Family Therapy Association.

Lindblad-Goldberg, M., & Dukes, J. (1988). Stress in black, low-income, single-parent families: Normative and dysfunctional patterns. *American Journal of Orthopsychiatry, 58*, 104–120.

Malson, M. (1981). *Black families and childrearing support networks*. Paper presented at the meeting of the Society for Research on Child Development, Boston.

Malson, M. (1983). The social-support systems of black families. *Marriage and Family Review, 5*, 37–57.

Marotz-Baden, R., Adams, G., Buccho, N., Munro, B., & Munro, G. (1979). Family form or process? Reconsidering the deficit family model approach. *The Family Coordinator, 30*, 5–14.

McAdoo, H. (1981). *Stress and support networks of working single black mothers*. Paper presented at the meeting of the Society for Research in Child Development, Boston.

Minuchin, S. (1974). *Families and family therapy*. Cambridge, MA: Harvard University Press.

Minuchin, S., Montalvo, B., Guerney, B., Rosman, B., & Schumer, F. (1967). *Families of the slums: An exploration of their structure and treatment*. New York: Basic Books.

Moynihan, D. P. (1965). *The Negro family: The case for national action*. Washington, DC: U.S. Government Printing Office.

Sameroff, A. (1975). Transactional models in early social relations. *Human Development, 18*, 65–79.

U.S. Bureau of the Census (1980). Washington, DC: U.S. Government Printing Office.

Van der Veen, F., & Novak, A. (1974). The family concept of the disturbed child: A replication study. *American Journal of Orthopsychiatry, 44*, 763–772.

Wahler, R. (1980). The insular mother: Her problems in parent–child treatment. *Journal of Applied Behavior Analysis, 55*, 459–470.

Weltner, J. (1982). A structural approach to the single-parent family. *Family Process, 21*, 203–210.

Wilkinson, C., & O'Connor, W. (1977). Growing up male in a single-parent family. *Psychiatric Annals, 7*, 356–362.

Willie, C. (1976). *A new look at black families*. Bayside, NY: General Hall.

Zajonc, R., & Markus, G. (1975). Birth order and intellectual development. *Psychological Review, 82*, 74–88.

7

Remarried Systems

MARY F. WHITESIDE, PhD

Alex stands at center stage in the school auditorium, ready to sing his solo with supreme 10-year-old confidence and self-assurance. His mother beams at him from one side of the audience. His father trips over Alex's duffel bag in the aisle, steadies himself, and starts the VCR camera. His stepmother, sister, stepbrother, and infant half-sister are in center seats in the front row. His teacher, hidden in the wings, thinks back 4 years to the confused, restless, worried little boy that Alex was in first grade, and silently thanks his parents for their persistence in creating a family that has attended to his needs so well.

The shape of the remarried family system is complex and highly variable. It is formed by membership and current living schedules, as well as by a complicated weave of many strands of developmental time. Membership includes the wide network of people and relationships created through divorce and remarriage. These ties include blood, in-law, former in-law, and step- relationships. The amount of everyday time spent in a household determines what feels like "home." Opportunities for time together affect the degree of intimacy, information exchange, and influence possible between and among household members. The form of scheduling influences the number of transitions with which the family must cope, the boundaries between households, the subgroupings emphasized or supported within households, and the degree of chronic loss felt by both parents and children.

Mary F. Whiteside. Ann Arbor Center for the Family, Ann Arbor, MI.

Developmental time includes the developmental phase of each of the household units on the divorce–binuclear–remarried continuum, as well as the developmental phase of each family member. As emphasized by Wallerstein (1983), the child of divorce faces not only the expectable tasks of childhood, but also the added challenges of the reorganization and readjustments stemming from the divorce and remarriage processes. The structure of the family changes at the same time as the child's developmental needs and abilities are changing. An accurate assessment of a child's adaptation has to take into account his or her current family structure, current developmental issues, and prior adaptations. Within the same family there can be considerable differences in adaptations achieved by siblings, depending on their age, sex, developmental position as it has interacted with family structure, and individual strengths and resources.

Despite the overwhelming complexity of the task of placing the various possible experiences of living in a remarried family system into an organized therapeutic intervention model, a framework has begun to emerge in the clinical and research literature within the past few years, and this has useful applications to most remarried families. The most important assumption about the remarried family is that the family system includes more than one household unit. All family members are affected emotionally, financially, or legally by the actions of the other household(s), and therefore must take them into account. Ahrons and Perlmutter (1982) describe this situation as the "binuclear family." Sager *et al.* (1983) refer to the network of relationships as the "REM [remarried family] suprasystem." Well-functioning remarried families find ways of negotiating these complex interrelationships that acknowledge the reality of the connections while maintaining comfortable subsystem boundaries.

One of the key elements for a well-functioning remarried network is the establishment of a successful coparenting team for the children. The coparenting team includes both biological parents and their respective spouses and/or committed live-in partners. Grandparents and stepgrandparents are included in this team if they are carrying major child care responsibilities. Siblings include both biological siblings and step siblings from both households. All these persons, in various combinations, constitute what can be called a child's psychological "immediate family." This is true whatever the legal custody and visitation arrangements may be. As discussed by Ahrons and Perlmutter (1982), "a continuing relationship between former spouses is necessary if they are to successfully co-parent their minor children," and "relationships between family members in the binuclear system are determined by the type of relationship established between the biological parents" (p. 40). What is evident from these assumptions is that the model of effective parenting for children in remarried families is different in several critical ways from the model of parenting in nuclear families. Suggestions for therapeutic interventions rest heavily on ideas about parenting within the remarried system. In therapy with families of remarriage, it is particularly important to establish with the parents a working model of a remarried family, and of a coparenting team that has the maximum opportunity to create a nurturing, appropriately disciplined, responsible, health-producing environment for the children. Without this background, therapist input directly to the children can be supportive, but not terribly powerful. The parents require a knowledge of the children's needs so that they can take appropriate action.

Figure 7-1 is a diagram illustrating the complexity of the role relationships for members of a remarried family system. It is important to note that all members have multiple roles, many of which have few societal guidelines. What, for example, is the proper relationship between a woman and the current husband of her husband's former wife? Some of the relationship chains pose logically perplexing relationships. For example, a mutual child may have a brother and sister who are not biologically related to each other. In addition, adult–child dyads in the same household may have similar generational structure, but different role structure. For example, a man may be a biological father to one child and a stepfather to another. If his child brings his half-brother with him for a weekend, there is no defined relationship between the man and his son's brother. Finally, each person in the family can have a different version of primary family membership. In order for individuals to feel normal within this confusing family shape, they need to construct a family paradigm defining an overarching family identity that crosses household boundaries. The content of the remarried family identity construct varies widely among families. However, attempts to think of the family in terms appropriate to a nuclear family violates the everyday reality of family members.

A second critical part of the remarried family model is that the shape of the family varies dramatically with changes over time that occur in the remarried family structure and in the children's growth and development. Thus the therapeutic implications of implementing the remarried family model will vary, depending upon family constellation, family stage, and ages of the children. The aim is to use the power of the therapist's intervention, combined with the motivation to change presented by the child's (or children's) pain, to help the family construct a way of living together that can flexibility adapt to changes over time, that accepts the realities of their family structure, and that maximizes the potential resources available to the children. The sequence of therapeutic interventions moves from a broad view of the remarried family suprasystem, to household subsystems, and only to individual child work if there are residual legacies for a particular child that are not attended to by an adequate coparenting team.

The model presented here is an organization of material from the family therapy clinical and research literature, illustrated with vignettes from my own clinical and research practice.

The Developmental Model

Within the concept of the "remarried family suprasystem," one needs to attend to developmental needs. Different stages of remarried family life have different characteristics, internal family structures, and parenting models. Children have different cognitive abilities and psychological needs at different developmental stages. Adults have both career and psychological issues of importance. These

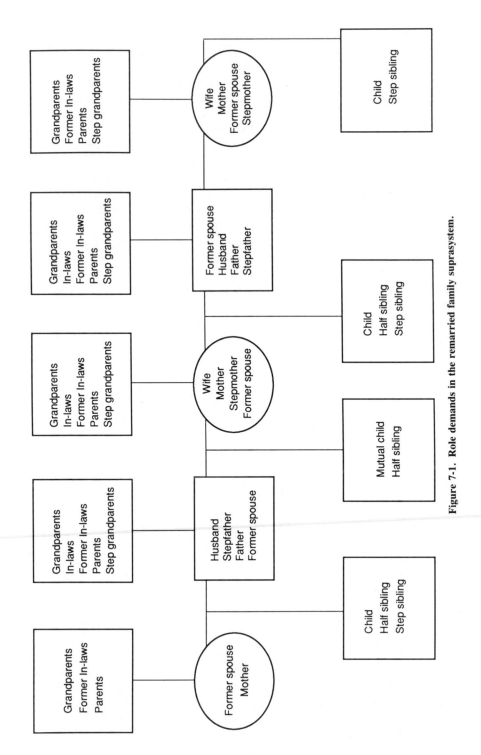

Figure 7-1. Role demands in the remarried family suprasystem.

138

time lines interact with one another. Some combinations are particularly difficult; others seem to go more smoothly. The experience of living in a remarried family will be different for different children in the same family, although family style may moderate this interaction. In addition, children may be moving back and forth between households in different phases of family development.

Papernow (1984) gives an excellent description of three phases of remarried family development, including seven substages for individual family members:

I. Early stages of family development
   a. Fantasy
   b. Assimilation
   c. Awareness
II.
   Middle stages
   a. Mobilization
   b. Action
III. Later stages
   a. Contact
   b. Resolution

These stages extended previous work in a manner that is extremely useful clinically.

Early Stages

In the early stages of remarriage, the structure of the family remains primarily divided along biological lines. Nevertheless, the commitment to form a new household represents a significant developmental shift that has ramifications throughout the extended family. This represents both a challenge for family reorganization and a reawakening of unresolved issues from previous stages. As stated by Wald (1981),

> Losses and discontinuities specific to earlier stages must be reintegrated in this stage and often require that one or more family members return to earlier "unfinished business" of never or only partially mastered tasks for further work. These may include issues related to continued emotional attachment between former spouses, unresolved mourning of one or more family members, children's hopes for parental reunion, identity issues, and feelings of lowered self-esteem because of the dissolution of the nuclear family. (p. 125)

Wallerstein (1983) suggests that the child must have completed a portion of this mourning process before he or she is emotionally available to form a relationship with a stepparent. The intensity of a child's sadness, anger, and loss of self-esteem is related both to the amount of contact with the noncustodial parent and to the degree of ongoing parental battling to which the child is subjected. The fact that themes of loss are so predominant in the divorce literature for children relates to the appalling statistics about noncustodial parents. For example, Furstenberg and Spanier (1984) report that nearly one-half of children from separated or divorced families have not seen one of their biological parents in the previous 5 years. When this is coupled with the observation that children with adequate contact with both biological parents form relationships with stepparents more easily (Crosbie-Burnett & Ahrons, 1985; Wallerstein & Kelly, 1980), the importance of supporting the coparenting relationship is obvious. The children who see a noncustodial parent most rarely will be perceived as needing a stepparent's closeness the most. There may be pressure on a stepparent to move into a parental role more quickly than appropriate, at the same time that a child may have more of a struggle accepting the contact.

The binuclear family model is heavily emphasized in this chapter because of my belief that therapists, as well as other societally sanctioned helpers, can have a strong preventive impact on a family structure through their vision of "normality." The problems of children in remarried families are typically exacerbated by absentee noncustodial parents and overburdened stepparents. If therapeutic interventions are conducted with the expectation that all the adults in a child's life must be attended to; if a repetoire of courteous and respectful patterns of coparenting exchanges is conceivable; and if ideas of long-distance, everyday contact between parents and children are available, a new, more resilient structure can be developed more often than not.

At the same time that old feelings are being worked through, the family must create opportunities for the development of new attachments and family cohesion. For many families, this stage begins before the actual wedding ceremony, during an extended period of courting and perhaps living together in the same household.

Middle Stages

The middle stages constitute the time when significant structural reorganization is possible. Although earlier discussions (McGoldrick & Carter, 1980; Ransom, Schlesinger, & Derdeyn, 1979; Stern, 1978; Visher & Visher, 1979; Whiteside, 1982, 1983) look at reorganization beginning from the point of remarriage, both Mills (1984) and Papernow (1984) emphasize that a much longer time may be necessary for a family to build up positive ties, to gain awareness about the characteristics of their new family system, and to build up momentum for change. Papernow (1984) describes the middle stages as a period filled with conflict and active negotiation. It is a time when the child is moved out of the couple relationship and boundaries around the marital couple are strengthened, as are boundaries around the step- relationships. If this is to be done, biological parental ties must be loosened. Differences between the two parental households are clarified, and boundaries around the stepfamily are strengthened in the extended kinship network. This is also a time when many remarriages founder. If the tasks of this

Table 7-1. Developmental Interaction Chart

Remarried family stage	Developmental stage of child			
	A. Preschool (0–5 years)	B. Middle years (6–12 years)	C. Adolescence (13–17 years)	D. Adult (18+ years)
I. Early stages (0–2 years)	IA	IB	IC	ID
II. Middle stages (3–5 years)	IIA	IIB	IIC	IID
III. Later stages (6+ years)	IIIA	IIIB	IIIC	IIID

phase are not mastered, either the family will move into a chronic stalemate divided along biological lines, or the new couple will move toward divorce.

Later Stages

By the time a remarriage is firmly established, patterns of relationship among family members are regular, reliable, and normal. Step-relationships allow for intimacy, authenticity, and true influence. Clear roles are established for stepparents and stepsiblings. The family structure is well integrated. In Papernow's (1984) study, her "fast" families reached this point in 4 years; "average" families took 7 years.

Possible Developmental Combinations

Using these three family phases, Table 7-1 summarizes the developmental combinations for one household subsystem and one child. Movement over time is represented by movement on the diagonals of the table. For example, if a 10-year-old boy's mother remarries, we have a combination of a child in his middle years, residing in a household in the early stages of remarriage (cell IB in the table). After 3 or 4 years, the stepfamily will have moved into its middle years or restructuring phase (Papernow, 1984), while the boy has entered adolescence (cell IIC in the table). What worked in the earlier years may now have to be modified, to take into account both the stepparent's demands for increased integration and the boy's needs for increasing independence and identity confirmation. In addition, recommendations for the parenting model for this boy will be different from the recommendations for his older sister, who was 15 at the point of remarriage (cell IC) and is now moving out of the household (cell IID). Finally, a relationship between the boy and his stepfather may be quite different from that with the stepmother in his father's household, a relationship that began when the boy was 4 (cell IA in the table). This developmental model of the stepfamily is discussed, taking each family stage and looking at the differing needs of children of different ages.

The Early Stages of Remarriage

A Time of Change and Reaction

The first years of the remarriage pose the challenge of the entry of new members into the household; the introduction of the stepparent into the coparenting team; and the creation of an interconnected kinship network, including former, step-, and family-of-origin relations. The fact that the family is responding to important changes needs to be carefully attended to in the type of therapeutic interventions selected. Normally, this is a time of increased stress. Lutz (1983), studying families with adolescents, found that stepfamilies in which couples had been married less than 2 years reported significantly more stress than others in her sample.

The remarriage causes a shift not only within the household, but also across households. What was formerly an established two-parent working relationship now includes a stepparent in some manner. This may cause strong feelings on all parts, and reactions in both households should be noted. Hetherington, Cox, and Cox (1985) report increased problem behavior in both boys and girls at the introduction of a stepfather. An unmarried custodial parent (often the mother) may feel her time and influence with the children threatened when her ex-spouse remarries, may increase her protective hold on the children, and may also experience strong feelings of anger and regret as she must say goodbye to the former marital relationship in yet a new way. At the same time, a noncustodial parent who takes on new responsibilities becomes less willing or able to sustain commitments to preexisting parental obligations (Furstenberg & Spanier, 1984). An adult with both noncustodial parenting obligations and stepparenting obligations in a custodial household has to negotiate a compromise distribution of time, money, and affection that weighs costs and benefits to both households (Clingempeel & Brand, 1985).

This shift was seen in a family in which an 8-year-old girl, living with her mother and younger brother, was referred because she was depressed and angry, resistant to discipline, and doing poorly at school. The mother reported that there had been no contact with the father for the last 12 months, since his remarriage. A critical intervention was for the therapist to support the mother in taking an assertive stance directly with the father—insisting that he see his children more, rather than expressing her anger on attacks on his incompetence and unreliability. An important corollary was work with the mother to deal with her own loneliness when the children were not with her, and to support her in finding independent satisfaction and adult stimultion.

Expansion of the Coparenting Team

A critical task in the early stages of remarriage is the development of a model for the functions each adult will perform as a part of the coparenting team. As discussed by Ahrons and Perlmutter (1982), there is a range of normal coparenting stances, both for biological parental dyads and for same-sex parent–stepparent dyads. Often a mother and stepmother will see each other with mutual respect and find a cooperative team in their common hearth-keeping concerns. The mother may have handled any feelings of jealousy and feel glad that her children have warm, competent caretaking when in their father's house. Alternatively, the mother and stepmother may feel intensely competitive, each vying to be the better mother and denigrating the other's efforts. Father–stepfather dyads are described as being usually less intense. They are less likely to have a great deal of involvement with each other, and less likely to feel that they are in competitive conflict. These differences may well reflect gender-linked socialization in the sense of responsibility for caretaking.

Families vary in the degree of responsibility assumed by the stepparent and in the degree of separation desired between households. What is key is (1) that all adults be acknowledged as being important figures in the children's lives, and (2) that the division of responsibilities be clear. In the early stages of remarriage, this new coparenting system is just beginning to develop. Normally, during this period, families will fluctuate among continuing the old system, adding in the new spouse's observations and opinions from an "advisor" role with little power, and creating a second-order change by including the new spouse directly in three- or four-way decision making. It is a time of experimentation and creation of novel parenting structures.

When a child is referred for therapy, it is important that the therapist's contacts confirm the importance of the entire coparenting team. In order to do so, at the point of the first phone call, the therapist begins to gather information that describes the shape of the family system. Thus, in addition to a description of the presenting problem, the therapist needs to know the membership in the various households, the child's schedule of time spent in each household, and the time since divorce(s) and remarriage(s). Sager et al. (1983) make efforts to see as many members of the remarried family suprasystem as possible in the first interview. Part of the therapeutic task is to work with the family members to extend their conception of family identity beyond household boundaries and to dispel the myth that the "normal family" is one that conforms to the model of the nuclear family.

An important intake question, then, is this: What has been discussed with the other parent about the difficulties experienced by the child? Has the request for therapy been agreed upon by both parent? This question usually reveals a great deal of information about the current status of the biological coparenting relationship. The therapist may hear that the other parent has not been notified; that the two parents never talk directly to each other; that the other parent does not care about the child; that the other parent does not believe either in therapy or in the fact that the child is experiencing problems; that there is a dispute over custody and that the other parent would only use this information in the dispute; and/or that the child spends so little time with the other parent that his or her input is assumed to be irrelevant. One may hear that the other parent might be interested, but that contact would be too upsetting. Responses range from established cooperation with joint concern, through carefully maintained distance with an information gap across households, to continued and accelerating high levels of bitterness and embattlement between households (including ongoing involvement with the courts).

The therapeutic task is to establish contact with both biological parents in a manner that is supportive of all involved. This must lay the groundwork for changes in the biological coparenting exchanges in a manner that avoids an advocacy stance for either household, and that honors necessary boundaries between households. Because the terms of involvement of the new stepparent are in the process of definition, it is essential that he or she also be a part of discussions involving the child. In requesting a joint meeting, the therapist has the opportunity to sanction contact between the former spouse and the stepparent. Frequently a biological parent is in the crazy, awkward situation of having his or her child spend a great deal of time with an adult about whom he or she has little knowledge. A parent sometimes has greater opportunity to find out about a nonfamily babysitter than about a new stepparent. One of the joining functions for the therapist, therefore, is to bring out positive attributes of each of the parents and stepparents during the interview, commenting on how lucky the child is to have such a powerful combination of important characteristics available to him or her.

A mother with sole legal custody of her adolescent daughter called following a series of screaming battles over homework and curfew, during which her daughter threatened to run away. She had not discussed the difficulties with the girl's father, because she feared it would prove to him, once again, that she was an incompetent mother. She also feared that her own anger and frustration would make it impossible for her to be rational with him. She was jealous of her daughter's increasingly close ties with her stepmother. The therapist gave her a choice of informing the father before bringing in the daughter, or of an interview alone without the daughter. She chose to come in alone initially. However, after her frustration was supported, the daughter's feelings about missing her father were pointed out, and the possibility that he might give some long-distance help with discipline was suggested, she was willing to call him. In the interviews that followed, she was able to give him information more openly, which helped him understand what she was experiencing. She also accepted the stepmother's useful observations about the daughter. The father and stepmother surprised the mother by their willingness to support her expectations for the girl. The father also agreed to take over responsibility for dealing with extracurricular activities. Feeling less overwhelmed, the mother was able to carry through a much firmer, less reactive stance.

A useful format for the joint meetings models the idea of boundaries between households. The emphasis is upon exchange of information; opinions must be carefully presented if at all; attempts to change the other household or evaluations of the other household are seen as nonproductive. What will work in one household may not be at all appropriate for the other. There needs to be differentiation between households, in that each one begins to build up its own routines and rituals that define it as a stable, cohesive relationship unit with an important and respected identity. At the same time, there needs to be acknowledgment of the common threads of values and shared history. Thus, for example, the adults in one household may have strictly held times during the day when children are supervised on their homework. The adults in the other household may emphasize the child's learning to organize his or her time, making choices independently. Both, however, agree that doing well in school is a high priority. If the differences are respected, children can profit from the diversity and find a style that fits their own temperament. A child may import useful routines from household to the other. If there is ongoing battling between households, with each household trying to change the other's beliefs, the child will become stuck.

Even if there is an ongoing child difficulty independent of the parental tensions, there needs to be coordinated parental intervention in order to address the difficulties most effectively.

A 6-year-old girl was referred because of enuresis. She lived in a joint custody arrangement, at one house during the weekdays and the other house on weekends. Her grandparents were her major babysitters. All the adults agreed that she had a problem; she wet the bed at all three houses. Each of the households had useful and appropriate suggestions for treatment of the symptoms. However, the continuing criticism and competition among the adults led to tension and arguments over which solution was the most appropriate one for her. Her mother accused her stepmother of being abusive. Her father accused her mother of being neglectful. The stepmother accused both the father and the mother of being inconsistent and negligent. Her grandmother disapproved of her contact with both the father and the stepmother and felt they were the cause of the problems.

The child described herself as being on a merry-go-round. The ongoing tension and uproar made it impossible for her to feel competent or relaxed; in addition, she could not respond to any of the parental interventions, because to be dry at one house would give validity to the accusations about the other households. The parents reported that in her mother's house they could set an alarm clock to wake her in the middle of the night to go to the bathroom. In the other household, she slept in a bedroom with stepsiblings, who would wake up if the same technique were used. What was needed was common agreement that she was expected to be responsible for bladder control, with different aids as required. What was also needed was an exchange of information on her successes as she moved from one parent to the other, so that acknowledgment and encouragement would be experienced throughout her week, even though she lived in different places.

A benefit of the exchange of information is the realization of how one household's actions affect the other. Sometimes simple adjustments can avoid the buildup of frustration and misunderstanding, even in the context of ongoing disagreement.

As the preceding example suggests, a second area of concern in engaging a coparenting team is that of the role of the stepparent. Although the evolution of the stepparenting role is discussed more fully later, discomfort over a meeting that includes both former and current spouses often surfaces early—both for the participants and for the therapist. First of all, because the child's biological parents are seen as the adults primarily responsible for the child, or because the child's difficulties are seen as reactive to the parents' divorce, the therapist may schedule initial interviews with biological parents alone. This stance ignores the changes in the coparental relationship that have occurred through the divorce and remarriage. It also discounts the importance of, and the resources available from, the stepparent(s).

One frequently hears stories such as this: "They couldn't possibly meet in the same room. The last time Jim [father] and Bill [stepfather] saw each other, Bill punched Jim out." Several points need consideration before the therapist abandons his or her plans to work with a coparenting team. First, people change over time. If the therapist asks, "When did this happen?", the answer may well be "Several years ago; they haven't seen each other face to face since." Incidents such as this carry much weight. They lead to the breaking off of communication and the buildup of stereotyped views of each individual. The parents remain stuck in a stressed, unproductive stance in relation to each other. At the time of referral, a new marital relationship may have become more settled and stable. The second husband may now feel less threatened by his wife's attachment to her first husband. He may be more cognizant of her ways of being irritating, perhaps more able to see the first husband's point of view, and tired of living with the continual tension. The first husband may have let go of the marriage more fully; perhaps he is involved in a more satisfying relationship himself, and therefore is less reactive to his first wife and has different aims in relation to the children. He may no longer want to re-establish the first marriage. He may now want only to have a deeper, more influential parental role for himself, separate from the mother. The mother also may have less need to distance herself from her first husband. She may feel more confident of herself, her judgment, and her influence over the children; less reactive to him; and more settled in her second marriage. All parties concerned may be fed up with living in an embattled zone where even minor discussions between households are unproductive and undertaken at great cost to everyone.

A second consideration is that most people act with more control when they are in public and when they are with their new spouses. Interviews in the office are quite different from loaded exchanges at the door of the former marital house. Once a new pattern is experienced in the presence of the therapist, it becomes more possible outside.

Third, involved in the punching-out incident described above is a pattern of the second husband's jumping into the middle of an argument between the former spouses. He is being protective of his wife in a way that perpetuates her helplessness and that does not speak to the underlying problem. It escalates the level of the dispute. An important intervention is to move his position from that of whiteknight protector to that of stable, strong backer. He can stand behind his wife, giving her positive emotional support in the emotionally difficult situation of negotiating with her former spouse. From this position, he adds his observations about the child's behavior and messages. He can give support for the other parent's position in a way his wife can hear. If there is a concern about safety (e.g., if the former spouse is alcoholic and has been drinking when he comes to their house), the power of his presence can be felt as part of a team, rather than in a fight between two men over their woman.

Once a beginning has been made toward parents' beginning to meet together face to face, the process of the common definition of the problem continues. Many times it will be agreed that the most important contributors to the child's stress have been the difficulties on the parental level. The adults may recognize the child's reluctance to speak of one household to the other. They may see the displacement of anger from one parent to another, or to a stepparent. There may be marked difficulties at points of transition or at times when members of both households are present at the same events. The child may have verbalized his or her wish to have the adults stop fighting. They may agree that having the child carry communications places a strain on him or her. They may see the child playing off one household against the other. Even if these observations are less clear to the parents, the child may show a dramatic lifting of spirits and relaxation of tension after the meeting, or after a civilized, planning phone call between parents. This, then, becomes self-reinforcing, and parents see the possibility and the benefits of their joint enterprise.

The basic model of coparenting teamwork is useful no matter how old the child is—whether he or she is a toddler who cannot convey much information verbally, or a young adult planning a wedding and stymied by the diplomatic complexities of the ceremonies. The model can be instituted at any point in the divorce–remarriage time line, even when there have been years of stalemate and bitterness. If it is introduced early, the family organization may be in flux, with emotions running very high, and new stepparents may be easily scapegoated. Attention needs to be paid to boundaries, containment of conflict, and modeling of civilized exchange; the therapist should be cognizant of the tremendous stress such encounters create. Later on, there may be more rigid barriers built up, and the interventions may focus on loosening boundaries and increasing contact. Most generally, a meeting of the coparenting team, whether in a therapist's office or in a restaurant over coffee, has a strong impact on the reorganization of the coparenting team from a two-parent dyad to a three- or four-person unit.

The Stepparent Role

The stepfamily subsystem begins with the structure of a weak couple subsystem and a tightly bonded biological parent–child subsystem. The stepparent remains an outsider initially as the biological parent continues to carry primary responsibility for his or her children. The biological parent needs to leave space for step- relationships to develop. The stepparent and children need to figure out a way of living together that does not require loving one another, but that allows the opportunity for becoming better acquainted. It is through the process of coming to know one another that desired roles can be discovered. Mills (1984) describes a number of possible roles for a stepparent, ranging from that of "star border," with little interest in or responsibility for a child, to a role approximating that of a biological parent. He emphasizes that the full parental role is the one least likely to be appropriate or successfully accomplished. It is rarely available in the period of early remarriage, but can sometimes be established by the later stages of remarriage with younger children who have spent most of their time in the household (i.e., cells IIIB and IIIC in Table 7-1).

It is not unusual to find that men have an easier time staying within a neutral stance with their stepchildren than do women. In three nonclinic families that I interviewed in the course of an ongoing study of families in their first year of remarriage, each of the women struggled throughout the year over her roles as stepmother. Even though none of the women defined herself as a homemaker or a traditional wife, each carried a strong sense of responsibility for the "hearth-keeping" functions of the family. Their sense of self in the roles of woman, wife, and mother was strongly affected by their stepfamily experiences. For example, one woman entered her marriage expecting to be more influential and closely tied with her husband's older children than they were willing to let her be. She had to accept that "it really is becoming more our marriage, instead of our family." Another wife bent over backward in the first few months to make their household an attractive, nurturing, and exciting place for her husband's noncustodial children to be. She finally realized that the backbreaking efforts were not that significant in their decisions to spend time with them. There was no question that her efforts made a positive impact on the boys' relationship with her; however, their willingness to commit themselves to a weekend stay was determined more by their father's clear insistence that it made a difference for him and that he expected them to come. In these three families, none of the husbands expected their new wives to take over mothering functions. In other families, expectations from both husband and wife about the proper division of labor between men and women may run counter to the practical exigencies of stepfamily life. If a woman's self-esteem depends upon pleasing her husband by obtaining a strong attachment with his children and by fitting into ongoing household rules without making waves, she is placed in a highly vulnerable position.

The Preschool Child

According to the research literature, children of different ages have different responses to the inclusion of a stepparent in their family. When there is little or no contact with the noncustodial parent, preschool children can readily bond strongly to a nurturing stepparent. It is in this situation that a role approximating that of a biological parent role has the best chance of success.

For example, Ms. M's son Joshua was conceived when her relationship with his father was breaking up. Joshua has seen his father only one or two times in his 2½ years of life; he is a stranger to him. Ms. M's fiancé, David, has been a constant figure for Joshua throughout the past 2 years, caring for him as a father would. Ms. M and David are considering obtaining permission for David to adopt Joshua after the marriage takes place.

On the other hand, when both parents remain connected for preschool children, introducing stepparents in addition, the living arrangements need to be carefully constructed so that the child is not caught in a situation that overwhelms his or her ability to cope. Although there is little research that explores the impact of a variety of coparenting arrangements for very young children, it seems essential that the opportunity for primary bonding with both biological parents, and the construction of two stable home bases for the child, be supported. In these situations, one is caught between weathering what may be short-term distress, in the hope of establishing an arrangement that will have long-lasting beneficial effects, and determining what is a harmful overload for an overburdened child. Two examples illustrate this dilemma.

Tom, aged 4, lived with his mother during the week. Before school he went to a neighbor's, who took him to his preschool program. He went to a different home for the afternoon. When his mother picked him up at 5:00, he was tired and cranky. She was exhausted from her long day of teaching. Over the weekend he went to his father's, spending some of the time with the father's new wife while the father pursued his activities. When the father and stepmother went out, a different set of babysitters was involved. Tom was confused, had trouble settling into the different settings, was aggressive with other children, threw temper tantrums at home, and had difficulty concentrating. When the therapist drew the map of Tom's daily schedule, listing all the different people he had to relate to, his mother got a new perspective on Tom's difficulties. Before this she was taking his tantrums very personally, either blaming herself for being inconsistent or worrying that his angry outbursts were "just like his father." With a different perspective, she and his father began to coordinate their babysitting plans, eliminating unnecessary transitions and increasing time spent with the father and stepmother together.

In a second example, when Scott was aged 2, his parents divorced and worked out a joint custody agreement, which involved Scott's residing at each house in turn for 3 months at a time (with visitation to the other house). But when his mother remarried, she moved across the country. Thus, every 3 months Scott now has to move to an entirely new situation. He responds with tantrums, loss of toilet training, crying, and trouble going to sleep. There is not enough consistency for him to handle the switch. Also, he misses the other parent, whom he cannot see for 3 months. Thus, the kind of schedule that an older child might be able to handle is too much for his coping skills. The task of establishing an everyday routine to the alternating schedule is too much for his understanding of time and ability to tolerate absence from a loving parent. The new caretaking arrangements have too many novel elements and are not assimilable.

When a remarriage occurs during the preschool years, it is likely that the child has had to make a series of living changes in rapid succession. If the child is in the typical situation of primary custody with one parent, the bonding with the noncustodial parent is at high risk. Many parents of preschoolers feel that it is a time when coordination between households needs to be high in order to establish continuity of everyday routines. In addition, the length of any separation from either parent needs to be relatively brief. These needs for the child may compete with the parents' needs to minimize contact and to differentiate their households. Because the caretaking demands of small children are immediate, new stepparents inevitably are drawn into primary care. This makes establishment of cross-household information exchange even more imperative if a child's needs are to be recognized.

In sum, the early years for the preschool child may initially be unsettling and confusing; the possibility that the child's basic needs may be neglected exists. The preschool child needs primary contact with both parents, but also can accept caretaking from a new stepparent.

The Middle-Years Child

Once children reach school age, they have an increased cognitive understanding of relationships and schedules, and an increased ability to accommodate to household differences with minimal developmental disruption. There are numerous opportunities for a child's parents to play out coparental cooperation publicly at school events in a way that supports the child, but that does not entail undue sacrifice on the part of the adults. Middle-years children remain home-based enough that there is a range of neutral, interesting activities through which stepparenting ties can be built.

On the other hand, the feelings of loyalty for one or the other parent can be most acute (Wallerstein & Kelly, 1980). Several authors suggest that if a close tie has developed between the child and his or her custodial parent during the single-parent period, the child experiences both a competitive loss and the loss of time and attention when the parent remarries. This seems to be particularly true for girls. Boys, on the other hand, although showing an upsurge of difficulties at the time of remarriage (Hetherington et al., 1985), tend to flourish when a stepfather joins a mother-custody household (Wallerstein & Kelly, 1980). Santrock, Warshak, Lindbergh, and Meadows (1982) found that boys in stepfather families scored better on both cognitive and psychological measures than boys in mother-only families. Clingempeel, Brand, and Ievoli (1984) found lower scores on love and higher scores on detachment for latency-age stepdaughters than for stepsons observed with stepparents of either sex.

Wallerstein (1984) notes in her follow-up interviews with school-age children (who were preschoolers at the time of divorce) that relationships with fathers and stepfathers were clearly distinguishable and held separate from each other: "The entire patterning[s] of attitudes and feelings, of real and fantasy expectations within each of these relationships, were often sharply different" (p. 57). It is likely that these research results reflect the outcome of a common, complex combination of interpersonal reactions. In relation to the developmental chart, there are differences in experience for children categorized in cells IB and IIB of Table 7-1. The children who experience the introduction of a stepparent in their middle years (cell IB) may experience a strong loyalty struggle. Those in cell IIB, although the same age, may accept a stepparent more as a matter of course. Their relationship includes early caretaking experiences with bonding implications for both adult and child.

Also, it is important to note that the children in the studies of Wallerstein and Kelly (1980), Hetherington et al. (1985), and Santrock et al. (1982) resided primarily in mother-custody homes and had infrequent contact with noncustodial fathers. The focus of the research highlighted difficulties in adjustment, rather than adaptive patterns of coping.

In my own clinical experience, latency-age children respond particularly well to interventions of implementing coparenting teamwork. However, if they come in with a well-established negative relationship with a stepparent, they may be particularly stubborn about publicly admitting a change in feeling after the stepparent has changed.

Heidi, aged 9, was referred because of temper tantrums and fights with her younger brother in her father's newly remarried household, as well as rude and resistant behavior to her teachers in school. Her stepmother had assumed responsibility for "teaching [her husband's] children some respect," and also was very concerned about Heidi's low self-esteem. Heidi's father felt very guilty whenever he found himself angry at Heidi and was reluctant to discipline her. He also felt that his wife overreacted to the children's boisterousness and fights; he felt that they needed to be listened to sympathetically. Both children lived in a joint custody arrangement, spending 1 week with their mother and 1 week with their father. Their mother had to work long hours at a low-paying job, and was also trying to finish a college degree. She identified with Heidi, thought of her as an especially talented girl, and gave her a great deal of independent responsibility. The father and stepmother felt that she did not spend enough time with the children. She had very different standards for strictness and protection. Tension and conflict centered on the children had accelerated dramatically when the father had remarried. The mother felt threatened by the children's positive feelings about their new stepmother, and became very critical of her to the children. In addition, she worried about the impact on the children of what she saw as inappropriately rigid rules at the other household, the anger they received from their stepmother, and the difference in treatment between them and their stepsiblings.

Early therapeutic interventions included parental meetings in which the stepmother was coached to support her husband, but to refrain from making inflammatory comments to his former wife. Both parents were coached to honor household boundaries and to attempt to exchange only information abut the children. Individual sessions were held for each household. With the therapist supporting the difficulty of her situation without passing judgment on her mothering, the mother was able to hear the children say how much they missed her when she was gone. She eventually was able to rearrange her schedule. The father and stepmother agreed to experiment with a system in which each was responsible for the discipline of his or her own children, and free to plan brief positive activities individually with the other's children. Once they felt comfortable arguing out their disciplinary differences, they were also able to institute family meetings, with some success.

The result of these interventions was a gradual settling down in each household, improved clear boundaries between households, and improved information exchange across households and with the school. Heidi was less tense and did better in school, but remained resentful at the changes in her life. Her stepmother implemented the therapist's suggestions by taking Heidi to buy a nice jacket and by working with her to crochet a pillow for her room. Heidi expressed her pleasure in private to her father. To her stepmother, she was unresponsive; thanks, if expressed, were monosyllabic. Even though her father reported the hidden pleasure, the stepmother was angry that Heidi was willing to talk to him and not to her. What eventually made a difference was her husband's appreciation of her efforts. She was willing to continue the experiment for him, although she was tempted to give up on Heidi. The limiting factors for this family seemed to be both the strongly held loyalty Heidi carried for her mother, which at her age felt incompatible with affection for a very different stepmother, and the continuing feelings of antagonism between the mother and stepmother. Each tried hard to give Heidi space for her relationships, but felt at heart that contact with the other woman was destructive. Heidi as yet was unable to gain enough outside perspective to detach herself from the father–mother–stepmother triangle.

Girls in families where there is mutual respect across households are freer to be open to a range of characteristics and to profit from affection received from a number of different sources.

The Adolescent

Adolescents have an increased understanding of their parents' human differences and a more sophisticated concept of the intricacies of human relationships. Therefore, they are more able to comprehend the idea of an inclusive family organization, and can in fact become active participants in its creation. Adolescents make a conscious choice about their commitment to the stepfamily and can be quite clear about desires to remain outsiders. They need the space to voice their concerns and opinions, the disciplinary firmness to be safely negative, and clear boundaries around sexual issues.

With some care, the binuclear family system can weave a firm, supportive umbrella for an adolescent, with continuity of expectations as well as islands of retreat. Experiences in both households can be helpful in the recognition of growing differences and competencies. One household can become a safety valve when complexity and stimulation from the other become too much. The remarriage of a noncustodial parent not infrequently becomes a time of change in custody and primary residence for an adolescent. Furstenberg and Spanier (1984) found that one-fifth of their sample reported custody changes at age 12, usually at the point of remarriage. Crosbie-Burnett and Ahrons (1985) report a similar finding. These moves can represent the recognition of the child's needs for more contact with a parent who at this point may be more settled and available. Alternatively, these moves can be precipitous, as a solution to problems in one household. Sager *et al.* (1983) describe severely dysfunctional forms of extrusion as a system problem, reflecting difficulties in integration of the remarried family.

A difficulty of conflicting developmental needs appears when the adolescent's need to become increasingly involved in the community of peers and adults outside the family competes with the stepfamily's need to build a cohesive household base. Parents become caught in the delicate balance of figuring when to insist on participation in a household event, when to insist on weekend visitation, and when to support healthy involvement outside the family. Teenagers with strong positive involvement in two households, as well as full academic and social lives, are very busy indeed. They complain about being pulled in too many directions and needing time to retreat and relax.

Findings from research on stepparent–adolescent relationships reports this combination as a particularly stressful time. Lutz (1983) found that the major issues reported in her study were those of divided loyalty (e.g., experiencing one parent's talking negatively about the other, feeling caught in the middle, and liking a stepparent more than a natural parent of the same sex) and of discipline from the stepparent. Again, gender differences were found to be important. Lutz (1983) found higher stress reported by girls in her sample and higher stress in stepfather–stepdaughter combinations.

In this combination of age and family stage, there should be no expectation that the stepparent will be able to assume an effective authoritative position directly in relation to the child. However, the added stability and love, as well as support given by the stepparent to the biological parent, can be invaluable. The parenting model that may be most effective is one in which the rules of the household are made explicit in a household family meeting. The stepparent can effectively support the adolescent by insisting that some of the child's points are valid and need to be attended to. Enforcement of rules comes from the biological parent, who is supported in his or her efforts by the stepparent. This support must be given directly to the parent, and not by taking over the enforcement with the adolescent. This is the difference between saying to the adolescent, "Do what your mother says," and saying to the biological parent, "I agree with your expectation that he come in on time. Keep at it." One woman described the process in these words: "He facilitates. He is an objective partner who can give me sound advice, but when there is a difference, he gives in.'' Similarly, in most cases, the decision making across households can remain in place as established in the double-single-parent phase. The stepparent can provide clarification, prodding, and/or reflection to the spouse as he or she negotiates with the former spouse. The interaction may go more or less effectively, but the structure may not effectively change.

The Middle Stages

If the tasks of the first 2–3 years have been attended to, the shape of the remarried family will have begun to change. One may see exchanges about the children going between mother and stepmother or father and stepfather on a normalized basis. The stepparent may have been able to achieve a special position, in which he or she has an intimate view of the child's adaptation as well as of the biological parents' exchanges, without being encumbered by their family history. A shared history has begun to be accumulated. Experiments in handling a variety of family events have been carried out.

A study by Anderson and White (1986) of functional and dysfunctional nuclear and stepfamilies (stepfather–mother–adolescent triads in remarried families for at least 2 years) found that functional stepfamily triads in the middle stages had achieved mutually positive stepfather-child relationships that were less intense than the biological father–child pairs in functional nuclear families. The dysfunctional stepfamily triads showed the marital subsystem existing separately from the rest of the family, with the stepfather excluded from a strong mother–child dyad. Both stepfather and child expressed a strong desire to exclude each other entirely from the family. They also found that functional stepfamilies were not different from functional nuclear families in their ability to make decisions that satisfied the individual needs of their members.

Papernow (1984) observes that it is in the middle stages that differences have been clarified and negotiation toward integration is carried out in earnest. There is tension among the former status quo, the expectations of society, and the necessity of dealing with the reality of family members who all want to be involved in an influential way. This entails change that goes farther than the accommodations of one person to the ongoing structure. It is more profound than resolving the loss of one person, but moving another into the same place. It is change in organization that affects all the members of the family.

It is during this phase that the stepparent tries most actively to change his or her outsider role and to implement some of his or her ideas for family patterns. The therapeutic interventions for families in the middle stages, thus are somewhat different than for families in the early stages of remarriage. The stepfamily household is somewhat more settled. When family members come for an interview, they act as if they belong together, in contrast with the confusing, more splintered feel of early-stage groupings. On the other hand, the patterns that are not working are more clearly evident, with a high buildup of frustration and resentment. Whereas in the early stages the continuation of the strength of the biological parent–child unit has been acknowledged and protected, in the middle stages, if the stepparent and child have begun to construct a positive relationship, the biological parent needs to be encouraged to stand back more and to allow more direct confrontations. In addition, the importance of the stepparent's observations needs to be supported, and the spouses need to be encouraged to struggle with their differences, altering each other's parenting styles.

On the other hand, the limitations of the parenting power of the stepparent must remain in view. The most difficult combinations of child stage and family stage are those represented in Table 7-1 by cells IB and IC moving to IIC—that is, the late latency-age child moving into early adolescence as the family moves into the unsettled middle phase, and the early adolescent moving into high school. These combinations are also the most likely to occur. It is not clear what happens to the flourishing middle-years child described above when he or she moves into adolescence. The research studies have been primarily cross-sectional, suggesting that there is more difficulty in adolescence, even when there has been a calm latency (see Dornbusch et al., 1985; Pink & Wampler, 1985). As described by Sager et al. (1983), entry into adolescence provides the family with a "second chance." Issues of identity, confidence, anxiety and depression about the divorce, anger, and guilt come back to the surface and provide another opportunity for mastery. this, of course, occurs in the midst of the emotion-filled negotiations between spouses about personal and family identity.

The satisfactions of negotiating these complicated interpersonal networks and the creative, healing outcomes are hinted at in some of the research findings. Crosbie-Burnett (1984) found that the establishment of "mutually suitable" relationships between stepfather and adolescent had a greater effect on family happiness than did the quality of the marital relationship. Anderson and White's (1986) findings point in the same direction, in that dysfunctional stepfamilies in their sample showed a relatively high level of marital satisfaction at the same time as a distant, hostile, excluding stepfather–child relationship. These findings speak both to the value of step- relationships that differ in form from parental ones and to the importance for all family members of attending realistically to the child's and stepparent's positions. Hetherington et al. (1985) found decreased problem behavior for 10-year-old boys at this stage of remarriage. Santrock et al. (1982) found that boys from families in which mother and stepfather had been married at least 18 months showed more competent social behavior than did boys in nuclear families. This corresponded with more competent parenting in these families. The role of a stepparent is not an easy one; the attention paid to the job in these families had important benefits for the boys. Again, the results were less encouraging for the girls. Their problem behavior increased in Hetherington et al.'s study. In Santrock et al.'s sample, they showed more anxiety and more anger toward their mothers. Clingempeel, Ievoli, and Brand (1984) found similar results, and added the distressing note that girls were visited less often by nonresidential parents than boys, whether the nonresidential parent was the mother or the father.

The Mutual Child

To complicate the picture further, children in the family who were very young at the time of remarriage, or who are children of this marriage (cells IIA, IIB, IIIA, and IIIB in Table 7-1), will most likely have relationships with the (step)parent that are very different from those of their siblings. These differences can be very confusing and difficult for both the parents and the older siblings. On the other hand, as described by Baker (1986), if a mutual child is the first biological child of a stepparent, he or she makes the stepparent feel more like a legitimate member of the family group. The mutual child may have the position of being responsible for peace and harmony in the remarried system, particularly since the birth symbolizes the love and commitment of this marriage. Baker (1986) suggests that this position may make the developmental tasks of separation more difficult.

Bernstein (1986) describes the cognitive developmental lens through which the mutual child tries to make sense of the remarried family. In interviews with mutual children, she found that definitions of family were based on residence and caring by preschool-age children, were explained in terms of history by school-age children, and were seen as reciprocal and contingent on other relationships by teenagers. She found that explanations of kinship were colored by their emotional loading and family structure. Children with both step- and half-siblings made more relationship distinctions. Those whose stepsiblings did not see their noncustodial parents made fewer distinctions than those who had to sort out more complex networks. Positive relationship tended to be interpreted as closer kin (e.g., "my brother" as opposed to "my stepbrother").

The School-Age Child

Children who are in early elementary school at this point will have been with the stepfamily nearly half their lives and will see all the adults as permanent and important members of their family, unlike their older siblings, who may have had to choose up sides with undying loyalty. For some school-age children, this is a time when they flourish. These are the children whose parents have from the start acknowledged competent parenting in both households. They have been allowed the gradual development of a relationship with a stepparent, which now has a solid history. The adults have achieved a workable equilibrium of coparenting styles, with some stability of expectations and routines. They have acknowledged from the start the pain and upset of divorce and the reality of the changed family structure, and have worked out some of the original differences. These children sometimes show levels of maturity, confidence, and ability to utilize varied resources beyond those of their peers who have not been forced to cope with similar challenges (J. Kleinman, personal communication, 1986). They are the children who have confronted very difficult living situations and coped successfully with them. Their parents describe them as adaptable and resilient; their stepparents describe their times together with pleasure; they are good friends with their stepsiblings. Rather than being caught in the descending spiral seen with children caught in chronic disputes, these children are in the midst of a reinforcing spiral of a network of positive relationships.

Sometimes at this stage a child will be functioning well within the stepfamily structure, but may carry over reactions to changes in the other household.

For example, a 10-year-old boy began to be forgetful and careless about his personal belongings, arguing with his father and stepmother when they asked him to do anything. His teacher reported that he was irritable and depressed at school. His stepmother expressed concern about what she saw as a deteriorating relationship with him, just when they had begun to be close. As the picture was enlarged, it was discovered that his reaction had begun at the point at which his mother was becoming deeply involved in a new relationship and was considering marriage. Absorbed in her own intense feelings, she had been less attentive to her son, and was unaware of the impact of her household changes on him. With the situation clarified, his mother could use the information from the other household in her conversations with her son, and the father and stepmother could remain supportive without taking the upset so personally.

The Later Stages of Remarriage

When a family has reached the point at which the remarriage is firmly established, they have worked out and accepted their model of a family that is different from a nuclear family. All members are included in relationships of greater or lesser distance, depending upon subsystem membership and developmental need. The family organization is integrated. Negotiations about relationship shape are no longer explicit; they have faded into the background of normality and everyday existence. There is intimacy in the step-relationships and strength in the marriage.

Types of Issues

When a family comes to therapy 6 or more years after a remarriage, the issues will be of two types. One is the distress within a family that, although established in terms of years, has not been able to deal with necessary structural reorganization. There may be chronic battles and crises from a never-resolved divorce. There may be rigid stalemates within the stepfamily along biological lines; a noncustodial parent may suffer from being cut off from biological children; or the stepfamily may be isolated within the families of origin. For these families, the therapist needs to explore early developmental issues, being mindful of the strength of the dysfunctional history.

The second type of distress is a crisis experienced within a family that has accomplished the tasks necessary for the established remarriage structure. As in nuclear families, life transitions or unexpected external traumas can strain a family's resources and lead to the appearance of symptoms. It should be noted, however, that the special issues of the remarriage structure and the demands for co-parenting contact continue to color the strains felt for life transitions involving children. When children begin to make college plans, there may be an upsurge of tension as negotiations about finances are made. Bar or bas mitzvahs, graduations, weddings, and funerals all pose complicated diplomatic challenges. The traditional rituals of formal ceremonies do not accommodate the needs of the remarried kinship network, and new ones must be devised.

Adult Children

The developmental issues for adult children of remarriage are seldom discussed either in the research or in the clinical literature. Clinical work with college students finds that they are certainly reactive to parental divorces and remarriages. Ahrons (1986) carried out an interview study with college students whose parents had divorced within the past 1–3 years. Among the issues mentioned were the students' feeling that they no longer had a home, that they had been abandoned by their parents, and that they had "lost a family." As parents gave up their responsibility for making decisions for the students, the students felt caught in the middle of loyalty conflicts. Supporting a theme found throughout the developmental time line, Ahrons found that women expressed more upset initially than men.

When parents remarry after a child has left the home, there is the task of establishing a mode of family connection, but without the advantage of time spent in close proximity. In my own research interviews, remarriages were observed on two generational levels: the parental generation and the grandparental generation. Efforts at building relationship came both from the remarried couple's reaching out to their children and from the children's actively making visits on their own schedule. The parents were informative about their plans, visited their children who lived farther away, and welcomed visits in their own home. At the same time, the establishment of a feeling of integrated family is expected to take at least as long at this age as at any other. One woman commented after 5 years of annual Christmas visits to her father and his wife, "This is the first year my sisters and brothers and her children feel like a group together."

Many adults do not acknowledge their relationship to a stepparent. They have little opportunity to establish a meaningful relationship with either the new stepparent or stepsiblings. Without active inclusion, there is a feeling that the biological parent has moved away and is preoccupied with other concerns.

As with all the earlier challenges, an emphasis on creative forms of family structure, an exchange of information with relevant family members, careful consideration of each individual's needs, and a great deal of sensitive support are necessary. It is important that remarried family members have opportunities to view themselves as adventurers in the territory of uncharted relationships, rather than as misfits in a second-rate, not-quite-normal, "not-quite-family" household.

REFERENCES

Anderson, J. Z., & White, G. D. (1986). An empirical investigation of interaction and relationship patterns in functional and dysfunctional nuclear families and stepfamilies. *Family Process, 25,* 407–422.

Ahrons, C. R. (1986). *Divorce when the children are older.* Paper presented at the meeting of the American Family Therapy Association, Washington, DC.

Ahrons, C. R., and & Perlmutter, M. S. (1982). The relationship between former spouses: A fundamental subsystem in the remarriage family. In L. Messinger (Ed.), *Therapy with remarriage families* (pp. 31–46). Rockville, MD: Aspen.

Baker, K. G. (1986, Winter). Issues for the mutual child leaving home. *Stepfamily Bulletin,* pp. 9–10.

Bernstein, A. C. (1986). *Stepfamilies with a mutual child.* Paper presented at the meeting of the American Family Therapy Association, Washington, DC.

Clingempeel, W. G., & Brand, E. (1985). Quasi-kin relationships, structural complexity, and marital quality in stepfamilies: A replication, extension, and clinical implications. *Family Relations, 34,* 401–409.

Climgempeel, W. G., Brand, E., & Ievoli, R. (1984). Stepparent–stepchild relationships in stepmother and stepfather families: A multimethod study. *Family Relations, 33,* 465–473.

Clingempeel, W. G., Ievoli, R., & Brand, R. (1984). Structural complexity and the quality of stepfather–stepchild relationships. *Family Process, 23,* 547–560.

Crosbie-Burnett, M. (1984). The centrality of the step relationship: A challenge to family theory and practice. *Family Relations, 33,* 459–463.

Crosbie-Burnett, M., & Ahrons, C. R. (1985). From divorce to remarriage: Implications for therapy with families in transition. *Journal of Psychotherapy and the Family, 1,* 121–137.

Dornbusch, S. M., Carlsmith, J. M., Bushwall, S. J., Ritter, P. L. Leiderman, H., Hastorf, A. H., & Gross, R. T. (1985). Single parents extended households, and the control of adolescents. *Child Development, 56,* 326–341.

Furstenberg, F. F., Jr., & Spanier, G. B. (1984). *Recycling the family.* Beverly Hills, CA: Sage.

Hetherington, E. M., Cox, M., & Cox, R. (1985). Long-term effects of divorce and remarriage on the adjustment of children. *Journal of the American Academy of Child Psychiatry, 24,* 518–530.

Lutz, P. (1983). The stepfamily: An adolescent perspective. *Family Relations, 32,* 367–375.

McGoldrick, M., & Carter, E. A. (1980). Forming a remarried family. In E. A. Carter & M. McGoldrick (Eds.) *The family life cycle: A framework for family therapy* (pp. 265–294). New York: Gardner Press.

Mills, D. M. (1984). A model for stepfamily development. *Family Relations, 33,* 385–372.

Papernow, P. L. (1984). The stepfamily cycle: An experiential model of stepfamily development. *Family Relations, 33,* 355–363.

Pink, J. E. T., & Wampler, K. S. (1985). Problem areas in stepfamilies: Cohesion, adaptability, and the step-father–adolescent relationship. *Family Relations, 34,* 327–335.

Ransom, J. W., Schlesinger, S., & Derdeyn, A. P. (1979). A stepfamily in formation. *American Journal of Orthopsychiatry, 49,* 36–43.

Sager, C., Brown, H. S., Crohn, H., Engel, T., Rodstein, E., & Walker, L. (1983). *Treating the remarried family.* New York: Brunner/Mazel.

Santrock, J. W., Warshak, R., Linbergh, C., & Meadows, L. (1982). Children's and parent's observed social behavior in stepfather families. *Child Development, 53,* 472–480.

Stern, P. N. (1978). Stepfather families: Integration around child discipline. *Issues in Mental Health Nursing, 1,* 50–56.

Visher, E. B., & Visher, J. S. (1979). *Stepfamilies: A guide to working with stepparents and stepchildren.* New York: Brunner/Mazel.

Wald, E. (1981). *The remarried family: Challenge and promise.* New York: Family Service Association of America.

Wallerstein, J. S. (1983). Children of divorce: The psychological tasks of the child. *American Journal of Orthopsychiatry, 53,* 230–243.

Wallerstein, J. S. (1984). Children of divorce: Preliminary report of a ten-year follow-up of young children. *American Journal of Orthopsychiatry, 54,* 54–

Wallerstein, J. S., & Kelly, J. B. (1980). *Surviving the breakup: How children and parents cope with divorce.* New York: Basic Books.

Whiteside, M. F. (1982). Remarriage: A family developmental process. *Journal of Marital and Family Therapy, 8,* 59–68.

Whiteside, M. F. (1983). Families of remarriage: The weaving of many life cycle threads. In H. A. Liddle (Ed.), *Clinical implications of the family life cycle* (pp. 100–119). Rockville, MD: Aspen.

8

Adopted Children, Adoptive Families:
Recognizing Differences

IRIS C. BUTLER, PhD

Death, illness, war, poverty, abuse, neglect, teenage pregnancy, unwanted pregnancy—each can compel biological parents to give up their children. Taken in by relatives or by strangers, these children may be told of their biological connections, or may be raised in ignorance of them. In some adoptions, little is known about the child's background, such as when the child comes from another country or is a foundling living at an orphanage. Often family secrets are scrupulously kept when a family member has a child, and shame surrounds the conception and birth.

Mrs. Harris spoke with much compassion about her mother, Mrs. Spaak, who had learned just months before the death of her "mother" that she had been adopted. In truth, the woman Mrs. Spaak knew as her mother was her grandmother, and her favorite aunt was her biological mother. Mrs. Spaak had been so stunned by this 67-year-old family secret that she never was able to get over it. She died within a year of receiving this news. Mrs. Harris was now trying to comprehend a part of her family history previously unknown, but the shadow had raised nagging questions.

Adoption is a story told and retold throughout human history. In clinical practice, I have seen many adoptive families with young children. Work with these families has raised many questions, among them the following: How does adop-

Iris C. Butler. Minneapolis Psychiatric Institute, Minneapolis, MN; Abbott Northwestern Hospital, Minneapolis, MN; University of Minnesota Medical School, Minneapolis, MN.

tion stress a family? How does it strengthen a family? How do adoptive families in treatment handle their children's ambiguous biological roots? How does an adopted child come to know acceptance? How do the child's adoptive parents come to know acceptance? What special rituals, if any, are used to mark the original loss and the coming of a new member into the family? How are the stresses of adoption increased when an adopted child is of another race or culture? This chapter explores how adoptive families have answered these questions. Lessons from the successes of adoptive families in and out of therapy are invaluable to the therapist who will work with these families.

Information about Adoption

Before the family therapist goes in and sits with adoptive families who have sought clinical help, there is some information with which he or she should be familiar.

General Statistics

About 4% of women in the United States adopt children; about 2% of these women eventually bear a child. The average age of an adoptive mother is 30; that of an adoptive father is 35. Adoptive parents are parents by choice, since it takes a great deal of effort and persistence, and sometimes considerable financial resources, to get a child. Each year an estimated 5000 babies are sold into adoptive homes for up to $25,000 each.

In 1984 there were 3,669,000 lie births in the United States, of which 1,790,000 were female, 2,924,000 were white, 583,000 were black, 42,000 were Native American, 347,000 were Hispanic, and 109,000 were Asian or Pacific Islanders. Within these varied groups, the U.S. Bureau of the Census (1986) reports the percentages of teen and unmarried mothers for 1984 as follows: among whites, 11% were teens and 13.4% unmarried; among blacks, 23.7% were teens and 59.2% unmarried; among Native Americans, 20.1% were teens and 39.8% unmarried; among Hispanics, 17% were teens and 28.3% unmarried; and among Asian and Pacific Islanders, 5.6% were teens and 9.6% unmarried. According to the U.S. Bureau of the Census (1988), since 1975 the number of petitioners related to adoptees has nearly doubled.

Most children adopted in this country are born here, but a growing number of adoptees come from overseas. In 1984, 8327 foreign-born children were adopted, and 62% of these were 1 year old or younger (U.S. Bureau of the Census, 1986). These adoptions are most often transracial; most commonly, a white family adopts a child of another ethnic background. At first, international adoptions were same-race adoptions (e.g., a white family would take in a white child from war-ravaged Europe). But due to war relief efforts, these adoptions have virtually ended. More recently, the majority of international adoptions have been Asian and South and

Central American, as reflected in the following statistics from 1984: 61.9% of these children were born in Korea, 7.1% in Columbia, 5.6% in India, 4.9% in the Philippines, and 4.4% in El Salvador (U.S. Bureau of the Census, 1986).

Public versus Private Adoptions

About 65% of the 141,861 reported children who are adopted in the United States are relatives of the families who have petitioned for the adoption. The remaining 35% are placed in nearly equal proportions through public agencies, private agencies, and independent sources. Since 1960, the percentage of unrelated children placed through independent sources has been decreased by half, from 22% to 11%, and those placed through private agencies has also decreased by slightly less than half, from 19.4% to 10.3%. The percentage placed by public agencies has increased by 1.3%. The major increase in adoptions has come from those families related to the adoptees (National Committee for Adoption, 1985). This increase has been 18.2% since 1960 and may be a reflection of the significant rise in teen pregnancy in our country since 1960; the decrease in the stigma attached to bearing and keeping a child born outside of parental marriage; and the difficulty that very young, single women have in raising a child with limited financial and educational resources. The increase in foreign adoptions coincides with the effects of war and ensuing cultural disruption, as well as of out-of-wedlock and interracial pregnancies.

Black Adoptions

The trend toward black adoptions had a modest expansion through 1977. Nonrelative adoptions did not increase for blacks between 1957 and 1974, despite the increased expression of need for black children. Feigelman and Silverman (1983) found that Afro-American children constituted 8% of the children adopted in their sample of adopting parents. Transracial adoptions, particularly those involving white families and black children, have been the target of much criticism since 1972, when the National Association of Black Social Workers took a public stand against such placements. Their position was that being placed with a family of different race robs black children of their racial identity and prevents them from learning adequate coping skills to deal with the realities of a racist society. The result, they postulated, is a person who experiences "serious psychological problems during adolescence and adulthood" (Leavy, 1987). In spite of this criticism, white families continue to adopt black children, and so the data that supports the positive effects of transracial adoptions continue to accumulate. The numbers of black families available to adopt black children is increasing, but there are still 140,000 black children waiting for placement in permanent homes (Leavy, 1987).

Disenabled Parents

When parents are physically or emotionally unable to take care of their child, the choice to give up the child for adoption may be the best option, albeit a painful one. This separation of parent from child is a wrenching experience for both. To get beyond the anger and hurt is a challenge to biological parents, adoptive parents, and adopted children, and family therapy may be extremely useful in assisting with this process.

Several studies, however, support the satisfactory development of children who are adopted after age 5. Older theories of child rearing emphasized that the first 5 years of life are crucial to adequate development of the child. The commonly held belief was that poorer outcomes of adoption are to be expected when a child is adopted later in life, and when the earlier experiences have been traumatic. For some children, however, removal from a neglectful or abusive home with the opportunity for adoption in a psychologically supportive and attentive environment can indeed lead to a more positive outcome, regardless of the age of adoption (Kadushin, 1967).

Adoption and Divorce

The rising divorce rate has had a decisive effect on adoption. Most immediately, it has resulted in an increase in single-parent families. It is estimated that 4 of 10 children born in 1970 will spend some part of their childhood in a single-parent-headed home (Feigelman & Silverman, 1983). Increasing social acceptance of divorce and of single-parent families have encouraged white unwed mothers to keep custody of their children, and child welfare agencies are willing to consider single adults as adoptive parents (Feigelman & Silverman, 1983). Until the 1950s adoption agencies focused on the needs of adoptive parents, seeking to match parent and child in ethnic, religious background, coloring, and temperament. They sought as close a match as possible between the adoptive parent and the adopted child. The effort was to minimize differences, "as if" the child were born of the adoptive parents. As the number of healthy white infants has decreased, there has been a surfeit of adoptive parents, such as single adults, infertile couples, and older couples.

Adoption agencies have re-evaluated their policies. Since the early 1960s, due in part to the rise of the civil rights movement, and more recently to that of the child rights movement, the focus is on serving the children needing placement. This has increased the numbers of special-needs placements, such as older, minority, and handicapped children who were previously considered unadoptable (Goldstein, Freud, & Solnit, 1973). Research data (Feigelman & Silverman, 1983) have emphasized the need and right of permanency in children's lives and the deleterious effects of the continuous changes that foster care often involves.

Family form, race, ethnicity, handicaps, and parental age are all factors that contribute to the responsibilities of the family therapist working with the adopting parents and their adopted children.

The Literature and Theories about Adoption

Adopted Children in Clinical Settings

There are factors involved in adoption that increase the vulnerability of the individual child to stress. The literature on adoption reports an overrepresentation of adopted children in clinical settings. In response to this observation, efforts have been made to characterize the psychological problems of adopted children. Some adoptees exhibit personality disorders with characteristic symptom patterns. These patterns include poor impulse control, sexual acting out, elopement, and conflict with authority (Schecter, 1960). A sizable number of adopted children are born prematurely and/or without adequate prenatal care. Problems in the neonatal period and subsequent disabilities, such as attention deficit disorders and antisocial disorders, are more likely in this population (Gossett, Lewis, & Bernhart, 1983; Schecter, 1960). In addition, adopted children may be preoccupied with concerns about abandonment—concerns to which are attributed the depressive affect and fragile self-esteem often observed when these children come into therapy (Brinich, 1980; Schecter, 1960). Although the classical literature on adoption has examined the individual responses of the children, as well as relevant issues for parents giving their children up for adoption and parents receiving children in adoption, descriptions of the types of family interaction in which these issues are played out, considered, resolved, or respected and fostered are not readily found in the literature.

Even though adopted children are overrepresented in clinics, more than 77% of adoptions are successful (Kim, 1985). Taking a child from one environment and one set of relationships to another is obviously stressful for both the child and the two sets of families involved; it is much like taking a cutting from a plant and trying to reroot it in another soil. Once transplanted, the cutting requires special tending if it is to adapt to its new environment. Successful adoptions appear to be those in which the adoptive parents and the adopted child learn to recognize, accept, and embrace their differences. Their ability to withstand the turmoil of the bonds between them gives rise to a renewed strength and recommitment.

The adoptive family needs to be secure. It must be able to deal with feelings about the adoptive parents' inability to produce their own children if this is the case, or with implicit slights to the adoptive child when a biological child is born, such as ''At least you have one of your own.'' The adoptive family functions best when relationships are patterned on a nurturing tie rather than on biological ties (Andrews, 1978). A sense of identity does develop within the adoptive family that is based on the child's importance to the family, even though the genetic roots are different.

Divided Loyalties

What aspects of adoption pull at the biocultural organization called "family"? The absence of biological ties compounds the complexity and developmental burden of the adoptive parent–child relationship (Boszormenyi-Nagy & Krasner, 1986).

Adults who adopt make the commitment to take a child who has been born to other parents and to raise this child to the best of their abilities, including consideration for the child's self-interest, as well as their own. Boszormenyi-Nagy and Krasner (1986) propose that the adoptive parents expect a return on their investment in this child, whether this is directly acknowledged or not. Adoptive parents expect the adopted child to offer them allegiance and loyalty similar to what a natural child might owe them. This expectation might be easily met if the child were not bound to both the biological and adoptive parents. The loyalty dilemma of adoptive children can fester and deepen in direct proportion to the split they sense between the biological and the adoptive families. The greater the barrier of contempt between them, the more exposed a child becomes to the dilemma of split loyalties.

There is growing discussion among child welfare groups and agitation among adoptee rights groups, fueled by increasing interest in genealogical information, on the question of opening previously sealed adoption records. From the 1930s until recent times, most children, when adopted, were "reborn" into their adoptive families; they were given new identities and new birth certificates. The old birth certificates with information about the biological parents, thought to be damaging information, were sealed. This practice was seen as protective for all members of the adoptive triangle; it guaranteed secrecy and anonymity. It also reinforced the idea of the adoptive parents as the only parents and facilitated the stories of the "chosen child." It is now being recognized that, although this practice may have served the needs of the adoptive and birth parents, it does not necessarily serve the needs of the adoptee (Feigelman & Silverman, 1983). Accessibility to both sets of parents would clearly help to diminish the destructive aspects of an adopted child's split loyalties.

Boszormenyi-Nagy and Krasner's (1986) concept of "loyalty" describes a person's dynamically obligated concern for family members. This concern or investment can be a response to early care, a return for benefits received. Contextual family theory addresses how loyalties can be denied, ignored, misused, and manipulated, leading to the need for a thorough assessment of family relationships to detect the operations of invisible loyalties, destructive loyalty conflicts, and split loyalties. What is at stake is an individual's capacity to form, develop, and maintain trustworthy relationships in the face of a third person's relational claims, rights, and needs. Loyalty implies that a person has a choice between two alternatives. The contextual premise is that eventually a person's loyalty has to extend to people who have made significant investments in his or her existence. In the situation of adoption, an adopted child is bound to be loyal to the biological mother, who went through the costs of the unwanted pregnancy and the risks of childbirth and who gave the child life. The biological father, by contrast, may or may not know of his child's existence, and so may elicit less loyalty. (This is Boszormenyi-Nagy's theory, but may or may not be how it is reflected in the mind of the child.) The fact of adoption places the child in an implicit split-loyalty configuration between the biological parents and the adoptive parents. How the issue is faced is critical in the family, and also in the family therapy process.

The increasing instances in which adoptive parents turn to disadoption when the going within the family gets rough, especially during a child's adolescence, can also be understood in these terms. For it is at this time that the child's awareness of split loyalties is greatest, while the adoptive parents' commitment to the child may be most tested (Boszormenyi-Nagy & Krasner, 1986).

Family Myths

Byng-Hall (1973) discusses the role of family myths, which are produced to rationalize hidden pathology and which originate in unresolved crises, such as failed mourning or desertion. These myths may be resurrected in a remaining family member and serve to increase the dysfunction of the family. Paul (1967) states that bringing to life the "ghosts of the past" is an essential element in family therapy. When they are not adequately mourned, given up, or truly internalized, these ghosts, which are the lost attachment figures, bind family members in a regressive way that prevents growth and renewal of life.

The relevance of these concepts of loyalty, family myths, and ghosts of the past to the issues of adoption lies in the links that such situations reveal about the family functioning and provide useful frameworks for assessment and family therapy. When the disturbing skeletons from unacknowledged losses can be located, their movement within the family system can be balanced.

Bonding and Attachment

Classical theories about attachment, separation, the separation/individuation process, and trauma have been cited to characterize the unique circumstances of the adoptive family. Furthermore, the adoptive parents' experience with infertility and the other factors that underlie their decision to adopt raises questions of projective identification. There is also pervasive realization of strangeness—the fact that neither the child nor the parents are "natural" to each other. Finally, there is the sense experienced by all members of the adoptive family that somewhere there is another family—the "real" family of the child, to whom the child really belongs, whom the child is really like.

Many developmentalists have tried to characterize the way in which parents cleave to the infant after birth (Kennell & Kennell, 1982) and the manner in which the infant identifies himself or herself with the caregivers (Bowlby, 1971). Maternal infant bonding is supposed to occur in the immediate neonatal period, where, as Kennell and Kennell have described it, the altered state of the new parent makes her uniquely receptive to accepting the infant as a part of her only within a critical period (much as a sheep accepts a new lamb). Since the mid-1970s, the concept of parent–infant bonding in this particular way has fallen into disfavor, and it is recognized that adults can "adopt" others at a variety of stages of life.

Attachment, as described by Bowlby (1971), is a concept drawn from several different sources—mainly from ethological studies and from observations of infants in secure relationships with caregivers, those in disrupted relationships, and those without relationships. Bowlby proposed that attachment is a fundamental necessity for the establishment of a secure identity in the child.

The establishment of an attachment relationship is commonly accepted as the main sociocultural issue in the first year of life and a process that continues throughout one's life. The classical theories on attachment emphasize the importance of a critical period of 0–12 months for this relationship to occur, and contend that it is then the prototype for all future attachment experiences. Stroufe (1979) has argued that this secure attachment influences later adaptation through increasing a child's confidence to explore his or her environment and develop more autonomy during the second year of life. Does this mean that the adopted child is forever "one down" in terms of his or her capacity to develop secure feelings or relatedness to another? This theoretical frame of reference places the major responsibility for relatedness on the mother, overlooks the importance of the father, and results in the mother's being blamed eventually for difficulties within the family.

Broadening the Systems Context: The Feminist Argument

Feminist theorists have criticized a unidimensional view of attachment, noting that the role of the mother is overemphasized and that the relationship between the parents, the role of the father, and the impact of the larger social system on the family and its members are all neglected (Goldner, 1985; Hare-Mustin, 1978). They explore a broader perspective of the family as not only a biosocial system, but a social system made up of people who are together by choice, even without biological connections. The individuals within these social systems are able to form lasting and significant attachments to one another and do so at varying periods of the life cycle. Most of the documented research on attachments has focused on the mother–child dyad, and has been done in the context of the biosocial family system. Examining adoptive families is an opportunity to develop another model of family organization, which can include the relatively neglected role of the father within the family and the virtually ignored consequences of gender. As already noted, the social and political realities of war, increased divorce rates, increased acceptance of single parenthood, and other factors have had profound effects on the family and have clearly influenced adoption practices. With this awareness, family therapists must have a broad perspective when sitting in a consultation room with families. When a family is stressed and comes for therapeutic intervention, it may be too easy still to look only at the dysfunctional relationship between mother and child or at the trauma of the loss of the biological parent. These theoretical models are most obvious, but since the family issues always reflect events at other systems levels, it is necessary to work with models that take a broader world view (Hoffman, 1981).

The Family Life Cycle

Another factor that influences attachments within the adoptive family is the interplay between the developmental stages of the child and of the family when the child enters. Zilbach (see Chapter 3, this volume) describes stages of the family life cycle. The first stage is called "coupling" and refers to the formation of a family identity and separation from the family of origin. The second stage, "becoming three," occurs when the first child is born and describes the shifts from a primary dyadic identity to triadic relationships within the family. The next several stages describe the gradual movement of dependents into the world outside of the family.

Adoption may occur at various stages of the family life cycle, and the inclusion of the adopted child will have different meanings and different effects on the family and child at these different stages. Generally, the adoptive child enters the family when parents are older than they are likely to be when bearing their own children; thus they may have had more time in Stage I, the coupling stage. A couple settled into the dyadic relationships of this stage may find it difficult to accept another member of the group and may experience the new member as an intrusion, in spite of their having wished to have a child.

The positive side of the entry point may be that the parents have had more practice at interdependence, and so may share more of the role decisions and nurturing aspects of child rearing. Perhaps this increased experience with couple interdependence facilitates increased sharing in the long and arduous fertility search, and then the paperwork, interview and child search. This process may increase the father's investment and commitment to the parenting. As this continues through the child's life within the family, the family is able to experience a more balanced and interactive father.

Formation of the Adoptive Family

Making the Child Their Own: Hera and Hercules

Adoption is a story told and retold throughout human history. According to Greek myth the goddess Hera, as an adoptive mother, concealed the baby Hercules inside her clothing and pushed him until he fell out between her legs. Through this ritual imitation of the natural birth process, Hera made it known that this infant was now her own.

The story of Hera and Hercules illustrates the ritual nature by which an adoptive family undertakes to make a child its own. Whether the child is a natural child or adopted, incorporating a baby into the family and the baby's reciprocal adoption of the family involve more than going through childbirth, as many developmentalists have studied. Attachment and separation appear to have the most relevance for understanding the processes by which an adoptive family forms.

Many adoptive parents report a sense of attachment to their adoptive child during the months that they wait for the adoptive process to be completed. They invest emotionally in the idea of being parents, and become attached to their shared fantasies about the child. For parents who travel to a Third World country and wait weeks or months for finalization of the adoption, there is much time to develop a connection and relationship with the newborn or young child.

One young mother stated, "We arrived in Chile after many hours of flight and several delays; we were exhausted. The uncertainty about the child actually being ours increased our stress; we worried how he would look, how his voice would sound, whether he would be healthy. It felt as if I went through the process of labor and that my husband was active in this process throughout. When we saw the baby, he was so little, so helpless, so willing to be cuddled. We felt so natural and at ease as we held him and fed him."

The stories of adoptive parents reflect the different opportunity for a mother and a father to share more equally in this initial attachment. But many adoptive parents do have a "prenatal" experience of their youngster—at first an intellectual one, developed through planning, paperwork, and discussion with the many people involved in the adoption process. Thus, the private, personal connection of the pregnant mother with her fetus yields to a shared experience between and among all of the family members anticipating the arrival of a child to be adopted. It is an opportunity for the father to become attached to the child at the same time and in the same manner as the mother.

Unique Aspects of Attachment

Some have emphasized the irreparable trauma of separation of a child from its natural family, contending that the initial bonding process between mother and child is critical to fundamental security and that adoption alters this process (Clothier, 1943; Wieder, 1978). If indeed the removal of an individual from his or her racial antecedents lies at the core of what is peculiar to the psychology of the adopted child, as Clothier has written, there are varying ways in which stages of the individual life cycle interact with this separation. Reese and Lipsett (1970) have indicated that there is no lasting harm when a child is separated from his or her primary caretaker between the ages of 1 and 8 months, because this is the period during which attachment normally occurs. Thereafter, however, attachment is thought to be a more perilous task for the child and the primary caretaker.

If the child comes into the family between the ages of eighteen months and 3 years, when the child is becoming developmentally involved in the separation/individuation process (Mahler, Pine, & Bergman, 1975), he or she may allow less cuddling and demand more time away from the parents. This moving close to and away from them may leave parents feeling less satisfied with the child and less rewarded in their efforts to care for the child, who has probably been more difficult to place. Families need preparation from adoption sources and extended families to cope with this period and their own frustrated wishes. The loss of or separation from significant figures is recognized as one of the most devastating experiences that an individual can sustain (Garmezy, 1985). This fact has clearly influenced many to study the impact of the loss of the mother on the child. Thus the adopted child has received attention relative to the sequelae of maternal deprivation.

Schwam and Tuscan (1978) noted that the fewer the intervening placements that a child has had prior to adoption, the fewer the incidents of disruptive acting-out behaviors that are seen in the family as the child grows. The quality of care children have had in placements prior to adoption is also critical to their mental and psychological well-being. Lack of stimulation, inconsistent and non-nurturing caregivers, and physical or sexual abuse are debilitating to the child and compromise the child's and family's attachment in an adoptive process. It may be that for some children, multiple changes in environment before there is adequate language to describe what is happening may leave the children more vulnerable and mistrustful and have profound effects on the adoptive process. It may also be that for some children, having to connect and disconnect repeatedly from caretakers, with a growing knowledge that they are excluded from permanent residency, may increase their anxiety and uncertainty as well as that of their adoptive families.

Yet several observations raise questions about these assumptions. As Garmezy (1985) has summarized, research has not demonstrated the dire long-range effect of the loss of attachment figures in most cases. There is a growing emphasis on individual differences with regard to vulnerability to stress and deprivation; furthermore, there is acknowledgment of a need to look at the contextual factors present during stress-arousing events. These observations also emphasize the need to look for protective factors that may be present. In the case of adopted children, the interrelationships and nurturing qualities of the families in interaction with the children must be stressed. As there is considerable plasticity in the adaptive capacities of children who have been lost or separated from significant figures, there may also be considerable plasticity in the families who take them in as well.

Entering the Family and Contract Acceptance

A couple may adopt because they can give birth only with difficulty, or not at all. Parents may also adopt when they feel needed by a child who has no living parents, or when the child's own parents are unable to care for him or her. Parents may also add to the children they already have by adopting another. Sometimes a father may adopt the offspring of his new wife when there is a remarriage, in order to feel more completely a father and to have the same legal obligations as the biological father (Smart & Smart, 1980).

How adopted children enter a family is very significant. A child may come, welcomed with anticipation and preparation from the parents, extended family, and community; or a child may come quietly wrapped in a blanket of shame, with his or her origins shrouded in secrecy because of the circumstances of birth. An adopted child may be originally welcomed, only to be moved aside with the birth of a biological child, or with the disappointment that the child is difficult to manage or seems ungrateful. The adopted child may enter the family as an infant with few memories of his or her earlier relationships, or the child may enter the family after several placements or harsh treatment within his or her biological family. Unresolved feelings of hurt and anger toward the biological family and/or the placement families may complicate the family's and the child's acceptance of each other.

Whatever the conditions of entry (the child's including age, previous life experience, and temperament, and the family's including reasons for the decision to adopt, life circumstances, and stage in relationship formation), there is a contract—one that is actually signed by the parents when the adoption is formalized, but one that is also implicit in the relationship. Basically, there is an agreement that the adoptive parents will act like parents to the child, nurturing, protecting, and educating him or her as if he or she were their own child. The child's side of the contract is to be parented, and to act as if he or she were a child of these parents. This "contract" is particularly apparent when it is breached by both sides, as in the following family:

Eleven-year-old Jenny and her biological sister, Mary, were adopted into the same home at the ages of 3 and 5, respectively. Both girls had memories of their biological parents. Their brother had gone to live with the biological father in another state. Their mother and father had relinquished custody of these girls and consented to the adoption because of their inability and unwillingness to continue caring for them. Physical abuse was a dominant theme in their family.

These youngsters early on had been very needy of attention, which the adoptive mother was able to give to both girls. However, about 2 years after the adoption, the mother gave birth to her own biological daughter; 3 years later, she had another daughter. Faced with a mother who now needed to divide her attention among four children instead of between two, Jenny began to act out. Her acting out included defiance, running away, capricious lying, stealing, and fecal incontinence. At times, the adoptive mother was extremely punitive in her anger. Although abusive of this child, she apparently did not abuse her other children in any way.

Through family therapy and some individual therapy, the mother's ambivalent feelings for Jenny and the fact that her efforts to be loving and caring had been rejected became clear. She interpreted Jenny's acting out as a sign that she was ungrateful for all that had been done for her. At the same time, Jenny felt free to express her own worries about her biological mother and her wish to be with her.

After some time in therapy, the adoptive mother came to realize that efforts on Jenny's part to contact the biological mother might be beneficial. She arranged for some phone conversations as well as a regular exchange of letters with the biological mother. This act precipitated a considerable change in the youngster's behavior. Her defiance and constant pushing against the adoptive mother ceased for the most part. She relished her contact with the biological mother but was not eager to see her, contrary to her initial wish. Instead, she seemed content to remain in the adoptive family, which led to an increased coalescence among the children and the family as a whole.

As a result of this adoptive mother's willingness to risk the loss of her child and to give up the intense power struggle, the contract within the family was clear: "You do not have to be a member of this family, but we choose to have you and you may choose to have us." The parents as well as the children had come to the edge of the cliff, looked over, and returned to the plateau. Clearly, the parents and child each made a choice to recognize the biological attachment without rancor.

Transracial Adoption

In Hans Christian Andersen's (1869–1871/1945) story "The Ugly Duckling," a swan's egg left on a duck's nest is hatched into a life of constant ridicule by the other barnyard animals, because the young cygnet does not look like his duck family. The feelings of shame and not belonging drive him to leave the duck family, searching for acceptance and peace of mind. When he eventually discovered other swans like himself, a powerful inner urge propels him toward these strange animals. He finally not only receives acceptance, but is accorded special attention because of his inner beauty, as judged by his own peers. This story illustrates the powerful urge to find one's own kind, to be accepted and loved.

Ayla, the heroine of Auel's (1983) *Clan of the Cave Bear,* is separated from her own people in an earthquake. She is found and adopted by another clan, and cared for by a sister and brother who take her into their hearts and become her family. However, Ayla's inherent differences from the clan bring her into conflict with its rules. As she grows, she gains greater personal skill and comes to understand that the differences are irreconcilable. Her adoptive family is able to recognize her advanced and unique skills and helps prepare her for a future they know will not be with their clan, especially after their deaths. Ayla then beings another journey to find others like herself, keenly aware of the many gifts she has been given by her adoptive clan.

These two stories emphasize two aspects of transracial adoption. The first emphasizes the added difficulty a family member may have when he or she does not look like other members of the group. There are obvious physical differences. The second story emphasizes the need people often feel when they are fundamentally different from others in the large group in which they grow and develop. There is a deep longing, a need to find others like oneself, a desire to fill in one's racial and cultural identity. This need alone does not negate the positive experiences that can result from growing up and developing among a group of people different from one's own racial heritage. The ugly duckling is unsuccessfully adopted; differences are emphasized and ridiculed, and the unfortunate cygnet finally has to leave the familiar to seek another environment, finally happening upon his own kind. Ayla has a successful adoption into the clan, being loved and learning the lore of the clan. But as she matures, recognition of her differences brings increasing tensions into her relationship with her adoptive family, leading to her eventual expulsion from the clan. In transracial adoptions, the issues of differences are always alive and need to be addressed.

When the parents look into the mirror of their adopted child's eyes, they see a reflected image different from their own. As Whitaker (1987) has observed, this difference complicates the connection between parent and child. If the image is one of a perceived promiscuous, irresponsible, or inferior demon, then the ability to connect on the "like me" continuum is diminished. There may also be complications from other family members, as the adopted child does not reflect the family heritage, either.

Tiffany, aged 12, was very hurt and jealous of the attention her family gave Matt, an adopted black child of 2. Matt's looks were different from the rest of the family, and they thought him to be rather exotic, with dark, curly hair and deep brown skin. He was treated like an adorable toy. This was the usual scenario in reverse.

Kim (1985) found that Korean adoptees were better adjusted than white adoptees, even though the Korean children were adopted at an older age. The Korean children, however, were quite uncomfortable about their physical appearance. They did not like their Asian look in contrast to that of their Caucasian parents.

Feigelman and Silverman (1983) found that Colombian adoptees were not uncomfortable about their physical appearance, and that they identified themselves and were identified by their parents as white in most cases. Their Hispanic origins were minimized. These authors speculated that because infertility was a significant aspect of the decision to adopt in most of these cases, parents tended to minimize the differences between themselves and their adopted children. Furthermore, these parents experienced little in the way of rejecting or racist insults to them or their children. The extended families and friends were as positive in social support and approval as, if not more so than, families and friends of parents of white, U.S.-born children. The social antagonism was least for the Colombian children; it was only slightly greater for Korean children, unless they lived in rural areas where there were few other Asian people; and black adoptees experienced the most social antagonism.

The adopted child's search for roots is a particularly salient issue in cross-race adoptions, because the differences are so apparent. As discussed earlier, there has been some controversy about transracial adoptions involving black children with white families, but research data have not supported the supposition that having white parents leads to personality problems in black adoptees. Simon and Alstein (1977) studied 200 transracially adopted children and found no special problems related to the racial issue. Their follow-up study (Simon & Alstein, 1988) indicated that the effects of cross-racial adoptions are positive. In my clinical practice, I see many white parents who are initially overwhelmed by the varied overt and subtle forms that racism takes, and they struggle with how to help their children cope effectively with this racism.

Bonnie, a black child, was adopted at age 8 by a white single woman. She had been sexually abused during one of several foster home placements, and she came to her adoptive mother with several significant issues unresolved. Her biological mother's inability to care for her, and her knowledge that her mother had kept her older sister, left Bonnie feeling unwanted; the sexual assault by a once-trusted adult further undermined her confidence; and she experienced uncertainty about her racial identity, which stemmed from the various foster placements. As she neared age 12, her confusion and conflicts about race became obvious. Her mother then married a white man. Bonnie's adoptive parents had few black friends, and the community, school, and church were predominantly white. Although the parents recognized the need for Bonnie to know more about her racial heritage, they had not developed a network to do so. Viewing her white parents as unreliable informants, Bonnie rebuffed any of their efforts to tell her about her heritage. Bonnie's trust in her parents was diminished, and she did experience some racial identity confusion and a denial of the opportunity to learn more about her roots. Her reliance on racial stereotypes was further damaging to her self-esteem. The family was caring and had some awareness of Bonnie's need for a fuller racial identity, yet their actions belied their stated intentions. This disparity was not overlooked by Bonnie, and caused her even more distress.

For some children, confusion about the racial identity is not a problem, but racism is.

Mary is the younger of two children in her family, and is adopted. Her older sister is the biological child of the parents, who are now divorced and remarried. Mary not infrequently experiences threats of violence from other black children and racial slurs from white children. She is sometimes able to share this experience with her parents. Mary's parents feel some sadness and guilt about not participating in a significant part of their child's heritage. They also feel helpless as they experience their own inability to protect their adoptive child from the racial prejudice in our society.

Such feelings that the parents and the child are different, and will continue to be so, are best openly acknowledged. When they are frankly discussed, the possibility exists that parents and child may find common ground to enrich each other—not in spite of, but because of, the differences. In Mary's family, although the parents have not experienced violence or racial insults, they have experienced rejection or been fearful of potential violence in other life situations. If Mary and her family can experience parts of their lives together, their connections to each other may be deepened, even though the differences may still be painful. Some families will need the consultation of a family therapist to assist them in sorting these things out. Others will do so on their own.

In some families in which adopted children are mixed with biological children, the parents may clearly favor the biological children over the adopted children, especially if an adopted child misbehaves. This increases the likelihood that the adopted child will not be included, as is true of the ugly duckling. Such scapegoating is particularly poignant in the racially mixed family, because of the racial overtones.

The Johnsons had two biological daughters and two adopted sons. One of the sons was Native American, and left the family during his adolescence; the other son, Mickey, was black. At about age 14, Mickey began to act out in school and to show some sexual interest in his younger sister. He made a peephole in the wall between his room and hers so that he could watch her undress, and made overt sexual remarks to her. The sexual behavior was most alarming to the parents and seemed very dangerous.

Mrs. Johnson was the primary nurturer in the family; she was the caregiver and the toucher. The father, a high-powered professional, was minimally involved with the children but had engaged in some play with them during their younger years. As the children got older, he became less physical with them and more and more occupied with his work. He was the breadwinner and the interpreter of society's rules, and displayed little tolerance for play and physical contact. Mickey exhibited not only antisocial behavior, but also signs of an attention deficit disorder. He enjoyed a lot of physical contact and was quite playful; as he got older, his efforts to maintain a connection with his parents became more and more frantic. Through his behavior, he seemed to be questioning their continued involvement with him. He interpreted their response cycle of worry and recriminations as rejecting.

Mickey was placed in inpatient treatment because the family was unable to exert influence on him, and his behavior had become increasingly threatening to others. Follow-up family therapy proved ineffective in changing Mickey's dark image in this white family. His unforgivable sexual sins were used to highlight the family's innocence and social posturing. His sexual transgressions had created too big a barrier to his being readmitted to the family, and eventually he was sent to live in a residential center.

In this family, incest was possible but never acted out. Denial of racial stereotyping and inability to talk within the family about racial issues and what they meant to each family member were obvious. Also, sibling rivalry was significant. Mickey felt very much out of place and sensed that he was not the favored child; he was competing with the younger sister without adequate means to be an effective competitor. He was a poor black child. Success would have been the family's, but the failure was his. Mr. Johnson was furious that the family's goodness for taking this child in could not make up the loss of the biological parents. Nothing makes up for that loss.

Cultural or racial stereotypes may be prominent in the thoughts of parents and extended-family members at times. If these stereotypes and prejudices are brought into the open, their power can be diffused; if not, their power intensifies. These may then be the families in which parents are afraid to be clear about limits, and enforce consequences with their adoptive children because of their unacknowledged prejudices. Some white parents shrink from expressing their honest, irrational anger to their black or mulatto children. This seems to stem from the parents' own unexplored racial attitudes and from their difficulty in facing their prejudice and guilt about it. It is as if these adults want to believe they could grow up in this country unscarred by racism. This dishonesty increases the insecurity, anger, and defensiveness of the children. In the more extreme clinical cases, the children are constantly testing the limits and meeting little or no resistance. A false sense of power grows, as does the reciprocal false sense of powerlessness within the parents, who seek therapy in a desperate effort to find someone who can bring the children under control. A family often searches for a therapist who shares the same racial background as the child.

The family therapist can be sensitive to the added dimensions that transracial adoptions bring to the consulting room:

1. The obvious physical differences and how they are experienced by the child, family, and community.
2. The effects of racism, whether experienced or avoided by the child and family.
3. The likelihood that the child will have a strong urge to expand his or her identity through contact with others of the same racial grouping.
4. The guilt adoptive parents may feel, due to very different life experiences and their own unrecognized prejudices.
5. The additional effort that may be required by families to develop and maintain contact within multiracial communities, and to learn about and share cultural traditions with their adopted children.

Family Balances—Critical Incidents

The decision period prior to finalizing the adoption, with both child and family waiting out this period, is likely to be a particularly critical time. Waiting prior to a definitive decision to adopt the child obviously places the attachment and formation of a trusting relationship ''on hold.''

After the induction procedures by which the adoptive family is formed, the family continues to be in a state of dynamic equilibrium in which the membership of the adopted child in the family group is balanced with the recognition of his or her membership in another family, at least in fantasy. How this is arranged will vary from family to family, but the older the child is when he or she joins the family and the greater the number of places the child has been, the more explicit this balancing will have to be.

There is a delusion that many adoptive families labor under and are perplexed when the adopted child does not accept it. The delusion is this: "We love you as much as our own children. There is no difference in our love for you and for our own children. Our love will make up for the loss of your birth mother and father." When some adoptive parents try to deny the differences between biological and adoptive children, several problems arise. Ignoring the reality causes confusion within the family. A constant comparison is set up by which the adoptive and biological families are in competition. The parents are setting up a cycle in which they try to prove themselves to the child and the child pushes the limits further and further to find out whether indeed the parents' statements are true.

Denying the difference between biological status and adoptive status encourages the denial of the existence of another set of people to whom the child has connections. The members of the biological family become ghosts. They are present, yet cannot be seen. They may become ever more powerful in the fantasy world of the child, especially if talking about his or her biological family causes great pain and disappointment in the adoptive family.

Many parents of adopted children who seek therapy report an aloofness that makes the longed-for closeness impossible. This is particularly true when a child's provocative behavior calls for discipline. When the parents make some effort to talk to or discipline the child, he or she stonewalls them; that is, the child either does not respond or responds inappropriately to the situation. Sometimes the child is contrite, but only momentarily, and then the forbidden act is repeated. This aloofness intensifies with age.

Such children usually report that their parents seem afraid and behave inconsistently. They feel able to apply sufficient pressure to force the parents' capitulation. Although this may be the manifest goal, it seldom is what the children really want. Often these children recognize that they really want their parents to be firm with them, to prove their commitment. Thus children and parents become involved in cycles that continue to leave the question of belonging in doubt.

Toussieng (1962) raised the question about whether the emotional distance many adopted children appear to seek is an attempt to identify with or maintain a loyalty to distant biological parents. He also proposed that adopted adolescents may have more difficulty than others in rebelling against their adoptive parents because their fear of abandonment is so strong. The family of Annie—or Mai Lee, as she later came to be known—illustrated an adjustment made in acknowledgement of the complex balance of wanting the child to belong and reconizing her other origins.

Annie, a 12-year-old Korean child, had been adopted by a childless white family at the age of 6 months. Her parents later had two biological children. As she approached her 12th birthday, Annie became increasingly preoccupied. She was distant and had trouble concentrating; she fantasized about faraway places in which she was active and lively. She stopped identifying with her adoptive parents, further isolated herself from them, and talked less. Finally, she insisted on being called by a different name. The name she choose for herself was a combination of a name she made up plus her Korean name.

Annie—or Mai Lee, as she called herself—then began to talk in therapy about her wish to know more about her Korean roots, her biological parents, and the reasons they had left her. She had a strong sense of being different from her adoptive parents in a negative way. She felt ashamed by this difference and initially attempted to handle her feelings in therapy by being distant and "above it all." Mai Lee's parents began to learn more about themselves as individuals and as adoptive parents.

The mother admitted that she hated her married name and had always wanted to change it. The father, somewhat bewildered by the strong emotional response to his family name, agreed to change it. He risked the disapproval of and isolation from his extended family, saying that if the mother and the daughter felt so strongly, it was reason enough for him to change his name.

Mai Lee's adoptive parents were willing to examine and even alter their identity to help support hers, hopeful that a new combination including her racial identity might form a different sort of family in which Mai Lee would feel a part. In a sense, by being willing to change their names, Mai Lee's family made itself available for adoption by her.

Search for Roots

The adopted child may long to find his or her biological roots, entertaining fantasies about the biological and the adoptive parents. Freud (1908/1950) described the "family romance," in which the child normally begins to sense that his or her own affections are not fully reciprocated; this awareness usually finds vent in the idea that he or she must be the stepchild or the adopted child in the family. For the youngster who is adopted, this is not a fantasy. He or she really has another set of parents out there who can be fantasized about at will. The child may dream of parents who will rescue him or her from being misunderstood, punished, or "unloved." The biological child has no such "reality" option. If the adopted child does not resolve a possible split perception between the good parents and the bad parents, and develop a more realistic picture of himself or herself and the adoptive parents, it can be damaging to both the child's and the family's development. If hostility toward the adoptive parents is not adequately resolved, it may be generalized to societal authority and increase the child's suspiciousness and oppositional stances.

Loving Is Not Owning

Adoptive parents have to grapple with the fear of separation. Will the child want to return to his or her own people? The issue of separation is further confounded in cross-racial adoption, where these roots may be very alien to the adoptive parents. Insofar as these roots may be unknown and the ways of the other people unclear, the adoptive parents may not be able or willing to help the child bridge this gap. Adoptive parents need to be clear in exploring their own attitudes about other racial groups, especially when they are involved in cross-racial adoption.

In a family in which separations work well, the adoptive parents exhibit a willingness to acknowledge the other set of parents and their importance to the child's life. They also help the child to search for his or her roots, if help is necessary. They may help the child make this transition. These adoptive parents hold and guide with open hands.

Jim and his wife, Peggy, have nine children, five of whom are adopted. Their oldest daughter, Marcy, is 21, and so far she is the only one who has expressed an interest in finding her biological family. Their 16-year-old daughter, Darlene, has steadfastly refused to read a letter that her biological mother sent with her. At this time, she wants no contact and no reminders of any life beyond the life in her adoptive home.

Marcy, with the help of Jim and Peggy, has made contact with her biolgoical family. Jim said that he was uneasy at first, because he thought that Marcy would distance herself from her adoptive family. In spite of his uneasiness, Jim felt it was important for his daughter to complete her search. He and Peggy talked to each other, but not to their daughter, about their reservations. With the additional help of the adoption agency, Marcy has been able to visit with her birth family and have some of them to meet her adoptive family. Marcy is now learning to live with the reality of knowing both families. She continues to come home to her adoptive family on school holidays.

Kip, their 9-year-old son and youngest child, is Korean. He is the only Asian member of the family, although he does have an older brother of African descent. Kip does not take much notice of his racial lineage at this time. He does have several neighborhood playmates who are also Korean and adopted. Kip has yet to ask much about his life before he was a member of the Rogers clan. Jim and Peggy are prepared to talk with him and their other children as questions arise, and to help him with his quest should he wish it.

Within the next several weeks, John and Ethel are expecting their first child, a son from Korea. They have photographs of their prospective child—healthy, sleeping peacefully. After 9 years of unsuccessful attempts to have a biological child, a fertility workup with its attendant stresses, and 2 years of waiting through an adoption agency, they are ecstatic; they are busily making plans for the new baby and anticipating changes in their family and daily life. Interestingly, they expect to travel to Korea as their son grows, so that he can see his country of origin at first hand. Ethel and John feel that this part of his life is so important to their family, they do not want to wait for questions to arise. The Brewsters are another example of a family willing to work with their adopted child to help him know his cultural heritage.

Losses

How parents deal with loss has a significant effect on how they relate to their adopted children, as well as to their biological children, and how they deal with loss is a function of where they are in their own development. Unresolved loss of a biological child profoundly complicates a subsequent adoption. The adopted child then faces a twofold dilemma: (1) the fact of his or her adoption, and (2) the unavailability or unsuitability of the adoptive parents, while the child is trying to form a stable and reliable internal picture of his or her primary caretaker.

Three-year-old Molly was adopted less than a year after her adoptive parents had lost their biological daughter to leukemia. Molly's mixed racial background had been too difficult for her previous family to accept. The new family had a biological son who was 4 years older than Molly; then, 2 years after the adoption, another son was born.

The essential unavailability of these parents largely stemmed from two factors. First, both parents had had painful childhoods; in particular the mother's relationship to her own mother was dominated by cruel ambivalence. Molly's mother had been suicidal as a child and was convinced her death would have pleased her mother. Second, the parents had never mourned the loss of their biological daughter, and they viewed Molly as a replacement. Their daughter had been a much-longed-for blond, blue-eyed child; the child they adopted was older than they had initially wanted and of mixed racial background. Not having adequately grieved for their biological child, they began to place many unrealistic expectations on Molly. The fact that her adopted child lived when her biological child had not provoked considerable resentment and rage in the mother. Molly had no way of knowing this. She could only feel the anger directed at her—and not just the anger, but the actual physical abuse that was part of her life from very early on. As this child grew, she was sexually abused by her older brother and grandfather. She did not tell either of her adoptive parents, feeling that she could not trust them with this information and that she would not be heard. It was not until she was in inpatient treatment for a series of problems involving chemical dependency and antisocial behavior that these abuses came to light. Only then did the parents begin to work on the long-delayed issue of the loss of their own child and their unavailability to their adopted child.

Expectations

Another problem seen in adoptive families seeking treatment is that of unrealistically high expectations. They are based on the parents' needs, not on
awareness of a child's individuality.

The Swensen family had two adopted children. Adopted at the age of $2\frac{1}{2}$,
Eric, now 12, was beginning to work out separation issues and clearly was not
available for much cuddling. He was active, lively, curious, and irreverent. In
contrast, Eric's adoptive father favored structure and order, tended to move at a
slower pace, and was much more deliberate and staid. The father felt that Eric's
active pace was "wrong" or "bad," and he sought therapy to get his son "fixed."
One focus of therapy was to delineate the varying personal rhythms in the
family. The parents came to understand that their son's active temperament was
not an attempt to sabotage their good parenting efforts. Another focus was to
explore whether or not the family could live with these differences. With the help
of the therapist, the family was able to look over the edge of the cliff and confront
the issue of whether or not to give this child up. They decided that they could
live together, although perhaps not 365 days of the year. Boarding school was
considered a viable alternative; with Eric coming home on holidays and vacations,
there would be less pressure all around for this child to be exactly what the parents
wanted and vice versa. Having had no clear picture of what a typical $2\frac{1}{2}$-year-old
is like, his parents had viewed his differences in temperament and his need to
separate from them as rejections or defects. His seeming rejection deeply hurt the
parents, but they had never openly addressed the issue. Thus, the hurt had built
up over many years.

Whitaker (1987) has said that we human beings have a strong need to see our
own faces reflected in the faces of our children. When a parent is angry at a child,
and looks into his or her face and sees someone unknown or someone sinful (i.e.,
an immoral parent) somewhere in the past, the parent's attachment to the child is
imperiled. When a parent is not able to maintain an attachment in spite of anger,
the child's overall development suffers. When the features of an adopted child
more closely resemble the physical features of his or her adoptive parents and
extended family, this facilitates a family identification, but it never eradicates the
differences between parent and child. When there is a cross-cultural or cross-racial
adoption, and the parents and child are significantly different in physical appearance, it is obviously harder to maintain a bond with the child, especially when
parents are angry and feel double-crossed.

Don remembered the pain he experienced as a child because he did not look
like either of his adoptive parents. He particularly sought out connections with a
female cousin, Helene, whom he felt he resembled in coloring and facial features.
All of his life, he had felt closeness to this cousin, in part because of the physical
similarities. He found some solace, some respite from the nagging sense of

strangeness that he experienced when he looked into the mirror of his parents' eyes.

Customs and Rituals

In adoptive families not in treatment, especially cross-cultural placements, parents often incorporate customs and food from an adopted child's cultural heritage. They may also invite other children and families of similar cultural or racial background to share their own family rituals.

Special holidays such as Christmas found the Walker family integrating many Mexican customs, including a *piñata* and some Mexican food, into their rituals as their part-Mexican child grew older. They also made an effort to meet and socialize with a few Mexican families, so that the child could see others who had his coloring and develop a sense of belonging to a multiracial environment.

The Extended Family

Functional adoptive families often have a good deal of extended-family involvement.

When the Mitchell's adopted child, a healthy boy, arrived from South America, the mother's extended family was available to help the new baby and parents settle in. The father's extended family lived overseas and had to wait to see their new grandson. These grandparents were involved, however, through letters and phone calls, so the early developmental milestones did not pass without their knowledge. The Mitchells and their adopted baby visited the grandparents during the summer, when a several weeks' vacation permitted travel abroad.

Family Therapy and the Adoptive Family

Do adoptive families come more readily for treatment? Clinical experience says "Yes." It appears that adoptive parents believe that the community is a place to come to for help when an adopted child shows a need for mental health care. After all, it was to the community that the adoptive parents came to when they were looking for a child. Furthermore, because the child is not biologically or genetically connected to the adoptive paents, emotional problems may reflect less negatively on this family, and therefore the parents may be more willing to seek help. Most often they focus on the "defective" child, and the adoptive parents are angry with the adoption agency for not revealing the child's problems. They feel that the agency did not adequately inform them of the child's background or give adequate information about what to expect when adopting this youngster. In some cases, the adoptive parents come into therapy with a "savior" attitude; they believe that their youngster is a "bad seed" that they are rescuing.

When things go awry, the adoptive parents often feel that the whole family is walking near the edge of a cliff. The specter of the family breaking up may lessen the family's resilience. Clearly, unlike a biological child, the adopted child can be sent to someone else; there is no clearly identified agency other than the court sytem where one can send one's own child. Contributing to this sense of walking near the edge of a cliff is the cultural fantasy that accompanies the idea of a "chosen child." Adoption, after all, is an improvement over a bad situation. The negative aspects of the choosing—disappointment and anger—may be denied. The adoptive parents may be disappointed that the child is not all that they had hoped for, and the child may feel the same way about the parents. Furthermore, neither the parents nor the child can safely express the feeling, "When I'm mad, I feel really sick of you and I don't want to be with you." When this blockage occurs in the family, it reflects the complex ties of the adoption process and the likelihood that parents may turn to this disadoption process, referred to by Boszormenyi-Nagy and Krasner (1986).

Adoptive families that are not in treatment talk more openly about their fears and jealousy and their need for constancy in the adopted children's lives as the children press for information and contact with their biological parents. In the clinical population, these feelings are often so covert, and therefore so powerful, that the adoptive attachment is severely threatened.

Summary

Although it is true that adoptive families are overrepresented in mental health settings, most adoptive families do not come to the attention of mental health professionals. Clearly, there are unique circumstances of the adoption process that predispose children and families to an intensification of stress. How these unique conditions are handled may make a critical difference for how successful adoptions are and who will seek treatment. To review, the unique conditions are these:

1. Loss of the child's biological parents and/or loss of the capacity of the adoptive parents to have biological offspring.
2. The child's having two sets of parents, with divided loyalties and the need for acknowledgment of the invisible family system.
3. Recognition that an adopted child is not the same as a biological child.
4. Anxiety about the bonding process among adoptive parents, members of the extended family, and the adopted child.

Information from nonclinical adoptive families and work with adoptive families in therapy provides the following guidelines for helping the adoptive family to survive as a strong, tolerant, and nurturing system.

1. Bring the invisible family out of the shadows with an open and generous heart.
2. Involve fathers and extended-family members from the preadoption decision onward.
3. Recognize that adoption is different from biological birth. It is a choice, a contract, a stewardship with the child.
4. Recognize the losses of biological parents, as well as the gains, which include opportunities to share in cultural rituals that may be new to both child and parents.
5. Acknowledge that transcultural and transracial adoptions intensify the differences implicit in all adoptions and add other racial and cultural issues that must be addressed.

REFERENCES

Andersen, H. C. (1945). The ugly duckling. In H. C. Andersen, *Andersen's fairy tales* (E. V. Lucas & H. B. Paull, Trans.). New York: Grosset & Dunlap. (Original work published in English 1869–1871)

Andrews, R. G. (1978). Adoption: Legal resolutions or legal fraud? *Family Process, 17,* 313–328.

Auel, J. M. (1983). *Clan of the cave bear.* New York: Crown.

Baker, F. (1987). Afro American life cycle: Success, failure and mental health. *Journal of the National Medical Association, 79,* 625–633.

Boszormenyi-Nagy, I., & Krasner, B. R. (1986). *Between give and take: A clinical guide to contextual therapy.* New York: Brunner/Mazel.

Bowlby, J. (1971). *Attachment and loss: Vol. 2. Separation, anxiety, and anger.* New York: Basic Books.

Brinich, P. M. (1980). Some potential effects of adoption on self and object representation. *Psychoanalytic Study of the Child, 35,* 107–133.

Byng-Hall, J. (1973). Family myths used in defense in conjoint family therapy. *British Journal of Medical Psychology, 46,* 239–250.

Clothier, F. (1943). The pyschology of the adopted child. *Mental Hygiene, 27,* 222–230.

Feigelman, W., & Siverman, A. R. (1983). *Chosen children.* New York: Praeger.

Freud, S. (1950). Family romances. In J. Strachey (Ed. and Trans.), *The standard edition of the complete pyschological works of Sigmund Freud* (Vol. 9, pp. 237–241). London: Hogarth Press. (Original work published 1908)

Garmezy, N. (1985). Development aspects of children's response to the stress of separation and loss. In M. Rutter, C. E. Izard, & P. B. Read (Eds.), *Depression in young people: Developmental and clinical perspectives* (pp. 297–323). New York: Guilford Press.

Goldner, V. (1985). Feminism in family therapy. *Family Process, 24,* 31–47.

Goldstein, J., Freud, A., & Solnit, A. J. (1973). *Beyond the best interests of the child.* New York: Free Press.

Gossett, J. T., Lewis, J. M., & Bernhart, F. D. (1983). *To find a way: The outcome of hospital treatment of disturbed adolescents.* New York: Brunner/Mazel.

Hare-Mustin, R. (1978). A feminist approach to family therapy. *Family Process, 17,* 181–194.

Hoffman, L. (1981). *Foundations of family therapy: A conceptual framework for systems change.* New York: Basic Books.

Kadushin, A. (1967). A follow up study of children adoptive when older: Criteria of success. *American Journal of Orthopyschology, 37* (3), 500–539.

Kennell, M. H., & Kennell, J. H. (1982). *Parent–infant bonding.* St. Louis: C. V. Mosby.

Kim, P. S. (1985). Adoption. In H. I. Kaplan & B. J. Sadock (Eds.), *Comprehensive textbook of psychiatry* (Vol. 4, pp. 1829–1832). Baltimore: Williams & Wilkins.

Leavy, W. (1987, September). Should whites adopt black children? *Ebony,* pp. 76–82.

Mahler, M., Pine, F., & Bergman, A. (1975). *The psychological birth of the human infant.* New York: Basic Books.

National Committee for Adoption. (1985). *Adoption fact book.* Washington, DC: Author.

Paterson, K. (1978). *The great Gilly Hopkins.* New York: Harper & Row.

Paul, N. (1967). The role of mourning and empathy in conjoint marital therapy. In G. Zuk & I. Boszormenyi-Nagy (Eds.), *Family therapy and disturbed families* (pp. 186–205). Palo Alto, CA: Science and Behavior Books.

Reese, H. W., & Lipsett, L. P. (1970). *Experimental child pyschology.* New York: Academic Press.

Schecter, M. (1960). Observations on adopted children. *Archives of General Pyschiatry, 21* (3), 45/21–56/32.

Schwam, J., & Tuscan, M. (1978). Adopted child: Part C, Varieties of family structures. In J. Noshpitz (Ed.), *Basic handbook of child psychiatry* (Vol. 1, pp. 342–348). New York: Basic Books.

Simon, R., & Alstein, H. (1977). *Transracial adoption.* New York: Wiley.

Simm, R., & Alstein, H. (1988). *Transracial adoption: A follow-up.* Lexington, MA: Lexington Books.

Stroufe, L. A. (1979). The coherence of individual development: Early care, attachment and subsequent developmental issues. *American Pyschologists, 34,* 834–841.

Toussieng, P. (1962). Regarding the etiology of pyschological difficulties in adopted children. *Child Welfare, 41,* 59–71.

U.S. Bureau of the Census. (1986). *Statistical abstract of the United States* (107th ed.). Washington, DC: U.S. Government Printing Office.

U.S. Bureau of the Census. (1988). *Statistical abstract of the United States* (108th ed.). Washington, DC: U.S. Government Printing Office.

Whitaker, C. A. (1987). Dynamics of the American family as deducted from twenty years of family therapy: The family unconscious. In J. K. Zeig (Ed.), *The evolution of psychotherapy* (pp. 75–83). New York: Brunner/Mazel.

Wieder, H. (1977). On being told of adoption. *Psychoanalytic* Quarterly, *46,* 1–22.

Special Families in Special Circumstances

Most parents think that their children are special, and most people would agree that every family is unique. Yet there are types of circumstances surrounding individuals in families that pose exceptional challenges, both to the families' functioning and to the development of the individual family members. Examining families who are coping with these special circumstances provides information about ways in which the difficulties threaten family functioning, as well as ways in which families do survive and perhaps surmount these difficulties.

This section covers six classes of special circumstances—three more directly affecting children and three more directly affecting parents, though of course all six affect all family members in some fashion. For those families coping with handicaps or illness in their children, the challenge is to maintain their integrity and to hold in dynamic suspension a sense of hope and expectation for the future, balanced with a sense of acceptance of limitations, chronic invalidism, or the possibility of untimely death. The special circumstance of childhood obesity is also included, because obesity in all ages is a major health hazard, resistant to treatment, and usually ignored by medical and mental health professionals alike. For those families where parents or other family members are affected with mental illness or substance abuse problems, or have died, the family environment must be radically readjusted to address the functions that support continued development of the nonafflicted or surviving members—particularly the children, who are the major concern of this book.

Chapter 9 provides a summary of a research project designed to investigate the coping patterns of families of children with a wide range of physical and cognitive handicaps. Beaver's research group used the Beavers Family Assessment model to evaluate the functioning of a number of such families with children of different ages; they found that the proportion of these families who could be described as functioning "normally" was the same as in families without the specific stress of a handicapped child. This is an extremely important testimony to the resourcefulness and adaptability of families. Beavers then goes on to detail the resources that were particularly useful to these families, and to contrast these with the specific difficulties in families who were not coping so well.

It is important to underscore that the well-functioning families, like the competent single-parent families described in Chapter 6, did not adhere to standard role concepts for either parents or children. It appeared, for example, that stepparents were often more able to cope with handicapped children than were natural parents; also, other children in these families were called upon to help with their disabled siblings in a way that gave them an important (often indispensable) role. Specific effective coping patterns included contextual clarity about the handicap; modification of family composition in response to the needs of a handicapped individual; high levels of activity and interaction; a problem-solving orientation; a consciousness about family processes that made family members open to positive self-evaluation; conscious balancing between acceptance and pushing; expressiveness; a focus on the lovable and enjoyable aspects of a disabled child; and an explicit sense of what was important and valuable to family members. These specific coping patterns were gleaned from what the families themselves reported about how they got along, and are contrasted with the dangers that are specific to the circumstance of raising a handicapped child. Furthermore, these coping patterns can become a guiding framework for treatment for those families not faring so well.

Children with special needs always involve the family with systems of experts outside the family. This is true for children with physical and cognitive handicaps, as it is true for children with physical illnesses. In Chapter 10, Libow tackles the complex system of the chronically ill child, the family, and the medical care system. Libow's approach to these systems involves an analysis of the specific issues to be managed by each subsystem, including the child, parents, siblings, and members of the medical care team. She presents systems for characterizing what it being coped with (such as the particular challenges of chronic illness, pain, deformity, and medical ambiguity), and an interweaving of stages of chronicity with individual developmental stages and stages of family life. This detailed examination of the internal issues of the family is a nice complement to the global family assessment presented in Beavers's chapter. Even so, from this different perspective, Libow echoes Beavers and colleagues' finding that families in these trying circumstances show an impressive degree of adaptability. For such a family, the family therapist is really a consultant to the child, the family, and the medical team. Libow's comprehensive consideration of the needs of these children and their families provides a rich guide to the complexities of assessing and assisting them.

Chapter 11, Harkaway's chapter on childhood obesity, brings this important and frustrating childhood condition into a working perspective. She notes, for example, that childhood obesity is a workable problem only when someone has defined it as such. That is, some children's obesity has been defined as problematic and others' has not. Furthermore, the degree of obesity is not necessarily correlated with the degree of distress about it. Therapy, she points out, usually comes at a time when there have been many failed attempts to help the child lose weight; thus, the focus of assessment is on what in the system keeps the child from losing weight. This level of evaluation leads to a characterization of how the concern about the child's obesity resonates with structural patterns in the nuclear family and with patterns of loyalty to extended families. This characterization then leads to a blueprint for treatment that combines structural and systemic approaches. It is interesting to note that problem families with obese children are similar in many respects to problem families with children with psychosomatic illnesses, including anorexia nervosa. Thus childhood obesity qualifies as a true eating disorder.

Harkaway's approach to assessing and treating families with a problem such as childhood obesity is an excellent model for the assessment and treatment of families with many childhood problems. However, she gives one grave warning. Usually family treatment with childhood problems is a short-term affair; after a few sessions, either the problem is resolved or the family members have gotten on a track that they can pursue independently. With the problem of obesity, Harkaway points out, progress is slow. No one can expect dramatic changes in the child's weight, and if one does, there are other problems in store. On the other hand, as she illustrates with an example, one does come upon dramatic changes in the family's organization in regard to the problem, and these changes can lead to the family's solutions.

Parents are vital to the secure and healthy development of children, yet many children have parents who have died or are impaired in some way. It is important to recognize that children who have lost a parent, or whose parents are impaired or ill, are at risk; to predict the kinds of emotional difficulties they will have; and to explain their difficulties on the basis of their parents' status. But by this time it should be clear that factors in the family environment may aggravate the liabilities of parents' death or disability, or may in some measure compensate for them. Patterns of family interaction and outside resources, as well as constitutional factors, contribute to what has been called "invulnerability" in children. The next three chapters explore some of the family contextual aspects of survival when a parent is compromised.

When a parent is mentally ill, the children may be in double jeopardy: Not only do they experience the confusion and inconsistency from the ill parent but they suffer the possibility of being vulnerable to the illness themselves. Unfortunately, though, adults with mental illness are often treated without consideration for their families, especially their children. Thus Guttman has had to assemble data about the lives of children of mentally ill parents from a variety of sources, and to move from there to the construction of an understanding of family systems interactions when a parent is mentally ill—both those that compensate for the illness and those that contribute to a more hazardous course for the children. She notes that probably the most disruptive factors in the families of mentally ill adults are inconsistency and unpredictability, and that often these are not compensated for by the "nonaffected" parent because of the extremely high incidence of mental illness or personality disorders in the spouses of mentally ill people. Furthermore, the patterns that often develop in such families—ones in which the children also participate—further disqualify the ill parent. Children in such families have been found to have a significant incidence of behavior disorders; these might be understood both as their response to a disturbed environment and perhaps as the precursor to some major illness to be manifested later in their lives.

Guttman advises that since it is much harder to construct new families for children who have already formed their attachments (even if to unpredictable parent figures), families should be supported in caring for their children, and she prescribes some treatment approaches. It is helpful to elicit the children's own interpretation of their experiences, and it is essential to provide them with a sense of continuity and security. It is also necessary to treat whatever symptoms of emotional difficulties they are experiencing, and, in particular, to understand these difficulties in terms of their experiences in the family. A combination of individual and family treatments, employing some approaches that have been specifically useful in treating families of mentally ill people, is recommended. In all of these approaches, Guttman stresses giving the children sufficient information so that they can manage better through understanding. One cannot be sanguine about the risks to a family when one of its members has a mental illness, but it is also important, once again, to learn from those individuals and families who have survived such stresses how these can be coped with.

This is true, too, for children in families where there is alcohol or other substance abuse. Again, most of the research on alcoholism has focused on individuals or on adult relationships (alcoholism in adolescents, couples, adult children of alcoholics, etc.), so that establishing the risks to children of alcoholics while they are still children in the family, and assessing how they cope with this form of parental incapacity, again require the effort of assembling data from many sources and piecing them together into a collage of the alcoholic family with young children. This is precisely what Copans has done in Chapter 13. He has assembled information from four sources: clinical experience, self-help group materials, research, and personal testimonials. Rarely do these sources illuminate the experiences of young (younger than adolescent) children directly, yet much can be inferred from such studies as Steinglass and colleagues' on the "wet" and "dry" phases of family life or Bennett and Wolin's on family rituals.

Copans takes a no-nonsense approach to this problem, emphasizing that therapists can be "enablers" if they do not confront the alcoholism directly as an issue that needs to be addressed before any lasting change can be expected in the family environment. His attitude is tough but optimistic. It is hard to treat these problems, but regardless of one's theories about whether alcoholism is a biological illness or a dysfunctional adaptation, many instances can be treated sufficiently to alleviate the oppresive atmosphere of secrecy and excuses that dominates the family life of alcoholics, and that seriously affects the young lives and the futures of their children.

When a parent dies, the whole family is turned topsy-turvy; this is the subject of Chapter 14. The surviving parent is usually torn among managing his or her own grief, trying to figure out the basics of keeping the family going without the other parent, and comforting and reassuring the children. This is a tall order, and, as Barth notes, it usually requires outside assistance. The best sources of this assistance, if available, are grandparents and other extended-family members who can immediately provide answers to some questions, such as "What will happen to us?" Barth presents a case example of a family that was coping with the death of one of the parents; she examines the family members' coping mechanisms and their particular strengths and vulnerabilities at the time of her interview, 13 months after the death of the father. She reports that there was a prevailing sadness affecting the older children and those who were closest to the father, coupled with a sense of movement and getting on with life. Each family member was in a different relationship to sadness and "getting on with it." The death of a parent is a circumstance in which time, in differing amounts for different people, is an essential healer.

Time is a healer, however, only if there is a base of security upon which the family expects to continue. As with the children of mentally ill parents, children of a parent who has died need explicit information—not only about death in general and the death of their own parent, but also about what is expected next. As in competent single-parent families and families with a mentally ill parent, these children will be called upon to assume other functions in the family (doing more chores, helping each other out, caring for themselves while the surviving parent works, etc.). These additional tasks need not be regarded as burdens, but as ways in which the children participate in the family's adaptation and ongoing survival. Barth's numerous vivid examples illustrate the long-lasting effects of not adequately addressing children's losses and the relieving effects of participation in exchanging information and ongoing family activity.

All six chapters in this section emphasize a number of common observations about families with young children who are coping with an exceptional challenge affecting a family member. The first is an observation that mental health professionals may find hard to keep in perspective: Most families do cope. This is demonstrated by Beavers and colleagues' research on families of handicapped children, but it can be inferred from the fact that even when environmental and genetic factors are combined (as when a parent is mentally ill or alcoholic), the rate of serious maladjustment in the children is far less than would be expected if families were not somehow managing to compensate. Because most families cope, we can learn about helpful processes from these successful families. Among these, the most crucial appear to be the following:

1. A degree of flexibility in role functioning, which, in particular, allows children to participate in ongoing family functions as contributing members.

2. The free exchange of information, given in a fashion that can be understood by and useful to family members of all ages.
3. The natural resourcefulness of the family—in particular, in relation to the extended family, but also in relation to the services of experts, used in a timely fashion and aimed at helping the family to function independently.

Family therapy cannot change the fact of genetic loading or physical disability, and it cannot bring back the dead. But family therapists, well informed by learning from healthy families, can help families to find ways of providing security and continuity to their children in spite of some of these circumstances.

9

Physical and Cognitive Handicaps

JEANETTE BEAVERS, ACSW

The Cultural Context

Families with a child having physical and/or cognitive handicaps are a numerically and socially significant group, whose experiences and needs have emerged from the shadows only recently. It is estimated that 1 child in 20 has an identifiable impairment at birth or after, and that 1.5% are severely handicapped. Readers of this chapter will probably have had more than one close personal or professional involvement with such families. In the past, they tended to keep their handicapped children sequestered and to reveal little about their lives with such children. The prevailing wisdom among medical personnel and laypersons was that a family should avoid claiming a handicapped child and arrange placement in an institution, for the sake of other family members. Although this assumption was modified for children with physical handicaps that did not affect cognitive or communicative abilities, even the families of these children kept a fairly low profile.

For many reasons (among them, medical advances increasing the survival rate and longevity of the handicapped; formation of parent groups, which became advocates for better services; the escalating costs of and horrifying deficiencies in institutional care), families with disabled children have become far more visible. Significant changes in social values and biases have shifted the usual family focus from shame or embarrassment to burden or responsibility. Placement away from the family is now more likely to be the last resort then first choice. Help for

Jeanette Beavers (deceased). Southwest Family Institute, Dallas, TX.

handicapped children and their families is provided by public schools, which offer programs that begin as early as the first year of life and expand to daily classroom placement from age 3 on through age 21. Reciprocal improvement in comfortableness and understanding between family members and outsiders can result from regular interchange.

Nevertheless, health professionals (especially physicians) and parents of the handicapped continue to report interaction that is unsatisfactory at best and hostile or depressing at worst. Fear, uncertainty, and anger about the disability tend to be projected between parents and professional helpers. The complexity and variability of the most severe handicapping conditions tends to influence physicians toward a pessimistic prediction; new parents frequently report having been told that an infant will never be more than a vegetable. The same complexity and variability tend to propel parents from one doctor and treatment facility to another, in search of something to treat (far preferable to accepting helplessness) or simply in search of hope. More information, experience, and cultural support are sorely needed to enhance the productivity of parent–professional communication.

Families of handicapped children have been regarded by professionals as somehow survivors of a calamity. The rarer opinion—that each family is successful, with particular strengths augmented by raising the disabled child—leads to a more useful approach to working with these families. This is an approach based on the expectation that the family being seen is the expert on its own experience, good and bad, and that the handicapped child is both part of the problem and part of the solution.

A Study of Family Functioning

The literature on handicapped children is replete with first-person stories written by parents, such as the excellent account by Featherstone (1980). Previous research with such families has been developed by means of interviews and questionnaires involving individual family members, most often mothers. Some of the data have been gathered retrospectively from siblings.

My colleagues and I carried out a longitudinal and cross-sectional study of family units of children enrolled in an urban public school district's special education program (J. Beavers & Gordon, 1983; J. Beavers, Hampson, Hulgus, & Beavers, 1986; Hampson, Beavers, & Beavers 1988). Southwest Family Institute, a private research and training organization, entered into a contractual agreement to serve families in the Dallas (Texas) Independent School District. We began with the assumption that these were ordinary families with an extraordinary task. This beginning attitude led us to our unique focus on what the families could teach us about coping as we concentrated on the current interaction of whole-family systems. We undertook the assessment of their structure, their capabilities at performing needed family functions, their ways of relating, and their observable feelings.

Our 5-year research (1980–1985) included 157 families of preschoolers (3–5 years of age at first contact) and 59 families of children at critical transition points previously defined in the literature (6–8 years, 12–14 years, and 18–21 year). Families represented the diversity of the school population with respect to race, socioeconomic background, and family composition. A wide range of physical and cognitive handicaps was included. Procedurally, the school provided a family coordinator who visited each family in its home, explained the project, and scheduled a videotape session at a school and time convenient for that family, with emphasis on participation of as many family members as possible. The first year's study focused on families with a child 3–5 years of age who was newly entering a classroom program, and encompassed 85 families. Each subsequent year, efforts were made to see these original families again, and new families were added. Over the 5-year period, 101 families were seen two or three times; 19 were available for four or five sessions at yearly intervals; and 32 sessions were conducted in families' homes, adding longitudinal and environmental dimensions. During the last 2 years, 59 additional families with children at critical transition points were interviewed, for a total of 408 interviews with 216 families.

The study of nonclinical or nonlabeled families as whole systems is a relatively new area of research. Because of the scarcity of data relative to current interaction of systems with a handicapped child, a description of our method and theoretical structure is provided. We utilized a structured interview (with questions modified as appropriate to the socioeconomic background of the participants), augmented by a 10-minute period of family play or picture drawing during which the interviewer withdrew. The approximately hour-long sessions were videotaped, making the interaction available for the family to watch if they chose, and for researchers and school personnel to view and analyze.

Analysis of the family sessions was based on the Beavers Family Assessment model of competence and style (W. R. Beavers, 1977). For readers not familiar with this model, the competence continuum measures family structure, boundaries, and the distribution of power among members; it also measures family members' autonomy, clarity of communication, ability to negotiate, feeling expression, overall mood, and conflict resolution. All observations are interactional and focused on patterns. The stylistic continuum of the model measures the family's tendency to pull members inward, emphasizing loyalty, closeness, and mutual interdependence (centripetal), or to push members outward, with emphasis on assertiveness, physical and emotional separation, and independence (centrifugal). On this model, the competence continuum moves from least to most capable; the stylistic continuum has extremes at either end, with a more desirable point in the middle.

Families were also asked to complete self-reports and to suggest advice to other families.

On the Beavers model, optimal and adequate families comprise those grouped as "healthy" (i.e., at the high end of the continuum of current capability). They have clear, flexible structure and rule systems; negotiate skillfully; encourage autonomy; allow a wide range of feelings; and have a warm, emphatic mood. Midrange families, located midway on the continuum, are clear but not very flexible in structure; negotiate with average difficulty; allow moderate individuation; are focused on control; and have more constricted feelings as well as more conflict. Borderline and severely disturbed families have either chaotic or rigidly inflexible structure; tolerate little or no individuation; are unable to negotiate or to resolve conflict; and operate in a hostile, cynical, or hopeless affective climate (W. R. Beavers, 1977).

Most Families Cope

In any family with an identifiably "different" characteristic (e.g., ethnic, extremely rich or poor, military) or member (e.g., schizophrenic, homosexual, celebrity), effective family coping is taken for granted or not noticed, while problematic family interaction is spotlighted. In our study, we discovered very early that families with a handicapped child are usually likable, always interesting, and not stereotypical; they have distinctive family personalities. Subjectively, we learned to appreciate their resourcefulness and their many strengths. Objectively, their distribution on the competence continuum was similar to that of other nonclinical families: 9% optimal, 33.5% adequate, 42% midrange, 14.5% borderline, and 1% dysfunctional. Scores of the cross-section of families with older handicapped children were higher than those of families with preschoolers, suggesting that with experience these families learn, adapt, and grow. By focusing on coping, we could validate the belief expressed by Wikler, Wasow, and Hatfield (1983) and others that chronic sorrow and increased emotional strength are by no means incompatible.

One of the interview questions in our study was a request for advice to other families in similar situations. A compilation of their responses follows (J. Beavers & Gordon, 1983).

- "Pay attention to the child. Be patient and let him know he is loved."
- "Treat the child naturally and expect her to do what she can."
- "As soon as you know your child has a problem, seek all the help available [information, programs, helping persons]. Keep looking until you feel satisfied."
- "Find things the child likes to do and work with him; the child's self-esteem grows with experience."
- "It's normal to feel anger and sadness about the problem, but you need not blame yourself or feel ashamed of the child."
- "Parents must help each other with feelings and responsibilities about their child."
- "Don't neglect the other children; spend individual time with them, too."
- "Talk about the disability naturally within the family and be open to each other's feelings about it."
- "Have as many outside experiences as possible to enjoy your life."
- "Find help and understanding wherever you can. Talk to other parents, join an organization, get counseling."

- "Don't rush things and don't give up. It takes time, and remember you and the child are learning."

These "inside views" are the foundation for our "outside" description of ways and means by which these families cope. Not only did we find that the information was instructive and useful, but the exercise of asking the families about what works invited them to reflect upon their successes and to offer some of their experience to others.

Effective Coping Patterns

Contextual Clarity about the Handicap

Beginning with the earliest recognition of something different about a child, a family's quest for clear understanding may continue over a period of several years. The need to know what is wrong, what it means, and what family members can do is a shared family task—one of varying difficulty, depending on the type of handicap. In our research sample, higher morale among families with a Down syndrome child was striking; these families have more clear and comprehensible information and feedback than do other families of the handicapped. Parental endorsement of open discussion about the disability within and outside the family, and some kind of consensus about how to describe it in words, what kinds of limitations are expected, and how to deal with those limitations, are essential for comfort and confidence. One parent often leads the way.

For example, the mother of a severely handicapped daughter described her approach when she noticed another child staring at Marie. Overcoming the temptation to say "You should't stare!", she offered, "Marie has cerebral palsy and can't talk, but she likes for people to talk to her." Thus the problem was named and its effect defined in a way that allowed both the disabled child and the stranger to get on. In the context of this kind of family clarity, the handicapped daughter's pleasant, interested facial expression during their interview seemed to be real participation.

In common with all important family tasks, becoming reasonably clear about a child's disability is largely a do-it-yourself process, and requires renewed efforts at different points in the life cycle and in response to different experiences. Out of general uncertainty reflecting society's lack of expertise about handicaps, families manage to develop needed clarity. The parents' needs for explicit understanding are amplified by the siblings' curiosity and confusion, which are in turn influenced by comments from outsiders. Foster (1986) refers to the ability of some handicapped children to explain their condition and adaptive equipment as an important social asset and means of coping with cultural prohibitions.

Structural Changes

Modification of family composition and organization is prominent in the adaptation of these families. The low percentage (36.5%) of families in our sample with both of the biological parents rearing the handicapped child suggests the frequency of restructuring after the birth of a handicapped child (though we acknowledge that the general population also shows decreasing numbers of traditional nuclear families).

What emerges with families of the handicapped are varied and distinctive kinds of parents who *choose* to assume this responsibility (i.e., stepparents or other parental figures). For some such parents, the element of choice and the absence of genetic linkage to the handicapped child can provide adaptive features. Among these are noncontamination of parental self-esteem with respect to the disability, a more objective view of the handicap, confidence in taking on a challenging parenting assignment, and a special sense of meaning and value in so doing.

In confronting the particular dilemma of parents of the handicapped—that is, "Is it that he or she *can't* or *won't* [eat unassisted, go to the toilet, follow the rules]?"—a stepparent may be more comfortable about pushing the inactive child to get past limited capabilities or setting limits for the obstreperous child who acts out. Some parents by choice—for example, grandparents—may have the luxury of total concentration on the handicapped child and less urgency.

Two other structural modifications are adaptive. First, decisions about having other children, whether negative ("We won't take on more than we can handle") or positive ("We will have a more normal family life—we and this child will have richer experiences by expanding"), affect the family's self-definition and sense of purpose. Second, involvement with members of the extended family can increase in a way that adds to all members' comfort and belief in being cared about. Although in our sample this development was described infrequently, its occurrence can be powerful and significant.

Finally, another structural change often observed in these families—increased involvement of siblings as parent helpers and substitutes—can be adaptive for families, particularly single-parent families and families with many young children. Though it might be expected that such responsibility would produce emotional distance, instead it appears to further the maturity and confidence of some older siblings.

High Level of Activity and Interaction

Families with multiple interests and involvements cope more effectively with the extra demands and the threat of "being different" posed by the disabled child. This pattern usually evolves after initial resistance to finding still more time and energy, and also after struggling with anxiety or guilt about choosing personal satisfaction if an activity does not include the disabled child. Complicated arrangements are necessary for almost any family outing, and it is difficult at best to find babysitting. Frustrating and embarrassing times in public are inevitable. Nevertheless, most families decide it is worth the effort to develop strategies for handling such situations, and they describe a dual victory: enjoying their own choices, and making a statement about the acceptability of having a handicapped child.

That family members need the satisfactions and confidence building available in the larger community may seem obvious. Fathers with more job satisfaction show less negative concern about their disabled children. For siblings, intense loyalty conflicts between endorsed attitudes of the family and expressed attitudes of peers wth regard to a disabled sister or brother can be more readily resolved by success experiences in the larger system. In one of our families (father, mother, two retarded sons, and a nonhandicapped daughter), despite extremely limited financial resources and social skills, the mother improved her own self-esteem (with corresponding elevation of the family's feeling tone) when she took on a job at her church nursery, where she was much praised for her skills with young children and was able to socialize with other adults. In another family, both parents used the term "fortunate" as they referred to their demanding but satisfying jobs, their interested extended families, their church groups, and their friends. Moving, trying, and doing are both the result and the cause of good family morale.

Problem-Solving Orientation

The absence of guidelines for assessing, rearing, and relating to the handicapped can be anxiety-producing and stressful, but it allows families to find out what works for them in their unique situations. A common successful pattern is the deliberate focus on the present and specific, concentrating on small gains and immediate responses. For example, many parents attest that appearances do matter more with these children. Attention to grooming, cleanliness, and physical fitness/ stamina, as well as to politeness and social routines, requires tremendous effort and patience but has definite payoffs.

In a family with a severely incapacitated daughter who was finally diagnosed as autistic at age 3, we initially saw the two parents (both highly capable professionals) making a radical adjustment to home life dominated by the erratic behavior of Kathy, then 2. They bent every effort to find and keep a housekeeper who was genuinely caring about Kathy; developed some new friends among couples who had young children; and concentrated their parenting on Kathy's current developmental stage of minimally responsive contentment, with occasional acquisition of partial motor skills. When we saw them a year later, they had a new, normal baby girl whose development was a delight. Kathy had regressed in temperament and capability, and they worked on surviving her unrelenting and insatiable demands. The third and fourth years found them relating to Kathy in a more direct, practical way—learning from the housekeeper, from Kathy's little sister (whose development was a powerful but not always positive influence on Kathy), and from school personnel what approaches and contexts produced better results, rather than expecting an upward progression of skills and maturity.

The problem-solving approach is also illustrated by allowing individual family members to perform in nonstereotyped ways. For example, fathers, if so inclined, can provide most of the nurturing for handicapped children, while mothers attend to executive functions with regard to siblings' outside activities. Siblings can choose and manage their degree of involvement with a disabled child differently at different times. Getting the job done (eating a meal, toilet training, arranging supervision for the disabled child) is the focus, and it can be accomplished in more than one way.

The manifestations of this approach include minimal guilt, tolerance for trial and error (and sometimes for failure), and a rather matter-of-fact stance seen in parents and siblings. These qualities, of course, in a circular fashion, are also contributors to successful problem solving.

Self-Consciousness as a Positive Element

Families under this kind of pressure appear to become more conscious of how they work. Members can usually describe roles played by each person and how they influence each other. They express pride in overcoming difficulties, in taking risks, and in charting their own paths. They also tend to compare themselves favorably with other families with handicapped children and with outsiders' ways of relating to handicapped persons.

Some of the parents in our sample articulated a belief that "I am [we are] somebody because of this needful child," or "I feel like a good person," or "We are a good family." There is a cheerleading aspect to this pattern—admittedly with a slight element of coercion, which places the noncompliant at risk of isolation. The overall result, however, is a kind of infectious optimism that appears to be stimulating, produces *esprit de corps,* and directs much of the anger generated by the problem of differentness toward "those other people who couldn't do as well."

Conscious Balancing

Many observers have described the delicate balance between acceptance and pushing, protectiveness and toughness, that is required of parents of the handicapped. Sometimes these opposite forces are split between two parents and are regularly negotiated. More often, various family members are advocates of one or the other approach at different times. The balancing also expresses twin understandings of how a disabled child is like the rest of us and how he or she is different.

Balancing of family cohesion and individual needs is also a prominent part of coping. Often arising from a sibling's complaint about essential unfairness of different family rules for the disabled member, this kind of balancing requires parental responsiveness and flexibility. The results of good balance are seen in increased autonomy for all family members, and in greater ability to manage life cycle transitions.

Expressiveness

Expressiveness, a problematic but vitally important aspect of family rules, assumes great importance when, in addition to the usual delights, frustrations, and losses of ordinary living, a mixture of feelings about the handicap must be managed. Freedom to acknowledge their resentment, sadness, and fears helps family members arrive at some resolution of their ambivalence and reduces loneliness and guilt. Siblings and handicapped children are notably less constrained in families that encourage expressive flexibility. A disabled child's difficult moods, angry opposition, and loneliness are recognized by family members as evidence that "this child is human like me."

A related coping pattern consists of enjoyment of the nonrational, play, and humor—often excellent outlets for aversive reactions to unchangeable circumstances. This includes the possibility that family members can make fun of their own futile efforts to produce a particular response from the disabled child; this was something we saw frequently in our sample.

Reframing the Role of the Handicapped Child

Here the focus is on the loveable or enjoyable. In a culture that measures children (and adults) by attractiveness, achievement, and talent the families of disabled children often experience an inverse ratio between their investment of resources, energy, and affection in the disabled children and the larger system's definition of the value of the children and the worth of their endeavors. A coping pattern developed naturally among subcultures that believe in the enjoyment and worthwhileness of caring for babies and young children; it can be enacted with mothers, grandmothers, aunts, adult siblings, and assorted children including the handicapped child, interacting in a manner characterized by easy give-and-take. This kind of family is seldom seen by (i.e., does not need) a therapist. What many families cultivate, however, is a pattern based on defining the child as endearingly fragile (if physical incapacity is prominent) or as family pet (if unpredictable behavior predominates). The child's unchangeable traits become a useful focus for relieving pressure and providing direct or vicarious pleasure derived from the child's innocence, mischief, clumsiness, and generally uninhibited behavior. (These patterns obviously diminish in usefulness as the child grows and matures.)

Other kinds of reframing appear to enable parents to develop a sense of meaning: "I protect this innocent child in a cruel world." "If not me [us], who would do this?" Difficulties presented by the child's deficits can also be viewed as evidence that the parents are uniquely capable and willing to do a hard job. The teenage mother who says she has come to realize that she must be an adult, or the single mother who says that because of her child she must carry on, are struggling with constructive reframing. Increased capabilities can develop from the inescapable dependency of a disabled child, and in circular response to the enlarged capabilities, family members can feel stronger and more loving. Parents frequently report that they have developed more patience than they believed they could possess. One mother, accustomed to defining herself as fragile (with a history of psychiatric hospitalization after the birth of the disabled child) and overdependent on her mother and husband, described learning to be and feel strong and brave enough to locate resources for her child and also to hold her own in parent–teacher conferences. The child in this family had visibly expanded and had become more competent.

Values

In addition to having a sense of purpose and taking pride in reaching out and going beyond, families with a disabled child appear to develop more explicit awareness of what is important and valuable to them. Foster (1986) comments that a developmental disability requires the family to deal with its core values. Parents and normal siblings verbalize and demonstrate concern for the less fortunate, compassion, tolerance, and patience. Many parents refer to "smelling the roses" (focusing on everyday pleasures), keenly appreciating their own and other people's normal children, being more aware of their partner's strengths, and being grateful for friendships. Religious beliefs were emphasized as essential by many families in our sample.

Pitfalls for Families

The degree to which a family is organized around a handicapped child is the key to successful or problematic adaptation. Similarly, the frequency of family members' viewing all events through the lens of differentness tells us much about their coping. Some more specific areas of difficulty are as follows.

Confused Context

As contextual clarity is the first coping essential, confusion about the nature and severity of the handicap is a major pitfall. Some handicaps are much easier to classify and understand; others, particularly the nonvisible ones, challenge the best families and professionals. Additional sources of confusion are cultural biases (e.g., religious beliefs that physical limitations are not real, or that proper religious faith will remove the handicap and blind spots in family traditions or in individual family members' emotional makeup. The uncontrollable child can be defined as not quite human; the severely incapacitated child can be defined as an invalid.

In a family with minimal or distorted understanding about the kind of handicap, its implications, and what can and cannot be done about it, one sees an atmosphere of unreality, depression (mixed with false cheerfulness), blocked communication, and isolation of the disabled child. The most dysfunctional parents ignore, do not recognize, or deny a child's problems, leaving that child at the mercy of whoever shows interest. In a slightly more competent family, rigidly authoritarian in structure, the dominant parent may subordinate the wishes and needs of all other family members to the goal of protecting or promoting the disabled child. Midrange families, striving for absolutes, show more strain in their efforts to arrive at the "right" way to develop and socialize their handicapped children. They may try to get answers from teachers and therapists, and some will be bitterly resentful if absolutes are not provided, or if the rules do not work with their children.

One such (midrange, control-oriented) family in our sample consisted of a recently separated father and mother whose daughter, aged 3, had a puzzling, hard-to-classify combination of physical and intellectual deficits. She related to family members and outsiders erratically. At times she was clinging or aggressive about making contact, but at other times she appeared indifferent. The mother, having carried almost total responsibility for the child after the father moved out of the home, sought advice desperately. Apparently becoming more dogmatic as the mother became more frantic, the father pontificated during the session that his daughter was really just the same as *he* had been all his life, "a square peg in a round hole." The paternal grandparents, who were usually involved only peripherally, participated in the session by vying with each other to demonstrate their keen interest, special knowledge, and intuition about the problem and how to treat it (e.g., "Steer her into drama or music"). In subsequent interviews, the father and his parents distanced themselves more and more, leaving a depressed mother with her frustrating search for a clear diagnosis and for an institution or resource that would tell her what to do. The child also became more inaccessible.

Another midrange family had a severely cerebral-palsied child and two normal younger siblings. The mother, the dominant parent, focused on the little girl's reportedly normal intelligence and denied the importance of her total inability to speak or to move. With phenomenal energy and determination, the mother pushed the other family members and the outside world beyond any reasonable limits— first immersing family and neighbors in exhaustive Doman–Delacato patterning, then coercing school authorities to mainstream the child, and feeling bitterly criticized and critical when these efforts failed to produce improved capability in the little girl. During this time, the parents' expressed differences became much sharper in tone; the mother's affect became more cynical and the father's more distant.

The parents sued the obstetrician who had delivered the child, and the father's concluding comment to us was this: "Knowing what I do now about her quality of life, I wouldn't have wanted the doctor to save her."

Parental Coalition Disturbances

Lack of clarity about the child's abilities and management increases the likelihood of unresolvable marital or parental coalition conflict (J. Beavers *et al.*, 1986). For a conventional married pair, cultural myths assume that a normal, healthy baby validates the marriage; an abnormal child raises irrational but troublesome doubts: "What does this mean about us?" "Did I do this to you?" "Did you do this to me?" Without shared acknowledgment that these feelings exist, numbing and distancing will follow, as with any unmourned loss.

The risks of projecting half of the conflicted feelings ("Don't expect anything of this poor little one, just be loving and supportive") onto the partner, while battling for the other half of the feelings, ("Pushing and firmness are what the kid needs to survive"), are substantial. One parent's overresponsibility for the handicapped child is often reciprocal with the withdrawal or acting out of the other parent. Clearly, the significance of parental interaction is intensified. Asked about the effect of the handicapped child on their getting along with each other, many parents give a conventional response: "It has brought us closer." Differences in philosophy and style can become either painful and alienating, or complementary and mutually reinforcing. The balance is not static.

Working with these differences as complementary can have beneficial effects, as it did with young, two-career parents whose first child was deaf and who also had two nonimpaired younger children. When first seen, the family appeared to be dominated by the mother's self-doubts; she expressed these in flat tones with a kind of pessimistic irony about herself and the deaf daughter, while the father remained pleasantly in the background. In the course of several sessions, the father, who showed better self-esteem and a preference for accentuating the positive, was encouraged to become more active. He had a lot to say about the assets of all three children and their family life, and during the sessions he demonstrated genuine enjoyment of the children. The mother then began talking about her reliance on the father's warmth and strength, while she continued to be the spokesperson for what they wanted to improve and change. Each parent spontaneously referred to very different models of child rearing in their families of origin, out of which they had developed a version distinctively their own. The deaf child became more confident and outgoing, and the younger siblings maintained competitive, lively, and apparently equal interaction with her.

On the other hand, a couple with two profoundly multiply handicapped daughters demonstrated progressive discouragement with the passage of time about their inability to do more than just stay afloat as they struggled with the overwhelming demands of the children. This father, like the father described above, made many efforts to play enjoyably with his daughters, despite their lack of response. When he repeatedly verbalized wistfulness about time out for some kind of recreation, play, or intimacy with his wife, her response hardened into a conviction that this was impossible, a dead issue. Apparently having functioned very capably prior to their double catastrophe, and with a history of energetic demands on the school and other systesm, she now felt too depleted to be a wife.

When the more discouraged or estranged parent withdraws, the handicapped child tends to become even less responsive. Disabled children with parents locked in unresolved conflict appear to be depressed.

Boundary Problems

The involvement of professional helpers from the time of a handicapped child's birth affects external boundaries in such a family. Combrinck-Graham and Higley (1984) note the prolonged and extensive need of the disabled child for a parent to accompany and assist him or her in outside settings, resulting in the delay or impossibility of independent movement that furthers differentiation. They also point to the more acute awareness of difference for the parents and the handicapped child when the child enters school. Alteration or absence of ordinary social rituals marking normative transition points for the handicapped, such as birth, school entry, adolescence, and leaving home, is described by Imber-Black (1987) as en-hancing family members' sense of differentness. When parents are more isolated from families of origin and friends, outside systems become more important, and agency control over vital services adds intensity and emotionality to these con-tacts. Hence, external boundaries are more permeable to professionals, who mod-ify family relationships for good or ill, and are less permeable to peers and social relationships.

A couple referred by their child's neurologist for help with the wife's depres-sion following birth of a microcephalic child reported their decision not to con-verse with other parents. The wife in particular felt that she had nothing in com-mon with other mothers now, and she wanted to protect herself from even more painful awareness of what she was missing. In therapy, the couple became freer to talk about their mixed feelings, and the wife agreed to venture first by making a clear statement to one neighbor about the baby's abnormality. As she was grad-ually able to reveal their dilemma to others, she not only learned that her experi-ences and reactions were not so aberrant, but also began to take responsibility for influencing their responses.

Within the family, generational boundaries are also vulnerable. Fixed alli-ances between a handicapped child and one parent are a risk. Often the mother concentrates on the handicapped child; the father focuses on other issues, with-draws, or acts out; and the siblings are relatively underparented. Combrinck-Gra-ham and Higley (1984) illustrate how a therapist can work toward strengthening the parental system and can increase the autonomy of the handicapped child and normal siblings.

In single-parent families, another boundary issue can develop: Rivalry between parentified older siblings and the parent can be as intense as that between conflicted mother and father.

Featherstone (1980) states that the handicapped child often remains outside the sibling subsystem. Only when siblings are very young (under 3 or 4 years of age) are the usual sibling-versus-parent alliances (to maneuver, communicate, or rebel) possible. Regardless of chronological age, the disabled child usually has the role of the youngest, and some of the family rules remain different for this child.

Problems for Siblings

Featherstone (1980) describes embarrassment, identification (with the differentness), and confusion as individual sibling pitfalls. Interactionally, with parents who may inadvertently or by choice be less responsive to the normal siblings, siblings may in turn try too hard to be good—to avoid making demands or causing problems of any kind. Some siblings become virtually invisible. Others are extruded or voluntarily go outside the family for the kinds of contact and experience they need; overwhelmed parents may ignore or even welcome this trend. Siblings can become scapegoats, the receptacle for parents' painful disappointments. The handicapped child can also be scapegoated, providing a ready explanation for everything that is unsatisfying in family life.

A frequently observed adaptation in families with other covert stressors (e.g., marital conflict, anger about a departed parent, conflict with family of origin), in addition to a handicapped member, is the pseudoadult behavior of siblings who try too hard and seem terribly self-conscious. Many of the families of the disabled have older or younger siblings who are unusually bright, outgoing, and confident; there is a qualitative difference between such children and pseudoadult siblings who feel responsible for holding things together, putting up a front, distracting unhappy parents, or the like.

Communicative Deficits

Basic cues and responses are impaired, missing, or radically altered between most of the developmentally disabled and the other family members. Coalitions (usually parent–child, less often siblings–child) are often formed out of one member's greater ability to communicate with a disabled child, and these can be used to distance other family members. Baker (1984) points to the limited effectiveness of verbal means of getting an autistic, retarded, or hearing-impaired child's attention. Family members must rely more on modeling and physical guidance, which require a more conscious, patient, and well-planned effort.

As indicated earlier, freedom to express a wide range of feelings is a key indicator of family competence. That families inhibit negative, resentful, sad, and aversive feelings toward and about the handicapped child has been described by Featherstone (1980) and others, and was documented in our research. Cultural prohibitions reinforce the controls on criticism or complaint about a central reality in the lives of these families. The members need to relieve their anxieties, and also need each other's understanding and problem-solving skills with regard to "telling it like it is" without feeling bad or mean.

Dealing with the stares, questions, or behavior of outsiders in response to a disabled member begins with the first family outing. Given the relative helplessness of the child in question, family members feel called upon to speak for that child, to present him or her in the best possible light, and to maintain their own dignity. In this, as in many problem areas involving strong emotions, intelligence is not necessarily a reliable guide to successful conduct.

Vulnerability to Additional Stressors

A family coping with the extraordinary assignment of a disabled child may demonstrate marked vulnerability to other major, ongoing family stresses, such as financial hardship, health problems, and cultural pressures. (As one example of cultural pressures, members of the black middle class in our study were often quite sensitive to the threat to their hard-won social security posed by this family phenomenon.) Family resources are indeed impressive, but finite. With multiple major stresses, one finds, under the surface, heavy anxiety or a kind of flat depression. Losses, such as death, divorce, or unemployment, will also hit these families harder.

One family, mother and stepfather of a boy with Down syndrome, had seemed to reach a workable partnership after a long struggle with the mother's timidity and the stepfather's overconfidence (about proper child psychology). Their delicate balance was destroyed when the stepfather lost his job, making it necessary for them to move in with the mother's family, where the maternal grandmother waged all-out war on the stepfather's disciplinary efforts.

Treatment Implications

In the light of this new knowledge about these families' abilities to find unique ways to manage their own particular problems, clinical work with such families takes an unusual turn. Instead of offering his or her expertise, the family therapist joins these families with acknowledgment of *their* expertise, derived from their own histories of experiences with physical and cognitive handicaps. These experiences encompass characteristic anxieties about dependency, differentness, and uncertainty—personal frameworks with which therapists are advised to be familiar. Helpers of families of the disabled must inevitably confront, at some level, their own feelings of consternation, pity, and (eventually) fears of chronic sorrow.

Family members join the therapist with histories of contacts with other helpers: physicians, teachers, and various kinds of therapists. Imber-Black (1987) refers to "critical incidents" with larger systems that shape families' beliefs. They have managed their dependency on outsiders for the definition of a child's problem and outlook and for the provision of services (special education, special medical care, special recreation). Such contacts may have been contradictory and confusing, or they may have been clear and helpful. They produce varying degrees of threat to family members' self-esteem in a culture that values independence more than almost any other trait. Family members are likely to be prepared for little or no positive feedback about the special child. Physicians in particular are often described by families as "treating the child like a case," failing to individualize and sometimes appearing to avoid physical touching of the child. (Physical contact may be particularly significant in therapy with such children.)

Families usually visualize professionals as quite powerful in either negative or positive ways. On their side, helpers frequently have genuine doubts about their power to change things for these families. Yet most helpers do want to respond to a family's expectations, and may have additional wishes to compensate for the family's previous unhappy experiences with professionals, or to atone for the blow dealt this family by fate.

The first principle of treatment is support for the family's coping, finding out (from each member) what the family does well. Families in our research avoided answering a direct question about this ("What do you feel you have done well in your family in raising _____ so far?"), but did offer comments and evidence of good coping as they talked about other things. Only the family can tell the therapist how it is to live with this handicapped child. Wikler (1981) suggest asking about the child's unique traits that give family members pleasure and asking for stories of familial successes in coping.

The therapist must, as always, assess the family. Assessment features distinctive for these families are extracted from our research findings and include the following:

1. How clear is the understanding of the handicap? The literature offers many ways to categorize handicapping conditions: physical factors, intellectual factors, appearance, mannerisms, seizures, speech, and others. In a child, these usually appear in combinations, and in a young child, most of the traits are hard to quantify. (The school district in which we worked had previously attempted a method of scoring that combined IQ, orthopedic, sensory, health, and other criteria, but found this so unsatisfactory that its use was discontinued.) From a family context, three elements appear most significant: overall dependency, physical incapacity (including sensory deficits), and difficult personality characteristics.

The therapist, then, needs to understand the family's definition of the handicap—probably the factor that most influences family members' adaptation. This therapeutic inquiry addresses not only their labels and their clarity about how the child is affected, but also their beliefs about the cause(s) and the meaning of this child's disability. Family members' blame or guilt about having caused the handicap or having failed to deal with it adequately has been linked by many observers to the most serious damage seen in family interaction. Therapists must therefore be alert to guilt and blame factors, and equipped with information as well as expertise in the resolution of guilt.

All family members, including the handicapped child, need acknowledgment of their feelings about the disability, and about family values (e.g., pressure to achieve) that contribute to distress in this family.

Helping a family select words to use that are comfortable and clear for that family is a valuable therapeutic task. Foster (1986) points out that the family members' interaction accurately demonstrates their understanding of the child's limitations. Their possible preference for a milder term than "mentally retarded," for example, is not evidence of denial. Foster also suggests using techniques such as drawings, mutual storytelling, or puppets to learn how the disabled child perceives the handicap and to modify misconceptions about it. With families who are stuck, it is probably necessary to spend considerable time on this issue—helping family members listen as well as talk, offering more active direction of who talks, and insuring that the disabled child has opportunity to get what he or she needs in the way of assurance and attention.

2. What social networks are available, and what has the family experienced with them? Current family and child involvements with extended family, friends, other helping professionals, and agencies affect the family's willingness to use a family therapist. Networks, which can be both supportive and intrusive, can be useful to the therapy—in fact, sometimes can be the channel through which change can best be accomplished. The family therapist is thus placed in more of a "case manager" role, which is then provided to the family with the needs of the whole family in perspective.

3. To what degree is the handicapped child the hub of the family wheel? Good coping means that this child is a significant but not an overriding feature of family life. Indicators include family members' activities at home and outside, as well as observed family interaction.

Family therapy can be directed at reducing the rather automatic overprotection of the disabled child that results from the family's usual experience. Since both child and parents contribute to this pattern, intervention may occur with either or both parts of the family system, via coaching, challenging, teaching, or playing. Foster (1986) reminds us that maximizing a child's energy for change minimizes the parents' resistance.

4. Are there unusual coalitions (parent with handicapped child, parent with sibling helper, sibling helper with handicapped child) and functions served by such coalitions? Their influence on other family members and on the whole system is the therapist's guide to whether and how they require challenging, unbalancing, reframing, and so on.

5. Is there permission to express varied feelings, ask questions, and talk about

important issues regarding the handicap? The therapist can be very useful in making implicit themes available for family negotiation. This is an area in which referral to parent support groups may be equally beneficial.

6. What are the family values and family morale in relation to the presence of a disabled child? The therapist's support for what the family has learned and accomplished is an integral part of their making sense of their extraordinary situation.

Clinical Example

A couple seen initially during a marital separation reunited and had their first child, who at age 3 was diagnosed as autistic and slightly retarded. (The marital therapist was aware of some sense of responsibility for the existence of this child.) The family was medically sophisticated and clearly understood what was wrong, without apparent guilt or blame. They were financially secure, possessed good social networks of friends, and had a significant religious affiliation, but their values and aspirations clearly pointed to unremitting excellence in appearance, achievement, verbal skills, and character traits.

The mother returned to the therapist after the diagnosis, with concerns about her inability to set limits. The child's behavior was so foreign to her high standards, and elicited responses that were so deviant from her ideal of herself as a loving mother, that she was in despair. She stated that their miserable home life caused her husband to stay away more and more.

With the therapist's help, the mother gained more assurance about managing the little boy, but soon went to the opposite extreme, using rigid overcontrol that demanded all her energy. The resulting tension produced no more inducement for the father to be a part of things than the previous chaos had.

Strenuous efforts to involve the father in the therapy resulted in a shared parental search for ways to enjoy their son, by any means agreeable to both. The father began to roughhouse with the boy, and, somewhat to his own surprise, did have some fun with their play. With the support of a husband/partner, and her own determination to enjoy mothering (vigorously endorsed by the therapist), the mother's morale improved markedly.

The parents subsequently adopted a daughter and returned to the therapist from time to time for reinforcement of their couple and parenting strategies. The adoptive sister, who was younger than the disabled child, began to behave in a rather self-conscious, prim, and cautious manner, reflecting in part the parents' overconcern about having chosen her and hence having placed her in an environment with this kind of chronic difficulty. The therapist helped the members come to terms with their real family, which had pluses and minuses and which offered a great deal to each of them, and the child became more childlike and appealing.

The families in our study were nonclinical families, and it was not our purpose to offer therapy to them. But the information gained about family functioning from the study has been helpful in approaching therapy for families who are not coping well. The clinical example illustrates the application of some of the principles learned from coping families, particularly the payoff from strenuous efforts to involve both spouses in the care of and interaction with the handicapped child, and the focus on a sibling as needing differential consideration as a child in the family.

Conclusion

Family therapists can best help families of children with physical and cognitive handicaps by identifying their unique experiences and coping patterns, and by directing efforts at (1) freeing families from constraints and misconceptions about the nature and cause of the handicap, and (2) utilizing the motivations, problem-solving skills, and values of all family members (including the handicapped children).

It is important for family therapists to keep in mind that most families do cope with this extraordinary experience, and to look within the families themselves for the strengths that can carry them beyond the moments of difficulty inevitably experienced by them. If therapists approach such systems without a proper respect for the unique ways these families find to handle their special situations, they stand a very good chance of becoming a part of the problem rather than assisting with solutions.

REFERENCES

Baker, B. L. (1984). Intervention with families with young, severely handicapped children. In J. Blacker (Ed.), *Severely handicapped young children and their families* (pp. 319–375). New York: Academic Press.

Beavers, J., & Gordon, I. (1983). *Learning from families*. Dallas, TX: Dallas Independent School District.

Beavers, J., Hampson, R. B., Hulgus, Y., & Beavers, W. R. (1986). Coping in families with a retarded child. *Family Process, 25,* 365–378.

Beavers, W. R. (1977). *Psychotherapy and growth*. New York: Brunner/Mazel.

Combrinck-Graham, L., & Higley, L. W. (1984). Working with families of school-aged handicapped children. In E. I. Coppersmith (Ed.), *Families with handicapped members* (pp. 18–29). Rockville, MD: Aspen.

Featherstone, H. (1980). *A difference in the family*. New York: Basic Books.

Foster, M. A. (1986). Families with young disabled children in family therapy. In L. Combrinck-Graham (Ed.), *Treating young children in family therapy* (pp. 62–72). Rockville, MD: Aspen.

Hampson, H., Beavers, J., & Beavers, W. R. (1988). Assessment of competency in families with a retarded child. *Family Psychology, 2.*

Imber-Black, E. (1987). The mentally handicapped in context. *Family Systems Medicine, 5* (4), 428–445.

Wikler, L. (1981). Family therapy with families of mentally retarded children. In A. S. Gurman (Ed.), *Questions and answers in the practice of family therapy* (Vol. 1, pp 129–132). New York: Brunner/Mazel.

Wikler, L., Wasow, M., & Hatfield, E. (1983). Seeking strengths in families of developmentally disabled children. *Social Work, 28* (4), 313–315.

10

Chronic Illness and Family Coping

JUDITH A. LIBOW, PhD

A child's chronic illness inevitably tests a family's emotional, organizational, financial, and adaptive resources. The unrelenting demands of medical treatment and adaptation to special needs and constant change take their toll on many families with vulnerable children. There is an extensive individual and family therapy literature focused on the damaging effects of illness on individual family members and the family structure itself. Problems such as family isolation (McKeever, 1983), overinvolvement of an ill child and a caretaker parent (Penn, 1983; Walker, 1983), maternal depression (Drotar, Crawford, & Bush, 1984; Velasco de Parra, Davila de Cortazar, & Covarrubias-Espinoza, 1983), and emotional problems in siblings (Spinetta & Deasy-Spinetta, 1981) as well as the chronically ill child (Brunnquell & Hall, 1982; Hughes, 1982) have been written about extensively. Interestingly, there is very little literature on the strengths of families with chronically ill children, their adaptive styles, or the elements of medical care most facilitative of effective family coping.

Yet many families with similar circumstances and hardships manage to successfully meet the challenges of the illness as well as the needs of their ill children and other family members, despite the ongoing problems of pain, disruption, uncertainty, family reorganization, and possibly life-threatening changes as the days go by. An examination of the relationship between chronic illness and family coping not only should help in the development of effective therapy approaches for families struggling with the demands of chronic illness, but also should sug-

Judith A. Libow. Children's Hospital Medical Center of Northern California, Oakland, CA.

gest useful preventive measures early in the identification of these families. The process of coping with serious illness shows us, in exaggerated form, the strengths and liabilities of all families. In addition, the study of families with chronically ill children highlights the significant multiple layers of systems in dynamic interaction with young families. And it points to the kinds of resources and social supports that larger systems can offer to families struggling with all kinds of adversity.

Chronic Illness and Children

It has been estimated that between 6% and 12% of all children in the United States have a serious chronic illness (Hobbs, Perrin, & Ireys, 1985; Hughes, 1982). An even more significant percentage of families are coping daily with chronic illness when we include adult members of the family, such as parents or grandparents. Although there are many definitions of "chronic illness," for the purposes of this chapter I use a very broad definition that includes lifelong diseases such as diabetes, cystic fibrosis, or sickle cell anemia; chronic medical problems accompanying genetic syndromes; and physical handicaps resulting from serious accidents, such as burns or spinal cord injuries.

Herz (1980) suggests that the greatest overall impact on a family is caused by the illness of a family member in the prime of life with the greatest family responsibilities. Clearly, the illness of the family homemaker or breadwinner can have devastating emotional, financial, and structural consequences for the family unit. However, a child's chronic illness has the potential of being the most emotionally devastating to the family unit. A range of factors will determine the effect of a particular child's illness on a particular family system, including aspects of the illness itself, developmental status of the affected child and family system, and the larger context of community and social supports.

Illness Dimensions

Rolland (1984) has established a very useful categorization of illness dimensions to help weigh the likely impact of a particular condition on a particular family. His major dimensions include onset (acute or gradual), course of illness (progressive, constant, or relapsing), outcome (fatal or nonfatal), and degree of incapacitation. Each of these illness dimensions and the many potential combinations of dimensions puts a different kind, intensity, and pattern of demands on the patient and family. For example, a nonfatal, gradual, nonincapacitating, but relapsing condition (e.g., ulcerative colitis) would clearly provide a different time frame and stress pattern than would a fatal, gradual, incapacitating, and progressive illness (e.g., AIDS). As Rolland points out, an analysis of these illness features helps us to organize our understanding of the psychosocial impact of a particular illness and the levels of adaptability, problem solving, role reallocation, and cohesion that are called for by that illness.

The illness of a child in a family generally requires a family to organize itself to be available on a flexible, unpredictable schedule, and to provide unlimited quantities of support and reassurance to allay the anxiety and emotional pain of its members. The family must develop creative means of integrating the ill child with the community and its institutions, and must develop its own ways of administering treatments and discipline. And the family must develop appropriate expectations for the child whose physical and emotional development deviates significantly from the norm for his or her peers.

Although Rolland's (1984) illness dimensions are designed for all age groups, several other dimensions are also significant for the particular impact of children's chronic conditions on their families. For example, three dimensions—pain, deformity, and treatment ambiguity—are also relevant to the emotional impact of a child's illness on the family system. In my own experience, conditions such as leukemia, where the chemotherapy treatments can cause the child great suffering, or juvenile rheumatoid arthritis, where the disease itself can be exceedingly painful, are likely to trigger more emotional intensity and parental response than chronic but essentially silent conditions such as cardiac disease. Suffering on the part of any family member is not easy for a family to tolerate, but it appears to be more successfully tolerated when family members are not overly enmeshed.

Physical deformity, such as that accompanying some genetic syndromes (e.g., trisomy 13) or severe burn scarring is often a powerful cause of parental shame (Wisely, Masur, & Morgan, 1983). Not only can the deformity cause injury to the child's own body image and self-esteem, but it can focus public attention on a child's differentness. The parent may perceive the deformity as an open wound and feel public shame for the failure to produce a "perfect" child or protect the child from suffering. Families that cope relatively well with physical deformity are often those with strong yet permeable boundaries with the outside community, and enough differentiation of family members to allow deformed children to represent themselves in the world outside the family. Effective boundaries with the community are particularly important for such a family, because the system needs to be able to provide adequate emotional protection for the child from the rejection of strangers, counterbalanced by acceptance within a well-defined family unit; exposure to the larger community can thus be gradually titrated.

"Treatment ambiguity" refers to the degree of parental judgment or discretion involved in administering treatments to the young patient. Whereas some conditions (e.g., some cases of epilepsy) involve a standard or unambiguous treatment for the child's condition, other illnesses (e.g., asthma) may involve a fairly complex regimen of multiple medications and considerable parental discretion as to when and how to respond to each new crisis. An increasing degree of parental discretion can be directly related to increasing parental vigilance, anxiety, involvement with the ill child, and sense of personal accountability for treatment "success" or "failure." Families that cope well with treatment ambiguity generally have a strong executive subsystem and a supportive relationship with their children's medical caregivers.

These three dimensions of pain, deformity, and treatment ambiguity can be usefully included in a formulation of salient illness features. Children's suffering, their physical differentness, and parental responsibility for treatment are very powerful emotional triggers for most parents. Especially when children are young, the important parenting task is to produce and nurture healthy children, protect them from pain, and help them adjust to their peer group. Chronic illnesses involving significant pain, deformity, or treatment ambiguity have a double potential for difficulty for families, in that they tend to encourage an even greater than usual degree of emotional dependency of children on the parents, while they provide fertile ground for feelings of parental failure. That so many families can weather these potential pitfalls is a tribute to the resiliency and adaptiveness of many family systems.

The Child as Patient

If we look for a moment at the child apart from his or her family unit, we see that chronic illness dimensions interact with equally complex features of the individual child responding to his or her illness. Chronic illnesses have their onset or first serious exacerbation at different ages and developmental stages, ranging, for example, from the early onset and identification of hemophilia in one child to the onset at adolescence of diabetes in another. Age at onset will be an important determinant of the degree to which the demands of the illness are integrated into the child's life style, self-concept, and family organization. Children who have grown up with restrictive diets, complex medication regimens, frequent hospitalizations, or dependency on machines from earliest memory are likely to have a very different relationship to their illness (and to families) than are children who are well until an acute onset of illness in middle childhood or late adolescence. One would expect the child who has been chronically ill from early life to have developed relationships and behavior patterns more compatible with the demands of the illness. This life style may serve the child relatively well, at least until the very new psychosocial stresses of later developmental periods (especially adolescence) demand new adaptations, particularly in the realm of increasing autonomy. And the same chronic lung, blood, or endocrine disease is likely to create a different set of challenges to children at different ages. For a 7-year-old it largely represents an upsetting interruption in peer activities and school life, or perhaps anxiety-provoking separations from family members. To a 16-year-old, the chronic disease is likely to generate issues of differentness from peers, a threat to a body image of intactness and attractiveness, and significant anxiety about prolonged dependency and shortened life span.

Paralleling the developmental needs of children at different ages is the issue of cognitive development and childrens' understanding of illness and body processes. The difference in childrens' understanding at different ages/developmental levels certainly is related to the age of onset of an illnesss and how it is conceptualized by a young patient. A substantial and interesting literature (Bibace & Walsh, 1981; Blos, 1978; Neuhauser, Amsterdam, Hines, & Steward, 1978; Steward & Steward, 1981) details the complexities for children of understanding how their bodies work, how illnesses affect their body functions, and how medical treatments relate to the healing process. This research utilizes a Piagetian framework of childrens' cognitive development. It demonstrates the evolution of childrens' concepts of health and illness along a developmental continuum from very global, primitive concepts at young ages to more fully elaborated, formal operational thinking in adolescence.

There is some limited but very interesting research suggesting that chronically ill children, despite their considerable medical experience and presumed sophistication, are in fact functioning at an unexpectedly lower level of cognitive understanding of illness than are well children (Whitt, 1982). Similar surprising findings are reported for the siblings of diabetic children relative to siblings of well children (Carandang, Folkins, Hines, & Steward, 1979). Whether this depressed cognitive performance in relation to understanding of illness reflects the stress and heightened affect associated with chronic illness, as suggested by Whitt (1982) and Carandang et al. (1979), or whether it indicates some sort of fixation of concepts acquired during an earlier developmental period of illness onset is difficult to determine. A more positive interpretation is that this limitation in comprehension of the illness process may reflect an adaptive response to the dependency and helplessness that some children experience in regard to their illness. At a minimum, it suggests that clinicians should not assume that chronically ill children or their siblings are necessarily operating with mature or appropriate conceptualizations of their illnesses, treatments, or bodies, despite years of living with their conditions and interacting with the medical system. In fact, Perrin and Perrin (1983) found that the medical caregivers they surveyed were quite inaccurate in their assessments of childrens' beliefs about and understandings of health and illness. This kind of misunderstanding of childrens' beliefs by medical care providers certainly poses problems for effective communication, as well as for development of a strong working alliance with young patients.

It could also be true in some cases that the caregivers' working relationship with relevant adults may be based on an inaccurate picture of the parents' level of understanding. It would be very interesting to examine the conceptualizations of caregivers about the parents with whom they collaborate, as well as the beliefs of parents of chronically ill children about the processes of healing or treatment facilitated by the different therapies they help administer. Parents' beliefs may be particularly distorted or idiosyncratic, given the high anxiety and emotionality of many parents with respect to their children's health. The invisibility and mystery of many conditions, such as pulmonary diseases and oncological diseases, can also contribute to distortion of understanding. Parents coping with conditions whose etiology or management is poorly understood even by physicians are certainly susceptible to superstitious or self-blaming theories of illness causation and to unrealistic expectations of outcome. Many parents experience at least as much

stress and affect as their chronically ill children; yet the majority actively collaborate in their children's care and perform elaborate and sometimes unpleasant
home caretaking functions (e.g., gastrostomy feedings, nasogastric feedings,
changing of tracheostomies) without professional training or even thorough comprehension.

Factors Affecting Family Coping

As Mitchell and Rizzo (1985) point out in their paper on families of handicapped
adolescents, it is inaccurate and naive to assume that the presence of a handicapped child in a family must necessarily result in parental maladjustment or a
"catastrophically negative influence" on the family. In addition to all the significant dimensions of each child's specific chronic condition and each child's individual development and cognitive level, significant factors in the family system
itself and in the larger systems with which families interact predispose the family
to effective or ineffective coping.

Stage of the Family Life Cycle

The age of onset of a child's chronic condition is significant, not only because
it determines the young patient's level of understanding and degree of dependency
on parents, but because it also determines the stage of the family life cycle at
which the family unit first confronts the challenge of illness. As Carter and
McGoldrick (1980) indicate, family members face different demands and stresses
at various points along the time line of family life. The intrusion of a serious
chronic illness at any point in the family time line is difficult, but families seem
better suited to handling the demands of certain stages. And if a chronic illness
happens to surface during an already stressful period in the family life cycle,
greater difficulties can be predicted. For example, young spouses who are having
significant problems with the redistribution of household tasks and the loss of time
and privacy due to their transition to parenthood are in danger of being overwhelmed by the additional demands of a baby's chronic heart condition. When
they have weathered the strain of early family life, this same couple may find
themselves considerably more competent at caring for school-age children, even
if this now includes a child with cardiac problems. On the other hand, some
families may be much more competent in handling the needs of very young, dependent, chronically ill children. Yet these same parents may first encounter serious family disruption if faced with the continuing dependency needs of a chronically ill teenager, superimposed upon the storms of adolescent autonomy battles.
A therapist assessing family coping will benefit from a thorough assessment of the
family's history of coping with normal life cycle/developmental crises. This will
help pinpoint the impact of the chronic condition on this family's time line. This,

in turn, will point the way to major issues for the therapeutic work at hand, and family strengths that can be built upon in the future.

Gender and Generational Boundaries

Women have traditionally carried the overwhelming responsibility of physical and emotional caretaking in families. Although this activity is consistent with the traditional maternal caretaking role, mothers cannot carry this burden alone without great cost. Families that conform to rigid, traditional notions of gender-determined family roles are in particular danger of problems when chronic illness ensues. A chronically ill child in a family often calls for a double dose of prolonged, nurturing, "mothering" behavior, as well as significant flexibility in timing and organization of family activities in response to the child's changing condition. The coparent of the child's primary caretaker (in most cases, the father) is a tremendous asset in such a family when he is flexible in sharing the broad spectrum of demanding caretaking tasks, such as administering treatments to the sick child, staying overnight at the hospital, cooking for the well siblings, attending to the subtleties in the sick child's symptoms, and providing sensitive support to the mother. In contrast, a father who reacts to the mother's or child's increased needs for flexibility and nurturance with extreme male-role-stereotyped emotional distancing and/or rejection of nontraditional family tasks risks exacerbating the difficulties in the family's daily functioning. In many cases, this dysfunctional behavior will be the focus of family treatment.

Rigid gender roles can also create difficulties for the chronically ill child. There can be a serious threat to the self-esteem of chronically ill boys unable to fulfill traditional expectations of male body strength, independence, athletic prowess, or detachment from their mothers. Fathers may contribute to the problem by rejection or perplexed avoidance of these less than "manly" sons, particularly in adolescence. Coping with a chronic illness may also prove distressing to a young female adolescent, in terms of impaired body image, diminished sense of attractiveness, and restricted opportunity for age-appropriate autonomy. Yet for young adolescent women, traditional concepts of femininity are less likely to conflict with the increased dependency and physical fragility often associated with chronic illness. Families with more flexible models of gender and roles have the great advantage of offering their vulnerable children a broader range of adult role models with whom to identify.

Maintaining the parental generational boundary is an essential element of effective functioning in all families (Minuchin, 1974); this is particularly true in families with chronically ill children. The caretaking demands of a child's illness almost invariably create an especially close, intense relationship between the young patient and the most involved caretaker (almost always the mother). Legitimate needs for greater time and emotional and physical involvement with the sick child must nonetheless be balanced with the need for protected time and intimacy for the parental dyad. Effective generational boundaries protect the marital dyad and serve as a critical counterbalance to the pull for a parent–child coalition at the expense of the less involved parent or other family members. Flexible roles for both parents that are free of gender-determined restrictions are an important element allowing for more sharing of the caretaking role. This sharing allows for a less exclusive role for the more involved parent; it also allows for greater empathy between spouses who are both experiencing the difficulties and rewards of caretaking. The availability of a geographically and emotionally close extended family is often a critical element protecting the parents' generational boundary. Grandparents, aunts, uncles, and other relatives in many families provide relief through babysitting as well as wise counsel to the parents in their observations of emerging family difficulties. They can also offer significant alternative relationships for a chronically ill child, which may also help free the more involved parent from a potentially overloaded relationship with the sick child.

Community Layers

The Hospital System

Next to the immediate and extended family, the hospital or specialized clinic is often the system most intimately involved with the child and family. The child and parent who spend a significant amount of time hospitalized or making repeated clinic visits develop long-term relationships with a large number of health care staff. Health providers often forget the fact that parents of chronically ill children are heavily dependent on them for ongoing emotional support and approval. Parents often feel that friends and family (if available) cannot possibly understand their concerns and daily dilemmas as can nursing and clinic staff. The attitudes and practices of hospital caregivers affect the parents' feelings about their child's illness and about themselves as competent caretakers.

Hospital personnel have definite, if often unspoken, beliefs about appropriate family visiting behavior, treatment practices, and family relationships. When parents do not live up to staff expectations due to real inadequacies or family cultural differences, insecure or sensitive parents may find it difficult to respond to the subtle disapproval they sense from nursing or medical staff, particularly when the criticism is not directly discussed with them. Parents may cope with this direct or indirect censure by withdrawing from active involvement in bedside care activities or daily visitation or feeling confused and betrayed by the loss of the support and approval they so need. On the other extreme, supportive and enthusiastic hospital staff members can successfully draw a parent more actively into the care of the child, through sensitive attention to the areas of success and competence exhibited by even the least skilled parental caretaker.

Rose was a 23-year-old Mexican-American mother of a 6-year-old son and a 2-year-old daughter. Her younger child, Marta, was severely neurologically impaired by meningitis at 8 months of age. This young single mother, with no family support and money only from public assistance, took care of the older boy as well as her now mentally retarded daughter with a seizure disorder. She also managed to attend a business program in the local community college. A new medical resident, unaware of this remarkable young woman's dedication to her children, confronted Rose with the fact that Marta's seizure medication levels were not under good control and suggested that the child would be better off in a foster home where she would not be neglected. Although this mother may well have benefited from more respite help or even outside placement of the child, the insensitive approach of this caregiver made it impossible for Rose even to consider placement, as it would have been an admission of failure. Furthermore, her fragile sense of competence was undermined. Rose, who was herself a foster child, had invested a great deal of her self-esteem in her role as a loving parent. Fortunately, several sensitive nurses who knew Rose and the context of her life circumstances were able to repair the damage and reinforce Rose's success at caring for two children, despite all the special demands of chronic medical problems.

The design of the medical caregiving institution itself contributes to the ways in which families organize around chronically ill children's needs. Hospital planners make crucial decisions about the design and use of space, policies on visitation, and the provision of supportive services that aid or deter families from involvement in patient care. Design practices that encourage active parental involvement in a child's medical care include space for parents to room in with their children overnight, comfortable parent lounges for respite from long hospital vigils, and attractive indoor or outdoor areas for family visiting. Daytime child care programs, when available, allow parents with other young children to visit their ill children more frequently, as do flexible visiting policies and facilities so that young siblings can visit.

Thoughtful policies regarding repeated hospitalizations of chronic patients can streamline the admissions process and save the families from having to repeat their long medical histories to each new medical student or resident they encounter. Flexible hours for parent conferences (including evening or weekend meetings) allow more parents to talk with their physicians as couples, rather than putting mothers in the go-between position of translating medical information to fathers and relaying the fathers' questions and comments back to the staff. Well-designed programs for chronically ill children and their families also provide regular preventive assessment of family coping by hospital-based family therapists, who are then available for brief, problem-focused treatment. All these services, while costly in the short run, are cost-effective in terms of encouraging faster patient recovery, smoother parent–staff communication, and earlier intervention in cases of potential family dysfunction.

Advisors to the hospital system could consist of parent–staff advisory committees, patient advocates, psychological consultants to the staff, or other professionals who retain some distance from the day-to-day functioning of the clinical units (e.g., pastoral counselors, child life staff). Ideally, some training in family systems theory and therapy would be optimal for an effective approach to the family–hospital relationship.

Home Care Services

The term "home care services" refers to the programs and services available in support of families who wish to provide some of their children's medical care in their homes. These services can range from the provision of monitoring equipment, to weekly injections administered by a visiting nurse, to round-the-clock nursing services provided for more seriously ill children. Intensive home support services can be provided to terminally ill children or to those requiring ventilator care or nursing care for multiple handicapping conditions. These services, generally provided by registered or licensed vocational nurses, are funded by private insurers, state Medicare, or hospice sources. The availability of these services as an option allows a family more freedom from the confines of the hospital building and more opportunity to take charge of some of the routine caretaking functions and decisions previously assumed by the hospital staff. It also allows the family unit to spend more time together in the home environment, instead of being divided between home and hospital. The noninstitutional setting, the reduction in the number of strangers in the child's immediate space, and greater contact with family members are all major advantages of home care services for the child's mental health. Institutions offering home care for their chronically ill patients allow a considerably greater range of choices to support the fabric of family life and allow greater inclusion of siblings and other relatives.

On the negative side, home care puts parents in the position of assuming a greater burden of personal responsibility for the child's care. As Lyman, Wurtele, and Wilson's (1985) study of families with home apnea monitoring indicated, a mechanical device allowing for home care of a child with a potentially fatal breathing dysfunction did not necessarily lead to better parental adjustment. They found that parents who used home rather than hospital apnea monitoring had higher anxiety levels, impaired sleep, and restricted social lives. Furthermore, mothers bore the brunt of this responsibility, responding to 85% of all machine alarms and being with the children 76% of the time. An additional problem noted was the sense of isolation, in that parents found it very difficult to obtain respite babysitting from adequately trained neighbors and family members. If a family has less than 24-hour daily nursing services (as is often the case, even for seriously compromised children), then parents have periods of time with sole responsibility for the child's survival. This is an ominous responsibility, and one that they would not have to shoulder at any time if the child were being treated in the hospital.

Another potential difficulty with home care services is the possibility that they will compromise the integrity of the remaining family in the home. Particularly in cases of in-home nursing, the daily presence of medical personnel in the home can feel intrusive and disruptive to normal family life. Family scheduling and intimacy may be affected by the changing shifts of nursing personnel. Although home care was designed to free families for more normalized family relationships, some parents may feel pre-empted in the parenting role even more by the presence of a nurse in the child's own bedroom than by a nurse in the child's hospital room. Or, conversely, assuming a greater role in administering treatments and therapies at home can lead some parents to feel that a pleasurable parenting role is slowly being transformed into a mechanical, unpleasant nursing role.

In extreme cases, the availability of home care services can also provoke a peculiar dilemma for families when their children are chronically ill as well as profoundly impaired. The possibility of taking a child home, when in earlier years there would have been no choice but permanent institutionalization, means that the family as a whole may undergo a significant change in life style that will alter the relationships of all family members.

For example, Maria was a 4-year-old who sustained severe head injuries in an automobile accident. After months of hospital care, she remained in a persistent vegetative state, with frequent infections and complications. Over the objections of the father, the mother (who had been driving at the time of the accident) decided to take her daughter home, with arrangements for 16-hour-a-day nursing care. This decision had a profound effect on the marital relationship, as well as on the behavior and affect of the 8-year-old brother. The brother and mother united to become a caretaking team, while the father increasingly distanced himself from the painful drama in the home through progressively longer hours on the job. The family was permanently altered by Maria's accident and by the decision to maintain her within the family unit. In this case, a certain degree of guilt fed the family's decision to put Maria's care as the top priority, even at the expense of the marital relationship and the sibling's needs.

The psychosocial staff members advising families such as these would be best equipped if they had access to more data on the coping successes and failures of families involved in home care. Perhaps of even greater value would be a clinician with considerable experience in helping families sort out issues of guilt, individual priorities, and realistic expectations in planning for home care of significantly impaired family members. In many cases, the critical element determining the success of a home care program will be that of ongoing support from several other layers of community services beyond the home and hospital.

Social Services

The availability of supportive social services is another important layer contributing to family coping. Beyond the emotional, logistical, and physical demands of chronic illness in the family, there is almost always a significant financial drain on the family's resources. Even families with comprehensive insurance coverage and/or supplemental programs, such as Crippled Children's Services (CCS) or Regional Center (for the developmentally delayed), find that their resources rarely cover all medical expenses. A few outpatient clinic visits for a child with a blood disease can cost thousands of dollars for blood products alone. As is often the case, families with incomes just a bit over eligibility limits for supplemental programs often find themselves the most financially strapped. Parents can even find themselves being advised to divorce in order to fall within income limits for single parents.

Beyond direct medical costs, there are numerous, unpredictable out-of-pocket expenses of caring for a chronically ill child. Transportation costs of repeated clinic visits; expenses of frequent meals eaten outside the home; babysitting for the well children; expenses of toys, trinkets, and special foods for the hospitalized child; long-distance phone calls to family members; and overnight motel expenses (if the home is a significant distance from the hospital) mount up on a regular basis, as do related costs of noncovered services (e.g., psychotherapy, hypnosis, special equipment, cosmetic devices, nontraditional treatments, massage, etc.). To compound the problem, families are doubly taxed by the need to keep one parent (generally the mother) out of the job market in order to be on call for home medical treatments or hospital duty. Hobbs *et al.* (1985) point out that not only is the mother of a chronically ill child often unable to pursue a career or take a full-time job, but the father too may restrict his career development and mobility in order to remain available to the family and close to the medical center. Single parents can lose significant amounts of money in days lost from work for periods of illness. Ironically, the working parent of a chronically ill child can easily find himself or herself "chained" to a particular job, due to the realization that a change of employment means loss of health coverage for the affected child. Commonly, the child with a serious pre-existing condition is refused by new insurers. The negative financial implications (as well as potential resentment generated by these involuntary restrictions) are obvious.

Well-coordinated and financed social services in the hospital and community can provide funds and programs to offset some of these extra burdens on families and patch up some of the holes in coverage. Respite babysitting care and foster homes trained and licensed to accept chronically ill and multihandicapped children help provide options for families temporarily unable to handle the multiple demands. Monies available on a short-term basis to families who rush their children to the hospital during the night or cannot stretch their funds till the end of the month can be very helpful, as are funds to help families maintain their telephone services, electric services, and so on. Advocacy services to help families through the maze of bureaucracies, parent support groups, and parent representation on hospital service committees can help reduce feelings of powerlessness and provide an extra margin of assistance to families of the chronically ill.

Lawrence was a severely asthmatic 6-year-old who spent 3 weeks in the hospital before a psychological consultation was requested for his increasingly apathetic, listless, and passive behavior. Evaluation of the family situation revealed that his parents had three other children at home younger than Lawrence; the father had just been diagnosed with terminal cancer; and the parents had not visited more than twice due to lack of transportation. A social service intervention mobilized a community hospice organization to provide support to the parents. Sufficient bus fare was provided, and hospital volunteers were located to offer daily child care for the three younger children so the parents could visit. The parents' and Lawrence's affect improved dramatically when the family was reunited in daily hospital visits.

Lawrence was reanimated by the reconnection with his parents. His parents seemed to benefit most from the opportunity to deal more directly with the fact of the father's cancer through family sessions and the hospice connection. The basic child care services allowed the parents the time and sanction to focus on the individual needs of this particular child.

The School System

The school system, as an extension of the larger society, is essentially designed to provide services to the average, healthy child who is able to attend and participate on a regular basis. Special services are also available to the learning-disabled, severly handicapped, or completely homebound child. Yet the chronically ill child often falls between the cracks because the child's educational needs vary with the changing circumstances of the illness. The chronically ill child commonly faces disruptive but unpredictable episodes of illness that frequently require bed rest, hospitalization, and disruption of the daily school routine. The school system can be most helpful to these children by being flexible and responsive. Most schools are able to alter childrens' daily programs without much difficulty to accommodate their needs for a shortened day, a reduction in physical activity, or breaks for medication. Periods of frequent but sporadic absence from school attendance are often less well accommodated. Special home teachers are generally available for children with chronic medical problems, but there are often administrative difficulties for the system in flexibly moving back and forth between home and school instruction.

Mickey was a 12-year-old sickle cell anemia patient who was hospitalized during one difficult year almost monthly for medical crises and complications. His hospitalizations lasted for periods of 8 to 15 days. His school district's regulations required that a child had to be too ill to attend school for 10 consecutive days with each new absence before a home teacher was assigned. They were willing to put Mickey on immediate home teaching status only if he withdrew completely from the rolls of active, school-attending students. Thus, Mickey was put in the position of having to choose between missing many weeks of the academic year without a teacher or withdrawing completely from school attendance even when well. Either choice was an unfair burden on this academically motivated child, for whom it was psychologically important to attend school as much a possible with his peers. It took many weeks of negotiation to reach a compromise with his school district.

Third-Party Payers

Insurance companies and government-funded health insurance programs cover the major expenses of the majority of chronically ill children in this country. Their designated patterns of reimbursement and active funding decisions for outpatient services play a significant role in the lives of many chronically ill children and their families. In many cases, the unwillingness of these programs to provide adequate nursing care and other home care services means that some children spend weeks or months longer in the acute care hospital setting than is really necessary. The consequences of keeping these children hospitalized for such long periods of time include not only the psychological effects of prolonged institutionalization, but damage to the development of the child and family unit. Some parents who endure long periods of uncertainty as to whether they will ever receive funding approval for the home care services they require respond to this frustration and disappointment by withdrawing from their child. Depending on the parents and the circumstances, this withdrawal can result in eventual total surrender of the child by the parents. Ironically, the private provider or public program that refuses a family 20 hours per day of home nursing services because of the expense often ends up paying significantly more money than the original request, in the cost of maintaining the child in the hospital unnecessarily or eventually sending the child to permanent, specialized foster care.

Decisions of third-party payers can have a profound impact on the life style and life choices of the young, chronically ill patient.

Andrea was an 18-year-old patient with chronic lung disease whose family prided itself on its success in encouraging her independence. In spite of, or perhaps because of, her shortened life expectancy, this young woman was eager to begin her life apart from her parents. As soon as she graduated from high school, she took a year-long secretarial course and found an apartment in another city. Yet her insurance company rejected her request to fund a daily home breathing treatment, stating that she was young enough for her parents to provide this service, or she could attend the hospital's daily clinic for treatments. Yet these options precluded living independently of her family or holding down her daytime office job, forcing her onto disability status. Fortunately, the existence of an alternative funding source finally allowed Andrea to pursue her new steps toward independent life, at quite a small cost.

The systems-oriented therapist can play an important role in evaluating the position of a particular family within the web of interacting systems, and can serve as a facilitator, family advocate, and agent of change. There are advantages to locating the systems therapist within a medical center for access to ill children and their families and ready referrals, but it is best for the therapist to serve as a systems consultant rather than as a staff member in a particular medical unit. Since so many difficulties involve interactions of direct medical caregivers with patient families, the consultant's outside position allows a freer, more objective stance and approximates a family's own position in relation to the larger hospital system.

Effective Family Coping

Defining "Normal" and "Dysfunctional" Families

Clinical definitions of family "normality" vary with the different schools of family systems theory. In a chapter of her edited book on conceptualizations of normal family functioning, Walsh (1982) has contrasted six major family systems models and the differences in their views of normal versus dysfunctional family systems. Although there is much overlap in the model's general views of average, nonclinical families, Walsh finds the major differences to lie in the selective emphases of the different models. For example, structural family theorists focus more on organizational aspects of effective family functioning (e.g., boundaries, hierarchy) and functional accomplishments of the system, as opposed to issues of differentiation of self (as emphasized by Bowenians) or communications processes (as emphasized by experiential/humanist approaches). The effects on family funtioning of a stressor as significant and pervasive as a child's chronic illness are examined for their interaction with these important family processes. Dysfunction is largely measured in terms of the processes emphasized by each model (e.g., dysfunctional family organization, impaired differentiation, communications dysfunction).

Research tools for the examination of family functioning have also been developed by several teams of researchers. These tools include Olson, Sprenkle, and Russell's (1979) circumplex model, with its emphasis on "cohesion" and "adaptability"; Reiss's (1971) model of family problem solving; and Beavers's model (Lewis, Beavers, Gossett, & Phillips, 1976) of competence and family style. All of these empirical models have been developed to help classify families as functional or dysfunctional in an effort to clarify the important dimensions of effective functioning. And many studies sidestep the issue by simply defining "dysfunctional families" as those found in a mental health clinic population, thereby allowing such families to designate themselves as dysfunctional by requesting therapeutic intervention.

In the medical setting, families identified as dysfunctional or coping poorly are generally those falling into one of two categories: overtly disorganized or difficult to treat. The overtly disorganized category is more similar to the general population self-defined by its search for treatment. Many families with chronically ill children make their coping difficulties known to their health care practitioners by direct requests for psychotherapeutic help and obvious family crises (e.g., a marital breakup or a child's running away, drug abuse, or school problems). Medical staff often turn to psychological consultants and therapists for direct intervention in these family problems, and the family dysfunction is often directly attributed to the impact of a child's illness on a vulnerable family system.

Many difficult-to-treat patients are eventually referred to therapists by sensitive physicians, although their symptoms are more indirect and are generally treated first by intensified medical intervention. Noncompliance on the part of patients or family members (e.g., altering medication regimens, pulling out intravenous lines, violating dietary restrictions, etc.) is often interpreted as a symptom of poor family coping. Patterns of hospitalization that are out of the ordinary (e.g., of unusual or increasing frequency) and not strictly explainable by the medical condition are also seen eventually as symptomatic of poor adjustment to a child's medical condition.

Poor family coping with the challenges of chronic illness can perhaps best be defined by the structural and strategic family systems model. This model takes the position that no one particular family style is inherently normal or functional; it can only be judged by its fit to the functional demands of the family's developmental and social context (Walsh, 1982). A family that is not accomplishing its tasks and meeting its functional demands, as defined by the child's particular illness and the adaptations it requires, can be considered dysfunctional for that particular context. In the context of chronic illness and the heavy demands for medical cooperation and family responsiveness to highly unpredictable and sometimes extraordinary circumstances, a family is expected to function at a very high level of adaptability. It is expected not only to meet the usual functional demands on family members at different developmental stages, but also to respond effectively, rapidly, sympathetically, and in an organized manner to the functional demands of the ill child's particular medical condition, with all its additional emotional baggage.

Not surprisingly, busy tertiary care centers for chronically ill children tend to direct their limited clinical resources and research efforts to helping the most overtly disorganized families and difficult-to-treat patients. With concerns appropriately directed toward these problem patients, it is easy to lose sight of the numbers of families—many of them poor or single-parent families—that manage to cope successfully with the significant extra demands of chronic illness. Even the crises that many families encounter at the period of initial diagnosis or during certain family developmental stages should not cause us to overlook the impressive degree of adaptability they demonstrate most of the time to the functional demands of life in and out of the hospital.

Idiosyncratic Coping Techniques

Many of the effectively coping families we encounter in our hospitals draw not only on basically healthy family systems and adequate networks of community resources, but on the idiosyncratic coping techniques they possess or acquire along the way. Many patients and families enduring a roller-coaster life of unpredictable changes successfully develop a "live for today" attitude that allows a shift in their time perspective but healthy cynicism about the limits of medical knowledge and predictions (Deaton, 1985). For example, the mother of a chronically ill 7-

year-old relished sending a yearly card on her child's birthday to the physician who predicted that her daughter "would not live to see her first birthday."

Strong religious beliefs, spiritual orientation, or the ability to surrender internal control proves helpful to many families faced with uncertainty and lack of control. The ability to attribute some meaning to a child's suffering and a family's special circumstances is often a great relief, even if the meaning itself is seen as inaccessible or known only to some higher being.

And some families with chronically ill children cope with their challenges through a style of toughened or crude humor that sometimes shocks caregivers in its bluntness, particularly when the child participates in this form of communication. For example, a grandmother bringing a young leukemia patient to undergo a painful procedure was overhead telling the child, "Look, kid, let's get this over with—we don't have the money to afford a funeral." Often the painful subjects of death, intimate medical procedures, and bodily dysfunction are the focus of open reference and crude jokes. This communication style, although blunt and defensive in nature, offers families a way of expressing real fears and making their concerns known to others.

If life with a chronically ill child can be thought of as a particular type of life style, then this group of families can be thought of as constituting a distinct subcultural group, with its own special interactional patterns, group norms, and values. Thinking in these terms requires an alteration in our expectations of "normal" family functioning along such systemic dimensions as enmeshment–disengagement, differentiation, and adaptability, because the social and developmental context of these families is far from "normal." Particularly when a chronically ill child is young and/or very debilitated, effective family coping with the child can be compatible with greater enmeshment, less differentiation, and higher adaptability, for example, than is considered functional in "normal" families whose daily context is quite different. As we further refine our definitions of "normality" for functional families with chronically ill children, we will move closer to identifying and supporting the strengths found in so many of these families. And these strengths, combined with effective social services, public policies, and community supports, should allow us to see many more families successfully survive the significant challenges of chronic illness.

REFERENCES

Bibace, R., & Walsh, M. E. (1981). Children's conceptions of illness. In R. Bibace & M. E. Walsh (Eds.), *New directions for child development: Children's concepts of health, illness and bodily functions* (pp. 31–48). San Francisco: Jossey-Bass.

Blos, P., Jr. (1978). Children think about illness: Their concepts and beliefs. In E. Gellert (Ed.), *Psychosocial aspects of pediatric care* (pp. 1–17). New York: Grune & Stratton.

Brunnquell, D., & Hall, M. D. (1982). Issues in the psychological care of pediatric oncology patients. *American Journal of Orthopsychiatry, 52* (1), 32–44.

Carandang, M. L. A., Folkins, C. H. Hines, P. A., & Steward, M. S. (1979). The role of cognitive level and sibling illness in children's conceptualizations of illness. *American Journal of Orthopsychiatry, 49* (3), 474–481.

Carter, E. A., & McGoldrick, M. (Eds.). (1980). *The family life cycle: A framework for family therapy.* New York: Gardner Press.

Deaton, A. V. (1985). Adaptive noncompliance in pediatric asthma: The parent as expert. *Journal of Pediatric Psychology, 10*(1), 1–14.

Drotar, D., Crawford, P., & Bush, M. (1984). The family context of childhood chronic illness: Implications for psychosocial intervention. In M. G. Eisenberg, L. C. Sutkin, & M. A. Jansen (Eds.), *Chronic illness and disability through the life span: Effects on self and family* (pp. 103–129). New York: Springer.

Herz, F. (1980). The impact of death and serious illness on the family life cycle. In E. A. Carter & M. McGoldrick (Eds.), *The family life cycle: A framework for family therapy* (pp. 223–240). New York: Gardner Press.

Hobbs, N., Perrin, J. M., & Ireys, H. T. (1985). *Chronically ill children and their families.* San Francisco: Jossey-Bass.

Hughes, M. C. (1982). Chronically ill children in groups: Recurrent issues and adaptations. *American Journal of Orthopsychiatry, 52,* 704–711.

Lewis, J. M., Beavers, W. R., Gossett, J. T., & Phillips, V. A. (1976). *No single thread: Psychological health in family systems.* New York: Brunner/Mazel.

Lyman, R. D., Wurtele, S. K., & Wilson, D. R. (1985). Psychological effects on parents of home and hospital apnea monitoring. *Journal of Pediatric Psychology, 10*(4), 439–448.

McKeever, P. (1983). Siblings of chronically ill children: A literature review with implications for research and practice. *American Journal of Orthopsychiatry, 53*(2), 209–218.

Minuchin, S. (1974). *Families and family therapy.* Cambridge, MA: Harvard University Press.

Mitchell, W., & Rizzo, S. J. (1985). The adolescent with special needs. In M. P. Mirkin & S. L. Koman (Eds.), *Handbook of adolescents and family therapy* (pp. 329–342). New York: Gardner Press.

Neuhauser, C., Amsterdam, B., Hines, P., & Steward, M. (1978). Children's concepts of healing: Cognitive development and locus of control factors. *American Journal of Orthopsychiatry, 48*(2), 335–341.

Olson, D. H., Sprenkle, D. H., & Russell, C. (1979). Circumplex model of marital and family systems: I. Cohesion and adaptability dimensions, family type, and clinical applications. *Family Process, 18,* 3–28.

Penn, P. (183). Coalitions and binding interactions in families with chronic illness. *Family Systems Medicine, 1*(2), 16–25.

Perrin, E. C., & Perrin, J. M. (1983). Clinicians' assessments of children's understanding of illness. *American Journal of Diseases of Children, 137,* 874–878.

Reiss, D. (1971). Varieties of consensual experience: III. Contrast between families of normals, delinquents, and schizophrenics. *Journal of Nervous and Mental Disease, 152,* 73–95.

Rolland, J. (1984). A psychosocial typology of chronic illness. *Family Systems Medicine, 2*(3), 2–25.

Spinetta, J. J., & Deasy-Spinetta, P. (1981). *Living with childhood cancer.* St. Louis: C. V. Mosby.

Steward, M. S., & Steward, D. S. (1981). Children's conceptions of medical procedures. In R. Bibace & M. E. Walsh (Eds.), *New directions for child development: Children's conceptions of health, illness and bodily functions* (pp. 67–83). San Francisco: Jossey-Bass.

Velasco de Parra, M. L., Davila de Cortazar, S., & Covarrubias-Espinoza, G. (1983). The adaptive pattern of families with a leukemic child. *Family Systems Medicine, 1*(4), 30–35.

Walker, G. (1983). The pact: The caretaker-parent/ill-child coalition in families with chronic illness. *Family Systems Medicine, 1*(4), 6–29.

Walsh, F. (1982). Conceptualizations of normal family functioning. In F. Walsh (Ed.), *Normal family processes* (pp. 3–42). New York: Guilford Press.

Whitt, J. K. (1982). Children's understanding of illness: Developmental considerations and pediatric interventions. *Advances in Developmental and Behavioral Pediatrics, 3,* 163–201.

Wisely, D. W., Masur, F. T., & Morgan, S. B. (1983). Psychological aspects of severe burn injuries in children. *Health Psychology, 2*(1), 45–72.

11

Childhood Obesity: The Family Context

JILL ELKA HARKAWAY, EdD

Childhood obesity is a serious problem affecting increasing numbers of American children. In a period of only 15 years (1963–1978), the prevalence of obesity in children between the ages of 6 and 11 increased by 54% (Gortmaker, Dietz, Sobol, & Wayler, 1987). It is a problem that is now estimated to affect 20–25% of American children (Gortmaker *et al.*, 1987). These data represent an increase in both male and female children, in both black and and white children, and in children of all ages. The increase has been attributed to a number of factors, such as increased food intake; the popularity of high-calorie foods; a change in eating patterns; decreased physical activity; and increased "passive" activity, such as television viewing.

Whatever the causes, the problem presents serious consequences for obese children. Unlike obesity in adults, childhood obesity does not directly affect life expectancy and has few critical or immediate medical complications. A few obese children do demonstrate medical complications of their weight: raised total cholesterol, lowered high-density lipoproteins, and elevated blood pressure. For most children the major health consequence is the risk of obesity later in life, with those complications associated with adult obesity. Of teenagers who are obese, eighty percent will maintain their obesity into adulthood, and they are likelier to be more

Jill Elka Harkaway. Departments of Psychiatry and Pediatrics, Tufts Medical School/New England Medical Center, Boston, MA; Brookside Hospital, Nashua, NH; Private practice, Cambridge, MA.

severely obese than those who gained weight as adults (Lloyd, Wolff, & Whelan, 1961).

By far the most serious immediate consequences of obesity in childhood are social and psychological. Obesity is one of the greatest social handicaps for children and adolescents in this culture. In a number of studies, children as young as 5 years old have demonstrated a prejudice against obese children, and have indicated an unwillingness to have them as friends (Goodman, Richardson, Dornbusch, & Hastorf, 1963; Staffieri, 1967). Obese children are frequently isolated, excluded from peer activities, and teased. They are viewed as deviant, not only by their peers, but by teachers and other significant adults as well. Well-meaning adults may attempt to "cure" the obesity by bullying, teasing, or publicly humiliating such children. Others, openly hostile toward obesity, may scapegoat the children. Unlike children suffering from other medical handicaps, obese children are blamed and punished for their condition and are considered subnormal in many ways (dirty, smelly, stupid, lazy, etc.).

This negative focus on obese children's weight has a tremendous impact on them at a time when they most want and need to conform, to be accepted, to define a place for themselves with peers, and to master social skills. How others respond to their appearance affects the children's body image, sense of self, and mastery of social skills. It is possible that psychological characteristics attributed to obese children (Hammer et al., 1972; Monello & Mayer, 1963; Nathan & Pisula, 1973) may develop as a result of the contextual response and constant disqualifying messages the children receive.

The question of etiology in childhood obesity is confusing and inconclusive; at this point obesity appears to result from a combination of individual susceptibility and environmental factors. Because the issue of etiology is so complex and confusing, for the purposes of treatment it is more useful to focus on the maintenance of the problem rather than its cause. The clinical question, then, becomes not "How did this child get fat", but rather "What keeps this child from successfully losing weight?" This shifts the problem from calories to context. Once an intervention (diet) has been prescribed, the problem is not what to eat, but how the diet is managed. Dietary interventions are generally effective, if followed. What prevents their being followed is the key.

Although treatment and research have examined physiological, behavioral, and psychological aspects of obesity, the interpersonal context has been largely ignored as a significant factor in the problem. The majority of authors who have addressed the interpersonal context of obesity have suggested that the family is the most significant of these contexts (Bruch, 1973; Bruch & Touraine, 1940; Dietz, 1983; Epstein, Wing, Koeske, Andrasik, & Ossip, 1981; Epstein, Wing, Steranchak, Dixon, & Michelson, 1980; Zackus & Solomon, 1973). On the other hand, very few have described the patterns of interaction that characterize families with obese children who fail to lose weight, and none have developed a treatment approach that focuses on family interactions. The family therapy field has been slower to work with obesity than with other eating disorders, but more recently the literature has reflected a growing interest in the application of family systems theory and practice to the problem of obesity (Barbarin & Tirado, 1984, 1985; Ganley, 1986; Harkaway, 1983, 1986, 1987; Loader, 1985; Marshall & Neill, 1977; McVoy, 1987).

The material presented in this chapter comes from family evaluations and treatment within a pediatric obesity program. The program exists as a specialty clinic within a tertiary care pediatric teaching hospital that is part of a major medical center. Patients range in age from 6 months to 24 years, and are fairly evenly divided between males and females. Patients are referred by pediatricians and other health professionals; many are self-referred. The degree of obesity ranges from 120% of ideal body weight and triceps skinfold measurement to 250%. We see families from many socioeconomic and ethnic groups. A large percentage of our patients have been treated previously for their weight, either professionally or commercially.[1]

In the development of a treatment model, we have found it useful to identify some patterns that occur in families with obese children who present for treatment and who have been unsuccessful in previous attempts at weight loss. Although it cannot be said that these patterns cause obesity, it is suggested that they may be associated with difficulty in losing weight. It is also important to remember that the families who served as the source of these clinical observations are those that have sought professional help with their children's weight problems, and therefore are not necessarily representative of all families with obese children. There are many families with obese children that are functioning well, and there are families that solve the problem of obesity without requesting professional help. Nor are all the patterns here to be found in every family we see. These are not intended to be conclusive or comprehensive observations; they are intended to suggest possible directions for clinical work and future research.

The Definition of Obesity

Althouth there are standard objective criteria for the definition of obesity in children (Dietz, 1981; Powers, 1973), the definition actually used by families is, in many cases, subjective and highly individualistic; it is frequently based more on aesthetic or emotional grounds than on medical considerations. There are individuals who, at 150% of their ideal body weight, function normally and without any noticeable impairment either socially or psychologically. Others, within 120% of their ideal body weight, see themselves or are seen by others as grossly impaired, and their functioning is severely hampered. In some families, many family members may be overweight, but only one may be defined as symptomatic. The degree of obesity alone does not determine the severity of the problem or its social and

---

[1] For a further description of this program, see Harkaway (1987).

psychological implications. Weight has different meanings for different families, as it does for different cultures, and the meaning is therefore determined as much by its context as by any scientific standard. The problem is not only the weight but also the organization of the system in terms of the weight, its function as an integral part of the system, and the development of a symptomatic identity and life style.

General Family Issues

Loyalty

If we assume that in every family there is necessarily a balance between autonomy and loyalty, the emphasis in many families with obese children is on loyalty to the family and family members at the expense of individual autonomy. There are difficulties with separateness, individuation, and differences. Members are expected to share beliefs, feelings, and experiences. Members frequently describe or refer to themselves in global terms, as a unit ("We like to eat," or "The Smiths have always been fat"), and there is often confusion and lack of individuation between members (when asked when her daughter's weight became a problem, one mother answered, "I've been overweight all my life"). This is particularly true among members perceived to share a weight problem. Family members defer to each other on questions regarding their own experience, and encourage others to answer for them by silence or other forms of cueing.

The following are excerpts from family interviews:

THERAPIST: *(To Carolyn, aged 14)* How much do you want to lose?
CAROLYN: *(To mother)* 18 pounds?
MOTHER: I thought it was 23.
SISTER *(aged 12):* No, 21.
CAROLYN: *(Shrugs)* I don't know.

THERAPIST: *(To Jenni, aged 12)* How is the diet going?
FATHER: Well . . .
MOTHER: *(Interrupting Father)* Do you want me to talk or Jenni?
FATHER: Jenni would be ideal. *(Mother laughs)*
THERAPIST: So how are you doing, Jenni?
JENNI: *(Shrugs, says nothing)*
BROTHER *(aged 8):* She always gets embarrassed when the camera is on.

In systems such as these, members are so accustomed to being informed by external cues ("I'm cold; put on a sweater") that they never learn to identify or trust their own experiences, feelings, or thoughts. Children may never learn to respond to their own sensations of hunger or fullness because they have learned to eat in response to external cues. Hunger can be confused with experience of other sensations or physical or emotional experiences, and therefore the children may learn to eat whenever they experience any sensation that leaves them uncomfortable.

Members are overinvolved with one another; they spend more time with one another than with social contacts. In some families, the overinvolvement includes all family members; in others, it unites some of the members and excludes others. Children tend to spend more time at home than out with friends. In many ways, the obesity "functions" to help a child stay loyal to his or her family by protecting the boundaries around the family, by preventing normal peer relationships and activities.

When seen in nuclear families, this is similar to what Minuchin, Rosman, and Baker (1978) describe as "enmeshment" of psychosomatic families. But it is a striking finding that in many of these families the problem and the patterns are of multigenerational standing—a factor that intensifies the relationship between loyalty and obesity. Obesity and attempts at weight loss become a multigenerational theme.

For some families, obesity is part of their heritage and identity. Family members have been overweight and have struggled with weight for many generations. Obesity has been a historical focus of attention, conflict, and concern, and has become part of their interpersonal transactions. In one family, when asked about his daughter's weight gain, the father answered, "I'm a compulsive eater. The whole family, we'd have bread and cake. Cathy has all these tastes. She's a Davis." He continued, "I come from a family that has weight problems. My father had terrific weight problems all his life; my sister is terrifically obese; my mother definitely has a problem. Poor Cathy"—he smiled—"she's just like us." Obesity, a visible mark of loyalty, can be one way in which members define themselves as a unit.

In families where there has been an exaggerated focus on and preoccupation with issues of weight, small weight gains assume meanings that differ from other families. In one such case, the mother brought her 6-year-old son for treatment in the obesity clinic when the pediatrician told her he was 2 pounds above his ideal body weight. When asked why she had decided to bring him to treatment, she responded, "I've been overweight all my life; Johnny is just like me. I was just waiting for the inevitable to happen." It is possible that the response to a minor weight gain, which is quite normal in preadolesence or at points of transitions such as loss, may be exacerbated by the heightened and intense response of the family. What may have begun as a simple "difficulty" can become a "problem" as a result of the concern about it (Watzlawick, Weakland, & Fisch, 1974).

Low Tolerance for Conflict

In families where there is a strong emphasis on loyalty, and differences are seen as threatening, conflict and disagreement can be viewed as dangerous. In these families, a strong taboo exists against open expression or resolution of conflict. If conflict is to be tolerated, there must be an acceptance of differences and autonomy, and an ability to sustain discomfort until the conflict is resolved. In these families, disagreement is felt as rejection, criticism, or betrayal. Conflict is experienced as a threat to the existence and integrity of the family unit. Therefore conflict is avoided whenever possible, or diffused if it emerges. In many families there may be an alcoholic parent or a history of alcoholism, and the family may have experience with explosive and unpredictable rages followed by distance. Conflict may be seen as the prelude to one of these rages, or parents may have learned from their alcoholic parents that conflict is to be avoided at all costs.[2]

There are many different ways in which conflict avoidance is managed: use of humor and laughter; framing criticism as "teasing"; topic shifts; shifts from the topic to a focus on the symptom; protective framing of statements ("This is for your own good" or "Don't take this the wrong way"); silence and professed ignorance; nonsequiturs and monologues; and, most importantly, the involvement of a third person in a dyadic conflict. Occasionally, frequent bickering masquerades as conflict, but it is rarely focused on the true sources of conflict, and rarely resolved; it just continues to recycle repetitiously. Conflict may center around eating or the obesity as a diversion from other sensitive subjects.

The following is taken from an annotated transcript of a family interview:

THERAPIST: I'm curious what your response is to what your wife just said.

FATHER: *(Long pause. He drops something; daughter picks it up. Father reaches for it and they smile at each other)* I have no response.

> Father avoids confrontation about daughter's weight, a source of conflict for the parents, by not responding.

DAUGHTER: *(Reaches for what ever Father is holding. They hold hands for a moment)*

> Daughter, his ally, distracts him, offers support.

SON: He wasn't listening.

FATHER: I was listening. I can tell you verbatim what she said.

> Son enters to attack father, support mother, diffuse conflict between them.

THERAPIST: Do you think—*(interrupted)*

MOTHER: Do you think my nagging her—*(interrupted)*

FATHER: I understand what she is saying, and I think when she turns into a teenager and her weight is a problem she'll do something about it.

> Father shifts the topic to end conflict.

One gets the impression that family members are walking on eggshells with one another, afraid to initiate a stressful or potentially dangerous situation. A constant level of tension exists because the expression of conflict is prohibited. Conflict remains at a constant low level; it is rarely resolved. One of the unfortunate results of this situation is that new solutions to problems are rarely found, and no action can be undertaken to make change.

[2] Although we do not have sufficient data, clinical experience suggests a possible relationship between obesity and alcoholic parents, particularly in women.

Within this framework, the individual's eating can be viewed as a way of both managing anger ("stuffing it down") and diverting energy and attention from the conflict. In fact, many descriptions of eating binges resemble uncontrolled rages or temper tantrums in their intensity and violence. This adaptation may be an attempt to protect the family by complying with the rule against open and direct expression of conflict.

Eating may start as an individual response to conflict and become a way of diffusing or distracting others from conflict. Many obese adults say they do not experience anger; they may have learned to identify all unpleasant experiences as hunger.

Rigid Extrafamilial Boundaries

While relationships within the family are overly close and overinvolved, relationships outside the family are frequently strained, weak, or nonexistent. Members are socially isolated or unsuccessful in school, work, or social contexts. The primary source of social contact outside the immediate family is often the extended family of one or both parents. Outside relationships are viewed with suspicion, and are often discouraged by other family members. Within the family's world view, the outside world is seen as dangerous; only family members are loyal enough to be trusted. Because of this belief, members rarely develop sufficient social skills to deal with peer groups. This situation potentially reinforces the belief that the outside world is dangerous; because the "outside world" frequently responds to obesity with abuse and ridicule, an obese child without adequate social skills is vulnerable to rejection and scapegoating.

The few relationships the child establishes outside of the family can be isomorphic to the family style. Frequently an obese child has one "best friend" who is also obese; this relationship frequently centers around weight ("you and me against the world") and eating, and can become a significant influence when one of the friends attempts weight loss without the other. This is the same kind of bind that can arise when one member of an obese couple attempts to lose weight. When questioned carefully about the effects of weight loss on their friendships, many children have confessed a concern that their friends would be angry or jealous and would abandon them.

Concern about weight and the diet may also support a pattern of social isolation. In some families, obese children are discouraged from playing outside the home or going to peer activities, because these pose a threat to the diet. In this way, the diet itself protects the family pattern or rule. Dieting as a solution can become a first-order change (Watzlawick et al., 1974) that protects rather than challenges the basic organizing premise. One very clear example was provided by a young woman who had lost over 100 pounds through her participation in a self-help group. When asked how her life had changed with weight loss, she answered, "When I was fat I had no social life at all. I spent all my time eating or thinking about food. Men never paid any attention to me, of course, and I thought

I would never even have one date in my whole life. Now I meet a lot of men, and sometimes they are interested in me and ask me out! I just met this great guy who I really liked who asked me out last week.'' When asked how that had gone, she answered, ''Well, I wasn't able to go out with him because I had group that night.''

It is important to add here that there are many obese children who are socially competent and successful. These observations are based on a clinical population. Obese children experiencing fewer social difficulties may not present for treatment as frequently.

Conflicted, Overinvolved Relationships with the Grandparent Generation

One or both of the parents may never have individuated successfully and may still be overinvolved with family of origin. This parent may maintain primary loyalties to his or her family of origin, and may be more ''married'' to one of his or her parents than to the spouse. This ''marriage'' may pose numerous problems: It can prevent the formation of a primary relationship between the spouses and leaves the other spouse emotionally abandoned. This may in turn lead to an overinvolvement between the ''abandoned'' parent and one or more of the children. It almost always leads to conflict and struggles among the three generations.

In a single-parent family, this same marriage between the parent and a grandparent may also exist, but may be intensified in both conflict and closeness. The parent and children often live with the grandparent(s) or within walking distance. Parenting rights and responsibilities are unclear, and the hierarchy is often confused. The child's obesity simultaneously unites the parent and grandparent, by giving them a common concern, and divides them, because of conflict over how and by whom it should be managed. The obesity can serve in this way as a boundary marker within the family.

In both types of families, a strong cross-generational alliance between a grandparent and a child frequently defeats parental authority. Grandparents may view the parents' attempt to put a child on a diet as a punitive attempt to create distance between them and the child (''She won't let me feed him any more''), and respond by undermining parental authority. Parents view the grandparents' involvement as undermining, but hesitate to confront them or attempt to establish their authority as parents for fear of upsetting or alienating their own parents. The child becomes triangulated—either involved in a cross-generational alliance with a grandparent, or constantly caught in triangles of loyalty.

The struggle between the grandparent and parent generations frequently revolves around giving and withholding food, as well as around the definition of obesity itself. Such struggles appear frequently in families where the grandparents and parents are of a different culture (as in an intermarriage or where the adult children are first-generation Americans), or where a single parent shares some or all of parenting responsibilities with grandparents.

Diffuse Interpersonal Boundaries

In addition to the overinvolvement and loyalty issues described earlier, there are patterns of intrusion and overprotectiveness. Family members are overprotective with one another in terms of both emotions and physical activity. They are careful about framing criticism or conflict, and may rush to soothe or comfort one another at any perceived hurt. Members seem uncomfortable with any unpleasant emotions, and either try to avoid them or cover them up for one another.

For a number of families, physical activity is seen as dangerous or boring, and is either not encouraged or openly discouraged. Although an increase in physical activity is useful in weight reduction, the prescription of increased activity is rarely enforced in families with pre-existing concerns or taboos against it.

In families with obese children, diffuse interpersonal boundaries may also be marked by intrusion, whether verbal or physical. Children may feel that they are constantly the center of attention, with all eyes focused on their bodies or behavior. Personal confidences may be shared inappropriately with outsiders, and members feel free to comment on one another without restriction. The children may become uncomfortable with this constant attention to their bodies, but at the same time they grow to depend on this "feedback." They may long for distance, and express a fear of "being swallowed up" by the others, but become panicked if they cease to be central. This dilemma becomes highlighted when children lose weight; many patients have confessed that although they feel "good" when people notice their weight loss and comment on it, they become anxious and even angry afterwards. The increased attention and vulnerability may be surprisingly more unwelcome than the obesity.

One additional aspect of the diffuse boundaries is the issue of incest. Clinical experience with families and with obese adult women suggests that there may be a relationship between obesity and incestuous relationships in childhood. This incest can be an actual overt history of sexual relations between a child and a family member, or a highly charged sexuality that is never enacted but presents a constant atmosphere of sexuality that is confusing, frightening, and overstimulating to the child. In either of these situations, obesity can be seen to function as an attempt to mark boundaries, to defend against the sexual impulses of others, and to manage one's own disturbing sexual feelings.

This description of diffuse interpersonal boundaries is again similar to what Minuchin et al. (1978) describe as enmeshment in psychosomatic families, but with some subtle differences. We do not always see the high affective reactivity and emotionality that is described in the families of anorexia nervosa patients. In a number of the families seen at our clinic, the members appear distant from one another and cool in their manner; an outsider might assume that they are very disengaged from one another. We have come to view this as personal or cultural style, not an indication of proximity or distance. Families can appear quite disengaged in their emotional style, and still be very overinvolved. Or they may appear to be highly conflicted, with constant bickering that keeps them overinvolved.

Marital Relationship and Involvement of the Obese Child

Although the parents as a couple may appear overly involved with each other, there may be a lack of intimacy in their relationship. There may be chronic unresolved conflict. They may have developed a comfortable distance that allows them to avoid conflict. Distance may also be related to a primary involvement of one parent with the grandparent generation. Frequently, dyadic interaction is difficult, and the couple appears to be more comfortable focusing on a third party, or including a third party in their interactions.

The child can become involved as a third party in the marital relationship in a number of ways. In one, the parents are in a struggle with each other. Each of the two parents (or parental figures) has different and mutually exclusive view on the nature of the problem, its cause, or the best approach for treatment. The child is caught in the middle, and cannot take the side of one parent without betraying the other. Thus, a mother may say that a daughter is too fat and should diet. The father may say she is fine the way she is. The daughter can neither diet nor maintain her weight without betraying one of them.

In another type of situation, the marital conflict may be masked as the parents unite in their attempt to make the child lose weight. The child may maintain this detouring by openly rebelling and refusing to diet, or by covertly rebelling by being "out of control" with the diet (e.g., bingeing secretly.) Failure, while frustrating to all, continues to unite the parents in frustration and annoyance.

If the child is in a stable coalition with one of the parents against the other, his or her weight can become part of that triadic relationship. In situations in which there is a stable coalition between the identified patient and a parent, it is usually the obese parent with whom the child is aligned, regardless of gender (Harkaway, 1986). The obese parent and child lack differentiation between them; they act and are perceived as if they were identical. The obese child, in such a situation, is in a difficult position. If the child loses weight, this implies a desire to be different that risks betraying and abandoning the obese parent. If a struggle exists between the spouses, weight loss can mean siding with the thin spouse against the child's "ally." If, for instance, the mother is fat, and the father has nagged her for years to lose weight and she has been unsuccessful, the child's weight loss can be an embarrassment and betrayal of the mother. If, on the other hand, the child tries to diet but fails miserably, this failure supports the mother in the marital struggle by proving that dieting is almost impossible.

This situation becomes even more complex if the struggle over the child's weight becomes a substitute for the conflict between the parents. In a couple in which one spouse is thin and the other obese, long-term unresolved conflict may be manifested in a struggle over the obese spouse's weight. Such a couple may be involved in "incongruous hierarchies" (Madanes, 1981), where the obesity serves to maintain a careful balance of power between them. The obese parent is simultaneously in a "one-down" position by virtue of being symptomatic, and in a "one-up" position by resisting the other's attempts to resolve the problem. The other spouse is in a "one-up" position by virtue of being symptom-free, but simultaneously "one-down" because he or she is powerless in attempting to resolve the problem. The weight serves as an analogical message about control: Although the obese parent overtly requests guidance and control, he or she covertly resists it. Because the resistance is covert, it takes the form of "involuntary" behavior (secret binges and losing "control"). As long as the couple is caught in this "incongruous hierarchy," the obese parent cannot lose weight without threatening the balance in the marital relationship (Harkaway, 1983).

This struggle, when it becomes too intense or threatening, can come to include the obese child as a third party in order to stabilize the relationship. The parents stop fighting about the obese parent's weight as they begin to focus on the child. This allows the parents to continue their conflict in a safer, more distant forum. They can communicate with each other on two levels simultaneously: on a literal level, about the child, and on a metaphorical level, about each other. In one family, the thin father warned the obese daughter, "If you ever want to get married, you'll need to lose some weight. Men don't find fat women attractive." To which the obese mother responded, "Well, I don't think you really need to worry; any man worth his salt will love you no matter what you look like." Clearly, it becomes difficult for a child to lose weight successfully in this situation.

Obesity is an interesting symptom because it is constant and visible. Unlike asthmatic or diabetic children, fat children do not have to act or be in crisis in order to affect the behavior of the family.

In a study following families through diet intervention (Harkaway, 1986), it was found that some obese parents began to lose weight when the focus shifted from the parents' failure to the children's struggle with weight.

Ineffective Parental Leadership

In a family where there is an obese child, the parents may well be unable to work together in a joint executive capacity. Perhaps because of the delicate balance in their marital relationship, or a general taboo against open and direct expression of conflict, they are too careful with each other to be able to negotiate differences and conflict openly and directly. In some cases parents appear to be in a symmetrical struggle over who is the better parent, who understands the problem of weight better, or who has the better solution. They can undermine each other, disqualify each other, and align with one or more of the children against each other. This kind of struggle is most frequently played out around the issue of the obese child's weight.

The parents are also unable to function in an executive role individually. Because of the taboo against conflict, they avoid taking stands. Cross-generational alliances between the obese child and one parent or grandparent can disempower both parents. Relationships between parent and child appear to be peerlike, rather than generational. Some families express an ethic of "the democratic family,"

where everyone has an equal voice. In many families, parents appear to be afraid
to enforce rules or confront the children (or the obese parents) about known
"cheating." Denial of "cheating" can protect the family members from the open
confrontation they fear. In other families, the parents may defer all authority to
the children and provide no guidance or structure ("She should want to do this
for herself," or "She needs to develop self-control and learn to deal with temptation"). Many parents do not work at managing the environment, do not enforce
rules, make unnecessary allowances ("have just one piece of cake"), and give
conflicting messages. Occasionally, in response to the lack of structure and authority, a child can be totally "out of control" in all areas of behavior, and yet
can appear to be the most powerful member of the family.

The Obese Child as a "Special Child"

Although some authors suggest that ordinal position within the family is related to obesity (Bruch & Touraine, 1940), it is our experience that obesity is
more likely to be idiosyncratic and related to the particular child within the particular family. Often the obese child is seen as a "special" child, necessitating, in
the family's view, special treatment. He or she may have been ill as an infant or
child, may have been born after a miscarriage or death of a significant family
member, may have special needs, or may be the "baby" of the family, born after
other children are grown. Whatever the reason, we see many families in which
the identified patients are treated as "special," and the special treatment is generally centered around eating. These children are also frequently pampered in other
ways, and can be uncontrollable in their behavior because of lack of adult controls. In these families, parents, grandparents, and occasionally siblings view diet
changes, no matter how minor, as deprivation of the "special" children and are
reluctant to follow them; they express concern for the children's feelings and/or a
fear of dealing with their rage if food is withheld.

Sibling Subsystem

There is frequently a hierarchical confusion within the sibling subsystem; the
identified patient, adult or child, is treated as young, incompetent, and helpless.
Siblings attempt to take a controlling role vis-à-vis the diet, which leads to a
power struggle. Sometimes there is no apparent sibling subsystem, with distance
or expressions of rivalry or hostility between siblings, who may harass, tease, and
scapegoat the obese child and refuse to help with the diet. This appears to be
maintained by cross-generational alliances and overprotectiveness of the identified
patient.

In many families there is little differentiation made on the basis of age or
hierarchical position. Older siblings are not given more or different privileges and
responsibilities than younger siblings. In one extreme example, a family in treat-

ment reported giving gifts and special treats to all their children on the birthday of any one of them so that "they wouldn't feel deprived or left out."

In some families, more than one child is overweight, but the attention is focused on only one of them as problematic. In one family, both adolescent daughters were obese, but the family only sought treatment for the elder. As they explained it jokingly, obesity was not a problem for the younger, for "she loves to eat."

Difficulty with Transition

Frequently families date the onset of the obesity to a point of transition. Families with obese children may have difficulty negotiating the changes that occur in normal life, whether they are developmental (a child's entering adolescence or going to school), involve membership changes (death, divorce, remarriage, or birth of a new baby), or are idiosyncratic (relocation or change in financial status). Rather than adapting to the new situation with the development of new interactional styles, the families respond by becoming more rigidly fixed in outdated patterns of interaction. Adolescence is particularly difficult for these families: There is a division of loyalties between an adolescent's family and the peer group, and the differentiating behavior is experienced as rebellion or betrayal. Death and loss can also be related to the development of obesity. Weight gain may initially occur as an individual response to grief, but may become a welcome shift in focus for other family members. Or the person may have been obese for some time, but treatment is sought after a family loss, either as a distracting focus or an attempt to pull the family together in order to work on a joint task.

Other factors reported frequently by families include geographical relocation, remarriage, divorce, and hospitalizations.

Treatment

Treatment for obesity has historically been a frustrating and difficult task, with high rates of dropout and relapse. No single form of treatment has proven effective over the long term. In addition, treatment for children and adolescents presents some risks. Ironically, it is possible that a traditional treatment approach to obesity can contribute to the problem in a number of ways. The attempt to help a child lose weight can activate a power struggle between parents and child, in which eating and "cheating" can become an attempt on the child's part to assert autonomy (Harkaway, 1987). Increased parental vigilance and focus on the enforcement of the child's's diet can lead to a pattern of "sneaking food" and secret bingeing as the child responds to restriction. The extreme focus on food, weight, and diet may lead the child to solidify his or her identity as an obese and symptomatic person. Finally, there is increasing evidence (Brownell, Greenwood, Stellar, & Shrager, 1986) that repeated dieting may increase the body's tendency to store fat, thereby creating a "diet-induced obesity." Bruch (1958) found in her follow-up of the children she had studied in the 1930s that the children who had the best psychological adjustment as adults, and who were most likely to have resolved their weight problems, were those who had the least amount of treatment for their obesity as children. Increasing attention is being paid to the aspects of dieting that contribute to the problem of obesity rather than resolve it (Bennett & Gurin, 1982; Harkaway, 1983; Polivy & Herman, 1983).

It appears that many of the problems in treatment for children arise from increased focus on eating, weight, and dietary restrictions. Another source of difficulty in treatment is the belief that all cases of obesity are the same. Despite the consistent argument that there are many different forms of obesity (Bruch, 1973), most treatment programs continue to treat all obese children as if obesity were a standard condition. Individual physiological differences and different family contexts create a different "obesity" for each child. For this reason, treatments that are standardized will only be effective in a certain percentage of cases. Although outwardly similar, each situation is idiosyncratic in terms of the difficulty of weight loss.

For these reasons, the focus in our treatment model is different from that of most weight loss problems. The emphasis is not on food, calories, or behavior, but on context—the relationships and interactional behavior that influence the individual's "freedom" and ability to lose weight. It addresses the interactions that maintain obesity, rather than the obesity itself. It is designed specifically for the particular system.

This is not to say that we do not discuss weight-related matters in therapy; because this is the issue the family brings to therapy, the content centers on this issue. We talk about instituting changes, and may even make dietary recommendations in order to see how the family responds. The treatment is ostensibly about weight, but the process occurs on two levels: It addresses weight on a content level, and weight-maintaining interactional behaviors on a process level. The concern is less about calories or compliance, and more about understanding the ways in which the system is organized around the weight.

Treatment is a lengthy and tedious process, with slow and nondramatic changes. Treatment must also address two problems, the weight-maintaining behaviors and the weight itself. The most elegant of interventions may "free" the child to lose weight, but he or she will not wake up the next morning having lost 60 pounds. Treatment becomes a two-level approach.

Although each therapy is designed idiosyncratically to fit each family system, there are some general guidelines:

1. All treatment should involve a thorough medical evaluation to rule out congenital (e.g., Prader–Willi syndrome) and acquired (e.g., brain tumor or Cushing disease) medical causes of the obesity. Consequences or complications of the obesity (hypertension, elevated cholesterol, etc.) should be considered. A family history for obesity, hypertension, diabetes, and other related problems should be taken.

2. An assessment of dietary history and eating patterns should be made, to

determine the particular areas of difficulty with food, and patterns that can be altered.

3. The therapist should identify and involve the significant members of the system. This usually involves parents or parental figures and siblings, but frequently involves grandparents and other members of the extended family as well. If they cannot be present in the therapy room, then, at the very least, the therapist should include them by asking questions during the sessions.

4. The therapist should maintain a position of neutrality (Selvini Palazzoli, Boscolo, Cecchin, & Prata, 1980) toward the problem, family beliefs, behaviors, and particular outcome (Harkaway, 1983, 1987). A focus on weight loss as the sole positive outcome of treatment can ensnare a therapist into becoming overinvested in weight loss. Such a position can lead to power struggles with patients, increased frustration, and an inability to understand the process of the family or the therapy.

5. The therapist should evaluate the "role" of the obesity in the organization of the family. What should be the consequences of successful weight loss? If there were good reasons for a child to stay overweight, what would they be? What is possible or prevented because of the "problem" with the child's weight?

6. The therapist should work with clear hypotheses about the ways in which the family patterns of interaction serve to maintain the problem. To be successful, a program of weight loss should address these patterns in ways that allow the family to develop new ways of interacting that allow for weight loss.

7. The therapist should use the issue of weight to address the interactions around it. The problem of losing weight is imbedded in family interaction; it is a problem of relationships, not pounds. To be successful, a program of weight loss should address the interactions between and among members that may serve to maintain the problem. Most treatment addresses the weight or the eating behavior without looking at the context of the obesity.

Case Study

Amy, aged 8, was referred for treatment for her obesity. She was the only child of Margaret, 39 years old, and Joe, 52 years old. James, Margaret's son by a previous marriage, lived with his mother and stepfather.

At the time of the referral, both Amy and her mother had been in individual therapy for 3 years, since the death of the maternal grandmother. Amy was in therapy for multiple phobias and violent, uncontrollable behavior. She was having difficulty in school because of her tantrums and inability to deal with authority. She had few friends because "no one will play with her because they're afraid of her." She had become involved with the Department of Social Services because of the school's concern over her behavior. Her mother was described as chronically depressed and "an inadequate personality incapable of mothering." She was not working; her husband was a salesman who was on the road from Monday morning to Friday afternoon.

Amy had had prior treatment for her obesity from a pediatrician, who, when this was unsuccessful, had referred her to a nutritionist. According to the family, the nutritionist had thrown Amy out of her office because of obscene language, tantrums, and violent behavior.

At the initial family interview, Amy sat on her father's lap and would not move to her own seat when asked to do so by the therapist. When the parents were asked to move her to a chair of her own, Amy became hysterical, screaming, kicking, and punching. Her mother cringed and moved away from her; her father threw up his hands in dismay and expressed his helplessness about making her do anything she did not want to do.

It became clear that this was a typical sequence within the family. When her mother would tell Amy to do something, Amy would throw a tantrum or yell obscenities at her mother, who would then back off. Her father would give in and placate Amy. This same sequence occurred in response to any issue, but was a particular source of difficulty for the parents in the area of eating and dieting. Whenever a professional suggested dietary changes and enforcement, Amy's mother became trapped between the professional and the alliance between Amy and her father, who, although he wanted Amy to lose weight, had a difficult time depriving "his" daughter of anything.

Over the course of the first two sessions, the following observations were made: There was a total lack of parental leadership, and neither of the parents was able to control Amy in any way. The father, because of his alliance with Amy, was uncomfortable asserting any authority, perhaps for fear of losing her loyalty. The mother, because of the cross-generational alliance between Amy and her father, did not experience any sense of authority with Amy; whenever she attempted to enforce discipline, Amy, having the father's covert support, was able to openly challenge and defy her. This situation was inadvertently exacerbated by Amy's individual therapist, who warned the parents not to put pressure on her in any way because she was "too fragile." Because of the lack of parental leadership, there were no limits set for Amy and no consequences for her behavior, and she appeared to be the only member of the family who possessed power and influence. In many ways, the real marriage in the family was between Amy and the father, for this appeared to be the intensely emotionally and intimately related dyad.[3]

The parents lived with great distance between them, which was maintained by the father's schedule, the mother's relationship with James and her depression, and the father's alliance with Amy. The only thing they appeared to share was the concern about Amy, at this time focused on her weight problem. There was a low tolerance for either conflict or proximity between them, and they appeared to

---

[3] Because incest is usually a concern in these situations, the therapist checked with the Department of Social Services, which reported that its investigation of the family provided no evidence of sexual abuse. In any case, whether or not there was actual physical abuse, a form of "incest" did exist in this family in the form of the inappropriate cross-generational alliance, and this was a concern of the therapy.

avoid each other as much as possible. None of the family members, with the exception of James, had social contacts outside of the family. The mother had had an extremely close relationship with her own mother, and had been depressed since her death. The father had no living relatives.

In the second session, on the basis of the information about Amy's previous treatments, the therapist raised the question as to whether or not it made sense to pursue treatment at this time. The parents were given a task: to decide how much weight Amy would have to lose "to prove that she really did want to lose weight and was ready for it." This paradoxical task was intended to address the previous failures and the possibility that Amy would similarly attempt to "defeat" this treatment. It defined the current weight loss behavior as a test and not a diet, challenging Amy to defeat the therapist. But it was primarily an early attempt to have the parents work collaboratively to negotiate a decision about Amy without her interference. This process took almost the entire session, and necessitated the therapist's constant blocking of Amy. After an extremely difficult and lengthy discussion, the parents decided on a number of pounds for Amy to lose. (In the therapist's view, this goal was unrealistic, but since the aim of the task was process-related, not content-related, it was accepted as a working goal.) In this way, no formal diet program was presented for Amy to reject; the framework involved Amy having to prove to the therapist that she could "earn" a diet before she was given one.

In the third session, a framework was developed that simultaneously addressed the weight and the dysfunctional interaction. The parents were told that Amy's problem with eating and weight was a result of the same core problem that led to all her other difficulties: her inability to control her behavior. The therapist suggested that she was unable to control herself because she was too young (a statement that Amy protested angrily), but that she was very bright and could learn well if the parents set out to teach her, and that the best way to teach her was to take charge and show her how.

For the next six sessions, spread over 10 weeks, the parents were asked during each session to choose one aspect of Amy's daily life that could be changed to help her (1) lose weight, and (2) learn to develop self-control. For instance, the first decision they made was to eliminate desserts; the next week they decided to limit her to one snack daily; and so on. (The therapist had provided a list of changes they could make, based on their descriptions of Amy's eating behavior and patterns.) The negotiations between the parents were so awkward and difficult that they frequently took the entire session to make a decision. In this way, the therapist attempted to build a stronger parental dyad, and to create a more appropriate boundary between parents and child.

Between sessions, the parents enforced each new rule they had made—at first with difficulty and extreme protest from Amy, but with increasing competence, assurance, and success. Amy was beginning to lose weight, and the parents, cheered by their success, were better able to enforce limits.

Two critical events in therapy happened in the eighth and ninth sessions. During the eighth session, the parents decided that Amy would no longer be driven to and from school, but would walk with all the other children. Amy became hysterical at this, perhaps because, unlike all the other decisions between the parents, this one was made swiftly and easily. She threw herself on the floor, kicking and pounding her fists on the floor, and screamed, "You're trying to kill me! This is child abuse! I'm going to report you to the authorities!" The therapist watched this performance briefly and waited for the parents to respond. Much to her dismay, the humor of the situation overcame her, and the therapist began to laugh. Of course, the more she tried to control herself and stop, the more uncontrollable it became. The mother, who had started to retreat and give in, gave the therapist a startled look and began to laugh herself, joined a few moments later by a very surprised father. Amy's tantrum began to lose steam when she realized no one was taking her seriously any longer. In this way, quite by therapeutic accident, the parents developed an alternative response to Amy's tantrums, which allowed them to respond by being amused rather than intimidated.

The ninth session was a key one, in which all the themes of the therapy were pulled together, and the changes the family had made were consolidated. During this session, the therapist learned that Amy slept in the father's bed during the week when he was out of town. This seemed to serve a useful function within the family, for although the parents complained about it, it was a way in which Amy could keep the mother company when she was alone, and perhaps prevent an intensification of her depression. It was also symbolic of Amy's somewhat ambiguous role in the family: Although ostensibly a child, she had assumed the role of authority of the father's wife. She had, through his alliance, the position of adult within the family, and it was no surprise that she alternated between her child's bed and an adult's bed.

The therapist asked, "What would happen if you [the parents] decided that she was to sleep in her own bed from now on?" The mother responded that they had only recently begun to discuss doing that. Amy smiled and said, "But it hasn't happened."

Since the mother appeared to be the one most in favor of returning Amy to her bed, and was showing an energy and authority that appeared to be quite new, the therapist aligned with her and pushed her to get her husband to make a decision with her. In the following dramatic sequence, the father wavered back and forth between the mother and Amy, taking one side and then switching to support the other. Amy put pressure on her father to stay loyal to her, pledging her love for him and her fear of his "betraying and abandoning" her by siding against her. The mother, with minimal support from the therapist, persisted in her attempts to get the father to join with her. As the conflict between the two females escalated and the father became torn between them, it appeared as if the family drama were being enacted and challenged at that very moment—as if the father were being forced to choose his "real wife."

At one very intense moment, Amy became agitated and yelled at her mother, "What does a bed have to do with a diet? You let her [the therapist] talk you into everything! First she talked you into making me walk to school, then she talked you into—" The mother interrupted Amy, asserting her authority, and explained that these were decisions they (the parents) were making. She took charge of the situation and insisted that the father join her in this task, which after a painfully long sequence, he did. From this session on, Amy slept in her own bed without protest, followed the parents' directives, and began to improve in all areas of her behavior.

The therapy lasted four more sessions over the course of 2 months. The mother continued to assert her authority successfully, undaunted by Amy's occasional protests, and retained the father's support. The parents continued to work together more effectively as parents, even though there was little change in their marital relationship. They were offered marital therapy, which they declined. Therapy was terminated when the parents were satisfied with the improvement in Amy's behavior and with her weight loss. Interestingly enough, diets were never discussed, and the achievement of the original goal was never referred to again. (It is worth mentioning that both Amy and her mother terminated their individual therapy voluntarily during the second month of family therapy.)

A follow-up on the family, offered by one of the professionals who had been involved with the family, revealed that the parents were divorced within a year after therapy terminated, and Amy chose to live with her mother. All family members were reported to be doing well, and Amy maintained her weight loss and behavioral changes.

Because the obesity in this case was viewed in terms of the family system, treatment was directed at the context, not the problem or the individual alone. Treatment, if it is to be effective, must address both the weight and its connectedness to family interaction and connectedness. This identification and description of interactional patterns is not meant to represent the "truth" about obesity, but to provide a framework for conceptualizing the problem so that effective treatment can take place.

Equally important, an examination of obesity in terms of interactional behavior begins to shift the focus from the traditional emphasis on individual pathology to the very complex and rich interactional context of which obesity is a part. It begins to suggest alternative, more useful explanations for failure in treatment. It is our hope that this examination will enable clinicians to develop more effective treatment and suggest areas for further study and systematic research.

ACKNOWLEDGMENTS

I gratefully acknowledge the help of William H. Dietz, MD, PhD, Director of the Weight Control Clinic, Tufts/New England Medical Center, Boston. An earlier version of this chapter was presented at the annual conference of the American Association of Marriage and Family Therapy, Dallas, 1982.

REFERENCES

Barbarin, O., & Tirado, M. (1984). Family involvement and successful treatment of obesity: A review. *Family Systems Medicine, 2*(1), 37–45.

Barbarin, O., & Tirado, M. (1985). Enmeshment, family process, and successful treatment of obesity. *Family Relations, 34,* 115–121.

Bennett, W., & Gurin, J. (1982). *The dieter's dilemma.* New York: Basic Books.

Brownell, K., Greenwood, M., Stellar, E., & Shrager, E. (1986). The effects of repeated cycles of weight loss and regain in rats. *Physiology and Behavior, 38,* 459–464.

Bruch, H. (1958, August). Obesity. *Pediatric Clinics of North America,* pp. 613–627.

Bruch, H. (1973). *Eating disorders.* New York: Basic Books.

Bruch, H., & Touraine, G. (1940). Obesity in childhood: V. The family frame of obese children. *Psychosomatic Medicine, 2.* 141–206.

Dietz, W. H. (1981). Obesity in infants, children, and adolescents in the United States: I. Identification, natural history, and aftereffects. *Nutrition Research, 1,* 117–137.

Dietz, W. H. (1983). Childhood obesity: Susceptibility, cause, and management. *Journal of Pediatrics, 103*(5), 676–686.

Epstein, L., Wing, R., Koeske, R., Andrasik, F., & Ossip, D. (1981). Child and parent weight loss in family based behavior modification programs. *Journal of Consulting and Clinical Psychology, 49*(5), 674–685.

Epstein, L. H., Wing, R., Steranchak, L., Dixon, B., & Michelson, J. (1980). Comparison of family-based behavioral modification and nutritional education for childhood obesity. *Journal of Pediatric Psychology, 5,* 25–36.

Ganley, R. (1986). Epistemology, family patterns, and psychosomatics: The case of obesity. *Family Process, 25,* 437–4451.

Goodman, R., Richardson, S., Dornbusch, S., & Hastorf, A. (1963). Variant reactions to physical disabilities. *American Sociological Review, 28,* 429–434.

Gortmaker, S., Dietz, W. H., Sobol, A., & Wayler, C. (1987). Increasing pediatric obesity in the United States. *American Journal of Diseases of Children, 141*(5), 535–540.

Hammer, S., Campbell, M., Campbell, A., Moores, N., Sareen, C., Gareis, F., & Lucas, M. (1972). An interdisciplinary study of adolescent obesity. *Journal of Pediatrics, 80,* 373–383.

Harkaway, J. (1983). Obesity: Reducing the larger system. *Journal of Strategic and Systematic Therapies, 2*(3), 2–16.

Harkaway, J. (1986). Structural assessment of families with obese adolescent girls. *Journal of Marital and Family Therapy, 12*(2), 199–201.

Harkaway, J. (1987). Family intervention in the treatment of childhood and adolescent obesity. In J. Harkaway (Ed.), *Eating disorders* (pp. 93–104). Rockville, MD: Aspen.

Lloyd, J., Wolff, O., & Whelan, W. (1961). Childhood obesity. *British Medical Journal, ii,* 145–148.

Loader, P. (1985). Childhood obesity: The family perspective. *International Journal of Eating Disorders, 4,* 211–226.

Madanes, C. (1981). *Strategic family therapy.* San Francisco: Jossey-Bass.

Marshall, J., & Neill, J. (1977). The removal of a psychosomatic symptom: Effects on the marriage. *Family Process, 16*(3), 278–280.

McVoy, J. (1987). Family fat: Assessing and treating obesity within a family context. In J. Harkaway (Ed.), *Eating disorders* (pp. 70–83). Rockville, MD: Aspen.

Minuchin, S., Rosman, B., & Baker, L. (1978). *Psychosomatic families: anorexia nervosa in context.* Cambridge, MA: Harvard University Press.

Monello, L., & Mayer, J. (1963). Obese adolescent girls: An unrecognized minority group? *American Journal of Clinical Nutrition, 13,* 35–39.

Nathan, S., & Pisula, D. (1973). Psychological observations of obese adolescents during starvation treatment. In N. Kiell (Ed.), *The psychology of obesity.* Springfield, IL: Charles C Thomas.

Polivy J., & Herman, P. (1983). *Breaking the diet habit.* New York: Basic Books.

Powers, P. (1973). *Obesity: The regulation of weight.* Baltimore: Williams & Wilkins.

Selvini Palazzoli, M., Boscolo, L., Cesshin, G., & Prata, G. (1980). Hypothesizing, circularity, and neutrality: Three guidelines for the conductor of the session. *Family Process, 19*(1), 3–12.

Staffieri, J. (1967). A study of social stereotype of body image in children. *Journal of Personality and Social Psychology, 7,* 101–104.

Watzlawick, P., Weakland, J., & Fisch, R. (1974). *Change: Principles of problem formation and problem resolution.* New York: Norton.

Zackus, G., & Solomon, M. (1973). The family situation of obese adolescent girls. *Adolescence, 8,* 33–42.

12

Children in Families with Emotionally Disturbed Parents

HERTA A. GUTTMAN, MD

The usual function of families is to promote and preserve the mental health of children. But if a family experiences events that impede its fundamental tasks of providing a child with shelter, nurturance, education, and a sense of continuity with history, the family itself may pose an obstacle to the child's development (Lewis, Beavers, Gossett, & Phillips, 1976). This is particularly evident in families in which one or both primary caretakers, the parents, are acutely or chronically impaired. This chapter addresses one kind of impairment—emotional disturbance in one or both parents, in families with school-age children.

The clinical and research evidence documenting the impact of parental emotional disturbance is first considered, and several pertinent clinical examples are offered. There is then a discussion of interventions that may be useful in mitigating the potential ill effects of a parent's mental disturbance. These remarks are based not only on the cumulative wisdom of clinical experience and research findings, but also on the retrospective reflections of adults who were brought up in such families. The chapter concludes by summarizing what seems to be conclusively known about this subject and by indicating those areas of knowledge that await clarification.

Herta A. Guttman. The Sir Mortimer B. Davis–Jewish General Hospital, Montreal, Quebec, Canada; Department of Psychiatry, McGill University, Montreal, Quebec, Canada.

The Family Environment

In seeking to identify those factors in families with mentally ill parents that are associated with morbidity in the children, one is struck by the disruptions; the role reversals between parents and children; and the periods of relative or actual neglect, abuse, or lack of clarity about the meaning of specific events. These may alternate with periods during which parenting is adequate or even overcompensates for previous neglect. Descriptions of families with parents who are mentally ill almost always emphasize the unpredictability and the frequent chaos of the family environment (Anthony, 1969; Steinem, 1986; Weissman, 1979). Another feature, less often described in subjective accounts but clearly evident in the remarks of independent observers, is the inconsistency of physical and psychological attention given these children. An impaired parent is preoccupied and unavailable at certain periods, and often demands the concentrated attention of the nonimpaired parent as well. Some parents require hospitalization and are entirely absent from their families. The medications prescribed to alleviate a parent's mental condition are not always immediately effective, and are also very often accompanied by side effects (e.g., drowsiness or extrapyramidal symptoms) that affect the parent's contact with the social environment.

The quality of a parent's attention may vary a great deal in terms of the type and intensity of affect directed at the child. Weissman and Paykel (1974) have demonstrated that depressed mothers may be very hostile at home, in spite of their passive, withdrawn behavior with mental health professionals, and that much of this hostility may be directed at their children.

Furthermore, it has been demonstrated that spouses of mentally disturbed persons are highly likely to be mentally disturbed themselves (Merikangas, 1984; Rutter & Quinton, 1984), thus dimishing the children's access to undisturbed parenting. The mental disorder most commonly concomitant with severe psychosis in one parent is a personality disorder in the other (Rutter & Quinton, 1984). In Rutter and Quinton's sample, the spouses' condition worsened over time—a finding that seems to fit with Weissman's (1979) observation that the marital relationships of the depressed women in her study continued being distant, hostile, and problematic long after the illness was no longer acute. These observations have usually been interpreted to mean that living with an impaired person exacerbates personality traits in the partner, but the systemically oriented observer would note that a circular process could occur, such that the illness in the one parent may also eventually be exacerbated in the context of the other parent's personality disturbance. Whatever the sources of the parents' personality disorders and the forces that perpetuate them, the fact that both parents may be involved contributes yet another element of potential discord and friction to the family environment. A spouse with a personality disorder either may be hostile himself or herself or may be an inadequate buffer against ill parent's hostility when it is directed against a child (Feldman & Guttman, 1984).

The family structure is of great importance. All indicators suggest that children in difficult environments, whether these are due to economic, health, or other adverse circumstances, do better when their primary caretakers are available and healthy. A one-parent family is, therefore, at particular risk if the solitary parent becomes mentally ill. The two-parent couple, closely bonded by strong emotional ties, can better compensate if and when illness strikes one of them. However, the illness itself creates tremendous stress on the parental bond, and the healthy parent also suffers from role overload. This is even more stressful when both parents suffer some form of mental impairment. In these circumstances, a larger supportive network—of extended family, school and other community institutions, and health care facilities—can partially mitigate the enormous problems that such families must solve (Werner & Smith, 1982).

The Child's Role

The study of the experience of individual children in families with mentally disturbed parents owes a great deal to Anthony (1969, 1975), who was among the first to conduct direct observations of the family milieu as well as interviews with the children. Anthony also coined the descriptive phrases, "the vulnerable child" and "the invulnerable child" (1974), to emphasize that children react differently to family pathology.

An important question is whether the children of psychotically ill parents are themselves more likely to develop psychiatric disorders, what kinds of disorders these are likely to be, and whether this familial transmission can be attributed to nature or to nurture. When considering evidence of mental disturbance in school-age children of psychotic parents, we must use indicators other than the usual data, based on adoptive studies, pedigree analyses, and family assessments, that are cited for young adults (Beardslee, Bemporad, Keller, & Klerman, 1983). This is because full-blown psychosis usually appears, at the earliest, in late adolescence. This discussion does not address a related question—whether or not there is a clear relationship between the early behavior of these children and their later propensity to develop an emotional illness—because this would go too far afield of our examination of the experience, coping, and adaptation of children with at least one mentally ill parent.

Most of the published studies of such children report on families with psychotic mothers; fewer include psychotic fathers. Some epidemiological explanations for this might be, first, that women tend to have children before illness onset or during the early years of the illness; and, second, that in keeping with the pattern in the general population, schizophrenic women tend to marry earlier than do schizophrenic men, who often do not marry at all. Furthermore, depression is more common in women and is also precipitated by childbirth in a certain number of cases (Weissman & Paykel, 1974).

Researchers have generally focused on finding cognitive defects in children of schizophrenic parents and affective problems in children of parents with affective disorders. However, Cohler, Grunebaum, Weiss, Gamer, and Gallant (1977) have demonstrated that children of both schizophrenic and depressive mothers have similar deficits in focusing attention. Whereas it is thought that the schizo-phrenics' offspring may be manifesting a genetically determined problem, the findings with the offspring of chronically depressed mothers suggest an interac-tional component to the observed deficit—perhaps the inability to reach out to a child and guide his or her cognitive development.

Rutter and Quinton (1984) find that school-age children of mentally ill parents most commonly suffer conduct disorders; these are more common in boys and are more frequent as children get older. Girls seem to be more likely to develop difficulties in adolescence, and these are more often personality disorders (Werner & Smith, 1982). Teachers' ratings of children's problematic behavior in school mirror the home situation. Studies further indicate that conduct disturbances are most common in situations in which the parents' mental illness is coupled with hostility toward the children, and in which persistent marital discord, foster place-ment of the children, poverty, and overcrowding compound the negative effects of the illness (Fergusson, Horwood, Gretton & Shannon, 1985; Rutter & Quinton, 1984) and are chronically stressful for the families and the children. A child's self-confidence and self-esteem are adversely affected if he or she is consistently and unfairly scapegoated. The child's inner life is also affected by preoccupation and worry about a parent who is ill (Ekdahl, Rice, & Schmidt, 1962). These findings corroborate the conclusion of Longfellow and Belle (1984) that mothers, more than fathers, seem to screen children from the negative effects of family adversity. Weissman's (1979) findings that young children of depressed mothers suffer more accidents and are often the targets of their mothers' hostility and withdrawal support these notions about the importance of mothers.

Vulnerability in the children of depressed parents is more frequently ex-pressed in behavior disorders and incipient personality disorders than in the small proportion of children who suffer early signs of obvious mental disorder (Beardslee et al., 1983; LaRoche, Cheifetz, Lester, et al., 1985). However, we should rec-ognize that obvious psychiatric diagnosis is a limited definition of vulnerability. Children who grow up in a consistently chaotic and inimical family and social environment are vulnerable to present and future difficulties of all sorts. They are constantly having to adapt, fend for themselves, and prepare for the unexpected; and they are missing the security or basic trust and expectation that they will receive protection and care, as well as guidance through the difficulties in their young lives.

In his study of children of psychotically ill parents, Anthony (1974) describes ''invulnerable children'' as follows:

[They have] a seemingly stubborn resistance to the process of being engulfed by the illness; a curiosity in studying the etiology, diagnosis, symptoms and treat-ment of the illness reaching to a level of knowledge that is quite surprising; a capacity to develop an objective, realistic, somewhat distant and yet distinctly compassionate approach to the parental illness, neither retreating from it nor being intimidated by it, but viewing it as something needing to be fully understood; an exposure to the stressful experience only after immunity has had time to build up;

and support, encouragement and candor from an adequately functioning other parent. (p. 540)

In a recent study of children of parents with chronic psychotic affective disorder, Keller *et al.* (1986) found that half (54%) of the children they rated were generally happy and able to cope adequately with their problems. Werner and Smith (1982), studying 29 Hawaiian children with parents who were either schizophrenic or psychotically depressed, found that those children who were "resilient" were more likely to have had good relationships with their primary caretakers during their first year of life, were well rated by teachers, had fewer cumulative life stresses than did the vulnerable children, and were more likely to have depressive than schizophrenic parents. Werner and Smith stress that constitutional factors play a large role in the development of infants, but that the availability in the family of other caring adults is important for later development. Like Rutter and Quinton (1984), they emphasize the cumulative impact of many family stresses on the child.

Clearly, invulnerability is not to be understood as an attribute that is determined solely by a child's constitution, a lucky escape from "bad" genes. Rather, it seems to result from some favorable constitutional factors coupled with an environment that helps the child to withstand the potential ill effects of a parent's illness. A corollary, although not overtly stated by any of the authors who have described the negative impact of direct hostility from a mentally ill parent, may be that the child who for some reason is not singled out for such attacks has a better chance of weathering chronic parental mental illness.

The literature also emphasizes the importance of marital harmony and the availability of another, nonpsychotic parent or family member in mitigating the development of psychopathology in children. Invulnerability should therefore be understood as being a relative rather than an absolute characteristic, and one that is associated with certain identifiable strengths within the family and the environment.

Family Response to Psychotic Illness of a Parent

For clinical purposes, the most important variables in a family with a psychotically ill parent are as follows: (1) the marital relationship; (2) the relationship between the identified patient and the children; (3) the relationship between the spouse and the children; (4) the adequacy of extrafamilial resources. A combination of these factors determines the ultimate impact of family life on the children and indicates the type of interventions that may be required.

All the data indicate that chronic marital discord, separation, and divorce are far more common among couples in which one partner has a psychotic illness (Rutter & Quinton, 1984). It is probably the exception rather than the rule to find mature intimacy, mutual self-disclosure, and reciprocal interdependence between these husbands and wives.

If a spouse can remain affectively involved with and attached to a depressed or schizophrenic partner, in spite of the mental illness, he or she will find it easier to avert marital discord and to provide a more harmonious environment for the children. To do so, the spouse must be able to identify and understand the partner's condition as an illness, and thus make a distinction between the spouse's disturbed behavior and his or her person. More often, however, the spouse finds it almost impossible to distinguish the "sick" from the "bad" partner. Then the mentally ill partner is shamed, blamed, avoided, attacked, or disqualified.

It is perhaps preferable for the well spouse to be able to be angry with and to expect "better" from the partner, because this at least reflects a kind of involvement. Too often, the mentally ill parent is gradually disqualified and peripheralized, so that spouse and children form an affectively united grouping that excludes the other parent. It is also possible for a particular type of recursive cycle to become established in these couple interactions, such that the "well" partner may identify any change in the spouse's behavior or demands as being evidence of illness, and the affected spouse may respond to these messages by maintaining "sick" behavior.

When one includes the children in the picture, one finds that the most difficult and problematic situations occur when one or more children are directly and consistently attacked by the impaired parent. Observers concur that it is less traumatic to have a parent who behaves in a generally bizarre and illogical fashion than it is to be the particular scapegoat of such a parent. This seems to be the case regardless of the diagnosis attached to the parent's condition. However, because the most frequent illness is recurrent depression in mothers, this condition has the greatest impact on children.

When evaluating the family relations of such a parent, it is important to be sensitive to the impact of the parent's potential hostility and the child's reactions. In some cases, the child will begin sharing the psychotic parent's perception of himself. If the children are treated differently, it is important to evaluate the impact of scapegoating not only on the victim but also on the other children. The latter can feel guilty and overburdened because of their preferred position; they can usually perceive the illness as an objective condition, and they can be concerned, saddened, or anxious about the parent's lack of judgment, as it affects many details of their everyday life.

The greater the number of conflict-free areas that can be fostered between the affected parent and the children—particularly the scapegoated child—the better the outcome in terms of the children's ultimate development. Sometimes such conflicts are absent only in certain situations, such as sharing a certain skill, activity, or interest. The greater the possibility of developing such conflict-free areas of interaction, the better the children's chances of developing a more multifaceted and not entirely negative identification with the psychotic, persecutory parent.

It is important, to be aware that recursive interactions are particularly frequent between a disturbed parent and a child who may have been singled out for scapegoating. In the assessment, it is particularly important to observe how the child encourages the parent's criticism by offering himself or herself as a scapegoat, by committing some disturbing act, or by demanding excessive attention from an already overburdened parent. Such behavior on the child's part tends to confirm the parent's own negative self-evaluation, making the parent feel worse and thus increasing the chances that the parent will do something hurtful or insulting to the child.

It is when most of a parent's hostility is directed against one particular child that therapeutic intervention may be most necessary and most difficult. The outcome depends heavily on the quality of the relationship between the unaffected parent and the children. The spouse who can maintain a positive image of the affected parent, yet can flexibly take over a large part of the parenting function as the need arises, will have the best chance of creating a healthy environment for the children. This can be an enormous task. Such parents find themselves assuming a great number of instrumental responsibilities, making constant shifts in child care arrangements as the situation dictates, and often operating almost as single parents for relatively long periods of time.

But since these parents are also often further handicapped by their documented propensity to suffer from mental disorder themselves, their availability and capacity to be effective parents may be far from optimal. The children thus have less chance of developing self-esteem and learning adaptive skills. If one child is particularly vulnerable or scapegoated in any way, he or she will be particularly affected by the family atmosphere.

The unaffected parent should serve not only as a model for the children, but also as a protective buffer between them and the other parent's irrationality or hostility. In some cases, he or she may even serve a prosthetic function, performing reality testing for the affected spouse and providing a corrective model for the children (Feldman & Guttman, 1984). The enormous difficulty of this task can only be appreciated if we recognize the humiliation felt by most psychotic parents at times when they realize that they are not functioning adequately and that their spouses are filling in for them. It may well be that for some, the hostility that Weissman and Paykel (1974) have described results from this knowledge but is directed against the children rather than at the spouse.

It is possible that families with particularly adequate nonpsychotic parents produce a higher proportion of "invulnerable" or resilient children. Werner and Smith (1982) stress the child's ability to attract nurturing care from the parent during infancy and the toddler stage. However, to date, the exact role and mode of functioning of the nonpsychotic parent in such a family has been insufficiently explored as an independent variable.

An understanding of the complexities of triadic functioning in this type of family, including the symptoms of the ill parent and the contributions of both the nonaffected parent and the children, may increase our understanding of the conditions that foster children's survival and adaptation versus those that increase their suffering. In the competent family with a mentally ill parent there is an interactional sequence in which the spouse is able to isolate the illness from the person's other characteristics, both for himself or herself and for the children.

Although actively stepping in to meet some of the children's needs, the spouse also involves the affected parent, to the degree that he or she can participate, so that the family does not close ranks without that parent. The children, adequately nurtured by the healthy parent, can spare their disturbed one, both through not being overdemanding and through showing affection.

In a dysfunctional family, the spouse not only demeans the ill parent, but also enlists the children both to feel sorry for his or her suffering as the spouse of a sick person and to disrespect the ill parent. These children are less available for relationships with their ill parent and are more likely to provoke his or her irritation and rejection, which may be seen as directed both at the children and at the spouse.

Many important strengths must be derived from outside the nuclear family. Although the nonpsychotic parent plays a key role in protecting the children and in fostering their healthy development in spite of the many imponderables of life with a psychotic parent, persons and systems outside the immediate nuclear family can provide supplementary support and attention, additional security, and a set of healthier potential models. Members of the extended family who are more or less permanently in the vicinity probably offer the most consistent and the most acceptable type of help. However, neighbors and friends can also defuse a difficult situation.

These same extrafamilial systems can, however, also worsen a bad situation by accentuating the psychotic parent's incompetence, moving in to take over areas where the parent still has competence and needs to maintain contacts, and aligning with the spouse and children if they are already tending to dismiss the psychotic parent. Clearly, this kind of response, which is common both among extended kin and among "helping" professionals, can promote the overall dysfunction of both the ill individual and the family.

If many families do not come to the attention of public agencies, it may often be because they have developed built-in support systems in the extended family or neighborhood network. Although the parents probably play the most important role in the child's identity formation and the development of self-esteem, we must not underestimate the importance of alternative models for development. Clinical experience constantly reminds us that such models, if they are consistently and reliably present during the crucial developmental years, can provide meaningful ideals and can counterbalance the potential damage wrought by inadequate parenting. This view is also congruent with a truly systemic approach to family functioning, inasmuch as it recognizes the many possible inputs to and outcomes of a particular set of events or circumstances.

The emphasis on the greater importance of the "natural" network, as opposed to the artificial network, is probably an acknowledgement that the former, in the long run, is more effective; the latter, painfully built up by a web of social institutions and their agents, may never "feel like home" and may always remain alien to the child and the family (Minuchin, 1984). Therefore, from a therapeutic point of view, mobilizing and assisting natural networks to help families with psychotic parents may be much more effective, both economically and in terms of the ultimate beneficial impact on the children and the families. Indeed, if we extrapolate from the finding that early and permanent foster placement is the only type of foster care that gives some prospect of truly resolving behavior disorders in vulnerable children (Rutter & Quinton, 1984), it seems clear that the original family atmosphere has such an "imprinting" effect that it must be countered by changes within the family, rather than by introducing a child into a world of strangers.

Examples of Families' Responses to Mental Disorder in a Parent

The Davidsons: A Family of Survivors

DESCRIPTION

Mrs. Davidson suffered her first hospitalization for depression at age 22, before her marriage. At 28, married and with a 2-year-old daughter, she suffered a second illness episode. Although depressive symptomatology predominated, she also presented with delusional symptoms and bizarre associations. She responded to a combination of antidepressant and antipsychotic medications.

Since that time, in spite of continuing psychiatric care and good compliance, Mrs. Davidson (now 45 years old) has had many illness episodes, of varying degrees of severity. However, with the exception of one that involved a severe suicidal attempt, with prolonged surgical hospitalization, Mrs. Davidson has not been hospitalized for more than 3 days at a time. Between illness attacks, she has always been an able and efficient office worker. Her mother has a history of depression. Her younger sister suffered a severe depression, necessitating medication, after moving to another city. Because of her symptomatology, family history, and work history, Mrs. Davidson has been diagnosed as suffering a schizoaffective disorder.

Mrs. Davidson has another child, a boy 7 years younger than his sister. Her husband was for many years an executive in a company. During the economic recession of the 1970s, the department in which Mr. Davidson worked was permanently closed, and he was dismissed with a year's compensatory salary. He has always felt that one of the reasons he was not transferred to another department was that he had previously missed many work days because of his wife's recurrent illnesses. For 5 years Mr. Davidson was at home full time. During that period, the family depended heavily on the wife's salary, and there was considerable economic hardship because she was not always able to work.

For many years, the Davidsons lived in a two-family home with the husband's parents. When the wife could not manage the household, the children would spend a great deal of time with their grandparents. This situation continued, even after the grandfather died and the families moved apart. Mrs. Davidson has always felt that her husband is more closely tied to his mother than to her. Her mother-in-law seems to pride herself on her long-suffering, uncomplaining devotion to the family, and disqualifies Mrs. Davidson's negative feelings about her on the grounds that she is ill.

The first signs of a new illness episode usually have consisted of delusional symptoms about the mother- or father-in-law or about one of the neighbors. Mrs. Davidson will feel that they are spying on her and her family. She becomes extremely angry, irritable, and attacking, with what her husband describes as a "motor mouth" that does not stop. She is usually particularly aggressive toward her 19-year-old daughter, Jane.

Jane did well in elementary school, but her grades began slipping in high school, and she finally dropped out in the 11th grade. She now works full-time, but still lives at home. Her mother described her as being "wild" when she was younger, meaning that she would play around in the neighborhood and spend a lot of time with friends and their families. This pattern continues, and she spends a good deal of her leisure time out of the house, with friends and neighbors. She has never been close to her mother or to her grandmother. Her mother feels bad about this, wistfully saying that she wishes they could go shopping together, like other girls and their mothers. Mrs. Davidson herself has never been close to her own mother. Jane has always felt close to her father, who has consistently protected her against his wife's attacks.

The son, Kevin, at age 12 is just beginning to move away from a close tie to both parents. He has always shared sports activities with his father, and these have taken them out of the house on weekends. His mother is very pleased with his schoolwork, and their relationship seems to center on his studies. During Mrs. Davidson's last illness, Kevin decided to spend the summer holidays at his paternal grandmother's home several blocks away, explaining that it was closer to his junior baseball activities.

Even during periods when she seems apparently normal, Mrs. Davidson can be struggling with delusions that she does not share until some time later. For instance, at one period she was convinced that her husband had won the Grand Lottery and that he was purposely not telling her about it because he wanted to surprise her some day. She found confirmation for this belief in various chance remarks made by her colleagues at work.

Mr. Davidson often becomes exasperated with his wife when she begins to be accusatory, voicing persecutory thoughts and feeling hopeless and depressed. He still treats her as if she could do better. As proof, he appeals to her exemplary record of receiving raises at work, in spite of her frequent absences. He is still puzzled by her illness and refuses to accept that she is entirely unresponsible for her behavior, even though her illness tends to be cyclical, occurring in the early spring. He usually does not immediately alert the treating psychiatrist when Mrs. Davidson's psychotic symptoms occur. He complains that she is too "selfish"— too preoccupied with herself, and therefore not available to the children.

COMMENTARY

This family has coped fairly well with chronic mental disorder in the mother, probably for several reasons: (1) the fact that the mother functions fairly well between illness episodes; (2) the fact that the husband actively serves a prosthetic and a buffering function, which was perhaps enhanced by his continued presence in the home during his many years of unemployment; and (3) the support provided by Mr. Davidson's mother (and father, when he was alive).

Mrs. Davidson is clearly somewhat emotionally peripheral to the family. There is a certain superficiality in her personality, even when she is well, that seems to preclude true intimacy. She is aware of and saddened by this. Her husband and children have reacted by bonding together and excluding her to some extent. The children will joke about times when she is "crazy." At these times, Jane will tell her mother she will discuss a sensitive subject with her "some other time," and the children will laugh together about these "crazy" periods. Mr. Davidson more openly expresses anger, disappointment, and frustration with his wife, and also with the medical profession for being unable to help her get completely well. Father and daughter openly express some concerns as to the possibility that this illness is genetically determined.

Jane's behavior shows that she has been able to use distance and humor, and has found other resources to help her deal with a mother who could not and cannot give her completely adequate parenting. She continues to seek close female companionship outside the home, neither bonding with her mother nor becoming caught in a loyalty conflict by bonding with her grandmother. She perhaps protects herself against a great sadness by joking about her mother's wishes for their relationship.

It can also be seen that Mrs. Davidson's peripheral status may be related to the way the family has organized itself to manage during her illnesses. Her superficiality, her lack of affective involvement, and, ultimately, the very nature of her breakdowns seem to accurately reflect the fact that the family members are largely aligned with each other and have excluded her. Furthermore, Jane's particular way of avoiding intimacy, possibly chosen to avoid involvement in her mother's illness, actually puts her at greater risk for similar management of relationships in her own future family. So, while the Davidsons have survived, they have done so at great cost, particularly to Mrs. Davidson and to Jane.

The Levines: A Family That Coped

DESCRIPTION

The Levine family began having difficulties when Mrs. Levine developed a postpartum depression after the delivery of her second child, a daughter. At the same time, Mrs. Levine's mother, who had had several previous depressions, required hospitalization because she became very agitated, thinking she was pregnant. Mrs. Levine responded to antidepressants, but continued to have a lingering lack of interest, energy, and enjoyment in her daily activities.

Although her husband had a rising position in her family's business, the couple felt that Mrs. Levine should continue working as a school teacher, partly for financial reasons and partly because they thought she would feel better in this role. This proved to be quite difficult, as she had to cope with recurring depressions as well as the burden of two demanding roles, at home and at work. The early years of the children's development were frequently quite chaotic. Maids came and went, housekeeping and child care arrangements were quite haphazard; the couple had reciprocal grudges, he because of the chaotic housekeeping, she because of his undemonstrativeness and perfunctory lovemaking.

Mr. Levine was basically quite content in the role of instrumental provider and rescuer, which he had also served in his family of origin. However, he openly attacked his wife for all her shortcomings and did not reprimand their son, Eric, when he sided with him. The daughter, Jessica, was consistently sweet, compliant, and self-effacing.

Mrs. Levine easily felt defensive, even when criticized by her 8-year-old son. She never sought to alleviate the role strain she experienced as mother–wife–housekeeper–professional, perhaps because she feared being disdained and identified with her own mother. She strove to emulate her older sister, also a school teacher.

During the children's school years, Mrs. Levine was discovered to have a malignancy, for which she was successfully treated. By then, she had had one manic attack and had begun receiving lithium, which helped her a great deal. She weathered her cancer and also was very supportive to her husband and his family when several family members successively died of cancer. Her husband had by then become financially successful. Mrs. Levine had had difficulties with her job during her successive illnesses and was happy to be able to stop working.

Eric had minor difficulties at school over the years, usually for not being well disciplined and for being rude and noisy in class. From school age on, he had many grandiose plans for getting rich quick, some of which involved being less than honest with his peers. At such times, Mr. Levine would intervene with prompt discipline and would be very disappointed and critical of Eric. Jessica consistently "stayed out of the way," remaining a model child who was concerned not to upset anybody.

At the end of high school, the children successively left home to go away to college. There, Eric became involved in a business, which he described to his parents in glowing terms. However, this venture failed, and it was not clear whether or not he had serious debts. His studies were affected and he had to repeat a year. Jessica studied very hard, was determined to become a lawyer, and had a disappointing relationship with a boyfriend, who did not want to be as "close" as she wished.

When the children both left home, Mr. Levine began to question his life and decided he wanted a marital separation. However, there were several reconciliations, always on his initiative; each time, his wife felt herself a passive recipient of his favor or disfavor. Finally, she felt she had been sufficiently humiliated by his ambivalence and insisted on divorce. This very much disturbed Eric. His studies suffered, and at the winter break he went to Florida on vacation and spent money quite recklessly. Jessica insisted that her parents' problems did not concern her, commenting, "They are both immature." And she continued to study single-mindedly for a future career.

In this case, the mother's aggressive feelings—never very strong—were mainly directed against her husband. She abdicated responsibility for the children's discipline; her nurturing was well-meaning but sporadic.

There was a clear connection between Mrs. Levine's illness and her relationship both with her family of origin and present family. In the former, she developed great sensitivity to others' feelings, which continued in the way she responded to any criticism from her husband: Either she became depressed and self-devaluing, or she behaved in an unrealistically euphoric manner.

Although the children were not victimized by an angry, attacking mother, they seemed to receive insufficient compensatory attention and consistent nurturance from their father, who confined himself to sporadically disciplining Eric and to criticizing and denigrating his wife's failings rather than supplementing them. However, Mr. Levine also provided his wife and children with structure and security.

As they reach young adulthood, the children are both functioning. However, a major cause for concern is that 20-year-old Eric may already have suffered at least one manic attack. This possibility has been denied by the family. Jessica's possible future difficulties may lie more in the realm of human relationships. She feels she has been unjustly deprived. Her career choice might partly compensate for this, but there is often less justice to be found in affairs of the human heart.

Eric, also highly criticized by his father, has adopted his mother's style of denial and method of escape from confrontation, which continues to be supported by the entire family's interactional style. Jessica, on the other hand, has adopted her father's style of lying low and blaming others, thus avoiding addressing her own responsibility for both the positive and negative sides of her relationships.

The Cohens: A Family with Difficulties

DESCRIPTION

The Cohen couple has separated each time the wife, now aged 33, has been hospitalized with a manic attack. These have occurred every year for approximately 6 years. As long as Mrs. Cohen does not require hospitalization, the husband leaves the home and she remains with the children. Should she be hospitalized, he takes over the household. These separations usually occur because Mrs. Cohen becomes convinced that her marriage is unfulfilling.

Mrs. Cohen's first illness, a postpartum depression, occurred after the delivery of Charlotte, now 6 years old. She has sporadically accepted medications from her physician, usually for short periods after she is hospitalized. She is very attached to her primary therapist, a nonphysician who does not administer medications. During her most manic periods, she has even slept on the doorstep of his home, with her children, to be near him.

The older child, Henri, is a quiet, rather insecure boy. He shows his need for attention by rather pedantically "showing off" his knowledge about scientific information. When the household becomes too chaotic in his father's absence, he appeals to his father, and Mr. Cohen has tries to have the children spend more time with him if this does not upset his wife. The little girl, Charlotte, is merry and excitable, readily joining her mother in her sudden enthusiasms or rejections.

Mr. Cohen is a quiet, intellectual, timid man, with a pronounced physical handicap that is the result of a childhood illness. He often appears unable to decide on a course of action when his wife is out of control and particularly aggressive toward him. He does not seem consistently to identify her behavior as resulting from an illness for which she is not responsible, and for which he must compensate by imposing his judgment of the situation. He behaves as if she were an "elemental force" against which he is helpless. He avoids any move that might provoke her rejection of him and has always eschewed the possibility of gaining sole legal custody of the children when his wife is ill. Usually, members of her own family seek to have Mrs. Cohen committed to hospital for treatment.

Thus far, the children do not have any major school problems, although Charlotte's teachers find her easily distracted and sometimes lacking in concentration. At home, they have a great deal of freedom; their mother does not believe in setting many limits, feeling that she was stifled by her own mother's limit setting during her childhood. The children seem to be aware of the unpredictability of meals, clean clothing, and routines in their home. However, they do not complain about this. They rarely spend time in other people's homes, except for visits to their father's parents and some of his siblings.

COMMENTARY

The Cohen children are growing up in a rather unpredictable, chaotic atmosphere as far as their instrumental needs are concerned. However, their mother does not scapegoat either of them. Their father, although a source of support, is weak in that he is unable to act either as a buffer or as an auxilliary ego for his wife when her judgment is impaired. One has the ominous feeling that worse developments are yet to come, as the children repeatedly experience their mother's mood swings and periods of paranoid thinking.

An additional problem is the hermetic atmosphere in which this family lives; there is very little input from the extended family. Even Mrs. Cohen's therapists are not permitted to communicate. In this rather closed system, there is little possibility for the children to experience mitigating influences.

In some ways, this family seems to be dealing appropriately with the mother's illnesses. For instance, Mr. Cohen takes his wife seriously and does not disqualify her as a mother. On the other hand, he fails to provide enough "reality testing" for his wife's flights of fancy; it is also likely that neither he nor his wife is providing the necessary grounding for Charlotte's work in school or Henri's appropriate view of himself as a child rather than a pedant. It appears that Mr. Cohen is much more focused on his wife as the family bellwether, and that she is much more focused on her internal needs, than either one is on the proper care of their children.

A Family of Victims

DESCRIPTION

Four-year-old Lisa is removed from home and placed in foster care by a social service agency, because she has been severely abused and starved by her alcoholic, psychotic mother. There are six other children who continue to live at home with the parents. The child lives continuously in the same foster home until age 11, when she returns home for 6 months and then again requires placement because of maternal abuse. However, even when she is in foster care, she is regularly sent home on the weekends. Her mother continues verbally and physically abusing her. The only protection her father can offer is to take her with him when he goes out for long gambling sessions. He cannot directly confront his wife in order to prevent her abusive treatment of their daughter. The mother has no extended-family members living in the city; the father's sister once vainly tried to gain custody of the children, after the parents involved them in making pornographic films. At adulthood, the patient and two other children have diagnosed major mental disorders.

COMMENTARY

On one level, this case is extremely familiar (Goldstein, Freud, & Solnit, 1973). It is described to illustrate the almost complete failure of the network of potential protectors surrounding this child. Neither the unaffected parent, nor the extended family, nor the social agency is effective.

A systemic assessment of this case shows that all the family members are victims. The mother is a victim of psychotic, addictive illness, neglect, and her husband's self-indulgent gambling; the father is a victim of his wife's drinking and psychosis; and the child is a victim of abuse. The family is a victim of a system that feels obliged to help only by separating family members, thus leveling blame and focusing on weakness, and undermining rather than strengthening any affective ties that could be sustained between family members.

Implications for Intervention

In thinking about the kinds of intervention that would be most effective for children in families with mentally ill parents, it may be helpful to begin with some naturalistic reports from adults who are themselves children of mentally disorderd parents, and who have not had any major pathology. Through their accounts of their experiences of growing up in such families, especially what has proved helpful and what has remained problematic, we may begin to construct a model of the type of family intervention(s) that may be appropriate. We must maintain awareness that young children may require different types of input at different stages. Moreover, we must never forget that a child "brings" his or her own temperament, personality, and potential to the situation. As Rutter and Quinton (1984) say, "children are not just passive recipients of environmental stimuli. The effects of family influences are dependent, in part, on their bringing about changes in children's self-concepts and in the styles of thinking and behaving" (p. 878).

Memories

In her essay, "Ruth's Song (Because She Could Not Sing It)," Gloria Steinem (1986) lovingly describes living alone between the ages of 10 and 17 with a "loving, intelligent, terrorized woman who tried hard to clean our littered house whenever she emerged from her private world, but who could rarely be counted on to finish one task" (pp. 146–147). Steinem's mother, Ruth, had been an accomplished young newspaperwoman who became increasingly withdrawn and helpless with her terrors and paranoid thoughts.

> an invalid who lay in bed with eyes closed and lips moving in occasional responses to voices only she could hear. . . . In many ways, our roles were reversed: I was the mother, and she was the child. Yet that didn't help her, for she still worried about me with all the intensity of a frightened mother, plus the special fears of her own world full of threats and hostile voices. (pp. 146–147)

What seemed to help the daughter was being able periodically to escape—to coffee shops and movie theatres, to the library full of books. She was also supported by the knowledge that her divorced father and older sister, although not in the same town, were concerned and would do all they could. What helped her as well were her mother's occasional periods of lucidity and the fact that even when she was very ill she seemed to have been proud and loving where Gloria was concerned.

Steinem finds much to admire in her mother, especially during her later years, when she was receiving psychiatric treatment and some of her original spirit and intelligence re-emerged. Just the same, the daughter ends her "song" with the remark, "I miss her, but perhaps no more in death than I did in life. Dying seems less sad than having lived too little" (p. 165).

A competent professional woman who grew up with a manic–depressive father, whose behavior was never explained as an illness (although several of his siblings had the same illness, and he had several courses of electroconvulsive therapy [ECT]), states that she knew there were periods when he was very irritable and had temper tantrums. Her mother would react to these by trying to keep everything at home on an even keel. The daughter had two alternative explanations for her father's behavior: that it was reality-based (e.g., that it resulted from business problems), or that these were "crazy periods," during which he had little control over his actions or feelings. These alternatives could not be discussed within the family. She describes some of this behavior with affectionate amusement, but does realize that it was a relief to have her mother finally put a medical name to it, once her father was receiving medications and the stigma of ECT was no longer a factor. Although she recognizes that her mother was trying to be a protective buffer, she is angrier with her than with the father, because she was somewhat distant and sometimes seemed ineffectual; the mother deferred to the father and sacrificed a close relationship with her children to her continued devotion for her husband.

A professional artist whose mother suffered severe manic–depressive illness from an early age remembers being taken to stay with family friends or being temporarily placed in a Catholic orphanage at times when her mother required hospitalization. She remembers being frightened by the nuns in the orphanage at age 4, wondering whether they would be angry with her for having some old candy stuck in her pocket. When her mother was well enough to be at home, there were also periods when the care of the children was largely in the hands of hired help. When her mother was well, and especially when she was hypomanic, the daughter remembers very happy times of great closeness between them. She was, and still is, quite angry with her father, whom she describes as having been selfishly preoccupied with his career, derogatory toward his wife, and neglectful of his children's development. To this day, she feels uncomfortable with the old family friends who would take her in when her mother was in the hospital. She feels she was a burden on their family life, a stranger at their table.

Lessons from Memories

These are the memories and histories of adults who have proven to be "invulnerable," in the sense that they have lived and are living lives that have been at least superficially unremarkable and in some cases truly exceptional. Yet their histories have some very important messages for us. It is certainly striking that these children, who seem to have been able to navigate quite well in the pain and chaos of their history, have often been more loyal to their more disturbed parents. It is as if such a child realizes that the ill parent is incapable of more effective parenting. The child's indignation falls on the nonpsychotic parent, who is experienced as affectively unavailable, perhaps in reaction to the strain of coping with life with a disturbed spouse. It is also clear that such youngsters accept and value what their disturbed parents have been able to give to them.

It is also striking that a disturbed parent's illness is easily made into a family secret, which is not discussed within the nuclear family. This gives the child the message that things are not to be discussed outside the family either. The result may be that other avenues of possible support, such as the extended family, the school, or empathic neighbors, are off limits to the child, and he or she suffers all the consequences of living in a closed system.

More objective research does not offer much more information about the conditions in which children thrive when a parent is ill. On the basis of a 4-year follow-up, Rutter and Quinton (1984) have concluded that only in the most favorable circumstances, where the home environment became much more harmonious, did the children's behavior markedly improve. They emphasize that once a child starts on a particular developmental pathway, it is very difficult to modify its course. Presumably the scapegoat's unappealing behavior "attracts" similar negative treatment in settings other than the home. The crucial variables are the general level of family discord and the extent to which the child is victimized.

These findings point to the obvious need to develop intervention strategies with *families* rather than with individual children. Yet the literature is not particularly rich in descriptions of such therapies, with the exception of cases of extremely destructive children such as those treated by Patterson (1975), mainly with a behavioral paradigm. The early work of Minuchin and colleagues is certainly relevant here, both in its emphasis on the reinforcement of family boundaries and in its concern with the double parental functions of nurturing and disciplining (Minuchin, 1974). However, it has never dealt explicitly and specifically with the approach to families in which parents are mentally disturbed.

No doubt the paucity of literature is partly due to the reluctance of family systems thinkers to acknowledge mental illness as a "thing in itself," since they have so avoided the medical model. They have believed that such a model is antithetical to systems theory, because it is linear rather than circular, and because it is unicausal rather than a multiply recursive model that does not attribute causality (Dell, 1982). This attitude has begun to change only in recent years, with the advent of the psychoeducational approaches in family therapy and the protests of feminist thinkers and others who have questioned this version of the family systems model (Anderson, Hogarty, & Reiss, 1980; James & McIntyre, 1983). Descriptions of family intervention strategies have been largely confined to multiple-family therapy and psychoeducational approaches in families in which the disturbed members are adolescents or young adults. The literature on family divorce therapy, although making frequent mention of family therapy intervention, usually does not specify the proportion of divorced parents who suffer from major mental disorders, although we know that such persons are at greater risk for separation and divorce (Briscoe, Smith, & Robins, 1973; Rutter & Quinton, 1984). Indeed, in many cases it can be demonstrated that the emotional illness preceded and, in fact, could have contributed to the decision to separate. We require greater documentation of the effectiveness of family therapy and must still largely depend on clinical reports that are not statistically validated.

By the same token, because of the identification of these disabling psychotic conditions as illnesses, symptomatic individuals tend not to be seriously examined in the context of family interactions. Whether or not family interactions cause these behaviors, they form repetitive sequences within the family, which, as we have seen, tend to maintain the illness as well as to contribute to the morbidity of the children. From the naturalistic reports of children grown up and from the descriptions of these family environments, as well as from the clinical studies reviewed in this chapter, it seems obvious that a systemic approach to working with these families can and should be formulated, not only in order to palliate the illness but also to help the entire family function on a healthier basis.

Therapeutic Interventions

The Child and the Family

As we have seen, about one-third of the children studied by Rutter and Quinton (1984) developed some form of conduct disorder, usually in a setting of parent–child or parent–parent hostility. In view of these authors' and Weissman's (1979) conclusions (that these disorders are continually self- and other-reinforced and that little spontaneous improvement occurs), such situations clearly require family intervention and therapy. Such efforts must be directed both at the child's behavior and at the parents' relationship.

Addressing the child's behavior and helping the parents deal with it involves assessing the role each member of the triad plays in its perpetuation. The ill parent's capacity to change his or her behavior and interaction with the other family members must be carefully assessed, and interventions should be designed to maximize this parent's strengths, so as to prevent disqualification by the other family members. The unimpaired parent's ability to be actively involved must be also carefully assessed and strengthened.

Although the therapist's direct intervention and modeling of more adequate methods and controlling and/or engaging the child may be helpful, this is usually not sufficient and may actually reinforce the family's tendency to enlist the therapist as a permanent caretaker. With a school-age child, an effective intervention is setting tasks that address aspects of the child's troublesome behavior and the parents' inadequate response. These can provide realistic goals that do not overwhelm the family by their vagueness or difficulty. The task can focus on behaviors, such as interrupting, being rebellious about homework, getting up on time, or table manners. The disturbed parent's complaints can be supported, but his or her hostile attacks can be modified; the spouse can be involved in a constructive manner, rather than continuing his or her criticisms and unsupportive behavior.

Another method is to give the child and the impaired parent a venue for sharing and enjoying each other's company (LaRoche, 1986). Tasks such as cooking together, playing board games, watching TV, or any other potentially enjoyable and relatively conflict-free activity should be encouraged. Sometimes this will work if the unimpaired parent is absent. In other cases, he or she should be on the sidelines, but present.

Whatever the form of family therapy, there should be some psychoeducational component. The affected parent's condition is explained to each family member at the level appropriate for that member. The usefulness of this method has been demonstrated with families of young adults (Anderson *et al.*, 1980; Falloon, Boyd, & McGill, 1984) and with couples in which one partner is depressed (Anderson *et al.*, 1986). Although psychoeducational procedures are usually described for family groups, there is no reason why explanation and education cannot also take place with single families. Indeed, this is perhaps preferable when preadolescent children are involved, as the illness can be more clearly explained at their level.

For some children—perhaps particularly for those whose ill parent is severely and chronically impaired and whose other parent is ineffectual or absent—it may be useful to hold individual or group child therapy sessions. One important goal is to strengthen and reinforce each child's perception and emotional differentiation from the parent's illness, to insure that more children become like the "invulnerable" children described by Anthony (1974). The child can share such feelings as anger, despair, fear, and helplessness, and can receive empathic guidance in handling the situation. However, it is important to be sensitive to the loyalty conflicts that these children so often experience. For this reason, it is always important to gain the parents' explicit consent for separate child therapy of whatever sort, and to embed it within concurrent ongoing family therapy.

Couple Therapy

Marital discord has been described as a key factor in creating the atmosphere of tension and hostility that so often exists in these families (Briscoe & Smith, 1973; Davenport, 1981; Grunebaum, Gamer, & Cohler, 1983; Rutter & Quinton, 1984; Weissman & Paykel, 1974). Moreover, spouses with bipolar mood swings may, during the hypomanic phase, deplore the very distance that they seem to prefer when they are depressed. Intervention with a couple in the child's absence may be more productive, because it is easier to preserve the child's respectful image of the impaired parent, to deal with issues of intimacy and sexuality, and to give the healthier spouse an opportunity to express his or her negative feelings without adding to the child's insecurity.

Activating Natural Networks

Many families benefit from the support of an extended network of relatives, friends, or neighbors. As we have seen, healthy coping on the part of latency-age children is reflected in their ability to reach out to people outside the nuclear family. However, this is predicated both on the presence of such a network and on the parents' approval for interacting in it. The capacity for such interaction in fact may be a fundamental sign of health on the part of both the child and the family, as it prevents the painful possibility of being shut up in a paranoid, a depressed, or an unrealistically manic system with very little rectifying input from the outside world. It is important to combat a process of reciprocal self-isolation between the family and the extended network, in reaction to the stigma of a family member who is mentally ill.

The unimpaired spouse should be encouraged to make or to sustain contact with other significant people on a regular basis. Sometimes this may involve excluding the impaired spouse, and raises issues of shame and doubt about the spouse. These must be worked through, so as to make it possible for the unimpaired spouse and the children to have external social contacts, even if they incur the other parent's irrational wrath or withdrawal.

Many families do not have a natural network, either because it has never existed or because they are geographically distant from their families of origin. In these cases, organizations such as the Association of Relatives and Friends of the Mentally Ill can be helpful to the unaffected parent.

Multiple-Family Therapy

Although few reports describe multiple-family therapy groups involving young children, Cunningham and Matthews (1982) have reported that this form of therapy enhances parent–child relationships and parenting skills in families with latency-age children. The experience of authors working with multiple-family therapy groups as part of the psychoeducational approach to severe mental disorders in adults indicates that this approach is beneficial (Anderson et al., 1980). There is a need to articulate the criteria and circumstances under which multiple-family therapy would be indicated for families of emotionally disturbed parents who have young children.

In our setting, a group for recently discharged patients with varied diagnoses and their families usually includes some cases in which the patients are mothers or fathers of younger children. Such a group offers children the possibility of receiving attention and affection from other adults and the chance to share certain issues with the siblings of younger mentally ill patients (Sigman, John, Levinson, & Betts, 1985).

Therapeutic Style

Anderson et al. (1986) have found that both the psychoeducational and the psychotherapeutic approaches seem to be valuable for families with depressed adult members. Family therapy, be it behavioral, psychodynamic, or structural, has grown out of the psychotherapeutic tradition. Although a great deal of research unequivocally demonstrating family therapy's usefulness remains to be done, there is no evidence that the psychotherapeutic approaches are completely useless (Smith, Glass, & Miller, 1980).

For young children, family psychotherapy should be congruent with their level of cognitive and affective development. It is necessary constantly to shift back and forth between the primary-process thinking of younger children, including the use of play and a focus on fairly simple cognitive paradigms, and the greater capacity for abstraction of older children and adults (Guttman, 1975; Zilbach, Bergel, & Gass, 1972).

Children of this age cannot comprehend the rather abstruse scientific explanations normally given for their parents' condition in the psychoeducational mode. Parents need help not only in mastering their own understanding of the illness, but also in explaining it appropriately to the children, as the following example indicates.

A young couple came to the first interview with two little girls, aged 7 and 5 years. The wife had always been energetic and good-humored. During the past 2 months, she had become withdrawn, preoccupied, tearful, and inattentive; was fearful about leaving the house; and showed a predominance of depressive and phobic symptoms. Her illness seemed to coincide with the discharge from a mental hospital of her own mother, who had been hospitalized for 25 years. The husband was baffled by his wife's condition, and was especially distressed at the prospect of having to explain to his parents that his wife was "sick," He responded well to reassurance that her condition would improve with time and medication. He was also reassured to know that he would receive homemaker support. The children listened intently to everything that was said and seemed happy to hear that "Mummy will soon be better"; that, meanwhile, she had to have rests; and that someone would be there to help take care of them.

Ideally, it is best to maintain intermittent contact with these families over a long period of time. The therapist who has known and shared with the family a deeply painful event is ideally placed to continue as a guide or counselor as the family faces particular crises (e.g., a parent's relapse) or more normative issues that may nevertheless pose difficulties. In view of the finding that cumulative life events have particularly adverse consequences, it is possible that periodic "family checkups" may be of some preventive help. This contact need not be continuous; it may occur only at times at which family members have come to some turning point in their personal or collective lives.

Conclusion

The reciprocal relationship between the child and the family is so strong that is almost impossible to intervene effectively with a mentally disturbed parent without some form of involvement with that person's family. Ideally, this involvement should be continuous, although not necessarily continual. It should be geared to foster natural development, the strengthening of natural supports, and the weathering of crises for which such families are often less well prepared than are others. Family therapy should be undertaken at critical points in a child's development and a family's life cycle.

The form and frequency of family intervention depend on such factors as the presenting problems, the quality of family relationships, and the personal resources of the family members. Family therapy can be conducted with single families or in multiple-family therapy groups. It can be combined with child therapy, child group therapy, and couple therapy, depending on the requirements of the particular situation. However, a systemic perspective should always be maintained by making family therapy the central therapeutic component.

A marked weakness in this as in many other areas of family therapy is the fact that the therapeutic outcomes of the various approaches have not been explicitly tested (Gurman & Kniskern, 1981). Therefore, although we are beginning to accumulate an authoritative body of observations regarding the impact on children of mental illness in one or both parents, there are almost no data demonstrating that our clinical beliefs are objectively valid. A most pressing future task is to ascertain whether family intervention makes a short-term and a long-term difference in children's ultimate development.

REFERENCES

Anderson, C. M., Hogarty, G. E., & Reiss, D. J. (1980). Family treatment of adult schizophrenic patients: A psycho-educational approach. *Schizophrenia Bulletin, 6,* 490–505.
Anderson, C. M., Griffin, S., Rossi, A., Pagonis, I., Holder, D. P., & Treiber, R. (1986). A comparative study of the impact of education versus process groups for families of patients with affective disorders. *Family Process, 25,* 169–184.
Anthony, E. J. (1969). The mutative impact on family life of serious mental and physical illness in a parent. *Canadian Psychiatric Association Journal, 14,* 433–453.
Anthony, E. J. (1974). The syndrome of the psychologically invulnerable child. In E. J. Anthony & C. Koupernik (Eds.), *The child in his family: Children at psychiatric risk* (pp. 529–544). Chichester, England: Wiley.
Anthony, E. J. (1975). the influence of a manic–depressive environment on the developing child. In E. J. Anthony & T. Benedek (Eds.), *Depression and human existence* (pp. 279–315). Boston: Little, Brown.
Beardslee, W. R., Bemporad, J., Keller, M. B., & Klerman, G. L. (1983). Children of parents with major affective disorder: A review. *American Journal of Psychiatry, 140,* 825–832.
Briscoe, C. W., & Smith, J. B. (1973). Depressive and marital turmoil. *Archives of General Psychiatry, 29,* 811–817.
Briscoe, C. W., Smith, J. B., & Robins, E. (1973). Divorce and psychiatric disease. *Archives of General Psychiatry, 29,* 119–125.
Cohler, B. J., Grunebaum, H. V., Weiss, J. L., Gamer, E., & Gallant, D. H. (1977). Disturbance of attention among schizophrenic, depressed and well mothers and their children. *Journal of Child Psychology and Psychiatry, 18,* 115–135.
Cunningham, J. M., & Matthews, K. L. (1982). Impact of multiple family therapy approach on a parallel latency age/parent group. *International Journal of Group Psychotherapy, 32,* 91–102.
Davenport, Y. B. (1981). Treatment of the married bipolar patient in conjoint couples psychotherapy

groups. In M. R. Lansky (Ed.), *Family therapy and major psychopathology* (pp. 123–143). New York: Grune & Stratton.

Dell, P. F. (1982). Beyond homeostasis: Toward a concept of coherence. *Family Process, 21,* 21–42.

Ekdahl, M., Rice, E., & Schmidt, W. (1962). Children of parents hospitalized for mental illness. *American Journal of Public Health, 52,* 428–435.

Falloon, I. R. H., Boyd, J. L., & McGill, C. W. (1984). *Family care of schizophrenia: A problem-solving approach to the treatment of mental illness.* New York: Guilford Press.

Feldman, R. B., & Guttman, H. A. (1984). Families of borderline patients: Literal-minded parents, borderline parents, and parental protectiveness. *American Journal of Psychiatry, 141,* 1392–1396.

Fergusson, D. M., Horwood, L. J., Gretton, M. E., & Shannon, F. T. (1985). Family life events, maternal depression, and maternal and teacher descriptions of child behavior. *Pediatrics, 75,* 30–35.

Goldstein, J., Freud, A., & Solnit, A. J. (1973). *Beyond the best interests of the child.* New York: Free Press.

Grunebaum, H. V., Gamer, E., & Cohler, B. J. (1983). The spouse in depressed families. In H. L. Morrison (Ed.), *Children of depressed parents: Risk, identification and intervention* (pp. 139–158). New York: Grune & Stratton.

Gurman, A. S., & Kniskern, D. P. (1981). Family therapy outcome research: Knowns and unknowns. In A. S. Gurman & D. P. Kniskern (Eds.), *Handbook of family therapy* (pp. 742–775). New York: Brunner/Mazel.

Guttman, H. (1975). The young child's participation in conjoint family therapy. *Journal of the American Academy of Child Psychiatry, 14*(3), 490–499.

James, K. B., & McIntyre, D. (1983). The reproduction of families: The social role of family therapy. *Journal of Marital and Family Therapy, 9,* 119–129.

Keller, M. B., Beardslee, W. R., Dover, D. J., Lavon, P. W., Samuelson, H., & Klerman, G. R. (1986). Impact of severity and chronicity of parental affective illness on adaptive functioning and psychopathology in children. *Archives of General Psychiatry, 43,* 930–937.

LaRoche, C. (1986). Prevention in high-risk children of depressed parents. *Canadian Journal of Psychiatry, 31,* 161–165.

LaRoche, C., Cheifetz, P., Lester, E., Schibuk, L., DiTommaso, E., & Engelsmann, F. (1985). Psychopathology in the offspring of parents with bipolar affective disorders. *Canadian Journal of Psychiatry, 30,* 337–343.

Lewis, J., Beavers, W. R., Gossett, J. T., & Phillips, V. A. (1976). *No single thread: Psychological health in family systems.* New York: Brunner/Mazel.

Longfellow, C., & Belle, D. (1984). Stressful environments and their impact on children. In J. H. Humphrey (Ed.), *Stress in childhood* (pp. 63–78). New York: AMS Press.

Merikangas, K. R. (1984). Divorce and assortative mating among depressed patients. *American Journal of Psychiatry, 141,* 74–76.

Minuchin, S. (1974). *Families and family therapy.* Cambridge, MA: Harvard University Press.

Minuchin, S. (1984). *Family kaleidoscope.* Cambridge, MA: Harvard University Press.

Patterson, G. R. (1975). *Families: Applications of social learning to family life.* Champaign, IL: Research Press.

Rutter, M., & Quinton, D. (1984). Parental psychiatric disorder: Effects on children. *Psychological Medicine, 14,* 853–880.

Sigman, M., John, R., Levinson, E., & Betts, D. (1985). Multiple family therapy with severely disturbed psychiatric patients. *Psychiatric Journal of the University of Ottawa, 10,* 260–265.

Smith, N. L., Glass, G. V., & Miller, T. I. (1980). *Benefits of psychotherapy.* Baltimore: Johns Hopkins University Press.

Steinem, G. (1986). Ruth's song (because she could not sing it). In G. Steinem, *Outrageous acts and everyday rebellions* (pp. 145–168). New York: Signet Books.

Weissman, M. M. (1979). Depressed parents and their children: Implications for prevention. In I. B. Berlin & L. A. Stone (Eds.), *Basic handbook of child psychiatry: Vol. 4. Prevention and current issues* (pp. 292–299). New York: Basic Books.

Weissman, M. M., & Paykel, E. S. (1974). *The depressed woman: A study of social relationships.* Chicago: University of Chicago Press.

Werner, E. E., & Smith, R. S. (1982). *Vulnerable but invincible: A longitudinal study of resilient children and youth.* New York: McGraw-Hill.

Zilbach, J. J., Bergel, E., & Gass, C. (1972). The role of the young child in family therapy. In C. Sager & H. Kaplan (Eds.), *Progress in group and family therapy* (pp. 385–399). New York: Brunner/Mazel.

13

The Invisible Family Member: Children in Families with Alcohol Abuse

Growing up in an alcoholic family is not a unitary phenomenon. Alcoholism manifests itself in many different ways, and has many different effects on both the alcoholic's behavior and that of the alcoholic's spouse. It varies not only from alcoholic to alcoholic and from family to family, but from phase to phase in a given family. For the child, each phase has its own traumatic effects (Ackerman, 1986). Whatever its particular manifestations, however, alcoholism plays a central role in the functioning and dysfunctioning of the family and of its individual members, and must not be overlooked or ignored.

During the past 5 years, as medical director of an adolescent alcohol and drug abuse treatment program, I have worked with many "alcoholic" families—that is, families whose way of being has alcohol consumption or avoidance as a major organizing force. Often these families have been in family therapy for extended periods of time, with little benefit either to the identified patients or the families. Treating a family with an alcoholic member without acknowledging, confronting, focusing on, and dealing with the alcoholism is generally doomed to failure.

In some ways, one can consider alcohol a key (and often secret) member of such a family. Failure to recognize and deal with the alcoholic's drinking and the nonalcoholic's denial and enabling is to function totally within the family's system of denial, and thus to be rendered ineffectual as a therapist. Attempts at structural or strategic therapy that ignore the alcoholism become a part of the family's de-

Stuart Copans. Department of Clinical Psychiatry, Dartmouth Medical School, Hanover, NH; The Brattleboro Retreat, Brattleboro, VT.

nial, and allow the family (and therapist) to pretend something is being done when the central problem is being ignored.

At the same time, conjoint family therapy and multiple-family group therapy have both been claimed to have beneficial effects when incorporated into treatment of alcoholics. Family therapists should not ignore family substance abuse, nor should they limit their role to identification and referral. Although they may wish to refer identified families and family members to substance abuse treatment programs, their continued involvement with such families can be essential for the success of the therapy.

It is imperative that family therapists learn to recognize substance abuse when it exists in a family, and to understand how it organizes families in general and their clients in particular. It is also imperative that they learn how to work with these families in collaboration with substance abuse treatment programs. This chapter cannot provide all one needs to know to accomplish this, but it explores existing frameworks for understanding the family context of alcoholism, including both the alcoholic and the nonalcoholic family members. It moves from such an understanding to indicate the directions one must pursue as a family therapist in order to work adequately with these families.

What We Know about Substance-Abusing Families

The literature on substance-abusing families and on children in substance-abusing families is rapidly increasing, increasingly confusing, and confusingly contradictory (Adler & Raphael, 1983; Deren, 1986). It springs from at least four different attitudes and four different bodies of literature; it describes poorly defined populations; and it often addresses different subsets of data in its descriptions.

One category of literature is personal and self-descriptive, at the same time claiming a certain universality to the experience—"This is what it was like for me, and also for many other people like me." There are two important components to this literature: the saga of the alcoholic himself or herself, and the stories of other family members. Together, these self-descriptions may begin to have a composite view of the family environment.

A second category is the clinical anecdotal report or the summary of clinical impressions—that is, the outsider's look at the alcoholic, which is usually strongly influenced by the clinician's background, personal experiences with substance abuse, or beliefs.

The third category consists of a slowly growing body of literature that seems to meet the current canons of acceptable scientific research, but at the same time may suffer from problems of either overgeneralizing from a limited sample, or leading others toward the temptation of such overgeneralizations.

Finally, there is a body of important literature from the self-help group movement—from the literature of Alcoholics Anonymous (AA), Al-Anon, and the National Association for Children of Alcoholics (NACOA). This consists primarily of "self-evident" statements, articles of faith, and quotations from founders or current leaders of these organizations. The prevailing attitude of self-help groups has been that the treatment applications of a biomedical approach are not adequate for the management of alcoholism. At the same time, there has been a tendency among mental health professionals to dismiss the contributions of the self-help movement. Thus there has been a general antagonism between self-help organizations and the mental health establishment.

Recently, however, more and more treatments have combined biomedically oriented therapies with self-help groups, as a kind of makeshift program addressing the biopsychosocial aspects of the problem. Self-help groups such as AA have been extremely effective, and the approaches derived from their work may be very helpful to many substance-abusing families.

Some acquaintance with each of these four bodies of literature is important, both because each contains important truths not addressed by the other areas, and because patients and families are likely to have had contact with and operated on the basis of data from all four areas. Some knowledge of each area is important in understanding these families. I review salient aspects of each and then attempt to construct a view of the alcoholic family as a context in which some children grow up. This model should help to clarify the context in which a child of an alcoholic may develop problems with alcohol, as well as the ways in which many children of alcoholics survive, manage to drink socially and in moderation, and lead productive and satisfying adult lives.

Werner (1986) points out that it is "not possible to predict a child's future adjustment solely on the basis of parental alcoholism" (p. 34) and notes that many offspring of alcoholics are quite resilient. It has been pointed out that several of the most recent presidents of the United States were the offspring of alcoholic parents, although Davis (1984) has suggested that many of our current foreign policy dilemmas can be attributed to the effects of the dysfunctional parenting of some of our leaders; this implies that worldly success is not necessarily an adequate measure of healthy functioning.

Certainly, as Jahoda (1958) suggested years ago, mental health is best assessed using multiple criteria; studies that use limited criteria to evaluate outcomes in offspring of alcoholic parents may overlook significant effects.

The Literature of Self-Description

The field of substance abuse treatment has until recently been dominated by "recovering" individuals—that is, by those with a prior history of alcoholism and addiction. Because of this, it is often difficult to separate the literature of self-description from the clinical literature, so, at times, what may be presented as dispassionate clinical impressions comes closer to autobiography.

A related though inadequately studied body of literature consists of the writings (biographical and autobiographical) in which substance abuse is present and described, but is not the central focus of the book. Jack London and John Berryman are among those who have written semiautobiographical novels describing their problems with alcohol (Gilmore, 1987). In addition, several movie stars or their offspring have focused on alcoholism in their biographies and autobiographies. Although such books are dramatic and appeal to our voyeuristic interest in the lives of stars, they are often written to attack or defend, and are hard to use as the basis for dispassionate analysis.

The Clinical Literature

The second body of literature, the clinical literature, seems in general agreement internally, although it does not necessarily agree with the research literature. A series of books and articles by Black (1981), Deutsch (1982), Wegsheider-Cruse (1981), Ackerman (1983, 1986), Cermak (1986), and others suggest that certain behaviors commonly occur in alcoholic families, and that certain "enabling" or "codependent" behaviors are common in the nonalcoholic members of alcoholic families.

The concepts of "enabling" and "codependence" are particularly important in working with alcoholic or substance-abusing families. "Enabling" or "enabling behaviors" refers to specific behaviors commonly seen in the nonalcoholic members of an alcoholic family that make it easier for the alcoholic family member to persist in his or her drinking. For example, when, on a Monday morning, the wife of an alcoholic calls her husband's supervisor to say that he is sick, and thereby protects him from the consequences of his weekend binge, she unwittingly enables him to continue his weekend binges without being called to account for them. In the same way, when a daughter chooses not to tell her father how sad and angry she felt when he was drunk and acted inappropriately during her friend's visit, she protects him from any awareness of the consequences of his drinking, and again thereby enables him to continue to drink and to maintain that his drinking is not a problem.

These enabling behaviors are not necessarily a sign of an unconscious desire to see the alcoholic persist in drinking. They result from the normal human impulse to care for and protect those one loves. One of the dilemmas in working with alcoholic families is that one must at times teach parents, spouses, or children to behave in ways that may seem harsh or unfeeling, in order to help an alcoholic family member come to terms with and stop his or her drinking.

It is not uncommon in alcoholic families to see young children taking care of their alcoholic parents, cooking meals, and calling the police when their parents get involved in violent fights. Often they resist and resent initial attempts to dislodge them from these parental roles.

The concept of "codependence" is a second approach to understanding the behavior of nonalcoholic members of the alcoholic family. Just as the relationship between the alcoholic and alcohol leads to a variety of deleterious effects on the alcoholic, including organic brain impairment, use of more primitive and less appropriate defense mechanisms, and appearance of a variety of psychiatric symptoms (including depression or disordered thinking), so the relationship between the nonalcoholic family member and the alcoholic family member may lead to a variety of symptoms in the nonalcoholic. These symptoms may include anxiety, isolation from others, depression, psychosomatic symptoms, shame, anger, denial, and projection. Typically, family members will deny the extent or seriousness of the alcoholic's drinking.

Codependence and enabling are seen in children in alcoholic families as well as in spouses and parents. Often these children will persist in these enabling behaviors after growing up and forming their own families. Daughters of alcoholic fathers, even when not alcoholic themselves, seem particularly likely to marry alcoholic or drug-abusing men, and to become the mothers of substance-abusing adolescents (Cermak, 1986)

The clinical literature also suggests that a limited number of relatively specific patterns of adaptation and defense can be seen in the children of alcoholic families, both during childhood and in their later adult lives. Children in substance-abusing families, according to the clinical literature, learn three rules—"Don't trust," "Don't talk," and "Don't feel"—as a way of protecting both themselves and their families (Black, 1981). A number of authors (Ackerman, 1983; Black, 1981; Wegsheider-Cruse, 1984) have also suggested that children in these families take on one of a relatively few stereotyped roles as a way of functioning despite high levels of anxiety and chaos. A typical set of roles described in the literature (Wegsheider-Cruse, 1984) is the following:

1. The "hero," whose task is to prove the self-worth of the family through accomplishment. "Hero" children frequently take on the parenting roles and responsibilities neglected by the alcoholic parent, and often those neglected by the nonalcoholic spouse because of his or her preoccupation with the alcoholic partner. It has been suggested that "hero" children of alcoholic families are overrepresented in the human service professions (medicine, nursing, and social work), and that this may contribute to countertransference problems in their dealings with alcoholic families.

2. The "scapegoat" or "problem child," who acts so as to divert attention from the parent's substance abuse problem. "Scapegoat" children are likely to come to the attention of a family therapist as a result of acting-out behavior at school. They are frequently given diagnoses of attention deficit disorder, conduct disorder, or specific learning disabilities. It has been suggested that these may on occasion be secondary to fetal alcohol syndrome, or that there may be some genetic connection between these disorders and alcoholism. Some theorists have even postulated that increased prenatal testosterone may represent a possible explanatory mechanism. It also seems likely, however, that some of these difficulties represent the children's response to the stress and dynamics of these families.

3. The "lost child," who passively adjusts to parental drinking and the attendant effects on the family. Unless detected by particularly alert and sensitive teachers, "lost" children rarely come to attention until adolescence, when they may develop substance abuse problems of their own. They often have learning disabilities, but frequently manage to scrape by and get passed on from grade to grade without being identified.

4. The "mascot" or "family clown," who provides the family with comic relief and detours aggression or hostility in the family.

Among the effects described in adults who have grown up in alcoholic families are the repression of feelings; harsh self-criticism; and feelings of anger, isolation, guilt, and abandonment. Eve (1986) suggests that these adult effects may be passed on in the absence of alcoholism by a nondrinking child of an alcoholic. Since only 5% of school-age children of alcoholics are identified and get help (Eve, 1986), and a similarly small percentage of adult offspring of alcoholic parents are identified or get help, it is hard to know what the relative validity of such clinical generalizations are.

One particularly helpful clinical approach is to consider family alcoholism as a disease with a developmental history. A variety of authors have described stages in the development of alcoholism and substance abuse. Although the initial descriptions of stages focused on the changes in the individual, Jackson (1954) proposed the following stages in the development of alcoholism in the family:

1. Denial
2. Attempts to eliminate the problem
3. Disorganization and chaos
4. Attempts to reorganization in spite of the problem
5. Efforts to escape the problem
6. Reorganization without the alcoholic family member
7. Recovery and reorganization of the home and family

These stages do not represent discrete, time-limited phases that all families pass through in an unchanging progress, but the framework of these stages may help in understanding the different ways in which alcoholic families present, their differing responses in similar interventions, and the differing behaviors of children in these families. It appears that certain families seem to "get stuck" in certain stages. The reasons for this are not clear, but may have to do with the behavior of nonalcoholic spouses. Some spouses tolerate their partners' drinking behavior, while others present their alcoholic spouses with the choice between separation and sobriety.

Paolino and McCrady (1977) suggest that Jackson's stages, which were developed on the basis of interviews with women active in Al-Anon, may not be the best way to conceptualize the developmental stages of the alcoholic family. They cite a variety of other studies and developmental conceptualizations of the alcoholic family, including that of Lemert (1960), who divided family coping approaches into two groups: the early adjustment phase, including overcoming denial, attempt to control the problem, and social isolation; and the late adjustment phase, including feelings of hopelessness, role changes, and divorce. James and Goldman (1971), who also studied wives of alcoholics, suggested that the wives' behaviors were related to the stages of the husbands' drinking, and that these could be conceptualized in five main categories: withdrawal within the marriage, protection of the husband, attacking the husband, safeguarding the family interests, and acting out.

The conceptualization of family substance abuse as a developmental process can help clarify the task of the family therapist. If a family is in the denial stage, the therapist can help the family recognize and acknowledge the problem. If the nonalcoholic members are making attempts to stop the alcoholic's drinking, they can be referred for substance abuse treatment, as well as to AA and Al-Anon. If they are at the stage of disorganization and chaos, they can be offered concrete help in structuring their lives and making necessary decisions; they can be referred to appropriate helping agencies; and, again, they can be put in touch with Al-Anon for concrete support and recommendations.

If the family has expelled the alcoholic member and is attempting to reorganize without him or her, the family therapist can help in the process of restructuring. At any stage, Al-Anon can provide support and practical help, through a connection with others who have dealt with many of the same issues and stresses.

The Research Literature

The research literature on substance-abusing families and children is less uniform in its findings than is the clinical literature. The largest body of data in this area comes from the Center for Family Research of George Washington University Medical Center (Bennett, Wolin, & Reiss, 1985; Bennett, Wolin, Reiss, & Teitlebaum, 1987; Steinglass, 1977, 1981, 1985; Steinglass, with Bennett, Wolin, & Reiss, 1987; Steinglass, Davis, & Berenson, 1977; Steinglass, Weiner, & Mendelson, 1971; Wolin & Bennett, 1984). It focuses on a variety of themes related to family functioning, including engagement and disengagement, family rituals, and the presence of alcohol abuse as an organizing principle for interactional life in certain families (Steinglass *et al.*, 1987). Among this group's experimental findings are the demonstration of different "family alcohol phases," including stable wet, stable dry, and transitional phases (Steinglass, 1981); the discovery that drinking serves a stabilizing function in some marriages (Steinglass *et al.*, 1971); and the discovery that the preservation of family rituals in an alcoholic family can help protect the children in the family against alcoholism (Wolin & Bennett, 1984).

The George Washington group's conclusions are based on direct observations of families, both in home settings and in the clinical laboratory. These researchers have both observed and described specific behaviors supporting their assertions. For example, one family cited in a number of their publications claimed that when the "identified alcoholic" drank, depression, fighting, and estrangement resulted. But family observations revealed that in fact drinking behavior resulted in increased interpersonal warmth, increased caretaking, and greater animation in the family (Steinglass *et al.*, 1977).

This finding helps explain the observation that often children in alcoholic families come to attention after the alcoholic member has *stopped* drinking. Children in these situations often complain about increasing limits, parental overin-volvement in AA and Al-Anon, or parental pressures to attend Alateen. It also helps explain why a higher rate of alcoholism is associated with being reared in an alcoholic family. Although one might expect children in these families to learn the dangers and ill effects of alcohol, Steinglass et al. (1977) suggest that what they may well learn is that alcohol makes things better—that enabling people to drink makes them warmer and more caring.

Steinglass et al. (1977) also suggest one reason for enabling and for the per-sistence of a family in the denial stage. In alcoholic families, life may feel better while the alcoholic member is drinking. Denial and enabling are then reinforced by the increased warmth and caretaking during the stable wet phases. The anger of the codependent spouse when the drinking and enabling are confronted may be surprising to the therapist who does not understand this feature of alcoholic fami-lies. The George Washington group's findings on the functioning of these families during their stable wet and stable dry phases helps explain the source of some of this anger (Steinglass et al., 1977). Attempting to move an alcoholic family from a stable wet to a stable dry state pushes its members toward a less comfortable equilibrium.

In AA, there is a great deal of both literature and folk wisdom about the "dry drunk." What both AA and Steinglass et al.'s (1977) data suggest is that cessation of substance abuse is only a partial goal in the treatment of the alcoholic family. While drinking persists, neither the family nor the alcoholic may be uncomfortable enough to work in family therapy. When the drinking ceases, the task is to pro-vide both the alcoholic and the family with the support they need to tolerate the added discomfort, and at the same time with the therapy they need to make struc-tural and dynamic changes to help alleviate some of that discomfort.

A second important body of literature is the work on the inheritance of alco-holism (Cadoret, Cain, & Grove, 1980; Cadoret, O'Gorman, Troughton, & Hey-wood, 1985; Cadoret, Troughton, O'Gorman, & Heywood, 1986; Goodwin, Schulsinger, Hermansenk, Guze, & Winokur, 1973). Generally, this literature supports the idea that there is a significant genetic component in alcoholism. Goodwin et al.'s data on adopted children, comparing those with and without alcoholism in their biological parents, strongly support the hypothesis of a genetic factor that contributes to the development of alcoholism in the offspring of alcoholics. Good-win and colleagues also found a threefold increase in divorce when the adopted-out sons of alcoholics were compared to a matched sample of adopted offspring of nonalcoholic parents; these divorces were apparently unrelated to drinking. An additional finding reported by Goodwin and his colleagues may speak to factors in the family environment in the presence of the alcoholic parent: They identified a twofold increase in depression in nonadopted daughters of alcoholics when com-pared to their adopted sisters.

Cadoret et al. (1980, 1985, 1986) have also carried out a series of studies of adoptees, and their series also supports the existence of a genetic factor in the transmission of alcoholism. In Cadoret et al.'s studies, childhood conduct disorder was related to alcoholic biological background, and also to the later development of alcoholism. Their early studies (Cadoret *et al.*, 1980; Cadoret & Gath, 1978) showed no relationship between alcoholism in the adoptive families and the later development of alcoholism in the adoptees. In a more recent study, however, in which they looked at the presence of alcoholism not just in the adoptive parents, but in their parents as well, a positive relationship was found between alcoholism in the adoptive families and alcoholism in the adoptees (Cadoret *et al.*, 1985). This recent finding is certainly compatible with clinical experience, and with recent emphasis on the role of codependence and enabling.

Another, more scattered body of relevant research literature is that which looks at the offspirng of alcoholic parents. Here there is a particularly striking contrast between many clinical reports and the research findings. The clinical and personal accounts present the experience of being a child in an alcoholic family as a devastating and traumatic experience, while the research literature often demonstrates few differences between the child in an alcoholic family and a matched control. On the one hand, personal accounts are not controlled studies and do not match the individual's experience of pain and trauma with another individual's, perhaps in response to other life factors. On the other hand, there are some factors that may explain why the research findings do not do justice to the emotional hardship of the the experience. Test batteries do not measure devastation and trauma; nor may they measure such symptoms as alexithymia, lack of trust, difficulty in establishing close interpersonal relationships, guilt, embarrassment, or even labile anger. In addition, much of the experimental literature is based on research with volunteer families, generally volunteer families that have identified themselves as alcoholic. In such families, one might expect that one factor described as particularly painful and traumatic would not be present—that is, the conspiracy of silence in which an alcoholic's problems are denied, hidden, covered up, taboo. It is this taboo, isolating children from their own experience and from any chance of external validation of their feelings or experiences, that is described as particularly painful by adult offspring of alcoholic families. In any case, one must be extremely careful about generalizing from any study of small numbers of self-identified alcoholics.

With these caveats in mind, some of the studies of particular interest are as follows. Marcus (1986) compared elementary-school-age children of middle-class alcoholic and nonalcoholic mothers who were comparable in race, education, and socioeconomic status (but differing in marital disruption, with more separation and divorce experienced by the alcoholic mothers). The offspring of the alcoholic mothers scored significantly lower on the Mathematics, Reading Recognition, and Reading Comprehension subtests of the Peabody Individual Achievement Test, as well as achieving a lower total test score. It was noted in the study that 65% of the offspring of alcoholic mothers and only 35% of the control group children were living in families in which the biological fathers were not present.

Bennett *et al.* (1985) compared children from alcoholic homes to a matched control group from nonalcoholic families and reported finding significant differences in self-concept, in psychological functioning, and in cognitive abilities and performance, but only marginal differences in behavior problems.

Werner (1986), as part of a longitudinal study of Hawaiian children, examined children in alcoholic families. She found more problems in male than in female offspring, and in offspring of alcoholic mothers than in children of alcoholic fathers. She also described a number of factors related to "no coping problems by age 18": temperamental characteristics that elicited positive attention from primary caretakers (including substitute parents); at least average intelligence an adequate reading and writing skills; internal locus of control; plenty of attention from primary caretakers in infancy; no prolonged separations from primary caretakers; no additional births into a family during first 2 years of life; and the absence of conflict between parents during the first 2 years of life.

In Werner's study, 59% of 49 offspring of alcoholics had no serious coping problem by age 18; however, since the usual age of onset of alcoholism is in adult life (occasionally as late as the 40s), it will be important to see the data at the next follow-up, when these offspring have reached 30 years of age. As mentioned above, female offspring fared better than males. Three-fourths of the resilient offspring were females, whereas two-thirds of the group that developed psychosocial problems were male. The offspring whose mothers drank during pregnancy were especially troubled. Of this subgroup, 44% had IQs two standard deviations below the mean, and 55% had criminal records.

The Self-Help Literature

The literature of self-help groups is probably best represented by two AA books, *Twelve Steps and Twelve Traditions* (Alcoholics Anonymous, 1952) and *Alcoholics Anonymous* (Alcoholics Anonymous, 1939), which have served as models for the whole range of groups, including Al-Anon, Alateen, Narcotics Anonymous, and Families Anonymous.

Alcoholics Anonymous began in 1935 with the meeting in Akron, Ohio of a surgeon and a New York stockbroker. Its antecedents included the Oxford religious movement and psychoanalysis. It is based on self-help and on the Twelve Steps, which trace the alcoholic's admitting his or her powerlessness over drinking; recognizing a higher spiritual power; placing himself or herself in a humble relationship to that power; openly admitting wrongs; and seeking a spiritual awakening.

The Twelve Steps for families in Al-Anon are almost identical with those in AA, and in both settings they serve a number of useful purposes. By accepting their own helplessness, both the alcoholic and the family are relieved of the guilt and the hollow grandiosity so pervasive in these families. The emphasis on the fellowship helps break down the isolation characterizing both the alcoholic family unit and its individual members, as does admitting one's faults to another individual. Making amends and routine self-evaluation and correction can help in restoring severely damaged self-esteem.

Bateson (1972) elegantly explains the success of AA by focusing on the alcoholic system and the effect of the Twelve Steps on this system. The Twelve Steps of AA, Bateson suggests, act through bringing about what he describes as "epistemological changes." That is, they change the alcoholic's transactions from ones of symmetrical escalation to ones of complementarity—from transactions that ignore or do not tolerate differences, to transactions in which differences are accepted and welcomed. This involves individuation and differentiation, concepts that are also consistent with Bowen's ideas. Certainly one of the most important aspects of Al-Anon and Alateen is the emphasis on the fact that the spouse or child has no control over the drinking behavior of the alcoholic. Any therapy with a child in an alcoholic family must confront directly the child's illusion that he or she is responsible for parental drinking.

Beyond these psychiatrically compatible explanations of the success of AA and Al-Anon, however, is the deep commitment of those in the fellowship to helping their fellow alcoholics. Individuals or families may ask for sponsors at a meeting, and these sponsors will be available to help 24 hours a day, 7 days a week, 365 (or 366) days a year, without any monetary reimbursement, whatever the individuals' or families' financial status.

Growing Up in an Alcoholic Family Context:
A Composite View

As I have already observed, alcoholic families are all different, and what I have tried to extract from the various literatures are family patterns that may help to clarify what growing up in such a family is like.

Denial is almost inevitably associated with isolation and shame. Disorganization and chaos lead to lack of nurturing and parental inconsistency, which in turn lead to insecurity and fear, and frequently to the premature assumption of adult roles by young children. Separation is often bitter and painful, and may be associated with unresolved guilt or with hatred and anger directed toward the alcoholic parent (or, in some cases, at the nonalcoholic parent, who is seen as abandoning his or her spouse). In many cases, these children have grave difficulty establishing appropriate heterosexual relationships because of the lack of role models.

Sexual abuse is common in these families, and often contributes further to unresolved anger and hatred of the opposite sex. Physical abuse is also common. Alcohol and drug abuse have been reported in 60–90% of cases of child abuse (Wertz, 1986). Sexual and physical abuse have been reported in 22.5% of alcoholic and addicted families, and neglect or abuse in 41% of these families (Deren, 1986). In addition, while relatively few alcoholics go on to become stereotyped skid row bums, the high incidence of divorce and the occupational side effects of alcoholism often result in financial difficulties in many of these families. Mothers may work full-time or in some cases hold down two or more jobs.

Steinglass (1981) suggests that what defines an alcoholic family is not the drinking behavior, but rather the centricity of the alcohol in the family's life. As previously described, such alcoholic families can experience dry phases, wet phases, and transitional phases, and as observed by Steinglass and colleagues in their laboratory studies, some of these families may appear to function better in their wet phases. Children in these families then learn a variety of lessons: Alcohol is the center of family life; alcohol can make things better; problems with alcohol are denied, covered up, and not discussed with those outside the family.

In addition, as Bateson (1972) has suggested, the children learn an epistemology: They learn to function and feel comfortable in an alcoholic system; they are taught to function in ways of symmetry, not complementarity; and this learning is not verbalized, intellectualized, or accessible to consciousness, but is rather bred in the bone, absorbed though the skin, taken in with the mother's milk and the father's rough play.

Bepo and Krestan (1985) have extended and amplified Bateson's ideas and incorporated them into their work with alcoholic families. They point out the self-corrective functions of alcohol for the individual, and the way in which "others in the [alcoholic] system begin to acquire the same types of attitudes, feelings and behaviors that are characteristic of the alcoholic, even though they don't drink" (p. 11). They also emphasize the intergenerational transmission of patterns of over- and underresponsible behavior and the role these may play in setting the stage for the intergenerational transmission of alcohol.

Work, then, with such families and such children requires an ability to enter into their system; to learn a new epistemology; and to behave in ways that may seem alien, strange, or uncomfortable, or appear to border on the unprofessional. Such work will evoke new feelings and behaviors in the therapist; it should not be done in isolation. Attending Al-Anon meetings can be of help. Working with a team of colleagues can be life-saving. Supervision by someone with experience with such families can be invaluable. Finally, reading the literature of AA, of Al-Anon, and of family therapy with substance-abusing families can help the therapist learn where to draw boundaries and how to intervene in systems that at times can mystify, enrage, or terrify him or her.

Some Clinical Principles

1. *Anyone working with children or children and their families who is never seeing alcohol and drug abuse is inadequately assessing and treating between 30% and 80% of his or her caseload.* Many authors have estimated the prevalence of alcoholism to range from 5% to 10% of the adult population at any given point in time, although it has been estimated that up to 18% of the population have significant substance abuse problems at some point during their lifetimes (Kinney & Leaton, 1987). Family prevalence is significantly higher, with estimates suggesting that up to 30% of families include at least one alcohol- or drug-abusing member (Hertz, 1986). Although there are few data on the prevalence of sub-

stance abuse in the families seen in child mental health clinics, most authors suggest a significant overrepresentation of children of alcoholics in these populations. Certainly, recent data suggest that over 50% of physically and sexually abused children come from substance-abusing families (Wertz, 1986).

2. *Alcohol and substance abuse must be directly addressed when they are present.* As stated in the introduction to this chapter, failure to deal adequately with substance abuse in a family, particularly in a family where substance abuse plays a stabilizing role, makes the chance of achieving lasting change in the family small. Steinglass (1977) suggests that part of the reason for the "singular lack of interest" in substance abuse on the part of family therapists lies in the fact that parental intoxication is most often not the identified problem, nor is an alcoholic parent the "identified patient." Family therapists may fear that focusing on the alcoholic parent's behavior will replace one identified patient with another, and shift the focus away from structural issues in the family. A second problem, Steinglass (1981) suggests, is that since substance-abusing families behave differently when the alcoholic family member is drinking, and since most therapists do not permit or at least strongly discourage inebriation during therapy, family therapists see only half of the interactional repertoire of such families.

Carol was a 13-year-old girl from a professional family; she was referred to a family therapist by her pediatrician because of increasing conflict with her parents, deteriorating school performance, and parental concern over her choice of friends. Her family therapist assessed the structure of the family and attempted to focus on areas of unacknowledged conflict between her mother and father, and on the family's reluctance to permit separation and individuation. There was little progress, and after 6 months the father refused to participate further in therapy.

Some time after this, Carol's parents discovered a variety of drugs in her room, and were referred by her pediatrician for evaluation by a substance abuse treatment program. At that time, evaluation revealed that both Carol and her father had significant substance abuse problems.

Because of the family members' position in the community, they were unwilling to participate in self-help groups. As a result, Carol and her father were each referred to individual therapists with experience in working with substance abusing patients. Marital counseling was also recommended.

At the time of follow-up 2 years later, Carol was doing well in school, her drug abuse had ceased, and the family was functioning in a more positive way. Although the family was able to make significant structural changes, it was only after the substance abuse was confronted and stopped that the family was able to follow up on the recommendations made earlier.

In understanding substance-abusing families, there has been an increasing emphasis on the behaviors of the nonabusing family members. These are the enabling or codependent behaviors, including denial (pretending that the substance abuse is not occurring), protecting (making excuses or covering up for abusing family members), rescuing (saving substance abusers from the consequences of their behavior), taking care (providing sustenance and support for substance abusers when they are unable to care for themselves because of their substance abuse), and projecting blame onto others ("He only drinks because it's so hard for him at work").

3. *The therapist must deal with the alcoholism or addiction at the beginning rather than waiting for a "good time."* To wait for a "good time" is to support the family's myth that substance abuse is too horrible to be talked about, and to run the risk that the family will leave therapy without having been confronted on the problems with substance abuse. At the same time, it is essential to support the drinking parent in his or her role as spouse or parent, and to avoid siding with the nondrinking parent in what may become an attack (Stanton, Todd, & Associates, 1982).

4. *As in other family therapy, it is important for the therapist to consider himself or herself only a part of an extended therapeutic process. Good therapy may result in a family's leaving treatment but being more accepting of the work with the next therapist.*

At the time of their daughter's preadmission evaluation, the members of the Jones family were informed that they would be expected to participate in family therapy on a regular basis, and to spend one weekend a month at their daughter's treatment program attending a variety of educational, self-help, and multiple-family groups. They initially refused admission, explaining that they had once participated in family therapy, and would never again allow themselves to be so abused. Mr. Jones brought out from his wallet a worn, ragged letter that he and his wife had received after they terminated family therapy. In this letter, their family therapist explained that their daughter's acting-out behavior kept him and his wife preoccupied with her behavior, and thereby helped make sure that he and his wife would not have to deal with their own disagreements.

It was explained to Mr. Jones that we were not particularly concerned with his marital problems. Our task was to help his daughter stop drinking, and stop behaving in ways dangerous to herself and upsetting to her parents. To do that, we needed their help; therefore, we needed to educate them about substance abuse, and to teach them the skills they needed to carry out the difficult task of helping their daughter maintain her sobriety. In addition, because that task was so difficult, the two of them needed to be able to work closely together, and that would require some effort on their part. The parents were assured that substance abuse was a genetic problem, and that it was not due to inadequate parenting or to hidden conflicts they were not telling us about. It was, however, a lifelong problem, and one that would require a great deal of effort on their part if they were to help their daughter in the best way possible.

The family participated actively in family therapy, family weekends, and Al-Anon throughout their daughter's hospital stay. At the time of discharge, permission was finally obtained to talk with their previous family therapists, who were informed of the family's progress; we assured them that although the family would probably never be grateful to them, we, the current treatment team, were.

5. *The therapist should know and use Al-Anon.*

The mother and two younger siblings of Philip, a 16-year-old boy, had been in family therapy for over a year while Philip had been confined to inpatient and residential placements because of violent, threatening, and self-destructive behavior. He had never been home for longer than 1 week, but continued to plan on returning home once his treatment was complete. After he was admitted to a substance abuse unit, his mother was encouraged to attend Al-Anon; the siblings were urged to attend Alateen; and the patient was expected to attend AA meetings five times a week.

In Al-Anon, his mother was able to develop a support group. The group provided her with support and encouragement in separating from her son, in beginning to focus on problems in her own life, and in setting more reasonable limits on her two younger children. In AA, Philip was able to develop a support network of his own, to displace his dependency onto someone other than his mother, and eventually to be able to move into an apartment on his own. Philip's two siblings attended Al-Anon and Alateen, and were able to confront their brother on the effect his behavior had had on them. Also, as they approached adolescence, they were able to work toward individuation in a significantly less ambivalent manner than their brother, both because of changes their mother had accomplished and because of their connections with supportive adults outside the family.

6. *Polydrug abuse is common; the therapist should beware of replacement addictions.*

After being confronted by his family because of his behavior, especially his stealing from family to pay for drugs, John was able to accept treatment in a cocaine rehabilitation program. Shortly after he returned home, John went out and got drunk. He protested loudly to his family that his drinking was not a problem, that he had learned never to use cocaine again, and that if they pressured him to cease alcohol use he would resume his use of cocaine.

7. *Alcoholic families do not necessarily contain an actively drinking person.*

Claudia G, a 6-year-old girl, was referred to therapy because of poor peer relationships, a variety of obsessive behaviors, and depression. Therapy had been recommended on two previous occasions, but her father had not allowed her to attend. Family evaluation revealed her father, an engineer at a nearby tool and die factory, to be distant, guilt-ridden, and controlling. In an individual meeting carried out as part of the evaluation, Mr. G revealed that his father had been alcoholic, abusive, and demeaning. Although he was not willing to obtain therapy himself, he hesitatingly permitted his daughter to begin therapy. The therapist was careful to meet with Mr. G at least once every 6 months, to answer any questions he had about the progress of the therapy, to support his decision to allow his daughter to continue in therapy, and to allay any anxiety he had about the therapist's "blaming" him for his daughter's problems.

8. *When drinking stops, alcohol-related problems may continue.*

When Ferris R, a 9-year-old boy referred for evaluation because of persistent behavioral problems at school, began to talk about his father's drinking problem, he stated that although he was glad his dad had stopped drinking, he saw little positive change in his family. Now, not only was his father gone to AA meetings, but his mother was at Al-Anon meetings. He had earlier imagined that when his dad stopped drinking, his family would be like other families, and he and his father would get to play ball together. Now he felt that he had not only not gotten his father back, but had lost some of his connection with his mother.

The Role of Family Therapy in the Treatment of Substance Abuse

A basic principle in promoting the emotional health of children and preventing the development of psychopathology is that family therapy should be a mandated part of the psychiatric treatment of adults. Family therapists would argue that family therapy has a beneficial effect on long-term prognosis of the condition being treated. Child psychiatrists would argue that involvement of the children in the treatment is a significant way of helping them understand what is happening to their parents.

Magical thinking and childhood egocentrism increase children's personal sense of responsibility for everything that happens in their family. One objective of including the children in family therapy for substance-abusing families, even when the children have not been identified as having behavioral or emotional problems, is the prevention of later substance abuse and/or psychopathology in the children. Since, as Spellman (1986) suggests, problems in children in substance-abusing families often do not appear until later in life, at which time they often present with problems in interpersonal relationships, depression or substance abuse, intervention before such problems are identified appears warranted. Furthermore, the research literature suggests that the childhood problems seen in children in alcoholic families are more often problems of self-esteem or of cognitive functioning than of behavior, and thus they may be more easily overlooked.

In some cases, substance abuse may skip a generation and then reappear. Although this may be explained as a genetic effect with mixed penetrance, Cadoret et al.'s (1986) recent study supports some family/environmental effects on the development of alcoholism. Certainly the concept of enabling can explain the phenomenon of skipped generations as economically as the genetic theories, and may be more helpful in encouraging appropriate interventions.

The role of family therapy in the treatment of substance abuse is not primarily conceptualized as help for children or as a preventive measure, however, but rather as part and parcel of substance abuse treatment. Stanton et al. (1982), combining research and clinical data, focus primarily on the family therapy of heroin addicts; their structural–strategic approach is heavily influenced by Haley and Minuchin. They point out both the difficulty and the importance of engaging these families in therapy, and stress the need to seek out and engage the families rather than simply sitting back and waiting for them to show up. Stanton et al. also comment on the relationship between substance abuse and unresolved family mourning processes, and on substance abuse as part of a family continuum of self-destruction.

Stanton *et al.* recommend not dealing with parental alcoholism early in the treatment of a heroin-addicted patient. First, this focuses on an area where the parents have not asked for help; second, this runs the risk that the nondrinking parent and other children may "gang up" on the drinking parent, and thereby weaken the parental subsystem and strengthen the intergenerational conflict—both changes directly contrary to the goals of the therapist. Stanton and colleagues suggest that the therapist join and support the drinking parent, to strengthen that person in his or her role as a parent. At the same time, however, Stanton *et al.* deals with the drinking problem in a nondisparaging way, and do, for example, draw up a contract whereby the drinker agrees to take no alcohol during weekends when the heroin addict is home.

Elkin (1984) focuses on alcoholic families and talks about the three contexts in which an alcoholic family may come into treatment: through the children, through the nonalcoholic spouse, and through the alcoholic. He points out that the first trap for many therapists is to see "abstinence as the goal of treatment, rather than as a condition which allows treatment to begin" (p. 76). He suggests that in treating an alcoholic family, a therapist may work toward five goals:

1. Stop the drinking, or if this is not possible, isolate the drinking member, lessening his/her impact on the other members (this is much less preferable).
2. Stop behavior that threatens the lives, health, or freedom of family members or others; this includes criminal activity and psychiatric symptoms, as well as behavior that facilitates destructive behavior in other family members.
3. Move children out of parental roles and sabotage inappropriate child–parent alliances.
4. Once the drinking is no longer an issue, help the parental alliance re-form so that parental authority will be effective.
5. Assist whichever family members are in need of help, or support them to obtain appropriate resources outside the family (A. A., Al-Anon, Alateen, counseling, women's consciousness-raising groups, sex therapy, and so forth). (p. 80)

Elkin also comments on several common pitfalls in working with alcoholic families, including "the rescue triangle." He focuses on the dynamics of power, and on ways to carry out a conjoint interview with an alcoholic couple; by using positive framing and paradox, the therapist is able to deal with the drinking, but to avoid allying with either the alcoholic or the nonalcoholic spouse.

Kaufman (1984) and Kaufman and Kaufman (1979) describe an approach to family therapy with substance-abusing families that integrates structural and psychodynamic family therapy approaches. They utilize multiple-family groups and couples groups, and at times specific groups for adolescents and children, as a way of having multiple impacts on a family system.

Bepko and Krestan (1985) extend the work of Bateson and focus on the use of alcohol in attempts at self-correction. They focus on three particular aspects of the alcoholic system: over- and underresponsibility, pride, and sex-role socialization, and on the therapeutic goals related to each of these. They divide treatment into three phases: the presobriety phase, in which the goal of treatment is to unbalance the system; the adjustment-to-sobriety phase, in which the goal of treatment is to stabilize the system; and the maintenance-of-sobriety phase, in which the goal of treatment is to rebalance the system. Particularly helpful are their differentiation of presobriety and postsobriety treatment and their listing of separate goals for involvement of children during each phase. During the presobriety phase, their goals are the following:

1. Educate children about drinking and convey understanding about life in an alcoholic family: relieve the child of a sense of guilt or responsibility.
2. Provide a safe environment in which feelings about drinking and the alcoholic parent can be discussed.
3. Assess the degree of neglect or emotional and physical deprivation occurring in the family.
4. Address any symptomatic behavior in the children themselves.
5. Establish what style of parenting is occurring in the family.
6. Map triangles, coalitions, and boundary positions.
7. Rule out potential unrevealed incest or abuse.
8. Attempt to restore or establish appropriate parenting to whatever degree is possible.
9. Take measures to counter the parent's tendency to scapegoat or attack the children for acknowledging drinking. (1985, 206)

During the postsobriety or adjustment phase, their treatment goals for children are the following:

1. Help parents to assume appropriate parental responsibility and to set limits in a calm, nonreactive manner. Have them practice or enact this process directly within sessions.
2. Encourage children to acknowledge their anger and sadness and to talk about the ways that things are different with the drinking stopped.
3. Normalize the family's reactions and responses.
4. Help the parents to evolve new ways of responding and relating to the children that will facilitate a process of "reparative nurturing."
5. Assess the roles each child has played in the presobriety family and work with the parent to establish new expectations, allowing each child a substitute reward to replace the power, specialness, or immunity inherent in the old mode of functioning. (1985, p. 211)

Whereas Bepko and Krestan focus on the false pride of the alcoholic family, Fossum and Mason (1986) focus on the role of shame. They suggest that shame in families is a crucial variable in all addictive behaviors, including not only substance abuse, but eating disorders, physical and sexual abuse, gambling and sexual addictions, workaholism, and compulsive spending and saving. They focus particularly on the dynamics of control and release behaviors in these families, and on the intergenerational transmission of shame. Fossum and Mason describe eight rules characteristic of shame-bound systems:

1. Be in control. (Control)
2. Always do the "right" thing. (Perfection)
3. Blame others when things don't happen as planned. (Blame)
4. Deny feelings, especially negative feelings. (Denial)
5. Don't expect reliability or constancy in relationships. (Unreliability)
6. Don't bring transactions to completion or resolution. (Incompleteness)
7. Don't talk openly and directly about shameful, abusive or compulsive behavior. (No Talk)
8. When shameful, abusive, or compulsive behavior occurs, deny it or disguise it. (Disqualification) (1986, p. 86)

Fossum and Mason, using this concept of shame-bound systems, are able to account for much of the behavior seen in codependent family members; for the multiple and changing addictions seen in these families and individuals; and for many of the commonly described behaviors observed in the children in these families. This concept also has important therapeutic implications, particularly for the "rebalancing" that Bepko and Krestan (1985) prescribe for the maintenance-of-sobriety phase.

Conclusion

The integration of knowledge and treatment in the areas of family therapy and substance abuse is long overdue. Although substance abuse treatment programs are becoming more aware of the importance of incorporating family therapy and education into their treatment programs, it is equally important that knowledge of substance abuse, its clinical course, its treatment, and its effects on the family be incorporated into family therapy training programs.

Given the ubiquity of substance abuse problems in our culture, every family therapist treats substance-abusing families. It is important that the ability to suspect, detect, and affect family substance abuse be part of the therapeutic armamentarium of every family therapist.

REFERENCES

Ackerman, J. (1983). *Children of alcoholics*. Holmes Beach, FL: Learning Publications, Inc.
Ackerman, R. J. (Ed.). (1986). *Growing in the shadow*. Pompano Beach, FL: Health Communications, Inc.
Adler, R., & Raphael, B. (1983). Children of alcoholics. *Australian and New Zealand Journal of Psychiatry, 17*, 3–8.
Alcoholics Anonymous. (1939). *Alcoholics Anonymous*. New York: Alcoholics Anonymous World Services.

Alcoholics Anonymous. (1952). *Twelve steps and twelve traditions*. New York: Alcoholics Anonymous World Services.

Bateson, G. (1972). Cybernetics of self: A theory of alcoholism. In G. Bateson, *Steps to an ecology of mind* (pp. 309–337). New York: Ballantine Books.

Bennett, L. A., Wolin, S. J., & Reiss, D. (1985). *Cognition, behavior and self esteem in young children of alcoholics*. Paper presented at the National Council on Alcoholism meeting, Washington, DC.

Bennett, L. A., Wolin, S. J., Reiss, D., & Teitlebaum, M. A. (1987). Couples at risk for alcoholism recurrence: Protective influences. *Family Process, 26* (1), 111–130.

Bepko, C. with Krestan, J. A. (1985). *The responsibility trap*. New York: Free Press.

Black, C. (1981). *It will never happen to me*. Denver: Medical Administration Corporation.

Cadoret, R. J., Cain, C. A., & Grove, W. M. (1980). Development of alcoholism in adoptees raised apart from alcoholic biologic relatives. *Archives of General Psychiatry, 37*, 561–563.

Cadoret, R. J., & Gath, A. (1978). Inheritance of alcoholism in adoptees. *British Journal of Psychiatry, 132*, 252–258.

Caroret, R. J., O'Gorman, T. W., Troughton, E., & Heywood, E. (1985). Alcoholism and antisocial personality. *Archives of General Psychiatry, 42*, 161–167.

Cadoret, R. J., Troughton, E., O'Gorman, T. W., & Heywood, E. (1986). An adoption study of genetic and environmental factors in drug abuse. *Archives of General Psychiatry, 43*, 1131–1136.

Cermak, T. L. (1986). *Diagnosing and treating codependence: A guide for professionals who work with chemical dependents, their spouses, and children*, Minneapolis: Johnson Institute.

Davis, J. H. (1984). *The Kennedys*. New York: McGraw-Hill.

Deren, S. (1986). Children of substance abusers: A review of the literature. *Journal of Substance Abuse Treatment, 3*, 77–94.

Deutsch, C. (1982). *Broken bottles, broken dreams*. New York: Teachers College Press.

Elkin, M. (1984). *Families under the influence: Changing alcoholic patterns*. New York: Norton.

Eve, S. I. (1986). *Children of alcoholic parents*. Paper presented at the First World Congress on Drugs and Alcohol, Tel Aviv, Israel; reported in *Clinical Psychiatry News, 14* (3), 1, 30.

Fossum, M. A., & Mason, M. J. (1986). *Facing shame*. New York, Norton.

Gilmore, T. B. (1987). *Equivocal spirits: Alcoholism and drinking in twentieth-century literature*. Chapel Hill: University of North Carolina Press.

Goodwin, D., Schulsinger, F., Hermansenk, L., Guze, S., & Winokur, G. (1973). Alcohol problems in adoptees raised apart from alcoholic biologic parents. *Archives of General Psychiatry, 28*, 238–243.

Jackson, J. (1954). Adjustment of the family to the crisis of alcoholism. *Quarterly Journal of Studies on Alcohol, 15*, 662–686.

Jahoda, M. (1958). *Current concepts of positive mental health*. New York: Basic Books

James, J. E., & Goldman, M. (1971). Behavior trends of wives of alcoholics. *Quarterly Journal of Studies on Alcohol, 32*, 373–381.

Kaufman, E. (1984). *Power to change: Family case studies in the treatment of alcoholism*. New York: Gardner Press.

Kaufman, E. & Kaufman, P. N. (Eds.). (1979). *Family therapy of drug and alcohol abuse*. New York: Gardner Press.

Kinney, J., & Leaton, G. (1987). *Loosening the grip*. St. Louis: C. V. Mosby.

Lemert, E. M. (1960). The occurrence and sequence of events in the adjustment of families to alcoholism. *Quarterly Journal of Studies on Alcohol, 21*, 679–697.

Marcus, A. M. (1986). Academic achievement in elementary school children of alcoholic mothers. *Journal of Clinical Psychology, 42*, 372–376.

McCord, J. (1986). *Family factors predicting alcoholism in children of alcoholics*. Paper presented at the First World Congress on Drugs and Alcohol, Tel Aviv, Israel: reported in *Clinical Psychiatry News, 14* (3), 1, 30.

Paolino, T. J., Jr., & McCrady, B. S. (1977). *The alcoholic marriage: Alternative perspectives*. New York: Grune & Stratton.

Russell, M., Henderson, C., & Blume, S. B. (1984). *Children of alcoholics: A review of the literature.* New York: Children of Alcoholics Foundation.
Spellman, S. A. (1986). *Learned dysfunctional behavior.* Paper presented at the First World Congress on Drugs and Alcohol, Tel Aviv, Israel; reported in *Clinical Psychiatry News, 14* (3), 1, 30.
Stanton, M. D., Todd, T. C., & Associates. (1982). *The family therapy of drug abuse and addiction.* New York: Guilford Press.
Steinglass, P. (1977). Family therapy in alcoholism. In B. Kissin & H. Begleiter (Eds.), *The biology of alcoholism* (Vol. 5, pp. 259–299). New York: Plenum.
Steinglass, P. (1981). The alcoholic family at home. *Archives of General Psychiatry, 38,* 578–584.
Steinglass, P. (1985). Family systems approaches to alcoholism, *Journal of Substance Abuse Treatment, 2,* 161–167.
Steinglass, P., with Bennett, L., Wolin, S. J., & Reiss, D. (1987). *The alcoholic family.* New York: Basic Books.
Steinglass, P., Davis, D. I., & Berenson, D. (1977). Observations of conjointly hospitalized "alcoholic couples" during sobriety and intoxication: Implications for theory and therapy. *Family Process, 16* (1), 1–16.
Steinglass, P., Weiner, S., & Mendelson, J. H. (1971). A systems approach to alcoholism. *Archives of General Psychiatry, 24,* 401–408.
Steinhausen, H., Gobel, D., & Nestler, V. (1984). Psychopathology in the offspring of alcoholic parents. *Journal of the American Academy of Child Psychiatry, 23* (4), 465–471.
Waite, B. J., & Ludwig, M. J., (1985). *A growing concern: How to provide services for children from alcoholic families.* Rockville, MD: National Institute on Alcohol Abuse and Alcoholism.
Wegsheider S. (1981). *Another chance: Hope and health for the alcoholic family.* Palo Alto, CA: Science and Behavior Books.
Werner, E. E. (1986). Resilient offspring of alcoholics: A longitudinal study from birth to age 18. *Journal of Studies on Alcohol, 47,* 34–40.
Wertz, R. (1986, November–December). Children of alcoholics. *Chemical People Newsletter,* p. 9.
Woititz, J. G. (1983). *Adult children of alcoholics.* Pompano Beach, FL: Health Communications.
Wolin, S. J., & Bennett, L. A. (1984). Family rituals. *Family Process, 23,* 401–420.

RESOURCES

For more information, readers may contact any of the following services:
1. National Clearinghouse for Alcohol Information
   P.O. Box 2345
   Rockville, MD 20852
   (301) 468-2600
2. Alcoholics Anonymous (AA)
   P.O. Box 459
   Grand Central Station
   New York, NY 10163
   (212) 686-1100
3. Al-Anon Family Groups
   P.O. Box 182
   Madison Square Garden
   New York, NY 10159
   (212) 683-1771
4. Children of Alcoholics Foundation, Inc.
   540 Madison Avenue, 23rd floor
   New York, NY 10022
   (212) 980-5394

5. National Association for Children of Alcoholics (NACOA)
   31706 Coast Highway, Suite 201
   South Laguna, CA 92677
   (714) 499-3889
6. National Council on Alcoholism, Inc.
   12 West 21st Street
   New York, NY 10010
   (212) 206-6770

14

Families Cope with the Death of a Parent: The Family Therapist's Role

JOAN C. BARTH, PhD

In 1984, 2,518,000 U.S. children under the age of 18 suffered the loss of a parent through death (U.S. Bureau of the Census, 1985). Of those, the majority, 98.9%, lost fathers; 1% lost mothers; and 0.1% suffered the loss of both parents. Since parents usually determine the shape of the family unit in which young children develop, the loss of one parent destabilizes the family and leaves the surviving parent to cope, not only with a personal loss, but with the re-establishment of family stability and security for the children. Such a crisis in the family requires extraordinary reorganization and restructuring, calling upon everyone, adults and children, alike, to respond in ways for which they are not prepared.

Despite the fact that the death of one of the adults in the household is a family crisis, there is very little literature on the issues of the family loss, the impact on the family as a unit, and the work the family does to reorganize. Rather, the literature focuses on individuals and individual losses. Thus most of the work concerning young children who have lost a parent concentrates on how children of different ages manage such a loss and on what adults (primarily the surviving parent) should do to help them with their loss. This approach, narrow as it is in its focus, tends to overlook the fact that the surviving parent is also in upheaval and may be looking to the children for extraordinary support during this time. It overlooks the fact that such a loss turns such a family upside down, with children tending to parents during the chaos of grief. It overlooks the need that such a family always has to utilize resources—extended family, community, and ulti-mately therapy—that it might not have needed in ordinary times.

In order to get more views on family coping and helping families to manage the loss of a parent, I have interviewed therapists and families themselves. The fact is that most families are not seen by a therapist immediately following a parent's death. Some are not seen until 1½ to 2 years later, when a child's behav-ior calls attention to the family's suffering. School personnel, pediatricians, or members of the clergy are commonly the referral sources at that time.

This chapter addresses the role of a therapist in helping a family with young children when a parent dies. Specifically, the chapter addresses several factors related to the impact of the death on children and their families: the family context before the death; "putting away" the body and the inclusion of children in this process; and the mourning, including family rituals and unresolved grieving. The most common adjustment problems of children are described, using clinical case examples. Some approaches to family treatment in these cases are described, lead-ing finally to some general conclusions about how therapists can work with fami-lies of young children who experience the death of a parent. A family's strengths, degree of closeness, ethnic background, and social network; children's ages at the time of the parent's death; and death as a relief are all important issues to be discussed.

Context of the Family before a Death

Before describing what brings families facing bereavement into treatment, let me provide a picture of one family that dealt with a death through the help of family and friends.

Mrs. Greene and her four young children nursed Mr. Greene at home for a year while he struggled with intestinal cancer. The mother, Alison, was a 36-year-old graduate student. Thirteen months after her husband's death, I set up an ap-pointment with her to discuss the last few months of her husband's life. She called me a few days later to say that her children insisted on being included. Mrs. Greene and her four children—Ashley, 13; Toni, 11; Samantha, 8; and Alec, 6—had not consulted with a therapist before, during, or since Mr. Greene's death. They were very willing to discuss their experiences, however.

Mrs. Greene began our interview by presenting me with pictures of the last vacation the family had taken together, camping at the seashore. All the family, including Mr. Greene, looked healthy. It was after that vacation that his remission ended and his condition declined.

Ashley, the oldest and most articulate of the children, told of how she and her father had exhibited champion dogs. They had discussed bloodlines and the future of their kennel. Since her father's death, she had dutifully taken care of the dogs, but she no longer had a zest for doing so. Her best friend, who had been helpful during the months preceding her father's death, had moved to another state since then; Ashley was mourning the loss of her friend also. She was uninterested in school. Nothing seemed to have any relevance for her. Ashley said that she no longer had a passionate interest in life.

Toni, the 11-year-old, had become the "responsible" child. She thought of all the potential needs of the family. She cooked all the meals, called the plumber, and remembered relatives' birthdays. Her grades were straight A's; she was captain of her soccer team; she monitored her younger sister's and brother's homework. It was she who had tears in her eyes during most of the interview.

The 8-year-old second-grader, Samantha, rarely spoke. Whenever an especially poignant memory was recounted by her mother or older sisters, she looked up at me from beneath her bangs but made no verbal comment. She did well at school but had gained a considerable amount of weight. A school counselor had asked whether she wanted to talk; Samantha had refused, but told her mother of the offer, and they then discussed Samantha's sadness.

The youngest child, Alec, the only boy, had been a preschooler at the time of his father's death. By the time of the interview he was very independent, getting his sneakers off and on himself, going to the bathroom alone down a dark hall, and sleeping in his own room.

Mr. Greene's parents lived near the family. It had been customary for them to "drop in" a couple of times a week, and for their son and his family to have supper with them every Friday night. When their son was no longer able to visit their home, his parents brought dinner over. Ashley said that she found it difficult to visit her paternal grandparents now, because they were so sad and she did not know how to console them.

The maternal grandparents lived further away from the family than the paternal grandparents did. They visited monthly and made frequent phone calls while their son-in-law was ill.

Mrs. Greene's sister and her family had opened up their home to any of the children when they needed to get away. Mrs. Greene had confided in her sister about her fears for her husband, herself, and children. The children freely visited their cousins.

Mr. Greene's brother visited frequently before the death and held long talks with his brother and with his niece, Ashley. On subsequent visits he spent time with each of the children, acting as surrogate father, and he attempted to maintain Ashley's interest in raising dogs.

Mr. Greene's friends had been a constant source of nurturance. An old friend had stopped at the house three or four times a week for short visits. His former "jogging buddy" had also stopped to visit each morning on his jogging circuit.

Whenever Mr. Greene's health allowed it, the family repeated activities they had done together previously. They went camping, bicycling, and horseback riding. And Mr. Greene spent time alone with each of his children. There had been much laughter and gentle teasing. Ashley recalled her father joking about his health.

Mrs. Greene's newly made friends at a food cooperative had organized a food chain. Each day for nearly 2 years, a home-cooked dinner was delivered to the Greene family by one of the co-op members.

Mrs. Greene had begun a master's-degree program before her husband became ill. Because of his urging, and with the help of family and friends who provided care for Mr. Greene and the children while she attended classes, Mrs. Greene continued her studies and had long-range professional goals. She had not begun dating yet, but did socialize with fellow students, old friends, and family.

The Greene family provided a good example of gradually mourning a father. They were aided in this by family and friends. Yet, after they had spoken with me for an hour and a half, Mrs. Greene recognized how much her children were still burdened by their grief and readjustment to life without their father, and she commented that she thought it would have helped to talk with a professional after her husband died.

A little more than a year after the death of Mr. Greene, the family was still recovering—not only from his death, but also from his final illness. There was a redistribution of responsibilities among the surviving family members, and there was a great reliance on the older children to carry on functions previously assumed by their father. The sadness of the group was pervasive at this interview, and yet there was much in this family that demonstrated effective coping and predicted an eventual good recovery.

Significant Factors for Families in Coping with the Death of a Parent

The example of the Greenes illustrates a number of important factors that contribute to a family's coping pattern. As noted above, a primary factor is that of the family's strengths and resources before the loss (Hilgard, Newman, & Fisk, 1960). With the Greenes, a close-knit family, reliance on family members for support following the death was expected. They had always shared their feelings with one another as well as with friends.

The family's connections with extended family and social networks before the death are crucial to its adaptation to the loss. Grandparents from both sides of the family who are involved with grandchildren before the death of a parent are likely to continue to attend to their grandchildren and the surviving parent after the death. Other extended-family members do the same. Their visits provide a sense of continuity and safety, and sometimes include financial security. Indeed, in my experience, when families of origin were integral parts of the family, the children ultimately made a good adjustment after the death of a parent.

The ethnic origins of the family often shape patterns of handling a death.

Different ethnic groups express their grief in different ways. Children growing up in specific cultural contexts have participated in ceremonies for a variety of life events, such as births, christenings, bar or bas mitzvahs, weddings, hospitalizations, leaving home, and deaths.

A large social network created before death from contacts at work, at church, or in the community provides a cushion of security, as do families of origin. One family, completely cut off from its families of origin, had virtually no community network either. The father was an alcoholic and the family moved whenever he lost a job, which was often. When he was killed in a motorcycle accident, no support system was immediately available to the family. The extended families had been cut off. The frequent moves of the family had prevented it from establishing long-lasting social ties. The remaining family members had great difficulty bouncing back from the death of the father.

Children who have spent time with a large network of adult persons in addition to their parents feel safe in many situations. Shopping with family friends, staying overnight with neighbors, or spending a week on vacation with grandparents are signs to children that they can be secure in many settings and with many people. These experiences and relationships established before a death in the family provide strong support for coping.

The degree of closeness children have with the parents is also an important factor in how the children manage the loss of one of them. A child who is especially close to the surviving parent adjusts more easily to the death of the other parent. Conversely, a child who has been especially close to the parent who died, and distant from the surviving parent, experiences a more difficult adjustment. How much the children resemble or are seen as like the deceased parent and how the surviving parent feels about the lost parent will also affect how the children and the surviving parent redefine their relationships.

Also important are children's ages at the time of death. The younger a child is, the more likely the child is to be upset. This is not due simply to the loss itself, but also to the massive family disruption that follows the loss. Younger children are more dependent on family routines and predictability of relationships than older children, who can often understand and participate in the extraordinary tasks that may need to be performed after a death. The younger children may also identify with their parents and assume they will die too, not having differentiated sufficiently to perceive the boundaries between themselves and their parents (Furman, 1974).

Although ordinarily we focus on the grief and loss experienced by a family in which a parent dies, sometimes the death also has positive effects. Families beset by continual strife may be relieved by the death of a major combatant. A parent freed from an unhappy marriage has more time, energy, and resources to devote to children of the marriage. Berlinsky and Biller (1982) observe,

> The death of a parent who has been sexually or physically abusive, rejecting, or merely disinterested may positively influence a child's self-concept and emotional adjustment. Even if the parent's death does actually represent a loss, a child's

development could be enhanced. She/he could become, of necessity, more independent and develop superior problem-solving skills. She/he could be prompted to work toward higher achievement in order to better serve the parent's memory. The few studies that have attempted to link parental bereavement with achievement indicate the potential for this line of research. (p. 129)

Other researchers agree:

The loss of a parent is quite positive: a relief from the real or potential burdens of caretaking, a welcome severing of destructive family ties, an opportunity to grow unhampered by parental expectations, and realization of the all too small reward of an inheritance. Yet our cultural proscriptions inhibit open expression of these feelings. (Moss & Moss, 1983–1984, p. 66)

Such thoughts are not commonly expressed, but they should be considered by a therapist who may encourage family members to express this aspect of the loss, so that the family is not additionally burdened by guilt about feeling relief.

The Death Itself

Giving Explanations and Support

The questions parents most often ask after the death of a spouse are "How can I tell the children? And what should I tell them?" Parents want to make the event as painless as possible, sparing their children "adult pain" (Grollman, 1967). Straightforward explanations of what has happened usually are best for everyone in the family. Both Grollman (1967) and Furman (1974) point out that young children, in particular, are likely to misinterpret explanations such as "God loved your daddy so much that He brought him to live in heaven," and may actually find such thoughts frightening.

A sudden, unexpected death or a suicide presents a particular crisis for the family and often leaves the surviving parent so absorbed with his or her own reactions that the children may not be attended to in the acute period. It is here that social contacts, extended-family members, or other helpers are urgently needed to offer support to the shocked and grieving family members.

One man finally sought help at age 43 for problems relating to having found his mother dead when he was only 5. No help had been available to him at the time. In contrast, a 4-year-old boy who had had to step across the body of his beaten, dead mother after his father had murdered her and left him cowering in a corner of the room was haunted by the memory of these events day and night. Because there was no parent available to the boy whose mother was murdered, mental health personnel worked with him immediately after the tragedy. Such assistance might have forestalled the older man's lifetime of unresolved feelings.

Circumstances: Chronic versus Acute

When a chronic illness such as multiple sclerosis has existed for a long time, children learn to make concessions as a matter of course in order to deal with the limitations it imposes. They are accustomed to the ill parent's undergoing periods of energy depletion and emotional outbursts. Their own lives exist parallel to that of the parent. When death occurs, they have done some anticipatory grieving.

In addition, when a parent dies at home after a long illness, some preparation has been made for the death.

In an acute illness, such as a heart attack, the family usually converges on a hospital, where control is located in people other than family members. Visiting hours are commonly set by fiat rather than on an individual basis, and young children may be denied admittance altogether. When death occurs in such places, resolving the loss may be much harder for children. There is a hint of unreality to it all. Some families have tried to relieve this sense of unreality by taking children to the hospital room, having them take along games, hobbies, and homework—things they would share with the sick parent if they were at home. Others who are not allowed admittance send crayoned drawings for the room or favorite photographs of themselves for the bedside. Some families insist on setting up house in the hospital rooms of dying parents who are ill for a long time (Furman, 1974).

There are researchers who advise anticipatory crisis training for children (Hart, 1976; Irish, 1971; Krupp, 1972). They believe that since most deaths occur in hospitals or nursing homes, children are ill prepared to deal with death as a normal life event. They are not involved or included. In fact, often neither are the adults in the family.

Finding Out

Children's report of their reactions to hearing about the death of a parent are most informative about the impact. One boy said, "It was like someone punched me in the belly. All my wind was gone."

"I was at swimming class when I thought I saw my father at the end of the pool smiling. I told my girlfriend I wanted to go home. I knew my dad was dead," a girl reported. When she arrived home, it was to find cars lining both sides of the street. Her mother met her at the door and was crying; the daughter cried too.

A boy whose father was a jet pilot in the Navy was met at the school bus, not by his mother but by an unknown Naval officer. He immediately knew that his father's plane had crashed and he was dead, but at that moment had to deal with the news by himself.

What May Happen and What Will Happen

After children are told that a parent is dead, they frequently ask very practical questions, such as "Will we have to move?", "Am I an orphan?", "What will happen to Daddy's body in the ground?", or "Are we poor now?" Those questions require answers. So do other, unarticulated ones.

It is helpful to forecast to children what they may experience—pain in the same area of the body where their parent had it; fear that they might die when they go to sleep; anxiety that every time they or someone in the family has symptoms similar to those experienced by the dead parent during the final illness, it means they will develop the same maladies and die from them. Children are frequently afraid to articulate such things or do not even know that they fear them. When adults they trust say what may occur, unstated fears that may create anxiety are anticipated and addressed.

Another anxiety that children experience develops from the need to know where they will live in the event of the other parent's death. A family of four told their mother they each wanted to live with a different family. The mother felt that they were symbolically telling her to stay healthy and laughed with them. She then assured them of her good health.

As soon as possible after family members have learned of the death, the surviving parent should discuss with the children what will happen next. This discussion should anticipate their anxieties about finances and worries about whether they will be poor, have to move, be unable to take vacations, or be unable to buy clothes or gifts. Expectations for future changes must be shared with the children, but without causing them alarm.

In the case of the fatally injured Navy pilot mentioned above, a large insurance policy allowed the widow to stay at home with her young children. It even provided college education for her and them. Telling the children of this financial support eased their fears.

Another widow, who had always been at home with her children, needed to find a job immediately after her husband's death, as there was neither income nor savings. She and her children experienced a great deal of stress. She had to take a job immediately, and her neighbors cared for the children after school until she returned from work. There was no time to consider a career, because bills for food and mortgages were pressing.

One child whose family had done a good job of explaining circumstances told me, "We never have a lot of money, but we always have enough." Her grandparents had made it clear that money was available to the newly single-parent family.

The Last Rites

The decision about disposal of the body usually does not include children, but it probably would be a good idea if it did. What is done, however, is important in how the family members cope. Levine (1982) suggests leaving the body in bed for a few hours to allow those closest to the dead person to make their farewells. Seeing the face freed of pain and peaceful, as it looks a few hours after death, creates serenity for the living, who may have spent months watching the agony of prolonged death consume their loved one.

In the Greene family, where the father died of cancer at home, the mortician did not arrive for nearly 8 hours after the death occurred. During that time, the children made repeated trips to his bedside and cried with siblings, mother, grandparents, and friends of their parents. In that way, the children were prepared to witness the more formal death rituals that followed.

By contrast, in a family where the mother died at home of cancer, the children returned from school to find no trace of her. Her body had been removed; the medical support devices were gone; all was tidy. This woman had also not allowed visitors to the home in the last phase of her illness.

After removal of the body to a funeral home or mortuary, the question of how much to involve children in family rituals of death must be faced. Those decisions can be made with the help of the children.

Attendance at "wakes" or "viewings" is a crucial question. Generally, there is much concern about the impact of death rituals on children. Many people who view young children as particularly vulnerable or fragile may fail to include them as a part of the family during these crucial rituals. Although many aspects of the viewing or funeral may be misinterpreted by and frighten the children, they are more likely to gain confidence through participation in the family's activity and the reassurance of being together with the family, even in grief.

Ethnic rituals such as "waking the body" or "sitting *shiva*" provide comfort to those familiar with such customs. But perhaps some special ritual can be developed and enacted by the family specifically to include the children. Children appear to need more rituals, not fewer. To deny children the chance to participate in important family events is to deny them important opportunities for therapeutic communication. It is though rites, rituals, and ceremonies that people work through their feelings. Although no child should be forced to participate, it would be wise to offer opportunities that are relevant to a child's needs. If participating in the funeral seems impractical, children could visit the funeral home with a mature and competent adult who would answer their questions.[1]

All studies in the literature report that children should be included in wakes and funerals as is age-appropriate. Explanations of what will happen in words that a child can understand should be made in advance of each of the rituals by the surviving parent or a trusted adult (Grollman, 1974).

1. See Zilbach, Chapter 3, this volume, for another example.

Furman (1974) asserts that children under 10 adapt successfully to the death even if they do not attend the funeral, whereas older children cannot. I do not agree, because I believe that young children's membership in the family is at stake, and when they are excluded from the family activities, they are more likely to suffer.

> To shut a youngster out of the funeral experience might be quite costly and damaging to his future development. He is an integral part of the family unit and should participate with them on this sad but momentous occasion. However, if a child is unwilling, he should not be forced to go or made to feel guilty because "he let the family down." (Grollman, 1967, p. xiv)

Young children who do not attend the funeral, however, should be included in other activities related to putting the body away, such as going to the gravesite afterwards to help in the planting of shrubs and flowers. They should not be hurried away from the location, but rather allowed to become familiar with the site. Some families even have picnics with their young children in the cemetery.

In addition, rituals can be developed to involve a child who does not attend the funeral in sending the parent off. For example, taking the child to some body of water—whether a lake, river, or ocean—where he or she can perform a ritual of release is healing. A child can place a photograph of the dead parent in a paper bag; can lay the bag in an aluminum pie plate; and, after talking about the parent and perhaps saying goodbye and shedding tears, can launch the plate onto the water. An older child can burn a photograph of the parent and watch the smoke become part of the earth's atmosphere. Some children and parents have tied balloons of the dead parent's favorite color together with ribbons, written notes to the person, tied them to the ribbons, said a prayer, released the balloons, and watched them float away. Such rituals acquire meaning from the significance of the objects and activities to the child.

In cases of accidents or suicides, memorial services often take the place of funerals. Children's inclusion in them are decided on the same basis as their attendance at funerals.

Mourning

During the mourning period, the whole family may revert to less differentiated styles of relating. Children's behavior may appear to regress to that of much younger children, encouraging adults to provide tactile, nonverbal comfort as is done with a baby. Children may be found daydreaming and need to be hugged often or otherwise touched rather then encouraged to talk. Seeing the deceased parent's belongings can provide either upset or nostalgia.

Thumbing through family photographs and reminiscing about times together is often healing for some families. Distributing personal items of the deceased parent to be cherished by the children may also be helpful. Rather than being viewed as morbid, fondling mementoes of the dead parent may provide a sense of security and peace.

While life at home without two parents settles into a routine, returning speedily to an outside routine once the funeral or memorial service is over is imperative. Children even need to eat the same cereal and drink their accustomed juice (Adams-Greenly & Moynihan, 1983). Returning to performance of homely chores, having arguments with siblings, and showing rebelliousness toward the surviving parent are all indicators of health.

Usually school-age children return to classes a few days after the burial. For young children, this may be the first time they face their peers. Their classmates may never have experienced a death, and the children will need to explain their loss to them. Some of their classmates may understand the loss of a two-parent home as the result of divorce. An older school-age child may have one best friend who has been somewhat involved during the formal mourning proceedings. That classmate often is a buffer for dealing with the other students' curiosity. He or she may have already explained to the class what has happened. When the bereaved child returns to school, a peer has prepared the way.

Teachers frequently lead discussion groups with the child's class before the child returns to school. These groups discuss death and its ramifications for the living. Such discussion precludes the likelihood of classmates' deluging the returning child with questions such as "Did you touch him? Was he cold?"

As extended family and social contacts are critical in supporting the family through the death and funeral and the time afterwards, teachers and peers are essential in leading the children of the family back into normal routines.

There seems to be a connection between the surviving spouse's resumption of a social life and his or her children's equanimity (Berlinsky & Biller, 1982). The parent's reinvolvement appears to signal the children that life is again safe and they are free to trust the future. When the parent does not become reinvolved in a social life, the children experience a continuing responsibility to him or her. This was true of a man, now in his 30s, whose father died 2 weeks before his birth. He says, "I always was sorry my mother didn't remarry. It placed such a burden on me."

After the death of a parent, children question the permanence of the remaining one. There is reluctance to leave the living parent's side. That parent may need some time alone or in adult activities, and may be impatient with the children's "haunting" him or her. The presence of other adults who are actively involved in the lives of the family members breaks up some of the intense clinging that the survivors are inclined to engage in. Thus, for example, short shopping trips with grandparents or adult friends often help children develop a strong sense of security even when away from the surviving parent.

When the family members re-enter their own social lives, children find solace in relationships other than those with their family and other adults, as happened with one 12-year-old girl whose best friend's favorite uncle had recently died. The two girls experimented with cosmetics, dressed up, went roller-skating. As they played, they also talked about being sad and lonely.

Adjustment Problems and Treatment

Problems at 18 Months to 2 Years

When problems do arise in families where a parent has died, these are commonly noticed 18 months to 2 years later. It is as if during the immediate bereavement period, family members are so preoccupied with soothing one another that individual needs may be overlooked. Often when a problem does surface, it is manifested in a child as it was in the instance of Jeff Montgomery.

Jeff was the only child of white Anglo-Saxon Protestant parents who had been relocated by his father's corporation three times before his fifth birthday. Mr. Montgomery was quickly climbing the corporate ladder and was as quickly becoming an alcoholic. He drank every night when he returned from work and most weekends. He and Jeff spent very little time together, while Jeff was very close to his mother.

When Mr. Montgomery died from cirrhosis of the liver, 5-year-old Jeff and his mother became even closer, with Jeff having no friends his own age. As a preschooler Jeff experienced no particular social problems, but when he was 7, his school asked the psychologist to see him because he was crying easily in class and hitting other children.

The school psychologist saw the mother and son in her office together several times. She discovered that Mrs. Montgomery had nightly periods of anxiety and brought her son into her bed to comfort her. She had not dated or gone out socially since her husband's death, although she was only 32 and quite attractive. She felt that no other man could mean to her what her husband had meant.

The psychologist set up several sessions with Jeff alone. She discovered that he felt enormous guilt for his father's death because he had frequently wished the father dead. He had resented his father's neglect of his mother and the disappointment he had caused her. At the same time, he was angry that his father had left him to tend to his mother.

The psychologist referred the Montgomerys to a family therapist, who slowly added more and more extended-family members to the psychotherapy sessions in order to give both mother and son others with whom to relate. Since the Montgomerys had moved so often because of Mr. Montgomery's frequent job relocations, their extended family lived a great distance from them. However, a great-aunt and two male first cousins lived nearby. The cousins, studying at a local college, enjoyed being "big brothers" to Jeff and made him a sort of mascot in their dorm.

The therapist believed that Mrs. Montgomery needed to feel needed and wondered whether her great-aunt needed her. The younger woman began to spend time driving the older one to meetings and church activities. Her great-aunt, a feisty woman in her 80s, encouraged her niece to go out with young people and even made some efforts at matchmaking. As the mother began to develop a social life, her son was freed from the need to nurture her. He became less depressed and stopped hitting other children.

The therapist encouraged Mrs. Montgomery to discuss her mixed feelings about her husband's loss with Jeff. After they told each other about their occasional wishes for Mr. Montgomery's death, they also expressed their anger with him for not taking better care of himself and them. Once their anger was released, the love they had for Mr. Montgomery was able to surface. They were finally able to grieve for his loss as well as theirs.

Finally, the therapist was supportive of Mrs. Montgomery's decision to return to her home state to be closer to family and old friends.

Another child exhibiting problems within 1½ to 2 years after a parent's death was an 8-year-old boy, Mark Morecambe.

Mark had become overweight and was referred to a therapist for that reason. During sessions with Mark alone, the therapist asked him to draw a picture of himself. He drew a head with eyes looking down at an unsketched body. He also drew himself as a stick figure standing next to a tree with a black hole in its trunk. He described how the tree felt: "It has a piece missing. It wants it back." When asked what was missing, he answered, "My dad." Mark expressed some guilt over his father's death. "Maybe I was a bad boy, and that made him die." His use of animal puppets allowed him to begin to express his feelings about his father's death.

The younger children are, the more likely they are to take responsibility for a parent's death. They believe that they have as much power over the life of their parents as the parents have over them. It is helpful for therapists to provide an opportunity for young children to express what they might consider unacceptable feelings without being in the presence of the remaining parent, similar to a dress rehearsal. When they finally do address the surviving parent, they no longer believe their feelings are unacceptable.

When the therapist saw Mrs. Morecambe, she gave her a prescription for her son. She was to contact a pediatrician and work with her on a diet for Mark. She was also to have him join Cub Scouts and Little League, and invite friends to stay overnight. At the same time, she was to go out socially. (She already was active in her church.)

About 6 weeks later, Mrs. Morecambe telephoned the therapist to report Mark's success with his diet and her support of his efforts. Mark was adhering to his diet, and she was being supportive of him as well as resuming a social life of her own. A year later, she again telephoned because the school was concerned with Mark's aggessiveness. Mrs Morecambe asked whether the therapist would see them and write a letter of assessment to the school. The therapist agreed.

What she met in her waiting room was a slender 8-year-old and his mother. Mrs. Morecambe no longer spoke for Mark, as she had previously done. Mark's behavior was appropriate for a boy his age. No longer did he let other children hassle him without giving them a shove or at least verbal assault. It seemed to the

SPECIAL FAMILIES IN SPECIAL CIRCUMSTANCES

therapist that what would not have been noticed in another boy was outstanding in the formerly overweight, unhappy child. His mother was overjoyed to see the changes in her son and found it exciting to support him in those changes.

Mrs. Morecambe had begun dating and was happy in her personal life also. The therapist congratulated both of them on their success. She later spoke to the school counselor about the aggressive behavior and found that, as she had thought, what was seen as age-appropriate in other boys his age was seen as aggressive in this formerly overweight, nonassertive child. The therapist suggested that the school counselor help Mark's teacher develop a new picture of him.

Chronic Maladjustment and Failure of the Family to Cope

Although it is common for crises to occur 18 months to 2 years after the death of a parent, sometimes maladaptation to parental death does not surface for years; it may not emerge until another developmental crossroads is reached. This was the case with Danny Guarino, whose father had died years before Danny was referred for therapy.

Danny Guarino was aged 9 at the time his father was killed in a motorcycle accident while drunk. It was not until Danny entered high school that he began to exhibit school problems.

The Guarino family had moved to a rural area from the south side of Philadelphia. They had no support system from their old Italian community. Their families of origin had also cut off regular connections with them. None of their relatives or neighbors approved of their itinerant life style.

Mrs. Guarino had always been promiscuous and became more so after her husband's death. She moved Danny and his sister into various homes of short-term duration with men with whom she was involved. When she could find work, Mrs. Guarino worked as a waitress. Her two children were streetwise in an area where most children lived stable, simple lives in a semirural community. The neighboring families did not allow their children to associate with the Guarino children, so the children had few friends.

The teachers in Danny's classes tried to encourage him in his schoolwork, as he was very bright. They were the only ones who were supportive of Danny. Aside from them, there were no dependable, nurturing adults in his life.

Children of the same sex as the dead parent benefit from a relationship with someone of that sex. When extended family or close friends do not provide these relationships, agencies like Big Brothers and Big Sisters, which match children with same-sex adults as friends, may fill that need. It was after Big Brothers proved unable to connect with Danny that his teachers became more insistent that he needed professional help.

The school counselor recommended Big Brothers to Mrs. Guarino as help for her son. She did not make use of the agency after an initial exploration. "Fucking nosey bodies'' was how she described them. She resented the questions she was asked at the initial interview and refused to cooperate with the social worker.

The teachers had been successful in keeping Danny out of serious trouble, and believed that if he had stayed in the city he would have become a juvenile delinquent. But they were unsure what might become of him in a middle-class, semirural community. They were insistent that he receive therapy. Since Mrs. Guarino would not pursue receiving therapy or any help outside of school, the school required that Danny attend group sessions for children with problems within the school setting.

Therapist Difficulties with Parent Loss

The issue of countertransference surfaced for at least two therapists I interviewed. Both of them had lost a parent through death at an early age. In cases involving the death of parents, they were drawn into empathic feelings toward the identified patients and felt antipathy toward the surviving spouses. Thus they tended to segregate the families in this very crucial time, rather than recognizing the families as the most significant units of healing.

An example of therapist countertransference occurred in a family with poor adjustment to the death of a parent. A boy's maladaptation was not apparent until he entered high school. Sam Bernstein is a good example of postponed mourning and its effects; unfortunately, the therapist's siding with the child alienated the parent and rendered the family inaccessible to further therapeutic assistance.

Sam Bernstein, a 15-year-old high school student, was recommended for therapy after his guidance counselor noticed his poor relationship with peers. Sam's father had died of cancer when Sam was 6 and his brother 2.

The high school recommended private therapy at this time because there was evidence of a strong mother–son conflict that the school felt unable to handle. The mother appeared to be anxious to keep the boy a child and opposed many of his social outreach behaviors, such as dating, going to parties, and going on ski trips with his class. Sam felt helpless to convince his mother that he should be permitted to attend teenage events. His mother had relied on him, her older son, to make her feel secure. When he began to move toward his own adult life, his mother fought his efforts.

The family, including the mother and both sons (Sam and his 11-year-old brother, Jason), attended 11 therapy sessions. As Sam became more assertive, his mother tried to develop a coalition with the male therapist so that he would pressure Sam to stop asserting himself with her. When the therapist resisted her attempts, she ended therapy.

Sam continued to make phone calls to the therapist, unbeknownst to his mother. The therapist encouraged him to mature, but did not advise him to tell his mother of the phone calls.

An indicator to a family therapist that he or she is becoming too subjective is finding himself or herself taking sides with any one family member. In Sam Bernstein's case, it was the therapist's taking the side of Sam and labeling his mother "controlling." It might have been helpful for the therapist to examine his own relationship with his surviving parent, so that he did not simply become the "good father" to Sam and continue to be distanced from his own father.

When Families Refer Themselves

Some families are self-referred because they themselves notice changes in the children. Mario Mantucci's mother was a social worker who felt she should be of more help to her son than she was.

Mrs. Mantucci felt concern for her 10-year-old son, Mario. Mario was very anxious and encopretic. His father had succumbed to bowel cancer 2 years earlier.

This Italian family had taken care of the father at home with only brief visits to the hospital. They had set up the playroom as a hospital room. There Mr. Mantucci slowly deteriorated over a period of 6 months. Originally, Mario had continued to use the room to watch television or play darts; as his father's health worsened, Mario spent more and more time in his own bedroom. By the time his father died, Mario had no contact with him and little with the other members of his family.

As Mr. Mantucci neared death, his widowed father moved into the house. The decision for the move was made among the adults; they did not include the children in the decision making. They decided that the senior Mr. Mantucci could take care of the yard and maintain the cars. His financial help would also be useful to the family. He gave up his home and moved into his son's house. He and Mario became close, both outsiders in a sense.

After her husband died, Mrs. Mantucci cast her father-in-law in the role of decision maker. She did not want to assume a strong role in the family, but rather a more traditional, passive one. She did recognize that Mario was experiencing depression and was becoming physically ill. She called a colleague for advice; that colleague recommended family therapy. The therapist entered the picture as Mrs. Mantucci and her father-in-law were working out their new roles. If Mrs. Mantucci's plans worked, Mario would lose the sense of camaraderie he shared with his grandfather. He would see him as the disciplinarian his father had been until he became ill.

The grandfather resisted the therapist's initial attempts to be supportive of his daughter-in-law. The therapist had one session with Mr. Mantucci alone, and shared with him his own mother's Calabrese background. Man to man, they discussed Mario's needs. Those needs included having a decision-making mother—a nontraditional role for Italian women. The senior Mr. Mantucci agreed that his grandson would miss out on the activities they had shared if he assumed the disciplinary role.

When the conjoint sessions resumed, the therapist had acquired a kind of cotherapist in the grandfather. The older man kept assuring his daughter-in-law of the good job she was doing in mothering her children. He refused to take over his dead son's role.

Mario's anxiety lessened and his encopresis ended. The therapist told him how people often develop physical ailments in the same area of the body where a loved one was ill. Mrs. Mantucci entered individual therapy.

When Parents Become Too Absorbed in Their Own Grief

Naturally, parents are preoccupied with reconstructing their own lives after the death of a spouse. They must resolve the issues of child care while they work, possibly make new financial arrangements, recover from the loss, and resume a single social life. They may easily overlook children who appear happy. Often, the depth of sadness children experience is not noticed at home, but rather in school. It was the school that recognized Barry White's problems with his mother.

Barry White learned of his father's death in a plane crash when he returned from school one afternoon and found a Naval commander waiting at his school bus stop. The officer put his hands on Barry's and his brother's shoulders and told them how proud they should be of their father, a Navy reserve pilot who flew fighter planes on weekends. Barry, 10, the oldest of three children, was in fifth grade. He had a younger sister, 8, and a brother, 6.

The church from which his father was buried was across the street from Barry's school. The cemetery next to the church was visible from Barry's classroom. It seemed to allow him to make peace with his father's death, as he often gazed out his classroom window at the gravesite. By the time he left elementary school and entered junior high, he appeared to have recovered from his father's death.

His father's brother became closer to his nephews and niece as well as to their mother after the death. He included them in holidays with his family and attended school events when he could. He and his wife encouraged Barry's mother to socialize with them, to no avail. She continued to wear black clothes 5 years after the death. She did not go out, and Barry felt much responsibility for her.

The School

It is unusual for children who have lost a parent through death to present behavior problems at school (Felner, Ginter, Boike, & Cowen, 1981). Instead, they are likely to display anxiety, shyness, or depression. Teachers are alerted to behavior shifts in children following a family crisis. In one school, "concern-a-grams" are sent to teachers and others involved with students; they inform school personnel of problems a child may be facing. Death of a parent is one reason why the forms are distributed.

One school runs groups for children who have experienced losses of any kind, including that of a sibling, a pet, an intact family, a neighborhood, or a home. The director of psychological services there hopes to provide a forum for children to discuss feelings of loss. Since all children experience loss at one time or another, this group validates feelings incumbent on loss (anger, fear, sadness, guilt, etc.). Discussing those feelings with other children allows group members to accept their own reactions. Even though one child has lost a home through fire and another has lost a parent through death, both children may be overwhelmed by feelings of powerlessness. Talking about it often lessens those feelings and makes a child feel more powerful.

Sadness in children who have lost a parent is commonly noticed by their teachers. As noted earlier in the description of the Greene family, an elementary school counselor was alerted to her weight gain and growing quietness by the second-grade teacher of Samantha Greene, whose father had died a year previously. The counselor invited the child to talk about her life. Although she refused the offer, the child told her mother about the invitation, and they began to talk. Her relating the counselor's invitation provided a catalyst for discussion between mother and child.

Some students may make even better grades than before the traumatic event; however, their siblings may react in the opposite direction, and their grades plummet. Their organizational skills vanish. Their minds wander when they attempt to study or read.

A 9-year old child in the primary grades, Matt Starkey, spent most of each school day gazing out the window after the death of his mother. His teacher became alarmed when his grades plunged and he showed no interest in improving them. The school system pointed out to the bereaved father the needs of his son.

Matt, 9, was referred to a school counselor, who in turn referred him to a private therapist. Matt was of concern to his teacher because he was so withdrawn. Matt's work had been consistent with his ability and age; it had deteriorated lately, and Matt seemed preoccupied. The family quickly responded to the counselor's recommendation to pursue family therapy. Matt, his older brother, and his father impressed the therapist with the kindness and love they expressed toward one another. Although David, Matt's 10-year-old brother, teased him, he also exhibited an underlying tenderness rarely shown by a boy that age.

Mr. Starkey was a pipefitter for the shipyards. He was well paid and enjoyed his work. He was raising his sons alone, but his wife's sister and parents provided emotional support for him and his sons. His sons stayed overnight with their grandparents and played with their first cousins a great deal.

Ethel Starkey had been active in church before becoming ill with cancer. David continued to sing in the same choir they both attended; Matt attended the Sunday school where his mother had taught classes. Mr. Starkey was less certain of the direction he wanted to take in the church. He and Ethel had attended so many of the church activities together that he felt uncomfortable when he attended them alone. Although church members invited him to events, he did not go to them.

The Starkeys' network was large and caring. Church, school, and family were all involved. But Mr. Starkey was uncomfortable doing things without his wife and stayed at home every night.

It is important for children to learn the specifics surrounding a parent's death. Without the facts, they create a false reality, often a maladaptive one (Adams-Greenly & Moynihan, 1983). The Starkeys had unwittingly created problems for their sons by silence about the facts of the mother's illness.

The first step the therapist took was to find out about the mother's death. The father and sons had not previously spoken together of the details of Ethel Starkey's death.

The therapist asked Mr. Starkey how his wife discovered she had cancer; his sons paid rapt attention to his description of their mother's calling him into the bathroom, where she had noticed a dimpling in her breast as she toweled dry after her shower. He related his attempt to soothe her fears as she told him of her recollections of her own mother's death from breast cancer. "Didn't she have any clothes on?" David wanted to know. He could not recall his parents as lovers. His only remembrance of his mother was as a sick and listless woman.

Mr. Starkey recounted details of the call to the doctor and the subsequent visit to his office. He sobbed when he told his sons of the doctor's actual telling his wife and him of her probable diagnosis, breast cancer. He described how he and his wife clung to each other in the car after leaving the physician's office. David and Matt openly wept as their father recounted the scene.

Mr. Starkey explained that his wife made him promise not to tell anyone the true reason for her hospitalization. She later refused to have visitors to the house while she underwent chemotherapy. Mr. Starkey could only speak to the one person who would not be present after his wife's death—herself. Because he was sworn to secrecy, Mr. Starkey avoided intimacy with any of the persons who might have consoled him. He especially avoided his sons; he was afraid he would reveal the secret if he spent much time with them.

"If the family does not discuss the child's experience, in the hope that he has not been aware of what has gone on, or if they contradict his observations in the hope of presenting a more palatable reality, a barrier is created in the parent-child relationship. The child then has to struggle alone with his frightening experiences and confused conclusions" (Furman, 1974, p. 20). The Starkeys were not talking about what was happening.

The boys, aged 8 and 9 at that time, were aware that their mother was getting sicker and sicker. She had no patience with them and could tolerate little of their youthful exuberance. When she died, her husband was home alone with her; the boys were at school. When they returned, their mother's body had been taken to the funeral home. Everything in the room she used was either missing or "tidied up." There was no evidence of her having been there.

Mr. Starkey described his wife's last few hours. She and her husband had looked over photo albums of their life together. Finally Ethel became comatose and her breathing slowed down. She just stopped breathing, and he continued to hold her in his arms. The effect of this description on his sons was elecrifying. They put their arms around their father, and all three of them cried softly.

Therapy consisted of eight sessions designed to encourage the father to resume an adult social life. He had not been out socially since his wife had been diagnosed as having cancer. The therapist encouraged him to attend church events and then other community social events.

Mr. Starkey and his sons drew sketches of their future life, a series of seagulls flying over a benign ocean. Mr. Starkey and Matt attended two sessions without David. At these sessions, Matt was free to act as young as he wanted to, without being teased by his older brother.

As his father resumed a social life, Matt became less withdrawn. His work improved and he made a friend at school.

Principles of Family Therapy with the Bereaved

"Anyone concerned with bereavement needs to appreciate the limits of his helpfulness and the unique impact of death" (Furman, 1974, p. 11). Therapists must respect the fact that each death is different and must realize that no one method of treating problems related to death is the best one. They may use strategic therapy, with its ideas of homework and age-appropriateness; Bowenian therapy, with its emphasis on the extended family; art therapy, with its use of the left side of the brain to educe unconscious healing; bibliotherapy, with its use of writings to foster discussion; and so on. There is no "correct" therapy for use with families who have suffered the death of a parent. The only correct approach seems to be to provide as few sessions as possible and leave the work of mourning to the family.

Involving Larger Networks

The needs of a family mourning a parent are determined by the support family members are receiving. The therapist must first of all discover what support is forthcoming. If that support is not from a person who has been and will continue to be included in the family network, it is essential for the therapist to set mechanisms in motion to include such people. A therapist can assess the amount of support available to the family by drawing up a genogram ("I see you have an aunt in Minneapolis. Could Johnny spend a week with her?"), finding out who comprises the family's network, and checking the school or church's support program.

Including the extended family in the treatment is one way to reduce the blaming within the nuclear family members; extended-family members can act as arbitrators. Inclusion of aunts, uncles, and grandparents also fosters a sense of security and permanence of family. Such inclusion has seldom been studied, yet clinical practice demonstrates that the presence of relatives seems to provide continuity and permanence. Children sense themselves as being part of a collective identity, the family.

In the absence of extended family, a network made up of church members, social friends, and friends from work can be included in family treatment. It is important that there be others outside the family to rely on. These others include special teachers, neighbors, church members, old family friends, peers, and even pets.

Addressing Individuals as Part of the Family Group

It is important for a therapist to work from the overview of family systems, but not to insist that the entire family attend all sessions. A family therapist must be willing to see individual family members for a session or two. Some of the feelings they possess have not been articulated by any adults because of the common occurrence of "canonizing the dead." After individuals have talked with a therapist about their sadness and possible guilt, it is essential that all the family members discuss their feelings together. Hearing other family members express what they themselves have hidden, because of the shame of having such feelings, provides forgiveness and normality. Therapists may need to tell families who are especially reluctant to express feelings what other families have felt in similar situations.

Children who often are reprimanded for being noisy or not doing well at school may believe that their behavior had something to do with their parent's death. Blame, especially in young children, may assume enormous proportions and influence them throughout life. A child may also believe that the surviving parent did not take proper care of the sick parent. This blame placing makes it difficult to receive comfort from that parent or to give comfort to him or her.

Employing the Familiar as a Transition

A home visit may be useful for a therapist. Children pointing out "Daddy's favorite chair," where their mother sat at the table, or the side of their parents' bed the deceased parent slept on may comfort them. It will also make concrete the fact that the parent is dead. Likewise, activities in the home are more likely to create opportunities for resolution of the death than sitting in an unfamiliar office is.

Making collages from tidbits of belongings of each member of the family, including the dead parent, is another method of eliciting healing conversation. So is placing photographs in albums.

Writing letters to distant relatives or friends describing the death and its after-effects allows the children to experience the sense of extended family and friends, as well as to be involved in the afterevent. Sometimes the immediate flurry of activity after a death make it impossible for grieving to take place. Participating in the homely activities mentioned here involves all family members, including the children, in direct ways after the death.

Bibliotherapy

Reading stories about families in which a parent has died give family members a sense of relationship with others who have suffered this loss. Classics include *Little Men,* by Louisa May Alcott; *Meet the Austins,* by Madeleine L'Engle; *Marged,* by Florence Musgrave; *The Big Wave,* by Pearl Buck; and *Rootabaga Stories,* by Carl Sandburg. Reading any of these stories within the family or giving them to an older child to read alone can also be a basis for further discussion (Ross, cited in Grollman, 1967).

Supporting Parents

Most parents are anxious to help their children cope with their loss, but need guidance in how to go about it (Adams-Greenly & Moynihan, 1983). In offering a family these techniques for recovery, the therapist must treat the surviving parent as a colleague. Directing suggestions to him or her and asking for feedback on their appropriateness with this family strengthens the parental role in the eyes of the children. The needs most children have after a parent's death, and methods found useful in meeting those needs, should be described.

A family therapist can give credence to the fact that this group of persons, minus a major member, still comprises a family. Frequent use of the word "family" is beneficial. Death does not end the life of a family, only that of one of its members.

Conclusions

In helping young children cope with the death of a parent, family therapists exert influence in the lay community by their articulated attitudes. Such influence should not be minimized. An attitude helpful to grieving families is that death is a natural occurrence, and as such can be handled by the family. Mourning the death of a parent is best managed by the surviving parent, the extended family, and close friends of the family. They must include the children of the dead parent as much as possible within the limits of emotional appropriateness.

When family members do not adequately address the loss and cope with the resultant changes in their outlook and the family life, problems may not surface in children until they are adults. Thus is better to make the planning of immediate family needs a whole-family enterprise that involves the children as well. In this way, all can observe the realities of the death and be party to providing a respectful farewell to their parent. "Healthy children will not fear life, if their elders have integrity enough not to fear death" (Erikson, 1963, p. 269).

REFERENCES

Adams-Greenly, M., & Moynihan, R. (1983). Helping the children of fatally-ill parents. *American Journal of Orthopsychiatry, 53*(2), 219–229.
Berlinsky, E. B., & Biller, H. (1982). *Parental death and psychological development.* Lexington, MA: Lexington Books.
Bertman, S. (1974). In E. A. Grollman (Ed.), *Concerning death.* Boston: Beacon Press.
Erikson, E. (1963). *Childhood and society* (2nd ed.). New York: Norton.
Felner, R. D., Ginter, M. A., Boike, M. F., & Cowen, E. L. (1981). Parental death and the school adjustment of young children. *American Journal of Community Psychology, 9,* 181–191.
Felner, R. D., Stolbert, A., & Cowen, E. L. (1975). Crisis events and school mental health: Referral patterns of young children. *Journal of Consulting and Clinical Psychology, 43,* 305–310.
Furman, E. (1974). *A child's parent dies.* New Haven, CT: Yale University Press.
Grollman, E. A. (1967). *Explaining death to children.* Boston: Beacon Press.
Grollman, E. A. (Ed.). (1974). *Concerning death.* Boston: Beacon Press.
Hart, E. (1976). Death education and mental health. *Journal of School Health, 56,* 407–412.
Herz, F. (1982). Jewish families. In M. McGoldrick, J. Pearce, & J. Giordano (Eds.), *Ethnicity and family therapy* (pp. 364–392). New York: Guilford Press.
Hilgard, G., Newman, M., & Fisk, F. (1960). Strength of adult ego following childhood bereavement. *American Journal of Orthopsychiatry, 30,* 788–798.
Irish, D. (1971). Death education: Preparation for living. In B. Green & D. Irish (Eds.), *Death education: Preparation for living.* Cambridge, MA: Schenkman.
Krupp, G. (1972). Maladaptive reactions to the death of a family member. *Social Casework, 53,* 425–434.
Levine, S. (1982). *Who dies?* Garden City, NY: Anchor Books.
Moss, M. S., & Moss, S. Z. (1983–1984). The impact of parental death on middle aged children. *Omega, 14,* 65–75.
U.S. Bureau of the Census. (1985). *Statistical abstracts 1986.* Washington, DC: U.S. Government Printing Office.

Managing Larger Systems of Childhood

The family grouping or household in which a young child is reared is the most crucial mediator of civilization, and therefore the most crucial mediator of bio-psychosocial forces in the child's life. As has been described many times already, the degree to which agents outside the nuclear family exert direct influence varies with the stage of family development and the conditions of the family. Most authors have observed that healthy families use resources outside the family freely, but in such a way that the family integrity is preserved. Families with handicapped children, with children with chronic illness, or with parents who are compromised need outside help. In the course of life, families naturally come into contact with other systems. Families are always embedded in the culture of their extended families, and children go to school, so these systems are constantly involved with families with young children. The placement process and child protective system are ones with which only some families become involved, and the same is true of the legal system. The purpose of the chapters in this section is to examine the interfaces between families and these larger systems and the ways in which the interactions affect children; once again, the intent is to describe a design for therapeutic intervention when necessary.

In Chapter 2 Hibbs has described, from the contextual point of view, the relational matrix of child development. In Chapter 15, Keith describes how the extended family actively participates in the entire family's symbolic experience of itself. He sketches the contributions of Bowen and Boszormenyi-Nagy, who have both elaborated theories of intergenerational transmission and ways in which troubled individuals in the present need to study and rework family patterns to release themselves from the inhibiting aspects of these same patterns. Keith's work, though, is directly derived from his long association with Whitaker; it emphasizes the contemporary influences of these patterns and the ways in which working with these entire family systems in the present enables them to rearrange themselves. This approach to work with several generations is the only one that explicitly directly involves children in the process. (In fact, Whitaker used to involve someone else's children in family sessions if there were none in the family!) The presence of the children in the session encourages the participants to get in touch with these impressionistic aspects of their family design. In focusing on the symbolic experience of the family rather than the analysis of specific relational forms and patterns, Keith's chapter is a companion piece to Kramer's work in Chapter 5. Both present the family as an organism, a team, a whole that must be addressed in its entirety, even if its entirety is only representational. In adding other generations to the direct family experience, Keith illustrates how the picture of the family shifts and fills out, dramatizing what Bowen and Boszormenyi-Nagy keep telling us about patterns of differentiation and legacies.

Next to their own families (whether in imagination or in real contact), and next to the daily interactions of the adults at work, families with young children have the most contact with their children's schools. As Rotheram discusses in Chapter 16, these contacts may facilitate progress in the children or may actually impede their progress in a way that may mistakenly be attributed to psychopathology in the children. Her descriptions of family–school interactions emphasize the presence or absence of fit in many areas. The most important areas, of course, are congruity about educational objectives, and these in turn are often related to ethnicity. Minority-group children, she observes, often come from families with cultural differences from the prevailing educational model. Children from these families are often caught in a conflict between the family culture and the school culture, and must chose a path that is either disloyal to the family or leads to failure in school.

More subtle differences in family and school styles, however, can be just as difficult; Rotheram emphasizes that it is not necessarily the peculiar qualities of family, school, or child, but the encounter between the family and school systems, that spells success or conflict. Thus there are overinvolved, centripetal, and enmeshed systems, and underinvolved, centrifugal, and disengaged systems. The most frequent type of interaction is that of an underinvolved family with an underinvolved school and treatment system, with the result that many agencies become involved in treating one case; this is usually perceived as the case of a single child or several "single" children in one family. The family therapist working at the family–school interface must have a clear picture of the nature of the interacting systems, as well as of the system that is created by the interaction of the two (and any others that may be involved). A clear definition of the problem, mutually agreed upon by all the parties involved, is essential to this therapist's work. Rotheram then goes on to describe school-based and family-based emphases in treatment; she stresses that the therapist who works well with both systems is rare, even though we now have a good theoretical basis and (thanks to her review) a range of experience for intervening successfully with both systems.

The subtitle of Chapter 17, "The Family Turned against Itself," expresses the bind experienced by families when children are involved in litigation, and the one in which a therapist/evaluator/consultant is likely to be trapped if he or she is not well aware of the shapes of systems formed by interaction between the family and the legal system. Mansheim refers to several different types of situations in which children are likely to be involved: custody battles, both between divorcing spouses and between families and state child welfare agencies; personal injury cases; and sexual abuse allegations. Although the reasons for involvement with the legal system may be quite different in each type of case, the effective conflicts of interest within the family are very similar. In each instance, the "best interests of the child" often become a battleground for other family agendas, and this situation works against the best interests of children. As Mansheim points out, the major reason for this is that the legal system is an adversarial, "either–or" system, based on conflict and the need to establish a right and a wrong position. The very nature of this process is very different from the "both–and" position of most family systems therapists, and, as Mansheim observes, is most likely to interfere with the therapist's effectiveness in working at the family–legal system interface. He recommends a practical approach in which the professional knows the legal system well (in particular, the peculiarities of the system in his or her locale), and works with it rather than against it. Much can be done with families to avoid a final battle in court; however, once a case enters court, the professional has to accept the rules of the legal process and do his or her best within these confines. To react or to protest amplifies the conflictual system, which has by now become the problem.

When children are placed, their custody may be temporarily assumed by the state, but they often stay emotionally connected to their parents. Urie Bronfenbrenner is said to have stated that every child needs an adult who is irrationally committed to his or her welfare. Itzkowitz, in Chapter 18, demonstrates that when agencies act as if children's parents are such adults, the placement process can be much less disruptive and much more productive. Welfare agencies and their agents who actually care for children are often put into the position of taking children away from their families and declaring themselves better than these same families. This is a terrible position for everyone to be in—the agents, the children, and the families. It is far better, Itzkowitz insists, when the parties work together. This means that a family is not judged and then dismissed for the conditions from which a child has to be placed. The story of Moses's placement in the bulrushes sets the tone for a mother's decision to place her child. Itzkowitz offers many examples of successful combined work with the placement setting and the family. The story of Larry, whose incarcerated mother, when contacted, was able to orchestrate a network of friends and relatives who could serve as support to Larry while he continued to grow up in a group home, is a particularly compelling illustration of the resourcefulness of family systems when they are taken into account. This and the other examples provided by Itzkowitz support the nation that placement can, indeed, be a place for family therapy.

The final chapter in this section takes a meta position on the interface between the family and the larger system when tackling the issue of family violence and the response to it. Miller, in Chapter 19, reviews the various kinds of family violence that traumatize children. She observes from the beginning that the responses of systems outside the family are gravely inadequate, emphasizing sexual abuse over physical abuse, despite the fact that the latter can be life-threatening. In addition, almost no notice is taken of the effects on children of violence against others in the household or against toys or pets belonging to the children—two types of childhood terrors that are not uncommon. The larger system's response to children who suffer family violence, then, is characterized by a moral bias; this is not necessarily the best way to protect children. The larger system, when there is a response to children who are experiencing family violence, tends to be polarized between those who espouse the victim–perpetrator dichotomy and the family systems theorists, who hold everyone in the family responsible. Miller examines the family environment, particularly commenting on the power differentials within the family, between males and females, and between adults and children. She also comments on the repetitive patterns within the family, and the ways in which these patterns are isomorphically reflected in the response system of child protective services.

What are we to do about all of these polarities, contradictions, and paradoxes? Miller proposes the development of conversation between parts of systems, using circular questioning. The construction of her chapter has this same circular feeling to it, as she suggests meaning systems through asking questions of the reader that involve wider and wider responses to the issues of violence and the protective secrecy surrounding violence. Miller ends the chapter with a provisional model consisting of (what else?) circles. The outer circle involves all of those who are involved in the problem—what Anderson, Goolishian, and Winderman have called "the problem-determined system." This circle also addresses the large questions of problem definition and of who is involved in what way. The middle circle focuses more on the specific issues of the violence; the inner circle is the most intimate, the one in which secrets may be yielded up. Through this process of developing ways in which the particular individuals involved in a particular instance of a particular family's troubles can develop a way of understanding difficulties and potential resources, a new experience can be evolved with a different outcome. If this sounds complicated and circular, it is; however, as Miller has so effectively argued, it may be the only way to break into the patterns that have existed for generations and that radiate out from the family into larger systems.

The chapters in this section, taken collectively, demonstrate that there needs to be a continuity between families and the other social systems that care for children. The other systems cannot substitute for families in authority or care, but there may be a constructive collaboration between them that enhances children's protection and welfare, when family-oriented therapists work with the larger systems created by families and social systems.

15

The Family's Own System: The Symbolic Context of Health

DAVID V. KEITH, MD

Truth is relatives.—Richard Miner, 1985

A child is reared by a family, and the meaning of "family" reaches well beyond the parents to include a multigenerational group, mostly biologically linked, of living and ghostly presences, who interact in nonrandom ways (Ford, 1983). Healthy families have four- to five-generation intrapsychic families that influence their living and their self-image.

Assumptions about human experience operate as guides for clinical action. This chapter is based on the belief that virtually all psychopathology is related to the multigenerational patterns of family functioning. However, the author knows that a multigenerational explanation of psychopathology is not comprehensive: The gaps and inconsistencies are endless.

There is no clinical problem for which an extended family interview is not a crucial contribution—if not as part of the treatment, at least for consultation. The very fact of a family's availablity for an interview, the history that can be obtained during the interview, the interactions that are observed and in which the therapist participates, and the sequelae of the interview are all vital to work with children and families.

For me, this pattern of working with children and families is based on my interest and investment in psychotherapy, not on the investigation of the causes of psychopathology. Involving the family increases the power of psychotherapy. The complexity and idiosyncrasy of each family and each family interview inspire a reverence that makes it necessary to involve as many family members as possible.

David V. Keith. Family Therapy Institute, St. Paul, MN.

This is because the family I am concerned with is not strictly a sociological phenomenon. It is an admixture (an odd mixture, if you will) of people, facts, fantasies, and distortions. Time and space are dyscalibrated. Let us think of this family as a symbolic or metaphorical formation. The family, with its history, is a metaphor for itself, an endlessly infolding system of symbols.

Picasso's work provides a particularly appealing analogy. His paintings present distorted views of the familiar and initiate a self-conscious process within the viewers to reintegrate the way they see their worlds. I try to send the family members away from the interview with a distorted, Picasso-like portrait of themselves. Their reality structure is challenged by the interview experience, and they must struggle to reintegrate it.

Many parents seem to feel better to discover that what is wrong with their child has a neurological cause. This attitude, which divides body from soul, keeping everything in its proper place, explains why Picasso can be disturbing. It also reflects a limitation in our cultural patterns of thinking about people, the ambiguity inherent in human distress, and the implications of change. The fear of craziness in our culture seems to be much stronger than the fear of death. I believe that the family that comes to the clinic with a child does not need a diagnosis. Instead, its members need a free-associative conversation about what their family is like, what might be wrong with the way the family functions, and on what their fears and doubts are based. Their shame, confusion, and despair may be fostered by preoccupation with guilt and interfere with their experiencing themselves. Often it is this deeply entrenched preoccupation that highlights and encourages the child's symptoms. A diagnosis of neurological or chemical imbalance takes away the despair that activates the initiative to change. But it also takes away the initiative for deeper human contact. The diagnosis interrupts the dialogue within the family that is necessary to establish a context for sharing ambiguity and frustration, and for repair. There is something powerfully healing about discussing areas of ambiguity, in making fun of what is sacred, in giving seriousness to what has seemed silly. Multigenerational dialogue gives the chance for delineating generations in a spirit of reconciliation (Stierlin, 1981).

This viewpoint is entirely clinically derived. There is no research basis for this practice, even though administration of a multigenerational family interview may be described clearly. What happens is informal; playful and meandering; accidental and reactive. The purpose in presenting this viewpoint here is not to describe families, but rather to encourage experimenting with adding extended families as consultants in family work with children. It would be nice to think that 20 years from now a diagnostic process that does not include a three-generation interview would be viewed as an incomplete workup. Of course, it has already been almost 20 years since this idea first occurred to me!

In this chapter, I review some of the background to working with extended families. Two levels of family interaction, the "historical/symbolic" and the "administrative," are described. Some details about the administration of such an interview are offered, followed by content areas to emphasize in the interview. Finally, I endeavor to describe the nonrational effect of an extended-family interview as a "family group psychosis," which, like Picasso's paintings, activates the process of examination, evaluation, and integration so critical to families' extending their resources for the benefit of their own members.

The Background of Multigenerational Family Work

Three major figures in the family field have made distinctive contributions to a conceptual framework for thinking about the working with the extended family. It is probably no accident that all three, Whitaker, Bowen, and Boszormenyi-Nagy, began their psychiatric careers challenged by psychotherapy with schizophrenics. It would suggest that interest in the deeply nonrational interpersonal qualities of schizophrenia leads to an interest in the complex, deeply personal, nonrational qualities of the extended, multigenerational family system. There is something in common between schizophrenia and the three-(plus-)generation family. My guess is that symbolic, unconscious reality is central to both.

Boszormenyi-Nagy and Bowen are best at describing the dynamics of extended families and multigenerational family processes. Each has a system for doing so, which is formulated in such a way that it can be taught and applied to the study of such families. In Whitaker's writing, on the other hand, concepts and clinical action are often inseparable.

Some family therapy patterns (such as the structural and systemic schools) diminish the significance of history in working with a family, especially in comparison to the impact of present dynamics. The importance of history is diminished in these approaches because facts can obstruct the spontaneity that leads to change. Boszormenyi-Nagy's work shapes family history as a "family ledger," a multigenerational system of obligations, which adduces the dynamic quality of the history. This form of history gives a new destabilizing meaning to the dynamics of present relationships. It is almost as if he were saying that time means nothing to families. His book *Invisible Loyalties* (Boszormenyi-Nagy & Spark, 1973) is an an invaluable clinical guide to this nexus of loyalties, obligations, and entitlements across many generations. It has the rich feeling of an Old Testament commentary. That is, the thinking and methods that emanate from it provide a means for finding the symbolic relational (interpersonal) meaning of historical facts, a symbolic history. Hoffman (1981) says of his contribution that it is a "rich and poetic metaphor of families as a multigenerational account book" (p. 251).

Boszormenyi-Nagy is especially important to those who work with children, because the pattern elaborated within his theoretical framework give special acknowledgment to the status of children in the family system. Crucial to this pattern is the "covenant" between the family and its children. The highest ethical priority in the family is that of the future life prospects of the young and as yet unborn children in the family, in generations forward. In order to belong to a family, children will suffer physical abuse, incest, self-abnegation, and admiration. "The struggle of countless preceding generations survives in the structure of the nuclear family" (Boszormenyi-Nagy & Ulrich, 1981, p. 162). Individuation can occur only in a context of responsibility to others. The family therapist will be entrapped and obstructed if he or she assumes that the deepest relational dynamic is adversarial. Anger is not the issue so much as the need for love (Boszormenyi-Nagy & Ulrich, 1981).

Bowen, widely acknowledged for his contribution to the theory and therapy of families, began as a psychoanalytically oriented psychiatrist. He began working individually with schizophrenics, and then advanced to studying the mother–child dyad. Inevitably, he had to acknowledge how the mother–child dyad was affected by the father's relationship to the mother–child relationship. He began to work with and think of this relationship triangle (father–mother–child) as the basic clinical entity. His clear clinical vision enabled him to make the jump to the complex system of interlocking triangles that comprises the multigenerational family. He has worked to develop a theory of the family system that includes three generations (Kerr, 1981). These theories about differentiation and interlocking triangles add a solid theoretical framework for thinking about the way a child (through identity and behaviors) is integrated into the larger family system.

Bowen was among the leaders of psychiatric thinking in the 1960s who looked upon psychopathology as an adaptation. He was convinced that it is an adaptation to a multigenerational family system. One of Bowen's most important contributions was first published anonymously; in it, he described using the ideas he was developing in the clinic to contribute to his personal growth by assessing and maneuvering to escape from the undifferentiated patterns of his own family (Anonymous, 1972). Significantly, his primary method of teaching thereafter was to guide trainees in the study of their own families as a prerequisite to doing clinical work with families.

Whitaker and I have been close colleagues for more than 15 years, so his work is most familiar to me and closest to my own. As my work mingles with his and his with mine, some of it is now hard to attribute to either of us, and therefore must be ours.

Thinking about the family in its vertical and horizontal extensions is very different from the experience of *working* therapeutically with extended families. They are two different levels of experiential activity—one analytical and cognitive, the other intuitive and responsive. Whitaker's early medical training in obstetrics and gynecology seems to have given him the action-oriented clinical freedom of the surgeon. This position is most clearly described in his paper "A Family Is a Four Dimensional Relationship" (Whitaker, 1976). Whitaker uses a series of case examples to describe the value of the extended family in therapy. He cites two basic reasons for including the grandparents. The first is to get their permission for the therapist to become the object of transference, much as real parents might give their blessing to foster parents. The second is to provide an expanded perspective on the family history. In the extended-family interview, there is no need to expose the reason for the nuclear family's being in therapy, nor is it necessary to discuss any of their issues. The interview establishes the facts that the family is a network and that the whole network is involved with the problem at hand. The therapist is given the responsibility for conducting the operation. Infrequently, the grandparents' behavior suggests that they are opposed to continued therapy by the nuclear family. Implicit in the benefit of inviting grandparents in is the fact that the children will also be there, so that the process will involve the *experience* of being a multigenerational group. This practice of including the children in the development of understanding of multigenerational family patterns distinguishes Whitaker's approach from that of either Bowen or Boszormenyi-Nagy and is essential to the impressionistic quality of the interview.

The response to an interview is unpredictable. Sometimes the interview opens up a new warmth in a family, especially if the members get beyond cautious overprotectiveness and are able to make even feeble efforts to express doubts, fears, and hopes. At other times, the coldness and isolation remain unchanged. But then the nuclear family members can see that little is available from the extended family, and they will be responsible for their own destiny.

A crucial point in the inclusion of the extended family is that its members are invited to come as *consultants*. They are not there to be patients, nor are they there to be blamed or attacked. However, they do have to mind their manners. They are not invited to give their family members instructions on how to conduct their lives and relationships, nor are they there to give the therapist guidance on how to run his or her practice.

The objective of such a conference is the discovery of who the other family members are, how they live, and how they operate with each other. The family members' separate realities are acknowledged. A side benefit of this process of discovery is often the resolution of rifts in family subgroups. One almost universal experience of a three-generation approach is a sense of dignity in the family as a whole, a sense that "we are the Smith-Johnsons!"

Whitaker diminishes the significance of the therapist in these family interviews in several ways. The therapist is important for guiding the planning for the interview, but during the interview itself is advised to keep a low profile. At the same time, however, the therapist has to maintain his or her own integrity. Some of the examples that follow later in the chapter illustrate the therapist's participation.

Implicit is the integrative influence of this consultation interview. This does not mean that the family is restructured, but rather that intrapsychic ambivalence is reduced. Pathological components are placed in a context of multigenerational family living and lose their divisiveness. Frequently, the long-range benefits outweigh the immediate impact of such an interview. The implication is that the interview experience plants seeds that come to fruition later.

Taub-Bynum's profound and complex book *The Family Unconscious* (1984) gives some other dimensions to this obscure terrain, which penetrates so far into time and space that an interview with an individual cannot begin to tap it. He includes material from family therapy, biological science, higher mathematics, physics, and the wisdom of Eastern philosophy. He stimulates conceptual development and provides a way of acknowledging family experiences that goes beyond a common-sense view of the world. For example, he discusses extrasensory perception, coincidence of physical illness in family members, and common dream themes in family members.

These perspectives on multigenerational processes and the extended family— that of a family justice and accounting system; of differentiation and interlocking triangles; and of the multiple levels of experience within the family and between the family and the therapist—set the scene for the multidimensional experience to be engaged in when the therapist invites the extended family into the consulting room.

Two Levels of Family Interaction

There are two levels of interaction pertinent to this discussion. The "historical/ symbolic" level is made up of stories and story fragments by which the family defines itself. Reviewing the stories simultaneously brings unity and raises differences. The "administrative" level pertains to how the family as "we" functions *vis-à-vis* the community. It is reflected in the way the family makes decisions.

The Historical/Symbolic Level

The most obvious use of an extended-family interview is to gain a clearer picture of the family history. The history has two components: the overt review of facts, and the implicit symbolic meaning of the facts and their arrangement. We cannot get a family history from an individual. We need the whole family to tell its story as a group. An error in modern, remedicalized psychiatry is to limit the history to the illness and the patient, and to ignore the symbolic context. The context includes the other family members, their relationships, the nonverbal components of the story, and the family unconscious. Facts are collected, but there is no sense as to how they are a circular system. As we shall see, the family history is laden with meaning that cannot be dissociated from the historical fact.

A cross-cultural example shows how the larger community is used for both diagnosis and therapeutic benefit. The Navajo Indians have a ceremony (the "Sing") for dealing with illness. It represents a prototype of a pattern that I wish to describe for working with the extended family. The identified patient is placed in the center of concentric circles; these are made up of the nuclear family, the extended family, and the community. The shaman sits in the center with the patient and chants and speaks with the gods. Then the assembled group, over a 24-hour period, talks about the person and what might be troubling him or her. In one instance, an important community leader drove off the road and rolled his pickup truck over. He fractured his pelvis and three limbs. After 6 weeks in traction in a hospital, he returned to his community, and a Sing was held to determine where his mind had gone when it almost let him be killed. In a second case, a woman had experienced an extended psychotic episode. By talking about her and what they knew of her prior to her psychosis, the members of the community made an effort to restore her fragmented mind. Imagine oneself in the center of that circle. Although it may be thought of as a threatening experience, one should not overlook the caring that can be available in such a situation.

The extended-family interview is a clinical method for evoking family spirits; good, evil, toxic, new, old. The method involves an interview with the family's own system—the vertically and horizontally extended family. The extended-family interview can be used as part of the diagnostic process, or it may be used in treatment.

The Administrative Level

A second important use of the extended-family interview is to facilitate administrative decisions in relation to the extended family's context. For better or for worse, the family is in charge of itself. When patients do not comply with our treatment, it is often because we do not have permission from the right people in the family, or are violating an important family rule with our treatment prescription. Advice from professionals does not always supersede family value patterns. As I have noted earlier, we find that one reason to get the grandparents or other important members of the extended family in for an interview is that if they favor the family's decision to seek psychiatric help, we are much more likely to be successful. Likewise, if the family elders are clearly opposed, it diminishes the likelihood of our having an effect. When I am faced with a family seeking an out-of-home placement for a child, it is crucial to bring the extended family in to help with the decision and to take the administrative initiative for the process, so as to disrupt the fantasy that I am (or the community is) taking the child away from the family.

I presented a paper to a medical conference describing the use of a three-generation family consultation interview in relation to chronic and catastrophic illness. The paper urged that families be convened to talk about the context of serious illness. At the luncheon break, a missionary nurse spoke to me about her experience at a hospital in Zaire, Africa. She found it amusing that I was encouraging urban American physicians to *include* the family to enhance the diagnosis and treatment process. She explained that in Zaire, Western physicians, in their effort to improve health care standards, were trying to get rid of the family. They were frustrated by their inability to separate patients from their families. A decision about a patient's treatment would not be made unless the grandmother was in attendnce, even if it meant a delay.

It is difficult for us as clinicians to work with families, because we cannot maneuver families in the way that we can maneuver individuals. Furthermore, it is not possible to work with families without being taken over by nonrational and symbolic processes implicit in human experience. We enter the realm of the sacred (combined effect of heart and mind, the blending of feeling and fact)

(Needleman, 1982). It is particularly important that we be mindful of the inadequacies in our knowledge when we turn to work with extended families.

The following case example illustrates how a three-generation interview stimulated administrative initiative in a defeated family, whose resources seemed exhausted after a series of failed therapeutic efforts.

The Klef family was brought in for a consultation by a therapist from an inpatient chemical dependency unit. A week before, the 17-year-old son had been discharged from his fourth admission. A daughter, 13, was suicidal and had run away from home four times. Another son, 6, was regarded as hyperactive. We learned in the first 15 minutes that the drug addict lived with the maternal grandparents, who were not present. Nothing of interest happened during the first interview. The parents were like zombies, defeated by their children and the series of helpers who had been involved with them. The children whined and sneered; the parents defended and floundered. We halted the interview early, because it sounded as if the family therapy had been a failure, and, likewise, it seemed that the consultation interview was headed nowhere. However, the family members protested that they wanted to return. We agreed to see them the next day, if they brought in the maternal grandparents.

The grandparents came, but even with three generations present, the family had no life. There were virtually no stories from the mother's growing up, no humor. "Are you certain these are the right grandparents?" I wondered to myself. The grandmother and grandson were having a romance that made the mother and father look like stooges. The grandfather had little idea about what was going on anywhere. We began to paint a portrait of doom, suggesting that the drug addict's brain would gradually fade. We wondered aloud whether the whole family was already brain-dead, and what they would be like after the daughter committed suicide. We were saying, for the second time, that the situation looked hopeless and any change seemed unlikely.

An interesting thing then happened. The grandfather and the father suddenly woke up, united by their anxiety. They could not believe that there were no options. We said that there were options, such as continuing in family therapy, or making three more runs through the drug treatment system. We just did not think there would be any *change*. The grandmother began to question whether her involvement with the grandson was helping or adding to the problem. The grandfather began to show concern for his grown daughter. That is, tenuous fibers of family morale began to emerge. A new subgroup in the family—the father and grandfather—was mobilized to active duty.

The effect of the interview was to stimulate the family members' initiative to take responsibility for themselves. The stimulus was despair, which appeared with our pressuring them through distortion and exaggeration of the situation. They began to see that things were even worse than they thought. The first interview was a standoff with no change. The next interview made it clear that the family was out of touch emotionally. The grandmother's "help" was obstructing the relationship between the parents and their drug-addicted son. The grandfather was being protected from the situation and had no awareness of the seriousness. The children, by having the grandparents' support, had too much influence. The grandparents' move to supporting the parents changed the power structure of the situation in a direction favorable to family health.

Administration of the Extended-Family Interview

Thus far, I have introduced some perspectives on multigenerational dynamics and the interview process. I have suggested the purpose for doing interviews with the extended family: to give the family members an expanded symbolic sense of themselves, and to augment the administrative adequacy of the family. Next, I consider some practical components of work with extended families. This segment has two components: administration of the interview and guidance in observing the content of the interview. The first is by far the more important and probably the more difficult.

Arranging for a multigenerational interview begins when the family first calls for an appointment. Over the phone, I find out what members are actively involved in the problem and suggest that they attend. If they are too far away or there is other objection, I agree that they could come to a later interview. Thus, a seed of expectation that the extended family will attend an interview is planted before the family comes in.

As noted earlier, when the family members in therapy are asked to bring in more of the family, they are told that the extended-family members are to come in as consultants (Whitaker, 1976). They are not expected to be patients. The purpose for framing their involvement this way is to relieve the outsiders' paranoia. They know that we have been talking about them, and can be assured that there is no intention to try to "fix" or change them. The consultants come in to help the therapists help the family. Although the consultants are to be treated like visiting dignitaries, they have no authority in the interview.

The family members in therapy are responsible for inviting other members to the interview. The implication is that the interview is for the family, not for the therapy team. If any of those invited want to talk with us about the purpose of the interview, they can phone us with their questions.

Even if a therapist is used to working alone with families, *it is important to have a cotherapist for the extended-family interview*. The family's anxiety is high, and the members have the power to seduce therapists into being educational, offering advice, or conducting a detailed history of the scapegoat's problems. All of these can eclipse the most important purpose, which is to induce a heightening of the family's anxiety about the way it functions as a group, so as to allow the blossoming of the family group psychosis (to be discussed later in the chapter).

When the grandparents arrive, it is important that the therapists provide social warmth and graciousness without being oversolicitous. The therapists should beware of being seduced into operating as if the grandparents are their own parents.

In this setting, the therapists outrank the grandparents. Symbolically, therapists should locate themselves a generation above the grandparents.

These consultation interviews, when they come after a series of family interviews, always begin awkwardly. The situation is similar to guests' arriving late for dinner. The conversation has to be interrupted temporarily to include them, then restarted. I introduce the purpose for the interview by saying that I am interested in getting families together so they can figure out a way to be more helpful to themselves. I am interested in supporting the family unity, but I believe that unity is enhanced by acknowledging differences. The cotherapist and I then guide those present into talking about the family as a system, as opposed to describing specific individuals or problems. The new arrivals are asked to talk first: "What was your son like when he was a little boy?" "What was the family like when the parents were growing up?" "Does it make any kind of sense to you that your daughter's daughter is having this kind of trouble?"

I routinely say that "crazy" or "half-baked" ideas get double credit. The effort to represent reality too carefully often misses the mark. "Do you have any *crazy* ideas about why things are as they are? You know, things that come to mind when you talk to yourself while driving to work, or when you wake up in the middle of the night." These idea fragments are frequently keys to crucial areas in the family.

After some initial questions or observations, I am quick to go to the sidelines, so that the family's anxiety can surface and provide the chief stimulus for the interview. The therapists' overactivity can easily get in the way of the family's ability to free-associate.

There is often an impulse to be too careful with the family, too polite. In order to counter our cautiousness, we are inclined to use words that are ambiguous in a way that expands emotional force. For example, when a grandfather stumbles at the beginning, I may ask, "I find myself wondering if you really don't know anything, or if you are just playing dumb." Or I may ask the grandmother, "Has he always had a habit of defeating you by playing dumb?" In regard to a single-car crash, I may ask, "Was anyone suspicious of suicide?" Or if the interview is deadening, "Do you have any awareness of when the family lost its sense of humor?" Whitaker (1986), when he describes the family to the family, amplifies deviance so that the family can see patterns more clearly. For example, the father's outburst to the mother might be characterized as a rage attack that occurred when the mother turned her back on him and went to visit her mother. Thus, pieces are amplified that the family might minimize or overlook. This kind of language, used nonchalantly, suggests to the family that we are assuming them to be much worse than they think they are. It begins a distorting process that allows access to the symbolic understructure of the family. The ambiguous, somewhat "nonprofessional" language throws the family off balance and disrupts their unconscious planning about what will be talked about.

In the case of the Klef family, above, I might have suggested that grandmother stole her daughter's son to get even for the daughter's having stolen the grandmother's husband 30 years earlier. As Whitaker (1986) suggests, purposeful distortion can help the family think more creatively about themselves. They take the lead and become playful in their self-description—a step toward family health.

By accident, I have found that mistakes made in reviewing the therapy or a bit of family history get the family members to be responsible for the interview. The impression is created that it is a relief to know how dumb their doctor is.

We work on two fronts—empowering the family, but at the same time questioning its integrity. It is important to keep pressure for honesty on the family, while simultaneously inducing an atmosphere of purposelessness that allows spontaneity. The purpose of the interview is simply for the family members to talk freely together about themselves. They are free to brag, but they will benefit more from expressing pain, doubts, fears, and confusion.

The interview fails when nothing happens. I make it part of my standard operating procedure to say after 20 minutes, "I have the feeling that you are trying to be so careful with one another that this interview will end up being a waste." Or, "It feels like you are all experts at beating around the bush. In order for this interview to be a success, you have to talk about whatever it was you want most to avoid talking about."

These gentle challenges, insults, and exaggerations may make the family angry. But anger in this situation is beneficial. It ruptures the assumption that the interview is just another social get-together, and facilitates the possibility of more honesty. The process begins with respect for the complexity of families, and an appreciation for the power of the status quo. Families are reluctant to get together because someone might get upset. Often these are the families that are affected the least by therapy. The status quo is powerful and blocks change.

It is important to include children of all ages in this extended-family interview. Not only do the children benefit, but they contribute to the interview with their play and nonverbal behavior (Keith, 1986). Families have an innate drive toward health; it is most clearly expressed in relation to younger children. Usually a child's symptom is a family theme that is being amplified in the child. With the whole family present, the theme can be more fully amplified and clarified. Treatment process requires confluence of symptom, underlying conflict, and relevant history. The family setting provides the necessary ingredients (Weltner, 1982).

Content of the Extended-Family Interview

What follows is a guide of issues to keep in mind. The implication is not that any of them be addressed specifically.

Is the family a biological intact whole? Do its members acknowledge their connectedness or deny it? This quality is best evidenced in their response to the invitation for a multigenerational family interview. A family member who blocks the interview or refuses to come suggests a division in the family that is likely to perpetuate the disturbance. Desire to participate without question is evidence of resilient family health.

What is the *esprit de corps* like? If the family were a baseball team, would it be a winning team or a losing team? Who is failing to cover his or her position? Where is there dissension? My assumption is that health is rooted in the family group morale; likewise, symptoms may be the result of team dissension, and/or may represent an effort for repair gone awry.

How do the family-of-origin cultures interact? What does one set of in-laws think of the other set? Had one set picked another family for the son or daughter to unite with? How do the family differences affect the present situation?

What are the present situational dynamics? What is happening in and around the family right now? A focus on a child's problem is usually a counterbalance to some more dangerous yet covert problem in the family. Some clues as to what pressures are present come from considering where individuals are in their life cycle. Therapists should keep in mind that the fantasies anticipating change are often worse than the process of accommodating to the reality of change.

For example, consider this family. Billy, aged 10, began having episodes of wetting his pants and bed. Evidence of depression came from the sudden drop in his school performance, and the fact that he was afraid of being bothered by some bullies on the way home from school. His parents were in their early 40s. His mother was making a new beginning in a career; his father's midlife crisis was blowing full force; a chronically dissatisfying marriage had erupted again. Behind the scenes, the father's father had disseminated cancer and was dying. The father's mother was blissfully pretending that nothing was wrong, but imposing endless controlling demands on her daughter-in-law. Thus, we saw three generations of psychological vulnerability in this family. The boy's symptoms were primarily reactive to more dangerous, covert troubles in the older generations.

Therapists should pay attention to changes of any kind as the family reviews its history (e.g., the father "got religion," the dog died, the mother changed jobs). Seemingly small changes may be amplified by the psychological stress field into larger troubles. The therapists should ask, "Why did a change happen then? How did this specific change tie into the family emotional network?"

What are the historical residues in the family related to deaths, illness, divorce, ghost members, or old religious or ethnic wars? How is the past present in the present?

In one instance, a young father, aged 35, had been seriously depressed for a year. His own father had died at age 39; he was 8 when his father died. His impression was that his father had been ill for a year. At the extended-family interview, we discovered that the father had become ill at age 34. He was ill for 4 years, then failed precipitously.

In another case, A 55-year-old couple, married 30 years, were moving toward divorce. Her family of German Catholics had been angry that she chose to marry a Norwegian Catholic, and had never given its blessing to the marriage. The religious differences continued to smolder.

What are the interpersonal implications of anything the family members talk about? How does it affect the family? To a grandfather whose mother died when he was 31, I may say, "What happened to you after your mother died? Do you think your father ever got over the heartbreak?"

Therapists should look for symbiotic relationship links within and across generations. The mother may be emotionally tied to her mother or sister. Father and daughter may be closer than father and mother.

Another very important consideration in working with the extended family is to pay attention to the culturally invisible pathology in the family. "Culturally invisible pathology" refers to unacknowledged behavior patterns that are burdensome or inhibit creative spontaneity for the family as a group or for individual family members. The behavior pattern is often an invisible complement of the scapegoat's behavior. For example, the parents of a child with a possible learning disorder may distort information when the girl is present. They may talk about what to tell her and how to tell her. Listened to in one way, this appears to be appropriate behavior for conscientious parents, but from another perspective it sounds like instruction not to know, not to understand. Other examples of culturally invisible pathology include heavy smoking, obesity, inability to laugh, or endless sarcasm. There is a reverse paranoia in the steady assertion that there is nothing wrong and never has been anything wrong. A constant smile is an upside-down sad mouth, or a camouflaged smirk. Pathological hope, the unrealistic belief that all questions have an answer, is yet another example of this pathology. If family members cannot find the answer at this clinic, they will find it at the next one, even though the preceding four clinics did not have one. Pathological innocence denies complexity. It does not believe in psychotherapy. It not only believes that innocence can be maintained despite experience, but that a person can be born more than once (i.e., born again).

One of the most valuable components of the extended-family interview is the perspective we get on themes and patterns that repeat themselves from generation to generation. It is uncanny to see the repetition. We can wonder why the repetition of themes is important. Perhaps it has something to do with maintaining resonance in the family unconscious. The mechanism is not understood, but it helps integrate the family in some deep way as the patterns surface.

The curious story of an encopretic 8-year-old boy illustrates this point. Treatment elsewhere had been unsuccessful. We expected an early impasse and invited the grandparents to the second interview as a way to avoid repeating the failure of the preceding therapy efforts. In this interview, the family learned that the maternal grandmother had been encopretic until age 8. The child's encopresis disappeared over the next 3 weeks. Strange but true!

The facts are usually the least important part of the interview. The almost invisible nonverbal and metaphorical components add the most significant access to the family unconscious. Therapists should listen for and make use of the family's metaphorical language and visual imagery. It is especially useful when the tone of the language fits the pathological themes. Eating-disordered families often talk about being "fed up," describe an experience as "nauseating," or are unable to "digest" what was just said. These, of course are not metaphors, but hint at the metaphorical structure implicit in their living (Keith & Whitaker, 1981).

Finally, therapists should pay attention to their own psychosomatic responses (body sensations and hallucinations) to the interview, and should describe them without interpretation (Keith, 1987).

Any interview with the extended family has implicit therapeutic benefit. The purpose is to see, hear, and feel what is there, and to get a fuller and more complex view of the family. The interview might be thought of as a biopsychosocial CAT scan. The CAT scan does not change or remove anything; it simply shows a shadow of what is there. The diagnostic/therapy team learns more about the family, and the family learns more about itself. So much happens on so many levels that the family interview is impossible to summarize fully.

Often, after a 2-hour consultation interview with a three-generation family, someone will ask that we summarize our thoughts about the family. Our reply is as follows: "No. By our questions and comments, we have said a lot about what we think. If I try to summarize this interview, it is likely to be tossed aside as just another learning experience, and nothing will happen from it. In order to get something out of it, it is important that you let your impressions cook inside your heads and hearts. In fact, our standard advice is that you not talk about this interview for the next 24 hours." By the way, this is a straight message; there is no paradox in it.

Some of the most important components of the experience are the family's preliminary discussions and organizational efforts, and postinterview ripples. The most significant components are deeply implicit and nonverbal. Often, the actual interview is not especially significant by comparison with the aftereffects.

For example, an orthopedic surgeon's son had been a serious problem in school. In the diagnostic interview, we learned of an old, congealed conflict in the marriage, plus a standoff between the surgeon's wife and his parents. Family therapy began with the two-generation unit. The boy's symptomatic behavior diminished and the marriage was showing signs of life after five interviews. The surgeon's parents and younger sister (aged 32) came for the sixth interview. We scheduled 2 hours. His family was rigid and self-admiring; the interview was boring and disappointing. It appeared that nothing happened. When my cotherapist and I discussed the interview afterwards, we thought we might have had them in too early in our work with the family.

At the next interview, the surgeon commented on his disappointment that nothing had happened in the interview. He was annoyed with us for not being more active and pushing harder. He went on to describe postinterview events in a free-associative way. His parents had stayed for the weekend. He had an unusual, extended discussion with his father; his mother interrupted them, and he objected. This led to a dispute, and his parents withdrew to their room. He went on to say that while they were pouting, he felt a great burden had been lifted from him. Since the argument, he had been sleeping better than he had in years. His demeanor was very different: He seemed larger, more full of himself, less obsequious. He had made a personal, existential shift. He did not know it, but we could see it. There were reasons for the change; there was just no way for us to know them. He was the subject of a family group psychosis, which is the crucial, albeit implicit, process result of the extended-family interview.

The Family Group Psychosis

There is something implicitly powerful about the three-generation interview. The "something" is powerful; I think it is common; yet it is difficult to acknowledge, let alone describe. It is difficult to acknowledge because of the power and the nonrational (crazy, creative) quality. It is a "something" I *feel* more than I observe. The preceding case example of the orthopedic surgeon and his family sketches some by-products of the "something." Families experience the "something" in relation to births, deaths, illness episodes, weddings, Christmas, family reunions, first communions, bar or bat mitzvahs, and other rites of passage.

There is no good word to describe the experience. I have called this experience the "family group psychosis," or, in relation to therapy, the "family group therapeutic psychosis." I use the term both playfully and seriously. It is an analogy. In using the word "psychosis," I am doing with readers what I have suggested that readers do with families: I am using words that exaggerate the experience as a way to bring the situation into better focus. Perhaps it is better to understand it as a poetic description of the experience.

I have not found a better word for the experience. Others I have tried include "family epiphany," where the face of the family spirit is revealed, or "existential arousal." Winnicott (1951) is helpful when he describes the transitional zone of experience, "a resting place for the individual engaged in the perpetual task of keeping inner and outer reality separate, but interrelated" (p. 230). In this case, the family is struggling with the interrelated realities of past and present, group and individual, family and community.

I attempt to compare the experience with the psychotic reaction that occurs in an individual. The psychosis is a socially identified experience in which the individual is overwhelmed (panicked) by subjective experience, personally isolated, ambivalently extruded from an intimate relationship (family), and objectified by the community. The experience is inordinately painful. If not placed in context, the episode's origins are regarded as mysterious and lead to ambiguity-absorbing explanations such as "chemical imbalance."

The family group psychosis (existential psychosis) refers to being in a powerfully subjective realm outside of the intellect, where social propriety is in abeyance and unconscious (preverbal) factors dominate. The subjective experience is powerful, but it is multipersonal, in the context of group experience. It is usually culturally invisible (i.e., blended into the fabric of the community). Even though the anxiety can be quite high, the situation is within the bounds of what the community regards as normal. To go further, the individual's psychosis begins in the same way. When the group anxiety or anger becomes too high, a scapegoat may be elected, extruded, and isolated. The crucial difference is that the family psychosis belongs to a group (Keith & Whitaker, 1988).

The family enters this multipersonal psychotic state almost any time it gets together. It is not to be viewed as dysfunctional, but simply as experiential fact. Individuals behave in the logic-bound patterns of the left brain, but families are always in the realm of the right brain. As an example of this mundane psychosis, readers may notice that when they get together with their parents, siblings, and children, names and pronouns become slippery. I call my mother by my wife's name; my wife I call ''Mother''; I call my younger brother by my oldest son's name; and so on.

Families both change and remain the same through these episodes of *normative* psychosis. They are part of the dynamic equilibrium that is family health. The prototype for this psychosis is a birth in the family. Family members are pushed together emotionally and physically at the birth. The marriage advances from a psychosocial relationship to a biopsychosocial relationship. The family past is welded to the future in the birth of the next generation. Child-rearing stories are brought out by the new grandmothers and shared with the new mother. Old rules are reactivated or revised, and new rules are made. Emotional vulnerability is heightened in the family. If for some reason the anxiety is too frightening, the family may pull back. The new mother can become isolated with her anxiety, and presto! A postpartum psychosis emerges.

Involvement of the extended family in clinical work can serve many functions, but always present in the background is this induced family group psychosis. For whatever reason the family members are convened, they have to deal with the resurrected family spirit. In some cases the resurrection is numbing and painful. But, even when it is upsetting in some way, the psychosomatic elements of joy are present and usually psychologically soothing.

For example, a normal family sought therapy because it was beset by a series of reality burdens. A crisis in the local economy increased the work demand on the father; the mother was depressed by the decreased income and the change in her husband's emotional availability. The second interview included the parents, their three children, and the father's parents. The interview clarified some residual conflict centering around borrowed monies, and there was some tearful resolution of old misunderstandings. When the parents and the three children returned for the next interview, the father described the family dinner after the extended-family session. The 10-year-old son wanted a second dessert, but could not finish it because his ''stomach felt full.'' He felt ''excited.'' The 13-year-old daughter said that she was feeling ''enthusiastic, like tomorrow was going to be Christmas.'' My understanding of the report is that it described a resuscitation and reintegration of the family spirit following the interview.

The effect of the multigenerational interview is nonspecific; usually some variation of this family group psychosis appears. The concept itself is inadequate, but it is intended to give a way to think about what is happening to the family as a result of one of these interviews.

Two Clinical Examples

Following are two descriptions of families with two common childhood clinical problems. In both cases, the interview experience with the extended family served as the treatment. There was no suggestion that the family do anything, but there was change. In both cases, the change was due to group psychosis or existential shift by the family.

Four months after his mother's death from cancer, Dick, 8, was given the diagnosis of attention deficit disorder (ADD), based chiefly on his behavior at school. The ADD clinic at the university child psychiatry clinic treated him with methylphenidate. Two months later the family doctor referred the family (Dick: his brother Paul, 11, and his father) to us when the boy took a small aspirin overdose. The father acknowledged distress about his wife's death, but said they could not grieve forever; it was time to move on. He also minimized the significance of his own hernia surgery, scheduled for 3 weeks ahead. The father did not grasp the fact that Dick was worried that he (the father) might die from the surgery. The father had all the affective range of a robot.

The father's father and sister, the most geographically available members of the extended family, were invited to the next interview. The father's mother was deceased. The grandfather was domineering and harshly matter-of-fact, indicating that his father had died when he was young, and he had managed just fine; the implication was that grieving was unnecessary self-indulgence. He encouraged *positive* thinking in such situations. We challenged his rigidity, saying that it appeared where was a rule against pain or sadness in the family, and Dick was bearing the brunt. In the manner of many accomplished positive thinkers, the grandfather belittled us, saying, "Psychiatrists don't know anything." We did not capitulate, but scolded the grandfather for being a narrow-minded bully. The father came to the grandfather's aid.

At this point, the father's sister, who had been suspicious of us initially, joined in, saying to the two men with tears and anger that she could not believe that neither had shed a tear at their wives' funerals. The father defended himself: "I needed to set a good example for Dick and Paul." Tears began to flow from all but the grandfather. Dick described his worries. He was afraid that his dad would not survive the hernia surgery. Dick thought that if the aspirin overdose had killed him, he would be able to go and find his mom so that he could help her if his dad died from the surgery. The grandfather smirked and said to some imaginary being that we had plannned the whole thing. We scolded him for his insensitivity; he tried to walk out, but his son and daughter prevailed upon him to stay until the interview ended. We saw the father and the boys once more before the surgery and twice after. Dick's hyperactivity was no longer an issue, and the robot's heart began to beat.

The following example, like the one preceding, was a consultation interview organized around diagnosis, but had profound therapeutic benefit. A 6-month-old baby was hospitalized for failure to thrive. She did well in the hospital with her mother's feeding under the supervision of the nursing staff. Our interview with the mother and father about what was wrong gave no obvious clues. We invited the father's parents in when we learned that the grandmother helped care for the baby. The grandmother was very critical (in that specially veiled manner of Minnesota grandmothers) of the way the mother took care of the child; the mother appeared infantilized and intimidated by the grandmother. The mother appeared significantly inhibited in this extended-family context. She seemed physically smaller, she stammered, and she did not complete sentences. It became clear that the grandmother was interrupting the mother's involvement with her baby.

During the 2-hour interview, we accused the grandmother of being jealous of the mother's relationship to the baby. At one point, we asked the father why he was afraid to stand up to his mother's intrusions on his wife. The grandfather timidly began to express his upset that his wife gave more attention and time to the baby and their married son than to him. The grandmother's anger with her husband's absence when their children were young then came to the surface. The triangular implications of the long-standing marriage between the grandmother and her son appeared. We suggested the possibility that the new mother and the grandfather run off together.

This review of the interview condenses the dynamics and gives an impression of more outward intensity than there was. There were emotional moments, but all had a context. At the end of the interview, the grandmother shook my hand and winked. I was left wondering what that wink meant.

A distored impressionistic portrait of the family emerged that strained their self-image. The resulting changes were massive. Past and future collapsed into the present as the family struggled to straighten out the generational confusion. The distorted portrait of the family was an accurate picture of dominating but covert relationship patterns. The experience was similar to what happens when we look at one of Picasso's distorted representations. We struggle to integrate the distortions into the reality we know; we do not succeed. We may be disturbed by what we see and repress the confused image. Right-brain domination induces uneasiness. Or we may experience our world differently as a result of the distortion. The family members were upset by our distortions of their image, but they were unable to disregard them.

The follow-up report from the pediatrician was that the baby moved back to the normal growth curve, and it appeared that the marriage was breathing on its own. He had no information about what happened to the grandparents.

Conclusion

Although the involvement of the extended family is very helpful to the family, we should not overlook the benefit to the therapist. Their involvement diminishes the view that there is something wrong that must be fixed. Invisible family patterns come into focus, albeit briefly. There are deep intuitive glimpses into how illness works in families in a multigenerational perspective. The literature of modern psychiatry, alleging chemical imbalance as the basis for mental illness, feels curiously imbalanced and implies a lack of awareness of the symbolic family context.

When a family is united, an administrative power often emerges. We come to see and feel the power of families. The aesthetic effect is like seeing an expansive landscape from a high place, or like hearing a large choral work performed. This aesthetic "feeling" has the implication of an emerging wholeness.

With more generations present, an expanded reality is possible. There is less capacity for intellectual understanding as the group grows in size. Unconscious themes dominate and the experience takes over. The expanded reality is related to the slippery time sense, the awareness of death, and the acknowledgment of failures survived. The potential for somatic impact is increased. In a multigenerational family context, all illness is psychosomatic. The mythic whole person is present. There is a magical and preverbal "force" (as in *Star Wars*) in the experience of meeting with the three-generation family group. The "force" that is with them is the implicit biological unity of the family. The power is grounded in the unconscious dynamics of five generations. The grandparents talk about their experience with their own grandparents in a tone of immediate experience. The past becomes a powerful component of the present—sometimes with anger, sometimes with delight, sometimes with sadness. The experience is reparative and creativity-expanding.

Although psychopathology can be explained as an adaptation ("I am like I am so that I can fit into my crazy family"), it has another dimension. Psychopathology also arises out of an aborted growth effort—out of the effort for self-realization, or more simply the effort to be more grown up. Or, to reiteratre a point made by Boszormenyi-Nagy (Boszormenyi-Nagy & Ulrich, 1981), it arises out of a hunger for love.

There is an impulse for health in the family that can be activated in time of need. Those of us who work with families too often overlook the symbolic integrity of the family, which leads to a capacity to function with administrative effectiveness on its own behalf. The impulse for health can be disrupted by family dispute, "holy wars," and the methods of mental health professionals. Grandparents can be very supportive to families, or they may be toxic to growth or change. In any case, convening extended families gives clarity to the patterns that affect our patients.

REFERENCES

Anonymous. (1972). On the differentiation of self. In J. Framo (Ed.), *A dialogue between family researchers and family therapists*. New York: Springer.

Boszormenyi-Nagy, I., & Spark, G. (1973). *Invisible loyalties*. New York: Harper & Row.

Boszormenyi-Nagy, I., & Ulrich, D. (1981). Contextual family therapy. In A. Gurman & D. Kniskern (Eds.), *Handbook of family therapy* (pp. 159–186). New York: Brunner/Mazel.

Ford, F. (1983). Rules: The invisible family. *Family Process, 22,* 135–145.

Hoffman, L. (1981). *Foundations of family therapy*. New York: Basic Books.

Keith, D. (1986). Are children necessary in family therapy? In L. Combrinck-Graham (Ed.), *Treating young children in family therapy* (pp. 1–10). Rockville, MD: Aspen.

Keith, D. (1987). Intuition in family therapy. *Contemporary Family Therapy, 9,* 11–22.

Keith, D., & Whitaker, C. (1981). Play therapy: A paradigm for work with families. *Journal of Marital and Family Therapy, 7,* 243–254.

Keith, D., & Whitaker, C. (1988). The presence of the past: Continuity and change in the symbolic structure of families. In C. J. Falicov (Ed.), *Family transitions* (pp. 431–447). New York: Guilford Press.

Kerr, M. (1981). Family system theory and therapy. In A. Gurman & D. Kniskern (Eds.), *Handbook of family therapy* (pp. 226–264). New York: Brunner/Mazel.

Miner, R. (1985). Personal communication.

Needleman, J. (1982). *Consciousness and tradition.* New York: Crossroads.

Stierlin, H. (1981). The parents' Nazi past and the dialogue between generations. *Family Process, 20,* 379–390.

Taub-Bynum, E. (1984). *The family unconscious: An invisible bond.* Wheaton, IL: Quest.

Weltner, J. (1982). One-to-three session therapy with children and families. *Family Process, 21,* 281–289.

Whitaker, C. (1976). a family is a four dimensional relationship. In P. Guerin (Ed.), *Family therapy: Theory and practice* (pp. 182–192). New York: Gardner Press.

Whitaker, C. (1986). Family therapy consultation as invasion. In L. Wynne, S. McDaniel, & T. Weber (Eds.), *Systems consultation: A new perspective for family therapy* (pp. 80–86). New York: Guilford Press.

Winnocott, D. (1951). Transitional objects and transitional phenomena. In D. Winnicott (Ed.), *From paediatrics to psychoanalysis* (pp. 229–242). London: Hogarth Press.

16

The Family and the School

MARY JANE ROTHERAM, PhD

An angry parent calls the school, complaining that a seventh-grade teacher has given too much homework and is ruining the family's time together over the weekend, asking too much of a young girl. The teacher is righteously indignant and counters that the parents are encouraging dependence and passivity in their child. She refuses to decrease homework. The next week, the daughter makes a suicide attempt, and the family wants to sue the school.

A school psychologist spends a month tracking down the kindergartener who smears feces over the bathroom wall. The culprit is finally identified as a bright, assertive girl, not a child who is having other problems in school. The parents do not believe their child to be guilty, except for the one time she is caught in the act. She must be imitating other children at school, and it surely will not happen again. The teacher begins taking tranquilizers, as the feces smearing was one of the minor behavior problems that the teacher has been attempting unsuccessfully to control.

Parents have been working successfully with a child diagnosed as hyperactive at age 2. They have developed strong behavior modification programs at home, and the boy is doing quite well; he is active, but responds to limits and rewards from others. Suddenly, in third grade, the teacher is calling the parents nightly about unruly behavior and is referring the boy for placement in a class for emotionally disturbed children. The parents call a therapist and want help.

Mary Jane Rotheram. Division of Child Psychiatry, Columbia University, New York, NY.

A fourth-grader writes an essay describing a violent fight that ends in a sexual assault. The teacher is concerned. The child appears withdrawn from peers, and there has been a gradual drop off in her academic performance over the school year (she is now getting C's, although she was solid B student earlier in the year). The teacher calls the mother (a single parent) regarding her daughter. The mother understands the teacher's concern on the telephone, but is unable to meet with the teacher, since she must work to support her three children. The mother thinks this is a phase that will pass and, since the teacher is so understanding, her daughter will do better soon. The mother agrees to talk to her daughter. The deterioration continues.

These vignettes show the types of problems that arise daily in the interface between the family and the school system. This chapter discusses the shifting and unclear boundaries between schools and families; contextual factors that influence how teachers, families, and therapists perceive and evaluate one another; and the role of a family therapist who might try to facilitate the interaction between these two groups. Since the family therapist may be a member of the school system, may be involved initially as the family's therapist, or may be a member of a third agency (e.g., social services), the chapter focuses on issues in the relationship between the family and the school.

The boundaries between schools and families have become blurred, as the importance of the school as a socializing agent for children has increased dramatically over the last 35 years. The shifts in family composition, structure, mobility, and geographic location, as well as in the labor market, have demanded a shift in the role of other major institutions, particularly the educational system. The school is often perceived as being equal to the family in determining a child's mental health. The school can be a way to contact families and elicit their participation in intervention efforts. Alternatively, since school touches every child daily, prevention and intervention programs for children with difficulties can be instituted at the school.

In this chapter, I will review factors changing the role of schools and discuss two main areas in which the family and the school interface. First, families and school personnel often do not agree on the identification of a child's behavioral problem. There are instances in which the school perceives substantial problems and the family does not. Likewise, there are many problems concerning the family that the school may not perceive as particularly bothersome. These two systems are more likely to agree if the child is demonstrating a pervasive developmental delay; if the cultural norms of the family and the school personnel are similar; if the community is middle-class and community agencies are fairly well networked; and if a systems approach is used to define the problem. These issues are reviewed in order to identify strategies for successful school–family interfaces. The final section of this chapter presents examples of various models for intervention at the school–family intersection.

A school-based family model is becoming increasingly common as a number of intervention programs have attempted to supplement the family's caring for children. The school is seen as serving as a substitute for the family, and thus may duplicate the problems in the family structure (e.g., an overinvolved or disorganized structure) or provide an alternative experience for children. A different approach is likely to emerge when a family therapist attempts to enlist the school as part of an intervention with the family. In therapeutic settings, the boundaries between school and family become blurred when either the school joins with the family as a cotherapy team or the school replaces the family (e.g., in a residential school setting). Each of these models has been used and, to some extent, evaluated. The decision criteria for when to implement different models are far less clear. Regardless of the type of model invoked, it is critical that the school become involved in most cases involving family therapy with children.

The Shifting Role of Schools in Children's Socialization

Shifts in the Social Demographics of Schools and Families

A number of forces have increased the socialization function of the school. First, the percentage of mothers working full-time with children under the age of 1 has increased dramatically in just the last 15 years, from 24% in 1970 to 49.4% in 1986 (Bureau of Labor Statistics, 1986a). The majority of children attend day care centers by the age of 3, in contrast to 30.3% just 10 years ago and 17% 30 years ago (Bureau of Labor Statistics, 1986a). Since the major analytic theories of child development emerged in a context where mothers had primary and almost sole contact with children under the age of 5, this shift in cultural patterns raises questions of how the developmental theories may need to be adjusted. Sullivan (1953) discussed at length the important role of the school in socializing children at age 6 or 7. These discussions must now be modified to consider how an institutional setting, such as school, will affect a younger child's development. The child who now enters preschool has far more limited cognitive, behavioral, and affective capacities and resources.

Second, the economic role of children has changed dramatically within the family. Whereas children were an economic asset to the family in an agrarian society, children are now an economic liability, with middle-class children costing parents approximately $124,000 from birth to high school graduation. These economic changes have shifted the functions of family and school. Children on a farm still have instrumental functions in the economic of survival of the family, but the school is currently the primary context in which children acquire a sense of industry. The process of acquiring a sense of industry, the primary task of middle childhood, has shifted from the family to the school (Erikson, 1968).

Third, the shifting demographics of the family in terms of its shrinking size, high mobility, increasing urban location, and the dramatic decrease in two-parent families have further modified the role of schools. Siblings were a major source of socialization, since the average family size until well into the 1960s was 3 children. This is less true today, with an average family size of 2.7 persons (U.S. Department of Commerce, 1986). The percentage of "only" children is also rising (Wetzel, 1987). Therefore, children learn about peer relationships at school, rather than at home. Simultaneously, there are fewer adult resources within the family, as 53.2% of all households with children have single parents. The fact that over 60% of all children under the age of 21 will live in single-parent households for at least 3 years during their childhood dramatically affects the impact school is likely to have. It is only within the middle class that a nuclear family model has been adopted; the lower and upper classes still are more likely to have large extended families or child care to support child care functions, but this is not true for the middle class (Wetzel, 1987).

Not only is the family context shifting, but the length of time spent in school is increasing dramatically (Bureau of Labor Statistics, 1986a, 1986b). There are clear ethnic differences in these rates. Among whites, 24.5% graduated from high school in 1940, compared to 74% in 1986. In contrast, 7.3% of blacks graduated from high school in 1940, compared to 58.5% today. Only 8% of blacks graduated from college in 1940, in contrast to 21% who graduated from college in 1986. The impact of the school increases as the school, rather than the labor market, becomes the major socializing agent during adolescence and early adulthood. In addition, labor market opportunities shrink with large birth cohorts, increasing the importance of school achievement in securing jobs. For example, as the children from the post-World War II baby boom generation reach middle age, there is increased competition for jobs and resources among this group. Each of these factors points to the increasing responsibility of school as shaping the next generation.

The Importance of the School in Children's Adjustment

Psychiatry has traditionally focused its attention on the role of the family, not the school, in shaping children's adjustment. This lack of interest in the school setting was justified by research findings that the school did not significantly affect achievement and job attainment, let alone socialization and behavior (Jencks *et al.*, 1972). More recent work leaves no question about the pervasive impact of the school experience (Reynolds, 1982; Rutter, 1983; Wolkind & Rutter, 1985), particularly on social adjustment in later life (Cowen, Pederson, Babigan, Izzo, & Trost, 1973).

School is a child's first exposure to corporate America—a hierarchical, competitive organization with its own norms, roles, and rules for the exercise of power. Schools vary substantially in their ability to have a positive impact on children's adjustment (Wolkind & Rutter, 1985). The evidence for the influence of the school comes from three sources. First, schools in which students are similar in socioeconomic and ethnic background show substantial differences in student achievement scores (Brookover, Beady, Flood, Schweitzer, & Wisenbaker, 1979). Second, epidemiological studies that control for students' achievement status upon entering school also demonstrate the importance of school ethos in affecting adjustment (Rutter, Maughan, Mortimore, Ouston, & Smith, 1979). Finally, the longer students stay in one school or classroom, the greater the impact of the school on the students' achievement and social adjustment (Good, 1983; Maughan, Mortimore, Ouston, & Rutter, 1980).

The factors associated with effective schooling are similar to those identified for effective parenting. Like family therapists' orientations, facilitative school environments can be characterized by their organizational features (as in structuralism), communication patterns (as in strategic interventions), and the roles assigned to students, with a set of values and meanings (as in psychodynamically oriented systems therapies). A positive school environment is defined *a priori* as one that encourages prosocial behavior, discourages misconduct, and enhances scholastic achievement. A review of the research on optimal school environments (Purkey & Smith, 1983; Reynolds, 1982; Rutter, 1983) indicates that a good school organizational structure is one in which the staff is encouraged to work together with agreed-upon goals for the students and school community; in which school-wide values and norms for student behavior are established, and students share these norms; in which there is a pleasant working environment, where a minimum amount of time is spent in setting up for learning and handling discipline problems; in which instruction is class-based, rather than individualized; and in which there are clearly assigned time sequences of activity, opportunities for students to take responsibilities, and established channels for students to receive feedback on their performance. Positive communication modes are identified as follows: High expectations are set for students; students are rewarded for small accomplishments; each student's strengths are reinforced with a variety of available rewards; there is frequent and consistent use of praise and encouragement; and teachers model positive behaviors for students. Finally, schools develop organizational climates with clear differences in norms, which are passed generationally among staff (Newcomb, Turner, & Converse 1969; Sherif & Sherif, 1969). Positive value systems address three types of norms: Subgroups of students are not alienated (e.g., by tracking students according to achievement level); commitment to educational achievement is high, with high expectations for students; and there is consistency across staff on the norms for appropriate student behavior and on discipline policy.

In 1986, the National Institute of Child Health and Human Development issued the first call for longitudinal studies of families. There is clear evidence from longitudinal studies that children's relationships with peers at school are predictive of later psychopathology (Cowen *et al.*, 1973). A line of research on social competence discriminates three types of children in terms of their interactional styles: rejected, neglected, and popular children (Asher, 1983; Dodge, 1983; Dodge, Schlundt, Schlocken, & Delgauch, 1983). When children enter new social environments, they carry their styles with them. Rejected children are quickly rejected by a new peer group, as they demonstrate high rates of aggressive behavior. Neglected children are not noticed by the new group. However, there have been no systematic analyses of the reciprocal influence of a child's peer group and the school environment on school adjustment.

The Family's Impact on the Child's Adjustment at School

Family therapists do not need to be convinced of the importance of the family to the child's school adjustment. In addition to the built-in bias, there is substantial empirical evidence supporting this relationship. First, the different types of family problems are reflected in different types of symptoms in children. For example, children whose parents are divorcing engage in more acting out and general maladjustment in school (Wallerstein & Kelly, 1974). In contrast, children in a family with a member who has a life-threatening illness engage in more anxious and withdrawn behavior in school (Felner, Stolberg, & Cowen, 1975). Children with health problems have more serious school problems and fewer competencies than healthy children (Lotyczewski, Cowen, & Weissberg, 1986). Likewise, children experiencing stressful life events are at risk for school adjustment problems over an extended period of time. (Brown & Cowen, 1988; Cowen, Weissberg, & Guare, 1984; Felner, Ginter, Boike & Cowen, 1981; Lotyczewski et al., 1986).

Parental behaviors have been identified as critical to school achievement in a recent multisite study of California schools (Dornbusch, Fraleigh, & Ritter, 1986)— a finding that has clear implications for therapists working with families. If parents speak a foreign language at home, children do better at school. Children from two-parent households achieve better grades than any other type of family structure. The most critical interpersonal process that has been identified is the parents' reactions to grades. Parents who do not become upset at poor grades and give modest rewards for positive grades have children with the best adjustment at school. Giving students large external rewards (e.g., money or the use of a car) for grades also decreases students' motivation and results in poorer grades. Families' making decisions as a group, rather than allowing the students to manage their school business on their own, also results in better adjustment on the part of the students. In addition, families that encourage high conformity in their children produce poorer students. Overall, authoritative parenting emerges as the optimal style associated with good school adjustment—a finding replicating Baumrinds's (1971) earlier work. In summary, there is substantial empirical evidence as to the family's impact on the child's school adjustment.

The Interaction of the Family and the School

Although there is substantial evidence that schools affect children's general adjustment and that families affect children's school adjustment, the literature on the interactive impact of schools and families is far more limited and comes primarily from the family therapy field. Empirical studies that examine factors of each system simultaneously are often too complex, too much like the real world, to execute or evaluate. Therefore, the evidence on interaction of systems has emerged primarily from descriptions of such interaction.

Schwartzman and Kneifel (1985) have reviewed the literature on how child care systems often replicate dysfunctional family patterns in attempting to help families. A large body of evidence indicates that there is often "context replication" between the family and the school (Aponte, 1976a, 1976b). For example, a fourth-grade boy fights constantly with older siblings at home; has a powerful, punishing father, with little affection in the relationship; and has an ineffectual, overwhelmed, protective mother. When the child fights with his siblings at home, the mother becomes overwhelmed, cries, and begs him to stop. Several hours later the father comes home and punishes the boy severely. The mother runs to the boy's aid, comforts the boy after his fight with his father, and fights with the father herself. When this boy goes to school, the scenario is easily repeated. The boy begins fighting with older peers at school. His teacher is overwhelmed and ineffectual in dealing with this problem. A powerful, punishing principal decides to resolve this issue, but is thwarted by the school pyschologist, who becomes highly protective, supportive and territorial with the boy. The child's behavior becomes a part of a dysfunctional interpersonal system within the school, much as it does in the family system. By recreating the dynamics of the family's organizational structure, the school insures that the boy's inappropriate behavior will persist.

Although there have been many different systems for classifying families, two major types of dysfunctional families emerge in the literature: the overinvolved and the underinvolved family (Schwartzman & Kneifel, 1985). The overinvolved family is one in which there is a sharp separation between the family and other systems in the environment (such as the school), a blurring of lines of authority and role relationships, and a fear of internal fighting or disagreements (Hoffman, 1981; Minuchin, 1974; Schwartzman & Kneifel, 1985). Every clinician has experienced such families, who have been described as "sticky glue" (Hoffman, 1981), "undifferentiated" (Bowen, 1960), or "consensus-sensitive groups" (Reiss, 1971a, 1971b).

School settings can also be typified as overinvolved systems. It should be easy to create such a system, following a few simple rules. A principal should deny the hierarchical structure of his or her organization, use a consensus decision-making style in staff meetings, assert the need for a close and family-like atmosphere among a group of highly diverse personalities, and verbally outline the high level of faculty autonomy, while simultaneously keeping close supervision over teaching content and style, and engendering a deep mistrust of central administration within the district or representatives of other social service agencies. Very soon there will be an overinvolved, rigid faculty within a school. The school staff will start fighting with the uncaring families of the students it serves; teachers will feel stifled and uncreative in their teaching, because one style predominates in the school. There will be no fights at staff meetings, and the staff will be afraid to gossip. Students are likely to be unappreciative of the sacrifices of the staff in this system; there will be high rates of alienation between students and staff, with constant punishment of the students by the teachers, who are eternally sweet and caring in their intentions. Once a student's reputation has been established by one teacher, this reputation will follow the student for his or her entire academic career. Perceptions, evaluations, and roles will be highly rigid in such an environment.

In contrast, families and schools may be underinvolved, centrifugal, disengaged, and disorganized in structure (Reiss, 1971a). Again, each clinician can clearly remember a family that could never keep appointments; various subunits of the family might attend a therapeutic appointment, but never the entire group; children were not required by parents to attend school; there were few exchanges of caring or loving acts among family members; there was significant dysfunction in many family members, but the unit could not get mobilized to get upset about this together; members felt hopeless in exerting control within the system.

Likewise, there are schools that mirror this disorganization. There are few personal ties among faculty members at the school and no loyalty to the school; there is little tracking of students in such a school; a child may have a positive experience one year and a very destructive classroom environment the next; programs that work well are not replicated, nor are programs that work poorly discontinued; there will be great diversity in the educational philosophies being implemented in different classrooms. One year, a student may have an open classroom with study in cooperative work groups and the next, a highly authoritarian environment with study in individual workbooks. Parents encountering such a system will feel overwhelmed. The school secretary will inform a teacher that a parent called; however, the teacher will claim that he or she never received the first six messages. A teacher will refer a child to a psychologist in September and the child may be evaluated in the spring. This is not a highly productive or warm system.

When families and schools of either of these types interact, few positive benefits result. The most frequent type of interaction is that of an underinvolved family with an underinvolved school. In such an instance, there are likely to be many social service agencies involved in treating the case; it is not an uncommon scenario to have over 100 agencies attempting to deal with one child. The problematic behaviors will continue as the child is rotated through agencies who continue to deal ineffectively with the presenting problem, largely due to their own inefficiency within an underinvolved treatment system.

When an underinvolved system encounters an overinvolved system, rejection is likely to occur very soon. A tightly knit group with high internal consensus is likely to reject any suggestions that change should occur within the system, and to blame the other party. Whether overinvolved or underinvolved, families and schools displaying such patterns need systemic intervention to resolve their difficulties.

The family therapist's goal is to help overinvolved families and schools to disengage and underinvolved systems to become better networked and integrated. The manner in which this is accomplished depends on the orientation of the family therapist. A behaviorally oriented family therapist models the behaviors he or she hopes to elicit from each system; that is, the therapist clearly outlines goals, defines ways in which he or she can act as a resource, sets limits on the therapeutic relationship, and congratulates school staff and family members who adopt new roles. More structurally oriented family therapists address the same goals in a very different manner.

The Context of School and Family Problems

Ethnic Differences

Ethnic differences in community norms often lead to ineffective interventions with children and adolescents. One's ethnicity will shape the development (Kitano, 1982), identification (Harwood, 1981), and conceptualizations of problems (Gallimore, Boggs, & Jordan, 1974). This is true both for schools and families, as well as for mental health practitioners. For example, Washington (1982) found that both black and white teachers had more negative perceptions of black children than of white children. Teachers' expectations of poorer performance from minority-group children often are reflected in children's poor attitudes and achievement (Gallimore et. al., 1974). However, teachers are often unwilling to acknowledge that racism exists (Milner, 1983), or they may even state specifically that racism should be ignored (Schofield, 1981). Teachers are often uninformed about variations in ethnic patterns and how these variations may influence relationships with children at school. For example, on a recent trip to an elementary school, I overheard a teacher complaining about the "sullen and devious" behavior of Mexican-American children who would not look her in the eye when scolded. Mexican-American children are taught to show respect by looking down when addressed by an authority

Reciprocally, families often misperceive teachers' and therapists' goals and intentions because of differences in cultural patterns. Kitano (1982) has shown how a differential emphasis on shame within Japanese-American families leads these families to ignore or attempt to hide children's difficulties, rather than to seek help from either mental health or school officials. The rates of families seeking services indicate that Puerto Rican families are underrepresented in services received, while other groups (e.g., black Americans) are overrepresented (Harwood, 1981). Back-to-school nights are often perceived as a threat by minority families, because they feel they are likely to be chastised or insulted, rather than given an opportunity to have input about their children's education. Teachers are then quick to interpet the families' nonattendance at these functions as lack of interest. The way such evenings are structured is perhaps a more important determinant of nonattendance.

Finally, there is substantial evidence that minority-group families are evaluated, triaged, and treated differently from those in the majority group by mental health professionals. Minority children are underrepresented in counseling programs, are diagnosed differently from white American children, have higher dropout rates from treatment, and tend to receive inferior-quality services (Atkinson, Morten, & Sue, 1983; Sue, 1977). Snowden and Todman (1982) have shown that a minority child is likely to be negatively stereotyped by both the clinician and the instrument when a traditional psychometric assessment is conducted.

To shift to the individual level for the developing child, ethnicity affects not only such obvious characteristics as language, style of dress, and celebration of holidays, but the fundamental ways in which children and families structure meaning, set interaction routines or styles, assign causality, and communicate feelings. Important differences in attitudes, values, and behaviors distinguish ethnic groups. The salience of ethnicity and the developmental acquisition of ethnic patterns by a child vary dramatically, depending on the specific ethnic group to which the child belongs (Aboud, 1977; Buriel, 1975), the ethnic balance of the school and the neighborhood (Brewer & Miller, 1984), the individual child's history (Rotheram & Phinney, 1987a), and the historical and sociocultural milieu in which the child is raised (Diaz-Guerrero, 1987).

A family's ethnicity will significantly affect the adjustment between the family and the school. Schools in the United States have traditionally been white middle-class institutions that propagate the values and attitudes of the dominant group. As such, they have not served the needs of children coming from different ethnic backgrounds. Minority-group children historically have lower achievement scores in school (Scarr, Caparulo, Ferdman, Tower, & Caplan, 1983), are over-represented in classes for children with learning disabilities (Spencer, 1985), and drop out of school more frequently (Borus, 1984; Savage, 1985). In the social arena, there is ethnic cleavage in friendships, which increases with age (Schofield, 1982; Singleton & Asher, 1977), and negative attributions regarding the intentions and behaviors of cross-ethnic peers are reinforced in schools (Kochman, 1981; Sagar & Schofield, 1980).

There is little indication that desegregation has been successful at changing either the academic or the socioemotional climate for minority-group children. Improved relations result only under highly atypical conditions: (1) when there is equal status for each ethnic group within the school; (2) when opportunities to disconfirm stereotypes of the other groups are available; (3) when there is mutual interdependence in achieving goals; and (4) when there are social norms that favor group equality (Brewer & Miller, 1984). These conditions are rarely met in desegregrated schools; however, when ideal conditions are established, it is easy for these conditions to disappear over time (Schofield, 1982).

The minority child, then, is confronted with a cultural system often quite unlike that of his or her family when attending school. Children raised in a pluralistic society may be bicultural or even multicultural in the norms, attitudes, and behavior patterns they acquire. There has been strong disagreement as to whether biculturalism has a positive or negative impact on development. Historically, it was presumed that acculturative stress had a negative impact on minority children, since each child must make a choice between his or her own culture and that of the dominant groups (Stonequist, 1935). This conflict or replacement model saw minority children as being required to replace their own set of ethnic patterns with those of another group. Being a "marginal" person was thought to be associated with anxiety, stress, insecurity, increased emotionality, and defensiveness (Child, 1943; Goodman, 1964; Lewin, 1948; Paz, 1961; Stevenson & Stewart, 1958).

However, since 1974, the benefits of biculturalism have been emphasized (Ramirez, 1983; Ramirez & Castenada, 1974; Ramirez & Price-Williams, 1974). A flexibility–synthesis model has been proposed, in which children raised in two cultures are seen as demonstrating greater role flexibility, flexibility in cognitive style, adaptability, and creativity. The norms of both cultural groups are assimilated and available to be used by a child, depending on the demands of the situational context. Current theories emphasize the benefits, rather than the liabilities, of socialization to more than one group (McFee, 1968; Ramirez & Castenada, 1974). Children with bicultural competence are thought to have higher self-esteem, greater understanding, and higher achievement than others (Ramirez, 1983).

However, there are few data in support of either theoretical position (Rotheram & Phinney, 1987b). The models are based primarily on retrospective histories, studies involving black and white dolls (which have been criticized for a number of reasons), and descriptive accounts of the socialization of minority children. Only recently have these issues begun to be empirically assessed.

The evidence suggests that there is no one clear effect of being raised in two cultures. Rosenthal (1987) indicates that the impact of biculturalism depends on a variety of factors, including the attitudes of the majority culture, the strengths and institutional integration of minority groups, and individual factors within the child. We (Rotheram & Phinney, 1987b) argue that there will be a differential impact, depending on the area being assessed. For example, being bicultural is likely to have a positive impact on a child's school adjustment. The child will have acquired the behavior patterns and orientation to authority figures that are likely to lead to success in school. If the child's parents are likewise bicultural in orientation, such flexibility will have a positive impact. The expectations, values, attitudes, and behavior patterns of the school and the family are similar. However, a bicultural child in a traditional family will develop problems. School adjustment will be fine, but the family will be a source of conflict.

On the other side of the coin, a child who has not acquired bicultural patterns is likely to have a positive adjustment within his or her traditional family setting. However, one might expect such a traditional child to develop problems at school as he or she encounters an institution with white middle-class values and behavior patterns. Minority children are easily caught between cultures. The disparity between school and family in the perception of a child's mental health problems is frequently based on the difference in cultural contexts between the groups.

The family therapist asked to consult in such a system is faced with this ethical dilemma: Is the therapist's goal to acculturate this traditional family? A child who is not bicultural may be at a disadvantage in competing in today's society, and will be denied substantial economic and social benefits. From this perspective, it is the therapist's responsibility to facilitate the family's acculturation, and thereby to facilitate the child's adjustment.

However, at what cost does this acculturation occur? In particular, there appear to be generational patterns of adjustment (Buriel, 1987), which highlight the long-term impact of adopting bicultural norms. Although acculturation, as reflected in ethnic labels, increases across first- and second-generation immigrants, a reverse trend occurs with the third generation (Buriel, Calzada, & Vasquez, 1982; Buriel & Vasquez, 1982; Lamare, 1982). For example, first-, second-, and third-generation immigrants use very different labels to describe themselves. In the case of those immigrating from Mexico, "Mexican" is more likely to be used by the first and third generations, while second-generation immigrants will be more likely to identify themselves as "American" or "Mexican-American." This process has been labeled the "deculturation" of immigrants (Berry, 1980).

The choices regarding ethnic identity are evident not only in ethnic labels, but in language preferences. Heller (1987) demonstrates that the language children choose to speak in Canada (French or English) is a critical aspect of ethnic identity. Differences in bicultural language patterns influence not only the child's school adjustment relative to his or her family adjustment, but the child's adjustment in the classroom relative to his or her adjustment with peers. Heller (1987) describes Eric, a bright, energetic third-grader who adjusts quite quickly within the English-speaking classroom environment, but is alienated from peers because he refuses to speak English on the playground. Speaking English at play is a symbol of surrendering his identity as a Francophone—too high a price for popularity. Would a school psychologist intervene with such a child?

When a family therapist attempts to acculturate a family, it is not clear what the cost of this will be within the extended-family network—a network that may well extend across thousands of miles. For example, in conducting a recent psychiatric epidemiological study of the entire island of Puerto Rico (Bird, 1985), it was found that 80% of the adult population had migrated to the United States for a period longer than 6 months at some point during their adult lives. They had now returned to Puerto Rico and were again living a traditional life style. What would the implications of acculturation be for this group? These questions remain unanswered, but therapists making choices regarding therapeutic goals must consider the broad ramifications of choosing to help families adjust to the norms of the dominant culture. School personnel and therapists who are quick to blame families for their "lack of cooperation" need to examine the assumptions and perspectives from which they are making this evaluation, in order to determine to what degree their evaluation is ethnocentric.

Other Contextual Factors

The size of a school and its geographic location also influence the adjustment of children to school (Wicker, 1968; Willems, 1967). There are advantages to both large and small schools. Students at small schools have more opportunities for leadership, can participate responsibly in more varied settings, and feel more involved in relationships with peers and family. In contrast, students at large schools receive more varied instruction and a larger number of out-of-class activities (Kelly, 1979).

Perhaps more important than characteristics of the child and/or the school is the degree of fit between the styles of each (Edwards, 1979). The degree of students' satisfaction and academic performance depends on the goodness of fit (Pervin, 1968). For example, Edwards (1979) has demonstrated that adjustment of students with poor person–environment fits will be worse in good schools than in poor schools. The contrast is greater between such a student's own adjustment and that of his or her peers in a positive school environment, making the student feel more atypical than in a less positive school environment.

These data suggest that transferring children and adolescents to new school environments may be a very effective psychotherapeutic intervention. Although a dysfunctional interaction may be recreated in a new environment, it is not *necessarily* recreated. School environments that enhance self-esteem, reward competence, and encourage positive relationships are likely to enhance the adjustment of students.

Definition of a Problem

Now that the importance of addressing both systems in any case involving a child has been demonstrated, the chapter addresses how such a case might proceed.

Who Says There Is a Problem?

Children do not define problems. Children signal that a school or family is dysfunctional by displaying symptomatic behavior. If a child does not become symptomatic, but has the resources to disclose problems and request action by a teacher or parent, it is the adult, not the child, who will act on the problem. Thus, although children are quite powerful change agents within a system, their power is usually indirect. Adults define problems and strategies for interventions until adolescence.

Second, a family therapist can play one of three roles. The therapist can be embedded within either the family system or the school system. For example, the family therapist can be a school counselor (Carlson, 1986; Connolly, 1986). If the family has initially contacted a therapist, a therapist approaching the school will be identified with the family by the school, regardless of the therapist's intent. A family therapist may also be outside both systems and become the coordinator of the interactions of the two systems.

If neither the school nor the family perceives a problem, both are likely to feel satisfied with a job of child rearing done well. The family therapist may not agree, however. Passive and shy children are likely to be neglected by family, teachers, and peers (Gottman, 1983), even though these children are demonstrating behavior patterns that have been associated with serious adjustment problems later in life. However, such patterns will often go unattended in young children.

There is likely to be mutual agreement on the existence of problems that involve pervasive developmental delays. In such a case, there is a strong motivation for both the family and the school to effectively coordinate services for a child who will need long-term supportive services. Likewise, symptoms that are clear-cut, limited in scope, and not necessarily reflective of deviance by adult caretakers are also usually mutually identified problems. Stereotypic behaviors and enuresis are likely to be undisputed by schools and families.

The gray areas will involve patterns of attention deficit disorder, conduct disorder, and anxiety symptoms. These cases necessitate judgment calls as to the appropriateness of intervention. At what point is an active 5-year-old boy labeled hyperactive? When a teacher perceives half of his or her kindergarten class as hyperactive, it is likely that the teacher has unrealistic expectations for kindergarteners. When a child hits others 35 to 40 times an hour and the parent feels that there is no problem, it is probable that the parent's expectations are inappropriate.

A family therapist is distinguished from intrapsychically oriented social agents by his or her attention to the reaction to information, the delineation of boundaries, the method of delivering and responding to feedback, and the maintenance of homeostasis within systems (Barnes, 1985). I advocate that the therapist must include attention to the school as an important system. Boissevain (1968) describes schools and families as members of each other's "effective zone," members of ongoing affective and instrumental relationships. Each system's response to information regarding a child's behavior (e.g., hitting others at school) reflects the operation of the system's organizational and communication structure. Do parents respond to the information as if they are about to be scolded by school personnel? How much information do they gather from the child? Do they instantly respond by disciplining the child even before visiting the school? Do they perceive this as an opportunity to get to know school personnel better? Likewise, does the teacher respond by calling parents the first time a child hits another, or does the teacher wait until he or she has already signed the referral papers to the committee on the handicapped? Does the teacher approach the parents in an accusing manner? Has the behavior of the hit child been considered in the evaluation of the incident? Answers to each of these questions provide valuable information to a therapist trying to intervene in any case involving a child, particularly at the stage of attempting to choose the point of entry in a case.

What Is the Problem?

The family therapist will define the problem on the basis of his or her theoretical orientation. A structuralist, a strategic therapist, a behavioral therapist, and a psychoanalytically oriented systems therapist will each focus on a different aspect of the child's network to facilitate resolution of the problem. Although the particular approach taken will not be important—the behavior of good therapists will look more similar and be more important than will their theoretical orientations (Parloff, Waskow, & Wolfe, 1978)—a systems orientation will be vital to successful interventions.

The participants' first agenda at meetings between the school and the family is typically to assign blame. School faculties spend much time in the conference rooms reassuring themselves regarding the uninterested, deviant parents who inflict small, undisciplined monsters on them. Parents, for their part, despair at the incompetent, uncaring teachers who are only interested in usurping parental authority through what they teach in the schools. A therapist must circumvent this blame-assigning tendency on the part of each party, in order to draw boundaries of an intervention system that includes school and family members.

A systems orientation facilitates this process, since no one party is targeted as causal and the process among interactants is the focus of the meeting. In such a context, the meeting will emphasize how change is to be executed rather than how inadequacies have developed.

Models of Intervention

School-Based, Child-Centered Interventions

School personnel often feel hopeless in controlling parents' behavior, find the prospect of networking with parents too costly, and receive state mandates to provide socioemotional services to students. A number of schools have initiated successful primary prevention and intervention programs for children. The programs that have been in existence longest and have most clearly demonstrated a positive impact on children's adjustment are those modeled after the Rochester Program of identifying and screening preschool and first-grade children at risk for psychopathology (Cowen, 1984, 1985; Cowen et al., 1975; Lorion, Cowen, & Caldwell, 1975). When supportive services are provided to children identified as being at risk, fewer children develop problems at school. This strategy has not been used with the general population of children in school, but has been used successfully to short-circuit the development of adjustment problems in children whose parents are experiencing divorce (e.g., Felner, Ginter, et al., 1981; Pedro-Carroll, 1985), significant life stress (Felner, Norton, Cowen, & Farber, 1981), or health problems (Lotyczewski et al., 1986).

The success of these programs gives pause to a family therapist, who is probably concerned that these programs do not address the family. How can these programs make any long-standing change when they do not address parenting behaviors or the function of the child's behavior within the family system? Surely, these family influences should lead to return of the maladaptive symptoms! Yet the gains are maintained across several years.

At least one of these programs has included the family in the design of the program. Snow and Grady (1987) have designed school-based alcohol and drug prevention programs for sixth-graders, which include parent training as a central aspect of the intervention. This program has had a very positive impact.

There have been some claims that the functions of the family can be replaced by bureaucracy (Litwak & Meyer, 1966, p. 35), and some believe that by training children in social skills, schools are passing the boundary into families' territory. Such claims will become even more controversial as schools attempt to implement the Surgeon General's recommendation for AIDS education and prevention in schools. If school personnel act without including families in such interventions, the schools will surely fail. At a community level, parent groups will be demanding the recall of school officials. At the level of the individual child, the child is likely to become triangulated in a conflict between the school and the family. Each system will perceive the other as having evil intentions and will act on the basis of mistrust rather than mutual help. The consequences outlined by Schwartzman and Kneifel (1985) will occur.

Parent-Centered Interventions

A variety of interventions have been successfully employed to help parents be better parents. Some of these programs have focused on helping parents listen better (e.g., Parent Effectiveness Training [PET]; Gordon & Sands, 1976), be more effective in shaping children's behavior (Dinkmeyer & McKay, 1976; Patterson, 1974), or deal more effectively with their own problems (Levy, 1976). Others have tried to reduce the stress of parenting through self-help support networks (Mitchell & Bergman, 1980; Lieberman, 1983; Pilisuk & Parks, 1980). Like the school-based, child-centered programs, each of these programs has been found to be effective, even though the entire family is not involved (Graziano, 1979; O'Dell, 1979; Tavormina, 1975, 1979; Tavormina, Hampson, & Luscomb, 1976).

These programs are most frequently offered through school districts to assist parents, and are typically delivered in a group setting. Two packaged programs have been widely distributed (Henry, 1981). STEP, a program theoretically based on an Adlerian model, teaches families over nine sessions to establish a more cooperative family structure, to listen reflectively, and to solve problems (Dreikurs & Soltz, 1972). The second program, PET (Gordon & Sands, 1976), trains parents to listen with greater empathy, to negotiate effectively with their children, and to make clearer requests and refusals. This program involves lectures, reading, role playing, and homework exercises. Although parents and schools have responded enthusiastically to these programs, there has been little systematic evaluation of them (Rinn & Markle, 1977). These programs suggest the diversity of intervention strategies that can be implemented by schools or therapists to facilitate children's adjustment.

Family Therapists Mobilizing the School in Treatment

Family therapists do not confine themselves to private practice and community mental health settings, but take their practice to the systems they are attempting to change. Connolly (1986) and Carlson (1986) have each presented excellent and well-documented case examples of school counselors' serving as facilitators of change in the family systems. In each case, an intervention by a school counselor was effective only when the rewards for a child's problem behavior were examined in the context of the family. In one case, a school-phobic child was getting so much attention form an overindulgent mother that the child would have been foolish to attend school. Although such cases are mundane for most family therapists, negotiating and establishing a relationship between a family and school personnel that will permit a systemic analysis of a child's behavior is not so common. Boundaries are typically drawn that do not include the two systems simultaneously. But systemic interventions do occur and are successful.

Far easier is the task of a family therapist who needs the cooperation of school personnel for a family with a troubled youngster. When a family therapist gets the assignment, the initial stigma is removed from school personnel. To the uninformed school counselor who is not a family therapist, the family has already admitted stigma and responsibility by the fact of having a therapist. The school is seen as guilt-free, so the attitude becomes "Let the consultation begin."

Why is it that skilled clinicians are reluctant to include both systems? School psychologists narrow their focus to the child's dysfunction and attempt to improve the child's skills. Family therapists increase the family's ability to respond to problems effectively by changing information flow, boundaries, feedback and the family homeostasis. When schools are involved in therapeutic plans, however, the intervention is heightened, and impact is optimal. This is particularly true with young children for whom behavioral programs are employed (e.g., to reduce the incidence of hitting).

Summary

Families affect children's school adjustment, and the school affects the families' adjustment. These two systems often mirror each other. Dysfunctional communication patterns or organizational structures will reverberate between the two systems, compounding a child's problems and leading the child to a chronic dysfunctional state. However, misunderstandings and disagreements regarding children's problems frequently arise between families and schools because of their different cultural or ethnic backgrounds.

The likelihood of conflict between these symptoms is small in two situations: when the child's symptoms are clear-cut and limited in scope (e.g., enuresis) or when there is a pervasive developmental delay. Symptoms such as anxiety, behavior problems, and attention deficits in a child provide ample opportunities for conflict between schools and families. The family therapist is particularly well equipped to deal with these issues through a focus on the interacting systems. Although child-based school programs and parent training programs have been demonstrated as effective interventions for children, the family therapist who utilizes both systems in addressing children's problems is most likely to succeed.

REFERENCES

Aboud, F. E. (1977). Interest in ethnic information: A cross-cultural development study. *Canadian Journal of Behavioural Science, 9*(2), 134–146.
Aponte, H. J. (1976a). The family–school interview. *Family Process, 15,* 303–311.
Aponte, H. J. (1976b). Under-organization in the poor family. In Guerin (Ed.), *Family therapy: Theory and practice* (pp. 432–448). New York: Gardner Press.
Asher, S. (1983). Social competence and peer status: Recent advances and future directions. *Child Development, 54,* 1427–1434.
Atkinson, D., Morten, G., & Sue, S. (1983). *Counseling American minorities: A cross-cultural approach.* Dubuque, IA: W. C. Brown.
Barnes, G. (1985). Systems theory and family theory. In M. Rutter & L. Hersov (Eds.), *Child and adolescent psychiatry* (pp. 216–229). Oxford: Blackwell.
Baumrind, D. (1971). Current patterns of parental authority. *Developmental Psychology Monographs, 4*(1, Pt. 2).
Berry, J. W. (1980). Acculturation as varieties of adaption. In A. M. Padilla (Ed.), *Acculturation: Theory, models, and some new findings.* Boulder, CO: Westview.
Bird, H. (1985). *A complete epidemiological sample of psychiatric disorder among Puerto Rican children.* Paper presented at the meeting of the American Academy of Child Psychiatry, San Antonio, TX.
Boissevain, J. (1968). The place of non-groups in the social sciences. *Man, 3,* 542–556.
Borus, M. (1984). *Youth and the labor market.* Kalamazoo, MI: W. E. Upjohn Institute for Employment Research.
Bowen, M. (1960). A family concept of schizophrenia. In D. D. Jackson (Ed.), *The etiology of schizophrenia* (pp. 240–370). New York: Basic Books.
Brewer, M., & Miller, N. (1984). Beyond the contact hypothesis: Theoretical perspectives on desegregation. In N. Miller & M. Brewer (Eds.), *Groups in contact: The psychology of desegregation* (pp. 281–303). New York: Academic Press.
Brookover, W., Beady, C., Flood, P., Schweitzer, J., & Wisenbaker, J. (1979). *School social systems and student achievement: School can make a difference.* New York: Praeger.
Brown, L. P., & Cowen, E. L. (1988). *Perceptions, experiences and sociodemographic differences in stressful life-events among children.* Manuscript submitted for publication.
Bureau of Labor Statistics. (1986a). *Labor and economic review.* Washington, DC: U.S. Department of Labor.
Bureau of Labor Statistics. (1986b). *Monthly labor review* (pp. 44–45). Washington, DC: U.S. Department of Labor.
Buriel, R. (1975). Cognitive styles among three generations of Mexican-American culture and sociocultural adjustments. In J. J. Martinez, Jr., & R. H. Mendoza (Eds.), *Chicano psychology* (2nd ed., pp. 417–429). New York: Academic Press.
Buriel, R. (1987). Ethnic labeling and identity among Mexican-Americans. In J. Phinney & M. J. Rotheram (Eds.), *Children's ethnic socialization: Pluralism and development* (pp. 134–152). Beverly Hills, CA: Sage.
Buriel, R., Calzada, S., & Vasquez, R. (1982). The relationship of traditional Mexican American culture to adjustment and delinquency among three generations of Mexican-American adolescents. *Hispanic Journal of Behavioral Science, 4,* 41–55.
Buriel, R., & Vasquez, R. (1982). Stereotypes of Mexican descent persons: Attitudes of three gener-

ations of Mexican American and Anglo-American adolescents. *Journal of Cross-Cultural Psychology, 13*, 59–70.

Carlson, C. (1986). *Eco-structural family therapy for school psychologists.* Paper presented at the meeting of the American Psychological Association, Washington DC.

Child, I. L. (1943). *Italian or American? The second generation in conflict.* New Haven, CT: Yale University Press.

Connolly, J. (1986). *Family assessment and intervention in school psychology.* Paper presented at the meeting of the American Psychological Association, Washington, DC.

Cowen, E. L. (1984). A general structural model for primary prevention program development in mental health. *Personnel and Guidance Journal, 62*, 485–490.

Cowen, E. L. (1985). Person centered approaches to primary prevention in mental health: Situation-focused and competence-enhancement. *American Journal of Community Psychology, 13*(1), 31–48.

Cowen, E. L., Pederson. A. A., Babigan, H., Izzo, L. D., & Trost, M. A. (1973). Long term follow up of early detected vulnerable children. *Journal of Consulting and Clinical Psychology, 41*, 438–446.

Cowen, E. L., Trost, M. A., Lorion, R. P., Dorr, D., Izzo, L. D. & Isaacson, R. V. (1975). *New ways in school mental health: Early detection and prevention of school maladaptation.* New York: Human Sciences Press.

Cowen, E. L., Weissberg, R. P., & Guare, J. (1984). Differentiating attributes of children referred to a school mental health program. *Journal of Abnormal Child Psychology, 12*, 397–409.

Diaz-Guerrero, R. (1987). Historical sociocultural premises and ethnic socialization. In J. Phinney & M. J. Rotheram (Eds.), *Children's ethnic socialization: Pluralism and development* (pp. 239–250). Beverly Hills, CA: Sage.

Dinkmeyer, D., & McKay, G. (1976). *Systematic training for effective parenting.* Circle Pines, MN: American Guidance Service.

Dodge, K. A. (1983). Behavioral antecedents of peer social status. *Child Development, 54*, 1386–1399.

Dodge, K. A., Schlundt, D. C., Schocken, I., & Delgauch, J. D. (1983). Social competence and children's sociometric status: The role of peer group entry strategies. *Merrill-Palmer Quarterly, 29*, 309–336.

Dornbusch, S., Fraleigh, M. J., & Rutter, P. (1986). *A report to the National Advisory Board of the Study of Stanford and the Schools on the main findings of our collaborative study of families and schools.* Unpublished manuscript, Stanford University, Stanford, CA.

Dreikers, R., & Soltz, V. (1972). *Happy children: A challenge to parents.* London: Collins.

Dube, B. D., Mitchell, C. A., & Bergman, L. A. (1980). Uses of the self-run group in a child guidance setting. *International Journal of Group Psychotherapy, 30*, 461–479.

Edwards, D. (1979). Coping preference, adaptive roles, and varied high school environments: A search for person-environment transactions. In J. Kelley (Ed.), *Adolescent boys in high school* (pp. 81–97). Hillsdale, NJ: Erlbaum.

Erikson, E. H. (1968). *Identity: Youth and crisis.* New York: Norton.

Felner, R. D., Stolberg, A. L., & Cowen, E. L. (1975). Crisis events and school mental health referral patterns of young children. *Journal of Consulting and Clinical Psychology, 43*, 305–310.

Felner, R. D., Ginter, M. A., Boike, M. F., & Cowen, E. L. (1981). Parental death or divorce in childhood; Problems, interventions and outcomes in a school-based project. *Journal of Prevention, 1*, 240–246.

Felner, R. D., Norton, P. L., Cowen, E. L., & Farber, S. S. (1981). A prevention program for children experiencing life crisis. *Professional Psychology, 12*, 446–452.

Gallimore, R., Boggs, J., & Jordan, C. (1974). *Culture, behavior and education.* Beverly Hills, CA: Sage.

Good, T. (1983). Research on classroom teaching. In L. S. Shulman & G. Sykes (Eds.), *Handbook of teaching and policy.* New York: Longman.

Goodman, M. E. (1964). *Race awareness in young children* (rev. ed.). New York: Collier.

Gordon, T., & Sands, J. (1976). PET in action: Inside PET families. In *New problems, insights and solutions in Parent Effectiveness Training*. New York: Wyden.

Gottman, J. (1983). How children become friends. *Monographs of the Society for Research in Child Development, 48*(3, Serial No. 201).

Graziano, A. M. (1979). Parents as behavior therapists. In M. Hersen, R. M. Eisler, & P. M. Miller (Eds.), *Progress in behavior modification* (Vol. 4, pp. 251–298). New York: Academic Press.

Harwood, A. (1981). *Ethnicity and medical care*. Cambridge, MA: Harvard University Press.

Heller, M. (1987). The role of language in the formation of ethnic identity. In J. Phinney & M. J. Rotheram (Eds.), *Children's ethnic socialization: Pluralism and development* (pp. 180–200). Beverly Hills, CA: Sage.

Henry, S. A. (1981). Current dimensions of parent training. *School Psychology Review, 10*, 4–14.

Hoffman, L. (1981). *Foundations of family therapy*. New York: Basic Books.

Jencks, C., Smith, M., Acland, H., Bane, M. K., Cohen, D., Gintis, H., Heyns, B., & Michelson, S. (1972). *Inequality: A reassessment of the effect of family and schooling in America*. New York: Basic Books.

Kelly, J. (1979). The high school: students and social contexts—An ecological perspective. In J. Kelly (Ed.), *Adolescent boys in high school* (pp. 3–14). Hillsdale, NJ: Erlbaum.

Kitano, H. (1982). Mental health in the Japanese-American community. In E. Jones & S. Korchin (Eds.), *Minority mental health* (pp. 149–164). New York: Praeger.

Kochman, T. (1981). *Black and white styles in conflict*. Chicago: University of Chicago Press.

Lamare, J. W. (1982). The political integration of Mexican-American children: A generational analysis. *International Migration Review, 16*, 159–188.

Lewin, K. (1948). Self-hatred in Jews. In K. Lewin (Ed.), *Resolving social conflicts*. New York: Harper & Row.

Levy, L. H. (1976). Self-help groups: Types and psychological process. *Journal of Applied Behavioral Science, 12*, 310–322.

Lieberman, M. A. (1983). Comparative analyses of change mechanisms in groups. In H. H. Blumberg, A. P. Hara, V. Kent & M. Davis (Eds.), *Small groups and social interactions* (Vol. 2, pp. 239–252). New York: John Wiley.

Litwak, E., & Meyer, H. J. (1966). A balance theory of coordination between bureaucratic organizations and community primary groups. *Administrative Science Quarterly, 2*, 31–58.

Lorion, R. P., Cowen, E. L., & Caldwell, R. A. (1975). Normative and parametric analyses of school maladjustment. *American Journal of Community Psychology, 3*, 291–301.

Lotyczewski, B. S., Cowen, E. L., & Weissberg, R. P. (1986). Relationships between health problems and school adjustment of young children. *Journal of Special Education, 20*, 241–250.

Maughan, B. M., Mortimore, P., Ouston, J., & Rutter, M. (1980). Fifteen thousand hours: A reply to Health and Clifford. *Oxford Review of Education, 6*, 289–303.

McFee, M. (1968). The 150% man, a product of Blackfeet acculturation. *American Anthropologist, 70*, 1096–1103.

Milner, D. (1983). *Children and race* (2nd ed.). Harmondsworth, England: Penguin.

Minuchin, S. (1974). *Families and family therapy*. Cambridge, MA: Harvard University Press.

Newcomb, T. M., Turner, R. H., & Converse, P. E. (1969). *Social psychology: The study of human interaction*. New York: Holt, Rinehart & Winston.

O'Dell, S. (1979). Training parents in behavior modification: A review. *Psychology Bulletin, 81*, 418–433.

Parloff, M., Waskow, I., & Wolfe, B. (1978). Research on therapist variables in relation to process and outcome. In S. L. Garfield & A. Bergin (Eds.), *Handbook of psychotherapy and behavior change* (2nd ed., pp. 233–282). New York: John Wiley.

Patterson, G. R. (1974). Retraining of aggressive boys by their parents: A review of recent literature and follow-up evaluation. *Canadian Psychiatry Association Journal, 19*, 471–481.

Paz, O. (1961). *The labyrinth of solitude*. New York: Grove Press.

Pedro-Carroll, J. L. (1985). *The Children of Divorce Intervention Program: Procedures manual*. Rochester, NY: University of Rochester, Center for Community Study.

Pervin, L. (1968). Performance and satisfaction as a function of individual-environment fit. *Psychological Bulletin, 69,* 56–68.

Pilisuk, M., & Parks, S. H. (1980). Structural dimensions of social support groups. *Journal of Psychology, 106,* 157–177.

Purkey, S. C., & Smith, M. S. (1983). Effective schools—a review. *Elementary School Journal, 83,* 427–452.

Ramirez, M., III. (1983). *Psychology of the Americas: Mestizo perspectives on personality and mental health.* New York: Academic Press.

Ramirez, M., III, & Castaneda, A. (1974). *Cultural democracy, bicognitive development, and education.* New York: Academic Press.

Ramirez, M., III, & Price-Williams, D. (1974). Cultural styles of children of three ethnic groups in the United States. *Journal of Cross-Cultural Psychology, 5,* 212–219.

Reiss, D. (1971a). Varieties of consensual experience: I. A theory for relating family interaction to individual thinking. *Family Process, 10*(1), 1–27.

Reiss, D. (1971b). Varieties of consensual experience: II. Dimensions of a family's experience of its environment. *Family Process, 10*(1), 28–35.

Reynolds D. (1982). The search for effective schools. *School Organization, 2,* 215–237.

Rinn, R., & Markle, A. (1977). Parent effectiveness training: A review. *Psychological Review, 41,* 95–109.

Rosenthal, D. A. (1987). Ethnic identity development in adolescence. In J. Phinney & M. J. Rotheram (Eds.), *Children's ethnic socialization: Pluralism and development* (pp. 156–179). Beverly Hills, CA: Sage.

Rotheram, M. J., & Phinney, J. (1987a). Definitions and perspectives in the study of children's ethnic socialization. In J. Phinney & M. J. Rotheram (Eds.), *Children's ethnic socialization: Pluralism and development* (pp. 10–20). Beverly Hills, CA: Sage.

Rotheram, M. J., & Phinney, J. (1987b). Ethnic behavior patterns as an aspect of identity. In J. Phinney & M. J. Rotheram (Eds.), *Childrens's ethnic socialization: Pluralism and development* (pp. 201–218). Beverly Hills, CA: Sage.

Rutter, M. (1983). School effects on pupils' progress: Research findings and policy implications. *Child Development, 54,* 1–29.

Rutter, M., Maughan, B., Mortimore, P., Ouston, J., & Smith, A. (1979). *Fifteen thousand hours: Secondary schools and their effects on children.* London: Open Books.

Sagar, H. A., & Schofield, J. (1980). Racial and behavioral cues in black and white children's perceptions of ambiguously aggressive acts. *Journal of Personality and Social Psychology, 39,* 590–598.

Savage, D. (1985). Door still revolves in inner city: High school dropouts. *Los Angeles Times,* Part 1, p. 1.

Scarr, S., Caparulo, B., Ferdman, B., Tower, R., & Caplan, J. (1983). Developmental status and school achievement of minority and non-minority children from birth to 18 years in a British Midlands town. *British Journal of Developmental Psychiatry,1,* 31–48.

Schofield, J. W. (1981). Complementary and conflicting identities: Images and interactions in an interracial school. In S. R. Asher & J. M. Gottman (Eds.), *The development of children's friendships* (pp. 53–90). New York: Cambridge University Press.

Schofield, J. W. (1982). *Black and white schools: Trust, tension or tolerance?* New York: Praeger.

Schwartzman, H. B., & Kneifel, A. W. (1985). Familiar institutions: How the child care system replicates family patterns. In J. Schwartzman (Ed.), *Families and other systems* (pp. 87–107). New York: Guilford Press.

Sherif, M., & Sherif, C. (1969). *Social psychology.* New York: Harper & Row.

Singleton, L. C., & Asher, S. R. (1977). Peer preferences and interaction among third-grade children in an integrated school district. *Journal of Educational Psychology, 69,* 330–336.

Snow, D., & Grady, K. (1987). *A social-cognitive approach to the prevention of adolescent substance abuse.* Presentation at the Northeastern Association of Community Psychology, Hartford, CT.

Snowden, L., & Todman, P. (1982). Psychological assessment of blacks: New and needed developments. In E. Jones & S. Korchin (eds.), *Minority mental health* (pp. 193–226). New York: Praeger.

Spencer, M. B. (1985). Cultural cognition and social cognition as identity factors in black children's personal-social growth. In M. B. Spencer, G. K. Brookins, & W. R. Allen (Eds.), *Beginnings: Social and affective development of black children* (pp. 215–231). Hillsdale, NJ: Erlbaum.

Stevenson, H. W., & Stewart, E. C. (1958). A developmental study of racial awareness in young children. *Child Development, 29,* 399–409.

Stonequist, E. V. (1935). The problem of a marginal man. *American Journal of Sociology, 41,* 1–12.

Sue, S. (1977). Community mental health services in minority groups. *American Psychologist, 32,* 616–624.

Sullivan, H. S. (1953). *Conceptions of modern psychiatry.* New York: Norton.

Tavormina, J. B. (1979). Basic models of parent counseling: a critical review. *Archives of General Psychiatry, 38,* 527–533.

Tavormina, J. B. (1975). Relative effectiveness of behavioral and reflective group counseling with parents of mentally retarded children. *Journal of Consulting and Clinical Psychology, 43,* 22–31.

Tavormina, J. B., Hampson, R. B., & Luscomb, R. L. (1976). Participant evaluations of the effectiveness of their parent counseling groups. *Mental Retardation, 14,* 8–9.

U.S. Department of Commerce, Bureau of the Census. (1986). *Statistical Abstract of the United States—1986* (106th ed., p. 36). Washington, DC: U.S. Government Printing Office.

Washington, V. (1982). Racial differences in teacher perception of first and fourth grade pupils on selected characteristics. *Journal of Negro Education, 51,* 60–72.

Wallerstein, J. S., & Kelly, J. B. (1974). The effects of parental divorce: The adolescent experience. In E. J. Anthony & C. Koupernik (Eds.), *The child in his family: Children at psychiatric risk.* New York: Wiley.

Wetzel, J. (1987). *Youth and America's future.* New York: The W. T. Grant Commission on Work and Family Relationships.

Wicker, A. W. (1968). Undermanning performances and students' subjective experiences in behavior settings of large and small high schools. *Journal of Personality and Social Psychology, 10*(3), 255–261.

Willems, E. P. (1967). Sense of obligation to high school activities as related to school size and marginality of student. *Child Development, 38*(4), 1247–1260.

Wolkind, S., & Rutter, M. (1985). Sociocultural factors. In M. Rutter & L. Hersov (Ed.), *Child and adolescent psychiatry* (pp. 82–100). Oxford: Blackwell.

17

The Family in the Legal System:
The Family Turned against Itself

PAUL A. MANSHEIM, MD

The Relationship between Mental Health and the Law

In the relationships between law and mental health before the 1960s, the relationship was one generally of mental health concepts' entering the law. Since the 1960s, however, the tendency has been increasingly for legal concepts to enter the world of mental health. For example, in the 1930s and 1940s, "mentally disordered sex offenders" statutes were passed by many states. These statutes provided for the indeterminate sentencing of a number of types of sex offenders, including pedophiles and exhibitionists. It was felt that sex offenders were individuals who, although they had committed crimes, had mental illness. Therefore, it made sense for the individuals to be kept in the "therapeutic environment" until they were able to be released and would no longer be dangerous (Brooks, 1974). By 1969, however, there was already much skepticism about whether indeterminate sentencing was realistic, given the available psychiatric technology. In the case of an appeal of a man "treated" for exhibitionism for 15 years and asking the court for his release, Chief Judge David Bazelon of the D.C. Circuit Court wrote,

> Predicting future behavior and evaluating its consequences is a uniquely difficult if not impossible task. It must be forthrightly confronted, not avoided by sugar-coating reality. There is no way on this record that we can escape the reality that

Paul A. Mansheim. Center Psychiatrists, Portsmouth, VA.

a "penal" incarceration would set appellant free in ninety days while the dissent's "non-penal' solution would likely confine him for years, if not for the rest of his life. *(Cross v. Harris,* 1969)

In the 1960s and 1970s, the legal system increasingly limited the prerogatives of mental health practitioners. One of the best examples in the family realm is what happened to the psychiatric hospitalization of minors, It had always been the law that parents could admit their children to psychiatric hospitals without the children's consent. In 1975, a three-judge district court declared unconstitutional the Pennsylvania Mental Health Procedures Act of 1966 *(Bartley v. Kremens,* 1975). As a result, a new Mental Health Procedures Act of 1976 was passed. This allowed minors 14 years of age or older to admit themselves to psychiatric hospitals. In fact, their parents would not even need to be informed for 24 hours (Mental Health Procedures Act of 1976).

From a family therapy point of view, the family is conceptualized as a functional organism that, in order to work harmoniously, must allow differences in functioning among the members of the various generations. In general, parents are the executives, and children are the directed. Children have generally been conceptualized as dependent upon their parents. The idea that children are able to actually make decisions about their lives is a new one. The Pennsylvania Mental Health Procedures Act is one example; youngsters' being able to consent to the use of oral contraceptives without their parents' consent is probably a more familiar example. The idea that children are not just dependent and not just directed and guided by their parents, but also to some extent have some independent "power," is a concept that largely comes from law and not from family therapy.

Certainly, family therapy has always made respect for children an important part of its mandate. The early efforts on behalf of physically and emotionally abused children, for example, have had the wholehearted support of family therapists. Family therapists have been in the forefront of the attempt to secure treatment for physically abused children and for families that are physically abusive. The idea that there should be respect for the individuals in the family is a hallowed concept in family therapy. However, the idea that children are independently functioning individuals with independent rights is a new idea. Family therapists will need to learn how to function in this climate, as individuals in other aspects of mental health have had to learn how to deal with the fact that the law is defining mental health parameters rather than vice versa.

Family therapy on the one hand and law on the other are both reasonably seen as methods of resolving dispute. In family therapy, the resolution is a process facilitated by the therapist. The goal is to meet the needs of all family members to the extent that family stability will allow. Family stability and family functioning are both the goals and the major limiting factors of the process.

The law's view of the resolution of conflict is very different. There are complicated rules that have to do with what evidence can be placed before the court. There is a finder of fact—namely, a judge or jury—that (or who) will make the decision. In some instances, there are rules of discovery, so that both sides have equal access to the data. The idea is that if both attorneys are given equal access to all of the data, the truth will ultimately be revealed by the adversarial process. It is possible in law to have a solution that does not meet the needs of some members of the family. One example is the awarding of a child's custody to one parent. It is possible to have legal solutions that do not end the sense of conflict, but they may be solutions nonetheless. An example is a pregnant teenager's right to seek an abortion over the objections of her parents.

The vision of a family working in functional harmony is that of any mental health professional who believes that the family is a child's most important natural resource. It is assumed that parents will work together to provide the optimum environment for the child. It is assumed that the child has an interest in having a sound relationship with both parents and with siblings and grandparents as well. This vision of harmony is in stark contrast to the adversarial dissonance promoted in families involved in legal actions (Levy, 1978). The following example is not atypical of courtroom interactions:

MOTHER'S ATTORNEY: Can you tell me what happened last Saturday night?
MOTHER: He . . .
MOTHER'S ATTORNEY: Do you mean the children's father?
MOTHER: Yes. He was bringing the children back from his weekend visitation, late as usual. The children were supposed to have been brought back to their home at 9:00, and it was already 9:45 when he pulled into the driveway.
(Father is seen gesticulating wildly, whispering hurriedly to his attorney)
MOTHER'S ATTORNEY: And what were you led to understand as to the reason for his being late?
FATHER'S ATTORNEY: Objection, Your Honor. My client is here and can answer that question directly.
MOTHER'S ATTORNEY: Withdraw the question, Your Honor. Now then, can you tell the court about how Brent behaved with you over the next 2 or 3 days?
MOTHER: Brent would do nothing that I told him to do. He jumped up and down on the sofa, and when I told him not to do this, he informed me that it was perfectly all right because his daddy had told him that he could do it. Brent said that Daddy had told him that he did not have to do anything that I said.
FATHER'S ATTORNEY: Objection, Your Honor. Hearsay!
JUDGE: Overruled.

Anyone listening to this sequence would be excused if he or she did not understand how this sort of interaction is supposed to be geared toward the resolution of conflict. Instead, it is easy to imagine that the issues could be much more easily solved in a therapist's office. Once the family has gotten as far as a court experience, however, the context of the family's interaction is changed, so that it is frequently impossible to use more ordinary forms of conflict resolution.

Jacobs (1986), in his proposal that the legal paradigm and the systems paradigms are in conflict, has characterized the dilemma that the family therapist will experience when confronted with such a court situation. The adversarial nature of the legal system implies that there will be a definitive and exclusionary answer to the questions brought before the court. Such questions are posed in largely either–or terms. The children will reside with either the mother or the father; joint custody is either good, or it is not; the mother is either the better caretaker, or she is not. The systems paradigm, on the other hand, is more consistent with the practice of mediation—a practice that focuses on the process of working things out, rather than on the establishment of truths that can then be weighed.

Furthermore, once a court action has been initiated, several new players are introduced into the system. These players have rigid roles, and all of them have a considerable amount of power (Burt, 1983). The judge, of course, has the power to make a decision. The attorneys have the power to cause individuals to be brought to court, under penalty of law, to testify as to what they know regarding the matter. By the time the hearing is actually conducted, both sides have committed so much energy and money to the undertaking that to withdraw from the case would cause a severe loss of face.

When a family-systems-oriented expert is called upon to enter the case at this stage, the legal system generally expects him or her to help one side or the other to "win" the case. Such a professional must recognize two issues fundamental to working with families in the legal system: (1) The questions being addressed are polarized and placed in the format of establishing fact; and (2) there are many other people involved in the system whose interests are not necessarily in how the family functions, or even in the "best interests of the child." Instead, they are invested in the legal action itself. The family system has swelled in number and is transformed by the many others now involved in pitting family member against family member as the legal process ensues.

The most vulnerable person in the situation, the child, is often represented not at all or by a guardian *ad litem* who views his or her role in the narrowest possible way. The guardian *ad litem* is an attorney, usually appointed by the court, whose job it is to be an attorney for the child and protect the child's legal rights. One can only sympathize with a guardian who must listen to two completely incompatible sides of the story and then try to come to some conclusion about what might be an appropriate way to protect the child's interests. More often than not, it is clear to the guardian that if the child's interests were really of paramount concern, the custody dispute would not have reached the courtroom.

Sometimes a department of social services finds it necessary to remove a child from a home because of serious child abuse or neglect. Under such circumstances, it is common for the department to request consultations about the child or the family from a family therapist. Here again, however, by the time this sort of consultation is requested, the therapist's usual function for the family has been co-opted by this new system. Although the therapist may want to consider such issues as whether it would be more emotionally harmful for the child to be removed than it would be helpful to protect him or her through removal, or whether the child could be protected while remaining in the family, the social services department may have already developed a very strong case to suggest that the child is so endangered that removal is necessary. At a hearing, the therapist may not be asked any questions as to whether it would be detrimental in any way for the child to be removed from the home. He or she may be asked only to present evidence of abuse or neglect: Did it happen or not? On other occasions, a therapist may be asked to do an evaluation of parents who have a history of engaging in dangerous or violent behavior toward their child, in order to assess whether or not they might be likely to engage in the same sort of behavior in the future. The therapist may understand full well that the family's balance is a delicate one and that the overall stability of the family is tenuous. However, he or she may not be asked questions about the interactions among family members and the way in which family members might manage to support one another. The therapist may be asked only those questions whose answer serves a clear, but polemicized, point of view.

The polarization involved in questions of removal of a child from a home may be very irritating to a therapist. That is, the city attorney may be arguing that the parents are extremely dangerous and that the child is highly likely to be dead in several days if he or she is not removed from the home. The parents' attorney, on the other hand, may be accusing the city attorney of 'trumping up'' an elaborate case based on little or not good evidence. The attorneys' questions to the therapist may not allow for a great deal of elaboration on the subtleties of the issues involved.

Although it is tempting for the expert to be caught up in the competitive spirit of the adversarial process, it is particularly important to maintain objectivity. The drama-like setting of the courtroom dispute lends itself to a false notion of resolution. The side that "wins" feels victory, and the side that "loses" feels that it has lost. Often it is only the family therapist who maintains enough perspective to realize that many of these disputes will continue long after the courtroom drama has concluded. A mother may lose custody of her child, but she has not lost the fact of motherhood. This may be forgotten in the heat of the moment.

The Therapist and the Legal System

When the family is involved in the legal system, the therapist, too, operates in a legal context. It is extremely important for the therapist to understand as clearly as possible all of the legal ramifications of the situation. The therapist should know the applicable law, at least to the extent that the law defines the scope of his or her role and functions. For example in a case of child sexual abuse in which the child has been removed from the home, it will frequently be necessary for the therapist to obtain formal permission from prosecuting and defense attorneys before the child and the alleged perpetrator can be seen together in the consulting room. The therapist who takes the time to understand such limitations will avoid a considerable measure of embarrassment.

Knowledge of the mental health laws in a given state is relatively simple to obtain. Most community mental health centers, mental health associations, and social service departments are willing to provide interested therapists with information as to where copies of the relevant state statutes can be found. Therapists may find it very useful to discuss the implementation of child abuse and neglect statutes with social workers from the social services department. Emergency workers and state hospital liaison personnel from the local community services board or base service unit are usually willing to discuss the operation of the state commitment act. The clerk of the local juvenile court is another good source of information with respect to the statutes, but also in particular with respect to the specific procedures employed in a given jurisdiction.

When it comes to understanding the legal ramifications of a particular case, any of the attorneys involved is a good source of information. Therapists should never see themselves as participants in the litigation. Therefore, there is no need for therapists to feel anxious or worried about speaking with any of the attorneys. Therapists should also never feel ashamed to ask questions that they regard as very basic. For example, it is not always immediately apparent to a therapist who is the plaintiff and who is the defendant. The therapist may need to ask about who has the burden of proof and what it is that needs to be proved. There are various standards by which evidence is judged. Civil cases are usually judged by a standard of "a preponderance of the evidence," which simply means that there is more evidence on one side than there is on another. Criminal cases are judged by a standard of "beyond a reasonable doubt," which translates roughly to a probability of 90% or greater.

In a situation in which the therapist has been explicitly contacted by an attorney for help in a given case, it is appropriate to ask the attorney to spell out clearly, preferably in writing, the exact nature of the legal question at hand and the precise help that is required of the therapist. In some cases, asking the attorney to cite the specific legal passages involved may also be appropriate. For example, in the case of the situation in which a therapist is being asked by a city attorney to come to court with evidence that may result in the termination of the rights of a parent accused of child abuse, it is important for the therapist to know what specific kinds of evidence are relevant and decisive in determining such questions.

Many therapists have a good deal of difficulty in accepting the realities of attorneys' roles in family problems. Therapists are inclined to think of themselves as facilitators of agreement. Attorneys can sometimes act in this role as well, if they feel that it is in the best interests of their clients. However, it is an attorney's role to function as an advocate for his or her client and to do whatever can be done to further the interests of the client. If the client's interests are in conflict with those of other individuals, the client's interests must be paramount. Understanding this will help a therapist to realize that the attorney's sometimes contentious tactics are in the service of his or her professional role.

It is best for a therapist to ascertain as soon as possible the presence of a legal question. Very often, a parent presents a child to the therapist as an identified patient with a request that the child be evaluated and that recommendations be given about treatment. Only after evaluation has been completed and treatment is under way does the therapist discover that there is an impending custody dispute. To avoid such surprises, in all situations in which a family is headed by a single parent, it is helpful to inquire as to the history of separation and divorce. One can ask directly whether changes in custody have been considered or whether such changes might be a possibility in the future.

Therapists' Rights Concerning Involvement in the Legal Process

It is probably impossible to guarantee that a therapist will never have to be involved in a legal case during a career of working with children. In the case in which family therapy has been an ongoing modality of treatment and in which divorce and custody litigation subsequently ensue, it is common to receive an inquiry from an attorney as to whether one has ever seen the parents interacting with the child in question, whether one has an opinion about the nature of the relationship during the time of the family therapy, or even whether one has an opinion as to the relative competence of either parent to provide supervision for a child. Sometimes, in spite of the therapist's protestation that the purpose of the therapy had nothing to do with these questions, the attorney may insist that the therapist is privy to useful information, and a subpoena may result.

Should the therapist be served with a subpoena to appear at a legal proceeding in which he or she does not want to participate, the choices are limited. He or she may file a motion to quash the subpoena, which is usually a costly and ineffective process. The result of such a motion is more often than not a private hearing with the judge, during which the therapist can present his or her reasons for not divulging information or testifying at the hearing. If records are involved, the judge may examine the records with no one else present, and then he or she will make a ruling as to whether the records are relevant. A second approach to responding to such an order is to ascertain the information that will be required and to appear at the hearing. Sometimes the therapist discovers that attorneys want to know information that the therapist simply does not have. If, for example, the attorneys ask whether one or the other parent appeared to be more competent, it is possible to disclaim information about the question, based on the reality that no specific evaluation was done that could answer that question. It is perfectly legitimate to respond "I don't know" to any question to which one does not know the answer. It is also reasonable, appropriate, and expected for the therapist to bill for the time lost in a court appearance. Should the therapist then be asked how much he or she is paid for the testimony, the correct response is that he or she is being compensated for the time (Belli, 1983). Sometimes, when there is little practical reason for the therapist's presence except to strike fear into the heart of the adversary, the attorney will release the therapist from the subpoena, or will at least try to inconvenience the therapist as little as possible when it becomes clear that the client will need to compensate the therapist.

Many therapists have the impression that they are protected by some sort of privilege shield. However, this shield exists only in those jurisdictions in which it is explicitly provided for by statute (Gumper & Sprinkle, 1981; Gutheil & Appelbaum, 1982). Privileged communication is communication that does not have to be revealed, even in court. Classic examples are a client's communication with his or her attorney and the communication between spouses. Privileged communication between patient and therapist is now generally construed to consist only of the "inner thoughts" of any patient or client in therapy. The fact of therapy's having taken place, the dates on which therapy took place, and the length of sessions are held not to be confidential information. The fact of third-party payment has contributed to this development to some extent, since individuals who are using insurance coverage to help with the cost of therapy must reveal a good deal of information to the insurance company.

Privilege is the right of the patient or client, and confidentiality is the responsibility of the therapist not to disclose information that is gained in the process of therapy. Patients and clients may waive their right of privilege; as a general rule, whenever one initiates some sort of legal proceeding in which one's own mental state is at issue, there is no privilege. This could readily be applied to the information gleaned from predivorce family therapy.

One way of categorizing the various ways in which a family may become involved in the legal system is to distinguish between voluntary and involuntary family involvement. Disputed custody, custody relitigation, personal injury suits regarding children, and one family member's accusing another of child abuse are examples of voluntary involvement. Examples of involuntary involvement include responding to a social services department's allegations of child abuse or child neglect.

Disputed Custody

The most comfortable way in which to become involved in family matters that relate to the court is as a "friend of the court," or *amicus curiae* as it is technically known (American Psychiatric Association, 1982; Westman & Lord, 1980). An example is the scenario in which family members are involved in a custody dispute and in which a comprehensive evaluation with recommendations is performed.

Where the therapist has the option of evaluating all parties, the evaluation process can become quite lengthy and expensive. It is critical to conduct one or more interviews with all of the adult parties in a custody dispute. Visits to each of the homes add to the weight of the evaluation. Interviews with all of the children involved helps the therapist to come to a conclusion about the alternative prospective nuclear family. Formal psychological evaluations are usually restricted to the parents and the children involved directly in the custody dispute. In addition to clinical interviews and psychological testing, videotaped interactions with family members can be done in the therapist's office or in the home. With so many evaluative interviews and tests to be performed, this kind of evaluation is generally done by a team of several clinicians.

Probably the most fruitful single area in which one can become involved in preventive child and family mental health is the process of mediation in divorce and child custody settlement. Whereas in former times it was felt that the decision to divorce was the result of failed family therapy, it is increasingly recognized that it is precisely at this point that some of the most useful interventions can be made for the long term (Pearson & Thoennes, 1986).

In the mid-1970s, the influential authors of *Beyond the Best Interests of the Child* (Goldstein, Freud, & Solnit, 1973) advocated a social policy in which one single parent would have incontrovertible control over the life of the child. A very short time afterward, however, new research into the impact of families on divorce (Wallerstein & Kelly, 1980) impressively demonstrated the virtue of a continuing relationship with both parents. In the wake of this, more and more states have considered a statutory preference in favor of joint custody. Although some see these new developments as naive, in view of the amount of bitterness and vituperation that is usually present during divorce (Derdeyn & Scott, 1984; Truiford, 1986), it would be foolhardy not to seize on the powerful hope for fruitful involvement in divorce and its aftermath that is offered by these new ways of conceptualizing a child's post-divorce needs (Ilfeld, Ilfeld, & Alexander, 1982; Irving, Benjamin, & Trocame, 1984).

Some localities have begun divorce mediation projects within the context of the juvenile court. In some of these, there is a requirement that parents enter mediation and fail in the process of mediation before they will be "allowed" to pursue a full-blown custody dispute through the court. Indeed, anecdotes are told of judges who occasionally lock parents in rooms and refuse to allow them to emerge until they have made an agreement between them about child custody. The principal task of the mediator is to find the common ground among all the parties, to appeal to the parents' desires for their children to do as well as possible, and to appeal to likely long-term gains at the expense of immediate short-term advantages (Campbell & Johnston, 1986).

Families' legal involvement takes place with varying degrees of angry affect and firmly set positions (Derdeyn, 1983). The amount of leverage that a family therapist has in helping to define an ultimate outcome differs from situation to situation. It will usually be the families' attorneys who are able to define the limits of the therapist's role. It is appropriate to ask attorneys directly whether the therapist may attempt to catalyze or facilitate an agreement concerning custody. Sometimes attorneys are concerned that questions of custody may ultimately affect questions of monetary disposition in a divorce. If this is the case, the attorneys may not be very interested in the therapist's becoming involved in this way, and ultimately there may be a clash between the therapist and the attorney or attorneys. It has been my experience that when these sorts of clashes occur, therapists are made quite uncomfortable. Sometimes, however, the attorneys themselves feel as though the custody dispute can be separated from other issues surrounding the divorce, and they recognize that there is no particular benefit to anyone in the family to continuing a custody dispute. In these cases, a full evaluation for custody may catalyze a resolution.

Custody Relitigation

With regard to custody relitigation, many therapists feel as though the most significant impact that they can have is when they are able to dissuade parents from reopening litigation. It would seem reasonable to take a position that custody relitigation is to be avoided except in circumstances in which there has been some obviously detrimental change in a custodial parent's life situation, or when a child has some discrete difficulty that will manifestly be relieved by changing custody from one parent to another. Sometimes it is possible to persuade parents by outlining for them the situation in which they find themselves and the way it would be perceived by an impartial, objective judge.

There are many tangential reasons for relitigating custody. The noncustodial parent may feel as though his or her affections have been alienated from the child as a result of the paucity of visitation. There may be ongoing disputes over child support payments. The noncustodial parent may become alarmed when the custodial parent remarries, and the child is in a new stepparent situation. The noncustodial parent may feel as though the initial hearing was not "fair," and that a different judge will see the custody dispute in a new and more just light.

One of the most important functions that the family therapist can play in evaluating such situations is to point out to families that even though the courtroom situation is dramatic, the dichotomies that are presented are often false and the resolutions illusionary. The dichotomy of one parent's having custody and the other's having visitation is false, because a noncustodial parent will not invariably lose the opportunity to develop a long-standing relationship with his or her child. Many parents forget that children grow and develop to the point at which they have an opportunity to take a more active role in their relationships with their parents. At age 18 a child is free to visit whomever he or she wants. A child is better served by the efforts of a noncustodial parent in continuing a relationship than by a regular round of custody relitigation that results in strained relationships between the child and both parents. If it is true that no child can survive a custody dispute with his or her affections for both parents completely intact, then how much more true must it be that the child who suffers repeated custody relitigations runs the risk of distorted attachments to both parents? In the home of one parent, the child must pretend to be inured to the charms of the other parent. He or she must pretend to enjoy Christmas at one parent's home more than at the other parent's home. He or she must pretend to be more excited by one parent's birthday gifts than by those of the other. Expressions of affection to each parent on such days as Mother's Day or Father's Day must be very carefully weighed, with unstated but very real negative consequences in the case of parental disappointment. Occasionally, it is possible to influence parents away from relitigating custody.

A 28-eight year-old woman consulted a family therapist in order to address the issue of relitigating custody of her daughter. The child, 8 years of age, was living with her father and stepmother. The child's mother felt that the home was unsavory, because the 8-year-old stepsister was described as a learning-disabled youngster, and the 12-year-old stepbrother was described as a "budding delinquent" who had spent a considerable period of time in residential placements for youngsters with acting-out behavior disturbances. However, the woman's daughter was an outstanding student who appeared to be functioning well in all major spheres in her life.

A complicating factor was that the child's mother had voluntarily given up custody of the child when the girl was 3 years of age, and the couple had been divorced for approximately 1 year. The mother had given up custody on a voluntary basis because she was accepted for a college program in a distant city, and it was her feeling that it would be best for the father to take care of the child on a temporary basis while the mother went to school. However, after the mother had been in school for about a year, the father went to court and petitioned the court for temporary custody. This petition was granted. The mother subsequently sued the father for custody on two subsequent occasions. Each time, she was unsuccessful.

The salient issues were outlined for the mother. It was pointed out to her that the child was functioning adequately; that she herself had already been in court on two previous occasions in order to sue for custody; and that there had been no significant changes in the interim. The therapist offered the mother a sympathetic ear and offered to interview the child in order to see what could be learned from interviewing the child.

Julie, the child, presented as an outgoing, friendly girl who spoke enthusiastically of the homes of both her mother and her father. She looked forward to the visits with her mother because of the intensity of the contact that was possible, in view of the fact that her mother was able to devote her attention exclusively to Julie during the visits. Julie also demonstrated a high level of affiliation with her stepmother and stepsiblings, and made it clear that she regarded her father's home as her home.

After two interviews with the child, the therapist reiterated to the mother his opinion that custody relitigation would be superfluous, and that the best thing for her to do would be to enjoy the visitation that she had and to pursue her career goals. During a discussion of the therapist's suggestion, the mother revealed to the therapist that she had been torn between continuing in school or using all of her available financial resources to sue for custody. The therapist pointed out to her that by doing the former, she could set an example of achievement and accomplishment for Julie while taking the opportunity to advance her own career goals. Opting for the latter appeared to be sacrificing her own career goals for a doubtful chance at obtaining custody. The mother was unhappy with the therapist's analysis and recommendations, but she was able to follow the logic. Ultimately, she agreed not to pursue custody litigation again.

The Therapist as Consultant to One Side:
Attorney Requests

Sometimes a professional is asked by an attorney to intervene on behalf of the attorney's client in a custody litigation. Attorneys frequently present these cases as situations in which many clear differences between the parents are in evidence. It is not unheard of for an attorney to indicate that his or her blameless, well-meaning, other-directed, noble client is fighting an unequal battle with a dissipated, alcoholic parent who will no doubt engage in many abusive and neglectful practices if the children are unfortunate enough to fall into his or her clutches. Although attorneys can be very persuasive in arguing the merits of their cases in order to convince expert witnesses to become involved, they are also perceptive enough to be incredulous at the zealous way in which expert witnesses occasionally take on such cases. It is very difficult to become involved in a custody litigation as an expert witness for one side or the other and come away feeling as though one has performed a valuable service. Perhaps therapists will feel best in those situations in which they can actively dissuade attorneys' clients from recklessly pursuing their own perceived interests at the expense of the interests of the children. Occasionally, however, there may be a situation so extreme that a therapist may opt to take the role of consultant to an attorney with the intention of doing what can be done to further the attorney's case.

In the event that a therapist decides to act as a consultant for one side, it is critical for him or her to begin by stating an interest in seeing all members of the family and insisting on cooperation in any testing procedures that are deemed appropriate. Videotapes of interactions between each contesting parent and the children, psychological tests, and interviews with grandparents or other interested parties can all be mentioned. Often the opposite side will refuse to comply except for the examination of the child. This will generally limit the therapist/consultant to stating that the parent on whose behalf he or she is testifying is an adequate parent and enjoys a good relationship with the child. It will not, however, permit the therapist to say that one parent or the other is a better parent. It is clearly unethical for the therapist to testify about what he or she has never seen, or has never had an opportunity to test for.

When involved in such a situation, it is critical for the therapist to say only what he or she can conclude on the basis of the evaluation performed. The attorney must take the burden of demonstrating the case to the court. It is perfectly acceptable to perform an evaluation on one parent and to testify that the evaluated parent is adequate, is competent, and enjoys a good relationship with the child; however, testifying that a parent one has never seen is inadequate or not to be preferred to the parent one has seen is risking one's credibility and reputation. On the other hand, in such circumstances, an attorney may attempt to make up for this incomplete evaluation by asking hypothetical questions.

"Hypothetical questions" are questions that the attorney puts to the expert witness after having established the facts underlying the questions. For example, if the attorney has established that one prospective home for a child consists of a one-parent family headed by a father and another prospective home consists of a two-parent family that includes the child's mother and stepfather, then it is possible for the attorney to ask the expert witness whether he or she is of the opinion that one home has an advantage over the other home. The therapist need not have evaluated any of the parties involved in order to be able to answer hypothetical questions. It is not unethical to answer hypothetical questions about people that one has never evaluated, because one is not being asked to form conclusions about specific individuals.

In the event that both parents are available for examination, it is extremely difficult to maintain objectivity. It is natural to look at the case from the point of view of the attorney who has made the referral and from the point of view of that attorney's client. Another problem is that if the therapist comes to a conclusion different from that of the attorney and the part of the family that he or she represents, the therapist may be called to testify on behalf of the other side. Anticipation of this anxiety-provoking possibility also tends to narrow one's sights and compromise one's objectivity. The two stories may be very different from each other, and the participants equally believable. Facts that may seem cogent when presented by the attorney (e.g., that the client, the father, is prosperous and remarried to a beautiful and devoted prospective stepmother) may pale when the therapist considers that the mother, however plain and impecunious, nonetheless appears to be a decent person and is, after all, the child's mother.

Personal Injury

Another aspect of voluntary family involvement in the court system is that of personal injury cases having to with children. Psychic injury to a child is a very difficult area for therapists, because it causes many conflicting feelings. On the one hand, all of us are sympathetic to children who have been traumatized. On the other hand, most of us feel intuitively that the best way to deal with any emotional trauma is to "get on with one's life." A certain amount of any kind of psychotherapy is exhortation, and we are accustomed to using some amount of persuasion with our patients and clients.

The child who has had an alleged psychic injury, however, is subtly or sometimes overtly encouraged by his or her family to appear injured. Family members will focus on all of those aspects of the child's behavior that appear to be inconsistent with the behavior of a child who has been injured. They are apt to overstate incompetency, to understate competency, and to repeat again and again all the signs and symptoms of regression that have occurred since the traumatic incident.

A family presented with a $3\frac{1}{2}$-year-old boy who had been struck by a car when he was two years of age. He had been playing in the street, and the car stuck him and dragged him several feet down the street. Almost miraculously, the physical injuries were limited to abrasions. However, the family maintained that since the accident there had been numerous emotional symptoms. To begin with, the child began to talk about how he was going to "kill" the man who had run him over with his car. Nightmares and enuresis began. The child "could no longer recognize all the letters of his name" and the family alleged that he had been able to do this before the accident. Although several evaluators concluded that these cognitive symptoms and statements about the boy's intentions toward the man with the car were particularly unbelievable, in view of the boy's cognitive functioning in the dull-normal range, the family members persisted in making their allegations.

It is not very difficult to ascertain that a family has a question about physical trauma. Usually the issue is related to the therapist within the first few minutes of the first session. However, families seem to sense instinctively that therapists are not likely to immediately grasp the issue of psychic injury and champion it enthusiastically. Accordingly, family members generally focus their concerns exclusively on all of the symptoms that the child is experiencing, and they speak with the therapist only about how concerned they are about these symptoms and what can be done about them. The therapist may inquire of the family as to whether legal action is under way or is being considered. The family's response often will be that legal action will be considered if there appear to be grounds for it. At this point, the therapist has the option of deciding whether he or she wants to become involved in the evaluation or would prefer to refer the family to someone else.

There are several potential sources of conflicting feelings and conflicting interests in situations involving childhood psychic trauma. To begin with, as is true in all legal situations, the evaluator who functions as a treating therapist may be accused of a conflict of interest. It could be thought, for example, that if the family is successful in persuing a legal claim for psychic trauma, the therapist is more likely to be compensated. Clearly, it is necessary to separate these considerations from the beginning. The concept of a therapist who is paid on a contingency basis is generally considered to be unethical.

A second problem that occurs is the differing focus of the therapist as evaluator and of the therapist as treating therapist. Evaluation requires an assiduous search for all the symptoms and all the possible implications of any given trauma. The family generally has no difficulty in being cooperative in this regard. However, when it comes time to begin formal and active treatment, the family usually has a good deal of difficulty in enthusiastically endorsing new forms of family interaction that may well lead to the recovery from emotional trauma. It is as though there is a perception that the better the child does and the shorter the time in which it takes him or her to recover, the less serious the injury will look, and the more dubious will be the family's claim for compensation. Frequently, the family members persist in saying that their only interest is for the child to get better and that they have absolutely no interest in magnifying the psychic injury to the child.

In attempting to resolve this dilemma, it is best not to confront the family directly with the evident conflict. Instead, a useful approach is to attend to all statements by the family members that relate to their interest in the child's continuing to improve, and to the family's interest in seeing the symptoms resolve. The problem of describing the injury should be dealt with by first describing the injury as completely possible. This will also help in establishing a relationship of trust between therapist and family. The second task is to help the parents differentiate between their concerns for themselves and their concerns for the child. Some time will need to be spent with the parents apart from the child and with the child apart from the parents. The most useful approach is to frame the child' needs into a developmental perspective. Very young children can be conceptualized as being in need of parents who will calmly take responsibility for assuaging insecurities, while older children need parents who will encourage functioning in academic and social contexts. Parents may need frequent reminders that children will need to get on with their lives; and therapists will have more credibility if they establish a solid base by having completed a thorough evaluation. Even, then, however families may have difficulty following through with a therapist's recommendation.

Allegations of Child Sexual Abuse

A family may also voluntarily involve itself in the legal system when one member accuses another of child sexual abuse. (Cases of sexual abuse that are uncovered by extrafamilial agencies are discussed in a later section.) Sometimes child custody cases become so heated that one parent accuses the other of child sexual abuse, even though there is no objective evidence of the sexual abuse's having occurred (Green, 1986). It appears as though sometimes parents consciously think of child sexual abuse as a quick way of resolving the custody or visitation dispute. On other occasions, however, the conscious basis of the apparently spurious accusations is not so clear.

A 29-year-old mother of three children (boys aged 6 and 4, and a girl aged 2) presented with the chief complaint that she was convinced that her 6-year-old boy was being molested by his father, and that the 2-year-old girl had also been molested by the father. The mother had taken the 6-year-old boy and the 2-year-old girl to hospital emergency rooms on 12 occasions within the 5 months preceeding the initial consultation. However, there were never any objective findings. The children were evaluated. The 6-year-old spontaneously and with a smile said that "Daddy messed with me," but could give no further details. This same child had been observed interacting with his father on numerous occasions. Experienced child care staff found no evidence of any irregularities in the relationship between father and son. The father was very concerned about his son's development, and took seriously the allegations raised, but denied ever having engaged in any sexual wrongdoing with any of the children. There were no signs of serious anxiety or depression, and the youngster appeared otherwise well adjusted. He further added that "Daddy slept next to my sister," but could give no more details about the father's alleged sexually abusive behavior with the 2-year-old girl. The 2-year-old girl, who was barely verbal, did not demonstrate any objective evidence of emotional or behavioral disturbance.

The fact of all the negative findings was presented to the mother, with the warning that perhaps an objective judge, disinterested personally in the results, might have a great deal of difficulty accepting as valid the mother's accusations about the father. In addition, she was confronted with her admission that the father had never demonstrated any sexual abnormalities during the couple's 7 years of marriage. She ultimately withdrew the accusations, albeit reluctantly.

Therapists often find themselves in very difficult positions when allegations cannot be supported by solid evidence. On the one hand, no therapist wants to "miss" a case of child sexual abuse. On the other hand, no therapist wants to be used in the service of a spurious claim. Unfortunately, there is no guaranteed way of arriving at the truth of any sexual abuse claim. It is always suspicious when the claim is reported to a therapist before it is reported to a social services department. If the child's story is invariant and is given in an extremely spontaneous fashion without much affect, this makes one wonder whether the allegations are true. Invariant and spontaneous recitation of the story suggest coaching, and it also suggests that there is little anxiety attendant on the child's reciting of the story. Inasmuch as anxiety and other painful affects are a frequent concomitant of actual sexual trauma of any sort, the absence of anxiety in the child's recitation of the story may suggest that the allegation is false.

A homosexual allegation against a parent who has had no previous history of a homosexual adjustment must also give one pause for thought. It strains credibility that a couple could be married for many years with no evidence that the father is a homosexual pedophile, and yet that the father should develop such symptoms and act them out upon his own son in the process of a divorce.

When children are in the presence of a parent falsely accused of sexual abuse, they are often very comfortable and may even discuss the alleged abuse, usually at the prompting of the accusing parent. Sometimes children who give spurious accounts of abuse use adult sexual terms. Sometimes the accusing parent presents with audiotape recordings of the child's account.

As a rule, children who report genuine sexual trauma do so with reluctance, with painful affect, and with immature sexual terms. They are characteristically very uncomfortable in the presence of the suspected parent. The children appear to keep their interactions with the suspected parent as superficial as possible, in order not to reveal that they have implicated that parent.

Child Abuse and Neglect

An example of involuntary legal involvement of the family in the court system is the area of child abuse and neglect. The simplest situation is one in which a family already in treatment is discovered to be engaging in abusive or neglectful practices. Reporting of child abuse and neglect is mandatory in all localities, and it is incumbent upon the family therapists to understand their obligations under the applicable statue. In the situation of a family already in therapy, the family can be told of the therapist's obligation to report the abusive or neglectful behavior. The family members can also be given the option of reporting it themselves. Reporting can take place in the presence of the family or outside the presence of the family. How precisely to accomplish the reporting is a matter of individual judgment that must be applied in the clinical setting (Racusin & Felsman, 1986). Sometimes there is a good deal of advantage to using the fact of the necessary child abuse report as material to be discussed in therapy.

A useful technique in discussing with parents the obligation to report child abuse and neglect is to depersonalize the reporting. That is, the therapist can make it clear to the family that his or her obligation, under the law, is to report examples of suspected child abuse or neglect. The therapist does not have discretion in reporting suspected child abuse or neglect; on the other hand, the therapist does not have an obligation to make a determination as to whether or not child abuse or neglect occurred. It is up to the department of social services to do the investigation and to come to a conclusion as to whether child abuse or neglect has occurred. Furthermore, it is almost always a point in favor of the family that the family has not only reported its own abuse or neglect, but is already in therapy. A family is never very happy about having to be reported, but if its members have a reasonable therapeutic alliance with their therapist, they are usual able to understand the therapist's obligation and to avoid concluding that the therapist is making a negative moral judgment about them by reporting the suspected abuse or neglect.

A more complicated situation is one in which a family is referred for treatment by a social services department specifically because of child abuse or neglect. It is very important to clarify the expectations that the social services department has for the therapist. Sometimes the department wants an evaluation with regard to whether or not a child should remain in the home. On other occasions, the department has already decided that the child will be removed from the home, but feels that therapy ought to be offered to the family as one part of the service plan that will eventually result in family reunification. Another possibility is that the department wants an opinion from the therapist as to whether the family will be able to be substantially helped by family therapy. Sometimes therapists must write reports that conclude reluctantly that family psychotherapy will not help, and that supervision and child care training are much more appropriate routes of intervention.

The decision to remove a child from the home is a judicial decision. In most areas, the social services department may obtain the court's permission to remove a child from a home for a short period of time without a hearing, in order to protect the child. Within a few days, a formal hearing must be held, and the judge will decide whether or not the child should remain in the custody of the department.

There is considerable room for disagreement among family therapists, social services departments, and juvenile courts in these situations. To begin with, most family therapists would argue strongly against the complete removal of a child from a home in all but the most dire circumstances. On the other hand, the first priority of the department of social services is to protect the child. The priority of the juvenile court is usually to pursue the "best interests of the child." Whereas the "worst-case scenario" for the family therapist is that a child will be removed from his or her parents for an inordinate period of time, the corresponding scenario for the social services department is the possibility that a child will be seriously injured or killed. Social services department workers frequently find themselves faced with situations in which family therapists simply do not believe that children's homes are as inadequate or even dangerous as the workers feel they are; by contrast, some family therapists feel that social services workers are too quick to remove children from their homes.

A helpful principle that may help resolve some of these situations is to remain as clear as possible about the roles of the various individuals involved. Family therapists may not always agree with the decisions of the juvenile court judge to remove children from their homes, but the therapists must respect the decisions in order to remain in a position to help the families as best they can. The maintenance of a detached and professional demeanor will help the therapists to avoid casting aspersions on the motivations of others involved in the process. As a result, the therapists may then decrease the probability that the social services department and the city attorney will see them simply as naive individuals who do not appreciate the grave danger from which the department has just saved the children by removing them from their homes.

The therapy of physically abused children and their families poses many complicated problems. To begin with, the parents themselves have frequently been subjected to a considerable measure of abuse as they have grown up. They may feel as though they are raising their children in a manner no different from which the way they were raised. It may be very difficult for them to realize that the way they were raised included unacceptable practices, and that their having been abused is not a license to abuse their own children.

Issues of relative degrees of socialization may also arise in the treatment of such families. Family therapists tend to subscribe to such middle-class notions as "Differences can be settled by reasonable discussion," "Corporal punishment is a last resort," and "The needs of children are absolute, and it is the responsibility of parents to meet them." Some families may have a good deal of difficulty subscribing to such notions, and the therapist must often spend a considerable amount of effort in joining with these families and making them feel as though he or she is really there to help them. It is necessary to maintain a delicate balance between being seen as a family's unquestioning ally, on the one hand, and being seen by the family as a judgmental authority figure who is unsympathetic to the family's point of view, on the other.

The image of an abused child in the popular literature and press is an image of a completely innocent youngster who is victimized by marginally socialized parents. The complicated dynamics involved in the rearing of chronically ill youngsters, mentally retarded youngsters, learning-disabled youngsters, and stepchildren, to name only a few of the groups of children at risk, are insufficiently appreciated. The amount of leverage that a child can gain by forming a coalition with one parent against another, or with outside agents against the parents, is also insufficiently realized. A common enough scenario is one in which the mother is indulgent toward the child but objects in the father's presence to some of the child's more flamboyant behavior. The father enters to discipline the child, and the mother then criticizes the father's discipline methods.

Cases of Child Sexual Abuse

More bizarre twists of family dynamics are seen in cases of child sexual abuse, which constitute another example of involuntary familial involvement in the legal system when these are discovered by agencies outside the family. Family roles are turned completely topsy-turvy. If a young girl is her father's consort, then she can be conceptualized as her mother's rival and her siblings' "mother," and there are many other confusing changes in the family dynamics (Justice & Justice, 1979).

There is usually a question as to whether or not the father will be allowed to remain living in the home. In a case of incest, he is frequently placed under a no-contact order and ordered to leave his own home. Sometimes an exception can be made if the daughter is removed from the home temporarily. The mother may then find herself in a position where she must choose between having her husband or her daughter at home.

Therapists frequently find themselves baffled by the relative leniency of punishment for intrafamily sexual crimes. The same sexual act perpetrated by a father against a daughter is seen in a very different light from what would be the case if a man did the same thing to an unrelated woman or child. For example, aggravated sexual battery, which could consist of one episode of kissing a child's breasts, is punishable in some jurisdictions by a sentence of 20 years in prison. Often the child's mother, without whose support vigorous prosecution is almost impossible, is reluctant to press for a breakup of the family. Sometimes, therefore, the notion of "treatment" is placed before the notion of "punishment." In such situations, it is possible for a family therapist to have major input into the question of under what conditions the family will continue to relate. Clearly, the decision will be made by a judge. However, if the family therapist is able to say to the court that he or she feels that treatment is very likely to be successful, then sometimes the court may be much less inclined to order the most severe penalty.

It is very important for a therapist to have a clear philosophy of treatment in cases of sexual abuse, and to make clear distinctions between treatment and punishment. Treatment is whatever may serve to remediate. It is recommended by therapists and sometimes ordered by courts. It may take place in inpatient, outpatient, or correctional settings. An argument that effective family therapy can only take place if the perpetrator is not in prison must be bolstered by cogent data that support a good treatment prognosis.

Different jurisdictions deal differently with incest situations and child sexual abuse. In some jurisdictions, the prosecuting attorney is willing to support levying criminal charges only if it is almost certain that a conviction can be obtained. In other localities, criminal charges are more routinely levied against the alleged perpetrator in the hope that, at a minimun, a plea of guilty to a lesser charge may be elicited and more control may then be exercised. Consequently, perpetrators themselves may find examples of unequal treatment. One man who has touched his child on the breast on one occasion can be given the same punishment as a man who has had repeated intercourse with his child, if both plead guilty to one count of aggravated sexual battery. If the sentence in each case is suspended, then neither will be incarcerated. The perception by the perpetrator that he is not being dealt with "fairly" simply tends to reinforce his denial—either denial that he has done that of which he is accused, or denial that it was a serious thing. Doing therapy with persons accused of such a crime necessarily involves a good deal of confrontation. Perpetrators tend to focus on their own needs rather than those of the children, and this must be changed. Perpetrators are likely to be more resistant to accepting responsibility if they feel that they have been treated unfairly, and this may complicate the therapist's work.

There are several useful roles that a therapist can play in a case of child sexual abuse. First, evaluating the victim is important in order to ascertain what (if any) actual emotional injury has been done, and what sort of treatment may be required. Second, the therapist can help the spouse of the alleged perpetrator to look realistically at issues of treatability and to take a wide view of the situation. The therapist can provide objective evaluative material about the alleged perpetrator, and can make recommendations about the realistic prognosis for improvement given the opportunity of psychotherapy.

A 14-year-old girl who had allegedly been molested by her father was referred to a family therapist. The father admitted to touching the girl on her breast. He said that the incident occurred one night when the child's mother was "out," and he later admitted that he was very angry at the child's mother for being away from the home that evening. The father had been arrested and had been placed under a no-contact order. He was living apart from the family.

The father's initial reaction to the sexual abuse was to deny it, and then later he became depressed, preoccupied with suicide, and convinced that he was an extremely bad person. The mother's response was to be horrified by the event at first, and then later to acknowledge that she had indeed engaged in a considerable measure of acting-out behavior during the marriage. She admitted to having had at least one affair, and she further admitted that there were times during the marriage when she had engaged in heavy drinking. The girl appeared to be a reasonably well-functioning youngster who did not show evidence of a great deal of anxiety or guilt about the event. She was appropriately angry with her father, and was able to utilize several sessions in which she talked with him about how angry and let down she felt.

Inasmuch as the father had a good work record and did not appear to be a primary pedophile or to be particularly dangerous to others in the community, he was allowed to enter a plea of guilty to a misdemeanor charge of taking indecent liberties with a minor. The couple was able to work meaningfully on the long-standing marital difficulties that contributed to a high measure of interpersonal stress. It remained unclear whether they would remain together or divorce, but they made strides toward talking about their interpersonal difficulties, rather than simply engaging in mutual recriminations about the father's sexual abuse and the mother's history of acting out.

Conclusion

Involvement with families in the legal process offers fascinating opportunities to struggle with new issues in a new forum. To see the once-arcane world of psychotherapy exposed to the larger world of law, social services, and even liability insurance is to see psychotherapy in a fresh and exciting way. Psychotherapists have in the past had the luxury of working in single offices with single families or clients. Whatever the psychotherapist has had to say has needed to be justified only to the family or to the individual client. Frequently, families and individual clients accept the psychotherapist's word as absolute truth.

Lawyers, judges, social services departments, and liability insurance companies do not accept the word of psychotherapists as if it were absolute truth. Consequently, in order for psychotherapists to interact with these individuals, they must be clear, consistent, and rational, and must make formulations in nondogmatic and nontechnical ways. This can facilitate a more realistic and ultimately more satisfying view of the role of psychotherapy.

The relationship between law and mental health before the 1950s was generally one of mental health concepts' entering the law. Since the 1950s, however, the tendency has been increasingly for legal concepts to enter the world of mental health. Psychotherapists, including family therapists, must see psychotherapy as a discipline and a profession that is encompassed by laws. Understanding the legal context and learning how to operate within it are ultimately much more productive than complaining helplessly about the constraints that are placed on our practices.

As if family therapy were not a sufficiently complicated discipline, families' involvement with the legal system brings additional complications. If the therapist can succeed in drawing distinctions among the roles of various participants in the legal process, can understand the legal questions, and can understand the limitations that will be placed upon his or her freedom of action in such situations, then working with families who are involved in the legal system can be an exciting challenge rather than a resented infringement upon the therapist's prerogatives.

REFERENCES

American Psychiatric Association. (1982). *Child custody consultation: Report of the Task Force on Clinical Assessment in Child Custody*. Washington, DC: Author.
Bartley v. Kremens, 402 F. Supp. 1039 (E.D. Pa. 1975).

Belli, M. (1983). The sparks of conflict: Advice to the expert witness. *American Journal of Forensic Psychiatry, 4*(2), 67–88.

Brooks, A. D. (1974). *Law, psychiatry, and the mental health system.* Boston: Little, Brown.

Burt, R. A. (1983). Experts, custody disputes and legal fantasies. *The Psychiatric Hospital, 14*(3), 140–144.

Campbell, L. E. G., & Johnston, J. R. (1986). Impasse-directed mediation with high conflict families in custody disputes. *Behavior Sciences and the Law, 4*(2), 217–241.

Cross v. Harris, 418F.2d 1095 (D.C. Cir. 1969).

Derdeyn, A. P. (1983). The family in divorce: Issues of parental anger. *Journal of the American Academy of Child Psychiatry, 22*(4), 385–391.

Derdeyn, A. P. & Scott, E. (1984). Joint custody; a critical analysis and appraisal. *American Journal of Orthopsychiatry, 54*(2), 199–209.

Goldstein, J., Freud, A., & Solmit, A. J. (1973). *Beyond the best interests of the child.* New York: Free Press.

Green, A. H. (1986). True and false allegations of sexual abuse in child custody disputes. *Journal of the American Academy of Child Psychiatry, 25*(4), 449–456.

Gumper, L. L. & Sprinkle, D. H. (1981). Privileged communication in therapy: Special problems for the family and couples therapists. *Family Practice, 29;* 11–23.

Gutheil, T. G., & Appelbaum, P. S. (1982). *Clinical handbook of psychiatry and the law.* New York: McGraw-Hill.

Ilfeld, F. W., Ilfeld, H. Z. & Alexander, J. R. (1982). Does joint custody work? A first look at outcome data of relitigation. *American Journal of Psychiatry, 139*(1), 62–66.

Irving, H. H., Benjamin, M., & Trocame, N. (1984). Shared parenting: An empirical analysis utilizing a large data base. *Family Practice, 23,* 561–569.

Jacobs, J. W. (1986). Divorce and child custody resolution: Conflicting legal and psychological paradigms. *American Journal of Psychiatry, 143,* 192–197.

Justice, B., & Justice, R. (1979). *The broken taboo.* New York: Human Sciences Press.

Levy, A. (1978). The resolution of child custody cases: The courtroom or the consultation room. *Journal of Psychiatry and the Law, 6,* 499–517.

Mental Health Procedures Act of 1976, § 201, Pa. Stat. Ann. tit. 50 § 7201 (Purdon).

Pearson, J., & Thoennes, N. (1986). Mediation in custody disputes. *Behavioral Sciences and the Law, 4*(2), 203–216.

Racusin, R. J., & Felsman, J. K. (1986). Reporting child abuse: the ethical obligations to inform parents. *Journal of the American Academy of Child Psychiatry, 25*(4), 485–489.

Truiford, J. R. (1986). Joint custody: A blind leap of faith. *Behavioral Sciences and the Law, 4*(2), 156–168.

Wallerstein, J. S., & Kelly, J. B. (1980). *Surviving the breakup: How children and parents cope with divorce.* New York: Basic Books.

Westman, J. C., & Lord, G. R. (1980). Model for a child psychiatry custody study. *Journal of Psychiatry and the Law, 8,* 253–269.

18

Children in Placement: A Place for Family Therapy

ANN ITZKOWITZ, MA

When the Biblical hero Moses was laid in a basket by the river, his mother weighed the precariousness of her baby's journey against the danger he would face if he were to remain at home. This is the same dilemma faced by families and social service agencies who are involved in placing children. The task is to weigh the relative risks of a child's remaining with the family against those of being placed out of the home.

For 5000 years, no one has questioned the mother's love for Moses, even in sending the baby away, for "only a . . . mother, in desperation to save her child from destruction, would thus expose it" (Hertz, 1968, p. 210n). And no one questioned the motives of Pharoah's sister in taking the child, for, when she saw "a boy that wept, she had compassion on him" (Exodus 2:6). But from this simple story of caring even when a child and family are separated, child placement has evolved over time into a controversial, conflictual, and often unwieldy process.

"Children in placement" here refers to children who are not living with their families. They reside in foster or group homes or other residential institutions. The children in these cases are categorized as dependent, having been abandoned, neglected, or abused. They are placed when their families are unable to provide adequate care and protection. The families are often overwhelmed by medical, economic, social, and/or emotional problems. They are unable to manage their

Ann Itzkowitz. Philadelphia Child Guidance Clinic, Philadelphia, PA, Private practice, Philadelphia, PA.

lives and have inadequate family or community resources to sustain themselves. Many of the children, coming from such dysfunctional families, are themselves symptomatic with severe emotional and behavioral problems; their difficulties both result from and contribute to the overall stress (Norman, 1985).

Under these circumstances, some parents may request placement for their children from welfare agencies. At other times, society, in the form of protective services, may insist on placement when children are considered endangered by remaining at home. In either case, the family system gets disrupted by the separation of child and parents and by an infusion of helpers—welfare case managers, therapists, courts, child care workers, and foster parents, among others.

At present, between 243,000 and 274,000 children are estimated to live in foster homes, group homes, and residential treatment centers (Norman, 1985, p. 1). Many more have been touched by the process but are no longer in placement. Still others live away from home in short- and long-term psychiatric hospitals and in settings for delinquents. Of those in dependent placement, many will experience relocation, either through unsuccessful return to the family followed by return into care or through moves between residential facilities. Some spend a brief period of time in care while their families reconstitute themselves; others remain in care much of their lives (Norman, 1985).

Background

The history of child placement has been richly described (Kadushin, 1974; Laufer, Laffey, & Davidson, 1974; Mayer, Richman, & Balcerzak, 1978; Norman, 1985). General trends in the field have been an expression of underlying societal values and social service know-how. Although, in general, there has been movement toward increased protection of abandoned and neglected children by society, the specific ways in which to do this have been varied and conflicting.

The roots of child placement may be traced back to the early 17th century. Prior to that, communal attention to unwanted children in the ancient period allowed for infanticide, abandonment, and child sale. During the Middle Ages, religious orders sometimes cared for abandoned children, along with sick, elderly, and homeless adults. However, in 1601 the Poor Law in England officially established public responsibility for poor, neglected, and handicapped children in the form of indenture and almshouses. These early efforts at care were motivated by public desire to save children from their poor and negligent environment. The placement also served the pragmatic purposes of clearing the streets of the homeless and possibly providing child labor.

In the mid-19th century, amendments to the Poor Law allowed for removal of children from their homes for reasons of neglect and for the separation of care of children from that of adults. In addition to almshouses, a variety of institutions, such as orphanages, custodial facilities for the handicapped, and trade schools, emerged. As interest in issues of child development and child welfare evolved, placement facilities sponsored by public and private agencies became increasingly differentiated.

Competition arose among the forms of placement—in particular, foster homes versus more institutional settings—as to which type of facility would be best suited for dependent children. Children were referred to and accepted in a particular living arrangement based on the perceived efficacy of the placement, without regard for the needs of the individual child. This ultimately resulted in inappropriate placements and failed cases. In general, however, placement reflected a long-term commitment to a child's growing up within the residence. At the time, families were not an integral part of the decision-making process or treatment of their children. Rather, parents were seen as negligent, incompetent, and best kept at a distance, with only their benign involvement tolerated.

In 1909 in the United States the White House Conference on Children declared that children were best situated in their own homes. There was little movement, however, to return placed children to their families; debate continued as to which type of placement would serve as the "best substitute" for the family. Then, in 1935, the Social Security Act provided aid to dependent children. Many children who would previously have been placed away from home because of financial need were able to remain with their own families. Those children who then entered care often had more problems and came from more dysfunctional families.

Dependent placements moved from a custodial model to increased emphasis on specialized services in the areas of education, socialization, and psychotherapy. Involvement of families, in the form of counseling and visits, also emerged. But this did not always meet the enormous need. Because of either their own lack of initiative or inadequate support by the caregiving agencies, families were found hard to reach, and parents and children frequently lost physical contact if not an emotional connection. But, unlike the situation in earlier times, the sense of commitment to see a child through to adulthood was no longer present. When the typical dependent residence or foster agency could not provide the care to meet their special needs, these troubled youngsters would be moved repeatedly from one place to another.

The situation was further complicated by variations in states and local communities as criteria for placement, standards of care, quality of treatment, and degree of family involvement that was expected and genuinely supported. With agencies not always able to meet the needs of the children they served, with uninvolved families, and with children falling through the cracks between or among multiple agencies, the original notion of societal protection of neglected and abandoned children was not always fulfilled; in fact, it may have become more a part of the problem than the solution.

More recently, the trend toward placing children away from their families is slowly being reversed. In reaction to the overtaxed child welfare system, the increased emphasis on deinstitutionalization, and renewed awareness of the importance of families, laws are being enacted to prevent unnecessary placements. They also provide for systematic review of the cases of children in placement, requiring specific treatment and disposition plans, so that children and families do not get lost in the system.

In addition to the new laws, programs such as Homebuilders in Washington (Kinney, Haapala, & Booth, 1986; Norman, 1985) are being developed to actively prevent child placement. The focus of these programs is on treating the family as a whole with brief but highly intense in-home services that include family therapy, parental skill building, and use of community resources to stabilize family life. With this treatment, the vast majority of families are reported able to weather their crises and remain intact.

A small percentage may refuse to participate in or cooperate with such programs, or simply do not benefit from this therapeutic approach. These become the treatment failures, and the children are considered for placement. The children who go to placement are usually the most severely symptomatic and come from the most dysfunctional families. They and their families are likely to need the most intense services.

Family Therapy: Place and Potential

Family therapy has given little attention to children and families disrupted by placement. Historically, child placement has emphasized social welfare and child-focused treatment. This contrasts markedly with family therapy's tradition of thinking about and working with two-parent families, and expanding to include variations in family configuration due to divorce, blending, single parenting, death, illness, and so on.

Beyond the disparate histories of the two traditions, however, child placement is still troublesome to family therapists. First, children tend to define a family. Before the advent of children there are couples, and before that there are individuals. In this regard, placement signals the termination of a "family," symbolically if not actually.

Second, placement may be seen as a treatment failure, in which the family therapist has participated in scapegoating, child rescue, parental blaming, and focusing attention on the symptom bearer rather than on the interactional patterns of the entire system. At the very least, the family therapist may feel that he or she has failed to support family functioning and competence, but, rather, has undermined it and contributed to its dissolution.

Third, placement runs the risk of taking on a life of its own and actually preventing family reconstitution. Although research is equivocal as to whether a particular presenting problem may lead to extended placement, it is clear that "the longer a child is in care, the greater is the probability that he or she will grow to maturity in out-of-home placement" (Stein, Gambrill, & Wiltse, p. 148).

Fourth, family therapists may also share a societal value that this unempowered population of multiproblem families, simply referred to as "placement cases," is impossible to treat. Rather, the children are left to get individual and milieu therapy in their placements, and the families to receive considerable casework from a myriad of social service agencies.

But even if a family therapist is inclined to take on this therapeutic task, with so many systems and changing contexts and without "the family," the question arises as to where he or she should intervene, and with whom. There is little in the family therapy literature to provide a framework for such treatment. The powerlessness of the child and family becomes the powerlessness of the helpers and of the family therapist.

It is generally believed by child experts that children are best raised within their own families. When circumstances make this impossible and the children go to placement, a family systems approach can provide a conceptual and practical framework for treating such children. Minuchin (1974, p. 4) points out that "theories and techniques of family therapy lend themselves readily to work with the individual in contexts other than the family." But doing this requires that the family therapist be flexible, focusing on and intervening with the child, the family, and the larger social system over time. This, in turn, requires the expanding and contracting of perceptions of the field and of specific treatment strategies as circumstances indicate.

Creating the Context(s)

A primary contribution of a family systems approach is seeing the individual within a context (Auerswald, 1971; Minuchin, 1974). For children in placement, identifying the context is a complex task. It requires that the therapist weave a contextual fabric from sometimes disparate, sometimes overlapping threads. For the fabric to be useful, it needs to provide continuity and a sense of integration in the face of the disruption that usually characterizes the lives of children in placement.

Placement as Context

Ideally, child placement should not be seen as the last resort for people who have failed at therapy and crisis intervention. Placement should be part of a larger and ongoing treatment picture in which the extended family, direct family therapy, intense in-home services, and other community resources are marshaled to sustain children and families. When these are not sufficient, other forms of treatment should be called upon. One such resource on this therapeutic continuum is placement of a child out of the home. When used as an intense therapeutic experience, placement can be an opportunity for the child and family to survive a particularly stressful life stage. But for this to be successful, such treatment must combat the serious risks of emotional (if not physical) cutoffs, a growing sense of failure, and abandonment of the child by the parents (as well as of the entire family by the therapeutic community). For child placement to function as an effective treatment modality, then, it needs to be seen as part of a larger treatment context, not as an isolated event, with continuity of care occurring at many levels. Such continuity should be reflected in overall planning and coordination of treatment; ongoing family involvement; and attention to the specific needs of the child before, during, and after placement (Mayer et al., 1978).

The decision to place a child away from home should be developed out of earlier therapeutic work (Mandelbaum, 1962). When intervention at home and/or in the community has not been sufficient to eliminate the problems or reduce them to a safe level, the family, in collaboration with professionals, should make the decision to utilize placement. The decision should be based on a set of criteria (Auerswald, 1969; Meddin, 1984), not on blaming the child, family, or therapist. Such blame is defeatist and will exacerbate an already existing sense of failure, which is counterproductive to treatment and undermines a family's self-value.

Rather, the criteria for placement should be translated into goals and purposes of such treatment, which describe clearly what needs to be accomplished by the child and by the family in order for discharge from placement to occur. Disposition planning should always be part of the admission process. To reach these goals, specific tasks are developed. Some are issues for the child to work on while in placement; some pertain more to the family; some tasks involve the child and family together. The roles of the placement agency and of other professionals are also delineated. Such planning should be clearly explicated in a treatment contract among child, family, and agencies (Stein et al., 1977). Goals, tasks, and disposition planning may change over the course of placement. What is important is that these changes be mutually agreed upon.

The points of admission to care and discharge from placement are important moments of transition to be considered. Within the specific placement context, however, possible slips in continuity may be more subtle, but need attention nevertheless. These include changes in staff shifts, and changes in staff more generally. They also include changes in peer groups due to admissions and discharges of fellow residents or foster siblings (Burch, 1984). Even a positive move (e.g., a "promotion" from a cottage for younger children to one for an older age group) can be a painful reminder to a child of earlier experiences of loss.

Continuity of care necessitates clinical attention to these points of transition and to the anxiety that such changes engender with a particularly vulnerable population. Interventions should occur on a programmatic level through rituals and general stability in activities and schedules. This can be supplemented by work on an individual's issues under the circumstances. It is important for such clinical work to deal with, yet not to get mired in, the experience of loss. While acknowledging such feelings, clinical work needs to include simultaneous focus on goals, growth, and opportunities to help children (and families) cope adaptively with such stressful experiences.

If a child is to go home following placement, the transition must be carefully planned, and a therapeutic support system for the child and family needs to be established (Mayer et al., 1978). Some children may remain in placement for a longer time, and some may not be able to return home at all. When one or the other of these is the case, therapeutic strategies should be developed to support the parent–child relationship, even when parent and child cannot live together (Mayer *et al.*, 1978; Tiddy, 1986).

The Larger System as Context

When placement becomes part of the treatment picture, the context of therapy expands. Work with a child and his or her family now includes professionals over the course of treatment, from the original referral source to those involved with aftercare. The professionals represent different disciplines and multiple agencies, such as the welfare system, foster care, the courts, residential treatment, and mental health agencies. They also represent different roles within a single institution, such as day or evening shift child care workers, teachers, recreation specialists, and so on.

The therapeutic task, then, is to establish within the larger, diverse system a flexible organization and hierarchy, with *someone* in charge and responsible for its overall coordination. Auerswald (1971, p. 266) points out that the "understanding of . . . human problems and effective remedial action is not possible within the linear framework of any single discipline." He develops a model of the "intersystems conference" that includes all the relevant professionals, community helpers, family members, and friends. A chairman is elected to coordinate the meeting and implement plans that develop out of it. The tasks are to share information and to develop a mutually agreed-upon treatment plan from which specific tasks emerge and are then carried out. Such a model is particularly applicable to treating children in residential care, and in a systemic way may reverberate to provide "community enhancement" as well (Auerswald, 1969).

When such collaboration does not exist among the professionals, or between professionals and families, and competing interests result in scapegoating and the pursuit of contradictory directions, the larger system becomes dysfunctional and nontherapeutic. This results in disenfranchised families and in children lost within and between interagency rifts and family–agency conflicts (Haley, 1976; Mandelbaum, 1961).

The Family as Context

The most important aspect of continuity, and that most threatened by placement, is family involvement. Many parents are considered resistant, hard to reach, and uncooperative. But professionals sometimes misconstrue the family's feelings of embarrassment, defeat, failure, and exhaustion (Mandelbaum, 1962) as signs of disinterest and disengagement (Hess, 1982). Parents may also be intimidated by professionals in charge of their children and by the institutions they represent (McAdams, 1972). Sometimes parents are, in fact, genuinely disconnected from their children. The process and fact of placement of a child away from home may support discontinuity to a degree that is nearly impossible for families to overcome. Parents have been shown to lose momentum in the treatment process as placement extends beyond 1 or 2 years (Shapiro, 1973).

For families and professionals to overcome such "resistance," treatment has to include joining the families, accepting them at their present level of functioning, and empowering them with a meaningful place in their children's treatment and in their lives throughout the course of placement. Ideally, the work with a child's family prior to placement should focus on forming this therapeutic alliance. To do this, professionals have to develop an appreciation for the significance of the parent–child bond; sensitivity to their developmental struggles; an emphasis on joint efforts to resolve the family crisis and avert placement; and attention to the meaning that placement may have for the family, if it becomes necessary. Even under hostile circumstances, one can assume that in most cases placement represents to parents a dashing of dreams for themselves and their children, accompanied by their own deep sense of failure and potential grief (Hess, 1982).

It is also true that despite the best spirit of collaboration and professional efforts at recruitment and joining, there are parents who will have limited or no contact with their placed children. Family contact, nevertheless, continues to remain important. From the beginning, contact should not be limited to parents. Regardless of whether parents are able to be involved, linkages between a child and the extended family and siblings need to be made as part of the child's natural context and history. The importance of such ties has been noted (Colon, 1978; Ward, 1984), as have ways to do therapy with siblings who are in placement (Lewis, 1986). Such efforts can extend to include members of the social community, to support ethnic and cultural ties (Colon, 1978).

The Child in Placement

Although the lens is enlarged to include a view of placement over time and the expanded context of treatment in placement cases, it also needs the flexibility to contract, to focus on the individual child.

Development/Clinical Issues

The developmental requirements and tasks of childhood need to be attended to (Leventhal & Dawson, 1984), regardless of where a child is living (Maier, 1979). The family is the most important source of nurturance and socialization of children. It gives a sense of personal history and continuity. And for most children it is in the family that these processes, in fact, occur. But what if a family is unwilling or unable to care for its young? What special issues exist for children who live away from their families?

For those placed in foster and group living situations, there are indeed special issues to be considered, in addition to the basic needs and tasks of childhood. Placement away from a family, usually as a result of severely symptomatic behavior in the child and/or serious problems in the home, is a wrenching experience. It may be accompanied by feelings of loss, confusion, anger, guilt, sadness, and possibly even relief at times (Fanshel & Shinn, 1978). A child may feel abandoned by his or her family, yet remain fiercely loyal to them (Boszormenyi-Nagy & Spark, 1984). Sometimes a child brings unresolved emotional issues from the family of origin to the new setting (Bowen, 1978). Mere physical separation does not preclude the power of the relationship (Jolowicz, 1946).

These highly charged feelings may be manifested in a variety of ways. A common phenomenon for children in placement is to refer to the biological parent as "my *real* mom." Children may also avoid their intense feelings of perceived rejection by their parents through denying any parental responsibility for the fact of placement (Rest & Watson, 1984). They would rather blame the courts, the social agencies, or themselves, even in the light of remembered neglect or abuse, or clear signs of parental abandonment.

A 16-year-old youth was recalling his childhood in placement. He vividly described the neglect he experienced with his mother. As a 4-year-old, he was often left hungry, dirty, and unsupervised all day with his younger and older brothers in the hallway of the apartment building where they lived. An elderly neighbor, whom he referred to as "Mom," felt sorry for the boys and with increasing frequency fed them and allowed them into her apartment to watch TV. Eventually, she agreed to take official custody of these three neglected little ones. Some years later, "Mom" felt that she could no longer care for the boys, and requested that the welfare department place the older two elsewhere.

The youth recalled the first instance as "Mom *taking us* from our *real* mother." In the seccond case, he claimed that the "welfare worker *took us* from Mom." He added that he and his older brother had had thoughts at the time of beating up the caseworker in retaliation. In neither situation did the boy hold his mother or the neighbor responsible for initiating the moves.

Allegiance to the family of origin, divided loyalties between family and caretakers, and the burden of emotional cutoffs and unresolved conflicts may be expressed by a placed child through difficulties in forming new relationships and in problematic behavior. Such behavior "proves" that the "professional" parents are not more successful than the "real" ones in raising children (Mandelbaum, 1962). Feelings toward members of the family of origin may be displaced onto adults and peers in the new setting. And without a means for resolving the old issues, a child in placement may remain emotionally stuck.

Children in placement also contend with the issue of impermanence, and lack even the security described in Robert Frost's "The Death of the Hired Man" (Frost, 1914/1950):

'Home is the place where, when you have to go there,
They have to take you in.'
                        'I should have called it
Something you somehow haven't to deserve.'

For a child in placement, this bond of security has been broken (Rest & Watson, 1984). The initial sense of rupture between child and family may be replayed through a series of placements, over which a placed child feels powerless (Fanshell & Shinn, 1978), with repeated losses and physical and emotional cutoffs.

A 16-year-old girl reviewed her life in placement. She knew that the court had removed her from her family when she was 1 year old because of repeated physical abuse she had received. She did not know whether the family had been offered treatment at the time, or whether they would have accepted it if it had been offered. She had had multiple placements and unhappy contacts with her mother, with whom she had a poor relationship. Now a teenager and a mother herself, she felt like a victim, powerless to control the tide of her life. Her child, aged 1½, was also in placement.

In summary, for placement to work, a number of ingredients are needed. First, the appropriateness of a particular placement should be considered. Although "goodness of fit" (Chess & Thomas, 1984)—that is, matching the temperament of each child with a context—may not be possible, some thought should be given to what a particular child needs. For example, it is generally agreed that younger children should live with a family. Those older children who are unable to tolerate the closeness that an intimate family setting demands may do better in a group living arrangement (Dinwiddie, 1974; Mayer *et al.*, 1978).

In either situation, there should be an ongoing commitment to the continuous care of the child, with few transitions and minimal disruption (Schaefer, 1977). The care involves providing for physical and emotional needs and for a sense of safety (Heard, 1982; Maier, 1979). In addition, placed children need the opportunity to maintain linkages to their significant networks, particularly their families—to assess these relationships realistically, to heal old wounds, and to develop ongoing connections and support (Colon, 1978; Tiddy, 1986). All of these can only occur under a clearly organized and planful social service system that does not allow children and families to get lost within its bureaucracy.

Underlying all of this is an attitude about children in placement and how they should be viewed and treated. Wherever they are placed, and whether they have direct contact with their families or not, children in placement need contexts and relationships that foster their development of basic trust (Erikson, 1959) and a sense of self-worth and empowerment. With such support, they have a chance to overcome the perceived stigma of placement and go on to lead competent and satisfying lives (Rest & Watson, 1984).

Finally, it needs to be recognized that most children in placement today are away from their families because they are sufficiently symptomatic that they cannot be managed at home, and/or they come from highly dysfunctional families that cannot care for them. The fact of placement itself is likely not to be the sole cause of the presenting problems nor to be adequate to remedy them. Various intense therapeutic services are also essential.

Treating Children in Placement

When children in placement present with symptoms, they are similar to those of children living in families. They may be suicidal, aggressive, or defiant, or may run away. Unlike children living in their own homes, however, the ability of placed children to relate to others is more consistently impaired. This problem usually takes one of two forms. Either such children become pseudoattached and clinging, draining anyone working with them because they are so needy, or they become very distant and aloof, pushing away anyone who tries to get close or be connected. This problem in establishing appropriate degrees of attachment exacerbates the other symptoms and interferes with the treatment process. Such behavior saps the energy of the staff and leads to feelings of burnout and ultimate rejection of these children.

A too frequent scenario in placement is that a child's behavior becomes intolerable. Efforts to help him or her within the setting do not work, and the child may be on the verge of eviction from the group or foster home. The referral often comes late in the sequence of problematic behaviors and curative efforts, when feelings of failure and burnout on the part of the child and "helpers" are pronounced.

At such a time, the goal of the referral source (usually a welfare department, foster care agency or residence) is to have the child evaluated to determine what is wrong with him or her, to have the child's symptoms eliminated, and to move the child on to yet another placement. If the symptoms are severe enough and the referral for treatment is made to an inpatient unit, the goal may be to use the hospital as the new placement, though a temporary one until something more permanent can be found.

From a systems perspective, the first goal of treatment is to *stop* the pattern of disruption, dislocation, and risk of emotional cutoffs that beleaguers children in placement. The second goal is to broaden the context of the problem by moving the "pathology" from inside a child to making the symptom into an interpersonal event (Montalvo, 1978). This implies seeing the individual child in context(s) and creating treatment strategies appropriate to the systemic definition of the problem and the level of intervention needed. Sometimes the therapy is done on an outpatient basis in conjunction with a local clinic or at the residential treatment center itself. When a child is at serious risk, the treatment may include psychiatric hospitalization. When inpatient treatment is required, the third goal is to acknowledge the risk and try to prevent the hospital from becoming merely another residential placement.

To accomplish these goals, the therapy needs to be inclusive. It should consider the stresses in the present that result from both usual and extraordinary development transitions (Haley, 1973). It should also keep in mind the historical messages and obligations that get passed down through families and affect present functioning (Boszormenyi-Nagy & Spark, 1984; Bowen, 1978). In addition, it should consider "the stress of living in *this* place at *this* time" (Carter & McGoldrick,

1980, p. 11). As such, it must recognize and contend with the mood of the larger social context, its philosophy, its resources, and its limitations (Nichtern, 1973).

The steps presented for such treatment are not mutually exclusive. Nor are they exhaustive. Rather, they are meant as general guideposts to the expanding ideas and imagination of the therapist (Itzkowitz, 1985).

DEFINING THE CONTEXT

Although family therapy deals with individuals within their social context, sometimes a child in placement is isolated and completely cut off from an ongoing social network or supportive relationship. In such cases, the family therapist first may have to help the child identify and develop such a context by locating at least one other person who will take an interest in the child and be willing to participate in treatment, and to whom the child can have a sense of belonging. An example of such extreme circumstances follows:

Larry, 11, had been living for a few weeks at a group home for delinquents. A judge had remanded him there after he was arrested for assaulting a teacher and for stealing a purse and a bicycle. In the home, Larry's "bizarre" behavior worried the staff. The boy was extremely withdrawn. He would not talk, eat, or change his clothing. He lingered at the second-story bannister, and the staff thought he might jump.

As a result, Larry was referred to a hospital for emergency admission. He arrived by ambulance with the driver, who did not know him. No one from the residence felt connected to the boy, nor was anyone willing to participate in his treatment. The staff at the group home thought that Larry might have a grandfather, but no further information was available. Larry was alone.

After several days in the hospital, during which Larry remained uncommunicative, the boy revealed the necessary telephone number and the grandfather was contacted. Unwilling to participate in the boy's treatment, the grandfather did appear one day, unannounced. He was intoxicated and disheveled, and requested placement for Larry's 14-year-old sister. (For this, the therapist referred him to the welfare department.) On the day of his visit, the grandfather reported that Larry had been living on the streets for years and managing to take care of himself. The boy rarely went to school, and only on occasion stayed at the grandfather's home. Larry's mother was in a prison a considerable distance away and had little or no contact with her children.

The initial step in treatment was to help Larry develop a meaningful context outside the hospital. Through prison social services, the therapist was able to get in touch with Larry's mother, who agreed to be involved. First, regular contact between the boy and his mother was established through telephone calls and letters. Second, the imprisoned mother took an active interest in the boy's therapy and disposition planning. Although no other relatives showed an interest in the boy, she was able to organize the members of her family sufficiently to have Larry and his sister stay with them for holidays. Third, the therapist also involved the welfare department, which took responsibility for the boy's care. Following Larry's discharge from the hospital, the mother continued contact with her son, the professionals, and the resident caretakers with whom Larry was placed.

Thus, an aspect of Larry's treatment focused on establishing a context for him—that is, a meaningful relationship that had the potential of being continuous and transcending a specific placement. Although far from the image of a young child warmly cradled in the bosom of the family, Larry was less cut off and isolated than he had previously been.

At a 6-month follow-up, Larry had made a successful adjustment to the residence. He and his mother, who was still in prison, had maintained contact through letters and telephone calls. She was due for early release.

THE PRESENT PLACEMENT

Usually a context is more readily identifiable. The child is living somewhere—a foster home, group residence, or shelter. And there is a welfare department or other social service agency overseeing the placement. The therapist begins by working with the patient and the adults responsible for his or her care. Added to these may be the other children living in the home. As with a patient living in a family, the therapist first assesses the pattern of relationships, determines the stressors and systemic issues in the present context that may be relevant to the child's symptomatic behavior, and then develops interventions to create change.

For such treatment to occur, the caregivers and agencies have to commit themselves to the child and the therapy. However, though there may be good intentions, surrogate families/agencies are often near the point of burnout and may not be willing or able to extend themselves as much in treatment as they may say at first. And the child, already sensitive to rejection, may sabotage his or her own therapy to avoid the risk of making a renewed commitment to a placement, only to face possible eviction again. Under such circumstances, it is not surprising that, after a period of what appears to be "successful" therapy, the child "blows it" and/or the family/agency gives up. The therapist, therefore, needs to be sensitive to the emotional and other constraints that exist during the therapy. These ambivalent feelings, in particular, need to be acknowledged and dealt with as they arise, so that the therapeutic goals will be realistic.

The risk that a child may be evicted from a placement, despite good therapeutic interventions, may make a therapist wonder whether he or she should bother getting involved. However, the intense work in the present context may be well worth the effort: (1) It gives the child and those in the residential setting a *chance* to relate in a way that is mutually satisfying and adaptive; (2) there is an opportunity to foster stability in the child's life, reduce the symptomatic behavior, and avoid a change in residence; (3) even if, at the end of treatment, it is decided that the child should live elsewhere, the therapy can be used to create a transition between residences and to avoid a sudden and often unexplained move; and (4) beyond the identified patient, the process may have a positive impact on the general functioning of the other children and staff in the home.

The following is a case example in which the child was able to remain in his present placement:

John, 12, was referred for treatment by the social worker at the group residence where he had lived for 6 years. Despite the agency's long-term commitment to the boy, the staff there felt that they could no longer manage his increasingly aggressive behavior and were on the verge of evicting him.

Within the residential setting, John experienced a number of stressors. He was approaching adolescence. He was living in the children's cottage, where he received a lot of nurturance from the staff (it had been "home" for 6 years). He was about to be "promoted" to the adolescents' unit—a move he was, at best, ambivalent about making. In addition, just prior to the referral for treatment, John's natural brother, who had also lived at the residence, was transferred to a foster home run by the same agency. No contact was allowed between the boys for several weeks, ostensibly to help the brother adjust to his new home." John probably missed his brother, and also was probably jealous of the younger boy's perceived opportunity. In addition, the staff disagreed about what to do with John. Some felt he should be allowed to stay in the children's cottage, where he felt safe and at home; others felt he should be transferred to the adolescents' unit; still others thought he should be evicted from the residence entirely. The social worker and her supervisor disagreed about whether John should be allowed contact with his brother during the period of adjustment.

Intervention at the residence included work with John and the staff to identify the stressors, to air their differing points of view with regard to the management of the case, and together to develop a treatment plan in which there was less unresolved conflict and more positive direction given to the boy, while also meeting his needs. As a result, John was able to experience a slower and more supportive transition to the cottage for older boys, insuring that he could maintain contact with the familiar staff and peers while developing new relationships; he was also able to resume contact with his brother. In this process John also had to learn to speak up more, rather than act out his feelings. And the staff was more available to attend to his needs as he became more capable of stating them.

The residence also felt ongoing support from the family therapist, who continued to work with the boy and the staff for some time. Although John still had some behavior problems, these were at a manageable level, and he was able to remain at the placement without threat of imminent eviction.

A second case illustrates a way of working when the caregivers view their involvement as temporary, ambivalent, or unsuccessful.

Loretta, 8, was referred to the hospital because of escalating dangerous behavior in the residential treatment center where she had been placed a few months earlier, following incidents of serious neglect and abuse in her family. Loretta had originally lived with her mother and brother, 11, in the homes of various relatives and with a number of the mother's paramours. The girl allegedly witnessed her mother's sexual encounters and was herself raped by one of these men when she was 6 years old.

At the time of the sexual abuse, Loretta was removed from her mother's care by the welfare department, and the father came forward to take custody of both children. About a year later, Loretta accused her father of beating her. She called a maternal aunt, who took her to the hospital to be checked. Once there, the doctor reported the incident of child abuse, and Loretta was removed from the father's home and placed at the residential treatment center.

At the residence, Loretta got into numerous fights with staff and peers. She was disruptive at school. She also ran away frequently. Once she was located several miles from her school. When driven back to the residence by her social worker, Loretta jumped out of the car into traffic, and had to be returned by police.

At the time of her admission to the hospital, it was made clear by the residence that Loretta could not return there, as they felt that they could not provide her with an adequate level of safe care. They did agree, however, to help provide a transition for Loretta. The child care staff remained in contact with the girl by telephone, and the social worker continued to visit over a number of weeks. (Loretta's mother came to hospital once to visit; her father's unannounced and erratic visits invariably left Loretta upset.) Although this transition was hardly ideal, it did offer Loretta a more gradual period of acclimation to the new setting (the hospital) while letting go of old relationships.

Given her parents' lack of involvement in her treatment and the irregularity and unreliability of their participation in her life, transitions were understandably excruciating for Loretta to deal with. This factor also was considered as her discharge approached. Over the weeks in the hospital, where she received intense treatment, Loretta had formed powerful attachments to staff and peers. She was referred to a special foster care program. In an effort to ease her transition from the hospital to her new residence, the foster parents, therapist, and others collaborated closely with hospital staff and spent considerable time in activities with Loretta prior to her discharge.

Following a stressful transition to the foster home, Loretta's symptoms abated somewhat once she was settled in the placement. But her mother's lack of involvement, her father's erratic contacts, and the numerous disappointments by extended-family members were continued sources of upset for her. Intensive therapy and coordinated efforts among therapists, foster parents, and the welfare agency were essential to maintain her in the community.

THE HISTORY

Working in the present context alone does not usually give a full explanation of the troubled behavior or an opportunity for complete treatment. The systems therapist should explore the child's history, looking for significant relationships, experiences, unresolved conflicts, and other issues that may be relevant to his or her present functioning. These may involve staff and peers in former placements, as well as professionals seen earlier.

For most children in placement, the most important aspect of this work is in the relationship between the child and the natural family. One can assume that for the placed child, the family is there—consistently, erratically, or in fantasy. When a family is involved, treatment with the entire unit can take place to deal with its particular issues and mutual goals. These include helping the child and family (1) heal a sense of loss and failure that placement may have engendered; (2) resolve earlier conflicts and restructure dysfunctional family patterns that may have contributed to the child's symptomatic behavior and to the placement; and (3) deal with loyalty issues among child and family and placement agency. Such treatment may result in the child's return home.

Tommy, 9, was referred for hospital treatment because of a dangerously escalating pattern of behavior that could no longer be managed by his group residence. Originally placed because of abuse by his mother, Tommy had been at the residential treatment center for approximately 3 years, during which time he visited home on weekends.

Over the years, the residence and the mother had accused each other of abusing the boy. Tommy's symptomatic behavior seemed to be a reaction to his long-standing mistreatment by *both* the mother and the residential staff, and especially to the ensuing battle between the two warring factions for his loyalty. The conflict between the mother and the agency appeared to take precedence over anyone's paying attention to the boy's real needs, or to his contribution to the ongoing battle. Tommy wanted to return home. His misbehavior and the difficulties in the residence activated his mother on his behalf and kept alive her interest in him. It also demonstrated the inadequate "parenting" he was getting at the residence.

Within the safety and the structure of the hospital Tommy was able to remove himself from the battle zone, and his behavior calmed down considerably. Initially, the therapy focused on reducing the conflict among the adults. Meeting with each side individually, the therapist had them acknowledge the inadequate and abusive care the boy had received both at home *and* at the residence. It also became clear that Tommy could not develop properly if the war continued. Eventually, the mother and the placement/welfare staff softened their hostile positions toward each other sufficiently to talk about their mutual concern for the child and to develop a treatment plan that would consider the boy's needs.

During the hospitalization, for example, it was learned that the boy was hyperactive, was learning-disabled, and had an attention deficit disorder. He responded well to the structure of the hospital program and to the use of medication. Such findings had important implications for developing an appropriate discharge plan.

During the hospitalization, it also became clear that Tommy wanted desperately to return home and that the mother wanted another chance at raising her son. She attended therapy sessions and the inpatient unit program regularly in an effort to demonstrate her good intentions and, in fact, her success in being with the boy, providing guidelines and nurturance. In this process, Tommy was encouraged to identify and express his feelings in positive ways, without having to resort to provocative behavior.

Despite the continuing conflict among the adults, Tommy was ultimately discharged into his mother's care. This was to be monitored by the court and the welfare department, which still saw the mother as hostile and abrasive.

Reunification is not always a realistic possibility. Family therapy must have the flexibility to focus on how the family and the child, with the support of the placement agency, can develop or maintain a caring relationship appropriate to their needs and abilities, even if they are not living together.

Margaret, 12, was referred for treatment because of her running away from home, placing herself in dangerous situations, engaging in sexual promiscuity, and making a suicidal gesture by pill ingestion.

The initial steps in treatment involved trying to soften the hostile relationship and improve communication between Margaret and her mother, in an effort to help the girl return home—a goal they both wanted. Within the treatment, it became clear that Margaret's behavior was a reaction to her relationship with her mother. It also served to reinvolve the mother's two former long-standing boyfriends with the family, both to provide paternal care for Margaret and to help reduce her mother's loneliness.

The therapy expanded to include these two men, as well as a cousin and maternal grandparents from whom the mother had been cut off. With the larger network, treatment focused on creating a familial context in which the mother and Margaret were not isolated, and in which the mother could receive support for herself and for her parenting efforts. Beyond the brief therapy contact, however, the extended network essentially abandoned Margaret and her mother.

Not long after the girl's discharge from the hospital, the symptomatic behavior reappeared, and Margaret was readmitted. The second phase slowed the treatment process. The primary focus shifted from the mother's learning to nurture and guide the girl, to the mother's receiving nurturance herself from the therapist. As this occurred, the mother gradually began to soften her attitude toward the daughter from one of abandonment and rage to expression of interest in the girl's well-being. In this situation, both mother and daughter would have to be cared for/ treated by others until they felt whole enough to form a solid connection with each other. This therapeutic work would need to continue while Margaret lived in a long-term placement, to which she was discharged.

When the family is very unreliable in its contact or is totally absent, the family therapist still must consider the child's longing for the family and the fantasies and idealizations about them. The therapist may need to support the child's reaching out, and then help the child anticipate and deal realistically with the family's reaction, which may be positive, ambivalent, or outright rejecting. In the following case example, a therapy session with the patient, the social worker from the group residence, and the family therapist focused on validation of the boy's feelings of attachment and loyalty for his mother, who had abused and abandoned him, while at the same time empowering him to move on.

John, 12 (previously described), had many issues to confront in his group residence. These were not believed sufficient, however, to account for his aggressive behavior. Among other things, he also missed and worried about his mother, whom he had not lived with or seen in years, and then only sporadically. He did not know where she lived—possibly somewhere in another state—and he had no way to get in touch with her. John longed for his mother, and thought about her much of the time.

When asked by the therapist where he would like to be, the boy quickly responded, "With my mother." When asked about whether he had ever lived with her and what that was like, he said that he and his siblings had last lived with her some 6 years earlier, when he was 6 years old. He remembered clearly that there was not enough food to eat; there was no regular place to sleep; his mother hit him and often left the children alone.

John was then asked to describe his present living situation. In the group residence, he was not beaten; he was fed and clothed, and generally received adequate care. The therapist again asked the boy where he would like to be. Unequivocally, he responded, "With my mother."

The therapist went on to acknowledge how much John missed his mother and wanted to be with her, but also asked whether this was a realistic possibility. When the boy said it was not, the therapist then asked John what he thought would be the next best thing if it were not possible for him to be with mother, even though that was what he clearly wanted. The boy thought a while, then said he guessed it was living in the residence where he had been for 6 years.

The interview further explored the details of what it would take for John to grow up at the residence, from the boy's point of view and from that of the staff. It was acknowledged by everyone that, for John, growing up in the residence was not as good for him as he imagined it would be with his mother. In this way, the staff could set reasonable expectations for John to succeed at the residence, while remaining aware and respectful of the boy's longing. And John could keep his loyalty and dreams about his mother, and, at the same time begin to be more invested in doing the things he needed to do for himself to grow up with the help of the staff.

THE LARGER SYSTEM

Treatment of a child in placement requires that the family therapist go beyond the child, family, and specific caretakers to include work with the larger ecological context. The therapist must intervene with the multiple systems that affect a placed child by (1) defining the problem within this larger context; (2) involving all relevant participants in the treatment; (3) establishing a sense of continuity of care, purpose, and organization that is interdisciplinary in order to avoid scapegoating, confusion, and further dysfunction; and (4) promoting a person in charge to see that the collective efforts of the helpers are coordinated, collaborative, and responsibly carried out.

Tommy, 9 (previously described), reappeared for treatment because of aggressive, provocative behavior several months following his discharge from the hospital. There was no indication of abuse by the mother, but clearly the discharge plan had not worked. There was no outpatient treatment at the local community mental health center, no prescribed medication for the boy, and no schooling. At the point at which mother and son reappeared, it was easy for the helping system to be disappointed and angry at the mother for *her* not following through with recommended treatment, and for the boy to be placed out of the home again.

Rather than simply scapegoating the mother for having failed, the therapist defined the boy's disruptive behavior as a dysfunction in the overall plan and within the context of the larger system. Included in the subsequent treatment were the boy, the mother, and the professionals already involved. The task was to identify the source of the plan's breakdown and to try to correct the problem through increased collaboration of all those involved.

It became clear that the mother had made considerable efforts to enroll her son in school. When the public school refused to place the boy in the needed special education class, and the special school had no opening, the mother kept the boy at home rather than have him in an inappropriate class. The family had no money. There were no funds for medication or for bus fare to go to therapy. There was no telephone, which only exacerbated the mother's already felt sense of isolation. She had no one to turn to for encouragement, support, or assistance with obtaining real services. This was seen as the breakdown in the original plan.

Treatment involved, then, creating a supportive network for the mother that would enable her to keep her son at home. Within this framework, the professionals collaborated with the mother to help her get the services that she felt she needed. The child advocate assumed responsibility for obtaining a list of special programs available to single parents, including homemaking help, crisis intervention, life skills training, and respite care, which could be used by the mother as she felt the need. The base service unit was to arrange necessary funding for these services. The welfare worker helped the mother get Aid to Families with Dependent Children, so that she could in fact support the boy. Family therapy and an after-school program were arranged to take place at the local community mental health center. The child advocate assisted the mother in getting the proper class placement for her son. The welfare department also provided supportive services in the home.

Although the infusion of services might have seemed overwhelming and possibly undermining of the mother's competence and authority, the spirit of the treatment was supportive to the mother and her son in an effort to keep the family together. The mother was able to call on the "helpers" as she felt the need, but an underlying goal for the treatment was for the mother gradually to create her own social supports and rely less on a professional network to manage her life. As this occurred, the professional network would decrease its involvement.

At a 1-year follow-up, Tommy continued to live at home and to attend special school. Medication was discontinued. The mother had requested crisis services once or twice in the beginning; now there was diminished contact between the family and the welfare department.

THE CHILD'S PERSPECTIVE

Treatment should include a focus on the child as an individual. Placed children have experienced multiple contexts, tenuous relationships, and disrupted histories. They feel the stigma of special living arrangements, and of being different from (and less than) other children. These factors have contributed powerfully to their symptomatic behavior, low self-esteem, and lack of trust. They see themselves as victims, overwhelmed by their circumstances.

Therapy should empower these children to take responsibility for their actions. They can learn to confront the reality of their situations, develop realistic goals, and use their networks and resources constructively to get their needs met.

In the case of Tommy (described earlier), the compelling features of his history—the abuse, the early placement, the extreme conflict between mother and agencies—could have rendered him merely a victim. In addition to dealing with the other issues, therapy challenged the boy to take responsibilty for his contribution to the ongoing problems, and to find more socially acceptable ways than provocative and disruptive actions to satisfy his needs. In doing so, it enabled the others in his network to see Tommy as a competent person. They could set reasonable expectations for him and hold him accountable for his behavior without their becoming abusive or his spiraling out of control. Tommy was not merely a victim.

The therapy can also nourish. It can provide a safe arena in which the therapist can validate the child's memory and history. And through this validation, it can provide for the child a sense of continuity, a sense of being whole. It can also be a place for a child to express sadness, anger, dreams, and hope. It is a place for a child to be encouraged to take risks, particularly in developing relationships.

In the case of John (described earlier), the therapy focused on acknowledging the boy's longing and grief. It also worked toward helping him move beyond such feelings to think of his present life and to free him to make new commitments.

In the case of Loretta (described earlier), the girl continued to relive the losses and earlier trauma with each failed visit by her parents and each unkept promise by the extended family. The therapy concretely focused on her learning to express her anger and disappointment in ways that would not hurt her or others. She was especially encouraged to look for support and nurturance from the hospital staff, and later from her new foster parents. This process of forming new attachments in the face of continued disappointments and abandonment by her family was a slow and arduous one.

Not often does a child in placement have the opportunity for such individual attention. It is an opportunity for the therapist to "whisper in the child's ear" that he or she is a worthwhile human being.

Conclusion

To work in the field of child placement in a meaningful way, a therapist needs a vision of the whole—the context(s), the history, and how the child and family fit into these. The therapist also needs the sensitivity and caring to attend to the individual child. Finally, the therapist especially needs a way to take care of himself or herself so as not to be overwhelmed and burned out.

Perhaps the most basic question is this: Who really cares—about the well-being of these children in our society, about their families, about the difficult dilemmas they face? Although grappling with such a poignant social problem may seem overwhelming to family therapists, the alternative—abandonment—is unthinkable.

ACKNOWLEDGMENTS

The author wishes to thank Martin E. Itzkowitz, PhD, and Deborah A. Luepnitz, PhD, for their review of the manuscript and for their helpful suggestions. She wishes to express special appreciation to Gordon R. Hodas, MD, for his ongoing collaborative work in this field. In addition, the author wishes to thank Suzanne Griffith, MSW, and Darlene Hewett, MSW, for sharing their perceptions of residential treatment and foster care, and Janet Hutchinson, MPA, for her insights regarding child placement at a national level.

Illustrative clinical material presented in this chapter is derived from cases of the Child and Family Inpatient Service of the Philadelphia Child Guidance Clinic. Identifying information has been disguised to protect the privacy of the patients and their families. In addition to presenting her own cases, the author wishes to thank her colleagues Neil Bonavita, MSS, Mary Boyle-Fox, MSN, Andy Fussner, MSW, and Beth Johnson, MSW, for sharing their clinical work.

REFERENCES

Auerswald, E. H. (1969). Changing concepts and changing models of residential treatment. In G. Caplan & S. Lebovici (Eds.), *Adolescence: Psychosocial perspectives* (pp. 343–357). New York: Basic Books.
Auerswald, E. H. (1971). Families, change, and the ecological perspective. *Family Process, 10,* 263–280.
Boszormenyi-Nagy, I., & Spark, G. (1984, rev. ed.). *Invisible loyalties.* New York: Brunner/Mazel.
Bowen, M. (1978). *Family therapy in clinical practice.* New York: Jason Aronson.
Burch, J. M. (1984). *They cage the animals at night.* New York: New American Library.
Carter, E. A., & McGoldrick, M. (1980). The family life cycle and family therapy: An overview. In E. A. Carter & M. McGoldrick (Eds.), *The family life cycle: A framework for family therapy* (pp. 3–20). New York: Gardner Press.

Chess, S., & Thomas A. (1984). *Origins and evolution of behavior disorders from infancy to early adult life*. New York: Brunner/Mazel.

Colon, F. (1978). Family ties and child placement. *Family Process, 17,* 289–311.

Dinwiddie, F. W. (1974). Reciprocity of emotional transactions: A crucial issue in residential care and treatment. *Child Care Quarterly, 3,* 119–124.

Erikson, E. (1959). *Identity and the life cycle*. New York: International Universities Press.

Fanshel, D., & Shinn, E. B. (1978). *Children in foster care*. New York: Columbia University Press.

Frost, R. (1950). The death of the hired man. In F. O. Matthiessen (Ed.), *The Oxford book of American verse* (pp. 548–554). New York: Oxford University Press. (Original work published 1914)

Haley, J. (1973). *Uncommon therapy*. New York: Norton.

Haley, J. (1976). *Problem-solving therapy*. San Francisco: Jossey-Bass.

Heard, D. (1982). Family systems and the attachment dynamic. *Journal of Family Therapy, 4,* 499–116.

Hertz, J. H. (1968). *The pentateuch and haftorahs* (pp. 209–210). London: Soncino Press.

Hess, P. (1982). Parent–child attachment: Crucial for permanency planning. *Social Casework: The Journal of Contemporary Social Work, 63,* 46–53.

Itzkowitz, A. (1985). Treating children in placement. *The Family Therapy Networker, 9,* 15–17.

Jolowicz, A. R. (1946). *The hidden parent*. Paper presented at the New York State Conference of Social Welfare, New York City.

Kadushin, A. (1974). *Child welfare services*. New York: Macmillan.

Kinney, J., Haapala, D., & Booth, C. (1986). *Behavioral Sciences Institute of the Homebuilders Program*. Private publication.

Laufer, M. W., Laffey, J. J., & Davidson, R. E. (1974). Residential treatment for children and its derivatives. In G. Caplan (Ed.), *American handbook of psychiatry: Vol. 2. Child and adolescent psychiatry, sociocultural and community psychiatry* (pp. 193–210). New York: Basic Books.

Leventhal, B. L., & Dawson, D. (1984). Middle childhood: Normality as integration and interaction. In D. Offer & M. Sabshin (Eds.), *Normality and the life cycle* (pp. 30–75). New York: Basic Books.

Lewis, K. (1986). Sibling therapy with children in foster homes. In L. Combrinck-Graham (Ed.), *Treating young children in family therapy* (pp. 52–61). Rockville, MD: Aspen.

Maier, H. W. (1979). The core of care: Essential ingredients for the development of children at home and away from home. *Child Care Quarterly, 3,* 161–173.

Mandelbaum, A. (1962). Parent–child separation: Its significance to parents. *Social Work, 7,* 26–34.

Mayer, M. F., Richman, L. H., & Balcerzak, E. A. (1978). *Group care of children*. New York: Child Welfare League of America.

McAdams, P. J. (1972). The parent in the shadows. *Child Welfare, 51,* 51–55.

Meddin, B. J. (1984). Criteria for placement decisions in protective services. *Child Welfare, 63* 367–373.

Minuchin, S. (1974). *Families and family therapy*. Cambridge, MA: Harvard University Press.

Montalvo, B. (1978). The family and child placement practices: Opening comments. *Family Process, 17,* 287–288.

Nichtern, S. (1973). The care of dependent children. *Journal of the American Academy of Child Psychiatry, 12* 393–399.

Norman, A. (1985). *Keeping families together: The case for family preservation*. New York: Edna McCornell Foundation.

Rest, E. R., & Watson, K. W. (1984). Growing up in foster care. *Child Welfare, 63,* 291–306.

Schaefer, C. E. (1977). The need for "psychological parents" by children in residential treatment. *Child Care Quarterly, 6,* 288–299.

Shapiro, D. (1973). Agency investment in foster care: a follow-up. *Social Work, 18* 3–9.

Stein, T. J., Gambrill, E. D., & Wiltse, K. T. (1977). Contracts and outcome in foster care. *Social Work, 22,* 148–149.

Tiddy, S. G. (1986). Creative cooperation: Involving biological parents in long-term foster care. *Child Welfare, 65,* 53–62.

Ward, M. (1984). Sibling ties in foster care and adoption planning. *Child Welfare, 63,* 321–332.

19

Family Violence and the Helping System

DUSTY MILLER, EdD

Nearly a fifth of all families in the United States experience a form of family violence, according to a recent study (Gelles, 1985). This staggering figure represents a condition of the lives of many more children than we usually identify as suffering the effects of domestic violence. Usually only those children who come to the attention of the larger helping system are seen as needing some assistance with their experiences of violence; these are the children who have been physically or sexually abused. In fact, children are affected by all forms of violence in the family, whether they are directly involved in sexual or physical abuse or are witnesses to violence inflicted on others, as in wife battering and rape, abuse of pets, and violence against personal property. The problem, then, goes beyond the immediate physical danger to the child, to the more pervasive emotional consequences of interpersonal patterns that characterize the system of violence.

The hierarchy of intervention in families where violence occurs reflects current societal values. Professional intervention is most active in cases of child sexual abuse, more moderate in cases of child beating and wife beating, and significantly less likely in cases where children are exposed to the traumas of violence against pets and personal property.

Families usually do not name violence as the problem for which they are seeking help; other problems, or pressure from outside the family, bring families to treatment. Violence frequently remains outside the immediate awareness of the family therapist.

Dusty Miller. Brattleboro Family Institute, Brattleboro, VT.

Description of the V Family

The description of a violence-involved family begins, often, with a description of the therapist's response to them. A therapist describing such a family says to his or her colleagues, "There's something about this family that really gets to me. I feel uneasy, I don't know what's going on here, but it feels—I don't know—it's a family I really dread seeing." The therapist wonders about the family's history with helpers, about secrets, about interactional patterns within the family, about danger. Is someone being abused? Are the children at risk? Where does the "evil lurk"?

Typical of this type of family was the V family (Miller, 1983). The therapist seeing this family asked the members about their history with the helping system and found that the family had a history of conflict with school personnel and social services over a period of approximately 10–12 years. Physical abuse had been suspected and investigated by the child protective services, but never adequately substantiated. The family's problematic patterns seemed to have been activated by confrontation with these other agencies; as the larger system intervened, always taking a stance of child advocacy against the family, the family grew increasingly reactive, tightening its defenses to the point of fortress-like impenetrability.

This therapist had begun seeing the V family at the request of the department of social services. At that time there was concern for all four children, ranging in age from 12 to 17. The schools, the local police, and the department of social services all speculated about the family. They saw Mr. V as tyrannical, old-fashioned, and probably physically violent with all four of his children. They suspected that Mrs. V was also alcoholic and physically violent, especially with her two daughters. The oldest child, a 17-year-old boy, appeared to be least at risk, but was considered a victim because of his parental role and the possibility that he was involved in abuse cycles. The 16-year-old boy was involved in delinquency and substance abuse, but he drew the sympathy of the professional community because they saw him as reacting to his father's unbending "old-world" rigidity and suspected violence. The two daughters, aged 14 and 12, were the focus of the greatest concern. They were seen as victimized by both parents. Physical abuse had been alleged and investigated, and there were suspicions of sexual abuse as well.

As noted, the family had been under surveillance over a period of 10–12 years. The children's schools, from elementary through high school, had repeatedly reported their concerns to the department of social services. Despite the numerous investigations, there was no proof. But, contrary to the principles of American justice, the V's were believed to be guilty until proven innocent beyond a shadow of a doubt.

The problems posed by this example are familiar. Whether the violence in question is threatening but elusive, or family violence has been clearly substantiated and addressed in treatment, the problem remains: How can one best empower all the family members to find their own healing solutions?

So far, the story of the V family illustrates several characteristics of violent systems. First, attention is called to the family through the plight of the victims (generally women and children), who, even if they are not physically injured, may be trapped in the dilemma of conflicting loyalties. Second, in cases where there is a long history of conflict between family members and members of the larger system, violence is often a tightly guarded secret. Third, it is often the case that the whole family, and particularly the women and children, may be reabused by the intervention of "helpers" when the professional network forces entry into the family system without addressing the historical context that has allowed the family's distress to be perpetuated.

This chapter examines the various forms of family violence that affect children and the roles that helping systems have played in working with these families. The chapter discusses the problematic consequences of either blaming one member of the family for the violence or, alternatively, holding everyone in the family equally responsible for the violence. The ways in which violence may be exacerbated in the process of treatment are identified, and a new model for the assessment and treatment of violence is offered as an alternative to the polarized positions of child advocacy versus family systems neutrality.

The State of Professional Response to Family Violence

As family therapists begin to consider the politics of family violence, a clear division emerges. At issue are the polarizing effects of our response to violence and the use and abuse of power in the definition of social roles.

> Violence compels us to take sides, the intensity and sense of urgency it creates is the arch enemy of perspective. It encourages us to think in terms of cartoons. . . . As therapists, we can't afford to substitute cartoons for the complexities of human relationships. Our job is neither to bemoan the spectacle of human cruelty nor [to] punish the wicked, but to help people find ways to open up possibilities in their lives. (Simon, 1986, p. 6)

Opinions vary as to how best to help people "open up possibilities," both within the family therapy field and in the larger helping system that includes family therapy. The cartoon images suggested by Simon are those of the victim–villain polarity.

Critical to the analysis of family violence is the way in which power is conceptualized in a broader social context. Family systems therapy has often dismissed the relevance of power differences in social relationships, while at the same time offering no other description for inequities in relationships that are characterized by domination and exploitation (MacKinnon & Miller, 1987). Child advocates often see parents as the villains, abusing their rights to exert control over their children. Feminists, on the other hand, are more likely to view family violence as a gender-defined issue: Men exert abusive physical and socioeconomic power over women and children. Violence toward children by women is explained in this framework as women's acting within social patterns created by men.

Critics of social control argue that intervention by state agencies is an issue of dominant professionals' threatening the rights and autonomy of the less powerfully positioned family. But feminists argue that this criticism overlooks the historical reality that women and children have appealed to protective agencies to defend them against the abusive behavior of male heads of families.

What seems to have emerged, as family therapy begins to consider the problem of violence, is a clear division between those in the helping system who are compelled by their jobs as well as their political perspective to take sides, and those who are more systems-minded and see a less hierarchial, less power-based social structure of relationships. It is becoming clear that in the larger helping system, the necessity for integration of both positions is imperative.

Defining Family Violence

Family violence is defined by how it comes to the attention of those who are attempting to define it. For example, a family coming to treatment specifically because of violence will usually be referred by a source outside the family, such as protective services, the school, the physician, or the criminal justice system. Usually these agencies apprehend the family's problem in such terms as "child sexual abuse," "child (or wife) beating," "offender," or "perpetrator," thus creating a victim–victimizer view of the situation. This kind of language reflects an intent to protect or rescue the victim and to punish the victimizer.

Unfortunately, the language of victim and victimizer may engender a blameful response in helpers. This is not useful in efforts to help the family (beyond simply removing the victim from immediate danger); it is also seen to perpetuate the cycles of violence in the family–helper system. That is, the victim–victimizer relationship is now experienced between the family and the helping agency representative(s). This is a characteristic dilemma in which "linear" (cause-and-effect) language dictates actions that seem to enforce symptomatic cycles.

In contrast, family therapists may try to define violence in more systemic terms, such as "the incestuous family" or "domestic violence." This conceptualization may lead to the description of a recurrent cycle of behavior, implying that the problem is a part of the way the system functions, rather than an interaction between two people with a power differential. In this way, the systemic reaction to the usual polarized position of helping professionals is to take an opposite (i.e., polarized) position in reference to blaming and rescuing.

Yet another version of the victim–victimizer position is taken by feminist critics of family systems language, who point out that it renders the gender-specific nature of violence invisible: "Husbands and fathers perpetrate the majority of sexually and physically abusive acts, while wives and daughters suffer the emotional and medical consequences" (Bograd, 1986, p. 35). Feminists critcize family therapists not only for obscuring gender-specific issues, but for cor.:tructing their views of families without considering this important aspect of social context (James & McIntyre, 1983; MacKinnon & Miller, 1987; Taggart, 1985).

Clinicians who diverge in their contextual perspectives (child protective workers vs. cybernetic-minded systemic therapists) may agree that violence on the personal level is directly related to violence affecting families on an institutional level. Unfortunately, the connection between family violence and the societal level of unequal relationships and attendant violence seems somewhat abstract when an individual appears to be in imminent physical danger. Yet the individual child (or woman) may be in greater jeopardy when helpers act against families without a map for understanding the larger social context, including the helpers. A framework is needed to provide both a description and an explanation for intrusion and coercion between family members and the helping system.

Beyond the Dichotomy

The issues discussed in this chapter are offered as illustrations of potential solutions to address the existing discontinuity between the victim advocate and feminist positions, on the one had, and the family systems position, on the other. This dichotomy has become a source of major conflict in current family therapy approaches to the problem of family violence. But perhaps the dichotomy is unnecesary, and we can dispense with "either–or" and begin to address the problem with a "both–and" perspective. Clinicians can address questions of power without losing their capacity to conceptualize family violence (and involvement of the larger system) from a systemic or "circular" perspective.

If the therapist seeing the V family were to approach the case from a perspective shaped by the larger social context, she could have addressed issues of power: How is power manifested in relational patterns within the family? How is power defined in the family? Can power be measured by degree of choice to leave the field—mobility to come and go from the family fortress? Is having power determined by exercising control through secrets? Is the secret of physical violence less powerful or more powerful than the secret of alcoholism? What about the power of controlling the secret pertaining to sexual abuse?

These questions are also relevant to the family–helper suprasystem. Isomorphic patterns between power and control in the family and power and control in the family–helper suprasystem show patterns similar to the power wielded by the parents over the children. When an agency violates a family's autonomy or independence from the professional network, a kind of boundary violation occurs, leaving the family with feelings that may be similar to the child's about loss of control over personal space, appropriate autonomy, and safety.

Is there also perhaps evidence that the children exhibit similar patterns of power and control in their relationships outside the family? For example, were the behaviors of the V children with each other and with their peers similar to the patterns of Mr. V's wielding power over his wife through economic and legal advantage as well as superior physical strength? A family's control of its secrets from the larger system may be seen as isomorphic to the patterns of control exercised in family relationships created and maintained through the keeping of secrets. Conversations about these isomorphic patterns could yield information about the process of maintaining power and abusing power as central themes in relationships.

Conceptualizing these problems exclusively in terms of power, however, may reduce the problem of family violence to a description that is distorted in its simplicity. Family interactions can also be conceptualized in terms of connections and loyalty. From a perspective allowing for the existence of multiple realities, it is possible to describe relationships that are simultaneously maintained through abuse of power and the dynamic of connectedness (love) and loyalty.

Forms of Child Abuse

As noted at the beginning of this chapter, family violence affecting children includes sexual abuse, physical abuse, and those situations in which children witness violence to beloved individuals, pets, or property. There are similarities among systems in which there is violence, regardless of the form the violence takes, but there are enough differences that each type deserves to be examined separately. Principles of assessment and treatment are presented after each general area of violence affecting children has been described.

Physical Abuse

Physical abuse is more likely than sexual abuse to be tolerated in contemporary society. Compared with children who are sexually abused, physically abused children are less likely to be removed from their families, and the helping system is generally less intensely activated, despite the harsh reality that children can die from physical abuse.

We have many questions and few adequate explanations as to why parents beat their children. In a society where violence is a central theme in daily television viewing, for example, it is perhaps not puzzling that there is violence in the family. Many experts in the area of family violence believe that the more physically powerful people in families abuse the smaller and less powerful family members simply because they can (Gelles, 1985).

When this somewhat simplistic explanation is favored, effective treatment focuses on building social control mechanisms into the family so that family members appoint their own "police officers." As in the situation of child sexual abuse, the first priority for the entire spectrum of larger-system members is to protect a child from further physical abuse. This may mean that agents of social control must go through investigatory and criminal procedures without eliciting genuine cooperation from the family itself. Generally, no attempt is made to explain why there is violence in this family but not another. That is, the investigation itself tends to decontextualize each family without seeking connections between patterns within the families being investigated and other related families.

Punishing and instructing parents about the evils of child abuse may constitute some measure of deterrent, but it is unlikely that patterns of physical abuse will change significantly when parents have no historical descriptions to inform their choice of conflict resolution. It seems likely that treatment must find a form in which each adult's experience of physical violence, both present and historical, can be voiced.

Violence against Parents, Pets, and Property

A child may be extremely traumatized by violence exerted by an adult against the child's mother, a family pet, or personal property belonging to the child or someone else in the family. In cases of repeated sexual abuse or physical abuse, children often develop a sort of protective numbness that allows them to distort the reality of what is happening to their own bodies, whereas when the children witness violence against someone or something dear to them, they may experience a level of terror or survivor guilt that is traumatic at a different level from violence experienced at first hand.

This sort of family violence is, quite unfortunately, least likely to be interrupted or treated by the helping system. Child advocates are currently overwhelmed with the vast numbers of children who are in need of protection from direct sexual and physical violence. Family therapists are most likely to view violence between parents as a marital issue; children are routinely excluded from the treatment of spouse abuse. Violence against pets and personal property is generally overlooked, no matter what the model of treatment.

If we could begin to comprehend these indirect kinds of violence as forms of terrorism against a child, we might find that our conversations with families would take on richer meanings. Where does this particular form of terrorism come from? When an adult destroys the property of a child or abuses a family pet, to whom is the communication directed? Often this is a complex form of communication that is an outburst of anger at or attempt to demonstrate power over the victim. It may be a destructive adult's message about roles in the family, and also a reverberation from the societal level of violence.

Often a child who has performed a sadistic act against a pet or another child is brought into treatment. The triad of firesetting, bedwetting, and cruelty to animals has been associated with extreme emotional disturbance and has been called a predictor of a future criminal. Because the other family members' violence against property and pets is more easily concealed from the purview of social services, school and/or medical personnel, and the various therapists who may be treating the child, it is understandable that a locus of pathology will be found within the child. It is imperative that therapists find better ways to participate with families in explorations of their mutual unhappiness, assuming that such violent behaviors in a child can be a manifestation of family patterns. "Mutual" does not, of course, mean "equal." A child may be devastated by an act of terrorism in the family; for instance, a girl may have seen her mother being beaten up by her father, or a boy may have unsuccessfully attempted to protect his dog or his bike from a stepfather's violent temper outbursts. The abusing adult may be simply guilt-ridden. Certainly remorse and devastation are different in experiential intensity. When helpers and families can discuss the unhappiness and frustration experienced by all members of the system, it becomes more likely that difficult questions can be asked and toxic secrets can be explored. In working with multiproblem (read "multiagency") families, layers of mistrust can often be penetrated by genuine compassion for the families's unhappiness and historical repetitions of inter- and intrafamilial violence.

Child Sexual Abuse

Child sexual abuse is the form of family violence that currently attracts the most public attention and agency involvement. It is worth an expanded discussion because it is a paradigm for examining the complex issues that involve larger systems and the family.

Many writers who have recently addressed the proliferation of reported child sexual abuse have commented on the controversial nature of the problem. It has been described as "the psychological equivalent of a disaster for victims, parents, and professionals alike" (Summit, 1986, p. xi). It is becoming increasingly clear that clinicians cannot easily separate the effects of the abuse itself from the repercussions of multiple-system involvement (e.g., courts, social services, and medical and mental health personnel). Lower-socioeconomic-status families may be more likely to experience the stigmatizing effects of multiple-system investigation and intervention, because they are overrepresented in public agency involvement. Researchers have documented enough evidence of child sexual abuse in middle- and upper-income families, however, to conclude that sexual abuse is not overwhelmingly relegated to one social class. The difference that counts, clearly, is how the problem is defined and treated, depending on the class, race, or ethnicity of the family.

THE LANGUAGE OF SEXUAL ABUSE

Child sexual abuse has been known to us, until recently, as something inflicted on children by strangers. Pedophiles have always been despised by society at large; neither the child victims nor their families were blamed in such cases. Treatment did not usually involve family therapy per se, for families of the child or of the offenders.

Now that sexual abuse is known to occur within the family as well as outside it, the helping system has taken on many new roles in beliefs about and involvement with these families. The language of the legal system—a language that assigns blame—has established the prevailing myths and stereotypes concerning individual family members as well as families as a whole. Fathers, stepfathers, uncles, grandfathers, and boyfriends are seen as "offenders" and "perpetrators," which gives them criminal status. The criminal is viewed as someone who should be removed from society as well as from the victims of his crime (i.e., his family).

STEREOTYPICAL DESCRIPTIONS AND CLASS PREJUDICE

In a society where criminals are judged according to their socioeconomic status—consider a low-income black man accused of rape, for example, versus Claus von Bülow, a wealthy socialite accused and twice acquitted of murdering his wife— the state may be more inclined to remove the lower-class male offender from the family than the less criminally implicated middle-class father, uncle, or grandfather. Low-socioeconomic-status families are also more likely to be viewed as incompetent in cases of alleged and/or substantiated child sexual abuse. It is assumed that a child from such a family will generally be better provided for as well as better protected in a setting away from the family.

Families that have histories of conflict with helping systems are especially susceptible to fragmentation by social service interventions. A symmetrical escalation emerges in which a family's mistrust of helpers is amplified, while simultaneously the helping system finds increasing evidence that the family is not "cooperative." The family is thus considered not capable of or not willing to utilize the resources offered by social services. In an attempt to "rescue" the children, the social representative scrutinizes and controls the family's mobility and choices; the family fights this intrusion, blaming helpers for family problems rather than attempting to find solutions to their violence-associated distress.

MOTHER BLAMING

Mothers of sexually abused children are defined by slightly less criminally influenced language, although they are implicated as "colluding" with the perpetrators or are viewed as accessories to the crime. The language of a referral source may strongly influence how the treatment involves a mother. If the mother is seen as chronically involved with social services (as many low-income mothers are obliged to be), she will be blamed either overtly or covertly for contributing to the situation that allowed the abuse to occur. She is seen by professionals and by society at large as failing in her biological role as mother. She is not placing her children's needs before her own; she is unnatural because she appears deficient in the necessary maternal qualities of fierce protectiveness, infinite accessibility to her children, and so on. When she is ambivalent, seeming to protect her husband or male partner more than her child, she is viewed as giving in to her own needs, being too weak or cowardly to confront actual or potential male violence, or being apathetic and self-absorbed. In fact, she may be severely debilitated or depressed by too much responsibility for family life, economic stressors, and/or a history of personal unmet emotional needs (Gelinas, 1983). Thus mothers in lower-income families are less likely to be involved in any sort of expert role of management or treatment than are middle-class mothers who have not previously been much involved with social services. It is a sad irony that women are traditionally held responsible for the well-being of the family and thus expected to seek help when the family's well-being requires it, while on the other hand they are blamed for becoming too involved and/or too dependent on helpers (Imber-Black, 1986).

Mothers who are known to be chemically dependent are doubly stigmatized if they are lower-income and/or single parents. Despite the well-known evidence that many mothers of sexually abused children are themselves incest survivors (Gelinas, 1983; Meiselman, 1978; Sgroi, 1982), helpers tend to see these mothers more as "bad" parents than as victims themselves. The helping system may offer various kinds of treatment, from substance abuse counseling to educationally focused groups for mothers of abused children. Overworked and understandably overwhelmed helpers often take on the principal support and protection of the children instead of involving the mothers in this role.

Children who have been sexually abused are usually seen by the legal system and by social services as victims of a crime, in need of care and protection from the helping system. This perception is especially strong if the child is young and/ or is from a lower socioeconomic background; if one or both parents appear to have a chemical dependency; and/or if the child is living in a single-parent family. Families in which sexual abuse is alleged to have occurred are generally characterized in the existing literature (and in the popular mythology of helping systems) by intergenerational transmission of abuse, lower socioeconomic status, significant social isolation, and higher-than-average social stress (Gelles, 1985).

Assessment for Change via Treatment

The parent or parents who are physically or sexually abusive generally develop a complex armor of defiance, fear, anger, and shame. Because women are socialized to be less physically violent than men, mothers are often more distressed than fathers when they have been physically abusive to their children. It may be difficult for an abusive parent, especially a mother, to voice the complexity of shame and distress and to experience a genuine relationship of connectedness with the therapist until the parent's own historical (family-of-origin) experience of family violence has been voiced.

In attempting to avoid a linear description, "*A* causes *B*," family therapy can fall into its own trap—that of focusing on reciprocal relationships and obscuring the differential in the individual family member's resources and options for defending himself or herself and/or leaving the field. And emphasizing structural rearrangements sidesteps the complexities of family loyalties and historical descriptions. Both approaches, the systemic and the structural, may overlook the importance of the evolving family–helper system created by the particular route that has brought the two systems together.

General Rules and Questions

A more flexible or useful way of assessing family violence should allow all family members and each part of the helping system more openings to join in a genuine and more richly layered description of the problem. One important way to assess the problem of violence is to explore the history of each family member's experience of violence and violation. By exploring the interactional patterns of violence, including violence of adults versus children, males versus females, and "professionals" (legal system, schools, social services) versus family, a language may be developed that goes beyond the cartoon dimensions of "bad guy–good guy" limitations.

There are several general rules for assessment of children in potentially violent families:

1. Actual danger to a child must be determined. Sometimes this can be accomplished through direct questions to the child and/or family members.

2. A family's capacity to allow nonmembers "in" must be explored. Can the family allow any secrets or unacceptable behavior to be known?

3. Beliefs about violence must be articulated by each member of the system. Does a family have religious or cultural beliefs supporting some types of violence, such as "A father has the right to beat a mother" or "Parents have the right to beat children"?

4. How has a family experienced outside "help" or "surveillance" over time? Some families feel victimized and labelled as "bad"; other families have long histories invoking outside "help" (clergy, social workers, the police) in times of family conflict.

5. Assessment of each family member's capacity to reveal shameful material is necessary in order to find "openings" in discussion of current violence (or its potential).

The asking of these assessment questions is, in fact, part of the treatment because the questions encourage the clients to join in mutual exploration of their own positions, creating, together with the therapist, a "mutually evolving meaning system." The therapist asks questions such as these: "Who was your mother, [father, grandmother] most likely to talk to if she [he] was worried or fearful about something? Would you be more likely to seek help outside the family for a medical problem or a problem involving conflict in the family? Who else would do the same? Who would be most likely to disagree with your solution?"

In the discussion of issues raised by general questions about secrecy, privacy, control, and authority, intervention has begun. The asking and answering of specific, necessary questions about current violence are more likely to lead to viable intervention if the therapist and family members are developing a genuine conversation about the meaning of their relationship. Hence, questions about control, privacy, and authority are critical to both the assessment and the treatment of family violence.

The V family described previously offered the therapist a rich, though distressing, history. The therapist learned their history because she took the trouble to listen, instead of attempting to pry out their "bad" secrets or to accuse them or to point out their inadequacies.

Mr. V, a Polish immigrant, had escaped the Germans during World War II. He had vivid memories of being a small child and running beside his mother through a nightmare of wounded and dead bodies. He also remembered the dreadful uncertainty of waiting for several years, alone with his mother, to find out if his father and brother were going to reappear, not knowing whether they were alive or dead. His fierce protection of his current family from incursions of a dangerous external environment become understandable in light of this history.

Mrs. V was herself the victim of an abusive family system. She was the oldest daughter of alcoholic parents; she was caught between them and their struggles with each other, and her struggle to keep them from hurting each other. She was both victimized and dependent on them, being overly close to her father at times and treated with cruelty and hostility by her mother.

Both Mr. and Mrs. V perceived themselves as outcasts in their communities, survivors of violent and traumatic childhoods. As their stories began to unfold with the therapist, it became clear that they were united in viewing the world outside their home as a dangerous place populated by an anonymous mass of untrustworthy people. By closing out the outside world, they had found a solution to their fears of the unknown and the unpredictable. Unfortunately, the solution created new problems for them.

Mrs. V grew increasingly overwhelmed by the isolation and boredom she experienced as the children went off to school and her husband left for his factory job. With no peer support, no friendship with neighbors, and no contact with family members, she began the process of self-medication through alcohol, which eased the immediate pain and loneliness of daily life. Alcohol seemed to fuel her anger toward the family members as both jailers and fellow inmates.

Because the children had learned the parents' beliefs about the dangers of the outside world, apparently neither they nor the father felt they could turn to anyone for help. Desperate and exhausted, the father and children drew closer together, episodically joining the mother in using alcohol and drugs (apparently attempting to alleviate the pain, fear, and frustration of their situation). Problems escalated as one child after another appeared at school dazed, bruised, or belligerent. The more the outside world of school counselors and social workers attempted to enter the family, offering assistance or escape, the more the family responded by closing ranks—a process that further increased the stressful internal atmosphere inside the home.

Asking about the "Unspeakable"

When the time comes to ask the direct and often threatening questions about physical or sexual violence, it is obviously much more useful to involve all family members, including designated perpetrators of the violence, in a cooperative effort to name the unacceptable behavior and to change it.

If treatment is going to help adults to manage their expectations of children (or their anger and frustrations), it is imperative that adults be also helped to voice their ambivalence and that the children be held accountable for respecting parents' efforts. Parents may, on the one hand, be defensive concerning their right to exert physical control over the children and at the same time may be ashamed that they are following in the footsteps of their own parents. Children may provoke parental violence out of the expectation that that is how things have been and will be.

In a conversation to create a mutually evolving meaning system, therapists and family members may be able to work profitably with the idea of the "abuser" and the "victim" being one and the same person. Naturally, this will have meaning for the family's and the therapy team's understanding of the family's historical description of violence.

The resource of time is a significant treatment issue. The "30 years' war" is too often the reality for families embattled with helpers over several generations. Families and helping systems who find themselves in an ongoing war need time and patience if old patterns are to be examined and altered. Working with "outlaw" families that have a history of conflict with helping systems may be seen as somewhat akin to the work of a naturalist who sits silently for hours, day after day, waiting until the natural inhabitant of a space is finally willing to allow itself to be observed (and has had the opportunity the observe the naturalist).

Do Problems Create Systems?

Systems theorists have begun to look at problem-determined systems rather than at the unit of the family alone (Anderson, Goolishian, & Winderman, 1986; Hoffman, 1985): "The problem is the meaning system created by the distress and treatment unit is everyone who is contributing to that meaning system" (Hoffman, 1985, p. 387). This system fits the currently evolving scenario of the treatment of abuse, particularly sexual abuse. The family is suddenly invaded and generally separated into various individual and group treatments. In addition, the accused "perpetrator" may be incarcerated. Certainly the family as a whole will be involved in an elaborate and often lengthy process of investigation. This leads to an expansion of the system, including not only the family members, but also a multitude of clinicians, protective workers, legal representatives, police, medical personnel, and so forth. If it is determined that the child (or children) should be placed in foster care or the home of a relative, then another family enters the "meaning system" as well.

What does this complex, unwieldy system mean to an abused child? The child has already experienced some degree of trauma, betrayal, stigmatization, and powerlessness. As the distress of the abuse becomes amplified to include the distress of the disclosure, the system created by the problem may present a new source of confusion, fear, guilt, betrayal, and powerlessness for the child.

In their eagerness to protect the child, those who extract the disclosure and determine the intervention may inadvertently force the child to silently endure the overwhelming guilt of disloyalty. The child may be more frightened at the imagined, or real, consequences of the disclosure than he or she was by the injunction to keep the abuse secret before the disclosure.

It is more the exception than the rule that an abused child is treated with any family members. If other family members are included, it is usually only the nonabusing parent and siblings. It is almost never the case that the child is treated in sessions that include both parents. Fear, confusion, and loss may escalate for the child. He or she not only is separated from the family for treatment, but is separated from it by being removed from the home. The "problem-created system" begins to take on a life of its own. The distress of the abuse may be buried beneath an avalanche of even more overwhelming problems: the family's separation; individual and collective shame; financial hardship; legal confusion; and the stigmatization experienced by victim, abuser, and nonabusing parent alike.

When members of the helping systems are at odds themselves as they try to manage all of these potentially incompatible relationships with the family, the family and the entire sprawling treatment system become stuck. No one is sure how to work with this large and now enmeshed system. The family quite often has become, or appears to have become, so dependent on the involved helping systems that there is mutual concern about the possibility of viable autonomy.

Researchers following the lead of Bateson have offered a point of view that may move us beyond the descriptions of both legally minded child advocates and "power-blind" family therapists in the search for more useful ways to approach the overwhelming epidemic of child sexual abuse. Hoffman (1985) describes how the thinking of scientific philosophers such as von Foerster, Maturana, Varela, and von Glasersfield allows us to consider the possibility that "objectivity" is "in the eye of the beholder" (p. 385). She suggests that the problem itself, not the family, is "an ecology of ideas." If we see that the significant system includes the family, the helpers, and whoever else is observing their situation, we begin to focus on an evolving meaning system.

Rather than accenting the potentially victim-blaming notion of positively connoting the sacrifice by the child for the good of the whole family, or simply describing what structures are in need of repair, the "second-order" cyberneticist may find ways to generate a fluid exchange of descriptions of the situation. As has already been stated, this "conversation" is the function of circular questioning; it allows each member of the family, along with protective agents of social services, child therapists, adult therapists, and observing commentators, to voice their experience and feelings, as well as to respond to the experiences and feelings of other participants. In such a forum, the evolving meaning system may discover a wider variety of modes for communication and change.

One such forum for conversation, for example, may allow family and helpers to collaborate in a description that will lead to a change in who needs to be further apart in the family and who needs to be closer. Another conversation may lead to an understanding that the family system needs more autonomy from helpers.

There are clearly limits to how and when such an approach may be workable. In cases where immediate protection of a child is the first priority, attending to this may precede any attempt to collaborate with family members and helpers to find helpful, healing meanings for a painful, injurious situation. On the other hand, considering the question of who can best protect the child with the family and helpers, at the time when removal is being contemplated, may result in another action's being taken or in the placement of the child's being at the request or consent of the parents. Although perhaps no method is as certain as legal consequences to protect children from continued involvement with abusive adults, it is also clear that "the children's verse, 'sticks and stones can break your bones, but names can never hurt you' must be questioned" (Hoffman, 1985, p. 391). If family members are named according to their perceived roles in the abuse—"victim," "offender," and "accessory to the crime" (the role the mother is often assigned in sexual abuse)—then, as we have seen, names can hurt. At another level, by calling the family a "structurally dysfunctional system" or a "system engaged in mutually maintained sacrifice of one for the good of the whole," we freeze richly complicated and dynamic beings into virtually one-dimensional objects, thus inhibiting any real possibilities for helping a complex human system to change and grow.

It is becoming increasingly clear that the child's experience of being physically or sexually abused by a family member varies greatly, depending on a complex web of factors, only some of which we can name (e.g., age of child, role of abuser in the family, secrecy factors; in sexual abuse, degree and type of coercion involved, type of sexual activity; etc). If a goal for the therapist is to find, with the family, a meaningful description of what has occurred instead of ascribing one type of preferred language or another to the family, we may enter a domain where genuine work for family and therapist together can begin.

The Dilemma of Getting the Secret

In any situation involving legal consequences, secrets are not offered up easily or willingly. In most instances of abuse, particularly sexual abuse, there are additional issues of shame, loyalty, fear, and confusion. In most cases these are issues for all family members, not the abused child alone.

Those who are charged with protecting the child from further abuse and with applying criminal procedures must work quickly, often without much regard for gaining genuine trust and cooperation from the family. However, those who are concerned with treatment must consider the context and process of building a cooperative relationship with each family member.

An important component of this task is the creation of a mutually constructed language or description of the situation, the family, the problem, and the potential changes. Can the family as a problem-determined system (a group of individuals with both discrete and connected beliefs) experience therapy as a series of "conversations"? Can each participant be allowed responsibility for constructing his or her own description of the abuse? In this kind of treatment, the process by which relationships are built up and a meaning system is constructed will be determined by several factors: What sort of possibilities for a therapeutic team exist? Is the therapist able to do this work without a team? Is each family member's contribution to the process respected? How long can the treatment system and the family work together?

In the instance of Ms. J, a single mother struggling to parent a 12-year old daughter and a 10-year old son, it appeared that the system had created a dangerous problem. When Ms. J had been with the children's abusive, alcoholic father, the children had been placed together in two successive foster placements to insure their safety while they were of preschool age. When the daughter was aged 8 and the son 6, the mother recovered them after leaving their father. The environment was then deemed "safe" enough for the children, despite an ongoing concern that the mother, too, had a drinking problem.

For a period of 3 or 4 years, a succession of social workers and school personnel experienced frustration in their attempts to help Ms. J gain control of her drinking and her children. She was especially worried about her daughter, who displayed temper tantrums; the family was on the brink of being separated once again by worried and disapproving workers.

During 6 months of family therapy, a more open relationship developed between the previously belligerently self-protective family and the professional system. Treatment included an actively participating team. The team had conversations about close, caring family relationships and questions that invited family members to express genuine descriptions of confusion, humiliation, and frustration.

Questions included the following: "What would happen if Ms. J was invited to design the family's treatment plan? Would Ms. J, her daughter, or the department of social services caseworker be most enthusiastic? Who would be most surprised if Ms. J could contain her daughter's tantrums? Who would be least surprised?" The process of developing a real "conversation" with this family was guided by periodically including the mother behind the one-way mirror and having her act as "supervisor" to the therapist in the treatment room with the children.

Following the cooperative connection between family and helpers, more openness developed between the mother and her daughter. The daughter was able to tell her mother that an adult male friend of the mother's had been sexually molesting her for approximately a year. Ms. J sought appropriate helping services, but also was able to be the principal source of support and protection for her daughter.

The successes in this case were multiple: The members of this family, previously paralyzed by the involvement of multiple systems and confused by too many conflicting professional voices instructing them on how to behave, were gradually able to find more productive, useful ways to describe their problems. As they found their genuine voices, they were able to tell each other about events that were engendering increasing fear and guilt. The daughter was able to tell her mother about the sexual abuse, breaking the silence that was a product of fear—fear of betraying herself, her mother's friend, and her mother. The silence had continued, at least in part, because the child was afraid that to reveal something "bad" would jeopardize her mother and the existence of their reunited family.

The therapist may discover that for genuinely open relationships to be created, therapy must take place both in the conversational domain of a group, including the family and the team or therapist, and in individual meetings. A recurrent criticism of family therapy has been its form. The conversational domain of team and family, together, may not be the most comfortable setting for an individual to expose his or her experience of shame or fear (Miller, 1988).

How does one begin talking about a family's experience of abuse when the rule of secrecy prevails? How can the therapist avoid replicating the experience of violation—that is, how can the therapist not violate the clients' control of the secret? If the therapist insists that an individual disclose his or her self-abusive behavior, or the abuse inflicted on him or her by someone else, is the therapist reabusing the client by this act of personal boundary violation?

Most of us who work regularly with substance abuse or with eating disorders have been influenced to think that we must confront clients with direct questions and direct statements about their eating or drinking or drug use. We have also been influenced to believe that the admission of the alcohol or drug or eating problem is the first and potentially most important step toward recovery. The field of abuse treatment, particularly sexual abuse treatment, shares some of these beliefs. Great emphasis is placed on getting the disclosure of the abuse, both in working with child victims and in work with adult survivors.

Here is the issue again of creating the safe space, the work of approaching the clients' silence. If we go back to the metaphor of the naturalist, we can clearly see the problem here of allowing clients to observe and evaluate the potential for safety with the therapist. If we approach the silence with a direct command to tell the secret (or secrets) of abuse, we will surely not be perceived as very safe.

Model for Mutually Evolving Meaning Systems

What I have been working out for myself is a sort of map of the treatment territory. My first concern is to try to explore how the setting for the conversation may feel to the clients. I ask myself, the clients, or whoever else I am sitting with: 'Are the right people present to hold this meeting or conversation? Who is missing? Is there someone who may also have something to contribute to our conversation, and, if so, how did it happen that he or she is not here? Who is absent from the conversation but feels present?"

When I explain to other people what I do, I describe the treatment as if they could actually see it drawn on a piece of paper, with an order and a shape to it. I explain it as a sort of series of concentric circles, in which parts of the treatment are separated from other parts. I describe the outer circle as distinct from the middle circle, both of which are separated from the core of the treatment (or the inner circle).

This map exists, of course, only in my head, and treatment never happens in such a neat, orderly, and compartmentalized way. For didactic purposes, however, let us pretend that this is actually how it happens.

The Outer Circle

The outer circle is where I begin the conversation. I go to this place no matter what kind of treatment has already taken place. I begin at the outer circle, for example, even when clients have already told a dozen other therapists about problems involving abuse. I begin there even when I have been working with a wife and her husband and teenage daughter for 20 sessions, in which all we have talked about is how upset everyone is about the daughter's truancy. I also begin at the outer circle when a client is meeting with me for the first time and says she wants to work on her distressing memories of being abused as a child.

The outer circle feels best to me when I have the opportunity to include the therapy team in this space. I also prefer to have more than one person who is part of the clients' life outside of therapy present for these conversations.

Outer-circle questions are about the issues of safety and control of information and space: Who wants to be participating in this meeting and who does not? How has it happened that these people came to therapy—whose idea was it, and who thought it was a good idea? I ask what might have changed or not changed if the clients had decided not to come to therapy.

While still in the outer circle, I ask questions about the history of the problem or issue the client's are describing. These questions are both historical and present-focused, and they are not so much about the content of the problem as about its meaning to everyone involved.

I spend a considerable amount of time exploring the theme of secrecy without ever asking to be told any secrets. For instance, I may ask historical questions about the keeping of problems inside the family: "If your mother was worried about your father for some reason, who would have known about it? Who would not have known? How are things different now if you are worried about someone in your family, like your husband or one of your children? How do you understand the difference between keeping problems to yourself and your mother's beliefs about that?"

The transactions that occur at this place in the conversation are a series of discussions about possible premises. The premises I am searching for are those that inform the clients about their relationship to the problem that has brought them to therapy. The problem, of course, may not actually be the stated problem. So the premises I am listening for are about something that may not yet have been named. I am also listening for the premises held by others who are in the conversation, possibly including the premises of other involved professionals, as well as all members of the family.

The issues we talk about in the outer circle are quite purposely not the issues of abuse. Here are some guidelines for the work of the outer circle:

1. The format for the conversation can include the clients and others who are part of their life or who they believe are connected to the problem they have brought to therapy. Also included can be the therapist and a team of colleagues.

2. The problems discussed should be expanded beyond the abusive behavior to include other life problems of significance to the clients.

3. The questions purposely avoid the problems of abuse, even if one or more of the clients have addressed the abuse or self-abuse directly themselves. This is because the therapist is allowing some space and time to occur in which the clients can be observing the therapist and making some internal decision about whether it really feels safe to discuss abuse. This is also because the therapist is learning the clients' story as it pertains to the issue of retaining control of secrets and to the experience of shame and fear, and is learning how close other people can come to the clients without overwhelming them and taking control away from them.

4. Premises about power, control, and age or gender privilege are being explored.

5. The use of secrecy as a form of protection is of special interest for conversations held in the outer circle.

The Middle Circle

The next phase of treatment involves moving to the middle circle, or "speaking about the unspeakable." At a point in the developing relationship between the therapist and the clients, it may begin to feel that the time has come to approach the silence (or the untold story). Sometimes the direct questions about abuse and self-abuse are asked by the therapist. These questions can be asked more indirectly by using a team of colleagues. Either way, the questions are less invasive if they take the form of wondering what it would mean to the clients to ask about abusive behavior.

Questions can include the following: "Who would be most relieved if I were to ask about situations of people in the family being hurt by each other? Would it be easier to talk about the problem of drinking or hurting someone else in the family? Would it be easier for this conversation to take place in X's presence or absence?"

At some point, I ask (or the team may ask) if the time has come for the clients to decide how they want to proceed with the conversation. We ask that they make some decisions about the direction we should go. We might ask, for instance, if a child would like to continue the conversation alone or with her mother present. We ask how each member of the family thinks he or she will react to that choice and how each thinks the other will react. This is important because it allows the family to have some feeling of control, but also allows us to assess how dangerous the conversation may seem to the child or a parent.

Despite careful preparation for both therapist and clients about what it will mean to tell secrets of both abusing and being abused, it is still a large and threatening step to take. In stepping into the inner circle, I have been very much influenced by the work of Denise Gelinas (1986), who emphasizes the importance of family loyalties and family resources. Even when the clients have decided to give up control of their secrets, they are generally tormented by the feelings of guilt and fear engendered by being disloyal to the family.

The Inner Circle

Generally, the inner-circle work happens in a conversational domain involving only one client and one therapist. This, of course, means that anyone in the problem-determined system may participate in the inner-circle point in treatment: Conversations/sessions may take place between the therapist and the child/victim, the therapist and the abusing parent, and/or the therapist and the nonabusing parent.

The rule for work in the inner circle is that the client must feel safe enough to be able to disclose the details of the abusive behavior. These disclosures are almost invariably both painful and shameful for the client. The therapist has become sensitive to this family's particular history in regard to the keeping of secrets, the meaning of violence, the experience of allowing professionals to be involved in family business, beliefs about "rights," and power dynamics. This sensitivity allows the therapist to support the telling of the most painful, shameful secrets.

When the abuse story has been told, many possible choices emerge for intervention. It is from working in the inner circle that the therapist is able to work with the family rather than against it in helping to facilitate necessary separations and to begin the work of building healthier family relationships.

During the period of time in the inner circle, it may become clear that the child victim is not the only family member in need of intensive treatment for posttraumatic stress. Both the offending and the nonoffending parent may also be in need of such treatment. Peer groups may also be necessary to help parents work on their own problems of substance abuse (including alcoholism), issues as adult children of alcoholics, or forms of addictive behavior commonly found in families where there is violence.

One family team, working over a period of 2½ years with the W family in which there had been sexual abuse, found that they were able to make a genuine connection with Ms. W, a single parent, when the therapist met with her individually after 2 years of family team meetings. It appeared that it was necessary to first explore layers of family history and beliefs. It was also important to allow a period of time for the family to explore the team's beliefs as well. It was only after this lengthy period of mutual exploration that the therapist was able to connect with the mother for the first time, in a more private, intimate setting of individual meetings. In this setting, the mother disclosed that she herself had been sexually abused; she then admitted allowing her youngest son to sleep in her bed until he was 15. This son had been placed in a residential facility after sexually molesting several younger children—the event that precipitated court-mandated family therapy. Gradually it became possible to address questions of substance abuse in the family, as Ms. W began to take charge of a chronically out-of-control situation.

The path to real openings for new description and explanations in this case was a long one, complicated by departures of therapists and team members, as well as the involvement of three different consultants. It seemed, however, that the increased richness of so many voices matched the complexity of the family's story, and this combined successfully with the more intense connection between the mother and the therapist created in individual sessions.

Conclusion

In working with families where any form of violence impinges on the rights and well-being of children, the helping system has not generally been able to approach the situation slowly and cautiously. Neither the legalistic language of the child advocate system nor the language of family therapy seems to have adequately addressed the complexity of the situation. This chapter addresses the need for a treatment context that allows each family member, along with involved helpers, to describe how the problem has created a "meaning system" of its own. When there is an immediate need to protect a child from further violence, those who are designated as agents of social control must, of course, follow their mandate. However, the family as a whole, as well as each individual within it, remains in need of treatment regardless of what must be done to protect the child. A conversational domain is needed in which family loyalties are respected; genuine descriptions of family unhappiness are revealed; distinctions are made between mutually maintained and equally maintained interactions; and new options for change, separation, and growth are created. The differences in power, resources, and freedom to leave the field, as determined by gender, class, age, and race, must be named.

This process may need to take place over several years. The form may alternate among family meetings, individual meetings, work with a primary therapist, work with someone helping the family and the helper system to work more cooperatively, and work with an observing team whose job it is to reflect what appears to be happening in the family and in the family–helper system.

REFERENCES

Anderson, H., Goolishian, H., & Winderman, L. (1986). Problem-determined systems: Toward transformation in family therapy. *Journal of Strategic and Systemic Therapies, 5,* 1–14.
Bograd, M. (1986). A feminist examination of family systems models of violence against women in

the family. In M. Ault-Riche (Ed.), *Women and family therapy* (pp. 35–45). Rockville, MD: Aspen.

Gelinas, D. (1983). The persisting negative effects of incest. *Psychiatry, 46,* 312–332.

Gelinas, D. (1986). Unexpected resources in the family therapy of incest. In M. Karpel (Ed.), *Family resources* (pp. 327–358). New York: Guilford Press.

Gelles, R. (1985). Family violence: What we know and can do. In E. Newberger & R. Bovine (Eds.), *Unhappy families* (pp. 1–9). Littleton, MA: PSG.

Hoffman, L. (1985). Beyond power and control: Toward a "second order" family systems therapy. *Family Systems Medicine, 3* 381–396.

Imber-Black, E. (1986). Women, families and larger systems. In M. Ault-Riche (Ed.), *Women and family therapy* (pp. 25–33). Rockville, MD: Aspen.

James, K., & McIntyre, D. (1983). Reproduction of families: The social role of family therapy? *Journal of Marital and Family Therapy, 9,* 119–129.

MacKinnon, L., & Miller, D. (1987). The new epistemology: Feminist and socio-political considerations. *Journal of Marriage and Family Therapy, 13* 139–154.

Meiselman, K. C. (1978). *Incest: A psychological study of causes and effects with treatment recommendations.* San Francisco: Jossey-Bass.

Miller, D. (1983). Outlaws and invaders: The adaptive function of alcohol abuse in the family–helper supra system. *Journal of Strategic and Systemic Therapies, 2,* 15–27.

Miller, D. (1988). Women in pain: Substance abuse/self-medication. In M. Mirkin (Ed.), *The politics of family therapy.* New York: Gardner Press.

Sgroi, S. M. (Ed.). (1982). *Handbook of clinical intervention of child sexual abuse.* Lexington, MA: Lexington Books.

Simon, R. (Ed.). (1986). Lifting the shade on family violence [Editorial]. *The Family Therapy Networker.*

Summit, R. (1986). Foreword. In K. MacFarlane J. Waterman, *et al., Sexual abuse of young children: Evaluation and treatment* (pp. xi–xv). New York: Guilford Press.

Taggart, M. (1985). The feminist critique in epistemological perspective: Questions of context in family therapy. *Journal of Marital and Family Therapy, 11,* 113–126.

The Local Community and the World Community

There has been a pattern in this book, starting in Section Two with individual nuclear families, and expanding through each section to include more and more layers of the ecology of children and families. By the time we come to examine the layers beyond the agencies that commonly interact with families, most of the theoretical frameworks that have been useful for understanding individual and family functioning seem to fall short of offering effective strategies for assessment and intervention. The chapters in Section Five address issues that involve families *and* the institutions with which they deal.

Poverty is more than just a low income. Rather, it is an encompassing life style of opportunism and survival. It is not a life style that therapists and philosophers know a great deal about; nor do developmentalists and psychopathologists. But, as Parnell and Vanderkloot describe in Chapter 20, the neighborhoods of the poor have an atmosphere that can be appreciated by those few professionals who care to make the effort, accompanied by residents of the neighborhood who will serve as guides. It is a dangerous life for those who live in poverty, and there is danger for those who look in from without. Many professionals who work with the poor complain that they are difficult to engage in treatment, often miss appointments, and are late for the appointments they keep. The question is, for what do these people need treatment? Not the usual issues of loss, disappointment, or maladjustment that bring families to most of our practices. Poor families, when they ask for help, need acceptance of their situation, recognition of their efforts to make life livable, and assistance in identifying and connecting with any additional resources the sociopolitical system may have to offer to them. Parnell and

Vanderkloot bring these clients to life in their chapter, as they have assisted them to stay alive and together as families.

In Chapter 21, Webb-Watson transcends the usual categorizations of ethnicity in suggesting that it is not just certain customs of various ethnic groups that are different, deviant, or defective, or any cluster of characteristics identified with a particular group, but epistemology—the shapes of meaning with which each family, with its unique history and its unique present, rears and educates its children, and that those children carry into their futures and the futures of their own children. Therapists will always encounter ethnic differences in the families with whom they work, though some differences will obviously be greater, as when there are racial, national, or (as described in Chapter 20) income-level differences. Thus it is essential that therapists place their own values, shaped by their own ethnic epistemology, on a shelf while they inquire about the unique experiences of client families. What this means, ultimately, is that therapists, unshielded by their own assumptions, will become much more vulnerable to the actual discomfort and desperation of their clients. Webb-Watson's argument is so persuasive that I was moved to tears in reading of the insensitive remarks made to Jamal, a 7-year-old black child in an all-white school.

Chapter 22 deals with another aspect of culture and ethnicity—the experience of immigration, when families attempt both to assimilate themselves into a new culture and to find expression of their particular ethnicity in the new country. Bullrich emphasizes that the patterns of immigration transcend any particular cultural blend; she uses Prigogine's and Maturana's observations about perturbation and entropy to characterize the ways in which family systems encounter the processes of emigration and immigration. Assessing family stress in these systemic terms provides a level of explanation that involves all members of the family in the struggle, even when, as is usually the case, only one member is symptomatic.

Finally, in Chapter 23, Greenwald discusses the issue that hangs over the entire earth: the potential for destruction through a nuclear holocaust. This particular issue has often been described as a conceptual challenge. Nuclear warheads cannot be properly called "bombs," and a nuclear encounter cannot be properly called "war," since there will be no exchanges of salvos and no battles if a nuclear confrontation were initiated. Thus the vocabulary needed to discuss the "nuclear threat" is one that has to be invented; it is like no other experience in human history in its implications. As Greenwald touchingly describes through the words of children and parents, there is concern and helplessness—a helplessness that levels the differences between nations (in spite of the arms race), as well as the those between children, who are supposed to be nurtured and protected, and parents, who are supposed to nurture and protect them. In facing the nuclear threat, they are equally resourceful and hopeful, and equally helpless. Nevertheless, Greenwald asserts that families are the children's most important resources in facing the anxiety and the helplessness, and he presents his own model for working with families—to help them have open discussions about their worries; to take sensible action; and, ultimately, to feel available to each other, which is the best comfort they can offer.

20

Ghetto Children:
Children Growing Up in Poverty

MYRTLE PARNELL, MSW, AND JO VANDERKLOOT, MSW

Children who grow up in poverty do so under the most handicapping set of circumstances. In this chapter, we examine the lives of children and families living in poverty in the inner city—the hardships, the limits poverty places on development and mobility, the violence, and the crime, as well as the caring and sharing, the laughter and dancing, the striving, the values, and the struggle to survive.

In order to have a frame of reference for working with these families, it must be understood that their lives all take place within the context of a domestic war zone. A representative example is a community in the Southwest Bronx in New York City, which is served by the clinic in which we worked. Its population is 60% Hispanic, and 40% black, most of whom are supported by entitlement programs or are underemployed.

If one enters a ghetto of poverty such as that in the Bronx, one is confronted by an onslaught of senses, an assortment of unfamiliar odors, sounds, and sights: vacant buildings in various stages of disrepair, abandoned cars, rubble in the streets, noise from "ghetto blasters," people, graffiti, and movement. This is the view most often portrayed, the shameful view—shame for the community and shame for the country. The strangeness and ugliness of the physical environment, along with different accents and languages and ways of dressing and moving, engender

Myrtle Parnell. Private practice, New York, NY; New York University Graduate School of Social Work, New York, NY.

Jo Vanderkloot. Private practice, New York, NY; New York University Graduate School of Social Work, New York, NY.

437

a deep-seated fear born of unfamiliarity and not knowing how to evaluate the environment and its people. For the person who is white, middle- or upper-middle class, and new to the neighborhood, these feelings are valid. There is a sense that the people here do not count—not the poor, and not those who take care of the poor. There is an overwhelming feeling of sadness, vulnerability, powerlessness, and, finally, anger.

This is what strangers to the area may feel on their first encounter with the life space of the urban poor. With time and exposure, one develops the necessary basis for evaluating the actions of the people and the meaning of the environment. Only then does one have a basis for evaluating one's own role in it, and one's own safety. The best opportunities to learn how to move through this world into the heart of the ghetto and the hearts of the people who live there come through extensive interactions with black and Hispanic professional and paraprofessional coworkers and with the clients. These are the best teachers, forming a bridge to a community often unseen by the press or public. The devastated buildings and graffiti are sharply contrasted with the sounds and life of the people. Children are everywhere, playful and energetic. Numbers of men of all ages are in the streets; the women are often leaning out of the window watching their children and exchanging gossip with each other. The voices are generally unrestrained, animated, and lively. Ethnic music can be heard spilling out of the many small shops, and children dance freely as they continue down the block.

Penetrating further into this community, one finds an emphasis on people rather than on material things. Family and friendship networks are very important for emotional and economic survival. There is a particular sense of caring and generosity, and a willingness to give freely of oneself and one's few possessions. One notices how hard poor people try to make a difference in their lives. Their resilience and lack of complaints about often overwhelming hardships are remarkable. They seem to be sustained by the ability to get pleasure from even small material things and life events—liveliness, music, dance, good ethnic food, and the companionship of family and close friends. They may be sustained by humility born out of religious roots, which implies an acceptance of their place in the universe: They are here for a short time, nothing is promised, and they are therefore able to enjoy what they do have in the present.

But humility here is not to be confused with passivity. The people in poor communities are just as persistent and determined in their efforts to provide better opportunities for their children and themselves as any other group. Poor children and families expect life to be difficult, in contrast with middle-class children, who expect life to go well. These differing expectations bring different kinds of satisfactions and problems. Finally, poor communities remain a stronghold for some traditional values that may be pushed aside as people reach for more and more material gains. As Robert Coles (1987) observed about the family of Ruby Bridges, the first black child to attend a white public school in New Orleans, ''What struck me about the Bridges family . . . was that they were hard working people, religious people, long suffering people but with a purpose. . . . They had, I think it fair to say, moral purpose which they offered their child.''

These contrasts in life style, values, and moral purpose of poor families require not only appreciation, but the development of alternative models for treatment, because traditional approaches have failed to respond to these special needs of the urban poor.

Who Are the Poor?

Sidel (1986, p. xvi) has observed that statistics are really people with the tears washed off. Statistically, the poor are predominantly women and children. According to the 1984 census, 14.4% of all Americans—that is, 33.7 million people—lived below the poverty line, currently defined as $10,609 for a family of four (Sidel, 1986, p. 4). Although the majority of the poor are white, blacks and Hispanics are disproportionately represented: 46.5% of black children and 39% of Hispanic children live in poor families; in black families headed by women the figure is 66%, while for similar Hispanic families the number is 70.5% (Sidel, 1986, p. 3).

The majority of poor people live well below the official poverty line of $10,609. An employed adult who is paid the minimum wage of $3.35 per hour has a yearly income of $6968. Aid to Families with Dependent Children (AFDC) maintains families far below the poverty line. In 1984 the average poor family had a cash income of $6477 (Sidel, 1986, p. 5).

How the poor get to be poor is a question with many answers, depending upon who is viewing the problem and under what circumstances a remedy is needed. The existence of the poor has been a concern throughout modern history, and the attitudes about it have changed only slightly since the Poor Laws were enacted in England in the 17th century. The Protestant work ethic, with its emphasis on self-sufficiency, continues to be a part of all thinking and planning for the poor.

When the Protestant work ethic is the prevailing attitude, the poor are seen as lazy, incompetent, and willing to let others pay their way. Economic measures are taken to provide the minimum to keep body and soul together, or emphasis is placed on helping the poor develop more moral character so that they can learn to care for themselves. Some actually believe that low-income people are not really suffering because the "safety net" of entitlement programs adequately provides for their needs.

In more liberal times, poverty is explained by environmental limitations imposed by social systems driven by greed and self-interest. Measures are then enacted to improve these conditions and increase access to mainstream opportunities, such as more scholarships for higher education.

In the end, however, how the poor get to be poor is irrelevant to the clinical problems of working with the poor. Although the effects of poverty are many, and are likely to produce great physical and psychological destruction in children forced to live in such circumstances, there are also competent, caring, effective adults among the poor who can create environments in which healthy children can develop.

The Impact of Poverty on Growing Up

Poor parents have the same job to do with their children as middle-class parents do; the difference is that poor parents have less money, less education, and less access to resources and alternatives. Most live under extraordinary stress, facing constant crises centered around food, shelter, and physical illness; these lead to feelings of helplessness, hopelessness, and powerlessness. These feelings are based in reality and relate to forces largely beyond the control of the poor family. Much of the time and energy of the poor is focused on getting through a day. Yet tomorrow they expect to have to do more of the same (Chicago Tribune Staff, 1986, p. 95). Decision makers are never seen and cannot be influenced (Ryan, 1976, p. 253).

The notion that childhood occurs in a protected, nurturing environment in which growth and mastery are fostered is a luxury that is generally unavailable in the ghetto. Usually this is not due to parents' lack of caring or competence. Deprivations and stressors attendant to poverty can so overwhelm a child that he or she cannot grow into a functional adult and will be found among society's discarded people, such as alcoholics, drug abusers, drifters, and prisoners. The major impact of poverty not only can deprive a child of the basics for healthy living in the present, but can also bankrupt his or her future. Learning to cope with the pressure of poverty may lead to adaptation but not to mastery of those skills that society values (Powell, 1983, p. 296).

The degree to which poverty, or the combination of poverty and discrimination, affects a child depends on circumstances. Poverty due to temporary unemployment may not produce permanent scars; the child may develop additional coping skills as a result of such an experience. For the most part, however, the impact of poverty in the child's earliest years depends on the strengths and coping abilities of the significant adults in the immediate and extended family, and the mutual help networks of the family's friends. Children born to parents who have maintained supportive family and kinship networks stand a good chance of reaching school age with an adequate self-concept. However, even if they have been sufficiently nourished, have felt the love and protection of the family, and have been presented with learning opportunities that have fostered age-appropriate physical, emotional, and cognitive mastery, poor children will soon become aware that the larger society devalues them and their families because they are poor and of different race or ethnic identity. Although this perception by others does not automatically result in lowered self-esteem, it does present yet another stress for these children as they move into the larger community (Powell, 1983, p. 296).

For poor children, entry into school may be their first encounter with adults who do not understand their life experience. These adults most often come from a very different world. The intelligence, curiosity, and creativity that children develop in the ghetto do not look the same as these same qualities developed by middle-class children. School is ghetto children's first experience with the realization that they are seen as less than they are. Many children find that school is a means of enhancing and expanding their world, but ghetto children find new constrictions and dissonances between the values of the dominant culture and what is available to them. At home they generally live in a very small space; at school there is a larger space; after school they return to the confined living area, as there are few recreational facilities and the streets are too dangerous.

There are other new challenges to be met by ghetto children entering the school system. They enter classes in which the program is based on children's previous school experience, but since they may not have attended kindgergarten, they may not have learned to relate and work cooperatively with peers, or to accept the authority of adults who are not their own parents. Ghetto children also often do not have the comfort of parents skilled in negotiating the school system and helping them to master the basic subjects.

These disadvantages are amplified as the children progress through elementary school. Hirsch (1987) reports that poor and middle-class students learn to read in roughly equivalent time frames, but as they move beyond third grade, differences begin to accrue. Since reading is based on assumptions about background knowledge, poor children are at another disadvantage. "Around grade four, those who lack the initial knowledge required for significant reading begin to be left behind permanently. Having all too slowly built up their cultural knowledge, they find reading and learning increasingly toilsome, unproductive, and humiliating" (Hirsch, 1987, p. 28). By the 10th grade, the knowledge gap is so wide as to be unbridgeable.

As the children approach the age in which they are freer to be in the streets, school and formal education often become less valued. A child who accepts the value that material success is important to pursue is then confronted with a moral dilemma: Being streetwise, being tough, knowing how to "get over," selling drugs, stealing, engaging in prostitution, and running numbers are ways to "make it" in the ghetto, and the electricity and excitement in the streets are not often matched in the classrooms.

Even a child who is motivated to learn has difficulty in succeeding, in face of the lack of discipline in the school and the constant threat of bodily harm. These youngsters often drop out of high school when it is clear that teachers and principals cannot maintain enough order for them to learn, and their safety becomes their own responsibility. Bright children may go unacknowledged or unmotivated by their teachers, while at the same time they are ostracized by peers for being studious. Their choices are often either to join a gang or drop out of school.

A Basis for Therapy with Poor Families

The politics of the larger social system are not something a family therapist can tackle directly. However, intervening to ameliorate the impact of the social and political system on the lives of the poor is an essential part of the initial engagement process with a poor family. Family therapists cannot work with poor nuclear families in ignorance of the concrete issues of housing, nutrition, and health, or the abstract issues of discrimination and oppression, that these families encounter daily. In the end, family therapists can activate the families' own resources and help them connect with resources in the community, often guiding them through a maze of social services while they learn to utilize those of importance to them. As these families are taught to advocate for themselves and their children in these ways, they provide better opportunities for their children.

Although the focus of this book is on children in family therapy, it is very clear to us that, in view of the innumerable forces that influence the lives of the poor, intervening only at the level of the individual child is rarely the best and most effective thing to do. Respect for the family, and the expectation that its adults are able to function in the role of parents, are key issues. Thus it is important to enter a collaborative relationship with the adults to enable them to do their job better. Poor children are not sheltered from adult problems. It is important to protect them through elevating their parents' abilities to care for them. To treat a child in isolation from the multiple interlocking systems that impinge on his or her life is to ignore the reality of the child's world. Each child needs at least one competent, enabling adult available to him or her on a regular, reliable, basis. Therapy should focus on a search for, and extensive and intensive support of, that one adult or kinship system.

What are the issues for poor families seeking treatment? The clients are usually very aware that their world is different from that of clinicians, and their dilemma is how to present their problems in a way that will be understandable to the professionals. A corollary to this is the prevalent attitude on the part of many middle-class clinicians that poor people do not know what they need. The form of questioning may also lead families to feel blamed for their problems. The families, therefore, are rightfully afraid of being misunderstood and put on the defensive. This leads them to seek help mainly in crisis/emergency situations when they do not know where else to turn.

Poor clients may feel the need to present themselves at a clinic as "crazy" or with a chronic physical ailment in order to get much-needed help with basic survival issues. For example, a client may show up periodically with a variety of chronic symptoms in order to get a required letter for public assistance. Poor families are more often than not deprived of privacy, due to the number of agencies that are of necessity involved. There are, in addition, broader implications for poor children and families in psychiatric treatment. Their records are rarely kept as confidential as those for other classes. Young children are often referred by the school system, which then may place them in special education classes. Children and families may also come to the attention of other agencies, such as the community's child protective agency. These multiple-agency involvements may compound the sense of disdain and blame felt by poor clients.

Preparing the Mental Health Professional to Work with Poor Families

To begin working with families of the urban poor, the clinician, particularly the white middle-class clinician, must receive an orientation to the neighborhood and its people. This is best accomplished with the support of multiracial, multiethnic teams. Teams are also essential to deal with some of the most complex family situation. It would be difficult if not impossible for one clinician to work alone with some of these families, due to the pervasive nature of the problems. Having achieved an appreciation of the people in the ghetto, and developed a reliable relationship with professional colleagues committed to the same endeavors, the professionals working with this population need to be directive and to become a responsible, stable force for these families.

Clinicians must make no assumptions that they know anything about their clients—not the clients' values, nor their life style. "Successful communication depends on shared associations" (Hirsch, 1987, p. 59). Therefore, "communication between strangers requires an estimate of how much relevant information can be taken for granted in the other person" (Hirsch, 1987, p. 4). But where strangers share little information in common, communication must be, of necessity, lengthy and simple. The awareness of a lack of a body of shared information prompted one young black woman to observe that the client needed some personal information, "not deep personal information," about the clinician in order to feel some sense of common connection.

Issues of closeness and distance need to be interpreted differently. For example, in work with Hispanics, after rapport has developed, a client will often move his or her chair over close to the clinician. It would be erroneous to interpret this as an inappropriate sense of personal distance on the part of the client. A corollary to this is how the clinician learns to deal with feelings of discomfort over violation of personal space, and of apprehension when a client is emotionally expressive.

A Model for Work with Families of the Urban Poor

Our theoretical framework is influenced principally by the work of Carter and McGoldrick, Auerswald, Scheflen, and Erickson. Use of a trigenerational genogram presents an important sense of continuity over time, with repetitive patterns that have a richness of meaning for a family's history (Carter & McGoldrick, 1980). In work with the urban poor, where three or more generations may be living with or near one another, the trigenerational model is very useful in understanding the meaning of family issues and behavior.

Auerswald (1971) pioneered work with macrosystems in his work with the urban poor in the 1960s. He recognized the ways in which the individual influences and is influenced by larger systems. For an understanding of the life of the urban poor, an awareness of the overlapping of the larger systems, including the family, is absolutely essential.

Scheflen (1981) has explored finding the salient patterns being played out through all levels of systems, from the cellular to the social system. His work enables us to recognize that patterns that take place in individuals and families are often played out at other levels of social organization.

Milton Erickson's unconditional acceptance of the person is of paramount importance to our way of working. Representing an interesting departure from Freud's view is his belief that symptoms become skills when a person feels good about himself or herself, as well as his view of the unconscious as the repository for all life's experiences and the source of creativity, change, and growth. Essential to our way of working are Erickson's two requirements for successful psychotherapy: "Observe at as many levels and with as many senses as possible" and "be flexible, behaving in a way formulated to meet the uniqueness of the individual's needs" (Zeig, 1982, p. 66).

Working with Urban Poor Families

As we have already stressed, working with poor families requires an ability to improvise and to respond to the needs of the moment, and this often prevents the following of any carefully devised map or treatment plan. Nevertheless, there is a certain method underlying our work that can be articulated.

Assessment

The primary focus of our assessment is on the organization of the information provided by the family. The family data must be appreciated at a variety of functional levels, including spiritual and physical health, and the functioning of individuals, the family, and larger social systems. Assessment of these levels is achieved through the following four areas of exploration: use of trigenerational genograms and ecomaps; intense observation of verbal and nonverbal behavior; tracking of behavioral sequences; and exploration of the family's relationships with macrosystems.

THE GENOGRAM

The trigenerational genogram depicts major patterns in the family over time, the solutions and coping styles of the family, and the highest level of functioning over generations. The effects of these past generational patterns can be identified in the current generation. Major past family problems are often not openly discussed, but may continue to exert a powerful unconscious influence on presenting behaviors. For example, the issue of premature deaths in the family may, depending on particular cultural norms, be reflected in particular ways, such as psychosomatic or chronic illnesses in one or more family members; stoicism, with incomplete mourning and denial of pain passed down to the next generation as strength; or total immersion in a religion to find solace. Each of these solutions will have an unconscious effect on future generations' styles of coping.

OBSERVATION OF VERBAL AND NONVERBAL BEHAVIOR

Intense observation of verbal and nonverbal behavior begins with the very first information the clinician receives about the patient, from whatever source. For example, if the waiting room of the clinic or the clinician answering the telephone seems to be formal when the client's style is informal, the information given is likely to be somewhat different than it would be in a context more suited to the client's comfort and liking. Here there is an incongruity between information gathering and information that will bias the information. Another level of incongruity is between the client's verbal and nonverbal behaviors. Particular emphases, facial expressions, or body movements that are not congruent with the words provide important clues to the meaning of the problem behavior in the individual or family.

A single mother brought in her 12-year-old son and said that she could not stand him. She further explained that she was a lesbian and that the child was the product of a rape by the male friend of her female lover. The observed relationship between mother and son was strikingly at odds with the mother's complaint, however. She and her son sat close together and seemed affectionate. The son listened calmly to his mother, without reaction to her statements. When the mother was asked about her beginnings, it was learned that she and her son shared an almost identical history. She was also a product of rape, as was her own mother. What emerged as the problem was the mother's concern that her son was going out in dangerous places at night and she did not know where he was. After discussion of this, he agreed to call his mother to let her know his whereabouts. Over the next couple of sessions there were some discussions about adolescence, but this was all the intervention that seemed to be necessary.

TRACKING OF BEHAVIORAL SEQUENCES

Tracking the sequences of behavior gives another kind of information about meanings. The sequences will reveal both who is involved in maintaining the problem (including those who participate inactively) and the meaning attached to it.

RELATIONSHIP WITH THE LARGER SYSTEM

With a poor population, we always begin by dealing with the most urgent and obvious problem, which for many is the difficulty in negotiating with institutions and agencies of the larger social system. The pattern that connects a patient and a larger system is usually the same one that operates on other levels as well.

After initial data gathering, and at every step along the way, it is important to develop a hypothesis in which all behaviors can be positively connoted. Hartman and Laird (1983) point out that as information flows, it needs to be punctuated to give it meaning, and it needs to be framed.

Often our clients have had their experiences framed in a negative way. Positive reframing takes into account the unconscious meaning of behavior, which is circular and concrete rather than linear and abstract. It brings out the positive intentions behind seemingly problematic or obnoxious behaviors. Two innocuous examples are (1) children's bickering and battling that mirrors parental behavior and serves to disrupt marital battles and (2) school phobia concealing a child's fear that if he or she leaves the mother something will happen to her; the child's staying home keeps the mother from being lonely and from worrying about her child's safety. Paradox, a restatement of the family dance or the family's own paradoxical situation, is another important tool. It is accompanied by a genuine cautionary prescription, which supports the family's cohesiveness and warns it of the potential threat to its stability if change should be attempted (Hartman & Laird, 1983). We spell out the persistent problematic behavior that serves an important maintenance function for the family; the warning against change acknowledges the importance of the symptom to the homeostatic balance of the family.

Engagement of Poor Families in Treatment

The clinician's initial moves to engage the family are crucial. Since the poor frequently experience judgmental attitudes in their contacts with various agencies, they often expect more of the same and withdraw from treatment unless the clinician has demonstrated that this encounter will be different. Ideally, this process is aided by an informal and inviting setting rather than the more customary medical one.

The clinician should introduce himself or herself in a friendly fashion using first and last names, thus encouraging the client to choose the degree of formality or informality with which he or she is more comfortable. It is important that there be congruity in the form of address. Using one's title while addressing the client by first name is an immediate signal that this is a one-up, one-down situation, and the client feels denigrated. Clearly, the message is not one of collaboration with the client.

Among black and Hispanic clients, coming for assistance is not generally seen as a one-to-one transaction. They may bring other people whom they consider either significant to the problem or potentially helpful in its resolution. The therapist should, therefore, check to see who has accompanied the client and invite him, her, or them into the session. This move is usually met with appreciation.

The goal of the session is to understand the problem from the client's point of view, which requires that the clinician understand the context in which the problem is embedded. It is wise not to make any assumptions about the world of the client, but instead to pay attention to the concrete needs of the family, lest the reality of its world be invalidated and the therapist lose all credibility. Immediate intervention in this area is possibly the most powerful and most connecting engagement skill, regardless of the discipline of the clinician.

To support the family hierarchy, information is gathered from the adult family spokesperson; the positive intent of behaviors is underscored through reframing. Family strengths and competence are validated by connecting aspects of the client's lives that they had not recognized before. In our experience, people are much more aware of their shortcomings and much less cognizant of what is positive in their lives.

While engaging the adults verbally in the session, we alternately engage the children nonverbally through playful eye contact, often terminating this with a nonverbal question mark to see which child feels most comfortable about responding. During this process, it is not uncommon, for children (particularly younger children) to approach us and lean up against us or climb into our laps.

When a child is the identified patient, his or her behavior should be positively framed and normalized within the context of the family dilemma. The clinician may seek permission from the child to take over the role of worrying about his or her mother or significant other, so the child can worry about school work, friends, and so on. The child cannot succeed at taking care of the adults, but his or her efforts to do so are acknowledged, and the therapist tries to free the child to be successful at taking care of age-appropriate tasks.

The following is an example of a typical presenting problem with the child as the identified patient.

Carlos B, a 9-year-old Hispanic boy, was referred by his school for behavior problems. He constantly disrupted the class, ran through the halls at every opportunity, and did not respond to the teacher or assistant principal who attempted to discipline him. He was described as a bright child who did not apply himself. His mother was at a loss as to how to change this pattern; she had told the school that she had problems disciplining Carlos.

Ms. B brought her family to the first session as requested. This included herself, Carlos, and his sisters, aged 6, 8, and 11, who gave their mother "no problems." The family was attractive and neatly dressed; the children were playful with one another and immediately responsive to their mother's instructions to sit and behave. She seemed pleased with her children, especially when the clinician remarked on how very appealing the family was.

Ms. B gave the following information: She was the only female in a sibship of 7, and the only one living in New York. She lived next door to her mother and the mother's boyfriend, and Carlos was his grandmother's favorite. He often slept at his grandmother's house, visited her daily, and received many special treats. Ms. B's daughters were also close to the grandmother, but it was clear that Carlos was *"numero uno."* (Favoritism toward the firstborn and/or the only male child is customary in Hispanic culture.)

Ms. B reported that she and her mother rarely disagreed on the discipline of the girls, but frequently differed over limit setting for Carlos; she had resigned herself to letting her mother make the decisions, although she did not like it, because the grandmother got upset and told Ms. B she was disrespectful. Ms B was hurt by the implication that she might be considered a "bad daughter," and was also fearful of losing Carlos's affection. She had tried talking to her son, promising him special gifts if he behaved.

The therapist observed that Carlos must feel very bad when he saw that he was the cause of problems between two people he loved very much. Carlos immediately acknowledged that he did not want his mother and grandmother to fight. He said that he tried to be good, "but somehow it just does not work out that way."

The therapist observed that it is not unusual for mothers and grandmothers to disagree over some things; most of the time they are able to resolve these disagreements, but at other times they may need some help from a relative, a friend, or even a therapist. The children were asked to think of some examples of their mother and grandmother's working out problems together, and had no trouble doing this task. The children were praised for being such good observers, and their permission was obtained to work on the adult problem, so Carlos could stop worrying. Their mother also appeared to be relieved.

The mother and grandmother attended the next two sessions, which focused on Ms. B's feelings about the different treatment she had received as the only female child. Whereas Carlos was singled out for special treatment, Ms. B had been singled out in childhood for extra work and responsibility for the house and younger children. (Again, both Carlos's and his mother's roles are culturally and stereotypically appropriate in Hispanic families.)

Ms. B and her mother were able to discuss discipline of Ms. B's children and the grandmother acknowledged that her daughter was a very good mother. This statement was accepted as a priceless gift by Ms. B. There followed a discussion of the roles of parents and grandparents, and negotiation of the authority each would have in relation to the children. Both adults understood the necessity of being consistent in their treatment of Carlos and felt they could work together.

The family was living on welfare, but there were no serious, concrete service issues. Ms. B was able to negotiate the agencies competently, insuring that her family received the appropriate financial assistance without interruption. Ms. B had elected not to work for several more years, because the neighborhood in which they lived was so bad that she thought the family needed her to be available. The grandmother was not well enough physically to have the full daily burden of care of four young children, and Ms. B did not want to rely on older children or other adults in the neighborhood for child care.

The issue of Carlos's behavior was quickly resolved through negotiation with the two adults. This case was closed after the third session, though the family had an open invitation to return if they chose.

When hyperactivity is the presenting problem, as is often the case in poor communities, the child's activity interests are explored, and the family is helped to identify and locate active after-school and weekend activities. Usually when this has been done, the problem disappears, but in the few instances when activity programs are provided and the child continues to be hyperactive, a more intensive neurological evaluation is done.

The experience of poor children in their schools and in their communities is one of a series of restrictions on physical activity. Play space in their homes often consists of a small hallway or a room crowded with beds. If children live in public housing, the common hallways and stairs may be their playground. Outside, safe play areas are almost non-existent. School athletic programs, likewise, are also almost non-existent.

In many cases, it appears that the diagnosis of attention deficit disorder is a euphemism for behaviors that are annoying to adults and appear intractable. Our consulting psychiatrist, Robert Neal, uses the approach that children's energy levels vary greatly, and that some children have extremely high energy levels within a normal range. For these children, structured activity and athletic programs are essential. He points out that the schools that used to provide such programs for children no longer have funding for physical education (R. Neal, personal communication, 1987).

Using Data to Identify Treatment Approaches

A significant proportion of the information we gather in our assessment is based on nonverbal behaviors. Who comes to the session, who sits where, how close or distant people are, how comfortable people are with the situation, and how they wait to be seen are important data. People living 'close to the edge" may have difficulty with control when pressed. This manifests itself in agitation, pacing, muttering, and requests about how much longer they need to wait. These clients should be seen immediately, without debating the possibility of whether the behavior is manipulative; if there are children involved, it is imperative to assess the home situation and the client's ability to control themselves at other times. Immediately seeing a client who manifests these signs is helpful in building rapport, and generally has a calming effect on the person.

How the family members look, how they interact with one another and with the staff in the waiting area, and what the children are doing are also crucial data. In addition, what is the clients' attitude toward the clinician, particularly if the clinician is from another racial/ethnic group or class? It is always important to deal with these differences.

Many of these observations take place before the session actually begins. In the session, we pay attention to who talks and who does not, what they say they want, and whether they agree on the problem. Who is in the family network? What are their living conditions, what is their source of income, and how adequate is it? Where do they live, who lives with them, and where does everyone sleep? A woman who sleeps with all her small children in one bed may not be incestuous or exploiting her children's companionship, but trying to protect her children from rat bites. Such questions are always foremost on our minds, although they are not specifically asked if the answers are inferred through other contexts.

Key questions in determining the highest level of functioning for individuals and families are these: How long has the family been in poverty? what is their immigration status, educational level, employment history, and prior mental health treatment?

Before we continue, it is important to realize that the questions we have raised deal with the social context in which the presenting problem is contained. Keeping the questions in mind is important, but it is not necessary to ask them all or frame them in this way. They are merely a guide for understanding the problems of the urban poor in a different light from the traditional medical psychiatric model.

What are the cultural and religious values that will affect the possible solution to the problem? For example, for a traditional Hispanic family, virginity still remains a significant value. Helping these parents deal with adolescent development is significantly different in quality from helping parents of adolescents in black or white population. The issue of abortion must also be carefully explored for religious reasons. Another issue to consider is the educational background of the parents; parents who themselves have dropped out of school may have a *laissez-faire* attitude toward their children's education, because they do not see it as an avenue for achieving a better life or as necessary for employment.

In the verbal interaction during the session, it is useful to listen for idiosyncratic phrases and repeated use of particular verbs, such as "hit," "smack," and "knock" as indirect indications of possible family violence. Picking up on this indirectly is not only helpful to the clinician, but also to the family members who may be reluctant to bring up this issue.

Assessment of the macrosystem in which poor families function is an essential part of evaluating a family presenting for help. What may present as an individual problem will have another meaning when the larger system is assessed.

Cookie R was a very obese black woman in her 20s, the mother of three children, all under the age of 10. She presented with depression of 1 year's duration following the burning of the building in which she lived. She had been treated with antidepressants and supportive psychotherapy, but 6 months into treatment her clinician noted what appeared to be an exacerbation of her symptoms, despite compliance with medication. Cookie had been relocated to one of the worst neighborhoods in the Bronx. She was too ashamed of her enormous weight to go out of the house except when absolutely necessary. Her children had presented with behavior problems in school, and Cookie was unable to go to school for her appointments.

The children, aged 8, 7, and 4, were shabbily dressed, not very clean, and somewhat lethargic; they looked tiny next to their mother, who weighed close to 500 pounds. Cookie was overwhelmed by the loss of her home and subsequent relocation. However, in spite of her preoccupation, she was attentive to her children; she was aware and concerned about their needs and about her ability to meet these needs. She reported that she had little energy and was irritable with the children.

When the therapist presented the client in her team meeting case conference, she was criticized for paying too much attention to concrete issues rather than the "underlying depression." But the therapist maintained that the most serious worry for the client was another fire. Cookie had reported that plumbing was being stolen from the building—a sure sign that the building would soon be torched.

There were several possibilities for intervention in this family—children, mother, family, macrosystem. When an ecomap was drawn, it depicted a basically isolated person who had minimal contact with society's major institutions, except for school and welfare. She had no supportive contact with extended family or friends, nor with courts or churches. And she had no work experience, having first become pregnant at age 15. Based on this information, the clinician determined that if this woman were to function as a mother for her children, she would need to broaden her contacts outside the home and learn to harness the major support systems in her community. For these reasons, the most powerful intervention would be with Cookie herself.

What needed to be done was to empower Cookie to make the necessary changes in her situation, in order to provide for the necessities of life and the safety of her children. The therapist helped Cookie to document her poor living conditions with photographs, and led her through the court process as she presented her case; the judge ordered the landlord to make the repairs. The therapist then helped her to appeal to her state representative for relocation to an apartment in public housing. Once relocated, and with her self-esteem boosted by her successes, Cookie returned to school for her high school equivalency diploma and started classes at a community college. Simultaneously, she lost 100 pounds over the next 3 years.

As her living environment improved, and as Cookie was able to take charge of herself and her children, she began to follow up on the children's school performances, keeping in touch with teachers. Their behavior improved, once it became clear that their mother meant business.

The example of Cookie's family illustrates that there are life circumstances to which depression, irritability, and low self-esteem are appropriate responses. The intervention in this case was with the mother and her relationship to the macrosystem; the assumption was that Cookie, given appropriate relief from and support in dealing with her overwhelming situation, could more than competently provide for her children's emotional and physical needs. Prior to the fire, Cookie had adequately cared for her family. Her doubts about herself and her children would have been greatly magnified if someone else—a clinician or the foster care system—had been placed in charge. Cookie's areas of dysfunction were practically viewed as inexperience in dealing with housing and the school system. Her own

lack of success and feelings about herself as a failure made it difficult to deal with
the teachers' comments and assessment of her children.

Working with a Team

We have found that one cannot work with poor, multiproblem families without a team of professionals. This means that these families have a variety of
people at the clinic with whom they are familiar and to whom they can turn. For
members of the team, the involvement of the other members spells relief from the
recurrent crises, the chronic problems, and the many occasions when it is necessary to devote whole days to individual clients. Furthermore, the team members
function as a support group to one another, and as the nucleus of a resource
network.

One of our longest-running and most complicated family cases provides good
illustration of the importance of teamwork in responding to the needs of poor
families.

The family of Mary T had been involved with psychiatric facilities and treatments since she was a young child. She had had multiple psychotic episodes, had
been hospitalized numerous times, and had been treated with a variety of medications. When she began treatment with us, she had already been a patient at our
clinic for a number of years. At that time she had three children, and a fourth was
born during the more than 5 years we worked with her and her family.

The two older children, Meurice, 12, and Tammy, 8, had been in foster care
with relatives, and both were competent students. They were loving toward their
mother, in spite of the fact that she had spells when she thought Meurice was a
demon and that she would have to kill him; that she was often harsh with them;
and that she had frequent fugue states in which she would disappear and wander
the streets or ride the subways. Tammy watched over her mother and reminded
her to take her medication.

The younger two children were Kathy, who was a year old when we began
to work together, and Tommy, who was born later. Initially a sociable toddler,
Kathy developed slowly and was seen to be functioning at a mildly retarded level.
Tommy's speech was slow in developing, and he, too, required special attention.
It was only some years into her relationship with us that Mary allowed us to work
with her children. It took that long for her to appreciate that we would not either
turn them against her or take them away from her.

INDIVIDUAL WORK WITH MARY

Our work with Mary and her family has had many chapters, and is a good
example of the improvisational work that must be done with this multiproblem-
ridden population. Mary was our central concern, as she was the center of her
family—a center of gravity whose holding force sometimes threatened to deterio-

rate and allow the children to fly off in all directions. Foci of attention included Mary's episodes of psychosis and our need to find solutions other than medications and hospitalization.

Typical episodes involved Mary's delusion, noted above, that Meurice was a demon and she must kill him. When Mary knew she was in trouble, she would come to the clinic requesting medication. Since the medication would not help immediately, she developed fugue-like states in which she would wander the streets, not being able to recall where she had been or whether she had been with anyone. She would first feed the children and ask a friend or family member to watch them, and then would go out to ride the subways or walk the streets alone until morning. Hospitalization was not really a viable alternative in these situations, because Mary herself would not agree to go voluntarily. When brought to an emergency room for psychiatric evaluation, she always had the ability to pull herself together so as to avoid involuntary commitment. Instead, she would walk out with some medication and a referral back to our clinic.

As it became clear that these fugue-like states were precipitated by her fear of loss of control and served to remove Mary from a situation in which she could do her children serious harm, or harm herself, we ceased for the time being to encourage Mary to stay at home; instead, we crossed our fingers, hoping that she would come to no harm while wandering the streets.

One approach to exorcise the demons involved attendance at a church, where one therapist spent the day with Mary while the minister and "sisters" (older female members of the congregation) prayed over her for the entire day. Mary was very calmed by this, and returned for the next day.

During another of these times, the psychiatrist employed a reversal of a hypnotic induction. This technique worked (for a longer period), and the fugue states all but vanished. Mary was given a suggestion that she could take her medication and close herself in her room to protect her children. She began to do this except on rare occasions when she would resume her wandering.

On still another occasion, Mary, in a paranoid psychotic state, crawled under a desk where she remained for the next 5 hours, whimpering whenever she heard footsteps in the hall. Mary was too afraid to allow anyone else in the office, so the therapist kept up a soothing flow of conversation as she attempted to write in her charts. Part way through the afternoon, Mary seemed much improved and felt she could go home, but after she left it was discovered that her chart was missing!

DEALING WITH MARY'S FAMILY EXPERIENCE

Mary's genogram reflected several generations of poverty, families on welfare, and involvement with drugs and alcohol.

At the level of her own parenting, Mary's strengths were her standards for her children; her attention to keeping them clean, sheltered, and well fed; and her fierce struggles to keep them with her. Furthermore, when she became aware that she might be a danger to them, she went away to protect them.

Early on in the treatment, we identified and met with all the competent, enabling adults who were involved in caring for Mary and her children. (Mary's mother was the only one of her generation who was on welfare.) We met with and spoke frequently with Mary's aunt, but had only one conversation with her sister, who was a frequent caretaker. It was important to Mary that she appear competent to the members of her family; she preferred to deal with them by herself as much as possible.

One of us kept in regular contact with the homemaking service to be assured that we had the most stable and competent people available. She was very cooperative. Frequent meetings were held with the homemakers, and they kept in touch by phone as problems emerged. Homemakers provided help to those clients determined by the physician to need help in the community due to physical or psychiatric illness. Almost all the women were warm and nurturing, quickly becoming absorbed in the family. They would also take the children home from time to time when Mary was having difficulty, or just to give her a break. Mary, in turn, took good care of the homemakers, giving them ample time off daily when she felt in control of herself.

One source of persistent grief and humiliation for Mary was the death of her fourth child as a young infant. The baby had never come home from the hospital and was unceremoniously given a pauper's burial by the hospital authorities.

For the first year or so, Mary dealt with the loss of her child as she dealt with all losses—namely, by becoming psychotic. It was during this time that she learned that her mother was terminally ill. She denied on and off that this was the case, but in the process began to think of life without her mother. With us, for the first time in her life, Mary had someone in whom she could confide about her struggle. This seemed to make it possible for her to talk about her baby daughter's death in a different way, without psychosis. She had never visited the graves of any of the people she had lost. Her family's way of dealing with the anniversary of a death was to ignore it and fight with each other. We thought this might be a good opportunity for Mary to learn that mourning is a normal part of living. We suggested a visit to the cemetery, which she immediately accepted.

The cemetery was more than an hour's trip by car from the clinic. Mary brought along her closest friend for support. Once at the cemetery, we were directed to an area of unmarked graves that was unattended and overgrown. As we approached the approximate gravesite, we noticed the mound of dirt alongside an unaccompanied, tiny pauper's casket awaiting burial. Mary took in the scene, became very quiet, and noted the similarity to her own child's burial. At this point she became quite hysterical, fell on the grave, and sobbed; finally, with time, she moved from tears to prayer.

During the period following the death of Mary's mother, the family was in turmoil. There were disagreements on religious grounds about the funeral, and one part of the family refused to attend the services. Mary was unable to attend the wake without the therapists. We accompanied her and remained through the first viewing. Mary was later able to attend the funeral in the company of family members without becoming psychotic. To everyone's surprise, the mother left her insurance policy to Mary. There was so much protest in the family about this that

Mary decided she did not want any of the money and turned the policy over to her siblings. The important thing for her was that her mother had remembered her in the end. Mary's relationship with her mother became an issue for treatment.

On the level of her own generation, Mary was the only one of her siblings not involved with drugs. She had a great attachment and loyalty to her siblings; she would take them into her home when they needed shelter, and would usually end up being exploited by them. On the other hand, the network of relatives who were relatively competent appeared to contribute to Mary's perpetual sense of being incompetent. There were several occasions on which we found ourselves drawn into a perception that the children were being abused or neglected; we ourselves would contact the child protective agency, only to realize that we had been inducted into the family pattern of scapegoating Mary.

After her mother's death, Mary took in her two brothers, both drug-addicted, and finally was forced to leave with her children for a shelter after she was raped by a friend of one of her brothers. The shelter experience was another serious episode in the work with Mary and her family, because it activated more of Mary's fears and bizarre behaviors, endangering her tenure in any shelter. The team, once again, had to become closely involved with shelter personnel in order to prevent eviction.

After 4 months, we were able to get Mary and her family into a family shelter consisting of apartments, where they would be permitted to stay up to 6 months. During this time the shelter staff was able to get the family an apartment in Harlem in a badly deteriorating building. There were (and still are) no decent apartments available in New York City for those on a welfare budget.

In the therapy of the last 5 years Mary has dealt with the loss of her baby; the death of her mother, uncle, and brother; the loss of her home; life in a city shelter; a move to a new area of the city; the launching of her 18-year-old son, Meurice, into independent living; and trying to help her daughter Tammy have a healthier adolescence than the one Mary had 25 years ago.

In the past 6 months Mary has separated from her boyfriend (the most supportive boyfriend she had ever had, but also an alcoholic), and lived through the brutal murder of another close female friend who lived in her building. She continues to have her extremes, and to require emergency psychiatric treatment from time to time, but she has come to see the members of the clinic team, led by us, as a basic resource for both her and her children.

Dealing with Resistance

If the clinician adopts the stance that he or she knows more about the client's needs than the client does, there will definitely be resistance, either covert or overt. When the clinician makes demands that do not fit the client's life style, or problem (e.g. "Come in once a week for 45 minutes and we will talk about why you are feeling so depressed"), he or she will also meet with resistance in the form of unkept appointments and/or lateness, or dropping out of treatment. If the client really needs concrete help and the clinician is reluctant to provide it because of fears of creating dependency, the client is unlikely to return.

Resistance is a red flag signaling the clinician that he or she is missing essential information about an alternate direction; it is necessary to enlist the family members' help as to how they might find it easier to cooperate.

When clients resist the therapist, what forms is the testing likely to take? We have already mentioned "no-shows" and coming late. In addition, clients will frequently mismanage a simple task to see whether the clinician is both interested in and capable of resolving the problem. They may withhold information, particularly if it shows the clients in a competent light and/or gives the therapist a small problem to deal with to test his or her competence and staying power. Clients who have had experience with generally unresponsive bureaucratic systems may not be willing to invest themselves in work with another clinician until they are certain he or she is not just going through the motions. Poor people have generally experienced clinicians as having very little staying power for the powerlessness and frustration of poverty. Usually if a problem is not resolved on the first or second effort, the clinician determines that the client has not tried hard enough, or in some way is at fault. He or she begins to quote agency policies and procedures as a way of discouraging the client from returning.

A classic example of this scenario is the woman who comes in requesting a letter for a face-to-face appointment with welfare that was scheduled for half an hour ago. The clinician informs the client that the agency policy states that such requests must be submitted 10 days in advance, to give the doctor time to sign it and make a copy for the file. One can certainly understand how easy it is to fail the client's test. We would propose two alternate responses. First, the clinician may fill out the letter, as requested, with full awareness that without the letter the client will have her welfare case closed. Second, the clinician may deal with the issue as one of testing and look for the smile of understanding. If no indication of understanding follows, the client has a much more serious problem in functioning and absolutely should not be sent away. What may be construed as being "too nice" to the client in these two responses in reality prevents the client from allowing her own frustration to jeopardize her benefits; also, the second response may provide the clinician with information about a severely dysfunctional client. In both instances the client, if given the letter, is likely to return for the help she needs.

An example of a resistant family that was enabled to engage and cooperate is the H family. This family was referred from the medical clinic, following discovery of venereal disease in the mother and her 20-year-old retarded daughter. None of the agencies that deal with abuse of adult children would intervene because of fear of violence on the part of the husband/father, who was named as the likely donor, since neither mother nor daughter left home unaccompanied.

Mother and daughter agreed to be seen by the author following the referral from the medical clinic. Mrs. H aged 51 but looking much older, arrived wheezing at the clinic. One glance revealed a very timid, frightened, and anxious woman.

She was accompanied by her obese 20-year-old daughter, who was sloppily dressed, grinning inappropriately, and obviously nervous.

Both women were very apprehensive about involving the department of psychiatry with the father, whom both described as very violent. The clinician explored their living situation and family network. The problems raised by these two consisted of the following concrete issues: There had been no heat or hot water for the past 6 months; the oldest son was in jail; the second son, who was named after the father, had been killed by the police under suspicious circumstances that had not been resolved during the past year; the father was an alcoholic and had lost his job as superintendent of the building 8 months ago; the youngest two children were retarded and in and out of special schools; the mother was severely asthmatic and in general felt unable to cope.

The family was invited to come in to work on the concrete housing issues, as well as to receive assistance in finding out what had happened to the dead son. Mother and daughter felt that the family would be very willing to come any time. An appointment was made for the following afternoon; the entire family arrived punctually.

The 54-year-old father was disheveled, unshaven, and tearful as he talked of the loss of his son and how it had happened. All family members had brought memorabilia (watch, wallet, pictures, etc.) to show the clinician, and they all took turns reliving what had happened almost exactly 1 year before. It was clear that this issue deserved high priority; until it was resolved, the family could not deal with anything else. In addition to the loss of the son and brother, the whereabouts of the firstborn grandson were also unknown. The family suffered a deep sense of having been violated and unrepresented by the police and the courts.

In subsequent sessions the family was connected to a Hispanic caseworker, who linked it to a Puerto Rican agency specializing in the kinds of legal cases in which foul play was suspected. In addition, work was begun on helping the family with its housing situation. At this time the family felt understood, and therefore had no need to resist. Because the clinician had respected and responded to the family's need, particularly that of the father, she became a respected authority to whom the family members readily turned for solutions to other problems, including, eventually, the issue of incest.

During the process of treatment, the father again became a dry alcoholic and found another job as a building superintendent. The two youngest children were doing well in training programs for eventual job placement in a medical setting, about which both were enthusiastic. The mother took her rightful place in the bedroom; the daughter was adamant that she was now capable of keeping the father at an appropriate distance. This was not a miraculous cure for this family. The family continued to function marginally in terms of the larger system, but was returned to what had been its highest level of functioning.

In this family, attempting to deal directly with the presenting problem of presumed incest between the father and his daughter would undoubtedly have been responded to by resistance from the family. The therapist's recognition of the factors most troublesome to the family, and her offer to address these, allowed the family to enter into a working relationship that was meaningful to them.

The S family is an example of one whose resistance was a major problem throughout our relationship to them. We recognized that it was based on the dignity and pride of Mr. S, and we continually struggled to make our services available to him on terms that he could accept without further humiliation.

Mr. S was 40, a single parent, and sole guardian of his 9-year-old son, Dennis. Our experience with Mr. S and Dennis spanned 2 years. Dennis's behavior in school was the initial problem, although it was immediately apparent that Dennis's father was suffering from an almost disabling depressive disorder. We quickly discovered that all of our efforts to address Mr. S's depression directly were rebuffed, whereas our involvement with him in the endeavor to make a better life for Dennis was usually successful.

In keeping with our principle of accepting the clients where they are, we evaluated Dennis's school situation by contacting his teacher. She confirmed what we appreciated during the first visit—namely, that Dennis's behavior problems were minimal. His teacher described him as a well-behaved child who occasionally got into mischief with two other boys. There had been a few incidents of pushing and shoving, which temporarily disrupted the classroom. He had been a consistently good student until recently, when his homework was occasionally incomplete. His teacher was concerned that Dennis sometimes looked sad, but generally saw him as a very likable child who responded well to adults as well as his peers and was consistently helpful in the class, often volunteering for various jobs as a monitor.

In contrast, Mr. S's situation was problematic on many different levels. He had immigrated from Jamaica and had done well initially; he had been employed as a manager of an auto supply store, which closed. He had been unable to find a comparable job since that time and had been too proud at first to accept a lesser position. He was used to having a well-furnished apartment, stylish clothing, and money for the many trips he took with his son. When he had money, he was generous to family and friends, but found to his disbelief that his generosity to others was not reciprocated. Since the loss of his last job 2 years ago, he had become increasingly despondent. Once in that state, he could not pull himself out, and things went from bad to worse. His relationship with his girlfriend deteriorated as he felt more stress, and he began "smacking her around—not really hurting her, just letting her know when she was getting on my nerves." After one such "smacking around" she filed a complaint and pressed charges. The more hurt he felt, the more his pride got in his way. He had some "discussions" with the judge that had led him to be found in contempt of court. He was sent to prison for a few days without having a chance to make plans for his son. Dennis, then 7 years old, had been left alone, and his father was not permitted to contact anyone for 24 hours. He was so devastated by letting his son down in this way that 2 years later he was tearful when he spoke of it; his rage and hurt were as intense as though the incident had happened yesterday.

Dennis reported that when his father had not come home he had been worried, but he had fixed himself something to eat and went to bed. The following day he got himself to school. Later, he stopped by a neighbor's house to tell her he was alone. She agreed that he could stay with her after school until his father returned.

Our assessment of this case was that Mr. S's personal pride was a resource to his son, but would also be a barrier to direct treatment of his psychiatric condition. The boy had several important resources: his father's consistent concern for him; his neighbor's continued caring for him; and his own strengths, including a pleasant personality, resilience, and a commitment to reciprocating his father's caring for him.

We attempted both directly and indirectly to address Mr. S's depression by involving black male staff members at our clinic. One was the team psychiatrist, who spent a long time with Mr. S and concluded in his assessment that Mr. S's depression required antidepressants. He also expressed his belief that Mr. S was not willing to connect with anyone and that possibly only a minister would be able to reach him. Mr. S refused the antidepressants; he also had no church connection and did not want one. Another staff member who tried to help was a mental health worker familiar with a West Indian church, who offered some culturally familiar healing, However, Mr. S, while acknowledging that this should be acceptable, was still too proud to ask for personal help. When he shifted temporarily from his focus on his son to his own problems, he insisted that the only way we could be of help to him was to reopen his court case and clear his record of the contempt-of-court charge. This, he said, would enable him to regain his dignity and manhood, which he must do before his life would be right again. We agreed to help him get a lawyer to reassess his case but found there was a $1\frac{1}{2}$ year waiting list for free legal services for nonemergency situations. This further depressed Mr. S.

Mr. S showed up at the clinic sporadically for the first 7 to 8 months. The more ashamed Mr. S felt about his situation, the more sensitive he became to real and imagined slights, readily challenging the offender. This frequently led him into fights with neighbors who had previously been his friends. On one occasion such a fight resulted in a leg injury that laid him up in bed and occasioned a home visit by the therapist. Living on a public assistance allowance did not work for Mr. S. He became even more depressed when he could not provide a "proper meal" for his son. He did not pay his rent, electricity, or any other bills. He also could not tell the clinician what was happening when he received an eviction notice. At that point he made a suicide attempt and was hospitalized for 8 days.

The therapist received a phone call from a social worker in a hospital asking for information about the patient, Mr. S, and reported that he had taken an overdose of medication. He had managed to take himself to the emergency psychiatric unit of the hospital and took Dennis to his neighbor.

We learned from this experience, with the help of an anglo colleague, that when a person of British West Indian background indicates that he is in pain he will usually do so in an understated way, often without emotion and without directly asking for help. However, the mere fact that he gives any indication that he is troubled should be taken seriously, and suicidal ideation should be explored. In working in the black and Hispanic community, where the affective component is usually very readily available, these minor cues can easily be overlooked.

Mr. S's hospitalization was not the first time that placement had been considered for Dennis. This had been an ongoing consideration between the therapists and the father, who felt that he was not doing justice to his son in his current situation. But Dennis was well cared for by the neighbor, whom he seemed to love; and, since the hospitalization was to be short, it was decided to make no changes in custody arrangements at this time.

During the months following Mr. S's hospitalization, he worked with the therapist almost daily to resolve his concrete issues (rent and utility bills). The biggest problem was the landlord's desire to evict Mr. S because of his quarrelsomeness. As the problems continued almost unabated, he made another suicide attempt and was again hospitalized. Dennis again stayed with his neighbor, and the possibility of placement was again considered. In a meeting with father and son together, Dennis admitted that he was afraid that his father would hurt either him or himself. He was less hopeful than he had been that things would work out, and admitted that he would like to be placed. Mr. S, however, refused to have his son placed, but after some further discussion agreed to think it over. In the meantime, the neighbor was still looking after Dennis; Mr. S gave her money, and she cooked for them daily.

A West Indian minister in the area was contacted and became involved with Mr. S. Mr. S was delighted to be able to talk to a fellow Jamaican whom he could respect, and he felt respected and understood by Reverend B. He was then able to connect with the clinician in a different way. At this time, he was more open about his finances; the clinician helped him file for Social Security benefits based on his years of employment. She also referred Mr. S to Special Services for Adults, with the hope that this agency could prevent his eviction; however, as his resources dwindled during the waiting period, he became increasingly angry with his circumstances. He also became worried that he might hurt his son and called us, saying that he had decided to place Dennis. He wanted to take charge of his life; he did not want anyone to help him. In conversation, Mr. S informed us that he had contacted the child protection agency to request placement. He said he planned to go home and wash and iron all of Dennis's clothes, so that his son would appear well cared for as he entered his foster home.

With Dennis securely cared for, Mr. S got to work on his own situation. With our help, he made appointments for physical and dental care and for job training. He enrolled in a home study course for truck driving.

Mr. S worked hard to get his life into shape for his child. He spoke with Dennis weekly, but refused to visit him, so ashamed was he of having had to place him. When it was clear that his employment as a truck driver was within reach, he had his first visit with his son and then made plans to take him out of placement as soon as he was established on the job.

We had no further contact with Mr. S after he received a retroactive disability check of $5000 from Social Security. With a very broad smile, he said that he felt like a man again. He was extremely pleased that he would be able to keep his promise to Dennis to buy the bike that his son wanted for Christmas. Dennis, he said, was going to have a very good Christmas.

He assured us that he would not squander the rest of the money, but had some plans to use it for a new start. He gave no details. At our last contact, Dennis was still in placement, with his father visiting regularly. Mr. S said that he had some friends who could use our help and he was sending them to us. This was his way of saying thank you and goodbye.

The S family is an example of a family that had fallen into poverty and found it an unexpected and humiliating state. The family was an unusual example of a single-father-headed household. The strengths of the child seemed related, in part, to his prior level of comfort and the general level of expectation that things would get better.

Conclusion

In this chapter we have endeavored to bring tears, strength, and dimension to the statistics on the poor. We have presented aspects of treatment of several families, emphasizing the principles we have enunciated about working with the poor, respecting their basic strengths, supporting adult networks, and activating the resources in the larger system.

We have presented a clinical model for working with the poor that is basically nonblaming and nonpathological. We have shown that helping the parents of poor children to do well what they most want to do has a powerful effect on the children and the family. We search for that part of the parents that fiercely wants life to be better for their children than it was for them. We validate the totality of the client's experience, and thereby form a powerful bond with the parents and children. We are seen as "we" rather than "they" when we work in this way. One of our patients (a convicted rapist), when he asked himself what was different in our treatment of him, said, "All the other people were nice and helpful, but it is as if I were out in a canoe in rough water. Everyone else was standing on the shore calling out directions. You dove into the water, swam out, got into the canoe, and showed me a new way to shore."

If we as clinicians are not prepared to "dive in," difficult as that may be, it will be hard if not impossible to capture the attention of poor children and their families. They are so busy struggling just to stay afloat that there is little energy left to focus on anything that is not immediately useful in the resolution of those struggles.

REFERENCES

Auerswald, E. H. (1971). Families, change and the ecological perspective. *Family Process, 10*, 263–280.
Carter, E. A., & McGoldrick, M. (Eds.). (1980). *The family life cycle*. New York: Gardner Press.

Chicago Tribune Staff. (1986). *The American milestone: An examination of the nation's permanent underclass*. Chicago: Contemporary Books.

Coles, R. (1987). *Moral purpose and the family*. Keynote address to the Family Therapy Networker Symposium.

Hartman, A., & Laird, J. (1983). *Family-centered social work practice*. New York: Free Press.

Hirsch, E. D., Jr. (1987). *Cultural literacy*. Boston: Houghton Mifflin.

Powell, G. T. (1983). Coping with adversity: The psychosocial development of Afro-American children. (pp. 49–73). In G. T. Powell, J. Yamamoto, A. Romero, & A. Morales (Eds.), *The psychosocial development of minority children*. New York: Brunner/Mazel.

Ryan, W. (1976). *Blaming the victim*. New York: Vintage Books.

Scheflen, A. E. (1981). *Levels of schizophrenia*. New York: Brunner/Mazel.

Sidel, R. (1986). *Women and children last*. New York: Viking Press.

Zeig, J. (Ed.). (1982). *Ericksonian approaches to hypnosis and psychotherapy*. New York: Brunner/Mazel.

21

Ethnicity: An Epistemology of Child Rearing

LINDA WEBB-WATSON, EdD

The TV is turned on during a typical weekday afternoon. A familiar refrain enters the room:

> Here's a story of a lovely lady
> Who was bringing up three very lovely girls.
> All of them had hair of gold, like their mother,
> The youngest one in curls.
>
> Here's a story of a man named Brady
> Who was bringing up three boys of his own.
> They were four men living all together
> But they were all alone.
> [You're supposed to forget they had a housekeeper.]
>
> Till one day when this lady met this fellow,
> And they knew it was much more than a hunch,
> That this crew should somehow be a family—
> That's the way they all became the Brady Bunch.

Mrs. Washington (her name could also be Chen, Rodriguez, or Ghiradelli) hears the music and knows she is about to be exposed to a half-hour of fairy tale. In fact, it's so fantastic that she is a little annoyed at herself for taking time to watch it What interests her about the program is that the parents are so wish-washy,

Linda Webb-Watson. Salesmanship Club Youth and Family Centers, Dallas, TX.

lacking the proper strictness to bring up children adequately. The children have too much to say in the day-to-day operation of the family. How would any mother manage six children with each of them being so individualistic? Of course, Mrs. Brady doesn't work and she has a housekeeper. Still, six children are quite a handful, as anyone knows. Mrs. Washington wonders how much easier raising her own four children would be if she could afford a housekeeper and enough space so they wouldn't have to spend all their time in the same room. She knows, however, that she would never allow her household discipline to become so lax. Her children would be more respectful, and they would be more careful in their contacts with the outside world. "You can never be too careful," she thinks. "The Brady children are just too free and don't take precautions against the dangers out in the world." Mrs. Washington also notices that the children are not really responsible for one another. The oldest son and daughter, Greg and Marcia, do not have any responsibilities for the care of the others. Somehow this seems wrong to her, but she can't quite put her finger on why. She wonders how Mrs. Brady can tolerate her children being so immature. They barely seem able to do anything on their own. She concludes that white people have strange ways and that their children are overindulged and self-centered. It's likely that they won't be able to do much of anything around the house, nor will they be any worth to others when they grow up, since they aren't getting any training now. She turns off the TV and prepares to go to work. She'll work on the 3:00 to 11:00 shift, as she has for the last 12 years. She cooked dinner earlier in the day. Tonya, her 10-year-old, is ready to take care of the other three children. "We're nothing like the Brady Bunch," she thinks, "and maybe that's good."

With her particular view of child rearing, it's fortunate for the Bradys that Mrs. Washington is not in a position to diagnose, treat, or write professional papers on the psychotherapy of individualism or the crippling effects of infantilization on children. It is also fortunate for the Bradys that Mrs. Washington is not in a position to influence public policy, because she might attempt to initiate social programs to counteract the negative effects of parental values and style on the Brady children. If Mrs. Washington had the power of position bestowed on mental health professionals, she could easily begin to take corrective actions on Brady behaviors that are cultural but that she misconstrues as pathological. Naturally, her opinions would be supported by a preponderance of professional literature and "scientific evidence"; consequently, it would never occur to her that there might be another kind of question to ask or another hypothesis from which to begin.

> . . . And now, a word about frustration, brought to you by the people at Constructivist Press. Constructivist Press, forging new inroads into the land of uncertainty . . .

The scene has changed. Mrs. Washington is finishing the final chapter of her dissertation on Brady family dynamics when she hears the commercial for Constructivist Press. She is distressed with their growing popularity and fears that one of her committee members may ask her questions about constructivist views that she is unprepared to answer. She is so sure of her conclusions. The Bradys are a pathological family; the pathology stems from a lack of parental discipline and the negative influence of affluence that has gone unchecked. She has been forced to conclude that the quality of the love relationship between parents and children is not healthy, since the parents do not take the time to be strict with their children. She also concludes that the severity of their individualism may be cause for national concern. On all of her tests, she has found the Brady children to be so internally controlled that they apparently have a perceptual screen blocking their attention from the impact of their behavior on others. What will be the fate of the nation with people like this in society?

She is shaken from her reverie with the closing jingle from the Constructivist Press commercial. "Why do they have to maintain such high visibility now?" She is just getting to the point of feeling that she knows what she is doing. When she has a family like the Bradys, she always educates the parents about the proper kind of parenting that will produce mentally healthy children. Of particular importance to her is making sure that the children learn interdependence. Rugged individualism is to be eliminated. Suppose someone on her committee asks her to describe the family's cultural strengths and how she might utilize them in therapy? No, that would be entirely too much! She thinks, "Who are these constructivists anyway, talking about multiple realities?" (Watzlawick, 1984). "Everyone knows there is only one reality, and, thank God, I know what that reality is. Besides, all of my colleagues in the office agree about families like the Bradys, so I know my ideas are real."

Mrs. Washington and the Brady Bunch live in a society created from a multitude of cultural groups, which, for the most part, rear their children to be contributing members of society. Each group offers to its members a sense of identity, direction, and explanation for the world around them, and each provides different processes for determining the meaning of life and how to achieve its goals. However, documentation of these processes is limited, and when differences are identified, they are often minimized or used inappropriately.

This chapter is organized to examine questions and assumptions as they relate to ethnicity, child rearing, and family therapy. The development of questions to bring focus to the discovery of useful distinctions in the cross-cultural encounter is stressed. There is no search for "truth," since that effort has not had a significant impact on improving cross-cultural relationships. Instead, the opportunity is offered to explore a world in which the only certainty is that we are all human beings making our way. Benefit from this exploration can be expanded if the reader selects a cultural group and identifies the assumptions that he or she holds about that group's child-rearing practices. The reader should ponder the questions that appear in each section and challenge his or her assumptions in light of different information. The distinctions offered here are arbitrarily developed to highlight certain points and illuminate certain questions. Attention should be paid to the pragmatic value of these distinctions as they manifest themselves in the reader's own context.

The exploration begins with a definition of culture and ethnicity. A review of the most prevalent ways of explaining differences follows. In describing escalating human relationships, Watzlawick, Weakland, and Fisch (1974) suggest that they ultimately deteriorate into charges of badness or madness. Two sections, "Culture as Deficit" and "Culture as Deviance," exemplify how these respective charges permeate the literature related to ethnicity and therapy. The next section, "Culture as Difference," discusses a rapidly developing area in the field—one that stresses the notion, "They're not mad or bad, just different." The final sections of the chapter offer another view of culture with implications for culturally informed therapy.

What Is Culture?

In reviewing the literature on culture and ethnicity, one discovers immediately that there is no universally accepted definition of culture. Nobles (1978) states,

> [C]ulture is a montage of specific ways of thinking, feeling, acting which is peculiar to the members of a particular group. Specific to a people's cultural montage is a particular "belief system." Conversely, it is the people's belief system which reveals their cultural montage, and in so doing, reflects their world view, normative assumptions, and frame of reference. (p. 682)

An ethnic group is a group possessing features that make it distinctive from the larger culture of which it is a part (McGill, 1983). In the United States, an ethnic group is usually identified by having its origins and roots in another country (this makes everyone, except Native Americans, ethnic). In other societies, ethnic groups may not be identified so much with a different place of origin as with different patterns of behavior derived from different belief systems and world views.

At least four phenomena of culture (Porter & Samovar, 1976) can be observed:

1. Every baby is part of a particular culture. No one is born free from other people who have more or less fixed ideas about how children should be brought up and what they should think and value.

2. The child's culture serves a very useful social and psychological purpose, in that it mediates the world to the individual and provides a sense of security, cohesiveness, and identity.

3. Culture is fluid, since it is constructed by people interacting with their environment. This has two implications: There are a multiplicity of cultures, given the diversity of environmental conditions on the planet; and cultures change in response to the changing environment.

4. Finally, culture is assumed, making behavior (which, by this definition,

must be cultural) seem natural and normal, and leading people to assume that their particular culture is right or best.

Consistent with the notion that people within a cultural group believe that the way they do things is natural and normal, the set of normative assumptions operating in society is believed to be "the reality" of how things are. Yet it is apparent that there is no definite, developed sense of what the national culture of the United States is. Instead, it is made very clear what it is *not:* It is not Nigerian, it is not Mexican, it is not Navaho. It becomes difficult for people whose origins are in these or other such societies to attach themselves to the national framework and hail the cultural similarities and overlap they experience with European-Americans.

Although all cultures believe in their inherent rightness (ethnocentrism), not all cultures have the power to dominate other groups by labeling the others' cultural behavior as "pathological" and by establishing research agendas to prove this assumption. In self-defense, professionals from dominated groups struggle to provide cultural explanations as a vehicle for positive intercultural understanding and identity building (Clark, McGee, Nobles, & Weems, 1975; Mindel & Habenstein, 1976; Nobles, 1974; Roger, Malgady, Constantino, & Blumenthal, 1987). Their work is reflective of a desire to highlight the distinctive, nonpathological elements of the group's essence. In this literature, African-Americans, Native Americans, Hispanics, and Asian-Americans, all of whom have been historically denigrated for their cultural heritage and values, are most often labeled as "cultural" rather than "ethnic" groups (Jones, 1980; LeVine & Padilla, 1980; Marsella & Pedersen 1981; Spang, 1971; Sue, 1981). In part, this is a response to the negative portrayal of minorities in the psychological literature, as well as a response to the ambiguity surrounding the essence of the national culture. In larger part, it is due to the fact that skin color is most often used as the defining feature of who is an "American" and who is not.

Many writers in the field understand, on some level, that people from the groups listed above also come from cultures that do not have Western ways of perceiving the world. For instance, Mbiti (1970) describes one distinction between Western and African thought.

> In western or technological society, time is a commodity which must be utilized, sold, and bought; but in traditional African life, time has to be created or produced. Man is not a slave to time; instead he "makes" as much time as he wants. When foreigners, especially from Europe and America, come to Africa and see people sitting down somewhere without, evidently, doing anything, they often remark, "These Africans waste their time by just sitting down idle!" . . . Those who are seen sitting down, are actually *not wasting* time, but either waiting for time or in the process of "producing" time. (p. 25)

These vast differences in non-Western and Western ways of perceiving and explaining the world (i.e., world views) also account for the "cultural" claim of the so-called "ethnic" minorities.

A flaw in the field is the homogenization of all European ethnics into one lump—the white lump. Cultural psychology often takes its point of departure from the white lump without ever describing it, thereby implicitly agreeing that the white lump is a legitimate starting point. For instance, Sue's (1981) book title, *Counseling the Culturally and Ethnically Different*, assumes the white-lump frame of reference and describes the points of departure. But the question remains, "Different from whom?" This chapter argues that the only legitimate point of departure is from where the client family is, and that a way of starting at that point is through the understanding of where the therapist, his or her theory, and society stand in relationship to that family. In other words, we cannot adjust our assumptions if we do not even know that assumptions are being made.

Thomas and Sillen (1974) state, "'Color-blindness' is no virtue if it means denial of differences in the experience, culture and psychology of black Americans and other Americans" (p. 58). The next two sections discuss forms of "color-blindness" that have different intents but similar outcomes. The case examples highlight the particular assumption under discussion. Each case is discussed from a culturally informed point of view in the section entitled "Implications for Culturally Informed Therapy."

Culture as Deficit

In the 1960s and 1970s, increasing social awareness highlighted a social problem requiring explanation: How could it be that specific groups in America were not "making it" and were remaining predominantly poor and disenfranchised? Though there were token efforts made during this period to change the most blatant aspects of institutional racism (system change), the primary focus was on finding an explanation that held the individual responsible for his or her failure to succeed in society. Genetic inferiority, the explanation that had formerly held a position of influence in the psychological and educational literature, no longer fit with the developing liberal posture of the period. The idea evolved that if the problem was not eminating from people's genes, it must be in their environment. Notice that this shift was consistent with what appear to be two themes in the national culture: the primacy of the individual and the dominance of personal responsibility (sometimes called "internal locus of control") for one's fate. This cultural stance precluded examination of the larger system and its role in problem creation and problem maintenance. Naturally, solutions that focused on individual change were supported.

Early in the century, Tylor (1903), defined culture as "that complex whole which includes knowledge, belief, art, morals, law, custom, and any other capabilities and habits acquired by man as a member of society" (p. 1). The educated class was considered cultured, and people who differed in beliefs and customs were seen as uncivilized and uncultured. Cultural deprivation theory, stemming from a similar attitude, became the explanatory construct of the Kennedy–Johnson era. It proposed that certain cultural experiences (in which "cultural" was synonomous with "white middle-class") were necessary for success in school, which ultimately meant success in society. African-American children lacked these experiences, and African-American parenting and home environments were seen as deficient, since these basic experiences were not provided.

Clift (1970) summarized many of the conclusions that appeared in the literature at this time. In all, he listed 169 traits of the deprived, including the following:

- African-American boys suffer from role confusion as a result of living in a matriarchy.
- The children suffer from lack of attention and affection.
- They depend more on external than internal control of things.
- The home situation is ideal for learning inattention.
- The lower-class home is not a verbally orientated home.
- The children are used to unsupervised play.
- There are no severe standards against aggression.
- Children and adults alike demand immediate gratification.

Federal programs, such as Head Start and Upward Bound, were designed to compensate for these early depriving circumstances and help children prepare for living in the white world. There was never a question that perhaps the white world was not the only world, let alone not the best world. Perhaps not surprisingly, compensatory programs have not accomplished what was expected. In fact, even a cursory evaluation of the effectiveness of the schools in educating African-American students using the compensatory assumption reveals an abysmal failure.

THE CASE OF Ms. SMITH. A young African-American mother, Ms. Smith, comes into therapy indicating that her baby is "slow." While she is waiting for her appointment, it is noted that she appears harsh and critical with her child. She repeatedly corrects the child and does not allow her to play with the toys in the waiting room. When questioned about the problem, she responds that LaTanisha is 24 months old and was slow to walk and talk. *(What are the reader's assumptions about this case? Do any of the assumptions Clift cited sound familiar?)*

The "culture as deficit" assumption is an assumption of "badness," and the conclusion drawn might be that Ms. Smith is in need of education about child development and parenting (the "culture as deviance" assumption, an assumption of "madness," might lead to the conclusion that she is not adequately bonded to her child). She might be given parenting information. However, all parenting materials begin from a particular cultural position. Since that cultural starting point is often implied rather than explicit, they advocate the "correct" way to parent, without regard for the possibility that there may be other ways to parent children effectively. Therapists narrow their manueverability when they use these materials, and may find that they lose their clients or are met with "resistance" when trying to get the clients to implement these parenting strategies.

Even so-called "universal characteristics" or "culture-free constructs" can begin with or be interpreted with "culture as deficit" assumptions. For example,

Piaget's concept of conservation is often thought to have cross-cultural applications. One assumption that arises from this concept is that children at about the age of 6 or 7 begin to demonstrate an understanding of conservation. The question arises as to whether this is a manifestation of innate human ability or a by-product of a specific experience.

Bruner, Olver, and Greenfield (1966) studied the concept of conservation in Senegal, West Africa. They found that Wolof (the Senegalese ethnic group they studied) children who attended school performed more like Western children on a conservation task than did their nonschooled peers in the same village. This experiment indicated that the conservation task is by no means culture-free and that perhaps Western schooling has more of an influence than some perceived cognitive switch that turns on at some stage.

Cole and Scribner (1974) conclude:

> [C]arrying such theories overseas without some awareness of their cultural roots and their very real limitations, *even in the cultures in which they arose,* carries with it the risk of experimental egocentrism—mistaking as universals the particular organizations of cognitive skills that have arisen in the historical circumstances of our own society, and interpreting their absence in other cultures as "deficiency." Perhaps this risk may never be entirely overcome until psychological science in non-Western countries becomes further advanced and generates its own theories and research methods—which can be tested on us! (p. 200, emphasis mine)

The therapist must ask himself or herself: What are my cultural yardsticks? What are the cultural yardsticks of my theoretical orientation? What do I think makes mentally healthy children? What do I believe is appropriate discipline of children? What is the source of my beliefs? How would people from different cultures view these questions? What might their answers be, and what might influence their answers? If I asked them these questions, how might their answers differ from those they would give someone from their own cultural group?

Culture as Deviance

From the "culture as deviance" position, groups are not seen as being from different cultures; rather, they are perceived as a deviant form of the dominant culture. For example, Kardiner and Ovesey (1952) reported their findings on the "basic Negro personality" derived from psychiatric interviews of 25 African-Americans. They stated that "our constant control is the American White Man. We require no other control" (p. 11). This way of thinking about culture and normality continues to influence many comparative studies of child rearing. A researcher identifies a "problem" for a particular ethnic group and proceeds to define that problem as the *group's* problem. The definitions of what the problem is, how it is a problem, for whom it is a problem, and what supports the problem are left entirely in the control of the researcher. Most importantly, the backdrop consists of the researcher's own cultural standards and values, which go unexamined and unchallenged.

Many textbooks written on child, adolescent, or human development are written in such a way as to imply the nonexistence of the impact of ethnicity on the development of the child. Papalia and Old (1981), for example, state, "Most of the studies of human development have focused on the white middle class, although an increasing amount of attention is being paid to development among members of minority groups" (p. 21). They further suggest that race, sex, ethnicity, and socioeconomic status are all aspects of development, just as heredity is. With this recognition, they proceed for nearly 600 pages to ignore these very factors and to present the view that *all* human beings develop in the same way, except when they make note of particular deviations. The authors recognize the differences in black adolescent development with references in the index to "juvenile delinquency," "school drop-outs," and "sexuality." Here "culture as deviance" can have a tremendous covert effect, particularly since what appears in the index is powerfully supported by what is *not* said in the rest of the text. The message is that African-American children develop in the same way as white children except for the deviations cited above.

THE CASE OF JAMAL. An African-American mother was referred by the school for family therapy. She called indicating that her 7-year-old son was fighting and school authorities had threatened to suspend him from school. *(What are the reader's assumptions at this point?)*

At the first interview, Ms. Johnson, a single parent, said that she was an accountant who moved from another city 2 years ago when she received a big promotion. Prior to the move, her son attended kindergarten in a school run by the Black Muslims. When he left, he was reading on the second-grade level. After the move, she enrolled him in a suburban school close to home. After 2 years, his teacher suggested that he be placed in a resource room for reading instruction; the teacher indicated that he did not stay in his seat. The school psychologist was also recommending testing to determine whether he was emotionally disturbed, since he was so aggressive in school. Ms. Johnson was very upset, unable to make sense out of the transformation of her son in the 2 years since the move. *(What are the reader's assumptions at this point?)*

Jamal sat quietly while his mother explained the situation. She asked him repeatedly why he fought at school. His reply was a shrug and an "I don't know." Ms. Johnson stated that she had tried everything from spanking to grounding; nothing seemed to work. The interviewer asked Jamal about his school. He said that he didn't like it very much. The rest of the dialogue went something like this:

THERAPIST: How many black children are in your class?
JAMAL: I'm the only one.
THERAPIST: Are you treated any differently than the other children?
JAMAL: Sometimes. Kids make fun of me.
THERAPIST: Kids make fun of kids. How is it different?

JAMAL: Today at lunch two kids sat down with me and one said, "How come you're black?", and the other one said, "I know. It's because a white person farted on him."

Jamal was crying by the end of his story and Ms. Johnson looked schocked. She said she never knew he heard such things in school.

A "culture as deviance" assumption might have led the therapist to say that the child's physical aggression was the problem, even though she might admit that it was terrible for the other children to say such cruel things. The referral source had already made the "deviance" assumption by its referral. If the referral had been accepted in the way it was given, the focus of treatment might have been on helping Jamal learn to direct his aggression in more "socially acceptable" ways and to walk away when children ridiculed him. The therapist might even have referred him for medication and agreed that testing for emotional disturbance was indicated.

Obvious questions emerge, related to how much a therapist uses the "color-blind" approach in his or her work. The therapist might ask: How am to I assess the ecosystem surrounding the problem (Auerswald, 1987)? Is it possible that the presenting complaint or the presentation of symptoms has a different significance within the context of the client's cultural group (LeVine & Padilla, 1980; Tseng & McDermott, 1981)? If this phenomenon has a cultural referent, how will that information change my assessment of the situation and what I recommend to do about it? What questions can be formulated to make this determination?

The next section deals with a departure from the color-blind point of view, as it introduces the notion of "they're not bad or mad, they're different."

Culture as Difference

Current developments in cultural psychology emerged at the convergence of several critical events. As a result of the civil rights movement, members of more ethnic minorities entered the field of mental health. With them came a sense of ethnic pride and an interest in developing new ideas about counseling minorities. The "social control" criticism of therapy (Chesler, 1972; Ryan, 1976; Szasz, 1970; Thomas & Sillen, 1974), with concomitant questions about the existence of mental illness (Szasz, 1974), all added together to provide a foundation for the broadening appeal of "culture as difference."

Simultaneously, the community mental health movement brought mental health services out of the hospitals and private psychiatric practices to the population at large. With this shift came an increasing recognition that members of ethnic minorities did not respond to treatment in the same ways as did their Anglo counterparts. One of the differences noticed was in termination rates after the first interview. In one study, African-Americans, Chicanos, Native Americans, and Asian-Americans were found to terminate after the first interview at a rate of approximately 50%, compared to 30% for Anglo clients (Sue, 1977). Explanations for

this phenomenon often ranged from deficit to deviance, until the option of difference was introduced.

The cultural psychology literature of the 1970s reflected the effort to account
for persistent treatment failures, with certain cultural groups using explanations
other than those from deficit or deviance constructs. This interest led clinicians to
identify certain redundancies of behavior in ethnic groups that were labeled as
"cultural." The apparent intent was to assist in the understanding and appreciation of diversity.

A growing number of authors (Falicov, 1982; LeVine & Padilla, 1980;
McGoldrick, Pearce, & Giordano, 1982; Sue, 1981; Tseng & McDermott, 1981)
have attempted to operationalize culture. Although these authors make a clear
statement about avoiding stereotyping, the idea of cultural traits, by its very nature, replaces old negative stereotypes with new positive stereotypes. These new
stereotypes are the most frequently recognized group behaviors occurring in the
bell of the normal curve for that culture. There must be an awareness, however,
that group data may not necessarily be appropriately applied to any specific individual within the group. There is often more within-group variance than variance
between groups (Porter & Samovar, 1976), particularly in cultures that coexist in
proximity to each other.

The emergent criticisms of this kind of work conclude that the new stereotypes do not offer useful information about working with different groups. Instead, the therapist may, through this cursory exposure to new stereotypes, be
likely to make errors of a different type. Maranhao (1984) states of family therapy, "Anthropology conceived as a taxonomy of cultures with its taxa defined by
value dimensions of stereotypical traits is unfortunately becoming the popular rep-
esentation of the discipline" (p. 275). He elaborates, "Nevertheless, lists of cultural traits could be helpful to family therapists if regarded as instrumental pieces
of information to establish the subject of discussion which is relevant for the
patients, not as cultural guidelines to pass diagnostic [judgments] or apply treatment" (p. 275). Therapists with only intellectual knowledge are like automobile
mechanics who know only how to fix a 1956 Chevrolet and must constantly return
to the book whenever a new model comes through the shop.

Montalvo and Gutierrez (1983) highlight the concept of the family's cultural
mask. Families can hide behind caricatures of their culture and fool themselves
and the therapist into thinking that these behaviors are cultural and are not subject
to change. A therapist with only instrumental knowledge of the culture will dismiss as "cultural" certain dysfunctional patterns of interaction.

THE CASE OF THE DIAZ FAMILY. A second-generation Mexican-American
family entered therapy because their 15-year-old daughter, Julia, had threatened
suicide and run away from home. Mr. Diaz had been on disability for several
months after injuring his back on the job. As a result, Mrs. Diaz got a job with
the local school district as a teacher's assistant in bilingual education. The family
lived in a predominantly Anglo neighborhood, and the girl's friends were Anglos.
Prior to coming into treatment the parents had had several conversations with the

priest at their church, who decided he would help the family by informing Julia that she could not have her *quinciañera* until she behaved (a *quinciañera* is a significant rite of passage in the life of some Mexican-American girls). This help did not accomplish the desired results. The girl did not behave, and the parents grew more anxious and upset that she would not go through this rite of passage.

In the first interview, the parents indicated that they wanted their daughter to behave, to show respect for them, and to stay at home rather than running away. Mr. Diaz showed his upset by crying during the session. Mrs. Diaz appeared aloof to the situation, stating only that she agreed with whatever her husband had to say.

When it came Julia's turn to speak, she began by complaining that her parents would never let her go anywhere without a chaperone. She complained that she could not go to the movies with her friends without her father's sister (a woman older than her parents) accompanying them. She was not allowed to be out after dark, but her brothers, who were younger than she, could do what they wanted to do. She had to do all the work in the house, and her brothers had no responsibilities. Both brothers confirmed their sister's statements. Her youngest brother (age 10) was not doing well in school, was grossly overweight, and whined to get his own way. These issues were not identified by the parents as problems. Near the end of the interview, Mrs. Diaz stated quietly that she had tried to tell her husband how other people at work let their daughters have more freedom, but he would not hear it. According to her, it was his decision. *(What are the reader's assumptions about this case?)*

A therapist with knowledge of the instrumental aspects of the culture, making the "cultural difference" assumption, might have decided that much of what the parents were doing with their child was cultural and therefore should be left alone. The therapist might have read that in some Mexican families men are dominant *(machismo)* and females are submissive (Falicov, 1982). In order to be respectful, he or she might have felt that this arrangement must not be challenged.

Although it is reasonable to recognize that knowledge of the redundancies of cultures can be useful, their utility is only as one of many starting points (and contrasting points) in the exploration of a patient's problem. Therapists must be able to flexibly discard rigidity masking itself as "cultural" when it is noticed that the rigidity may be part of the problem. So, just as quickly as a possible solution emerges—to raise clinicians' awareness of culture through the identification of differences—significant problems are also found that can greatly inhibit therapeutic maneuverability. How is the dilemma to be solved?

Culture as Epistemology

> *Every family has elements in their own culture which, if understood and utilized, can become levers to actualize and expand the family members' behavioral repertory. Unfortunately, we therapists have not assimilated this axiom.—Minuchin & Fishman, 1981, p. 262*

Let us consider for a moment two very different philosophical tenets: the Western position, "control of nature," and the Native American position, "one with nature." It would be inconsistent with the second position to establish a Bureau of Wildlife Management, whereas it is perfectly consistent with the first position. In the human sciences, consistency with "control of nature" leads to compartmentalization of human experience into discreet units, so that a group's psychology is separate from its sociology, its history, its physiology, and its relationship with nature. In cultures emerging from the "one with nature" position, the separation is much less clear when mind–body distinctions fade. For example, we treat patients in therapy whose own view of their "psychological/medical" problems is that they may have a natural or supernatural explanation (Harwood, 1981). This basic incompatibility often leads to early termination or noncompliance. If we better understood the epistemologies of cultures, more effective treatment would develop.

THE CASE OF THE *CURANDERO*. Juan was referred by a physician for several psychosomatic complaints, including esophageal spasm and stomach pains. He had been seeing the physician for several months, but his condition seemed to be worsening. Judging by appearance alone, he was very healthy. He had left his family in Mexico and believed that someone there wished him to be ill. After assessment of the relationships at home and a discussion of his beliefs about his physical problems, a *curandero* (Mexican folk healer) was called to consult on the case. He burned candles, said prayers, read stones, and told Juan about his problems. At the end of the session, he told Juan that the unhappiness at home had been resolved and that his pain would disappear. Juan left and in the next interview was relieved of his symptoms. He was seen a couple more times, then discharged from treatment.

Epistemology can be defined as "the rules one makes for making sense out of the world" (Hoffman, 1981, p. 342). The question of epistemology in family therapy has begun to be widely debated (Bateson, 1977; Dell, 1980; Keeney, 1979, 1983) as family therapists search for those concepts that help organize the world of therapy and provide meaningful explanations of people and their problems. The search for an appropriate epistemology has been undertaken in the same way as all traditional science has been: objectively. That is, it has been approached as if an epistemology is somehow outside of a culture's creation. But is it? And if we transcend the bounds of our culture, what are the far-reaching implications? These questions must be considered, even though the consideration must be limited within the scope of this chapter.

The idea of accounting for the client's world view (an element of culture) is not new to family therapy. Other authors have previously pointed out the importance of accessing world view (Haley, 1976; Minuchin, & Fishman, 1981; Watzlawick *et al.*, 1974)—an idea that was particularly prevalent in the work of Milton Erickson (Haley, 1973). Among these authors, Minuchin (1984; Minuchin & Fishman, 1981) is most explicit about the issue and use of culture in the context of therapy. Yet we seem unable to make the quantum leap to understanding that epistemology and culture are one and the same thing. We want to discuss the epistemological issues of family therapy as if our shifted position can reside comfortably within the context of current culture. And we want to play it safe by contemplating epistemology apart from culture. This does not seem possible.

From what has been discussed up to this point, it is obvious that psychology and therapy emerge from a particular cultural montage and are, therefore, subject to the biases of their normative assumptions, world view, and frame of reference. von Foerster's (1981) thinking on second-order cybernetics offers a useful metaphor as we consider theory building as a cultural activity. Just as the distinctions between the observer and the observed become blurred as we identify recursions in the process of observation, so too do we notice the influence of culture on the development of theory—most particularly, psychological theory. Groucho Marx may have said, "I would never belong to a club that would have me as a member," but theorists must say, "I would never develop a theory apart from the normative assumptions of my culture or a theory that identifies me as abnormal." Since psychological theory emerges from a cultural referent, perhaps this explains the difficulty in the field with accepting ecosystemic notions of people's problems. These notions are simply not culturally syntonic, since they do not emerge from the same philosophic base upon which the rest of society lies.

With this in mind, the questions to consider are these: In the absence of a Western idea of the "self," do other cultures even construct psychological theories? If not, what are their explanations for human behavior? If so, how does a specific cultural group describe its useful psychological constructs? What are the variations within the culture that are seen as acceptable?

Implications for Culturally Informed Therapy

From the act of conception, the pregnancy, the foods that are eaten during the pregnancy, and the birth ritual, cultural and economic factors are at work in a child's life. When we talk about cultural influences on child rearing from this point of view, we realize that child rearing is in and of itself a cultural activity. In order to accomplish making the distinction between culture and child rearing (or culture and any behavior), a notion of "child rearing" that is objective or acultural must emerge. To develop an understanding of our acultural notion of "child rearing," we have to superimpose aspects of cultures upon one another and see the differences between and among groups. This view leads to "cultural difference" and the inevitable list of cultural traits that hinder our flexibility rather than enhance it. Therefore, when the distinction is drawn between child rearing and culture, there is a limitation on possible ways of thinking about the issues. The drawing of the distinction is in itself a cultural act.

To appreciate the shift from therapy as an objective "thing" out there to understanding the unity of psychological thinking and cultural assumptions is to begin to appreciate the implications of culture as epistemology. The search for the epistemological basis of culture in therapy is just beginning. At best, a therapist can develop a method of operation that is culturally informed.

In the United States, culturally informed therapists understand their own culture and the values both stated and implied in their theory of therapy (Pedersen & Marsella, 1982) They understand that not all clients share their views or their interpretations of the clients' behavior. In their assessment of families, they acknowledge their blinders and ask questions that help them delineate the families' distinctions. They appreciate that people are products of not only their personal but also their group's history. They recognize that inequities in society are a part of the clients' problem, just as such inequities are a part of their own problem. (In the case of white therapists, the "white lump" has been as dehumanizing—perhaps in more benign ways—to them as it has been to people of color.) Finally, the culturally informed therapists know that transitions in culture are often painful processes, fraught with a sense of loss and disorientation. Some families reel from the shock; some have heard that they are no good for so long that they seem numb. These therapists know that not all people want to be absorbed into the dominant culture, and that many people from other cultures want to be respected and have an opportunity to be successful (by their own standards) without having to give up so much of themselves.

An examination of the cases presented in earlier sections may serve as guides to culturally informed therapy.

The Case of Ms. Smith

As I work with various groups on issues of cultural sensitivity, I encounter a common question. At one meeting of public health physicians, the question from the audience was stated this way: "I know I should respect people's differences, but when I see a black mother in the waiting area and she is so controlling of her children, it's all I can do to keep from telling her to back off of them. Don't I have a responsibility to the children to get this domineering mother to stop correcting them so much?" The assumptions made in this statement are clear: The physician believes that children should be afforded a certain degree of freedom. Children who are "too well behaved" are the products of controlling mothers, and will therefore suffer in the future. In contrast to this way of thinking, an African-American world view is the view that strict discipline is equated with love (Nobles, 1976). Regardless of social class, African-American parents believe that discipline is mandatory to insure their children's survival in a world that allows very little "freedom" for black people. To the African-American mother, her competence as a mother is revealed in how well her children behave in public settings.

Ms. Smith's complaints about LaTanisha's slow development may come from a cultural expectation. Awareness of varying cultural expectations for the development of the young child (Bartz & LeVine, 1978; Hale-Benson, 1986; Morgan, 1976; Young, 1971) will influence the therapist's view of the problem. Without

THE LOCAL COMMUNITY AND THE WORLD COMMUNITY

knowing that a pervasive African-American expectation is that a child should walk at about the age of 9 months (an expectation that is validated in the literature; Geber, 1958), the therapist may conclude that this mother's expectations are simply unrealistic. To depart from the assumption of deficit, certain questions may help to determine whether the mother's presenting complaint emanates from a cultural expectation: "In your family, how old were people when they started to walk and talk? Besides yourself, who else thinks this is a problem? What does he or she say about it?" The intervention may include validation of the cultural standard so as to legitimize the mother's cultural view while helping her to appreciate individual differences.

The Case of Jamal

In a case such as Jamal's, there should be a question for the therapist: What is the problem? Is it the child's fighting, or is it the emotional violence that he must face on a daily basis? The culturally informed therapist understands the position that the public schools take when educating children of color, and always assesses the ways in which that larger system is affecting the child, the family, and their behavior (Webb-Watson, 1988). In some sense, accepting the referral perpetuates the idea that the family is the problem and is what needs changing. The system supports cruelty in children by letting it go unchallenged and supports racism by pretending that it does not exist. In some cases, school personnel are amenable to change (except that they only seem open to first-order change), because they recognize a problem but do not know what to do about it. Larger-system assessment and interventions (Imber-Black, 1983; Webb-Watson, 1987) can be useful. In Jamal's case, the school was convinced that he was becoming a sociopath. Since his mother had the financial means, a private school for African-Americans was found. Jamal was enrolled there and is doing well.

The Case of the Diaz Family

If the Diaz family had lived in a area with a strong, traditional Mexican community, the parents might have been better able to maintain the idea of chaperones and specific gender-based role definitions, because those would be commonly held beliefs. However, they were living in a neighborhood that supported an entirely different belief system. Many people who move from their ethnic communities are unaware of the powerful effects such moves can have on family relationships and family functioning. The stress that is generated is often surprising to such families. In certain neighborhoods, the stress often increases as children develop and reach the age when there is interest in dating. Some families manage this by sleeping at their residences but really living back in their old communities through family visits, church involvement, and club memberships.

Not only was Julia upset with the strict nature of the rules, but she was actively expressing her mother's concerns about the usefulness of the traditional way of doing things. Since Mrs. Diaz had begun working outside the home, she had been exposed to other ideas about family relationships. On one level, the child's symptoms could be understood as the expression of the tremendous stress this family was facing as its cultural mandates responded to new information and to the pressure of shifts desired by individual family members. On another level, she may have been protecting her father from experiencing the loss of his former status as breadwinner in the family. Mr. Diaz was attempting to maintain a certain cultural tradition in an environment that would not support it. The less able he became to control his daughter with cultural prescriptions, the more he insisted on their value. They became magnified, blocking the way to problem solving. The process of cultural transition was supporting conflict and turmoil that the family had never before experienced. The treatment included both hypotheses mentioned above. The family did well and resolved not only the presenting problems but also the problems of the son. The validation and recognition of the cultural transition seemed particularly helpful.

Concluding Comments

The realization that everything is relative to other things, and that context cannot be assumed or trivialized, can be very distressing. It requires attending to information on several levels, as well as slowing down and checking out our assumptions. As therapists, it is often easy to get wrapped up in our work and rarify it without realizing that it has no significance for those who do not know about it. Parents, from all cultures, want the same things for their children: They want shelter, food, clothing, and a degree of contentment. However, the process for getting those things may be different. Culturally sensitive therapy, above all else, recognizes that there are many roads from point A to point B (Adler, 1976; Lappin, 1983). Each of these roads has ruts, holes, and impassable places, but most of life's travelers seem to make the trip, in their own way and in their own time.

ACKNOWLEDGMENTS

My appreciation to Delane Kinney, PhD, for her helpful comments, and to Graciela Montani, MEd, for her collaborative work with Hispanic families.

REFERENCES

Adler, P. S. (1976). Beyond cultural identity: Reflections on cultural and multicultural man. In L. A. Samovar & R. E. Porter (Eds.), *Intercultural communication: A reader* (pp. 362–378). Belmont, CA: Wadsworth.
Auerswald, E. H. (1987). Epistemological confusion in family therapy and research. *Family Process, 26*(3), 317–330.

Bartz, K. W., & LeVine, E. S. (1978). Childrearing by black parents: A description and comparison to Anglo and Chicano parents. *Journal of Marriage and the Family, 40*(4), 709–719.

Bateson, G. (1977). The birth of a matrix or double bind and epistemology. In M. Berger (Ed.), *Beyond the double bind* (pp. 41–64). New York Brunner/Mazel.

Bruner, J. S., Olver, R., & Greenfield, P. (1966). *Studies in cognitive growth.* New York: Wiley.

Chesler, P. (1972). *Women and madness.* New York: Doubleday.

Clark, C., McGee, D. P., Nobles, W., & Weems, L. (1975). Voodoo or I.Q.: An introduction to African psychology. *Journal of Black Psychology, 1*((2), 9–29.

Clift, V. A. (1970). Curriculum strategy based on the personality characteristics of disadvantaged youth. In A. C. Ornstein (Ed.), *Educating the disadvantaged* (pp. 139–149). New York: AMS Press.

Cole, M., & Scribner, S. (1974). *Culture and thought.* New York: Wiley.

Dell, P. F. (1980). The Hopi family therapist and the Aristotelian parents. *Journal of Marital and Family Therapy, 6*(2), 123–130.

Falicov, C. J. (1982). Mexican families. In M. McGoldrick, J. K. Pearce, & J. Giordano (Eds), *Ethnicity and family therapy* (pp. 135–161). New York: Guilford Press.

Geber, M. (1958). The psychomotor development of African children in the first year and the influence of maternal behavior. *Journal of Social Psychology, 47,* 185–195.

Hale-Benson, J. (1986). *Black children: Their roots, culture and learning styles* (rev. ed.). Baltimore: Johns Hopkins University Press.

Haley, J. (1973). *Uncommon therapy: The psychiatric techniques of Milton H. Erickson, M.D.* New York: Norton.

Haley, J. (1976). *Problem-solving therapy.* San Francisco: Jossey-Bass.

Harwood, A. (Ed.). (1981). *Ethnicity and medical care.* Cambridge, MA: Harvard University Press.

Hoffman, L. (1981). *Foundations of family therapy.* New York: Basic Books.

Imber-Black, E. (1983). The family and public sector systems: Interviewing and interventions. *Journal of Strategic and Systematic Therapies, 5,* 88–99.

Jones, R. L. (1980). *Black psychology* (2nd ed.). New York: Harper & Row.

Kardiner, A., & Ovesey, L. (1952). *The mark of oppression.* New York: Norton.

Keeney, B. (1979). Ecosystemic epistemology: An alternative paradigm for diagnosis. *Family Process, 18,* 117–129.

Keeney, B. (1983). *Aesthetics of change.* New York: Guilford Press.

Lappin, J. (1983). On becoming a culturally conscious family therapist. In C. Falicov & J. C. Hansen (Eds.), *Family therapy collections: Vol. 6. Cultural perspectives in family therapy* (pp. 122–136). Rockville, MD: Aspen.

LeVine, E. S., & Padilla, A. M. (1980). *Crossing cultures in therapy: Pluralistic counseling for the Hispanic.* Belmont, CA: Wadsworth.

Maranhao, T. (1984). Family therapy and anthropology. *Culture, Medicine and Psychiatry, 8,* 255–279.

Marsella, A. J., & Pedersen, P. (Eds.). (1981). *Cross-cultural counseling and psychotherapy: Foundations, evaluations, and ethnocultural consideration.* New York: Pergamon Press.

Mbiti, J. (1970). *African religious and philosophy.* Garden City, NY: Doubleday/Anchor.

McGill, D. (1983). Cultural concepts for family therapy. In C. Falicov & J. C. Hansen (Eds.), *Family therapy collections: Vol. 6: Cultural perspectives in family therapy (pp. 108–121).* Rockville, MD: Aspen.

McGoldrick, M., Pearce, J. L., & Giordano, J. (Eds.). (1982). *Ethnicity and family therapy.* New York: Guilford Press.

Mindel, C. H., & Habenstein, R. W. (1976). *Ethnic families in America.* New York: Elsevier.

Minuchin, S. (1984). *Family kaleidoscope.* Cambridge, MA: Harvard University Press.

Minuchin, S., & Fishman, H. C. (1981). *Family therapy techniques.* Cambridge, MA: Harvard University Press.

Montalvo, B., & Guiterrez, M. (1983). A perspective for the use of the cultural dimension in family therapy. In C. Falicov & J. C. Hansen (Eds.), *Family therapy collections: Vol. 6. Cultural perspectives in family therapy* (pp. 15–32). Rockville, MD: Aspen.

Morgan, H. (1976). Neonatal precocity and the black experience. *Negro Educational Review, 27,* 129–134.

Nobles, W. W. (1974). Africanity: Its role in black families. *Black Scholar, 5,* 10–17.

Nobles, W. W. (1976). *A formulative and empirical study of Black families.* Research conducted under a grant by the Administration for Children, Youth, and Families, Washington, DC.

Nobles, W. W. (1978). Toward an empirical and theoretical framework for defining black families. *Journal of Marriage and the Family, 40*(4), 679–688.

Papalia, D. E., & Olds, S. W. (1981). *Human development* (2nd ed.). New York: McGraw-Hill.

Pedersen, P. B., & Marsella, A. J. (1982). The ethical crisis for cross-cultural counseling and therapy. *Professional Psychology, 13*(4), 492–500.

Porter, R. E., & Samovar, L. A. (1976). Communicating interculturally. In L. A. Samovar & R. E. Porter (Eds.), *Intercultural communication: A reader* (pp. 4–24). Belmont, CA: Wadsworth.

Rogler, L. H., Malgady, R. G., Costantino, G., & Blumenthal, R. (1987). What do culturally sensitive mental health services mean? *American Psychologist, 42*(6), 565–570.

Ryan, W. (1976). *Blaming the victim* (rev. ed.). New York: Pantheon.

Spang, A. T. (1971). Understanding the Indian. *Personnel and Guidance Journal, 50*(2), 97–102.

Sue, D. W. (1977). Barriers to effective cross-cultural counseling. *Journal of Counseling Psychology, 4*(5), 420–429.

Sue, D. W. (1981). *Counseling the culturally and ethnically different.* New York: Wiley.

Szasz, T. (1970). *The manufacture of madness.* New York: Harper & Row.

Szasz, T. (1974). *The myth of mental illness* (rev. ed.). New York: Harper & Row.

Tseng, W., & McDermott, J. F. (1981). *Culture, mind and therapy.* New York: Brunner/Mazel.

Thomas, A., & Sillen, S. (1974). *Racism and psychiatry.* New York: Citadel Press.

Tylor, E. B. (1903). *Primitive culture* (4th ed.). New York: John Murray.

von Foerster, H. (1981). *Observing systems.* Seaside, CA: Intersystems.

Watzlawick, P. (1984). *The invented reality.* New York: Norton.

Watzlawick, P., Weakland, J., & Fisch, R. (1974). *Change: Principles of problem formation and problem resolution.* New York: Norton.

Webb-Watson, L. (1987). Larger system interviewing: Expanding resources for change. In E. Lipchik & J. C. Hansen (Eds.), *Family therapy collections: Vol. 24. Interviewing* (pp. 119–130). Rockville, MD: Aspen.

Webb-Watson, L. (1988). Women, family therapy and larger systems. *Journal of Psychotherapy and the Family, 3*(4), 145–156.

Young, V. H. (1971). Family and childhood in a southern Georgia community. *American Anthropologist, 72,* 269–288.

22

The Process of Immigration

SUSANA BULLRICH, PhD

It is true, no doubt, that in this great physical and psychic migration some of the old household gods are carefully packed up and put with the rest of the luggage, and then unpacked and set up on new altars and new places.—Lippman, 1929

Immigration and its inevitable precursor, emigration, are paradigmatic of a family crisis in its truest sense of danger and opportunity. It is easy to see that a family preparing to emigrate is undertaking many risks, regardless of the risks from which it may be escaping by taking this step. Emigration is an enterprise that will transform a family's way of life. The success of the enterprise rests in immigration—the arrival in the new country and adoption of the new way of life in a way that both brings the enterprise to fruition and also preserves the family's sense of identity, relationship, and value as a group.

Acculturation is the ultimate goal of immigration. Acculturation represents the new, complex pattern of family organization that is the outcome of successful immigration. The fact that successful immigration leads to new and more complex elaborations of family structure and relationships can be best understood through considering Prigogine's ideas about open systems that exchange energy with the environment—systems he calls "dissipative structures." Central to understanding these processes are the traditional concept of entropy and Prigogine's discoveries that as structures dissipate according to the second law of thermodynamics, they do not do so randomly, but indeed form new organizational patterns along the way (Prigogine & Nicolis, 1982). Thus, a random disturbance (a perturbation) of

Susana Bullrich. Department of Mental Health Sciences, Hahnemann University, Philadelphia, PA; Centro di Terapia Sistemica e di Ricerca, Milan, Italy.

a system will cause it to disorganize, only to reorganize in a new way. For the immigrant family, this new way will be realized in its particular form of blending old and new, its acculturation.

The broad systemic patterns of emigration and immigration can be understood in these terms: A perturbation occurs in the family, or in the system in which the family is embedded, introducing entropy. Entropy requires the system to change, and one of the changes to be made is emigration, leaving the old and moving to the new. In the new area, old ways, already modified by the process of emigration, are now further modified in exchange with the new culture. A particular blend of old an new propels each family to a new order of organization and structure and definition of values.

At this level of defining the processes of immigration, it is clear that along with the opportunity for system elaboration, there are serious risks. These risks are related to the changes in a system's balance of the forces of morphostasis and morphogenesis. Entropy is change. If the family changes so completely that it retains nothing of its previous coherence, it disintegrates. On the other hand, if it remmains essentially conservative in the face of the challenge of the new culture, it fails.

The process of a family's emigration and subsequent assimilation into the new country is essentially a perturbation of the system and an opportunity for the system to elaborate new and more complex structures. Although this process is unique to each family, in combination with each culture of origin and of relocation, there are certain large patterns that appear in the competent management of the emigration–immigration process. A functional response to the perturbations surrounding emigration is for the family to become centripetal—to draw itself out of involvements with aspects of its attachments to people and experiences in the old culture, into itself. Upon arriving in the new country, however, the family must become more centrifugal, sending its members deep into the new culture while maintaining a center that holds the system togetether. In the new country, assimilating itself into the new culture, a family experiences the tension between morphostasis and morphogenesis—between the need to perpetuate familiar structures and relationships, and the demand for accommodation to new life styles. It is in these tensions that families become dysfunctional and children may be compromised. Understanding these larger systemic issues can direct therapeutic interventions with immigrant families in trouble.

This chapter elaborates these systemic principles in examining the circumstances of immigration and its impact on young children.

Emigration

The act of emigration can have almost as many variations of process as motives for initiation. These variations are manifested uniquely in each family according to its character, and are expressed according to the particular way in which that family's process of emigration and subsequent accommodation within its adopted country (immigration) unfolds.

There are many reasons why a family emigrates, ranging from wanting to improve the quality of life to needing to escape death. Prior to the event itself, a detailed and complex process takes place: coming to terms with the decision to emigrate. In some instances, this process is experienced as a split-second decision between life and death, whereas in others there may be months of organization and preparation for the move.

Yet for all the deliberations that may take place, a larger systems view, taking Maturana's ideas into consideration, makes it clear that a measure of entropy is introduced into the system (Maturana & Varela, 1973; Maturana, 1983–1984). Entropy, in human systems, can be defined as the amount of energy unavailable for useful work in a system undergoing change. It can also be defined as the degree of disorder in a system. Families, like all living systems, have a certain amount of energy available for work. The more energy that is needed for change, the less energy is available to maintain order in that system, thereby increasing entropy. An excess of entropy can threaten the family with disintegration (Maturana, 1983–1984).

Without a doubt, the events leading to emigration, and emigration itself, introduce entropy into the family system. Indeed, many changes in traditional family values have been found to occur prior to emigration. In some cases, the decision to emigrate is a conscious attempt to regain order; in others, the focal energy of the family preparing to emigrate re-establishes order in the form of clarity of family identity and family members' functions.

Emigration affects the entire family, even if the perturbations that have engendered the thinking about emigration appear to affect only one individual in the family. In very few other instances must the family's membership and identity be so clearly defined as in the deliberations about who will go and who will be left behind. The boundaries between the nuclear family and the extended family, friends, and work systems—are sharply drawn at the family's departure.

Take, for example, a husband with a wife and two small children who is considering a better job offer in a different country. His doing so introduces a perturbation into the family system. (I begin this account at the point at which a better job offer is made, but it is clear that many events surround this one.) Many decisions and assumptions that will have an important impact on the family must be made. If the husband accepts the offer, he has to take responsibility for relocating his wife and children, and thereby separating them from their own country, extended family, school system, work, and friends. He is expected to provide the same, if not better, living conditions for the family. The wife, in turn, has to decide where her loyalties lie and what she believes to be in the best interests of the family. The children, who have no choice once the decision has been made by the parents, will be asked at an early age to make a tremendous contribution to the family effort, emphasizing their roles as family members above the other roles to be assumed by school-age children—socialization and learning the industry as well as the culture of their country. In the new country, the children will of course go to school, but they will learn to speak a different language from the family's language, and will be exposed to different social mores. Prior to emigration, preparing to sever ties with the systems in which it has been embedded, the family tends to focus all available energy on keeping itself together. The movement is centripetal. When emigration is accomplished, the family will be able to utilize the available energy to move away from the center and to assimilate itself into a new environment. For successful adjustment in a new country, the immigrant family must retain the strong family identity consolidated by the centripetal movement in the emigration process and must also shift its primary forces to centrifugal movement, allowing family members to assimilate in the new country.

The fact that it is not at all clear which aspectes of one's culture of origin will remain the same and which will change is central to a systemic understanding of the process of these transitions. Similarly, it is not clear how these changes are made; at what level of the systems they are made; who makes the decisions; when they do appear to have been made; and whether they are true decisions. Are such decisions made by one person, and, if so, how is this person selected? Is the selection a part of the process that has initiated the emigration process? Whatever the process, it unfolds at the expense of the established code of norms and conduct of the whole group. The distinctive changes that follow from this process are those that, in the end, determine the nature and course of each family's saga.

The Cultural Context of Immigration

Culture is the totality of language, knowledge, and technology passed on from one generation to the next as defined by a given society. It is a way of life of a group of people, an integrated pattern of responses learned and transmitted among those people. Different cultural patterns guide the members of each respective culture through life tasks in ways that differentiate them from members of other cultures (Williamson, Swingle, & Sargent, 1982). They promote and affirm one's cultural identity. They provide guidelines not only for insiders but for outsiders as well, helping them to recognize what makes a culture different from their own.

The specific impact that a change of cultures has on a family in transition depends on many factors. Some of these include the nature of the family traits and cultural patterns, and the degree of fit with the new culture. How a recipient culture responds to the differences between its patterns and those of immigrating families becomes pivotal to the measure of how well a person or group will survive the transformation and adopt the new culture. The process itself is further complicated if the culture of origin and the culture of adoption lie at oppositie ends on a continuum of values and norms—for example, if one culture values independence, competitiveness, and aggressiveness, and the other culture values closeness, cooperation, and nonaggressiveness.

Other factors influencing acculturation are the type and extent of the resources a family can count upon to absorb the pressure and assist with the multiple requirements of the situation. These factors include legal, social, economic, and educational family status; language, specific stage of the family life cycle; and support from the extended family. All of these are interdependent with the available resources in the host culture, such as job opportunities, cultural tolerance, flexibility, and community and governmental support. This interdependence illustrates the way in which two cultures in "cultural contact" (Bateson, 1983), incoming and dominant, reciprocally influence each other; it demonstrates the dialectical nature of this phenomenon.

Each culture has its own rules and norms, which are different from the laws of a particular locality. Hans Kelsen (1960) writes that laws are not enforceable unless the legal system provides sanctions for noncompliance. Cultural norms do not operate in this fashion. A violation of cultural norms will challenge some group, be it the family, the peer group, or the culture in general, thereby eliciting sanctions but of a different order from legal sanctions. Cultural sanctions may include being considered deviant or being shunned by the family and/or the community, rather than being punished by society as a whole. The existence of these sanctions has a profound effect on the identities of individuals and families who reside within and participate in a particular culture.

One rule common to all cultures is that children must be socialized. Almost everybody agrees on the basics: Children must be taught how to behave. While socialization is a lifelong process, the period of childhood is perhaps critical in this process. It is in childhood that cultural patterns are incorporated and begin to be expressed in actual behavior. The nuclear family, the extended family, the neighborhood, the school, and the community all have a very strong influence on how things are done and what things are to be valued (Escovar, 1982). Families are responsible for educating their children in the ways of their own culture; in immigrant families, however, children are often the leaders, educating their families about the new cultural mores and norms (Vasquez, Avila, & Morales, 1984; Wakil, 1981).

Being called "foreigners" or experiencing themselves as "foreigners" brings immigrant family members face to face with the information about cultural differences and the personal choices to be made. To say that one is a foreigner is to state that a difference exists (Bateson, 1979). The statement has denotative and connotative meanings. It denotes that one does not belong, is alien, uncharacteristic, and disconnected from the mainstream. This experience may induce family members to abandon previous identities and cultural norms and to take on the costume and manners of the new country so as not to be identified as foreign. School-age children are usually more adept at this than other family members, and teenagers have a particularly keen need to belong to their peer group. In either case, such a reaction to being foreign may be seen as disloyal within the family and produce difficulties. The connotataive meaning of being foreign includes subjective expectations and a degree of acceptance or rejection of the new environment. One may *choose* to be called foreign, clinging to one's own ways rather than joining in the practices of the new culture. Ethnocentrism is a perpetual threat to immigrants, both when it reflects the attitude of the immigrants and when it prevails in the host culture.

The entire process of adaptation to a new and ever-changing culture implies a reorganization of familial interactions and dynamics. According to Prigogine and Nicolis's (1982) ideas, this is a reorganization to a higher order of complexity, which in this case is called "acculturation." The accommodation of old values to new cultural mores often requires the family to reorganize its structural components without losing its coherence. If accommodation does not occur, there is a serious risk of disintegration. There is no satisfactory way of maintaining sameness after immigration.

Immigration: Basic Tasks

One of the basic tasks that immigrant families face is to connect with and integrate themselves into the new culture. As noted above, this implies a reorganization of familial interrelations to a higher order of complexity. The more able a family is to connect with and integrate itself into the new culture, the more flexible the family structure becomes. This acts like an ongoing spiral that enables the family structure to adapt and change more readily (Morin, 1980, 1985; Shands, 1971).

A traditional middle-class family that, in immigrating, faces the need to adapt familial roles and responsibilities is a reasonably typical example. Although the father may continue to function as head of the household and main provider, the mother, hitherto a housewife, may now have to seek employment to supplement the father's income. Children who previously were responsible only for going to school may now have chores to perform to help out now that their mother is working. The family way may also experience a concomitant change in social status. These adjustments will change the complex family structure, but, ordinarily, will not dissolve it (Kagan, 1981).

The demand for flexibility in the family may be understood as coming from the increased flux of energy that results from the interaction with the new culture—that is, entropy, driving the family system to change rather than to concentrate energy on preserving its forms. Rigidity, or the inability to adapt in this situation, leads to family dysfunction. The energy available for useful work is consumed in preserving its integrity, and, in the face of new challenges, appears in maladaptive behavior. The period of adjustment is a long and difficult one, during which movement toward a new equilibrium takes place; this movement is complicated by a tension between the need for maintaining an identity and the need for change and adaptation (Falicov, 1982; Selvini Palazzoli, Boscolo, Cecchin, & Prata, 1978).

It is critical for sound adjustment that the attitudes, beliefs, and actual responses of a particular culture afford to the immigrant family some hope for the fulfillment of its needs and dreams. If this does not happen, members of the family begin to wonder what has been gained by their immigration. Some degree of fulfillment is needed to assuage the family's sense of loss and the frustration brought about by the need to postpone many gratifications. Family members may make tremendous sacrifices for the sake of acculturation by doing things or acting in ways that are deemed necessary, regardless of their belief in or commitment to these new ways. This takes its toll on the family, but more so when there are no personal rewards or satisfactions of any kind forthcoming.

Movements to Adapt

A systemic view of families suggests the permanent coexistence of two forces, morphostasis and morphogenesis. The changes affecting the immigrating family are incorporated into this ever-present struggle for balance between the two forces.

The environmental and interrelational demands can be so stressing and overwhelming that the family will succumb to them and be precipitated into a crisis. The needed balance between the past and the present is much more difficult then. Under those circumstances, it is essential for family members to come to terms with the new reality they have to live in. They have to go through a mourning process. Not being able to accomplish it may alter and disrupt the process of adaptation.

The family's ability to respect its own pace of adaptation and acculturation can also help it adjust successfully while maintaining a sense of balance. It is easy to succumb to pressures to adapt at too rapid a pace. A sense of loss of control over time, or of running out of time to change, can draw family members into difficulties with this issue.

The impact of the cultural shock and the degree of emotional unsettlement involved in the immigration process cannot be anticipated. Knowledge and accurate information can help family members to tolerate and accommodate to the disruptive feelings of sadness, isolation, hopelessness, alienation, uprootedness, and fear. It is clear that any effort to help an immigrant family with its transition from one culture to another can be maximized by highlighting and focusing upon those goals and values that are shared (Lappin, 1983).

Loyalty Issues

If one of the major reasons why a family emigrates is to improve the level of education and opportunities for the children (Korazim, 1985), the pressure on these children can be immense. Not only do these children have to adapt to a new culture, perform well in school, and be grateful to their parents, but they also have to maintain loyalties to their family and culture. Children's performance will be measured by two very different groups and by two sets of criteria. Are they going to be given credit for their loyalty to family patterns or for their success in coping with the adjustments? The children's success may become the markers by which parents measure their own success in becoming part of the new culture, but the parents may simultaneously resent this success.

The inability of children to balance the demands posed by the new culture with demands coming from their families can result in cognitive and social paralysis. The children may feel trapped between the conflicting levels of the messages they receive from the family and from the culture (Haley, 1979). They are told simultaneously to adapt to the new culture and not to adapt (Yao, 1985).

The Yao-Liangs, recent immigrants from Vietnam, brought their 11-year-old son for therapy because of a dramatic decline in his school performance and withdrawal from his friends. Initial information cited no apparent reason for the child's sudden drop in grades. He was the oldest of three children, and his family had immigrated to the United States the preceding year.

It was discovered in the initial interview that although the parents spoke some English, the burden of translating from and to the family fell on the boy's shoulders. The parents explained that they did not understand the recent change in their son's behavior. According to them, there was no change in the family. They were proud of their son—of his adjustment to the school system, as well as his rapid learning of the language. When further questioned about any new developments within the family, Mrs. Yao-Liang mentioned that she had begun working 3 months ago in order to save enough money to send for her mother. Her decision to work came up after, with the son's help as interpreter at the Immigration Office, the parents learned that they could send for her mother. Now that his mother was working, the boy had to care for his younger siblings until late in the evening, when she came home.

At the end of the session, Mr. Yao-Liang, who up until then had been very quiet, mentioned how happy he was to be in the United States, especially because of the educational opportunities for his children. He pointed out that his son had been selected for a special after-school program on computers, and although the boy wanted to participate he would not be able to, due to the family's need for him to care for the younger children. The father hoped that the boy would be able to attend the program during the next year. When questioned about this program, the boy was silent and became tearful.

The oldest boy was experiencing something that has been described in Vietnamese immigrants (Hussain, 1984; Lin, Masuda, & Tazuma, 1982). Assessing the situation from the perspective of the family system, the therapy team appreciated several conflicting and contradictory messages the boy was receiving. His excellent grades and ability to speak English put him in a privileged position at school and at home, making him the spokesman for the family and a measure of the family's successful adjustment to the new country. The important and unique role he played within the family gave him power; however, this power was subject to the needs of the family, and consequently he was not always able to utilize it for his own individual benefit and development. On the one hand, he played an adult role in being a translator for the parents and finding out ways for them to maintain family ties. On the other hand, when he was offered the possibility for individual growth, the family's wishes to be together took precedence over his personal aspirations.

The Yao-Liangs had come to the United States seeking freedom and a better education for their children, emphasizing that all of the hardships they endured were for the younger generation. The situation appeared to be quite the opposite for the boy. In fact, he was deprived of his freedom and educational opportunities. Furthermore, his sacrifice was for the oldest generation, that of his grandmother—a not uncommon occurrence with resettling Indochinese families (Nicassio & Pate, 1984). He responded to this confusion by withdrawing and giving up his investment in progressing, since he ended up being restricted instead of rewarded (Nguyen, 1984).

A systemic assessment of the movements in the family found that, not atypically, the child had moved smoothly and centrifugally into the culture of his new country, while his parents maintained a centripetal stance, working to draw yet other members into the family and opposing their son's movement by requiring him to be at home as well. The balance between morphogenetic energies (those of the child) and the morphostatic ones (those of the parents) was tipped in favor of morphostasis, and the boy's failure in school could only be seen as his joining the conservative forces of his family.

As part of the treatment, the family was advised to contact the services of an agency that provided consultation for immigrants. There they learned that the process of bringing the grandmother in would take no less than 2 years, and that therefore the family could slow down the pace of providing for the grandmother's immigration.

For ongoing treatment, the therapy team decided to work only with the parents, selecting the part of the system that appeared to be most conservative in order to support the parents' leadership in the family's adaptation to the new culture and to readjust the system's predominantly morphostatic energies. In discussion, the parents realized that now that they were in the United States, priorities had changed for them. As their own need for support and closeness with their families of origin had prevailed, their children's best educational opportunities—for which they had ostensibly made this move—had been postponed.

The parents were seen once every other week, and therapy focused on the couple's inability to deal with the difficulties arising from changes inherent to their immigration. On the one hand, they had survived the Vietnam War, demonstrating their toughness and adaptability. The effort necessary to adjust to the new country would also be demanding and painful, but in a different way. In addition to adjusting to a new country and new language, they also had to adjust to a less critical situation—to learn to live in peace, rather than in deprivation and fear. It was also discovered that excessive work on the part of the parents was a means for both spouses to avoid sadness and isolation, especially for the mother. This overinvolvement with work, convenient and justified for the adults, had occurred at the expense of the children's social life.

In exploring their living situation, it was discovered that the Yao-Liangs had settled in a neighborhood where there were other Vietnamese families who had been in this country for varying amounts of time, as well as families of other cultural and ethnic backgrounds. Their next-door neighbor had offered to watch the two little children while the mother worked. Furthermore, the family attended a local Catholic church among whose congregation, again, was a mixture of families, including many Vietnamese. Thus there were many opportunities within their own community for continuity and variety. The parents were directed to take advantage of these resources in their community. They enrolled their small children in the church nursery school, where the little ones joined children of many backgrounds. They worked on building new social relationships by assuming specific tasks in different areas. The father was asked to help at home and to offer an hour a week for community services. The mother was encouraged to join a group and take English lessons.

When the neighbor's offer to care for the little ones after school was mentioned, the mother said that she could not accept it, since she had no way to pay her back. Her worry about foreigners looking after her children was balanced by her concern that others would reject her and her family because they were foreign. With considerable urging from the therapeutic team, the parents worked out an arrangement with the neighbors in which they took turns taking care of the little ones and preparing meals. The neighbors were appreciative of the subtleties of Vietnamese cuisine, and the family felt comfortable implementing the suggestion that they have dinner with their neighbors once a week.

These steps were taken successfully, and 7 months later the family was functioning and showed evidence of progressive adaptation. The oldest boy was again achieving very well at school, and the other two were in kindergarten. The parents were still saving money in order to bring the grandmother to the United States, but the pace at which this was being accomplished ceased being disruptive to the family life. In a follow-up session 8 months later, the family continued to be positively engaged in their process of adaptation.

Time Orientation

Another manifestation of the tension between morphogenesis and morphostasis is in the tension between future orientation and past orientation. At some point in the process of immigration and acculturation, the demands for change and adaptation are made more explicit by the family members most advanced in the adoption of the new culture. Everybody in the family, therefore, should become future-oriented, abandoning the possibility of satisfying ambitions dreamed of in the old country.

But, of course, not everyone in the family adjusts at the same time. Indeed, the fact that some family members cling tenaciously to traditional modes while others rush headlong into the new society can be seen as critical to maintaining family cohesion, even though it may also result in symptoms in one or more family members (Grant, 1983).

This type of difference in time orientation among family members was seen in the Castros, who had immigrated from Colombia to the United States 16 years earlier. The reasons for their decision to leave Colombia were political instability and the effects of economic decline on the husband's business. In addition to the parents, there were three daughters and a son. Nine years after the immigration, another daughter was born. The reason for the family's seeking consultation was the mother's concern about the youngest daughter's destructive behavior. The mother reported that her daughter had been an aggressive child since she was two years old. At that age she destroyed her toys, but they thought it was a phase and she would grow out of it. But instead of disappearing, this behavior had gradually increased. Quite recently the child had begun tearing apart her dresses, newly made by her mother.

During the initial interview, Mr. Castro emphasized how well the family had adjusted and progressed in the new country over the 16 years they had been here. He spoke of his successful business and how he was able to keep the family together by having his son and son-in-law working with him. His older daughters had gone to college and married professionals. He also said he was grateful to this country for providing him with an opportunity for developing his talents and achieving financial security. He felt that his youngest daughter's behavior was the result of her being spoiled by her mother. But when the therapist said that she wanted everyone in the family to attend the sessions for an extended evaluation, he became quite resistant and made it clear that he had no time to spare. He believed that the problem concerned only his wife and the child.

Mrs. Castro kept silent during his report, but finally said that she felt helpless to stop the child's misbehavior. When she was asked to express her opinion further, it became apparent that her English was not good and she was embarassed by this. While she was speaking, Mr. Castro appeared exasperated. He apologized for his wife's poor English and explained how he had struggled with her about the immigration. She had not wanted to leave her family, especially her mother. He pointed out how her refusal to learn the language kept them from socializing and developing a network of friends. She was always expressing her desire to return to Colombia to live.

In the second interview, with the entire family present, it was noted that the youngest daughter, who came to the interview just after school, was impeccably dressed in an elaborate and fancy way. When a remark was made about the daughter's dress, her mother spoke with pride about it, saying that this was the way nice girls from good families dressed for school. A heated discussion then ensued between the mother and the older daughters, who felt that dressing up the child just to go to school was ridiculous and inappropriate. They said, "Mother, we are already in the 21st century!" The child said that she agreed with her sisters and wanted to wear jeans and a T-shirt to go to school.

It was evident that there were strong conflicts surrounding different time orientations within the family. The father and older children were clearly present- and future-oriented, while the mother clung to the past, refusing to make the adjustments to the new situation even after 16 years. The child was caught within these extremes. Her paradox was that though she was the only native-born American in the family, she was asked to look, dress, and behave as if she lived in another century and at a different time.

Treatment involved the parents and all of the children. When the therapy team explored further the family's attachments to Colombia and to the new country, it was learned that the entire family flew "home" to Colombia for Christmas each year. This was a tradition enjoyed and affirmed by all the family members, and it allowed the team to question the family's presentation of itself as fully assimilated, thus narrowing the apparent gap between the old-fashioned mother and the new-fashioned father and children.

It seemed to be a relief for all to recognize how important their Colombian roots were for them. One of the daughters, married to an American, decided to give her soon-to-be-born infant a Spanish name, realizing that she could move into the 21st century with her roots intact; her husband was very enthusiastic about this.

As the children began to achieve a better balance between their Colombian backgrounds and their American life styles, they began to appreciate their mother's role in maintaining traditions from which they had been tempted to turn away. This shifted the balance in the family, leaving only the father protesting that his wife's old-fashioned ways were an embarrassment to him. Because of her dress and her imperfect English, he claimed that he could not include her in his business-connected social life. The team wondered why, since the father was so financially successful, he had not arranged for his wife to have English lessons—at a school, or even with a private tutor. His protests in response to this question revealed, finally, his own reliance on her maintenance of the connection with their Colombian roots. Another shift took place, in which he acknowledged the importance of their heritage, and she was at last freed to make her own claims for a place in this country. She wanted to work outside the home, and it was finally settled that she would take a job at his office, working with him.

Because the child's misbehaving had had a function of occupying the mother and keeping her at home, these changes in the larger system, integrating the old and the new, allowed her to engage in school and and with her friends in an American way while still participating in a family with a very distinctive character—a special blend of Colombian and American.

Role Changes

Over time, families learn to recognize the cues for determining which of the old norms and standards are permitted and which are prohibited, as well as the reasons for each. This means re-evaluating the familiar myths, ideologies, and conceptions. Some norms are destined to preserve the cultural saga and familiar patterns; others are destined for revision or replacement within the new culture. It is likely that in the reorganization of familial behavioral patterns, those that aid the family in adapting to the new culture are reinforced, while those that create more dissonance with the dominant culture are modified or extinguished. The disparity between the two sets of norms—old and new—implies a need for reconceptualization of concepts and roles as basic as those of husband and wife, father and mother. The need for flexibility in the conceptualization of these concepts and roles is made more difficult by the linear, black-and-white quality of Western languages which compartmentalizes the world in terms of good or bad, normal and abnormal.

One problem commonly found in working with immigrant families is the multiple effects that arise from the language barrier. Language is essential. Immigrants would list their being competent with the spoken language of the adopted country as a turning point for their feelings of belonging. The ability to communicate and to express oneself appropriately remains a basic mechanism of survival and ultimately of integration into society. Isolation is one of the most devastating effects of not speaking the national language of the adopted country. It results in distancing the family from the mainstream society, and also in separating family members who have progressed further in acculturating (usually the children) from those who have not been able to adapt quickly because of difficulties in learning the language. This could be the case with a mother who is called to her child's school regarding his or her behavior; she may be unable to understand what the teacher is pointing out, or even to explain what the family situation is. In this respect, family roles of children and parents become confused, as we have already seen, with the children becoming interpreters for the family. At some points these different levels of mastery of language and culture may produce what some (Karrer, 1986) have called "acculturation dissonance" within the family—a situation that can lead to children's actually making major decisions for the parents.

The topic of paternal and maternal roles is very important in this respect. Although basic patterns of parenting may not change very much from one country to another, some differences in these roles among different cultures do exist. What it is to be a good mother or a good father in one culture may be very different from the criteria established in others. Many subtle manifestations of so-called good mothering and fathering, plus the meaning of being a good child, are challenged.

Acculturation may be particularly difficult for the mother of the family if, as is frequently the case, she remains at home. Sluzki (1979) writes that if families split the instrumental and affective roles, "usually the female" takes care of the "affective activities" (p. 385). Because she is the caretaker of the emotional and spiritual background of the family's saga, she is also often the locus for the problem of integrating the new and the old. Thus, mothers in acculturating families who stay at home much of the time may be at risk for depression and isolation (Williams & Carmicheal, 1985). This is all the more so when they do not speak the language of the new country and rely only on their husbands and children for communication with the surrounding world; this situation is a starting point for a rigid attachment to the past and a halt in the process of acculturation for her. As we have seen, life in the new country may begin for some members of the family and seems to end in a cul-de-sac for others. A crisis may be precipitated when these roles become mutually escalating.

This same exaggeration of difference may affect therapeutic intervention when the therapist is not sufficiently attentive to gathering information concerning the culture of the immigrant family (Lappin, 1983). For example, an emphasis on personal independence and individualism for a family whose culture encourages the maintenance of family ties and cooperation may result in the failure of the therapy or in the family's dropping out of treatment. A seemingly successful adaptation to an individualistic culture may require that the child break away totally from his or her culture or origin (Shorter, 1977); this may also aggravate the child's inner struggle to conciliate and to establish an acceptable balance between what is gained and what is lost. Emphasizing the cultural advantage of individualism in such a family will undoubtedly contribute to the maintenance of the problem. Thus, the therapist must help the family find ways to balance these conflicting demands on behavior.

For example, the case of a 12-year-old girl who obtained a babysitting job after school and whose mother wanted her to help at home was solved when the therapist suggested a compromise—namely, that the child contribute a small amount of the money earned from babysitting toward the household budget. The girl's adaptive behavior in assimilating to the dominant culture was supported, as was her obligation to help support her family and respect maternal authority.

Challenges to Morals and Values

In a situation of shifting cultures, nobody knows which norms are going to prevail. In this context, the family is deprived of its power to be the first to enforce rules and to punish.

Compare the acceptability of physical punishment of children in many cultures with the stringent regulations about child abuse in the United States. Over time, several different institutions from the adopted culture are going to usurp parents' authority at the very moment when they are themselves struggling to adapt to these new norms and maintain both an identity and a sense of self-esteem. Others, whether institutions or public officers, are going to establish limits regarding what is right and what is wrong behavior for the children. The parents no longer are the primary source of authority.

Putting It Together: An Immigrant Family in Treatment

The Amharans were referred to a community outpatient clinic by a school psychologist, following the truant and "inappropriate" behavior of their 13-year-old daughter. The family consisted of Mr. Amharan (42), Mrs. Amharan (30), and their daughters Farah (13) and Shamil (11). They were originally from Turkey and had lived in the United States for the past 3 years. Both Mr. Amharan's parents and Mrs. Amharan's father still lived in Turkey; Mrs. Amharan's mother had died when she was 14. The family had some relatives and friends living in nearby cities, with whom they maintained infrequent contacts.

Mr. Amharan had been employed as an optician in his country, and Mrs. Amharan had been employed as a nurse's aide. Mrs. Amharan had come to the United States first when her sister found her a job in a nursing home. Mr. Amharan followed her a year later with their two daughters. He was not able to find a job in his field because of the language barrier; consequently, he worked as night watchman in a factory. He was laid off from this job about 5 months prior to the family's contact with us. Since then, he reported having difficulty sleeping because of the change in sleep patterns.

The family had immigrated to the United States in search for better opportunities and a better way of life for their children. The two girls appeared to have adopted the American way of life quite easily, talking, acting, and behaving as most other American children would.

Mr. and Mrs. Amharan had come from large rural families. Their marriage was arranged by her father soon after her mother died. She was the youngest of six children. He was the oldest of three boys, and his family was well respected in their small community.

Family Evaluation

During the initial evaluation, Mr. Amharan expressed deep concern over Farah's behavior. He explained that the principal of the school had called him to say that his daughter, who had not attended classes, was found kissing and hugging a boy from the senior class in the gym. Mr. Amharan related all of this with much embarrassment. He spoke about how shocked he felt, how ashamed he was of his daughter, and how afraid he felt of the bad example that she was providing for her younger sister. In fact, the therapists learned that Shamil was already defying her father's authority, wearing makeup and aligning with her sister.

Mrs. Amharan spoke in a quiet voice. She expressed more concern over her older daughter's truancy than over her inappropriate behavior, which she saw as a minor misdemeanor. She viewed her husband as too strict. The mother was also worried about her younger daughter, Shamil, who was beginning to have difficulty falling asleep; in addition, her performance in school was dropping.

Farah, who had just turned 13, was rebellious and oppositional. She spoke of how she had no freedom. Her father did not permit her to make phone calls or go out with female friends, nor did he allow her boyfriends to visit her. She spoke openly about being angry with her father. She said that since he had been laid off from work he was overcontrolling and strict, constantly questioning her whereabouts.

Shamil was very bright and spoke calmly about her father's concern over her sister's behavior; at the same time, she supported her sister's desire for more independence. She explained that because of her father's unemployment her mother had recently taken an additional part-time job to make ends meet, and so four times a week she did not come home until midnight. She was noticeably upset and became tearful when talking about her mother's having to work at night.

The problems presented by the Amharan family lay in two major areas of conflict: cultural clash accentuated by the father's unemployment, and cultural clash aggravated by the phase the Amharans had reached in the family life cycle.

Cultural Clash and the Father's Unemployment

The Amharan family had migrated to the United States seeking only a selective portion of the American dream—that is, material wealth, better employment opportunities, and a higher standard of living. At the same time, the Amharans wanted their cultural traditions and values to remain untouched, to at least some extent. They were denying the existence of obvious differences between sets of values corresponding to alternative cultures. This was particularly true of Mr. Amharan, who wanted to adhere rigidly to the traditional authority granted the man in Turkish society, and was consequently appalled by his daughter's behavior and ashamed of the possibility of his family and friends' finding out about it.

Mr. Amharan's unemployment played a crucial role in the turmoil the family was experiencing. Since he was unable to fulfill his parental role as wage earner, he was relegated to the job of caring for the household. This was a blow to his authority and masculinity. He reacted with anger, frustration, and rigidity.

In contrast, his wife played an instrumental role in the family and appeared future-oriented. This role reversal—her being the provider and his staying at home—further exacerbated the difficulties and challenges Mr. Amharan encountered in responding to cultural demands for change. His wife, instead, seemed to be calmly adapting to the changes. She was younger than her husband; had a better command of the English language; was more actively interacting with her environment because of her two jobs; and had an easier time balancing traditional values from her own culture, especially those dealing with male–female roles, and the more egalitarian American values. Obviously, the more comfortable and successful she felt, the more it seemed that she easily abandoned the Turkish cultural mores, and the more desperately Mr. Amharan needed to cling to them and to insist on his family's respect for them.

Because he was not able to display these feelings to his wife (she was financially supporting the family, after all), his only avenue of ventilation was to try to keep his daughters true to their Turkish heritage; in doing so, he become overcontrolling and unreasonable with them. He perceived their disagreement with him as a defiant act of direct aggression toward his already fragile authority: "They are putting me down." His appearance as a defeated man reflected his feelings of worthlessness and helplessness.

His wife attempted to alleviate his burden by working harder, but this only succeeded in further distancing him from the rest of the family, which had begun to feel more and more integrated and at ease with the new country's mores.

The Family's Stage of Development

The second conflict experienced by the Amharans was the phase of the family life cycle they were in—that in which the children begin to expand their identities in relationships outside of the family. The normal readjustment families make at this time were escalated into serious conflict, both by the need to adjust to the child's adolescent striving for independence, and by the fact that these strivings were expressed in clashing cultural forms (Sharma, 1984) and the resulting behaviors were thus experienced as inappropriate by the parents (Arredondo, 1984). Furthermore, this was occurring in the context of the parents' polarized positions because of their different levels of acculturation.

Farah's interest in boys, her oppositional nature, and her rebelliousness are common in adolescent girls. Specifically, Farah's attempt to be more like her friends clashed with the way Turkish girls are expected to behave at that age— that is, to relate almost exclusively to the family, to help with the chores, and to wait for the father to authorize a previously approved boyfriend to visit at home on chosen days. But Farah's turning away from these expectations was supported by her mother, so that the behavior reflected a deep split in the family.

She seemed also to be very angry at her father, whom she considered old-fashioned, and she tried to gain support from her mother in this respect as well. Farah and her sister were not only struggling through their own conflicts, but were also trying to impose liberal American views concerning child rearing on their family. Their parents' reaction, particularly the father's, was strong. In Turkey the father has a far more important role in regulating, controlling, and mediating the needs of children, especially females.

Mrs. Amharan was distressed in Farah's attitudes about school, skipping school, and ignoring her school work, for she was anxious for her daughters to succeed in this new country. In some way, even her dissatisfaction with Farah's behavior was at odds with her husband's. He wanted Farah to remain Turkish; she wanted Farah to become American. Clearly, Farah was trying to do both.

The Amharan family was suffering from all of the stresses specific to the immigrant family. The first were the loyalty conflicts expressed between Farah's behavior and Mr. Amharan's concerns about the opinion of his family and friends. Unlike the Yao-Liang boy, who gave up his friends and his investment in school to serve his family, Farah defied her family to persue her comfortable place with her American friends. The second was the difference in time orientation, although this was not as dramatic as in the Castro family. The Amharans also suffered from the tension between the father's expectation that his daughters would behave like good Turkish girls, and their own desire to do otherwise. Role changes were particularly problematic for this family, as the Turkish mother became the bread-winner, while the proud Turkish father was at home and unemployed. Furthermore, of course, the daughters, in their quicker grasp of life in America, challenged their father's authority. Farah's behaviors, especially those with boys, challenged the morals and values of her family, whose initial extremely controlling response probably contributed to her more desperate acts (such as snatching moments of intimacy with her boyfriend in a place where they were bound to get caught).

Treatment

Treatment began by trying to attenuate the stress that immigration had brought to the family relations. The therapist offered a redefinition of the family's problems, thereby switching the attention from Farah's present symptoms (which also covered for Shamil's, as well as for the father's unemployment) to all the differences and changes they had to become aware of and had to adjust to.

With respect to the chief complaint, the father and mother were united by bringing together their partial reactions to their daughter's behaviors. The mother's concern about Farah's not attending classes and the father's concern over her inappropriate behavior in the gym were both given equal support and reformulated as being complementary. The therapist emphasized that *both* parents were concerned about Farah's behavior. In so doing, the therapist returned authority to the father, and at the same time supported the mother in her attempt to play a more egalitarian role in keeping with American values. Clearly, this therapeutic intervention decreased the potential coalition between the mother and Farah against the father.

After psychological testing of Shamil ruled out the presence of any learning problem, and her pediatrician found no physiological basis for insomnia, Shamil's difficulty with sleep and declining grades were defined as responses to the father's unemployment and the mother's overemployment. The parents were urged to shift their attention from their own problems to those of Shamil, to offer her more comfort and reassurance. This meant, for example, that Mr. Amharan would have to pay more attention to her than to his own sense of failure, or even to Farah's carrying on.

Farah's behavior was explained as a means both of getting her family to discuss her needs as an adolescent and of bringing to the surface other family problems, particularly her own and her younger sister's concern about their father's depression. Farah's behavior was looked at as a failed attempt to separate too early from parental authority. The conflict between her loyalty to her parents and to her peers, as expressed in her behavior, was pointed out. Had her comportment continued, she would have risked suspension and ultimately would have had to stay home, thereby indirectly complying with her father's desires and with what was expected from a Turkish girl. She would have lost the opportunity to attain her freedom.

Farah's problems were also reframed as protective for the whole group, especially the father, whose concern and anger over his daughter's "irresponsible behavior" depicted his own feelings of having failed to be responsible as a Turkish father. Farah's expression of sadness over her bringing shame to her family helped the therapist to work with the father's own sense of shame for not being the provider for the family. His strong need to be responsible for finding a job in his field of expertise were explored and discussed with him, along with his desire to improve his knowledge of English. He committed himself to the prospect of looking into possible agencies.

An agreement was reached between the parents and Farah. In exchange for her helping with the household chores, she was given permission to bring friends (both girls and boys) to the house and to go out with them on the weekends. A 10:00 P.M. curfew was established.

The parents had now found some areas of agreement and had been confirmed in their authority in the family by the therapy team and the response of their children. They were thus prepared to follow the therapist's directives to pursue relationships with relatives and friends, and to develop lives of their own, independent from their daughters. In order to encourage her parents to take these social steps, Farah agreed to stay at home while they went out.

Finally, all four of the family members worked together to plan the family rituals for the celebration of the next Turkish holiday, happy in the reflection that this was a distinctive custom for them. Farah asked, and was given permission, to invite a friend to share in this special occasion with her family.

Conclusion

The opportunities provided to a family through immigration are many. There are the consciously appreciated opportunities for the family system, afforded by the system's opening itself up to assimilate new information and to reorganize itself accordingly—in other words, acculturation. These opportunities are accompanied by risks; these risks, while suffered by all family members, are often expressed through the children, who are both the ready bridges to the new culture and the probable victims of a family's failure to acculturate.

Understanding the experience of immigrant families in terms of these global systemic movements can provide therapists with a framework for appreciating the processes in which the families are engaged and for assisting them in regaining effective momentum.

ACKNOWLEDGMENTS

The author wants to express her warm appreciation to Lee Combrinck-Graham for her sustained encouragement, to Betty Karrer for her valuable feedback, and to Janet Edgette and Gloria Crespo for their help and comments.

REFERENCES

Arredondo, P. M. (1984). Identity themes for immigrant young adults. *Adolescence, 19*(76), 977–993.
Bateson, G. (1979). *Mind and nature.* New York: E. P. Dutton.
Bateson, G. (1983). *Steps to an ecology of mind.* New York: Ballantine Books.
Escovar, P. L. (1982). Cross-cultural child-rearing practices: Implications for school psychologists. *School Psychology International, 3*(3), 143–148.

Falicov, C. (1982). Mexican families. In M. McGoldrick, J. K. Pearce, & J. Giordano (Eds.), *Ethnicity and family therapy* (pp. 135–161). New York: Guilford Press.

Grant, G. (1983). Immigrant family stability: Some preliminary thoughts. *Journal of Children in Contemporary Society, 15*(3), 27–37.

Haley, J. (1979). The family of the schizophrenic: A model system. *Journal of Nervous and Mental Disease, 129,* 357–374.

Hussain, M. F. (1984). Race related illness in Vietnamese refugees. *International Journal of Social Psychiatry, 30*(1–2), 153–156.

Kagan, S. (1981). Ecology and the acculturation of cognitive and social styles among Mexican American children. *Hispanic Journal of Behavioral Sciences, 3*(2), 111–144.

Karrer, B. M., (1986). Families of Mexican descent: A contextual approach. In R. Birrer (Ed.), *Urban family medicine* (pp. 228–232). New York: Springer-Verlag.

Kelsen, H. (1960). *Teoria pura del derecho.* Buenos Aires: Eudeba.

Korazim, J. (1985). Raising children in ambivalent immigrant families: Israelis in New York. *Children and Youth Services Review, 7*(4), 353–362.

Lappin, J. (1983). On becoming a culturally conscious family therapist. *Family Therapy Collections, 6,* 122–136.

Lin, K. M., Masuda, M., & Tazuma, L. (1982). Adaptational problems of Vietnamese refugees: III. Case studies in clinic and field: Adaptive and maladaptive. *Psychiatric Journal of the University of Ottawa, 7*(3), 173–183.

Lippman, W. (1929). *A preface to morals.* New York: Macmillan.

Maturana, R. H. (1983–1984). *Biologia del conocimiento.* Unpublished seminar, Buenos Aires.

Maturana, R. H., & Varela, F. (1973). *De maquinas y seres vivos.* Santiago de Chile: Editorial Universitaria.

Maturana, R. H., & Varela, F. (1984). *Las bases biologicas del entendimiento humano: El arbol del conocimiento.* Santiago de Chile: Editorial Universitaria.

Morin, E. (1980). *La methode: Vol. 2. La vie de la vie.* Paris: Seuil.

Morin, E. (1985). Le vie della complessita. In G. Bocchie & M. Ceruti (Eds.), *La sifda de la complessita* (pp. 49–59). Milan, Italy: Feltrinelli.

Nicassio, P. M., & Pate, J. K. (1984). An analysis of problems of resettlement of the Indochinese refugees in the United States. *Social Psychiatry, 19*(3), 135–141.

Nguyen, S. D. (1984). Mental health services for refugees and immigrants. *Psychiatric Journal of the University of Ottawa, 9*(2), 85–91.

Prigogine, I., & Nicolis, G. (1982). *Le strutture dissipative.* Florence, Italy: Sansoni.

Selvini Palazzoli, M., Boscolo, L., Cecchin, G., & Prata, G. (1978). *Paradox and counterparadox.* New York: Jason Aronson.

Shands, H. S. (1971). *The war with words.* The Hague: Mouton.

Sharma, S. M. (1984). Assimilation of Indian immigrant adolescents in British society. *Journal of Psychology, 118*(1), 79–84.

Sluzki, C. (1979). Migration and family conflict. *Family Process, 18*(4), 379–390.

Shorter, E. (1977). *The making of the modern family.* New York: Basic Books.

Vazquez, N. E., Avila, V. Z., & Morales, B. G. (1984). Working with Latin American families. *Family Therapy Collections, 9,* 74–90.

Williams, H. E., & Carmicheal, A. (1985). Depression in mothers in a multiethnic urban industrial municipality in Melbourne: Aetiological factors and effects on infants and preschool children. *Journal of Child Psychology and Psychiatry, 26*(2), 277–288.

Wakil, F. A. (1981). Between two cultures: A study in socialization of children of immigrants. *Journal of Marriage and the Family, 43*(4), 929–940.

Williamson, R., Swingle, P., & Sargent, S. (1982). *Social psychology.* Itasca, IL: E. Peacock.

Yao, E. L. (1985). Adjustment needs of Asian immigrant children. *Elementary School Guidance and Counseling, 19*(3), 222–227.

23

Nuclear-Age Children and Families

DAVID GREENWALD, PhD

> *The idea of any human future becomes a matter of profound doubt. In that image we, or perhaps our children, are the last human beings. There is no one after us to leave nothing to. We become cut off, collectively self-enclosed, something on the order of a vast remnant. . . .*
>
> *The fact is that we can't yet know how to evaluate the psychological consequences of this extraordinary image of biological extinction. But we must assume that every relationship along the great chain of being is in some degree affected. This specifically includes generational relationships, already existing and imagined, between parents and children, grandparents and grandchildren, and . . . great-grandparents and great-grandchildren.—Lifton, 1982, pp. 67–68*

There are several generations of nuclear-age children today. All of us who grew up since Hiroshima are children of the nuclear age. Even those parents and grandparents who came of age before the release of atomic energy often feel childlike before the overwhelming power that has been unleashed. There is no historical precedent for the place that the possibility of nuclear destruction has in our lives today. And it is clear that this situation in which we find ourselves, this threatening shadow under which we live, specifically affects children, families, and the development of both children and families. We are only beginning to ask the questions that will enable us to understand the profound implications of the potentiality for total destruction.

Children today are growing up increasingly aware of the present reality—that human beings, through their own actions, have the capacity and seem prepared to exterminate life on our planet. How this awareness affects the development of children is still the subject of speculation, investigation, debate, and concern. The fact that children do have this awareness has only recently been widely acknowledged.

Early indications from a variety of studies, as well as from a wealth of anecdotal data, are that children's feelings on this subject are considerable. Their predominant emotion in regard to the nuclear issue is fear—fear that they will not grow up, fear of family separation, fear of chaos and destruction. Children also express bewilderment about the adult world, and specifically about how a state of

David Greenwald. Private practice, Philadelphia, PA.

affairs like this could have come to pass. They question the fairness and rationality of the adult world. Some children experience anxiety about the matter, and others attempt to master the problem through constructive activity.

Adults today find it difficult and painful in several ways to acknowledge that children do have feelings about the nuclear threat. They find it even harder to approach and help children on this issue. Adults' own fears and uncertainties are tapped; childhood memories about growing up with fallout shelters and air-raid drills are evoked. Especially poignant for parents is the sense that their abilities to protect the next generation are profoundly limited. Furthermore, confronting this fact often raises disquieting issues for parents as to how they live their lives and where their responsibilities lie. Unfortunately, the avoidance of adults and the reverse protectiveness of children (not wanting to raise an issue that profoundly unsettles their parents) have led to a conspiracy of silence on this most important issue. This continued silence leads to further isolation and mystification, and interferes with the development of coping strategies. Coping strategies are needed to help children understand their world, as well as to support the community of families that seeks a more secure future.

For the past several years, disparate groups of family therapists have taken their clinical skills—their experience in interviewing families, in supporting children within families, in understanding contexts, and in realizing the power of secrets—and have brought these skills to bear on this subject. In this work there have been tremendous resistances, both personal and professional; the tribulations of hearing painful stories; and, at times, despair. But there has also been the sense of learning at the cutting edge, of making connections and seeing patterns, and of reading literature and doing research on an issue of vital importance to all. In this chapter I try to give a sense of the field of inquiry: the responses that have been evoked in my colleagues' and my interviews with families. Finally, I note how children can be helped in regard to this issue, how families can engage the issue with their children in a positive way, and even how therapists and other professionals can help to engender hope and counteract hopelessness and helplessness in the face of questions about the survival of the planet.

An Illustration: One Family's Thoughts on Nuclear War

The subject of the impact of the nuclear age on children (and tellingly, also, on researchers, therapists, and parents) is illustrated by the unfolding of a story we came across in our own research.[1] Several years ago a friend of my family, a divorced 37-year-old mother of three, told us that she was angry. She had just

---

[1] The initial Philadelphia team, consisting of myself, Forman, Garfield, and Perlman, discovered the existence of the Boston team of Zeitlin and Reusser. We discussed mutual findings, and the eventual division of labor was that the Philadelphia group focused on families with children between the ages of 5 and 12, while the Boston group studied families with teenagers. Eventually this research and its implications were presented in a book (Greenwald & Zeitlin, 1987).

watched the film *In the Nuclear Shadow: What the Children Can Tell Us,* an Academy Award-nominated documentary that showed children discussing what they knew of nuclear weaponry. At times during their conversation they were angry, tearful, or uncomprehending. This mother's anger was directed at those adults who, in her view, had filled children's heads with information, fears, and notions of nuclear catastrophe. She was aghast that adults would use children by upsetting them so greatly. Finally, she declared that she was sure that her own children, then aged 12, 10, and 8, were totally unaware of and unconcerned about such threats themselves. Furthermore, she wanted to keep it that way. She would initiate no discussion that would shatter her children's innocence.

About 3 months later her children, friends of my children, were spending the weekend at our house. At one point during conversations, the two younger children, particularly the 10-year-old girl, talked about their worries that the world would blow up and that they wouldn't have a chance to grow up. When we queried whether this child had discussed this with her mother, she stated that she had not because she felt that her mother had enough on her hands, with the divorce and its consequences. She was protecting her mother, as her mother was protecting her, from the obviously upsetting topic.

By the following year, our team in Philadelphia was studying how families communicated about the entire range of nuclear issues through analysis of videotaped interviews. At that time we remembered this family's conflicting statements, and offered our family interview as a forum where the mother and children would explore these taboo subjects in a direct and possibly helpful manner. We were a little surprised when the mother readily agreed to participate in the interview. Apparently her attitude had changed in the intervening year, and she anticipated that the interview would not necessarily upset the children, but that it would be an opportunity to discuss the topic and to comfort them.

During the family interview the boy, now aged 10, and the girl, now $11\frac{1}{2}$, expressed themselves as many other children we interviewed did, openly and eloquently; they showed that they had given this topic a great deal of thought. The boy repeatedly returned to possible solutions to the dangers of these weapons: "Maybe we could bury them; maybe we could shoot them into space; maybe we could deep-freeze them [a child's literal understanding of 'nuclear freeze']," he proposed. This approach, solving the problem through some technical or technological solution, was quite common among boys between the ages of 8 and 12. His mother was patient and attentive, explaining that some of these ideas might not work, but that it was a very good thing that he was using his mind and his creativity to address the problem.

The $11\frac{1}{2}$-year-old girl related a dream, sharing it with her family for the first time. "Once I had a really scary dream about nuclear war: Everybody was running around and going crazy. But I didn't tell Mom. I worry before I go to sleep about what if there were a nuclear war. And what if there really weren't but everybody thought there was? Then people would send the bombs, just because they thought there was, and everybody would be screaming and lost? Sometimes I worry how to prevent it from happening."

This family had moved from the mother's conviction that her children did not worry about it at all to the interview, where the dream and the possible solutions were shared. Just as the boy's technical dreams were typical, so, too, the girl's fears of chaos, of a system out of control, and of mayhem unleashed accidentally were typical of many children we and others have interviewed. Parents as well as children feared being lost or separated from other family members.

In families, as in the culture at large, many approach the subject of the nuclear threat through initial denial—the belief that "my children don't worry," and the possible protection from encountering some of the painful images subsequently revealed that such a stance allows. But the denial forces an isolation on this important issue and allows neither children nor parents the contact and community with each other necessary to encounter the issue in a way that can lead to more hope.

The Context: Psychological Impact of the Nuclear Threat

In 1947, a year and a half after the bombing of Hiroshima, Lewis Mumford, the social critic and historian, considered how a future with nuclear weapons might affect human development:

> The young who grow up in this world are completely demoralized: they characterize themselves as the generation that drew a blank. The belief in continuity, the sense of a future that holds promises, disappears: the certainty of sudden obliteration cuts across every long-term plan, and every activity is more or less reduced to the time-span of a single day, on the assumption that it may be the last day. . . . Suicides become more frequent . . . and the taking of drugs to produce either exhilaration or sleep becomes practically universal. (Mumford, 1947)

Is this a prescient view into a future that has come to pass, or an alarmist overreaction that has its echoes in the warning cries of countless antinuclear activists? To us, it is uncanny in the late 1980s to read such a sweeping prediction about social trends that was made over 40 years ago, and to ponder possible connections between today's suicide and drug use crises and the sense of inevitable nuclear obliteration. To a great extent, we must approach this topic through such ponderings and imagination, for it is impossible to do "hard" research on a subject so broad and so emotional. There is no way to control innumerable variables, and where, at this point in history, do we find a control group of non-nuclear-age subjects? Indeed, as Mumford predicted, the cynicism about future and continuity may be so pervasive that people may not even connect it specifically with the nuclear threat.

Several thinkers have approached the question of how we manage to continue our daily lives amidst such an incredible threat. Frank, in *Sanity and Survival* (1967), writes of the psychological unreality of the danger, for nuclear weapons are not part of our daily life, being neither seen, felt, tasted, or smelled (p. 30). He posits that people have adapted to this threat either through avoidance (ranging from outright denial to avoiding exposure to disturbing information or its implications) or acceptance (as people have remarked to me, "It's going to happen, and there is not a thing that you or I can do about it").

Lifton has studied the psychological consequences of life in the nuclear age since he began his extensive interviews of Hiroshima survivors in 1962. He noted that the survivors, out of shock, guilt, loss, and particularly their overwhelming confrontation with death and overwhelming death imagery, seemed to walk around in a state of perpetual numbness; they were greatly impaired in their capacity to respond in an emotional way. His chronicle of this research encapsulates his findings in its title, *Death in Life* (1982).

More recently, Lifton (1983; Lifton & Falk, 1982) has suggested that perhaps we all cope with our fears about nuclear war through psychic numbing. He argues that humankind's traditional forms of symbolic immortality have been especially disturbed in the nuclear age. According to Lifton, five modes of symbolic immortality have provided human beings with ways of managing death anxiety. The first of these five modes is the biosocial, or the sense that individually we may perish, but that our children and their children will continue the "great chain of being." This attachment may also be present for us with the tribe, clan, nation, organization, movement, or even species. The second is theological, wherein we transcend death, either directly through an afterlife, or through reincarnation or spiritual attainment. The third is creative—the sense of living on in one's works or achievements, discoveries, students, or good deeds. The fourth is that nature itself is a part of the timelessness of the natural world. The fifth is experiential transcendence, which relates to those times of intense, peak experiences through mysticism, childbirth, sexual intimacy, and other states in which time and death disappear.

Our relationship with all of these modes has been rationally altered through the novel reality of confronting absolute extinction. Lifton speculates that the rise of fundamentalist religions and the increase in experiential transcendence are popular responses to this radical alteration. For family therapists the biosocial mode, wherein our family lives take part, is of particular interest.

Issues of authority and obedience are crucial to the views of another nuclear theorist, psychoanalyst and psychiatrist Joel Kovel. Kovel views the helplessness and powerlessness that many people express regarding the nuclear threat as similar to the terroristic threats of abusive families. He sees that we are coerced into submission by the father figure of the modern state:

> For nuclear terror is the means by which a citizenry becomes intimidated into accepting the paranoid system of states. It takes our primordial fear of the bomb, which is rational—since it is an expression of the unutterable degree of barbarity expressed by nuclear weaponry—and makes us accept that bomb, and the order which constructs it, which is paranoid and irrational. (Kovel, 1983, p. 85)

Kovel says that our psychological responses to the bomb are extremely vulnerable to manipulation by managers of the nation states, with a resulting profound sense of isolation. This isolation, he asserts, is the worst pathology of the nuclear age. Because the threat is intangible, it often feels unreal, and we are forced to rely on our imaginations to confront the possible reality. This reliance on our inner worlds limits our abilities to act publicly: "Whether we escape in fantasy to a desert island or move in the direction of imagining the real, we end up isolated" (1983, p. 11). Such dreaming is a private activity that forsakes the public domain of language. To survive and make history, we have to overcome our passivity and find ways to share these ideas with others, to develop a shared reality. The nuclear experience is inherently isolating to a greater degree than has been the case with any collective calamity before faced by humankind. According to Kovel, the "fatal irony here [is that] the one threat which should objectively bring us together since we will all go together, when we go, is the threat which subjectively keeps us apart" (1983, p. 11).

Kovel's points are especially relevant to therapists, who spend much of their professional lives working at the intersections of private inner worlds and outer public ones. As therapists, we need to help people encounter these private imaginings and help them to apply and express their private thoughts in a public realm.

The Literature: Children's Reactions to the Nuclear Threat

For many years of the nuclear age, very few examinations of the effects of the age on its children were produced. This lack of research seems attributable both to the difficulties that such research entails and to the feelings evoked by such inquiry—hearing children express themselves on topics that are so painful and that make us all feel so vulnerable.

Some critics claim that it is the researchers and teachers who have frightened and upset children by bringing the subject up in the first place. In Congressional hearings in 1983 on the subject of children's fears of nuclear war, some conservatives were intensely critical of any courses on nuclear issues in the schools. As psychiatrist Harold Roth put the case against teaching children about these matters, "These programs only scare the wits out of young people, challenge them with unsolvable problems, provoke a reaction of despair and hopelessness, ultimately lead to a sense of hopelessness about the future and possibly result in a reaction to aggression of any kind" (Roth, 1983, p. 13). This logic of "don't scare the children" blames those who bring the message that children are already scared.

Even so penetrating an interviewer as Robert Coles has demonstrated how prone we all are to blame someone as an outlet for the intense discomfort that this subject raises. In an article titled "Children and the Bomb," Coles (1985, p. 44) tells the story of his discussion with a young girl he calls Susan. Susan, while working on a painting of a city after nuclear attack, spoke knowingly of potential aftereffects. Susan said she was "worried because a lot of people are sticking their head in the sand." Coles answered that it is "quite possible we won't be witnesses to such a tragedy." Susan refused to be reassured, and Coles felt "intimidated, maybe even judged by this child, reprimanded for my reassurance."

Coles looked at the painting that Susan completed and commented that he "had never seen such an unremittingly raw, lifeless painting." A discussion ensued of things they would miss (e.g., ice cream, tennis)—a discussion that Coles admittedly tried to steer away from the pain of the topic. Coles once again honestly reports his emotional response: "I was reasonably sure Sue was not someone in need of treatment, though I was beginning to realize that her fears were prompting at least one psychiatrist to stop and think—to see. . . . I believe I was angrier with Sue than I dared acknowledge to myself."

In the article, Coles goes on to speculate that nuclear fears among children are solely among the offspring of the privileged, professional, and well-to-do. He condemns some particular self-absorbed activists who spent time at meetings instead of taking their asthmatic son to a physician. This tendency to blame the "bad parent" is familiar to family therapists as a reaction to stressful situations. In fact, in our own interviews on nuclear issues and in nuclear discussions, blame has emerged as a frequent emotional response (Greenwald & Zeitlin, 1987). It may be blame of the Russians, Reagan, or antinuclear activists.

We have heard children tell their parents that they did not want them to cut back on political activity but, if anything, to do more. One boy told his mother, "Get arrested, but be home for supper." Also, neither we nor other researchers have noted any class bias among children about nuclear concerns. Babette Jenny, who has worked with inner-city children in Philadelphia, says that she found a greater ability among children who have witnessed violence to accept the possibility of ultimate nuclear catastrophe.

Ultimately, the children themselves will answer the critics. The degree of their awareness was highlighted to us when we asked a 10-year-old boy in our own study whether other children knew about nuclear weapons. He responded, "Yes, unless they don't have a TV or radio, don't get a newspaper or magazine, don't have a phone, and don't go to school." Thus, although the temptation to accuse the researchers of creating the nuclear-age stress that is being studied is evident, it is hard to ignore the fact that children do know and express or repress their concern in varying ways. More difficult to confront is the effect that this awareness, anxiety, or fear has an personality development. If children are so aware of the nuclear threat, then we are obligated to examine this effect.

Schwebel (1965, 1982) was an early investigator into the question of whether the nuclear threat contributed to trends toward family disruption, drug abuse, heightened loneliness, and declines in scholastic performance among teens in the early 1960s. During the Berlin crisis of 1961 and the Cuban missile crisis of 1962, he administered 3000 and 300 questionnaires, respectively. He asked for a response in writing to the following question: "Do I think there is going to be a war? Do I care? Why? What do I think about fallout shelters?"

Schwebel (1982, pp. 609–612) reported that widespread among his several thousand respondents was an anger about "having the most to lose." They often felt that "they would be denied a chance to live, to love, to work, to bear children, and raise a family." He found that most of these youths did not want to survive a nuclear war, largely because they envisioned their families being destroyed. He delineated the primary emotional reactions to the subject as denial, resentment, and powerlessness. As a clinician, he was concerned about the effects of such emotions on developmental issues.

We found ample corroboration of Schwebel's findings in our own interviews. Today, the themes that Schwebel found in adolescents are also raised by children and parents. In fact, during the course of these interviews and other discussions we have had, it has rarely taken much probing for someone's nuclear story to change from "I never think about that," to a memory of a time when there was an anxious reaction or a response that chilled in its powerlessness or resentment. One mother from a housing project in North Philadelphia asked only that her children be allowed to reach adulthood. "If only that, I would be eased," she said.

On nuclear concerns, not all that much has changed in the 20 years since Schwebel's interviews. "If I allowed myself to think about it, I'd be miserable," remarked one teenager to Schwebel (1982, p. 612). Another one commented, "It's terrifying to think that the world may not be here in a half-hour, but I'm still going to live for now." Children told us, "It's like, what if there is a nuclear war, and I'm at school, and Mom is at home, and Dad is at work?" or "I guess if I did think about it more, I'd have to think about dying all the time."

Schwebel identified a reactive, "macho" pose that greatly fears any weakness as a psychological defense from feelings of powerlessness. This appears to be an increasingly popular stance at present. The belief that it is unmanly to hold any but a superior, controlling position in any encounter has culturally been embraced through Rambo and other such heroes. This belief leads to a dangerous trigger-happy pose. The attractiveness of offense as defense among preadolescents was illustrated by the report of a guidance counselor in an elementary school. She mentioned that she was conducting a group for acting-out boys, and that shortly after the bombing of Libya in 1986 there was a widespread excitement among the boys. One after the other exclaimed about the need to fight and generally boasted of how "we would show them." One boy hesitatingly demurred that he was afraid that the bombings could lead to war and that he didn't want to be bombed and die. After his comment, there was lengthy and absolute silence.

Another early investigator, Escalona (1965, 1982), tried not to bias her subjects by raising the subject of nuclear war, and asked open-ended questions instead. She asked 350 teenagers in the mid-1960s to think about the world as it might be 10 years later. She found that 70% mentioned the bomb or war spontaneously. Escalona focused on developmental issues; she has argued that growing up in a social environment that tolerates and ignores the risk of total destruction by means of voluntary human action tends to foster those patterns of personality functioning that can lead to a sense of powerlessness and cynical resignation (Escalona, 1982).

She concluded that although few children or adolescents lived in actual fear of the threat except during acute crises, there was nonetheless an impact on interpersonal relationships, stemming from authorities' assertions that the only way to survive and prosper is for the nation to have the most and biggest weapons. Escalona found a weakening of the readiness to invest energy and long-range planning, and felt that this was a developmental effect of awareness of the nuclear threat. She also found that the ability to participate and carry through with the momentum of organized collective activity was also threatened. Instead, children seemed to reflect that might is all and that the self is paramount.

The early studies by Schwebel and Escalona, then, conclude that some of the effects of the nuclear threat on development include a tendency to isolation, reduction in long-range planning, and the encouragement of an illusion of bullying personal power.

Currently, there is a rapidly emerging professional literature that consists largely of survey studies of children aged 12 and older. This literature consistently concludes that young people are acutely aware of the possibility of nuclear war and consider it high among the issues of greatest concern to them (Bachman, 1983; Beardslee & Mack, 1982; Berger-Gould, Moon, & Van Hoorn, 1986; Chivian et al., 1985; Goldenring & Doctor, 1985; Solantaus, Rimpela, & Taipele, 1985). Although the existence of this concern does not reveal the impact of such concern on development, surveys do inform us that television is children's main source of information about nuclear issues and that discussion with parents and other adults is rare (Chivian et al, 1985; Holmberg & Bergstrom, 1985). A study of adolescents in Toronto (Goldberg et al., 1985) found that those who talked with parents were significantly more hopeful that they and others could do something to prevent nuclear war than those who did not speak with parents and other adults.[2]

Several studies examine the question of the extent to which children are really upset. There is a paradoxical conclusion to these studies: Apparently, many of those respondents who described themselves as quite anxious about the threat of nuclear war were nonetheless more hopeful about the future than children who said that they were not anxious or worried. In a study where nuclear fears were included in a questionnaire that addressed many other subjects as well, Goldenring and Doctor (1983) concluded that the group of youngsters (about a third) who were most concerned about the effects of the nuclear threat appeared to be more aware of other potential dangers and to show greater maturity and higher leadership abilities than their peers.

In a similar study of about 1000 metropolitan Toronto students, Goldberg et al. (1985) found that although those students who stated that they worried very often about nuclear issues were from all socioeconomic groups, they reported a greater faith in their own abilities to affect the future than did those who stated that they never worried. The worriers' reported confidence in their own abilit-

---

[2]For an analysis and review of the literature of studies of nuclear effects on children and adolescents, see Eisenbud, Van Hoorn, and Berger-Gould (1986).

ies extended to other areas of their personal lives and goals beyond the nuclear issue.

Although a very small group may worry intensely about nuclear war and may have given up because of that, for most children this worry and anxiety is associated with a constructive approach to problem solving. We cannot say which came first, the sense of personal efficacy or the willingness to confront this frightening prospect, but there does seem to be a relationship.

For anyone who has ever worked with adolescents or children, this corroborates a clinical impression—that cynicism and apathy place the young at greater risk than overt anxiety about the future. Avoiding the entire dimension of hope and despair leads to a dimmer sense of the future and to passive resignation. Confronting the nuclear issue, along with its attendant hope and despair, at least enables the participant to engage seriously with the question.

There has been very little research on preteens' attitudes regarding the nuclear threat. Part of the reason for this was commented on by Alvik (1968), who noted that bringing up this subject made even seasoned researchers anxious. Had it not been for the mutual support of our own research group, we might well have avoided or given up the goal of our study. Even with support and with professional and personal commitment to this work, we each encountered significant moments of fear, uncertainty, and depression.

Rothman (1987), in one of the few studies of preadolescent children, investigated 8- to 12-year-olds within the context of a general investigation of spontaneously generated and ranked fears, intergenerational communication, parental political activity, and media exposure to the topic. She found that 20% of the 22 children mentioned nuclear war spontaneously, but that when asked directly they ranked it second among their fears. Contrary to expectation, this fear was related neither to parental political activity nor to media exposure to the topic.

Thus, since there are so few data about children under 12, we need to extrapolate some of the findings from the research with older children to see which findings are pertinent.

Results from the variety of studies with adolescents indicate remarkable consistency on adolescents' perceptions of the possibility of nuclear war. Repeatedly, it has been reported that by the teen years the overwhelming majority of youngsters are aware of nuclear war and its potentialities. Furthermore, many are pessimistic about the chances of avoiding that war, while others report deep despair, a sense of living for today, and/or an anger at adults for creating such a situation. The most striking concern of researchers, and a refrain we have often heard from parents, is the worry that adolescents' ability to commit themselves to a future and confidence in their own abilities to do anything about the future are impaired.

The results of these probes indicate a great deal of awareness from an increasingly early age, focused on several key concerns. There are many vivid and upsetting images of the devastation that nuclear weapons may cause. Beardslee and Mack (1982) concluded that thoughts of nuclear annihilation had penetrated deeply into the consciousness of the children and adolescents they studied. There were expressions of unease about the future. There were severe doubts that nuclear war could be limited, and most of their subjects did not expect to survive if it happened.

What Did the Children Tell Us?

Clearly, we may concluded that children's awareness of nuclear developments is widespread and that it has significant implications for child development. Our own research, based on this literature, was focused on having children express their feelings and thoughts within the setting of a family discussion. We hoped thereby that we would hear children's comments in a more naturalistic, even supportive, setting. We reasoned that we might hear a more honest accounting of the children's thoughts in this setting, and we further hoped that a somewhat therapeutic milieu would be established in which these concerns might be addressed.

We, the Philadelphia group, began our study by finding (through our many contacts with colleagues, clergy, activists, educators, parents' groups, etc.) families that would consider an interview with us. We approached parents first, explained what we were doing, and asked whether they would invite their children to participate with them. Interestingly, for our Philadelphia team, which was focusing on families of 5- to 12-year-olds, there were more refusals than acceptance. Parents were very uneasy about their own abilities to participate in such a discussion with their young children, and were often unwilling even to ask their children whether they wanted to talk about the subject. In the family discussions in the Boston area, parents of adolescents were more willing to at least ask their offspring whether they would be interested. We were especially surprised that we received so many refusals, because the vast majority of parents in our earlier study had endorsed the importance of family discussions on this topic (Greenwald, Garfield, Perlman, Forman, & Rothman, 1985).

The actual family interviews lasted from 20 to 50 minutes. The role of the interviewer was to ask questions, but more importantly to facilitate the flow of discussion among family members. Any time that there was a topic-related interaction, the interviewer would take a background position. Basically, we attempted to adopt a clinical interview model, in which questions would stimulate discussion and elicit follow-up questions. We also were very conscious of our skills as clinicians and were poised to intervene should a discussion become overwhelmingly anxious or debilitating. At no point was such intervention necessary.

There were a few questions that we used to promote discussion: "What comes to mind when you think of the terms 'nuclear,' 'nuclear war,' or 'nuclear weapons?' " "How likely do you think a nuclear war is in your lifetime?" "Do you think you and your family would survive such a war?" "Who do you talk to about any concerns you have about this subject?" "How can nuclear war be prevented?" "Do you think there is anything you could do to prevent nuclear war?" These questions were asked of most of the families, but since our goal was to encourage each family's own discussion, every question was not asked of every family.

Ultimately we interviewed 12 families in our study; all but 2 came from the Philadelphia metropolitan area. Three of the interviews included grandparents who happened to be there or were especially invited.[3] Of the 20 parents interviewed (there were 3 single mothers and 1 single father with joint custody), 5 had either signed a petition, written a letter, demonstrated, or devoted time to "activism" on nuclear weapons. This was a skewed sample, but, again, even among activists, many parents refused to involve their children in the research. There were 5 boys and 7 girls between 5 and 8 years of age, and 6 boys and 7 girls between the ages of 9 and 12. There were also 2 teenage girls, included because they had younger siblings in the target age group. The families were largely suburban and upper-middle-class, but included several blue-collar, two inner-city, and two very different families. In summary, this was a pilot study organized and carried out to begin a field of inquiry. It made no attempt to do rigorous random sampling. The most important characteristics of the families were good communication skills and their beliefs that open communication can be constructive.

Some development a lists have pointed out that children are less well defended psychologically than older people, and are therefore more susceptible to upsetting nuclear imagery and awareness. In our work, we found children to be open about their wishes to avoid the subject. They often struggled with whether to allow themselves to think about it or to acknowledge their fear. An 8-year-old girl told us, "I sort of forget and sort of remember." A 9-year-old girl told us, "I do something to put my mind off of it—I'll go into my room and play with dolls and stuff. It comes into my mind once in a while."

In a particularly telling passage, a first-grade boy said that he was scared of nuclear war, because the "school can fall down when the bomb comes, and it can come straight down on it. It can." When replied about his parents, "They could tell me not to think about it, or find an easy way for me to get to sleep somehow. My dad can get me to sleep. I can't think about it when I'm sound asleep." How much do we all share this child's wish for escape?

Very few children are totally naive about nuclear terrors. One study (Friedman, 1984) found that even preschoolers at play, after an experimentally induced frustrating experience, expressed nuclear and bomb imagery. This means that nuclear bomb consciousness begins at an early age. The option of protecting our children from any encounter with this imagery and information no longer exists, and seems to vanish at increasingly young ages.

The inevitable confrontation with this imagery means different things at different parts of the life cycle. For very young children, we agree with those developmentalists who argue to wait for the children to bring up the subject. However, we agree with them less because of a fear of overwhelming small children than because the children probably will not pay much attention to the conversation.

---

[3] The presence of the grandparents seemed to take the parents off the hook a bit, and they could talk more freely of their own misgivings, feeling that their own parents were there as an additional support.

Information is processed when a child is ready for it, and children in this age group have demonstrated the ability to efficiently compartmentalize a great deal of this material.

In our study, we did have one 5-year-old and several 6-year-olds. Two of these children did not talk, and one asked to leave the room out of lack of interest. One child, having just come from Mass, attempted to reassure her family by saying, "If we did all blow up we would meet together again in God." This child also replied, when asked what the word "nuclear" meant, "It's like *The Never-ending Story*. The whole world would be made nothing."

Other 6-year-olds, twins who engaged in bitter contests over their clothes, found it hard to understand why the adult world was not using the oft-stated advice that they talk it out, work it out, or share without fighting. One girl of 7 asked why countries could not get along without fighting, and her father responded by bringing up her fights with her brother. He was implying that if they couldn't get along, how could they expect that countries would?

These days, children aged 5 to 8 often have already been exposed to the concept or image of nuclear war. Their understanding, although limited, is part of the texture of their understanding of other issues. With this age group, it is most important to try to understand in what way the children have processed and integrated nuclear imagery. As two Piagetian child educators have pointed out (Carlsson-Paige & Levin, 1985), children of this age actually have some crucial defenses for protecting themselves from overwhelming anxiety. The combination of concrete thinking (in this case, a greater ability to envision explosions than radiation or even arms control), compartmentalization (the tendency to talk about an upsetting subject one minute and a totally different one the next), and egocentricity (the belief that one's own or one's parents' actions are omnipotent) characterized the way these younger children handled the subject.

The significant time in development for the appearance of nuclear issues appears to be the period from 8 to 12 years of age. At 8, children appear to be just beginning to take the threat of nuclear war more seriously. By "seriously," we do not mean that younger children are frivolous, but that the emotional aspects of the issue—the increased understanding of implications and possibilities—seem far greater at the later age. Although one younger girl did speak of her fantasy/fear that a nuclear war would separate her from her family, and of a dream of walking in the graveyard after a nuclear war, this child was calmly munching granola as she related these images. Openness to nuclear imagery in the younger children did appear to be associated with an ability to isolate the feelings. It was in later childhood that isolation broke down and there was a greater congruence between affect and the content of disturbing images.

Children aged 8 to 12 began to integrate nuclear awareness with their own emotional responses and (of crucial importance) with their need to feel competent, industrious, and in control. This age group had fantasies and dreams of chaos, and envisioned more specific grotesque consequences reminiscent of horror movies. These children were often amazingly eloquent and quite well informed. Several children said that they would rather die quickly than survive and suffer radiation sickness. A number of children in this age group mentioned their fear of being separated from their families. Repeatedly, children remarked that they thought it was all unfair: "Why can't they get along without blowing each other up?" and "Why can't we be allowed to live out our lives?" These questions were repeated often enough that we questioned whether the children's entire sense of justice and fairness; of the rationality of the adult world; and of the efficacy of personal, social, and long-term actions was not in some important ways affected by grappling with this subject.

This group of children often evinced great fear, but they also had the greatest hope for actively solving the problem. This impression is corroborated by the studies (e.g., Goldberg *et al.,* 1985; Goldenring & Doctor, 1985; Van Hoorn, 1986) that have elaborated the relationship between anxiety/concern and hope. Nuclear anxiety and concern in several studies peaked at about 11, 12, and 13 years of age; older adolescents had more concern with life tasks of work and identity, but correspondingly higher scores of hopelessness. Once again, paying attention to this issue correlates rather paradoxically with hope for the further. Perhaps our clinical impression that preadolescents were especially hopeful is related to the fact that their characteristic approach to this concern was through the application of the industry that is the developmental focus of this age group.

Parental Responses

Parents in our study confessed that their greatest concern was that they felt unable to protect their children from the nuclear danger. Some had considered how or when they might engineer the suicide and death of their family members upon hearing of the outbreak of nuclear war or immediately after the first impact. Parents stated to us that they felt a sense of failure and guilt that they could not promise their children protection and a chance to live out their lives.

It seemed that parents were generally relieved that their children were not overwhelmed by terror or fatalism and felt enough hope and strength to go on with their lives. The relief and hope were felt more on a parental than a personal level, for by and large the adults had their own insecurities about the future. Adolescents, if anything, were the most pessimistic about the survivability of the planet.

When parents expressed their pessimism to the children, although they were probably motivated by wanting to "tell it like it is," they left their children with few options. If an adult believes that there always will be fighting, and equates that thought with nuclear weaponry, then clearly that person must have a rather dim view of the possibility of avoiding calamity. If fighting is seen as "human nature," and evidence is presented from within the sibling relationship, then there can be few grounds for hope; the bomb becomes internalized.

Berger-Gould, Eden, and Gould (1984) pointed out that adolescents and adults who do not internalize the bomb, but view it rather as an ego-alien entity, tend to feel more hopeful. And although there seem to be few if any young children who do internalize the nuclear issue in this way, the risk of just this internalization is far greater during the emotional maelstrom of adolescence. Perhaps this is why younger children have more hope about avoiding nuclear catastrophe, even though their awareness of this threat seems to fall on less well-defended psyches.

Parents in dialogue with children who used their imaginations, creativity, and problem-solving capabilities were most helpful when they encouraged such capabilities. At times some adults did seem to need to point out why a particular solution would not work. One grandfather replied to his granddaughter's plaintive remark, "There must be another way than war," with a mocking question: "What would you suggest? Soccer?" But, by and large, parents wanted to walk the line of encouraging their children to approach this subject through their own capabilities without spelling out too emphatically why each particular suggestion might be impractical. It does seem most important, as one mother noted, to encourage children to think about it using their intelligence and desire for mastery. As one boy in this age group put it, "I don't want to think about it in a bad way."

We often do not know what our children are thinking, or whether they are upset about nuclear war, because we do not ask them. This lack or limitation of discussion is due to several circumstances. First of all, we do not want to upset the children. Much of the hue and cry attending the television movie *The Day After* was a misplaced attempt to protect children. We all need and want to shield our children from pain. Although it is impossible and potentially crippling to try to protect them from any and all pain, we certainly want to spare our children pain that is not inevitable and part of life. Today's children are inevitably aware of nuclear terror and its attendant pain.

Parents themselves have often not worked through their own feelings about the bomb left over from their own childhoods. Each time we would hear during interviews, workshops, and discussions that "I never worry about the bomb," we almost inevitably heard a story that told of a specific time in that same person's life when he or she experienced a great deal of anxiety through dreams, memories, or fantasies. This happened even on a trip to Moscow: I met a scholar, and after telling him of the work I was doing, I heard from him, "If it happens, it happens. It's like worrying about the weather." Yet he proceeded to tell of a time in the early 1960s when he was very, very scared of a nuclear war and even talked to his father, who pooh-poohed his fears. People's reactions to this subject are seldom what they first seem and are the combination of many different emotions and thoughts.

Repeatedly, we heard parents discuss their difficulty with the realization that they could not protect their children. One mother said that she had such great difficulty with this that she tended to try to distract herself with other thoughts. Another parent reflected, "With other things, even frightening things, it's possible to tell them what to do. 'Don't talk to strangers,' 'Don't get in any cars,' but, with this, what can I say?"

One thing that parents did do, although it did not feel like much to them, was to affirm their children's reactions. One mother told her children that of course she was afraid, and that it was normal to be afraid. Other parents, by describing their own fears (either in childhood or in the present), indicated tacit understanding of and sympathy with their children's own worries. We have talked with children who have had their nuclear anxieties defined as pathological, and these children especially need reassurance and affirmation that such anxieties are not abnormal. As one mother put it, "It's normal to be afraid. It wouldn't be normal not to be afraid."

In general, our study supported those objective studies that demonstrated that children who had adults to talk to were doing better than children who could not discuss this with a receptive adult audience. A mother and father told us that their daughter's upset after seeing *The Day After* was something they could not handle, and so they told her not to bring it up any more. We found that children who could bring up such fears felt better about their chances to do something about it than those who could not bring up their concerns, or who had those concerns labeled as pathological.

An Eriksonian Framework

In understanding our data (Greenwald & Zeitlin, 1987), we found that Erikson's (1963) typology of life stages was most pertinent. His description of the task of industry versus inferiority proved apt and useful for the children, and his description of generativity versus self-absorption was helpful in understanding the parents' reaction.

The children we interviewed with their families definitely seemed to relate to the nuclear issue on the axis of industry versus inferiority. Those who took an active, competence-based approach to this issue spoke far more readily, less fearfully, and with a great deal less resignation than almost anybody else we spoke with.

Most of the parents of these youngsters were in the Eriksonian stage of generativity versus self-absorption. The adult task is to take responsibility for the nurturance of new ideas, new lives, and a new generation. The parents' confidence in this ability was profoundly shaken in a world of hairtrigger nuclear capabilities, and they experienced the nuclear threat as an assault on their generativity. This frustrated generativity—the dread of powerlessness and helplessness regarding one's own children—was a theme we heard again and again. With this assault on generativity, how much to today's parents and those of the age to be parents retreat into self-absorption?

Repeatedly, children spoke of their need to approach their concern with problem-solving strategies. But, even more importantly, they viewed the overall issue as one in which their sense of inferiority or industry was itself at stake. Parental messages, such as "You don't need to trouble yourself with that," were received as comments on their inferiority rather than as reassurances. Likewise, parental encouragement of the children's potential solutions was most beneficial and appreciated. In this regard, more knowledge and information, rather than further fright-

ening the children, usually gave them both a sense of participation and competence in understanding the problem, and the tools to begin to construct solutions.

One 8-year-old boy told us that he felt privileged to know about this, and a
9-year-old girl said that I was "like a test; the more you know, the more you are
prepared." Other children were more specific in their attempts to master the subject through their industry. Thus 10-, 11-, and 12-year-old boys were remarkable
for their schemes and plans. There was the boy with his wish to "freeze" the
weapons or to shoot them into space, and the boy who wanted to construct a time
machine that would permit "the rebuilding of the world" after the radiation went
down, by saving scientists, leaders, and architects.

The scariest way to think about this subject was to be stuck in helplessness
and hopelessness. Industry was therapeutic for children and for adults as well,
because it enabled them all to feel that at least they were working on something.
As a grandfather put it to his family, the worst feeling is that of not being able to
do anything; "we may not win [i.e., prevent wars], but at least we will feel
better." An 11-year-old girl who was especially hopeful envisioned that demon-
strations and committed people would do for this cause what the civil rights activists did for the cause of desegregation. Interestingly, this child, who pinned her
hopes on widespread public outcry and activity, had never been to a demonstration, and her parents had never taken part in any such action. One father reassured
his children by telling them that they could use "whatever skills they have" to
deal with this issue. As a developmental psychologist has said regarding children's
sense of loss and helplessness, "Action is the best therapy" (Elkind, 1983, p.
55).

Whether expressing their fears, positing possible solutions, or sharing fantasies of destruction or escape, the children we studied overwhelmingly felt better
when they were able to communicate with adults about this subject. The lack of
a forum for their concerns leaves children with no means to exploit their innate
drive for mastery. Obviously this is not an issue we can expect them to master
completely or to solve for us, but efforts at control and mastery must begin somewhere; since they have already begun to wrestle with the issue, we need to encourage any attempts they make to comprehend and solve the problem.

Family Patterns

Families had certain recognizable patterns in dealing with the subject of nuclear
war. Parents responded to children's concerns through either blame, affirmation,
or protection. We found that when families did bring the subject up, conversations
seemed to arrange themselves on particular dimensions that suggested themselves
as polarities, in keeping with the Eriksonian typology we found useful for understanding life stage reactions. We found that these dimensions provided a framework both for assessing where families were in their discussions and for helping
them move forward. We have elaborated four basic dimensions that overlapped
but appeared throughout the interviews (Greenwald & Zeitlin, 1987).

The first of these dimensions we termed "contact versus separation," which defined how families first encountered the subject. The second dimension, "community versus isolation," was related to the first, but broadened it by beginning to prescribe a course of action, while also noting the leveling or lack of hierarchy around this issue. The third, and perhaps crucial, dimension we called "hope versus despair." It is the most obvious area that is aroused by any discussion about nuclear weapons. The final dimension we termed "commitment versus emptiness," a category that brought forth conflicts and possibilities for the family in the future.

Contact versus separation was demonstrated by families through both the content and process of their encounters with the material. Certainly the greatest for all family members was that of being separated during a nuclear attack. One blended family had gone so far as to make plans of where to meet in case of attack, but the son said that he would leave his father and stepmother and find his mother. For "she would have nobody, and at least you guys would have each other." Berger-Gould et al. (1984) have speculated that the phenomenon of increasing numbers of adult children residing with their families of origin may be attributable to the fear of separation in case of nuclear attack. When family members spoke of their fears of separation in our research, they were often touching each other, emotionally, physically, or hopefully.

Contacting each other through this issue rather than keeping it to oneself had further positive effects on those who so chose, in that it allowed children's questions to be addressed. These questions were as diverse as "Where are the bombs kept?" "Can they actually blow up accidentally?" "Can one bomb blow up the whole world?" "Why build them anyway?" Children hearing answers to these questions often found them both reassuring and troubling, but in either case they were experiencing contact.

The second dimension, community versus isolation, extends this concept by considering the family as a whole and its relationship with its social environment. Every clinician is familiar with individuals who form no attachments for fear of being hurt or abandoned. In the nuclear age, this fear may encompass all of humanity. Also, if we are "all in the same boat"—if, in fact, parents are as vulnerable as children, and interviewers as vulnerable as interviewees—then we are all united in this community that is threatened. The alternative, isolation, may make us feel less vulnerable for the short term, but ultimately cannot lead us from the edge of destruction.

Hope versus despair, the third dimension, was the topic of much family discussion. Parents were very upset that their children might in fact give up hope. Again and again, we heard parents tell their children that they must not give up, that they must be hopeful. The greatest parental fear was that children would become discouraged and decide to give up on life or live solely for the moment. Much of this lecturing seemed to reflect the parents' own hopelessness. Parents found it very difficult to admit their own serious doubts about the future to their children (there is a real question whether such admissions would have harmed the children, since in the few instances in which parents did admit their own pessimism, the children seemed to balance this with a greater sense of hope). We would not recommend that parents tell young children of these feelings, especially if the children are under 8, but when parental despair prevents any discussions at all, each member of the family will be isolated with his or her own fears.

Both hope and despair, when they came up in the discussions, sounded more beneficial than the often prevailing fatalism. Parents did preach hopefulness, even when they did not feel so hopeful themselves. Children often see through the adults' attempts to convey hope. One teenage girl asked her father incredulously, "You really feel hopeful that nuclear war can be avoided?" At a talk we gave at a local high school, the students were scornful to the point of hostility that we actually felt hopeful that human beings, through their actions, could prevent the final holocaust.

Macy (1983) has pointed out that despair not only is very real but can be ultimately mobilizing. Most people avoid a difficult encounter with this dimension and opt for facile hopes. Our culture bombards us daily with messages of hope; this is one of the most promoted and perhaps one of the least deeply felt emotions in the nuclear age.

One major reason why both hope and despair are not confronted is that a full encounter would force a decision on the issue of commitment. The last dimension we found in families, commitment versus emptiness, raised a great deal of conflict and uneasiness among the adults. There were questions about responsibility, such as "What can I do?" or "What should I do?" Usually, these questions were accompanied by guilt or the feeling of being overwhelmed. Certainly all parents at times feel that what they already do in terms of livelihood earned and children raised takes virtually all their available energy. However, the opposite of commitment in many aspects of life is emptiness. If we do not risk commitment to all of life, which is threatened, do we risk feeling a sense of emptiness about life itself?

Families Address the Threat

Because it has often been difficult for children and adults to address this topic together, the isolation for children has been greatly increased. Many children report that they have very few, if any, places to bring their concerns about this subject. A crucial finding in various research studies was that children who did have outlets for discussions about this were in some key ways in better shape than children who did not have ways to discuss any fears or thoughts they might have. The children in our study surprised us by how much they expressed an appreciation of being included in the discussion. They were relieved that adults were listening to them.

Our research provided, through family discussions, relief and an appreciation that there was at least a momentary break in their mutual isolation on this issue. Clearly, what is needed for both children and adults is a public realm where our private fears and images can be shared, so that we may begin to identify and build community forums to enable private fears and concerns to be brought to bear in a public way. Our view now is that family discussions are a particularly apt place to start the process of moving from isolation to community (Greenwald & Zeitlin, 1987).

There are several ways in which children and families can interact in respect to the nuclear threat. By interviewing families as a whole, rather than focusing on children, we wanted to avoid the charge of children being force-fed values and prejudices regarding nuclear weapons. It is perfectly acceptable and necessary for values and fears to be dealt with within the family as part of its necessary functioning and roles.

We interviewed families because we also believed in the healing abilities of family process in regard to difficult and emotionally charged issues. We were particularly drawn to analogies of family rites and processes of grieving, because even in this grieving process there is an imaginary or future reality. Furthermore, such family discussions, like any broaching of the topic, must be undertaken with a view to preventing such a tragedy. As one father told us, he was grateful for the chance to discuss this subject with his children, because it was like an illness: "It doesn't go away by not looking at it. By paying attention, one can learn what needs to happen to get well."

We realized from our earlier parent questionnaire (Greenwald et al., 1985) that many parents saw the importance of family discussions, but avoided these at times for fear that they would make their children more anxious. In fact, children, by and large, emerged from our interviews appreciative and somewhat more hopeful, while adults usually had a more anxiety-provoking and somewhat depressing experience.

However, the actual process of family members' sitting down together and discussing a subject that is of mutual concern is a unique one for many families. This is a subject as important for children as for adults—in some ways more so, since we heard several cries from children that the old people in Washington or Moscow had already lived their lives and they wouldn't care if the young didn't get their turn. The social issue of fairness and the question of what kind of world the children have been brought into, together with parents' attempts to teach alternatives to violence and force, are thrown into question when this subject is confronted. For family members to confront these questions together, from the standpoint of being all in the same boat in one sense, allows the children to express themselves on an issue of great importance to them; to hear from adults some of the information they need; and to get a sense of the family's attempting as a whole to take responsibility for its survival.

Death and Dying in the Nuclear Age

One way in which generational arrangements have been altered in the nuclear age is in respect to death. Throughout the ages death has been a natural part of life, a necessary end stage, optimally occurring after a long and productive life. Old age, then, has traditionally been the province of death and dying; although there were certainly exceptions, through disease, war, and accident, death was primarily dealt with as a day-to-day reality only by the aged. Today, this situation has necessarily changed in a way that all ages understand. The images of death through nuclear war have reached our families and have altered families' relationship with death. Now family members of all ages must confront both their individual deaths and the threatened deaths of all those near and dear, as well as of the entire supportive culture. Thus death assumes the intimacy and importance for us all that it has traditionally had primarily for the old.

This greater overall confrontation with the reality of death, however, does take place within the context of massive death. Children in our study did not envision their families surviving a nuclear war, or could only poorly envision what such survival might entail. By the ages of 7–10, all the children in our study and many of the children in larger studies had become aware of certain nuclear realities. Included in this was a sense that weapons of enormously destructive force exist; many children did envision such power as potentially world-destroying. Children we interviewed either over- or underestimated the bomb's potential. One 7-year-old girl said that a single bomb would kill maybe thousands of people, while another said, "A single bomb could break the planet."

If we are all made children in our feelings of smallness before the threat, depending on the beneficence of parental authority for our very survival, we arrive at a dependence that goes even beyond that of early childhood. If we are all old suddenly in the ways in which we must confront our own and other's mortalities, in the seriously real and immediate threat of death, then we all need to be adults in response to the threat as well—competent, able to plan, organize, and join together with like-minded others.

Where Do We Go from Here?

As therapists, as parents, and as citizens, we must do what we can to facilitate a change from separation, isolation, despair, and emptiness to contact, community, hope, and commitment. These processes, apparently basic to life in the nuclear age, are especially important for children as developing creatures. Could it be that there is an interaction between any change for the better on these dimensions and an overall improvement on the nuclear issue as well? Certainly hope, community, or commitment anywhere can provide skills, investments, and necessary preconditions for the possibility of change in this most threatening dimension as well.

At a recent meeting of the American Orthopsychiatric Association, I met a woman who had clearly moved through these dimensions. She had been divorced from her son's father, who was in the military. When her son was 9 or 10, he began to have dreadful nightmares of nuclear bombings, and he would avoid sleep. Therapy did not prove helpful, but this mother's own study on the subject of nuclear issues and her commitment to educate other parents finally ended the boy's terrors. Her own actions of contacting the subject, finding and forging community around it, making a commitment, and encountering hope and despair as a live issue provided her child with great relief.

Obviously all children are not as terrified as this child, but we cannot ignore the fact that many children are afraid and are silent. As therapists, we must recognize this metacontext and understand its importance. We must use our skills at helping people face difficult issues and communicate about them. We must recognize the healing effects of action, for children and adults.

> We would prefer to know nothing of the atomic menace . . . we want to live, not to die—but this catastrophe would finish everything, so there is no point in thinking of it. It seems to be one of these things which decency forbids mentioning, lest it make life unbearable. And yet, nothing but this very unbearableness can cause the event that might change it.
>
> Today the constant presence of the cataclysm as a possibility—indeed a probability—offers a signal opportunity for reflection as such, and at the same time, the one chance for the political rebirth that would avert the cataclysm. The stakes of the game should be part of everyone's life, as a call for reflection. There lies the horizon of reality in which we must stand. A refusal to know is already part of the disaster. (Jaspers, 1961, p. 6)

It is of vital importance that we know and that we ask our children what they know, for only then can we begin to say how we feel about this threatening reality. Only then can we form communities that can sustain our common desire for generation following generation. Only then can children experience that basic human optimism that growing things know. Only then can adults impart their skills, abilities, and dreams to their children.

When we reflect on this subject enough, we feel its importance. It appears increasingly that this weight does affect us in the here and now. We share Norman Cousins's observation (1981) that, in a sense, in part of our consciousness, we are living in a postnuclear war of all against all. Certainly our despair and anxiety take their toll in ways strikingly similar to Mumford's early prognosis.

But it also becomes obvious that in very important ways we are all alike. We are alike in the threat under which we live our lives. All of us express our wishes for safety and protection in different ways—from wishes for a perfect space shield that will provide total protection, to attempts to change the policies of the superpowers. Researchers and subjects, parents and children, we are all in the same boat. We all feel enormously threatened, and we cannot bear such feelings for long.

Children are afraid. Adults feel vulnerable. Parents feel unable to protect children. Yet we must begin where we are. In our own research (Greenwald & Zeitlin, 1987), we found that when people do reflect on these feelings in the presence of significant others, important affirmations and the beginnings of life-sustaining commitments take place.

REFERENCES

Alvik, K. T. (1968). The problem of anxiety in connection with investigations concerning children's conceptions of war and peace. *Scandinavian Journal of Educational Research*, pp. 215–233.

Bachman, J. G. (1983). American high school seniors view the military: 1976–1982. *Armed Forces and Society, 10*(1), 86–104.

Beardslee, W. R., & Jack, J. E. (1982). The impact on children and adolescents of nuclear developments. In R. Rogers (Ed.), *Psychosocial aspects of nuclear developments* (Task Force Report No. 20, pp. 64–93). Washington, DC: American Psychiatric Association.

Berger-Gould, B., Eden, E., & Gould, J. (1984). Children and the threat of nuclear war. *Alberta Psychology, 13*(5–6), 28–29.

Berger-Gould, B., Moon, S., & Van Hoorn, J. (Eds.). (1986). *Growing up scared?* Berkeley, CA: Open Books.

Carlsson-Paige, N., & Levin, D. (1985). *Helping young children understand peace, war, and the nuclear threat*. Washington, DC: National Association for the Education of Young Children.

Chivian, E, E., Mack, J. E., Waletsky, J., Lazaroff, C., Doctor, R., & Goldenring, J. (1985). Soviet children and the threat of nuclear war: A preliminary study. *American Journal of Orthopsychiatry, 55*, 484.

Coles, R. (1985, December 8). Children and the bomb. *New York Times Magazine*, p. 44.

Cousins, N. (1981). *Human options*. New York: Norton.

Eisenbud, M., Van Hoorn, J., & Berger-Gould, B. (1986). Children, adolescents and the threat of nuclear war: An international perspective. In B. Berger-Gould, S. Moon, & J. Van Hoorn (Eds.), *Growing up scared?* (pp. 183–219). Berkeley, CA: Open Books.

Elkind, D. (1983, September 20). *Hearing before the House Select Committee on Children, Youth, and Families*, Statement. In *House of Representatives, 98th Congress*, p. 54. Washington, DC: U.S. Government Printing Office.

Erikson, E. H. (1963). *Childhood and society*. New York: Norton.

Escalona, S. K. (1965). Children and the treat of nuclear war. In M. Schwebel (Ed.), *Behavioral science and human survival*. Palo Alto, CA: Behavioral Sciences Press.

Escalona, S. K. (1982). Growing up with the threat of nuclear war: Some indirect effects on personality development. *American Journal of Orthopsychiatry, 52*(4), 600–607.

Frank, J. (1970). *Sanity and survival*. New York: Random House.

Friedman, B. (1984). Preschooler's awareness of the nuclear threat. *California Association for the Education of Young Children Newsletter, 12*, 2.

Goldberg, S., LaCombe, S., Levenson, D., Parker, K., Ross, C., & Sommers, F. (1985). Thinking about the threat of nuclear war: Relevance to mental health. *American Journal of Orthopsychiatry, 55*(4), 503.

Goldenring, J., & Doctor, R. (1983, September 20). *Hearing before the House Select Committee on Children, Youth, and Families*, Statement. In *House of Representatives, 98th Congress*, p. 61. Washington, DC: U.S. Government Printing Office.

Goldenring, J., & Doctor, R. (1985). California adolescents' concerns about the threat of nuclear war. In T. Solantaus, E. Chivian, M. Vartanyan, & S. Chivian (Eds.), *Impact of the threat of nuclear war on children and adolescents: Proceedings of an international research symposium* (pp. 112–113). Boston: International Physicians for the Prevention of Nuclear War.

Greenwald, D., Garfield, R., Perlman, D., Forman, W., & Rothman, L. (1985). *Parental attitudes and frequency of discussion about nuclear war with children*. Paper presented at the meeting of the Society for Research in Child Development, Toronto.

Greenwald, D., & Zeitlin, S. (1987). *No reason to talk about it: Families confront the nuclear taboo*. New York: Norton.

Holmberg, P., & Bergstrom, A. (1985). How Swedish teenagers think and feel concerning the nuclear threat. In T. Solantaus, E. Chivian, M. Vartanyan, & S. Chivian (Eds.), *Impact of the threat of nuclear war on children and adolescents: Proceedings of an international research symposium*. Boston: International Physicians for the Prevention of Nuclear War.

Jaspers, K. (1961). *The atom bomb and the future of man*. Chicago: University of Chicago Press.

Kovel, J. (1983). *Against the state of nuclear terror*. Boston: South End Pres.

Lifton, R.. (1982). *Death in life: Survivors of Hiroshima*. New York: Basic Books.

Lifton, R. (1983). *The broken connection: On death and the continuity of life*. New York: Basic Books.

Lifton, R., & Falk, R. (1982). *Indefensible weapons*. New York: Basic Books.

Macy, J. R. (1983). *Despair and personal power in the nuclear age*. Philadelphia: New Society Publishers.

Mumford, L. (1947, March). Social effects. *Air Affairs*, pp. 370–382.

Roth, H. (1983, September 20). Statement. In *Hearing before the Select Committee on Children, Youth, and Families, House of Representatives, 98th Congress*. Washington, DC: U.S. Government Printing Office.

Rothman, L. (1987). *Fear of nuclear war among pre-adolescent children and family communication*. Paper presented at the annual conference of the American Orthopsychiatric Association, Washington, DC.

Schwebel, M. (1965). Nuclear cold war: Student opinion and professional responsibility. In M. Schwebel (Ed.), *Behavioral science and human survival*. Palo Alto, CA: Behavioral Sciences Press.

Schwebel, M. (1982). Effects of the nuclear war threat on children and teenagers: Implications for professionals. *American Journal of Orthopsychiatry, 52*, 608–618.

Solantaus, T., Rimpela, M., & Taipele, V. (1984). The threat of war in the minds of 12–18 year olds in Finland. *Lancet, i*, 784.

Van Hoorn, J. (1986). Facing the nuclear threat: Comparisons of adolescents and adults. In B. Berger-Gould, S. Moon, & J. Van Hoorn (Eds.), *Growing up scared?* Berkeley, CA: Open Books.

Index